Cambridge Handbook of Institutional Investment and Fiduciary Duty

The *Cambridge Handbook of Institutional Investment and Fiduciary Duty* is a comprehensive reference work exploring recent changes and future trends in the principles that govern institutional investors and fiduciaries. A wide range of contributors offer new perspectives on dynamics that drive the current emphasis on short-term investment returns. Moreover, they analyze the forces at work in markets around the world which are bringing into sharper focus the systemic effects that investment practices have on the long-term stability of the economy and the interests of beneficiaries in financial, social and environmental sustainability. This volume provides a global and multifaceted commentary on the evolving standards governing institutional investment, offering guidance for students, researchers and policymakers interested in finance, governance and other aspects of the contemporary investment world. It also provides investment, business, financial media and legal professionals with the tools they need to better understand and respond to new financial market challenges of the twenty-first century.

JAMES P. HAWLEY is Professor and Senior Research Fellow of the Elfenworks Center for Responsible Business at Saint Mary's College of California. He is the author (or co-author) of well over thirty scholarly articles, as well as four books, on a variety of topics, including corporate governance, responsible investment, the international monetary and financial system, and environmental issues.

ANDREAS G. F. HOEPNER is an Associate Professor of Finance at the ICMA Centre of Henley Business School at the University of Reading, where he directs the i-finance laboratory. He is also currently serving as the Senior Academic Fellow to the United Nations supported Principles for Responsible Investment and as Senior Associate to the University of Cambridge's Programme for Sustainability Leadership.

KEITH L. JOHNSON represents pension funds and institutional investors globally on fiduciary, investment, corporate governance and related litigation matters. He chairs the Institutional Investor Services Group at Reinhart Boerner Van Deuren, s.c. He is also co-chair of the Fiduciary Duty Working Group for the Network for Sustainable Financial Markets, an international think-tank.

JOAKIM SANDBERG is Associate Professor of Practical Philosophy at the University of Gothenburg, Sweden. He is an internationally acclaimed expert on ethical issues in finance in general and also in pension management. His PhD work (from 2008) was the first ever comprehensive philosophical treatment of the concept of socially responsible investment.

EDWARD J. WAITZER is a Professor and the Jarislowsky Dimma Mooney Chair in Corporate Governance at Osgoode Hall and the Schulich School of Business at York University. He was Chair of Stikeman Elliott LLP from 1999 to 2006 and remains a senior partner whose practice focuses on complex business transactions. He also advises on a range of public policy and governance matters.

When people agree to become members of boards of pension organizations, what duties do they take on? This new book on fiduciary duty makes clear there is no simple answer to this question. It examines the subject not just from a legal perspective, but also from its implications for board behavior, investment policy, and the consideration of societal issues beyond the immediate confines of the pension plan. [It is] a valuable new tool for trustees.

Keith Ambachtsheer

Director of the International Centre for Pension Management at the Rotman School of Management, University of Toronto

Eight years after the Freshfields report, this handbook is a much needed in-depth analysis of the fiduciary duty of institutional investors. It is sharp, thoughtful and inspiring, and takes an interdisciplinary approach, ranging from finance, investment and law to philosophy and psychology. It is a must read for institutional investors wishing to understand and fulfil their fiduciary duties in a modern era.

James Gifford

Executive director of the United Nations-backed Principles for Responsible Investment

A focus on fiduciary standards in the investment chain is critical to the reform of the financial services sector to meet more effectively the needs of the non-financial economy. This book places the issue where it needs to be – on the centre of the stage.

John Kay

Professor at London School of Economics, journalist, and author of The Kay Review of UK Equity Markets and Long-Term Decision Making

This book is a thrice-blessed treasure: it meets society's needs to understand how the eclipse of fiduciary precepts has impoverished our commercial life; it meets the needs of governance professionals in providing a single repository of scholarly analysis of the various aspects of fiduciary duty; and it meets

the needs of everyday citizens in describing a world in which their expectations can reasonably be met. It is the right book at the right time by the right people. Congratulations to the Cambridge University Press and the Editors for timely bringing to the public such an essential contribution to public discourse – this book is instantly the must have for all who are interested in corporate governance or who invest money on behalf of others. The authors of the 36 component articles are such a luminous lot that one should not single out individual contributions. In brief, this is an instant classic – no finance or governance library should be without it.

Robert A. G. Monks

Author, entrepreneur, governance expert and former US pension and welfare benefits regulator

Fiduciary principles are under enormous pressure to narrow their reach; at the same moment in history forces shifting the ownership of assets from individuals to institutions argue for greater fiduciary scrutiny of investment decisions. By any measure, the importance of fiduciary principles has never been greater [than now]. The essays set forth in the Handbook are timely and deserving of becoming the intellectual North Star as the discussion of this centuries-old doctrine proceeds.

Knut A. Rostad

Founder and president, Institute for the Fiduciary Standard

This groundbreaking handbook is an insightful look into the real-world challenges of an investment industry navigating the ever-changing waters of the global economy. It shines a light on the risks that fiduciaries may face if they don't understand how the world is changing around them. The handbook is a must read for any investment fiduciary interested in a comprehensive interdisciplinary perspective.

Anne Stausboll

Chief executive officer of the California Public Employees' Retirement System (CalPERS)

Cambridge Handbook of Institutional Investment and Fiduciary Duty

Edited by

JAMES P. HAWLEY

ANDREAS G. F. HOEPNER

KEITH L. JOHNSON

JOAKIM SANDBERG

EDWARD J. WAITZER

CAMBRIDGE
UNIVERSITY PRESS

University Printing House, Cambridge CB2 8BS, United Kingdom

Published in the United States of America by Cambridge University Press, New York

Cambridge University Press is part of the University of Cambridge.

It furthers the University's mission by disseminating knowledge in the pursuit of
education, learning and research at the highest international levels of excellence.

www.cambridge.org
Information on this title: www.cambridge.org/9781107035874

© Cambridge University Press 2014

First published 2014

Printed in the United Kingdom by Clays, St Ives plc

A catalogue record for this publication is available from the British Library

Library of Congress Cataloguing in Publication data
Cambridge handbook of institutional investment and fiduciary duty / edited by James P. Hawley,
Andreas G. F. Hoepner, Keith L. Johnson, Joakim Sandberg, Edward J. Waitzer.
   pages   cm
Includes bibliographical references and index.
ISBN 978-1-107-03587-4 (hardback)
1. Institutional investments.   2. Trusts and trustees.   I. Hawley, James P., 1944–
HG4521.C257 2014
658.15′5–dc23
2013046225

ISBN 978-1-107-03587-4 Hardback

Contents

Figures

Tables

Contributors

Editors

James P. Hawley Professor and Director, Elfenworks Center for the Study of Fiduciary Capitalism, School of Economics and Business, Saint Mary's College of California.

Andreas G. F. Hoepner Associate Professor of Finance, ICMA Centre, Henley Business School, University of Reading; Senior Academic Fellow, Principles for Responsible Investment, United Nations.

Keith L. Johnson Head of Institutional Investor Legal Services, Reinhart Boerner Van Deuren s.c.; Program Director, Wisconsin International Corporate Governance Initiative, University of Wisconsin Law School.

Joakim Sandberg Associate Professor of Practical Philosophy, University of Gothenburg.

Edward J. Waitzer Professor, Jarislowsky Dimma Mooney Chair in Corporate Governance, Director of the Hennick Centre for Business and Law, Osgoode Hall Law School and Schulich School of Business; Partner, Stikeman Elliott LLP.

Contributors

Jane Ambachtsheer Partner and Global Head of Responsible Investment, Mercer, Toronto; Adjunct Professor, Centre for Environment, University of Toronto.

Ralf Barkemeyer Lecturer in Corporate Social Responsibility, Sustainability Research Institute, University of Leeds.

Larry W. Beeferman Director, Pensions and Capital Stewardship Project, Labor and Worklife Program, Harvard Law School.

Aaron Bernstein Senior Research Fellow, Labor and Worklife Program, Harvard Law School.

Christine Berry Former Head of Policy and Research, ShareAction.

Anders Biel Professor of Psychology, University of Gothenburg.

Tim Cadman University Research Fellow, Institute for Ethics Governance and Law, Griffith University; Research Fellow, Earth Systems Governance Project.

Gordon L. Clark Professor and Director, Smith School of Enterprise and the Environment, University of Oxford; Sir Louis Matheson Distinguished Visiting Professor, Faculty of Business and Economics, Monash University, Melbourne.

Rebecca K. Darr Senior Fellow, Aspen Institute Business & Society Program, New York City; Cofounder of Atayne LLC, Brunswick, Maine.

Stephen M. Davis Associate Director and Senior Fellow, Harvard Law School Programs on Corporate Governance and Institutional Investors; Nonresident Senior Fellow in Governance Studies, the Brookings Institution.

Ivan Diaz-Rainey Senior Lecturer in Finance, Department of Accountancy and Finance, University of Otago.

Robert G. Eccles Professor of Management Practice, Harvard Business School.

Arman Eshraghi Postdoctoral Fellow in Finance, University of Edinburgh Business School.

Frank Figge Professor of Sustainable Development and Corporate Social Responsibility, Kedge Business School, Marseille.

Andrea Finegan Lecturer in Corporate Finance, Norwich Business School and Tyndall Centre for Climate Change Research, University of East Anglia.

Alison Fox Lecturer in Financial Accounting, School of Business, University of Dundee.

Tommy Gärling Emeritus Professor of Psychology, Department of Psychology and Center for Finance, School of Business, Economics and Law, University of Gothenburg.

Dieter Gramlich Professor of Banking, Baden-Wuerttemberg Cooperative State University; Graduate School of Business, Cleveland State University.

Danyelle Guyatt Investment Manager, Catholic Super; Visiting Fellow, University of Bath.

Tobias Hahn Associate Professor for Corporate Sustainability, Kedge Business School, Marseille.

Ian Hamilton PhD Candidate, Umeå School of Business and Economics, Umeå University.

Tessa Hebb Director, Carleton Centre for Community Innovation, Carleton University.

Jock Herron Senior Research Associate and Co-Head of the Digital Cities and Societies Research Initiative, Harvard Graduate School of Design.

Liaw Huang Consulting Actuary, TTerry Consulting LLC, Chicago.

Gbenga Ibikunle Lecturer in Finance and Climate Change, University of Edinburgh Business School.

David Ingram Executive Vice President, Willis Re, New York.

Magnus Jansson Research Fellow, Gothenburg Research Institute, School of Business, Economics and Law, University of Gothenburg.

Michael P. Krzus Founder of Mike Krzus Consulting and co-author, with Robert G. Eccles, of *One Report: Integrated Reporting for a Sustainable Strategy*.

Andrea Liesen Lecturer in Finance, Umeå School of Business and Economics, Umeå University.

Steve Lydenberg Founding Director, Initiative for Responsible Investment; Partner, Strategic Vision, Domini Social Investments.

René H. Maatman Professor of Asset Management, Institute for Financial Law, Radboud University Nijmegen; Partner, De Brauw Blackstone Westbroek, Amsterdam.

Tek Maraseni Deputy Director Operations, Australian Centre for Sustainable Catchments, University of Southern Queensland.

Claire Molinari Visiting Research Associate, University of Oxford.

Agnes L. Neher PhD student in Financial Ethics, Department of Catholic Theology and Business Ethics, University of Hohenheim; Visiting Scholar, School of Management, University of St Andrews.

Jonas Nilsson Assistant Professor of Business Administration, School of Business, Economics and Law, University of Gothenburg.

Gordon Noble Director of Investments and Economy, Association of Superannuation Funds of Australia Ltd.

Michael Perino Dean George W. Matheson Professor of Law, St John's University School of Law, New York.

Ryan Pollice Associate – Responsible Investment, Mercer, Toronto.

Douglas Sarro Law Clerk, Court of Appeal for Ontario.

Charles Scanlan Former Head of Pensions, Simmons & Simmons.

George Serafeim Assistant Professor of Business Administration, Harvard Business School.

Sebastian Siegl Researcher, School of Business and Economics, Åbo Akademi.

Richard Taffler Professor of Finance and Accounting, Warwick Business School, University of Warwick.

Thomas Terry Consulting Actuary, TTerry Consulting LLC, Chicago.

Raj Thamotheram President, Network for Sustainable Financial Markets; Cofounder, Preventable Surprises and the Positive Deviants Club.

Michael Thompson Research Scholar, International Institute for Applied Systems Analysis, Laxenburg, Austria.

Daniel J. Tulloch Doctoral Researcher, Department of Accountancy and Finance, University of Otago.

Roger Urwin Global Head of Investment Content, Towers Watson, London.

Stephen Viederman Grandparent; retired President of the Jessie Smith Noyes Foundation, New York City.

Christopher W. Waddell Senior Attorney, Olson Hagel & Fishburn LLP.

Aidan Ward Organizational Systems Consultant, author of *Trust and Mistrust: Radical Strategies in Business Relationships*.

Christian E. Weller Professor, Department of Public Policy and Public Affairs, University of Massachusetts, Boston; Senior Fellow, Center for American Progress, Washington, DC.

Jay Youngdahl Senior Fellow, Initiative for Responsible Investment, Hauser Center, Harvard University.

Jayne Zanglein Professor of Business Law, Western Carolina University; ERISA attorney, formerly with Vladeck, Waldman, Elias and Engelhard, New York.

Stefan Zeume PhD student in Finance, INSEAD.

Foreword

The world currently faces increasingly complex governance challenges. While there is a growing recognition that we urgently need to take a longer-term view in order to deal with them successfully, many of the incentives that shape the thoughts and actions of leaders encourage myopia in the private and public sectors alike. Strategies with a high probability of success are available but not pursued because powerful short-term incentives are increasingly misaligned with the timeframes required for the solution of growing problems with profoundly destructive inter-generational impacts.

Thus far, legislators have not adequately addressed these inter-generational issues. In previous eras, when obvious and invidious injustices grew to intolerable scale due to the protracted paralysis of leaders, the necessity for action has often found its venue, by default, in the judiciary. Now, once again, courts – responding to specific fact situations – may well play a critical role in breaking this logjam. One likely legal strategy is based on the concept of fiduciary duty – the legal obligation to act in the best interests of others.

With the growth of specialization and interdependence, our increasing reliance on the services and expertise of others has given rise to the concept of a "fiduciary society" – a classic non-zero-sum game in which all can benefit. But if fiduciary obligations are betrayed and trust is eroded, it becomes a game in which all can lose. As a result, the values of *loyalty* and *trust* – shaped by "reasonable expectations" – have come to form the basis for broad fiduciary standards.

These developments have occurred in the context of a historically dramatic change in the ownership of almost all asset classes: public equity and debt, real estate, private equity, infrastructure assets and others. In the past, these types of investments were generally held by individuals. In the last thirty to forty years they have come to be held mostly by institutional investors (e.g., pension funds, mutual and other retirement vehicles) – which, in turn, are fiduciaries for the majority of the adult population. As fiduciaries, they have duties of care and of loyalty which, many are coming to believe, should be extended to encompass attention to inter-generational fairness. In other words, the outcomes of fiduciaries' decisions should reflect due regard for the best interests of future (as well as current) beneficiaries.

Meeting this challenge of fair treatment assumes a level of proficiency with respect to long-term value creation and risk mitigation. Arguably, these fiduciary standards impose obligations:

- To demonstrate respect for social norms;
- to give beneficiaries (or in the case of future beneficiaries, perhaps their proxies) a voice in decisions that affect their interests; and
- to think and act strategically and collectively.

To date, such standards have not been tested in the courts, but there is good reason to believe that they soon will be.

Investing is a means to ensure our future well-being. This requires a broader consideration by fiduciaries of systemic effects – for example, consideration of how investments can create better markets tomorrow, rather than simply focusing on "beating" the market today. Incentives that encourage fiduciaries to take advantage of asymmetries have frequently seduced fiduciaries to succumb to a self-destructive cycle of short-termism and have clearly generated unhealthy outcomes for the system as a whole.

It is only a matter of time before our courts (or regulators) will find opportunities to better define and protect the public interest. This is likely to lead to the imposition of public stewardship responsibilities throughout the financial services supply chain. We see elements of this today in the UK, and in the recent set of "investment beliefs" that CalPERS (the largest public pension fund in the US) recently adopted. Another example is the adoption of Regulation 28 in South Africa that requires that prudent investing should give consideration to "any factor which may materially affect the sustainable long-term performance of a fund's assets, including factors of an environmental, social and governance character."

Core to the stewardship idea is that human beings are the beneficiaries of their retirement funds. While this sounds obvious to many, far too often the funds themselves (and their relative, benchmarked performance) have been the primary or sole focus of short-term investment strategies. In order to better realize the goals of stewardship, the core concepts of fiduciary obligation will have to be rebalanced. For example, a rebalancing might shift at least some of the weight presently given to "prudence" (often defined as short-term performance relative to "peers") to put greater weight on "loyalty," including a duty of impartiality to current and future beneficiaries.

Those who want to shape the process of fiduciary reform, rather than simply be subject to it, should read this volume of essays. This Handbook highlights the role that fiduciary duty plays in determining how managers of the world's financial capital impact the sustainability of the economy, environment and society, as well as our future financial success.

Those large global financial institutions that are subject to fiduciary duties can and must play a crucial role in solving today's most serious sustainability challenges. This volume brings together some of the leading practitioners, academics and policy makers confronting these issues. We hope and expect many of these ideas and lessons will have significant impact.

Al Gore
Former Vice President of the United States and Co-founder and Chairman of Generation Investment Management

CHAPTER 1

Introduction

JAMES P. HAWLEY, ANDREAS G. F. HOEPNER,
KEITH L. JOHNSON, JOAKIM SANDBERG AND
EDWARD J. WAITZER

Introduction

This *Handbook* responds to the evolution in the ownership of companies and financial assets over the past thirty to fifty years. It also is concerned with the more recent widespread failure of pensions and other long-term savings vehicles to deliver on sustainable financial security goals for the individuals whose monies they are investing.

The volume highlights important changes in the landscape of finance, especially with regard to institutional investors: those large financial institutions entrusted to manage most of our savings, pensions, retirement funds, insurance assets and national wealth reserves. It primarily focuses on the changing legal understanding of the role and purpose of these institutions in many countries. This includes recognition of the influence that collective investment practices of institutional investors have on society and the greater economy, as well as the corresponding influence that economic health and social stability have on the sustainability of institutional investors' performance and their ability to succeed in meeting long-term goals for the beneficiaries who depend on them and who collectively constitute the societies in which they exist. The *Handbook* is also a testament to the rapidly evolving nature of academic research and public policy discourse concerning institutional investment and financial markets.

These changes are significant, are interrelated and are likely to greatly influence the way in which financial intermediation is conceived of and practiced in the coming decades. Fiduciary duty provides a legal and practical framework that guides the development and implementation of institutional investor practices in response to these changes. While a single volume could not cover all of the relevant dynamics that are shaping

the evolving understanding of fiduciary duty, this *Handbook* features some of the most significant trends.

Institutional investment and fiduciary duty

Over the past few decades, global capital markets have come to be dominated by institutional investors – pension funds, banks, mutual (unit) funds, insurance companies, sovereign wealth funds and other collective investment vehicles. These institutions control the majority of financial assets in most industrialized countries, and are thereby central to the financial well-being of both corporations and individuals. It is almost impossible in contemporary society to find a person or enterprise without a significant relationship to banks, insurance companies and investment funds alike. Furthermore, as the recent financial crisis demonstrated, the activities and inaction of these institutions matter greatly to the well-being of both local and global economies.

The traditional legal understanding of the purpose of institutional investment is predicated on the concept of fiduciary duty. Institutions or individuals, who are the trustees or fiduciaries of funds, are mandated to manage (or organize the management of) assets in the best interests of the individual beneficiaries or investors: the ultimate recipients or owners of the funds. The obvious (but far too often ignored, trivialized or overly simplified) fundamental question is: what are the "interests" of these ultimate investors and beneficiaries?

Their "interests" have over time become equated with short-term "financial interests" as captured by prevailing finance theories. This has led to a widespread and mistaken belief that fiduciary duty is essentially a duty to maximize short-term returns; an almost mathematical approach to institutional investment. One significant consequence is that jobs in the industry have been reserved mainly for financial professionals with narrow analytical training. This has fostered an institutional investment approach that is confined almost exclusively to econometric analyses of risk and performance against artificially constrained benchmarks that do not reflect a full measure of their impacts on, and alignment with, the interests of end beneficiaries in the real world. These developments have resulted in a disconnect between institutional investor practices and a balanced application of fundamental fiduciary principles.

Understanding of fiduciary duty in the current economic, social and academic context is changing. It is important to note that we are hardly the first to notice and highlight these legal and attitudinal changes. Nor, may we add, is this the first time that the landscape of institutional investment and fiduciary duty has gone through significant changes in regard to both theory and practice. Finally, it should be noted that a broader conceptualization of risk (and externalities) is becoming more widely prevalent, with governance implications that extend well beyond the realm of institutional investment.

A changing legal landscape

Fiduciary duty principles have been around for a long time and are well established in common law. However, the understanding and application of them regularly evolve in response to changes in knowledge, as well as in social, financial and economic circumstances and structures. In civil law and mixed civil law/common law jurisdictions, the idea of being a fiduciary (in theory bound to uphold the interests of the ultimate beneficiary or investor based on the idea of a "trust") has in recent decades come into its own via legislation. The consequence is that there is a growing global congruence in the understanding of fiduciary duty across common law and civil law and mixed civil/ common law countries.

A number of local circumstances are affecting the application of fiduciary duty in specific countries. For example, the Kay Review of United Kingdom Equity Markets and Long-Term Decision Making has highlighted the need for clarification of fiduciary duties in response to changing circumstances. But there have also been global developments, reflecting the common human challenges involved in fiduciary relationships.

In the last half of the twentieth century, the interpretation of fiduciary duty principles evolved in response to the efficient market hypothesis and resulted in implementation of new finance theories by institutional owners and investors. This evolution reflected a variety of factors, including the growth of assets under institutional management, innovations in economic theory, the professionalization of financial traders and advisers, and the influence of a variety of stakeholders with material interests in how these relatively recent large institutional owners managed their funds. Many observers today take the financial theory view for granted and feel that "this is the way it always has worked."

This volume argues that we appear to be at the cusp of another fiduciary evolution. There are many causes, such as computerization of the investment industry, globalization of capitalism and financial markets, changes in communication technology, concentration of assets managed by fiduciaries, increasing experience of economic shocks, resource limitations and challenges to key assumptions underlying the application of accepted finance theories posed by recurring market failures and looming externalities.

It is increasingly argued that prevailing finance theories give an impoverished and deeply skewed view of financial value that is focused too much on short-term gains at the expense of sustainable growth over the longer term. Financial industry participants have also focused too much on the individual company, forgetting how companies are interdependent and exert influence on each other throughout the economy. We suggest then that institutional investors do better financially for their beneficiaries by taking a longer term view and also considering systemic issues regarding the sustainability of markets and the interaction of all firms in the economy. This increased emphasis on achieving a balance between short- and long-termism is supported by the fiduciary principle of impartiality: when there are both current income and future interest beneficiaries, fiduciaries should act impartially and not arbitrarily favor the interests of one over the other.

Furthermore, both academics and practitioners increasingly stress the importance of looking beyond what are today's financial concerns (indeed, often too narrowly conceived) to consider wider environmental, social and governance (ESG) matters. What are sometimes called "extra financial" are often "not yet financial." Some institutions have begun to take this to heart and adopted "responsible," "socially responsible" or "sustainable" investment approaches. Indeed, "sustainability" and ESG are rapidly becoming the "talk" of both financial and nonfinancial firms. But "walking the walk" consistently is still very far off. Arguments for an emphasis on ESG factors have been mounted from the fiduciary principle of impartiality, but also from an appeal to beneficiaries' broader interests in a healthy society and planet, as well as from general ethical and precautionary principles. Views of a particular issue can and often have become transformed into a broad social norm and as such can become "material" factors that affect asset prices.

Finally, it is also increasingly argued that fiduciaries need to focus more on their beneficiaries, who are the ultimate investors. For too long, the direction of investment funds has been set by professionals in the finance industry who are likely to have a rather different world view and set of priorities than the average investor or beneficiary. Personal interests and behavioral biases have also affected the perceptions of investment professionals and how they implement responsibilities, often without an understanding of how those factors influence the process. This *Handbook* includes contributions from authors who encourage further recognition of these effects and from authors who seek greater clarity in understanding of the interests of beneficiaries and end investors, perhaps even with some input into the investment decisions of their fund.

A changing research landscape

A parallel development has been a surge in academic interest in issues related to institutional investment and fiduciary duty from a broadened range of disciplines and perspectives. Over the past few years, we have seen highly relevant research from such diverse academic fields as finance, management, organizational design, behavioral economics, sociology, anthropology, geography and philosophy. These fields, new to previously established canons of finance, can add a lot. Jean-Claude Trichet, former President of the European Central Bank, noted: "as a policymaker during the crisis, I found the available [economic and financial] models of limited help. In fact, I would go further: in the face of the crisis, we felt abandoned by conventional tools." Trichet goes on to appeal for inspiration from a multitude of disciplines – physics, engineering, psychology and biology – to help better explain the economic landscape (in Davies 2012).

Economics professor and former IMF chief economist, Raghuram Rajan argues:

> three factors largely explain our collective failure [in predicting the crisis]: specialization, the difficulty of forecasting, and the disengagement of much of the profession from the real world. Like medicine, economics has become highly compartmentalized – macroeconomists typically do not pay attention to what financial economists or real-estate economists study, and *vice versa*. Yet, to see the crisis coming would have required someone who knew about each of these areas – just as it takes a good general practitioner to recognize an exotic disease. Because the profession rewards only careful, well-supported, but necessarily narrow analysis, few economists try to span sub-fields (Rajan 2011).

Purpose and use of this *Handbook*

The *Handbook* is an attempt to collect current information and thought on the application of fiduciary duty principles and insights into factors that will shape evolution of fiduciary practices over the next decade. It contains both global and local market perspectives, in recognition of the roles that each plays in shaping understanding and application of shared fiduciary principles. Current thinking from related fields is surveyed, and the *Handbook* intentionally presents forward-looking, interdisciplinary perspectives, with the recognition that institutions guided by fiduciary principles have experienced declining success in meeting their goals and are facing challenges that extend beyond the boundaries of finance theory.

The *Handbook* reflects the belief that social, demographic, economic and physical changes in the environment in which fiduciaries operate (and in the knowledge base available to them) have presented an opportunity for introspection, learning and evolution in understanding and implementing fiduciary practices. The starting point is a focus on intergenerational equity, which recognizes that fiduciary duties extend to the human beings who are intended beneficiaries rather than to an inanimate collective legal entity. This provides a foundation for application of interdisciplinary advances in the understanding of human behavior and of environmental and human systems to fiduciary practices, within the context of current circumstances.

The volume presents a unique collection of input from various perspectives that we hope will be helpful for scholars interested in a broad range of issues connected to institutional investment and fiduciary duty. It should also be instructive for students who are new to the area and unfamiliar with current changes in both theory and practice regarding financial institutions. Finally, and perhaps most importantly, we hope it will be a good read for investment professionals, asset owners and corporate investees alike, who might not have considered current changes in interpretation and application of fiduciary duty principles to institutional investment. The *Handbook* attempts to provide tools for fiduciaries to better meet the challenges of their journey from the world of the twentieth to the twenty-first century.

A brief overview of the contents

The *Handbook* is organized into six parts with different but complementary themes.

Part I provides a global outlook on current (changes in) interpretations of the fiduciary duties of institutional investors, highlighting many similarities between countries but also some significant differences. Waitzer and Sarro (Chapter 2) review the efforts of the Supreme Court of Canada to develop a broader conceptual framework for fiduciary obligations and consider steps that might be taken to address them in the context of pension fund administration. The chapter concludes by considering the trajectory of the law and how it appears to be positioning fiduciaries with public responsibilities. Youngdahl (Chapter 3) provides an overview of current fiduciary duty principles in the United States, including those contained in common law and in the Employee Retirement Income Security Act (ERISA), with an eye to identifying evolving standards and challenges faced by fiduciaries. Fox (Chapter 4) considers the governance and accountability mechanisms that operate in United Kingdom pension schemes and, in particular, analyzes the central role that trustees play in the fiduciary relationships that they have with a variety of stakeholders. Noble (Chapter 5) reviews the development of Australia's "hybrid" superannuation system, with special emphasis on recent reforms and current governance and investment challenges. Sandberg, Siegl and Hamilton (Chapter 6) survey and discuss the Swedish regulatory environment for institutional investment and are particularly interested in whether, and how, it promotes responsible investment practices. The chapter also includes a case study of the AP funds. Finally, Maatman (Chapter 7) provides an overview of the structure and regulation of the Dutch pension system and associated fiduciary duties.

Part II presents a selected landscape of fiduciary institutions and their practices in a variety of contexts. Johnson and Viederman (Chapter 8) examine the relationship between the charitable purposes of nonprofit organizations and fiduciary obligations, including how they relate to trust and endowment monies. Beeferman (Chapter 9) argues that the current dominant understanding of fiduciary duty is overly narrow regarding defined benefit pension plans. He concentrates on the role of trustees in understanding the prudent person rule and argues for a more comprehensive view of the scope of fiduciary duty to encompass broader issues beyond narrowly defined portfolio returns. Hebb and Zanglein (Chapter 10) focus on economically targeted investments (ETIs) under ERISA in the United States, suggesting that over time and in spite of apparent interpretive changes by the regulator, the application of fiduciary duty in regard to ETIs has not changed significantly. Diaz-Rainey, Finegan, Ibikunle and Tulloch (Chapter 11) explore the role of institutional investment in the European Union Emissions Trading Scheme, arguing that investment in carbon increases portfolio diversification benefits while carrying some unusual risks. Perino (Chapter 12) looks at investors' rights in the United States under the 1995 Private Securities Litigation Reform Act (PSLRA), examining how the involvement of institutional investors has impacted outcomes of corporate fraud lawsuits. Finally, Molinari (Chapter 13) looks at fiduciary duty in the United Kingdom, focusing on the shrinking space for fiduciary obligation to beneficiaries at the very moment when they are in need of it the most.

Part III develops several of the themes underlying the previous parts by challenging conventional wisdom about fiduciary duty. Bernstein and Hawley (Chapter 14) question whether the search for alpha (above-market, risk-adjusted returns) is a breach of fiduciary duty when sought by institutional investors pursuing an active stock picking strategy. They argue that the alpha hunt is a zero or negative sum game when practiced on a large scale. Hoepner and Zeume (Chapter 15) examine the relation between so-called "sin stocks" (tobacco, alcohol) and fiduciary duty, suggesting that real world "sin stock" portfolios do not outperform their benchmarks and that hence fiduciary duty does not legitimize or even encourage overly sinful investment. Thamotheram and Ward (Chapter 16) develop the idea that "risk" as traditionally analyzed is far too narrow. They suggest that a clear focus on the end beneficiary would remedy this situation. Gramlich (Chapter 17) examines problems of both financial and other forms of sustainability in terms of systemic risk and argues that, without an ethical compass, sustainability is not likely to succeed. Huang, Ingram, Terry and Thompson (Chapter 18) look at the fiduciary duty of impartiality through the lens of cultural theory and from the vantage point of stakeholder analysis in order to understand how stakeholders with different views respond to uncertainty. Eshraghi and Taffler (Chapter 19) look at financial and market behavior from the perspective of emotional finance, focusing in particular on how such

a perspective explains behaviors of institutional investors and what that implies prospectively.

Part IV highlights scholarship that aims to develop (or critically discuss the possibility of) a broader interpretation of fiduciary duty to include environmental, social and governance (ESG) dimensions. Clark (Chapter 20) rereads pivotal court cases on fiduciary duty in order to reveal the historical origins and function of the concept. He suggests a reconceptualization of the practice of investment that further emphasizes sustainability. Urwin (Chapter 21) considers how the evolving application of fiduciary duty affects pension funds' investment exposures to ESG factors. He specifically highlights broader interpretations of fiduciary duty that lead to the inclusion of ESG policy in practice. Lydenberg (Chapter 22) seeks a broader interpretation of fiduciary duty that replaces the prevalent focus on rational activity (maximizing what is in one's self-interest) with a standard of reasonableness (activity guided by principles needed for societal cooperation). Sandberg (Chapter 23) reviews attempts at reinterpreting fiduciary duty and takes a more pessimistic stance about the possibility of justifying socially responsible investment in this way. Instead, he proposes an alternative legal framework with independent social and environmental obligations. Darr (Chapter 24) relates the results of a set of interviews with fiduciary "insiders," which demonstrates that broader societal expectations of institutional investors are increasing, although these societal expectations may not yet constitute an enforceable legal duty. Finally, Guyatt (Chapter 25) argues that a combination of new tools, evolving beliefs and industry conventions is integral to supporting a broader interpretation of fiduciary duty. While some challenges remain, she thinks the building blocks are in place for change to be meaningful and sustained.

Part V aims to give voice to the viewpoints of the ultimate fund beneficiaries or investors and discusses potential roles for them in investment decision-making. Berry and Scanlan (Chapter 26) outline the legal case for pension fund beneficiaries to have a greater say in investment policy – both proactively, by having their views taken into account in the formulation of policy, and reactively, by being empowered to hold fiduciaries to account for decisions made on their behalf. They also address common legal and practical objections to such involvement and explore how these play out in practice through real-world case studies. Sandberg, Jansson, Biel and Gärling (Chapter 27) present the results of empirical research on the attitudes of beneficiaries, specifically on how beneficiaries define their own "best interests" and whether they think that fund managers should include social, ethical and environmental concerns in investment decisions. Correspondingly, Barkemeyer, Figge, Hahn, Hoepner, Liesen and Neher (Chapter 28) present the results of empirical research on the sustainability-related perceptions and priorities of practitioners in socially responsible investment, and argue that the general mismatch with such perceptions in society creates a "nonfinancial fiduciary duty problem." Finally, Nilsson (Chapter 29) discusses what current knowledge regarding retail investors' views and preferences can indicate about the likely attitudes of the beneficiaries of large institutional investors, with a particular focus on whether one can expect such beneficiaries to have stable and reasonable preferences in the complex context of financial investment.

Part VI concludes with chapters on fiduciary duty and governance. Ambachtsheer and Pollice (Chapter 30) examine the role and growth of multi-stakeholder paradigms as a form of "soft law" in regulating and influencing corporate behavior by various types of financial institutions. Eccles, Herron and Sarafeim (Chapter 31) look at the fiduciary roles of corporate board members, suggesting that investment fiduciaries have something important to learn from corporate boards, which extends beyond "shareholder primacy." Krzus (Chapter 32) explores the role of private sector initiatives to promote integrated reporting and sustainability accounting, arguing that there are significant business benefits from such approaches. Weller (Chapter 33) looks at the detrimental impact of short-term corporate practices in the nonfinancial sector of the US economy. He argues that they undermine many corporate governance activities. Waddell (Chapter 34) examines the role of pension fund trustees in implementing their fiduciary duties, focusing on recommendations of

the Stanford Institutional Investor Forum. Cadman and Maraseni (Chapter 35) analyze survey data that suggests the governance of institutional investors needs to take account of a broader range of principles and stakeholders than it typically does. The part concludes with Davis (Chapter 36), who takes these themes further by arguing that dominant institutional investor governance practices are characterized by widespread failures that impede effective investor monitoring, stewardship and governance activities, making some of their actions perverse. He proposes a number of remedies.

Acknowledgements

Putting together this *Handbook* has been a significant task, both in terms of time and complexity. It would not have been possible without the support of several organizations and individuals, whom the editors would like to thank. Three organizations have jointly encouraged and supported this substantial undertaking. In alphabetical order they are the Network for Sustainable Financial Markets (SFM), the Principles for Responsible Investment Academic Network (PRI AN), and the Sustainable Investment Research Platform (SIRP). The editors would like to thank all authors who contributed to this *Handbook*, especially for their patience during a prolonged submission process. We are indebted to James Bezjian, Woomin Kang and Arleta Majoch for their editing assistance, as well as to Paula Parish and Claire Poole for helpful editorial feedback. Last but not least, we want to thank all colleagues and friends whose insightful comments have been invaluable in helping to shape the book.

References

Davies, H. 2012. "Economics in Denial," *Project Syndicate*, August 22, 2012.

Rajan, R. 2011. "Why Did Economists Not Foresee the Crisis?" *Project Syndicate*, February 7, 2011.

PART I

Fiduciary duty: a global outlook

CHAPTER 2

The public fiduciary: a Canadian perspective

EDWARD J. WAITZER AND DOUGLAS SARRO

Introduction

Fiduciary duty is a dynamic concept – one that has responded to changing contexts and worldviews but is firmly rooted in clear and enduring legal principles. As society faces governance challenges, there is a growing recognition of the need to take a longer-term and more systemic view of fiduciary obligations. This challenge is particularly acute in the financial services sector.

The Supreme Court of Canada (the "Court") has focused on developing a coherent view of the nature of fiduciary relationships and the consequences thereof. In doing so, it has extended the scope for fiduciary duties and consequential remedies. After a summary discussion of how fiduciary duties have been applied in the pension fund context, this chapter reviews the efforts of the Court to develop this broader conceptual framework. We then consider, in the context of pension fund administration, steps that might be taken to address and mitigate liability in respect thereof. We conclude by considering the trajectory of the law – why pension fiduciaries are increasingly required to look beyond the immediate "imperatives" of the market to longer-term, systemic concerns, such as intergenerational equity and sustainable development. So positioning fiduciaries with public responsibilities will further alter legal and governance precepts.

The fiduciary obligations of pension fund trustees

Pension trustees are subject to a range of fiduciary obligations, including duties of care, loyalty to the interests of beneficiaries, and obedience to the purposes of the fund. Unlike corporate law (directors' duties are to act in the best interests of the corporation as a whole), trustees' duties are to present and future individual beneficiaries.

Following the collapse of the "South Sea bubble" in the early eighteenth century, English courts of equity required trustees to restrict their investments to government obligations and mortgages. In 1830, an American court took a different approach, instructing trustees "to observe how men of prudence, discretion and intelligence manage their own affairs."[1] The flexibility of this objective behavioral standard was quickly circumscribed.[2] As recently as the 1970s, stock investments were widely viewed as imprudent for trust fiduciaries.[3]

Over time, the market environment made this restrictive approach impractical. Trustees needed to hedge against inflation and the superior performance of equities (and foreign securities) favored diversification. So, too, did growing acceptance of modern portfolio theory, which suggested a portfolio-level approach to investment. With the reintroduction of the "prudence standard" came the repeal of rules prohibiting the delegation of investment responsibilities, recognizing the growing complexity of managing financial assets and the need for trustees to rely on professionals.[4] The prudent person standard was refined in the 1990s by recognizing that prudence should be measured on an overall portfolio basis (rather than by discrete consideration of particular investments), and by

---

[1] *Harvard College* v. *Amory*, 9 Pick. (26 Mass.) 446 (1830).
[2] In *King* v. *Talbot*, 40 NY 76 (1869), a New York court limited trustees to investments in government bonds and mortgages.
[3] See *Restatement (Second) of Trusts* §227, Comment (f) (1959).
[4] See, for example, *Restatement (Second) of Trusts* §171 (1959).

imposing a higher standard of care when a trustee is an investment professional.[5]

Events of the past decade have challenged the narrow application of modern portfolio theory as the basis for prudent investment and risk management practices. For example, it is now broadly accepted that most funds' returns come from general exposure to the market (beta) rather than seeking market benchmark outperformance strategies (alpha) (Ibbotson 2010).[6] This makes systemic market factors critical to fiduciary responsibility. Pension fiduciaries are increasingly expected to consider questions of future value and "to assess the impact of their investment decisions on others, including generations to come," with all the uncertainties so entailed (Lydenberg 2013: 11). Risk management for pension funds extends well beyond that which is captured by market benchmarks, extending to market integrity, systemic risks, governance risks, advisor risks and the like. There is a growing recognition that projects (and asset classes) of longer duration often yield the highest private (and social) returns.

To the extent it is unlikely that current governance frameworks will facilitate a smooth transition in the pricing of externalities, there are likely to be inflection points that trigger rapid repricing, with severe consequences for various types of assets (e.g., when a realistic price is placed on carbon emissions). Pension trustees should be considering ways to mitigate consequential risks. A renewed focus on the duty of loyalty – acting in the best interests of beneficiaries (including responsibility for the oversight of supply chain conflicts of interest, precautionary risk management, intergenerational impartiality and the incorporation of sustainability factors into investment management processes) – helps address these concerns.

[5] See, for example, Uniform Prudent Investor Act §§ 2(b), (f) (1994); *Pensions Act 1995* (UK), 1995, c. 26, ss. 33(1), 35, 36(2).
[6] While this concept is widely embraced by academics and market professionals, there remains a significant gap in practice. We suspect that many pension trustees would be hard pressed to explain the difference between alpha and beta in this context and that most continue to assess their managers in relation to benchmarks.

Mapping fiduciary duties: the supreme court of Canada's heroic quest

To determine the relevance of the duty of loyalty, it is useful to examine the principles and purposes that have motivated its development. This is a task that common law courts have generally avoided, preferring a category-based approach, under which relationships are recognized as fiduciary if they fall within (or resemble) the historically recognized categories of fiduciary: trustees, solicitors, corporate directors and partners.

The Court has been an exception. Its singular focus and unique perspective on fiduciary duties can be traced to its need to address Crown liability to Aboriginal peoples. It did so in its 1984 decision *Guerin* v. *The Queen*, where the Court recognized a new class of fiduciary relationship between the Crown and Aboriginal peoples. In doing so, the Court rejected a category-based approach to fiduciary law, stating instead that a relationship is fiduciary in nature in any case where one party (the fiduciary) has discretionary power over the interests of another (the beneficiary), and is obligated to use that power to serve the other's best interests.[7]

In *Hodgkinson* v. *Simms* (1994), the Court offered two related justifications for regulating the use of fiduciary power. First, fiduciary law compensates for beneficiaries' inherent vulnerability to abuse of power by fiduciaries. Because of the often highly specialized nature of fiduciary services, beneficiaries cannot meaningfully monitor the fiduciary's work and must trust the fiduciary to exercise care and look after their best interests. Such a relationship, the Court noted, cannot be "characterized by a dynamic of mutual autonomy," and for this reason, "the marketplace cannot always set the rules."[8] Instead, fiduciary law imposes a higher standard, rooted in norms of loyalty and good faith, to protect clients' interests.

In protecting the interests of individual clients, fiduciary law also seeks to further the interests of the public as a whole. The Court noted that

[7] *Guerin* v. *The Queen*, 2 SCR 335 (1984). See also *Galambos* v. *Perez*, 3 SCR 247 (2009), paras 70, 76.
[8] *Hodgkinson* v. *Simms*, 3 SCR 377 (1994), 422.

fiduciary services are vital to our economy and society at large. Individuals will not trust fiduciaries with their property, or to provide specialized advice, unless they have reason to be confident that fiduciaries will not abuse this trust. This is the second and principal justification for fiduciary law: to bolster public confidence in fiduciary services, and thus secure the economic and social growth these services promise, by "reinforc[ing] the integrity of [the] social institutions and enterprises" through which fiduciaries provide their services.[9]

In defining the social purpose of fiduciary duties, the Court has relied heavily on scholarship chronicling the rise of the "fiduciary society" (Frankel 1983: 802), the central aspect of which is a high degree of specialization in the professions (which is intended to spur knowledge creation and generate wealth for individuals and society as a whole). Specialization makes us more interdependent – it requires us increasingly to trust and rely on the expertise and services of strangers. The rise of the fiduciary society, in this sense, is a classic nonzero-sum game, where every player can benefit, but only so long as these players cooperate with one another. If beneficiaries lose trust in fiduciary services, the game fails and everyone loses.

The Court's understanding of the growing public importance of fiduciary services, along with its belief that fiduciaries serve a public purpose and that fiduciary law exists to respond to changing social needs, has led it to adopt a dynamic approach to determining not just when fiduciary obligations arise but also to their nature and scope. Values of trust and loyalty, shaped by "reasonable expectations," form the basis of the broad fiduciary standards set by the Court. This helps fiduciary law achieve its objective of instilling confidence in fiduciary services in two ways. First, open-textured standards can be more easily adapted to changing social needs. Second, refusing to set bright line standards for fiduciary conduct ideally encourages fiduciaries to err on the side of caution, holding themselves to higher standards as a means of avoiding liability.

The two primary duties flowing from the concept of the fiduciary relationship are the duties of care and loyalty.

[9] Ibid.

The duty of care

A fiduciary's duty of care, skill and diligence has been held to be "at the heart of the fiduciary obligation."[10] One means of achieving the broader purpose of ensuring public confidence in social institutions is to protect beneficiaries from the careless, inept or inattentive exercise of a fiduciary's discretionary power. The Court has articulated the requirement that a fiduciary exercise the same degree of care as "a person of ordinary prudence in managing his or her own affairs."[11] In the case of pension trustees, this standard of care has been elevated by statute, requiring the exercise of the same degree of care that "a person of ordinary prudence would exercise in dealing with the property of *another person.*"[12]

Critics of the prudent person standard include the Ontario Expert Commission on Pensions, which was led by Professor Harry Arthurs (the "Arthurs Report"), which called the standard "very vague," adding that it fails even to "lay down at least the main principles involving investment decisions" (Ontario Expert Commission on Pensions 2008: 85). For instance, the prudent person standard does not make clear who bears the risk of liability when pension trustees delegate their responsibilities, a practice that is commonplace in today's investment environment. The longer the supply chain, the less effective the fiduciary constraint becomes. Legal uncertainty creates perverse incentives for trustees to avoid liability by delegating responsibility, while the delegates in turn try to avoid liability by contracting out of it, by providing advice but not making final decisions, or by seeking indemnity. The result of these actions "can be a circular system in which no one takes responsibility and the interests

[10] *Blueberry River Indian Band* v. *Canada*, 4 SCR 344 (1995), para. 38.
[11] *Ermineskin Indian Band and Nation* v. *Canada*, 1 SCR 222 (2009). See also *Fales* v. *Canada Permanent Trust Co.*, 2 SCR 302 (1976), which sets the standard as that of "a man of ordinary prudence in managing his own affairs."
[12] *Pension Benefits Standards Act, 1985*, RSC 1985, c. 32 (2nd Supp.), s. 8(4), emphasis added. Provincial pension benefits statutes use similar language. This standard is presumed to be a higher one because a person is expected to be more prudent when managing another person's property than when managing his or her own.

of agents trump those of pension beneficiaries"
(Hawley et al. 2011: 9).

In response to such ambiguities, the Arthurs
Report called for the replacement of the prudent person standard with a set of clearer investment rules imposed by statute (Ontario Expert
Commission on Pensions 2008: 86). Such an
approach was adopted in the UK Companies Act
2006, requiring corporate directors to have regard
for the long-term consequences of their decisions,
including their likely effects on stakeholders, the
broader community and the environment.[13] Many
have advocated similar guidance in the institutional
investment context.[14]

The point is that the prudent person standard,
like all aspects of the fiduciary relationship, will be
elaborated and adapted as necessary to meet changing social and economic challenges and expectations. Anticipating how this principle could develop
over the coming years is thus a critical exercise for
pension plan trustees seeking to discharge their
legal duties and minimize legal risk.

The duty of loyalty

With the ascent of modern portfolio theory, the
duty of care came to be interpreted as a convenient
benchmark (and liability shield) for pension fiduciaries insofar as it encouraged them to adhere to
common practices. The hazards of this approach
became evident during the financial crisis. Herding
behavior created market volatility. Excessive reliance on peer comparisons resulted in a shift towards
relative performance metrics rather than a focus on
intergenerationally sound, risk-adjusted returns.

While the duty of care has been the focus of legal
liability in recent years, the duty of loyalty is the
central duty flowing from the fiduciary relationship
(Laby 2004: 78). The social institutions that fiduciary law is intended to protect can function only if
there is reason to trust that fiduciaries will serve the
best interests of their beneficiaries. As the Court
has observed, a loss of this trust will also harm the

public at large, given the significant social interests
served by fiduciary services.[15]

Given the open-textured nature of the duty of
loyalty, courts may develop new rules to respond to
changing social and economic needs. For example,
courts have increasingly held that, in assessing the
best interests of the beneficiary, a fiduciary must
consider not only the beneficiary's narrow pecuniary interests, but the beneficiary's status as a
responsible member of society.[16] This implies
compliance with the law and generally avoiding
conduct that is unethical or otherwise does not
reflect social norms.

The challenge of the duty of impartiality

Assessing, and acting in, the best interests of multiple beneficiaries can be challenging, especially
when the interests of different classes of beneficiaries conflict. In these cases, the duty of loyalty gives
rise to a duty of impartiality or even-handedness.

Impartiality does not mandate equal outcomes,
or even equal treatment. Rather, the duty of impartiality mandates fair treatment, holding that "conduct in administering a trust cannot be influenced
by a trustee's personal favouritism … nor is it
permissible for a trustee to ignore the interest of
some beneficiaries merely as a result of oversight
or neglect."[17] The duty of impartiality also imposes
procedural requirements. Not only must outcomes
reflect due regard for different beneficiaries' interests, but the "process of administration itself,"
including communication with beneficiaries, must
be impartial (Ascher et al. 2006: §17.15).

The duty of impartiality assumes a level of proficiency (and, hence, implies a heightened duty
of care) with respect to long-term value creation

---

[13] Companies Act 2006 (UK), s. 172.
[14] See Getzler (2009: 245), advocating qualitative and quantitative investment restrictions "to recover the public dimension of trust institutions – serving society's financial needs
fairly and effectively."
[15] *Hodgkinson* v. *Simms* (1994), 420–2.
[16] *BCE Inc.* v. *1976 Debentureholders*, SCR 560 (2008)
defines a director's duty of loyalty as being "to act in the best
interests of the corporation *viewed as a good corporate citizen*" (emphasis added). See also Singer (2008); Gold (2009);
Waitzer and Jaswal (2009: 475–7). This emerging standard
may not apply where a pension fund's governing legislation
redefines the trustee's duty of loyalty as a duty to act in the
"best *financial* interests" of plan members.
[17] *Restatement (Third) of Trusts: Prudent Investor Rule*,
§78, Comment (b) (1992).

and risk mitigation. Peter Drucker recognized this challenge in his epilogue to the 1996 edition of *The Unseen Revolution*. Drucker argued for a shift away from short-term thinking in favor of a focus on defining performance (and results) as "maximiz[ing] the wealth-producing capacity of the enterprise" (Drucker 1996: 218); he argued that this should define the role of institutional investors (as well as managerial accountability). This means paying closer attention to reputational and sustainability concerns, which are key to investee companies' ability to generate wealth in the long run, and which often have an intergenerational dimension.

Leaving aside issues regarding adequate tools and incentives to think and act with a view to the long term, there are fundamental concerns about the balancing of competing interests. The question of whether a fiduciary can owe a duty to the interests of multiple parties whose interests may not coincide is not novel, however. As William T. Allen suggested, "anyone trying to understand how our law deals with corporations must have in mind that they are the locus of many conflicting claims, and not all of those claims are wholly economic" (Allen 1992: 280).

These conflicting claims became the focus of the Court's decision in *BCE* v. *1976 Debentureholders*, which reviewed a decision by the directors of BCE Inc. that bondholders alleged was unfairly prejudicial to their interests. The Court held that there is "no principle that one set of interests … should prevail over another set of interests. Everything depends on the particular situation faced by the directors and whether … they exercise business judgment in a responsible way."[18] This means treating stakeholders "equitably and fairly," in accordance with their "reasonable expectations."[19] As previously noted, the meaning of "reasonable expectations" is highly malleable (indeed, somewhat tautological).

The balance of this chapter canvasses legal theories and tools that may assist in breathing life into this duty of impartiality in the context of pension administration. We argue that the result of these theories include obligations on pension fiduciaries to demonstrate respect for social norms, give beneficiaries a voice in decisions that affect their interests, and think and act strategically and collectively. This effectively positions pension fiduciaries with public responsibilities to address long-term social concerns and imposes on them a duty to collaborate with each other in so doing. While this outcome may sound somewhat radical, it reflects fiduciary law's overriding concern with protecting public confidence in fiduciary services. It also reflects the personal and direct (i.e., to beneficiaries with social as well as economic interests) nature of pension trustees' duties and the systemically important role pension funds play in our society.

Respect for social norms and the duty of obedience

Not unlike the duty of impartiality, the legal currency of the "duty of obedience" has waned over the years. However, the concept has been revived in a series of recent US cases focusing on the obligation of corporate actors to have due regard for non-corporate norms. *Caremark*[20] addressed directors' failure to oversee corporate legal compliance systems, finding an obligation to ensure "corporate information and reporting systems" exist to provide "timely, accurate information sufficient to allow management and the board … to reach informed judgments concerning the corporation's compliance with law and its business performance." In *Stone* v. *Ritter*,[21] the court found that the directors will have breached their duty of good faith if they "knew or should have known" of violations of law (in this case, suspicious bank transactions).

The duty of obedience has become "the animating 'ghost'" behind such regimes as the "reasonable expectations" and "good faith" doctrines (see Palmiter 2010–11). The Court's decision in *BCE* reflects this logic, requiring directors to act in the "best interests of the corporation *viewed as a good corporate citizen*" (emphasis added), shaped by

---

[18] *BCE Inc.* v. *1976 Debentureholders* (2008), para. 84.
[19] Ibid., para. 64.

[20] *In re Caremark International Inc. Derivative Litig.*, 698 A.2d 959 (Del. Ct. Ch. 1996).
[21] *Stone* v. *Ritter*, 911 A.2d 362 (Del. Sup. Ct. 2006).

"reasonable expectations."[22] This conception of the duty of obedience furthers the broader public aim of fiduciary duties, by requiring fiduciaries not to undertake unethical actions that would shake public confidence and trust in fiduciaries and the services they provide.

Giving beneficiaries a voice

While our legal systems are infused with the notion of equity and fairness between contemporaries, they have yet to embrace the notion that justice should be facilitated between members of different generations. One exception has been in environmental law, where "sustainable development" legislation is designed to improve environmental decision-making. "Sustainable development" is defined as meeting present needs without compromising the ability of future generations to meet their own needs.[23]

How can we expect better, longer-term decision-making processes when our legal frameworks are still largely reactive and short-term focused? One possibility is to strengthen the voice of beneficiaries in fund governance (Richardson 2011: 597). The OECD Principles of Occupational Pension Regulation suggest that beneficiaries in defined contribution plans should be allowed to have a voice in the choice of their investment options (OECD 2004).[24] Likewise, several jurisdictions require plan member representation on trustee boards in certain circumstances.[25] While not "representative"

in a literal sense, they can play an important role in linking plan beneficiaries to plan governance.

The idea of giving beneficiaries a voice accords with fiduciary law. It helps fiduciaries to fulfill their duties of loyalty and care by improving their understanding of the interests and preferences of beneficiaries. It can reinforce public confidence in pension administration by creating a transparent process by which beneficiaries can learn about and help inform important decisions that affect their interests.

The duty to inform and educate

If beneficiaries are to hold trustees to standards of care and loyalty, they must know what the trust property consists of and how it is being managed. There must be enough information provided so that beneficiaries can make informed requests. The duty should extend as broadly as possible, to protect against the "danger of partiality" (Gallanis 2007: 1627).

In *Froese* v. *Montreal Trust Company of Canada*,[26] Mr. Froese (a pensioner) was not made aware of the fact that his former employer had ceased to make regular contributions to the plan, which, ultimately, resulted in the plan being wound up. He claimed against the trustee for the plan's shortfall. The British Columbia Court of Appeal held that the trustee had a duty to inform the beneficiaries that the pension fund was at risk – this "duty to warn" was simply an aspect of the trustee's general duty of care owed to beneficiaries.

One means of fulfilling this duty to inform, in a way that answers concerns regarding intergenerational equity and sustainable development, may be to embrace concepts such as the intergenerational reports that are required by law in Australia.[27] To

---

[22] *BCE Inc.* v. *1976 Debentureholders* (2008), paras 64, 66, 84.

[23] See, for example, Canadian Environmental Protection Act 1999, SC 1999, c. 33, s. 3; Federal Law on Sustainable Development Act, SC 2008, c. 33, s. 2.

[24] While studies have shown that individuals faced with unstructured investment choices tend to choose overly conservative investments, a plan trustee can correct for this tendency by (1) setting default options for beneficiaries depending on their age and other relevant factors and (2) supplying a "simplified menu" highlighting a limited number of investment options that may also be appropriate for the beneficiary (while giving the beneficiary the option of requesting information on all available alternatives). See Mitchell and Utkus (2006); Huberman et al. (2007).

[25] See, for example, Supplemental Pension Plans Act, RSQ, c. R-15.1, s. 147; The Pension Benefits Act, CCSM c. P.32, s. 28.1(1.2); or Pensions Act 2004, s. 241 (UK). As discussed

below, providing beneficiaries a "voice" can be achieved without board representation, thereby avoiding duty of loyalty concerns.

[26] *Froese* v. *Montreal Trust Company of Canada*, 137 DLR (4th) 725 (BC CA 1996).

[27] Charter of Budget Honesty Act 1998 (Cth.), s. 2(4) ("The Treasurer is to publicly release and table an intergenerational report at least once every 5 years"). For an example of such a report, see Commonwealth of Australia (2010).

be relevant to concerns about distributive fairness, such reports would also need to focus specifically on the needs and perspectives of prospective beneficiaries.

The duty to consult

In a fiduciary relationship, ultimate decision-making authority must rest with the fiduciary alone. But this does not mean that a fiduciary cannot consult with beneficiaries as part of its decision-making process. On the contrary, communication with plan members has long been recognized as a strategic imperative for pension trustees (Hall 2003: 12), and the Arthurs Report argues for both greater transparency from plan trustees and more involvement by plan members in plan governance (Ontario Expert Commission on Pensions 2008: 86). This recommendation echoes calls for a statutory "duty to consult" plan members before trustees take actions that affect plan members' interests.[28] When faced with difficult choices likely to deeply affect beneficiaries' interests, consultation can evidence trustees' prudence and loyalty to the best interests of beneficiaries.[29]

The concepts of consultation and accommodation are closely connected with the concept of the fiduciary relationship developed by the Court. Other fiduciaries that are required to balance competing interests have been required to consult with beneficiaries or stakeholders before taking action that might impair their interests. The Crown, for example, is generally permitted to balance Aboriginal interests against broader public interests.[30] But before engaging in a balancing exercise that may harm Aboriginal rights or title, the Crown must fulfill a formal duty to consult and accommodate those Aboriginals who may be affected by its actions.[31] This is not tantamount to a duty to agree. Rather, it requires that both sides negotiate in good faith and that the Crown take reasonable steps to accommodate Aboriginal interests.

The concept of consultation is familiar to pension law. Pension trustees must look to the interests of different classes of plan members before making decisions that affect their interests. Ontario pension legislation requires trustees to consult with beneficiaries before applying to amend a pension plan in a way "that would ... adversely affect the rights or obligations of a ... person entitled to payment from the pension fund."[32] Federal pension legislation, along with pension legislation in Ontario, British Columbia and Nova Scotia, allow current and former members of a plan to establish an advisory committee to monitor and make recommendations regarding the administration of the plan.[33] Federal legislation provides that, where the trustee is a pension committee, plan members may be represented on that committee if a majority of them so request.[34]

Applying a duty to consult gives existing beneficiaries a voice in pension plan decision-making. The more challenging question is how to provide a voice for contingent beneficiaries. Edith Brown Weiss has suggested giving standing to representatives of future generations in technical and administrative proceedings or appointing a public office charged with "ensuring that positive laws conserving our resources are observed" (Brown Weiss 1989: 120). Sunstein's principle of intergenerational neutrality (i.e., that "the decade of one's birth has no moral relevance any more than

---

[28] See, for example, Watt (2006); Richardson (2011).

[29] In any consultation process, trustees should be alert to the possibility that the plan members they hear from may not be broadly representative of the plan membership as a whole. Plan members close to retirement, for example, may have more time and motivation to make their voices heard than others. Trustees must take care to ensure that any decisions they make are not unduly influenced by any particular group of plan members, but rather reflect the best interests of plan members generally.

[30] *Wewaykum Indian Band* v. *Canada*, 4 SCR 245 (2002), para. 96.

[31] *Haida Nation* v. *British Columbia (Minister of Forests)*, 3 SCR 511 (2004). In *West Moberly First Nations* v. *British Columbia (Chief Inspector of Mines)*, BCCA 247 (2011), the BC Court of Appeal adopted a broad interpretation of the duty to consult, holding that it must include consideration of "cumulative effects" of "past wrongs" and the impact of future developments extending beyond the immediate consequences of the mining exploration permits that were in issue.

[32] Pension Benefits Act, RSO 1990, c. P.8.

[33] Pension Benefits Standards Act, 1985, RSC 1985, c. 32 (2nd Supp.), s. 7.2.

[34] Ibid., s. 7.1.

does one's skin colour or sex") (Sunstein 2007: 269) may be a helpful norm for such surrogates to advocate and monitor, as could the Great Law of the Iroquois, which requires that decisions be made with regard for the impact on the next seven generations (Clarkson et al. 1992).

Existing trust law instruments may be instructive. The use of a "trust advisor," typically to work with the trust's asset managers in reviewing their decisions, dates back a century. A more recent phenomenon is the advent of trust protectors,[35] which gained popularity for investors who seek to use offshore trusts but are reluctant to cede full control of their assets to a foreign trustee. To address this problem, legislation legitimated the concept of a domestic "trust protector," who can have limited powers over the trustee, as well as the trust itself, without defeating the original purpose of the offshore trust (by giving control over the trust assets to the settler or beneficiary).

Consultation and accommodation is a critical element of perspective taking – seeing issues through the eyes of others. Allowing plan members (and representatives for future beneficiaries) to play a role in the decision-making process increases the likelihood that they will see the decision reached by the trustees as fair. It reduces trustees' risk of being held liable by providing strong evidence that the trustees made their decision in accordance with their duties of loyalty and care.

The duty to be strategic

One of the unintended consequences of the intense regulatory focus on risk management and compliance has been to distract attention from the (complementary) need for strategy management and oversight. Ensuring that organizations achieve their purpose (i.e., satisfying their obligations to beneficiaries) requires as much attention to developing and executing strategies as on risk management and operational issues. The challenge may be to refocus legal norms on managing strategy, as well as risk. One commentator has gone so far as to recommend clarifying the fiduciary duties of cor-

porate directors specifically to reflect this role and responsibility.[36]

Institutional capacity to plan for change and understand and adapt in the face of increasing interconnectedness, complexity and accountability requires strong leaders who can think strategically and contextualize and manage expectations as to what may be achieved and in what time frame. In times of stress, it is human nature to adopt a narrow, short-term focus. Underinvestment by fund fiduciaries in broader, longer-term analytic capacity (for example, thinking about the collective macro impacts of their funds' micro-investment decisions) is analogous to underinvestment in physical infrastructure where the consequences are not immediate.[37] Both diminish institutional and systemic resilience, transfer costs to a future cohort and create cascades of collateral damage when there is a failure.

Conclusions: the pressing duty to collaborate

In outlining the Court's extended effort to develop a broader conceptual framework for fiduciary duties (and the public interests so served) and exploring how it might be applied to pension trustees, we have tried to identify emerging and potential obligations (and consequential liabilities) as well as steps that might be taken to effectively address them.

Very few crises respect institutional mandates or jurisdictions. A classic immune system response is swarming – blood clotting when we cut a finger or sneezing when our sinuses are congested. This type of self-organization, the ability to pull an "all hands on deck" reaction, is critical to building resilient institutions and systems. Achieving this level of intelligence and "response-ability" requires extensive networks, within and across organizations, which have to be built up over time,

---

[35] See, for example, Sterk (2006); Ruce (2010).

[36] Grossman (2013) linking this duty to the duty of good faith held to exist in *Caremark* and *Stone* v. *Ritter*.
[37] Martin (2012), arguing that while stock lending by pension funds increased annual returns, it will immeasurably reduce long-term returns.

invested in and nurtured. This is the logic underlying the Court's promotion of the "fiduciary society" concept.

The obstacles to such collaboration have been the subject of academic research since the publication almost fifty years ago of *The Logic of Collective Action*, in which Mancur Olson challenged the "democratic" notion that groups would form and take collective action when doing so would serve their common interests. Instead, he asserted that, absent coercion or direction, "rational, self-interested individuals will not act to achieve their common or group interests" (Olson 1965: 2).

As societies become more complex, self-organized governance regimes that can find nonzero-sum solutions to social problems are not only possible but, increasingly, imperative (Wright 2001). The responsibility of, and opportunity for, pension trustees (and other institutional investors) to have an impact when acting collectively (both among themselves and with asset providers) is great, as is the opportunity cost of defaulting. This reflects the dominance of institutional ownership as well as the challenges of retirement income provision. The scale of such investment pools and the demands on them will attract increasing expectations and scrutiny.

There remains considerable distance between academic and regulatory ideals and the present reality. Institutions remain rationally reticent (see Gilson and Gordon 2013: 867). While shareholder activists fill a gap in governance markets, they often exacerbate the myopic consequences of existing institutional competencies and incentives. They may also help to mask the underlying problem by suggesting that institutions can and will play a more proactive role in corporate governance. The general acceptance of principles of responsible investment, engaged ownership and similar initiatives can easily become a façade to hide behind.

Similar hazards arise from the growing subscription (but not necessarily meaningful commitment or adherence) by institutional investors to "best practice" standards – too often giving rise to an appearance of stewardship by "ticking boxes" with respect to the features (rather than the functions) of good governance. An additional risk is that such standards often presume, incorrectly, "a unique set of appropriate institutional arrangements *ex ante*

and view convergence toward those arrangements as inherently desirable" (Rodrik 2008: 100). By definition, governance is contextual. Worse yet, such standards tend to be backward-looking – based on and reacting to past failures, rather than anticipating where markets will be going. This invites gaming, reactive (politically motivated) regulation and the petrifaction of governance processes. The costs of such reactive governance – both in tangible terms and in public trust – can be immense.

Given the lessons learned, as well as the impact of "universal owners" (Hawley and Williams 2000), it is intuitively compelling that pension fiduciaries should be focusing on ways in which their investments can benefit the whole and, in so doing, mitigate risk and increase return. It is imperative to move beyond a focus on portfolio-level benefits to a consideration of systemic effects – considering how investment can be used to create better markets tomorrow, rather than simply "beating" the market today. This means taking into consideration how investment decisions will affect the stability of financial systems, the direction of the economy and the sustainability of our environment. Put differently, the fact that an investment decision may result in positive relative financial returns over the short term (in which performance management is typically measured) has no bearing on whether such an investment will yield benefits to current or future pension beneficiaries.

Investing is a means for pension fund trustees to ensure the future well-being of beneficiaries. Financial returns are a necessary element but, in considering the interests of beneficiaries, so, too, are other questions. It is in this context that pension trustees become "public" fiduciaries. Given the mission, size and systemic significance of pension funds, this suggests a "duty to collaborate" (and consequential behavioral shifts). This goes beyond seeking cost advantages to the heart of effecting systemic reform.

Acknowledgements

Earlier versions of this chapter appeared in the *Canadian Bar Review* 91 (1): 163–209 and the *Rotman International Journal of Pension*

Management 6 (2): 28–37. The authors thank Keith Ambachtsheer, Peter Chapman, Gordon Hall, Jim Hawley, Steve Lydenberg, Ben Richardson and two anonymous reviewers for providing helpful comments. The authors bear responsibility for all views and errors.

References

Allen, W. T. 1992. "Our Schizophrenic Conception of the Business Corporation," *Cardozo Law Review* 14: 261–81.

Ascher, M. L., A. W. Scott and W. F. Fratcher. 2006. *Scott and Ascher on Trusts*, 5th edn. New York: Aspen Law & Business.

Brown Weiss, E. 1989. *In Fairness to Future Generations: International Law, Common Patrimony, and Intergenerational Equity*. Dobbs Ferry, NY: Transnational Publishers.

Clarkson, L., V. Morissett and G. Régallet. 1992. *Our Responsibility to the Seventh Generation*. Winnipeg: International Institute for Sustainable Development. www.iisd.org/pdf/seventh_gen. pdf.

Commonwealth of Australia. 2010. *Australia to 2050: Future Challenges*. Canberra: Commonwealth of Australia.

Drucker, P. F. 1996. *The Pension Fund Revolution*. New Brunswick, NJ: Transaction Publishers.

Frankel, T. 1983. "Fiduciary Law," *California Law Review* 71: 795–836.

Gallanis, T. P. 2007. "The Trustee's Duty to Inform," *Northern Carolina Law Review* 85: 1595–628.

Getzler, J. 2009. "Fiduciary Investment in the Shadow of Financial Crisis: Was Lord Eldon Right?" *Journal of Equity* 3: 219–50.

Gilson, R. J. and J. N. Gordon. 2013. "The Agency Costs of Agency Capitalism: Activist Investors and the Revaluation of Governance Rights," *Columbia Law Review* 113: 863–928.

Gold, A. S. 2009. "The New Concept of Loyalty in Corporate Law," *UC Davis Law Review* 43: 457–528.

Grossman, N. 2013. "The Duty to Think Strategically." *Louisiana Law Review* 73: 449–508.

Hall, G. M. 2003. *20 Questions Directors Should Ask about their Role in Pension Governance*. Toronto: Canadian Institute of Chartered Accountants.

Hawley, J. P., and A. T. Williams. 2000. *The Rise of Fiduciary Capitalism: How Institutional Investors Can Make Corporate America More Democratic*. Pittsburgh: University of Pennsylvania Press.

Hawley, J. P., K. L. Johnson and E. J. Waitzer. 2011. "Reclaiming Fiduciary Duty Balance," *Rotman International Journal of Pension Management* 4–17.

Huberman, G., S. S. Iyengar and W. Jiang. 2007. "Defined Contribution Pension Plans: Determinants of Participation and Contributions Rates," *Journal of Financial Services Research* 31 (1): 1–32.

Ibbotson, R. G. 2010. "The Importance of Asset Allocation," *Financial Analysts Journal* 66 (2): 18–20.

Laby, A. B. 2004. "Resolving Conflicts of Duty in Fiduciary Relationships," *American University Law Review* 54: 75–149.

Lydenberg, S. 2013. "Reason, Rationality and Fiduciary Duty." *Journal of Business Ethics*. Published electronically February 4, 2013. http://dx.doi.org/10.1007/s10551–013–1632–3.

Martin, R. L. 2012. "The Gaming of Games," *Drucker Society Europe Blog*, October 17. www.drucker-forum.org/blog/?p=190.

Mitchell, O. S. and S. P. Utkus. 2006. "How Behavioral Finance Can Inform Retirement Plan Design," *Journal of Applied Corporate Finance* 18: 82–94.

OECD. 2004. *Recommendation on Core Principles of Occupational Pension Regulation*. Paris: OECD.

Olson, M. 1965. *The Logic of Collective Action*. Cambridge, MA: Harvard University Press.

Ontario Expert Commission on Pensions. 2008. *A Fine Balance: Safe Pensions, Affordable Plans, Fair Rules*. Toronto: Queen's Printer for Ontario.

Palmiter, A. R. 2010–11. "Duty of Obedience: The Forgotten Duty," *New York Law School Review* 55: 457–78.

Richardson, B. 2011. "Fiduciary Relationships for Socially Responsible Investing," *American Business Law Journal* 48 (3): 597–640.

Rodrik, D. 2008. "Second-Best Institutions," *American Economic Review* 98 (2): 100–4.

Ruce, P. J. 2010. "The Trustee and the Trust Protector: A Question of Fiduciary Power. Should a Trust Protector be held to a Fiduciary Standard?" *Drake Law Review* 59: 67–96.

Singer, J. W. 2008. "Corporate Responsibility in a Free and Democratic Society," *Case Western Reserve Law Review* 58: 1–11.

Sterk, S. 2006. "Trust Protectors, Agency Costs and Fiduciary Duty," *Cardozo Law Review* 27 (6): 2761–806.

Sunstein, C. 2007. *Worst Case Scenarios*. Cambridge, MA: Harvard University Press.

Waitzer, E. and J. Jaswal. 2009. "Peoples, BCE and the Good Corporate 'Citizen'," *Osgoode Hall Law Journal* 47: 439–96.

Watt, G. 2006. *Trusts and Equity*, 2nd edn. New York: Oxford University Press.

Wright, R. 2001. *Nonzero: The Logic of Human Destiny*. New York: Vintage Books.

The basis of fiduciary duty in investment in the United States

JAY YOUNGDAHL

Introduction

Any person concerned with issues of institutional investment must understand the various roles that apply to those who undertake financial responsibilities in this field. Such a project should begin with an understanding of fiduciary duty in investment.

At its core, the concept of fiduciary duty is simple. Whatever the particular duties with which a fiduciary may be charged, the basis of all fiduciary responsibility is found in a common human sense, emanating from the nature of the relationship that the fiduciary has with a *beneficiary*. The fiduciary, who often works under the moniker of *trustee*, takes on a responsibility to look after assets belonging to beneficiaries. Viewed from the outside, the fiduciary appears to be the owner of the assets, but in fact, his or her leeway for activity is significantly constrained. Each and every decision made by the fiduciary must be made in the interests of the real owner of the assets, the beneficiary. The fiduciary must be loyal to the beneficiary alone and is obliged to be impartial in protection of his or her interests.[1] The fiduciary's action may not be contrary or adverse to the interests of the beneficiary, whether for his or her own benefit or for the benefit of any nonbeneficiary, and must avoid any situation in which the personal interests of the fiduciary and the interests of the beneficiaries could clash. Other attributes of common sense apply, especially as fiduciary duties must always be exercised in certain historical, investment and political climates.[2]

While circumstances vary in many locations in which fiduciary relationships are found, there is an unbending rigorousness to the basic fiduciary duties. The seminal exposition of this concept can be seen in this quotation from the famous American jurist Benjamin Cardozo:

> A trustee is held to something stricter than the morals of the market place. Not honesty alone, but the punctilio of an honor the most sensitive, is then the standard of behavior. As to this, there has developed a tradition that is unbending and inveterate. Uncompromising rigidity has been the attitude of courts of equity when petitioned to undermine the rule of undivided loyalty by the "disintegrating erosion" of particular exceptions. Only thus has the level of conduct for fiduciaries been kept at a level higher than that trodden by the crowd.[3]

Any consideration of fiduciary duty must begin with this basic understanding.

However, even given this seemingly simple and clear foundation, the application of fiduciary duty to any particular situation today can be complex and problematic. The scope and meaning of fiduciary duties vary widely depending on the location and circumstance of their operation, and this often leads to practical confusion. Two confounding factors are especially important in this regard. The first

---

[1] For commentary and case citations to these duties, see Ascher and Scott (2011); Bogert (2013); *Restatement (Third) of Trusts* § 227, comment e (1992).

[2] Some in the United States argue that the duty of impartiality, which applies to fiduciaries should receive more recognition. "Although ERISA does not spell out the duty

of impartiality to successive beneficiaries ... the courts have occasionally derived it from ERISA's duty of loyalty" (Langbein 2003: 1327); see *Struble* v. *NJ Brewery Employees' Welfare Trust Fund*, 732 F.2d 325, 333 (3d Cir. 1984); "In the rare case in which the conflicted trustee does seek improper advantage, the law responds by enforcing a fairness norm, derived from the duty of loyalty, called the duty of impartiality, which places the trustee 'under a duty to the successive beneficiaries to act with due regard to their respective interests'" (Langbein 2005: 939); see also *Morse* v. *Stanley*, 732 F.2d 1139, 1145 (2d Cir. 1984).

[3] *Meinhard* v. *Salmon*, 164 NE 545, 546 (NY 1928), p. 546.

is that there are many classes of fiduciaries, with each class having different duties. To be successful in navigating the area, any examination must begin with a clear understanding of the nature of the relationship. Only a successful exploration of this relationship will allow a transparent view of how duties should apply. For example, in and around institutions and corporations, there are a number of uses of the term "fiduciary duty." Corporate directors are subject to fiduciary duties, although the duties to which they are subject are significantly less demanding than those held by institutional trustees in investment. Corporate directors' fiduciary duties are also more flexible than those of benefit fund trustees. As a court decision stated more than sixty years ago, "[a]cts which might well be considered breaches of trust as to other fiduciaries have not always been so regarded in cases of corporate officers or directors."[4]

The second important factor for the application of fiduciary duty in investment today is that the application and definition of fiduciary duty in investment have unfortunately become battlegrounds for different interests, different views of the effects of investment on society and different interpretations of the effect of institutional investment on the growth in the financialization of globalized economic activity. As such, claims made in connection with fiduciary duty may reflect an interested stance rather than a dispassionate view.

In addition, within the investment arena itself, the fiduciary duty of certain types of financial advisors has historically differed in regulation and in practice from the fiduciary duty which applies to trustees.[5] For example, a controversy that involved financial advisors and differing interpretations of fiduciary duty to which they are subject from certain regulatory authorities, such as the US Department of Labor and the Securities and Exchange Commission, erupted in 2012 (Schoeff 2012).

While much could be written about these two factors, for the purposes of this overview the result of these definitional difficulties and political considerations is that any consideration of fiduciary duty must begin with a comprehension of the law and regulation which applies to the particular place in which the duty arises and the particular person who wields such duties (DeMott 1988; Smith 2002; Stabile and Zanglein 2007).

The birth of fiduciary duty and a brief history of American trust law

To understand the common sense underpinning of fiduciary duty, a brief overview of the history of the concept and operation of trusts is constructive. This area of law and regulation began in a legal entity known as *trust*, a legal structure in which money or property is held and managed on behalf of another. "Fiduciary" originates from the Latin words *fides* and *fiducia*, meaning faith and trust (*American Heritage Dictionary of the English Language* 2004). While a number of accounts of the origin of the concept exist, the most well-known is that the first trusts that resemble those of the present day were established in the Middle Ages (Krikorian 1989).[6] To protect and preserve wealth while away from his property, a landowning knight often transferred legal ownership of his estate to a close friend or agent. During the absence, the transfer of legal title allowed the friend or agent to have full rights and management responsibilities. Upon the return of the knight, full ownership and control would revert to him.

The separation between equitable ownership and legal ownership is critical to understand the concept of a trust. Many argue that this particular divide began in English courts. Legal ownership was identified and enforced through the common law courts; courts of equity recognized and enforced the equitable ownership. Today, while the

---

[4] *Paddock* v. *Siemoneit*, 218 SW 2d 428, 432 (TX 1949).
[5] Subsequent to the passage of the Employee Retirement Income Security Act (ERISA), which gave certain regulatory authority to the US Department of Labor, the Department issued a number of pieces of regulatory advice defining fiduciary duties, or the lack thereof, which apply to various types of financial professional who work with trustees. See Department of Labor Interpretative Bulletin (1996); Department of Labor Advisory Opinion (2005).

[6] The history has been traced back farther to Roman and Salic law, and precursors of modern trusts can be found in Islamic law. See Avini 1996.

two concepts remain distinct, the same court generally enforces both interests. The legal owner of the trust, the *trustee*, retains the right to possession, the privilege of use and the authority to transfer those rights and privileges. However, the trustee looks like the owner of the property.[7] Beneficiaries continue to be recipients of the benefits of the assets in the trust and retain the equitable title of trust assets.

The first institution chartered in the United States in the business of trusts was the Farmer's Fire Insurance and Loan Company of New York, in 1822 (Edwards and Willis 1922).[8] The need to raise money for new business ventures produced a need for corporate trusts. The number of trusts and institutions with trust departments grew in the following years.

The regulation of various matters involving Native Americans led to the next major expansion of the use of trusts. The relationship between sovereign native peoples residing in the United States and local, state and national governmental entities in the country has always been complex. In 1906, Congress passed the Burke Act, which was intended "to accelerate the assimilation of the Indians by truncating the length of the trust period and benefits derived there from for Indians determined to be competent."[9] While the Act was directed toward the real property rights of Native Americans, the legislation also enabled banks to serve as trustees in unrelated areas (25 USC § 349). By 1920, more than a thousand banks offered trust services (Shenkman 1997).

The realization of the importance of work-related benefits for workers produced the next spurt of growth for trusts. In the 1940s, in the years after the Great Depression, employment benefit

trusts became exceedingly popular (Wooten 2004). Money for pension and other benefits for workers was pooled to allow certain economies of scale and protection for promised entitlements. However, concerns over the operation of these trusts soon grew. In response to the concerns, in 1974 the US Congress passed the Employee Retirement and Income Security Act (ERISA), which codified the general responsibilities of trustees managing funds (29 USC § 18). By the early 1980s, thousands of banks, trust companies and other entities were managing more than $220 billion in employee benefit trusts (Wooten 2004).[10]

The employment retirement and income security act of 1974 (ERISA)

Today, trustees of pension and employee benefit funds are responsible for trillions of dollars held to provide benefits for American workers.[11] The most important single legal and regulatory source for their fiduciary and other duties can be found in a federal statute, the Employee Retirement and Income Security Act of 1974 (ERISA).

Prior to the passage of ERISA, American policymakers became more and more troubled by the paucity of adequate federal regulation of employee pension plans. An NBC Reports television documentary titled *Pensions: The Broken Promise* (1972), which aired on September 12, 1972, detailed the inadequacies of pension fund regulation and the loss of benefits by many who had counted on them. This television program has been credited with helping to bring national attention to the issue and leading congressional hearings that

---

[7] Under the Uniform Trust Code (UTC), forms of which are applicable in certain states, the term "beneficiary" is defined as a "person that a) has a present or future beneficial interest in a trust, vested or contingent; or b) in a capacity other than that of a trustee holds a power of appointment over the trust property" (UTC § 103(3)).

[8] The first important American case defining the duties of trustees was decided a few years later. *Harvard College* v. *Amory*, 26 Mass. 446, 9 Pick. 461 (1830).

[9] *County of Thurston* v. *Andrus*, 586 F.2d 1212, 1219 (8th Cir. 1978), p. 1219.

[10] ERISA applies only to certain classes of benefit plans. For the purposes of this overview the major classes of funds which are not subject to direct ERISA strictures are state and local public benefits plans.

[11] Globally, the monies accumulated for workers' benefits are extraordinarily large. Before the stock market decline in the last quarter of 2008, just one class of trust entity, defined benefit pension funds in the United States that are affiliated with unions or unionized public employers, held assets in excess of $3 trillion (Investment Company Institute Research Fundamentals 2006).

enacted ERISA.[12] As noted in a report of the US Pension Benefit Guaranty Corporation:

> Until 1974, there was little or no protection for pensions. Because of shocking instances of workers losing their retirement benefits (most notably in 1963 when 4,000 Studebaker auto workers lost some or all of their promised benefits), Congress in 1974 took action to prevent such tragedies by enacting the Employee Retirement Income Security Act (ERISA) (Pension Benefit Guaranty Corporation 2010).

ERISA does not direct the establishment of pension plans, or require a minimum level of benefits. What it does is to decide which plans are covered by federal oversight and provide a scheme of regulation covering the administration of a pension or employee benefit plan once it has been established. For example, ERISA provides direction as to the necessary governing documents of the plan, the information that must be included therein, and identifies which individuals hold legal responsibility for the operation and administration of the plan (ERISA § 402(a)(1)). Such mandates may seem mundane, but ERISA gives the US Department of Labor broad leeway to regulate the area.

ERISA Section 404(a) defines the meaning of fiduciary duty in investment for plans it covers. The relevant language is as follows:

(a) Prudent man standard of care.
  (1) Subject to sections 403(c) and (d), 4042, and 4044 [*29 USCS §§ 1103(c)*, (d), 1342, 1344], a fiduciary shall discharge his duties with respect to a plan solely in the interest of the participants and beneficiaries and –
    (A) for the exclusive purpose of:
      (i) providing benefits to participants and their beneficiaries; and
      (ii) defraying reasonable expenses of administering the plan;
  (B) with the care, skill, prudence, and diligence under the circumstances then prevailing that a prudent man acting in a like capacity and familiar with such matters would use in the conduct of an enterprise of a like character and with like aims;
  (C) by diversifying the investments of the plan so as to minimize the risk of large losses, unless under the circumstances it is clearly prudent not to do so; and
  (D) in accordance with the documents and instruments governing the plan insofar as such documents and instruments are consistent with the provisions of this title and title IV.

As the financial arena has gotten more complex, compliance with the US Department of Labor rules has increased the cost and complexity of plan administration. And, where it applies, ERISA is a powerful statute, as it pre-empts or supersedes "any and all State laws insofar as they … *relate to* any employee benefit plan covered by ERISA" (ERISA § 514(a)).[13] Legal action of "relating to" has been found in numerous areas in which states have attempted to act in areas of insurance and employee benefits. Many find these to be positive developments.

ERISA is not without critics, however. These voices generally focus on the argument that its seemingly simple words have produced an undulating maze of legal and regulatory interpretations. Many claim that the American judiciary has given the law authority not intended by legislators. As a recent legal critic wrote, the history of ERISA "is also a study in the power that legislative words do not have over judges" (Stumpff Morrison 2011: 101). A second concern is whether

---

[12] This television report won a prestigious Peabody Award and praise from the American Bar Association. For more information on the documentary and its influence on Congress, see Raphael (2005). Interestingly, one review credits the infamous murder of Joseph Yablonski, Sr., a prominent American labor leader for much of the impetus that propelled ERISA through Congress. It argues that Yablonski's death gave pension reform advocates, such as influential Senator Jacob Javits, an opportunity for legislation (Schneider and Pinero 2011).

[13] See also *Cal. Div. of Labor Standards Enforcement* v. *Dillingham Construction, NA*, 519 US 316, 324–5 (1997) (stating that state law relates an ERISA-covered plan if the law specifically refers to such a plan; "acts immediately and exclusively upon" the plan; or if the plan's existence "is essential to the law's operation"). The extent of this relationship remains an unsettled issue in the United States and is sure to be subject to judicial scrutiny in the near future.

protection against dubious investment decisions, a central concern of the drafters, needed such a sweeping statute. Embezzlement of plan funds was already illegal under state and previously existing federal law. The principal problem that Congress perceived, and which led to a new regime under ERISA of *prohibited transactions* and related fiduciary requirements, seems largely to have been one of uneven enforcement. And many argue that its application produced, "the anomaly of interpreting ERISA so as to leave those Congress set out to protect – the participants in ERISA governed plans and their beneficiaries – with less protection ... than they enjoyed before ERISA was enacted."[14]

As mentioned above, ERISA applies only to certain classes of private employee benefit trusts. Many such funds that appear to be similar and that generally cover public employees are not subject to this federal statute, but are subject to state and local law and regulation. This situation produces varied notions of fiduciary duty in investment and thus causes consternation to trustees and fund attorneys alike.[15] In 2000, noting the resulting complex matrix of fiduciary duty in state and local based plans, the National Conference of Commissioners on Uniform State Laws made the first attempt at codifying these common state and local law practices relating to American trusts and estates into a uniform statutory code, the Uniform Trust Code (UTC).[16] Today, more than twenty states have adopted some form of the UTC. The UTC followed the preparation by the same body of a related model statute, the Uniform Prudent Investor Act (UPIA), which has been adopted by the vast majority of American states (76 American (Second) Jurisprudence 2011, § 477).[17]

But in spite of the lack of universal reach or the merits of the opinions as to the need for ERISA, the statutory language of ERISA, the regulatory and judicial interpretation of it and the advice given to fund trustees as to its meaning remain the most important sources for understanding of fiduciary duty for investment decisions undertaken by trustees.

Modern portfolio theory and the twentieth century evolution of the concept of fiduciary duty in investment

While, as Judge Cardozo observed, the basic concept of fiduciary duty in investment must be rigid and consistent, the practical application of the concept itself has been quite malleable. Attention to this history is useful as one thinks about the potential future of the concept. Further, as with many areas of American jurisprudence, the law and regulation of the trustee investing function have been interpreted and reinterpreted as new situations have led to new analyses and rules.

Before the prudent investor rule was adopted in 1992, with its basis in modern portfolio theory, fiduciary duties looked very different.[18] The *Restatement (Second) of Trusts*, a book of legal precedents produced by the American Law Institute, which became effective in 1959, contained the prudent man rule, which served to guide decisions made in investment.[19] This rule mandated

---

[14] *Mertens* v. *Hewitt Associates*, 508 US 248, 267 (1993), p. 267.

[15] For example, the largest funds in the United States, such as the California Public Employees Retirement System are not subject to ERISA, but to laws and regulations promulgated by the state of California. Many employee benefit funds exist in the United States are not subject to ERISA. However, as discussed herein, the main language and interpretation of ERISA cast a long shadow over state and local laws and regulations, which apply to these non-ERISA funds.

[16] The Uniform Trust Code is available at the website of the National Conference of Commissioners of Uniform State Laws; http://uniformlaws.org/Act.aspx?title=Trust%20Code.

[17] For an interesting view of the UPIA, see Taibbi (2010). In addition, many state legislatures have promulgated legislation, which regulates practices and activities of pension funds in their states. However, it must be observed that in spite of these diverse legal frameworks, differences in conceptions of fiduciary duty in investment between ERISA and non-ERISA covered funds are seldom crucial for the discussion herein.

[18] There can be no doubt about the influence of modern portfolio theory on the drafters of *Restatement (Third) of Trusts*. The explanatory article by the reporter contains dozens of references to this investment theory (Halbach 1992a).

[19] After ERISA, the *Restatements of Trusts* are the most influential source of legal analysis when considering fiduciary duty in investment.

that trustees invest trust assets as a "prudent man" would invest his own estate (76 American (Second) Jurisprudence 2011, § 360). This standard was a significant alteration of the old rules that had previously directed that trust asset could only be invested in safe financial instruments, such as US government bonds. The prudent man rule required trustees to protect the needs of the beneficiaries by maintaining the "corpus of the trust" – the principal, and the amount and reliability of the income.[20]

The investment duty as defined under this prudent man rule would appear quite odd at present. For example, using this standard, the *Restatement (Second) of Trusts* contained language defining the following as improper investments:

> The (1) purchase of securities for purposes of speculation, for example, purchase of shares of stock on margin or purchase of bonds selling at a great discount because of uncertainty where they will be paid on discount because of uncertainty whether they will be paid on maturity; (2) purchase of securities in new and untried enterprises; (3) employment of trust property in the carrying on of trade or business; (4) purchase of land or other things for resale.[21]

Thus, today a perusal of the assets in any significant employee benefit fund will show all manner of investments that would have been prohibited under the prudent man rule. Trustees and investment committees today invest in junk bonds, speculative securities, property, stock in start-up companies and even on the purchase of entire shaky enterprises.[22]

The *Restatement (Third) of Trusts* was issued by the American Law Institute in 1992. Recognizing the divergence between modern Wall Street practices of investment management and the commands of the *Restatement (Second) of Trust*, the authors of the new *Restatement* – judges, academics and lawyers – wrote that the prudent man rule in the *Restatement (Second) of Trusts* improperly constrained the opportunities of investments by trustees, and exposed the trustees to liability if they chose "impermissible" investment vehicles. The definition of *duty* in their previous volume, they found, conflicted with "modern asset management practices."[23] And, as part of this significant movement, *Restatements (Third) of Trusts* enshrined adherence to modern portfolio theory as the test of fealty to proper fiduciary duty in investment (Halbach 1992a).[24] Investment techniques that had been considered forbidden just a few years before were now the preferred method of action.

In the aftermath of the change, "[t]he trustee is under a duty to the beneficiaries to invest and manage the funds of the trust as a prudent investor would, in light of the purposes, terms, distribution requirements, and other circumstances of the trust."[25] Today, as well, there is a requirement that a trustee employ "reasonable care, skill and caution."[26] Today's common standard often evaluates prudence by assessing the actual volatility of return – or *risk*, as it is commonly referred to in economic literature – with respect to the proper level of such return in relation to the risk in each

---

[20] *Restatement (Second) of Trusts* (1959), § 227. The recognized overarching principle behind this rule is that a trustee must "observe how men of prudence, discretion and intelligence manage their own affairs, not in regard to speculation, but in regard to the permanent disposition of their funds, considering the probable income, as well as the probable safety of the capital to be invested." *Harvard College* v. *Amory*, 26 Mass. (9 Pick.) 446, 461 (1830).

[21] *Restatement (Second) of Trusts* (1959), § 227 comment f.

[22] In addition, all manner of derivatives of investment vehicles are purchased with trust funds, including such inscrutable products as "structured investment vehicles" and "synthetic CDOs." Many such investments failed during the crisis of 2008 and the financial consequences remain the subject of litigation today.

[23] *Restatement (Third) of Trusts* (1992), § 227.

[24] Halbach further expanded his writing on the topic (Halbach 1992b). See also *Restatement (Third) of Trusts* (1992), § 227 comment e. While modern portfolio theory was enshrined into the legal duty of a fiduciary in 1992 in the *Restatement (Third) of Trusts*, it had been the subject of vigorous debate and growing acceptance in the investment community for over fifteen years. In 1977, just after a particularly difficult investment period in 1973–4, *Institutional Investor* magazine published an article entitled "Modern Portfolio Theory: How the New Investment Technology Evolved." The magazine considered modern portfolio theory a "revolution," arguing that it proved that previous investment strategies were "inefficient, illogical, ill-conceived and frequently erroneous" (Bernstein 2005: 256).

[25] *Restatement (Third) of Trusts* (1992), § 227.

[26] UPIA (2002), § 2(a).

investment portfolio. A leading legal hornbook on ERISA describes the investing duties of trustees as follows: "[f]iduciaries must choose investments based upon financial analysis, taking into account the risk of loss and the opportunity for income or other gains associated with the investment."[27] Interpretations of ERISA section 404(a) generally follow this prudent investor interpretation, in spite of its use of the term "prudent man." But the dominance of modern portfolio theory, which underlies the prudent investor rule, is now being called into question. Many wonder why strict adherence to this theory is often a sole touchstone for proper application of fiduciary duty. As with the upheaval in investment theory after the troubles of 1973 and 1974 which helped lead to the adoption of modern portfolio theory, the financial difficulties of 2008 exposed serious problems in today's predominant theory of investing and risk aversion. In 2010, Professor Paul Woolley wrote that, "[m]uch has come to pass in financial markets in the last ten years that has been at odds with the prevailing academic wisdom of how capital markets work" (2010: 121). For example, the systemic risk to a portfolio has been shown to have been unanticipated by drafters of this theory.[28]

Paradoxically, like other areas in which an ascendant theory conquers all others, a number of serious and harmful unintended consequences have arisen.[29] Steve Lydenberg of Domini Social Investments (2009) wrote the following:

> The dominant theory of investing today, Modern Portfolio Theory, is based on a definition of success that fails to acknowledge the extent to which investments at the portfolio level can affect the overall financial markets. In particular, its

techniques for controlling risk at the portfolio level – diversification, securitization, and hedging – can actually increase market-level risks to the detriment of finance and the economy as a whole. In addition, the benefits that accrue from the practice of this theory are at best part of a zero-sum game and available to only a limited number of investors. In addition, the more investors that adopt its practices, particularly risk-control techniques, the less likely these practices are to succeed. Reform of this theory is not sufficient. Alternatives are needed (Lydenberg 2009).[30]

Other difficulties seem to exist as well. "Short-termism" in investment outlook is contrary to the long-term duties trustees have to beneficiaries, as the core duty of benefit funds involves the provision of benefits over the long term. Unfortunately, the current practices of investment theory and measurement have led to a singular focus on quarterly results. John Bogle (2011), the former leader of the Vanguard investment company, argues that in the recent era the culture of long-term investment has been swamped by a culture of short-term speculation. Further, the Center for Financial Market Integrity, an arm of the CFA Institutes, the body that regulates many financial professionals, has recognized that:

> The obsession with short-term results by investors, asset management firms, and corporate managers collectively leads to the unintended consequences of destroying long-term value, decreasing market efficiency, reducing investment returns, and impeding efforts to strengthen corporate governance (Ethics World 2006).

Business leaders have concerns as well, with one of their trade groups, the Business Roundtable, criticizing short-termism in 2006, decrying it as "excessive focus of some corporate leaders, investors, and analysts on short-term, quarterly earnings and a lack of attention to the strategy, fundamentals, and conventional approaches to long-term value creation" (Hess 2007: 224).

Thus, unyielding allegiance to modern portfolio theory appears to be inadequate to engender superior activity by trustees in their investment duties.

---

[27] In addition, under this "whole portfolio" approach, the prudence of an investment is judged not in isolation, "but with reference to the role that the investment plays in the entire fund" (Serotta and Brodie 2007: 542).

[28] This is recognized by practitioners as well as academics, and efforts are underway to deal with this omission (White 2012).

[29] Examples might include problems associated with widespread use of common antibiotics, which have resulted in viruses that are immune to these medicines, or the burgeoning problems associated with certain herbicides and pesticides, which are resulting in unwelcome chemically resistant weeds and plants.

[30] See also Bernstein (2005).

It is time for operative conceptions of fiduciary duty today to reflect this reality.[31]

The current upheaval in the environment of fiduciary duty in investment

In response to this environment, there has been a small eruption of political and regulatory ferment. The center of major concerns regarding the question of permissible investment practices is located in the universe of trust funds regulated by ERISA. Pursuant to ERISA, the controlling regulatory agency, the US Department of Labor, has issued several rounds of guidance, which are essentially political in nature, cautioning against certain behaviors in trustee investments.

The controversy in this area often involves multi-employer pension plans. Such private sector labor-affiliated benefit plans are authorized by the Taft-Hartley amendments to the National Labor Relations Act. Trustee power is shared equally between labor and management.[32] Since their enactment in the first half of the twentieth century, these legal amendments have produced a system for pension coverage for workers covered by a collective bargaining agreement who are employed by various employers within one industry, such as construction workers.[33] While these Taft-Hartley amendments guide many areas as to how plans

under the act must operate, other important matters, including fiduciary responsibility, were not specifically regulated until the enactment of ERISA. Today these considerations are examined within the context of ERISA.

Thus, the issue of fiduciary duty in investment, especially under ERISA, has become a site of struggle for the allies of labor and those of capital. While the US Supreme Court has held that "ERISA's legislative history confirms that the Act's [UPIA] fiduciary responsibility provisions codify and make applicable to [ERISA] fiduciaries certain principles developed in the evolution of the law of trusts,"[34] on more than one occasion corporate influence has attempted to obstruct what it regards as pension fund activism, under the guise of a strict definition of fiduciary duty. Yet, at the same time trustees are allowed and encouraged to invest in exotic investments, the failure of many of which contributed to the problems in 2008.[35] Because of the gargantuan size of the reservoirs of capital held by employee benefit funds, the guidance of the US Department of Labor as to how trustees should interpret ERISA's rules on investing is of supreme importance. The US Department of Labor is skeptical of any approach that does not follow a strict Wall Street narrative. Unfortunately, such government guidance has the effect of ignoring the reality of the investment universe today, as well as the history of the evolution of fiduciary duty.

The result is that life is difficult for thoughtful trustees as they determine how to invest benefit fund assets. The collapse of the certainty of modern portfolio theory, the growing understanding of the effects of investment practices on the long-term real economy and the political battles in this sector have created an unstable environment in which trustees must exercise their fiduciary duty. The situation is in flux.

---

[31] Halbach and his fellow drafters recognized the likelihood of further refinements in the duty. "The prudent investor project was undertaken with a clear recognition that trust investment law should reflect and accommodate current knowledge and concepts in the financial community. While seeking to incorporate the lessons of modern experience and research, a scrupulous effort was made to avoid either endorsing or excluding particular theories of economics or investment. In addition, an important objective in drafting the prudent investor rule was to preserve the flexibility necessary for the incorporation of future learning and developments" (Halbach 1992a: 1154).

[32] 29 USC §§ 151–69.

[33] 29 USC § 302(c)(5). Without the security of Taft-Hartley plans, it would be nearly impossible for mobile union employees to find portability within their employee benefits. The authority for Taft-Hartley plans is hidden in the text of the Taft-Hartley Act, as these plans were actually created as an exception to the general proposition that employers

cannot give money, or anything else of value, to employee representatives.

[34] *Firestone Tire & Rubber Co.* v. *Bruch*, 489 US 101 (1989), pp. 110–11.

[35] The US Chamber of Commerce has been especially active in this area. See US DOL (2007). A similar situation exists for funds that desire to use economically targeted investments (ETIs). See, for example, Griffin (1998).

One major issue that remains unresolved is how and when trustees, in their investment activities, may consider so-called "ESG" considerations – the environmental, social and governance activity of entities in which trustees invest. A fair assessment, when scrutinizing legal rules and regulations to consider how to engage ESG considerations, is that such principles may be accorded weight so long as they are motivated by appropriate purposes and do not affect, in a negative way, the economic performance of the portfolio as a whole (Asset Management Working Group of the UNEP Finance Initiative 2005: 109). Prudence is especially important in ESG, keeping a close eye on procedural strictures. And, as always, trustees must keep the interests of the beneficiaries foremost in mind. While political considerations within the US Department of Labor might occasionally counsel a different path, studies continue to mount that ESG considerations need to be applied to investment activity if one employs a powerful and thoughtful exercise of this fiduciary duty. And, contrary departmental regulation is always subject to potential judicial oversight in American jurisprudence.

In fact, such a position is consistent with many American legal principles. For example, in *The Law of Trusts*, the authors wrote:

> Trustees in deciding whether to invest in, or to retain, the securities of a corporation may properly consider the social performance of the corporation. They may decline to invest in, or to retain, the securities of corporations whose activities or some of them are contrary to fundamental and generally accepted ethical principles. They may consider such matters as pollution, race discrimination, fair employment, and consumer responsibility (Scott and Fratcher 1988: 500).[36]

[36] The Uniform Management of Public Employee Retirement Systems Act (UMPERSA), adopted in two states, states that a trustee "may consider benefits created by an investment in addition to investment return only if the trustee determines that the investment providing those collateral benefits would be prudent even without the collateral benefits" (UMPERSA § 8(a)(5)). The view of the Department of Labor can often be seen as a similar mandate. UMPERSA was heavily influenced by the UPIA. See UMPERSA Commission's Prefatory Note (1997); Simon (2006).

Conclusions

American ideas of fiduciary duty are, at their core, a rigid set of common sense concerns emanating from the relationship between the trustees and the beneficiaries. The application and definition of the concepts will continue to evolve, while the basic considerations remain stable. Over twenty years ago, those who wrote the *Restatement (Third) of Trusts* understood the need for flexibility by well-meaning trustees attempting to serve their beneficiaries. As Edward C. Halbach, Jr., the reporter for the volume, writes:

> The rules are designed to be general and flexible enough to adapt to the changes that may occur over time in the financial world. They are also designed to be flexible enough to allow prudent use of any investments and techniques that are suitable to the different abilities of different trustees and to the varied purposes and circumstances of the diverse array of trusts to which the prudent investor rule will inevitably apply. Accordingly, the prudent investor rule is intended to liberate expert trustees to pursue challenging, rewarding, non-traditional strategies when appropriate to a particular trust. It is also designed to provide unsophisticated trustees with reasonably clear guidance to practical courses of investment that are readily identifiable, expectedly rewarding and broadly adaptable (Halbach 1992a: 1154–5).

Given the need for productive capital in facing the long-term problems of society, as well as the need for responsible investment practices that can produce sustainable and significant investment returns, the manner that trust investments are managed is crucial. For the prudent and thoughtful trustee, legal definitions of fiduciary duty of investment must not constrain an ability to employ the most up-to-date techniques and to avoid unhelpful and unnecessarily complex investments. A fair and cautious reading of the current legal and regulatory framework of fiduciary duty is consistent with this mandate. Such investment activity, which employs conceptions of sustainability and other long-term investment criteria, is the only way to provide for the well-being of the beneficiaries.

References

Ascher, M. L. and A. W. Scott. 2011. *Scott and Ascher on Trusts*. New York: Aspen Publishers.

Asset Management Working Group of the UNEP Finance Initiative. 2005. *A Legal Framework for the Integration of Environmental, Social and Governance Issues into Institutional Investment.* UNEP Finance Initiative.

Avini, A. 1996. "The Origins of the Modern English Trust Revisited," *Tulane Law Review* 70: 1139.

Bernstein, P. 2005. *Capital Ideas: The Improbable Origins of Modern Wall Street.* Chichester: John Wiley & Sons.

Bogert, G. G. 2013. *Bogert on Trusts and Trustees.* Eagan, MN: Thomson West Publishing.

Bogle, J. C. 2011. "The Clash of Cultures," *Journal of Portfolio Management* 37: 14–28.

DeMott, D. 1988. "Beyond Metaphor: An Analysis of Fiduciary Obligation," *Duke Law Journal* 37: 879.

Department of Labor Advisory Opinion. 2005. www.dol.gov/ebsa/regs/AOs/main.html#2005

Department of Labor Interpretative Bulletin. 1996. www.dol.gov/ebsa/regs/fedreg/final/96_14093.pdf

Edwards, G. W. and Willis, H. P. 1922. *Banking and Business.* New York and London: Harper & Brothers Publishers.

Ethics World. 2006. *Breaking the Short-Term Cycle: "Short Termism," Its Threats, and What Can Be Done to Reform It.* www.ethicsworld.org/corporategovernance/PDF%20links/Shortterm.pdf.

Griffin, T. 1998. "Investing Labor Union Pension Funds in Workers: How ERISA and the Common Law Trust May Benefit Labor by Economically Targeting Investment," *Suffolk University Law Review* 32: 11.

Halbach, E. C., Jr. 1992a. "Trust Investment Law in the Third Restatement," *Iowa Law Review* 77: 1151, 1154–5.

 1992b. "Trust Investment Law in the Third Restatement," *Real Property, Probate & Trust Journal* 27: 409–65.

Hess, D. 2007. "Public Pensions and the Promise of Shareholder Activism for the Next Frontier of Corporate Governance: Sustainable Economic Development," *Virginia Law and Business Review* 2 (2): 221–63.

Investment Company Institute Research Fundamentals. 2006. "The US Retirement Market, First Quarter 2009." www.ici.org/pdf/09_q1_retmrkt_update.pdf.

Krikorian, B. L. (1989). *Fiduciary Standards in Pension and Trust Fund Management.* London: Butterworth Legal Publishers.

Langbein, J. H. 2003. "What ERISA Means by 'Equitable?' The Supreme Court's Trail of Error in Russell, Mertens, and Great-West," *Columbia Law Review* 103: 6.

 2005. "Questioning the Trust Law Duty of Loyalty: Sole Interest or Best Interest?" *Yale Law Journal* 114 (5): 929.

Lydenberg, S. 2009. "Beyond Risk: Notes Toward Responsible Alternatives for Investment Theory," *Domini Social Investments.* www.unpri.org/files/Lydenberg_PRI2009.pdf.

Pension Benefit Guaranty Corporation. 2010. *A Predictable, Secure Pension for Life: Defined Benefit Pensions.* www.pbgc.gov/docs/a_predictable_secure_pension_for_life.pdf.

Raphael, C. 2005. *Investigated Reporting: Muckrakers, Regulators, and the Struggle over Television Documentary.* Urbana, IL: University of Illinois Press.

Schneider, P. J. and B. M. Pinero. 2011. *ERISA: A Comprehensive Guide*, 3rd edn. New York: Aspen Publishers.

Schoeff, M., Jr. 2012. "Dueling Fiduciary Standards from SEC, DOL 'Not Workable,' Says Industry Expert," *Investment News* June 18. www.investmentnews.com/article/20120618/free/120619924#.

Scott, A. W. and Fratcher, W. F. 1988. *The Law of Trusts*, 4th edn. New York: Little, Brown.

Serotta, S. and F. Brodie (eds.). 2007. *ERISA Fiduciary Law.* Edison, NJ: BNA Books.

Shenkman, M. M. 1997. *The Complete Book of Trusts*, 2nd edn. New York: John Wiley & Sons.

Simon, W. S. 2006. "Trusts," *The Prudent Investor Act: A Guide to Understanding.* Camarillo, CA: Namborn Publishing.

Smith, G. 2002. "The Critical Resource Theory of Fiduciary Duty," *Vanderbilt Law Review* 55: 1399.

Stabile, S. and J. Zanglein. 2007. "ERISA Fiduciary Litigation: A Three-Part Primer Part I: Who Is a Fiduciary?" *Journal of Pension Planning & Compliance* 33: 56–75.

Stumpff Morrison, A. 2011. "Darkness at Noon: Judicial Interpretation May Never Have Made Things Worse for Benefit Plan Participants

Under ERISA Than Had the Statute Never Been Enacted," *St. Thomas Law Review* 23 (2): 101.

Taibbi, M. 2010. *Griftopia.* New York: Random House.

UMPERSA Commission's Prefatory Note. 1997. www.uniformlaws.org/ActSummary.aspx? title=Management%20of%20Public%20 Employee%20Retirement%20Systems%20Act

US DOL. 2007. "Letter from Robert J. Doyle to Thomas J. Donohue (Dec. 21, 2007)." www.dol. gov/ebsa/pdf/ao2007-07a.pdf.

White, A. 2012. "Academics and Industry Unite." www.top1000funds.com/news/2012/08/03/ academics-and-industry-unite/.

Woolley, P. (2010). *The Future of Finance: And the Theory that Underpins It.* London: London School of Economics Press.

Wooten, J. A. (2004). *The Employee Retirement Income Security Act of 1974: A Political History.* Berkley: University of California Press.

Governance and accountability in UK pension schemes

ALISON FOX

CHAPTER 4

Introduction

Relatively little is known about the governance of UK pension schemes (Epstein 1992; Clark 2004; Evans et al. 2008) except that they are administered by trustees who have a duty to act in good faith on behalf of their members. Such an admission is surprising since pension schemes play an important role within the UK economy. For example, in 1993 the Pension Law Review Committee (PLRC) suggested that "[f]or most people, their pension rights are likely to be one of the most valuable assets they have"[1] (Pension Law Review Committee 1993: 358). UK pension schemes are also large institutional investors in the capital markets (Solomon 2007) and so their success is important to many companies that rely on them for funding.[2] However, in January 2009, The National Association of Pension Funds (NAPF) reported that the UK faced the prospective closure of nearly 50 percent of existing defined benefit (DB)[3] schemes over the next five years (National Association of Pension Funds 2009). By February 2010, only 23 percent of all UK pension schemes remained open to new members compared to 88 percent ten years ago (National Association of Pension Funds 2010). In February 2012, the UK's Pension Protection Fund (PPF) reported that the aggregate deficit of the 6,432 schemes in its PPF

7800 index was £222.2 billion and that 81 percent of these schemes were in deficit (Pension Protection Fund 2010).

The failure of some UK pension schemes, such as the Mirror Group in 1991,[4] has been attributed to poor governance (Stiles and Taylor 1993), however, this is not surprising as the literature suggests that the success (failure) of a company is also positively (negatively) associated with its governance practices (see, for example, Pike et al. 1993; Barker 1998; Bell and Jenkinson 2002). Indeed, recent corporate governance guidelines (Financial Reporting Council 2010) have sought to influence the behavior of company directors as they discharge their fiduciary duties by addressing issues such as their leadership, effectiveness, remuneration and how they should discharge their accountability to stakeholders; thus accountability can be viewed as a subset of governance (Keasey and Wright 1993). Given that the role of a trustee has often been associated with that of a company director (Myners Report 2001; OECD 2002), this chapter considers the governance and accountability mechanisms that operate in UK pension schemes. Specifically, it summarizes the nature of UK pension schemes and describes the central role that trustees play in the fiduciary relationships that they have with a variety of different stakeholders. The development of UK pension scheme governance is explored alongside the role of the Pensions Regulator in that context and an analysis of the various ways that

---

[1] The Office for National Statistics reported that, in 2008, an estimated 27.7 million people in the UK (45 percent of the population) were members of occupational pension schemes.

[2] The Myners Report comments that "Institutional investors – in particular pension and life funds – now manage the savings of millions of people. They also 'own' and control most of British industry. They have come to play a central – if low key – part in our national economic life" (2001: 1). Solomon (2007) maintains that the four main types of

institutional investors are pension funds, life insurance companies, unit trusts and investment trusts.

[3] A DB scheme is defined by FRS 17 as a "pension or other retirement benefit scheme other than a defined contribution scheme" (Accounting Standards Board 2000: para. 2).

[4] Other pension scheme failures that occurred around the same time included Lewis's Group (1991), Belling (1992) and Burlington International Group (1992).

trustees can discharge accountability for their fiduciary duties. It concludes by suggesting opportunities for future research.

The nature of pension schemes in the UK

This section discusses the main objective of pension schemes and demonstrates how trustees are central to their governance structures. Clark (2008) suggests that the main aim of most pension schemes is to provide the beneficiaries with income on their retirement. This is often referred to as "the pension promise" and, to fulfill that promise, Clark (2008) suggests that pension schemes have three main functions: (1) to administer the financial contributions made by members of the scheme; (2) to determine and value benefit eligibility; and (3) to manage the assets of the scheme. Historically, in the UK, companies have provided two types of pension scheme for the benefit of their employees: (1) defined contribution (DC) schemes[5] and (2) defined benefit (DB) schemes. Regardless of whether a pension scheme is DC or DB, similar characteristics exist in terms of their administration, governance and the stakeholders involved. Figure 4.1 illustrates the flow of funds in a UK pension scheme and the wide variety of stakeholders who are involved in its control (see also Asher 2008).

Funds are initially generated by employee wage deductions and employer contributions to the pension scheme. The employer usually deducts the employees' pension contributions from their wages and pays them directly to the pension scheme, although employees can also pay additional voluntary contributions. In consultation with sub-committees, actuaries and advisors, the trustees decide upon the investment strategy for the pension scheme contributions and allocate the funds to appropriate fund managers who invest them in accordance with the chosen investment strategy. The fund managers are therefore usually responsible for managing a variety of assets including bonds, equities, deposits and property. A contract normally exists between the trustees and the fund managers to determine how the investments should be managed (Myners Report 2001). The return earned by these investments and any liquidated assets are used by the pension scheme to: pay pensioners; make transfers to other funds on behalf of employees that leave the pension scheme and become deferred members; or return any surplus to the sponsoring employer (alternatively, schemes can take a contribution holiday [Napier 2009]). Further, the administration of the scheme can either be outsourced to a third party or can be conducted in-house, either by dedicated staff or by the human resources department of the sponsoring employer (Myners Report 2001).

Schemes such as those described in Figure 4.1 are usually based on trust law (Clark 2006; Nöcker 2001) and, as far as the governance of the pension scheme is concerned, the trustees administer the pension scheme and safeguard its assets in accordance with the terms of the trust deed. The Pension Law Review Committee (1993), which was commissioned in the aftermath of the Maxwell scandal, clarified the fiduciary duties of trustees stating that they should include: a duty of good faith and loyalty to the trust beneficiaries; a duty not to profit from their position; a duty to preserve the trust assets and to deal with them in what they honestly believe to be the best interests of the beneficiaries; a duty to act impartially; a duty to fairly balance the interests of different classes of beneficiary; and a duty to exercise care in the performance of their functions. These duties are normally specified in the trust deed and, although trust deeds are not normally available to the public, Cocco and Volpin (2007) suggest that they will: address procedures for the appointment of trustees; describe the powers of the trustees in relation to the financial recordkeeping of the scheme; outline the process for the appointment of advisers; specify the

---

[5] FRS 17 defines a DC scheme as a "pension or other retirement benefit scheme into which an employer pays regular contributions fixed as an amount or as a percentage of pay and will have no legal or constructive obligation to pay further contributions if the scheme does not have sufficient assets to pay all employee benefits relating to employee service in the current and prior periods" (Accounting Standards Board 2000: para. 2).

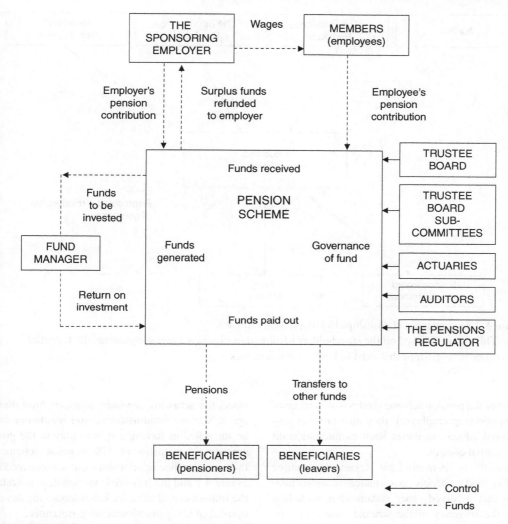

Figure 4.1 The nature of pension schemes in the UK.
Adapted from: BPP Publishing (1999: 105).
Note: The following stakeholders have been added to the original diagram: The Pensions Regulator and
Sub-committees to the Trustee Board.

investment strategy of the scheme; and establish
of a schedule of contributions by the sponsoring
employer. Therefore, the trustees perform a crucial
role in the governance of UK pension schemes and
the trust deed is an example of a formal governance
mechanism.

However, UK pension scheme governance is
not an issue that is exclusive to trustees; other

stakeholders, such as the sub-committees to the
trustee board also play an important role (Myners
Report 2001). In addition, the actuaries assist in
the determination of the contributions required to
be paid by the sponsoring employer to maintain
the solvency of the scheme. Similarly, auditors
are important to the governance of UK pension
schemes because, not only do they audit the annual

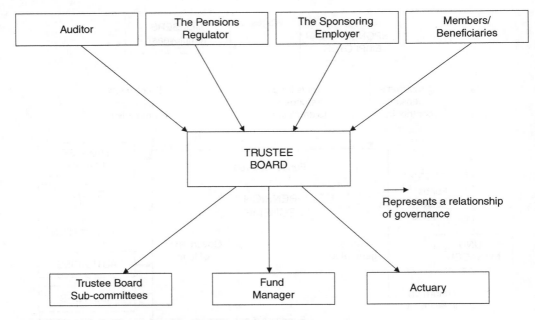

Figure 4.2 Governance relationships in UK pension schemes.
Note: This figure is based on the stakeholders identified in Figure 4.1 and summarizes the potential governance relationships that exist in UK pension schemes.

report of the pension scheme (and possibly those of the sponsoring employer), they also provide professional advice on issues such as internal audit and internal control.

Indeed, the Pension Law Review Committee (1993) made specific governance recommendations that involved other stakeholders including that: the solvency of the scheme should be certified by the actuary; the scheme actuaries and auditors should report any irregularities to the regulator; the fund managers must be explicit regarding who they are acting for and from whom they should take instructions; the fund managers must be provided with a well-defined brief of their duties and investment strategy; the scheme administrator should provide the regulator with an audited statement that pension fund contributions have been received and invested in a timeous fashion; a bank account must be maintained separate from that of the employer; there should be a statutory requirement to keep proper books and records; and the trustees should submit an annual return to the regulator. Clearly, from a very early

stage, the actuaries, advisers, auditors, fund managers, scheme administrators and regulators can be identified as having a role to play in the governance mechanisms of UK pension schemes; these governance relationships are summarized in Figure 4.2 and the following section demonstrates the importance of these stakeholders to the development of UK pension scheme governance.

The development of UK pension scheme governance

The death of Robert Maxwell in 1991 exposed the scale of the Mirror Group pension scheme financial scandal and in 1993, the PLRC reported that almost 30,000 Mirror Group pensioners were affected by the loss of "some £298 million of assets ... from CIF [the Mirror Group's pension scheme] and a further £155 million from individual pension schemes" (Pension Law Review Committee 1993: 359). A subsequent Department of Trade and Industry report, *Mirror Group Newspapers*

(Thomas and Turner 2001), claimed that Robert Maxwell was, in the main, responsible for the financial scandal and evidence presented to the PLRC drew attention to "a number of accounting control weaknesses" (Pension Law Review Committee 1993: 360). Stiles and Taylor (1993) provide a detailed analysis of the Maxwell case and attribute the scandal to a failure of governance in three main areas: (1) the lack of intervention by regulatory bodies; (2) Maxwell's dominance of the board of directors; and (3) poor investor relations and meaningful debate.

The Maxwell case demonstrates that there can be significant consequences when fiduciary duties are breached and highlights the risk whereby trustees, the sponsoring employer or fund managers can act to benefit themselves at the expense of employees and pensioners. Although corporate governance for UK companies has managed to avoid statutory regulation, the same cannot be said for the regulation of UK pension scheme governance, which is grounded in both statute and professional self-regulation.

Following the Maxwell scandal in 1991, the then Secretary of State for Social Security, Peter Lilley, commissioned a report under the chairmanship of Professor Roy Goode "to review the framework of law and regulation within which occupational pension schemes operate … and [to consider] the accountability and roles of trustees, fund managers, auditors and pension scheme advisers" (Pension Law Review Committee 1993: iii).

The report was motivated by concerns over:

> the qualification and disqualification of trustees; the degree of employer control over their appointment and removal, and the composition of the trust board; the distribution of powers between the employer and the trustees; trustees' conflicts of interest; outdated restrictions on the power of trustees; their inability to meet claims against them for loss caused by their breaches of duty; and the level of knowledge of trustees about their role and responsibilities (Pension Law Review Committee 1993: 17).

Thus, the purpose of the Pension Law Review was to ensure adequate governance and accountability of UK pension schemes and to protect the interests of scheme members and beneficiaries.

The PLRC recommended that: the grounds for trustee disqualification should be similar to those of company directors; auditors, actuaries and administrators should not be permitted to act as trustees; employers should not have sole power to appoint or veto a trustee; pensioner trustees and member-nominated trustees (MNT) should be encouraged; members should be entitled to appoint at least one third of the trustee membership; there should be no minimum or maximum term of office recommended for trustees; and the sponsoring company should not be able to remove member-appointed trustees. Further, an investment standard was required of trustees; it was recommended that they would:

> exercise, in relation to all matters affecting the fund, the same degree of care and diligence as an ordinary prudent person would exercise in dealing with property of another for whom the person felt morally bound (Pension Law Review Committee, 1993: 30).

The PLRC also permitted the incorporation of the trustee board as a limited company to administer the pension scheme. The effect of incorporation of the pension scheme is that the trustees become directors of the pension company which is then subject to corporate law and corporate governance requirements.[6] The remaining recommendations of the PLRC (1993) are summarized in Table 4.1 and most of these recommendations have since been included in a number of subsequent statutory instruments (including the Pension Schemes Act 1993, the Pensions Act 1995, the Welfare Reform and Pensions Act 1999 and, most recently, the Pensions Acts of 2004, 2007 and 2008).

The Pensions Schemes Act (1993) saw the creation of the Occupational Pensions Board (OPB) whose main function was the registration and certification of occupational and personal pension schemes. There was also provision made for the protection of scheme members in the event of them leaving their scheme early or in cases

---

[6] However, despite the availability of this option, the Myners Report (2001: 5) commented that, at that time "most occupational pensions [were] organised on a trust basis" and therefore would not be subject to corporate law and corporate governance requirements.

Table 4.1 A summary of the PLRC (1993) recommendations.

1.	The enactment of an Occupational Pensions Schemes Act
2.	The appointment of a Pensions Regulator
3.	The statutory regulation of the primary duties of the trustees in relation to the pension promise
4.	The introduction of a minimum solvency requirement for all funded schemes
5.	The empowerment of the regulator to give consent to and oversee scheme amendments and wind-ups
6.	The adoption of specific rules regarding early leavers from the pension scheme
7.	The implementation of flexible guidelines
8.	The disclosure in the annual report by the trustees that they have carefully considered the investments and are satisfied that they conform to the statutory criteria
9.	The required contribution by the employer to secure the scheme's liabilities where a pension scheme is in deficit
10.	The establishment of a compensation scheme to protect members against the defaults of those dealing with pension fund assets
11.	The enactment of specific rules regarding disputes; the assignment and loss of pension rights; retirement on grounds of ill health, public sector pension schemes; the establishment of pension rights on divorce; and Inland Revenue and Social Security requirements.

where the sponsoring employer was insolvent. An Ombudsman was also created by this legislation to investigate and determine any complaint made by a stakeholder who had sustained injustice as a result of maladministration. Thus, the 1993 Act was the first to engage external parties in monitoring the behavior of trustees.

The Pensions Act (1995) created the Occupational Pensions Regulatory Authority (OPRA), which replaced the OPB. OPRA reported directly to the Secretary of State and its main aim was to increase the supervision and direct monitoring of schemes and their trustees. Whilst the 1993 act concentrated on pension schemes themselves, the 1995 act addressed the eligibility (and exclusion) of individuals to act as trustees and clarified their functions and duties. The 1995 act also created the Pensions Compensation Board to whom applications for compensation could be made where an employer became insolvent or the value of the pension assets diminished. Thus, pension scheme monitoring became more formalized as the 1995 act reinforced trust law affecting how pension schemes were administered and increased the security of members' benefits (Pensions Regulator 2007a). The Welfare Reform and Pensions Act (1999), which followed four years later, concentrated less on the

governance of pension schemes and addressed the protection of pension contributors, creating provisions to be applied in the event of divorce and other welfare issues.

The Myners Report, which was published in 2001, was a seminal piece of work that reviewed institutional investment in the UK and focused on the governance of the investing activities of UK pension schemes in particular. It was motivated by the increasing concentration of pension schemes among the institutional investors grouping and aimed to encourage shareholder activism. Thus, the Myners Report was commissioned to investigate whether the investing decisions of institutional investors such as pension schemes are "rational, well-informed, subject to the correct incentives and, as far as possible, undistorted" (Myners Report 2001: 4). The report made several recommendations which influenced the legislation that subsequently followed. Most significantly, in relation to governance, it recommended a review to clarify who owned any pension scheme surplus and highlighted that, although the expertise of trustees was a key governance issue, there was no legal requirement for them to develop the skills needed for investment decisions. These concerns were based on evidence that:

Table 4.2 A summary of the Myners Report (2001) principles for investment decision-making.

1.	Decisions should be taken only by persons or organizations with the right skills, information and resources needed to take them effectively.
2.	Trustees should set out an overall investment objective for the fund, in terms which relate directly to the circumstances of the fund and not to some other objective such as the performance of other pension funds.
3.	The attention devoted to asset allocation decisions should fully reflect the contribution they can make to achieving the fund's investment objective.
4.	Decision-makers should consider a full range of investment opportunities across all major asset classes, including private equity.
5.	The fund should be prepared to pay sufficient fees for actuarial and investment advice to attract a broad range of kinds of potential providers.
6.	Trustees should give fund managers an explicit written mandate setting out the agreement between them on issues such as the investment objective, and a clear timescale for measurement and evaluation.
7.	In consultation with their investment managers, funds should explicitly consider whether the index benchmarks they have selected are appropriate. Where they believe active management to have the potential to achieve higher returns, they should set both targets and risk controls to reflect this, allowing sufficient freedom for genuinely active management to occur.
8.	Trustees should arrange to measure the performance of the fund and the effectiveness of their own decision-making, and formally to assess the performance and decision-making delegated to advisers and managers.

Source: Myners Report (2001: 15).

62 per cent of trustees have no professional qualifications in finance or investment; 77 per cent of trustees have no in-house professionals to assist them; more than 50 per cent of trustees received less than three days' training when they became trustees; 44 per cent of trustees have not attended any courses since their initial 12 months of trusteeship; and 49 per cent of trustees spend three hours or fewer preparing for pension investment matters (Myners Report 2001: 5).

The report therefore recommended that trustees should be:

> familiar with the issues concerned ... if trustees do not feel they possess such a level of skill and care, then they should either take steps to acquire it, or delegate the decision to a person or organisation who they believe does (Myners Report 2001: 14).

It also recommended eight principles, which it believed codified best practice for pension scheme investment decision-making and these are summarized in Table 4.2.

This table highlights that, in 2001, the governance of pension schemes was being scrutinized at a micro-level. However, the Pensions Act 2004

refocused attention on UK pension scheme governance at the macro-level and contained provisions to create the Pension Protection Fund (PPF) and the Pensions Regulator (PR) to replace OPRA.[7]

Whilst the Pensions Act (2007) addressed arrangements to be put in place to resolve potential disputes between the pension scheme and its beneficiaries, the Pensions Act (2008) concentrated more on the employer's responsibilities as far as their employees were concerned. Although the 2008 act addressed some issues of compliance in relation to unpaid contributions, it concentrated mostly on encouraging greater private saving. More recently, the Pension Act (2011) increased the state pension age and required employers to automatically enroll their employees in a pension scheme. Thus, the regulation of UK pension scheme governance has significantly altered since 1993 and one of its most important developments

---

[7] All companies that have a pension scheme now pay a levy to the PPF, and employees can claim compensation from the PPF in the event of the insolvency of the sponsoring employer (McCarthy and Neuberger 2005).

was the creation of the PR by the Pensions Act (2004). Consequently, the following section summarizes the main aims of the PR, and codes of practice and regulatory guidance that have been issued to achieve these aims.

The Pensions Regulator (PR)

The Pensions Act (2004) established the PR as the regulatory body responsible for issuing codes of practice and regulatory guidance. These guidance documents give practical information about compliance with statutory requirements and set desired standards of conduct; they are indicative of how a well-run scheme should be administered. The PR claims to be a risk-based regulator whose objectives are achieved by a process of education and enablement and, where necessary, enforcement (Pensions Regulator 2008a); this regulator also argues that governance underlies all of its statutory objectives (Pensions Regulator 2007a).

To date, twelve codes of practice and twenty-two pieces of regulatory guidance (see Table 4.3) have been issued to support the PR's three main objectives, which are: (1) to protect the benefits of the pension scheme members; (2) to encourage schemes to develop administration practices that are of high quality; and (3) to minimize claims on the PPF (Pensions Regulator 2007a). In relation to the first objective the PR states that:

> Trust-based pension schemes have a separation of beneficial ownership and day-to-day control of assets ... Potential risks to members' benefits arise from this separation. In well-governed schemes, however, where trustees or managers act in accordance with their fiduciary obligations to members ... the separation of ownership and control means that a level of skill may be brought into the management of assets beyond that which the beneficiaries could provide on their own behalf (Pensions Regulator 2007a: 11).

With regard to the second objective, the PR maintains that "[a] well-governed scheme will have systems in place to achieve a high standard of administration" (Pensions Regulator 2007a: 11) and, as far as the third objective is concerned, the PR argues that trustees should be aware "of the

scheme's funding position and of the employer covenant" (Pensions Regulator 2007a: 11).

Thus, the PR recognizes that pension scheme governance is a significant issue and in April 2007 a discussion paper titled *The Governance of Work-based Pension Schemes* (Pensions Regulator 2007a) was issued; while that document referred to a definition of governance that was previously used by the National Council for Voluntary Organisations,[8] it acknowledged that pension scheme governance is not easy to define and that it is often difficult to distinguish governance activities from other activities in pension schemes. Instead, the PR chose to identify several components of the pension scheme that were considered to be part of its governance. First, it highlighted the appropriate composition of the governing body, the supply of trustees and the requirements made of MNTs and directors. Second, it considered trustee knowledge and understanding to be important to the governance of the scheme. Third, it identified the sponsoring employer, advisers, administrators, scheme members, regulators and investment managers as important stakeholders in pension scheme governance. Fourth, the procedures required of the governing body were also considered to be central to the effectiveness of its governance practices.

These procedures included: how trustees carry out their work; how the scheme is administered; the frequency and effectiveness of meetings; recording decisions; and the management of risks as well as internal controls. Finally, the constitution of the governing body, including keeping an up-to-date trust deed, set of rules and other key documents were also identified as being key components of governance. Therefore, although the PR does not define pension scheme governance, the discussion document was used to illustrate fundamental areas of pension schemes that the PR considered to be important to their governance.

In October 2007, the PR issued its response to the discussion paper: *How the Regulator will Promote Better Governance of Work-based*

---

[8] This document defines governance as "the systems and processes concerned with ensuring the overall direction, effectiveness, supervision and accountability of an organisation" (Pensions Regulator 2007b: 7).

Pension Schemes (Pensions Regulator 2007b); the PR confirmed that it would prioritize its future work agenda in relation to pension scheme governance in eight different areas: (1) knowledge and understanding;[9] (2) conflicts of interest;[10] (3) monitoring the employer covenant;[11] (4) relations with advisers;[12] (5) administration;[13] (6) processes for investment choice;[14] (7) governance during wind-up; and (8) contract-based schemes (Pensions Regulator 2007b). The PR also stated that a three-pronged approach would be used to address these priorities: (1) education, guidance and enabling;[15]

[9] Knowledge and understanding relates to the education of trustees and the PR has since issued code of practice (number 7), practical guidance and an e-learning program (also known as the trustees' toolkit) to address this issue.

[10] The PR maintains that if conflicts of interest between different stakeholders are not managed appropriately, trustees could make decisions that are not in the interests of members. The PR recognizes that many different stakeholders can be affected by a conflict of interests and has since issued regulatory guidance on this matter (Pensions Regulator 2008b).

[11] The PR maintains that those trustees who do not monitor the employer covenant will not be in a position to make appropriate funding decisions or decide any recovery plan that might be deemed necessary. The PR has now issued regulatory guidance on the clearance of company transactions which incorporates guidance on assessing the employer covenant (Pensions Regulator 2009a).

[12] The PR advocates that trustees should have the confidence to ask questions of their advisers and challenge the advice they are given; it suggests that the establishment of clear aims and objectives for meetings with advisers should facilitate such questioning. In May 2008, the PR issued regulatory guidance identifying some key issues for trustees to consider in their relations with advisers (Pensions Regulator 2008c).

[13] Both code of practice number 7 and the trustees' toolkit address the administration of the pension scheme, however, the PR emphasized the need to develop, promote and share good practice in this area by providing examples of good practice and developing "closer relationships with administrators and those who work with them such as auditors" (Pensions Regulator 2006: 18).

[14] With regards to processes for investment choice, the trustees' toolkit addresses these issues and identifies the need to provide good examples of effective processes and different approaches in relation to these matters.

[15] The PR argues that it aims "to combine existing initiatives with new initiatives, primarily good practice guidance including case examples" (Pensions Regulator 2007c: 4).

(2) working in partnership;[16] and (3) intervention[17] (Pensions Regulator 2007b). Consequently, although the PR's approach to the regulation of UK pension scheme governance is strategic, these regulations are not contained in a single document as they are for companies (Evans et al. 2008) in the UK Corporate Governance Code (Financial Reporting Council 2010) (see Table 4.3).

The accountability of UK pension schemes

Some authors suggest that the discharge of accountability is influenced by the organizational context within which it operates and so have called for context specific studies of accountability (Otley 1984; Scapens 1984; Laughlin 1990). Using Figure 4.2, Fox (2010) identified seven different potential accountability relationships in UK pension schemes and these are described in Table 4.4.

Specifically Table 4.4 demonstrates how each of the stakeholders identified in Figure 4.2 adopts either the role of accountee or accountor (Gray et al. 1987). For example, in the first three relationships described in Table 4.4, the Board of Trustees adopts the role of the accountee to whom its sub-committees, the fund manager and the actuary are accountable. However, in the last four relationships described in Table 4.4, the Board of Trustees adopts the role of the accountor and is accountable to the scheme auditor, the PR, the sponsoring employer and the scheme members. Concentrating on the final relationship in Table 4.4, and using the results of twenty-one interviews with a variety of stakeholders, Fox (2010) discovered that five documents

[16] The PR suggests that "central to the successful delivery of proposals, this included working with the pensions industry, the FSA and the Government in the development of good practice guidance. It also involves identification of future initiatives and consistency of approach, whilst taking current initiatives and working practices into account" (Pensions Regulator 2007c: 4).

[17] In line with the PR's risk-based approach it maintains that it "will focus on areas posing most risk to the regulator's objectives, and any intervention will be proportionate to the level of risk" (Pensions Regulator 2007c: 4).

Table 4.3 A summary of the PR's governance pronouncements.

Panel A: Codes of Practice	
1.	Reporting breaches of the law
2.	Notifiable events
3.	Funding defined benefits
4.	Early leavers
5.	Reporting the late payment of contributions to occupational money purchase schemes
6.	Reporting late payment of contributions to personal pensions
7.	Trustee knowledge and understanding
8.	MNT/MND – putting arrangements in place
9.	Internal controls
10.	Modification of subsisting rights
11.	Dispute resolution – reasonable periods
12.	Circumstances in relation to the material detriment test
Panel B: Regulatory Guidance	
1.	Abandonment of DB pension schemes
2.	Clearance
3.	Conflicts of interest
4.	Corporate transactions
5.	Cross-border schemes
6.	DC schemes Q&As
7.	Effective member communications
8.	Incentive exercises
9.	Lump sum death benefits
10.	Member retirement options
11.	Mortality assumptions
12.	Monitoring employer support
13.	Multi-employer withdrawal arrangements
14.	Record keeping
15.	Relations with advisers
16.	Scheme funding and clearance case studies
17.	Scheme funding FAQs
18.	Transfer values
19.	Trustee guidance
20.	Trustee knowledge and understanding
21.	Voluntary employer engagement
22.	Winding up

Note: This table summarizes the Codes of Practice and Regulatory Guidance issues by the PR as at April 3, 2012.

are used to discharge the accountability of UK pension schemes: (1) the Statement of Investment Principles; (2) the Summary Funding Statement; (3) the Popular Report; (4) the financial report of the pension scheme (to a limited extent); and (5) the annual report of the sponsoring employer.

The Statement of Investment Principles (SIP) is an internal document that is required by the

Table 4.4 Potential UK pension scheme accountability relationships.

Accountee	Accountor	Regulation of the accountability relationship
Board of Trustees	Sub-committees	Trust Deed
Board of Trustees	Fund Manager	Letter of Engagement
Board of Trustees	Actuary	Letter of Engagement
Auditor	Board of Trustees	Statute and Letter of Engagement
The PR	Board of Trustees	Statute
Sponsoring Employer	Board of Trustees	Trust Deed
Members/beneficiaries	Board of Trustees	Trust Deed

Note: All of the potential relationships of accountability identified in this table are suggested on the basis of the governance relationship identified in Figure 4.2.

Pensions Act 1995 and its main aim is to describe the principles governing the investment policy adopted by the trustees. As the SIP is an internal document, it is not automatically distributed to stakeholders, however, there was evidence to suggest that some pension schemes have made their SIP available online while others have included them as part of their annual report. The SIP is therefore a document that is used in conjunction with the trust deed to regulate the investment practices of UK pension schemes. The SIP addresses issues such as: the types of investment held; the balance between different types of investment risk; the expected return on investments; the realization of investments; and the extent to which social, environmental or ethical considerations affected the investment decisions taken.

The Summary Funding Statement (SFS), a second document identified by the interviewees as a mechanism used to discharge accountability for UK pension schemes, is required by all schemes that have at least one hundred members. The PR states that it must comprise of "a summary of the funding position of the scheme based on its last 'ongoing' actuarial valuation" and most interviewees in Fox (2010) concluded that the SFS was a useful document. However, an auditor interviewee explained that this document, far from providing an account was potentially very confusing for members because the SFS is calculated on a minimum funding requirement (MFR) basis, which is very different from the basis used to calculate the FRS 17/IAS 19 accounting numbers. A finance officer of a sponsoring employer in Fox's study described how his SFS included an actuarial valuation (which is calculated

every three years) and calculations based on buy-out, MFR, FRS 17 and IAS 19. He declared:

> It must be very confusing for the lay person. I mean it's hard enough to explain to a board of directors for, you know a PLC, the different methods and of course they're all guesses at the end of the day (in Fox 2010).

Some pension schemes voluntarily produce a Popular Report and this was a third document cited by the interviewees in Fox (2010) as a mechanism used to discharge accountability. One of the Pension Scheme officers explained that the Popular Report produced by his pension scheme is:

> [a] four page document ... [and is] a summary of [the] trustee account and reports, it'll be sent out to members ... that is one of the more important [documents] as far as members are concerned.

This document typically contains: highlights of the Members' Report from the trustee; a report on the funding of the pension scheme and its funding position; a report on how the risk of the fund is spread; details of the fund's investments; information on the trustee directors; a description of how the fund is valued; and details of the scheme's membership. Another interviewee indicated that it might also contain biographical details of the trustees.

The fourth document cited by the interviewees in Fox (2010) was the financial report of the pension scheme itself which the Statement Of Recommended Practice (SORP): *Financial Reports of Pension Schemes* (PRAG 2007) requires should contain: a trustees' report; an investment report; a compliance statement; statements by the actuary and the auditor; the financial statements; and other disclosures in the annual report. However, these financial statements do not require the liabilities of the pension scheme, in respect of its future pension payments to members, to be brought onto the Statement of Financial Position and this was clearly an issue for some of the interviewees in Fox (2010). According to several of these interviewees, the pension scheme financial statements, as a list of assets alone, did not provide all of the information that members wanted to see. For example, interviewee AU1 argued that:

> In theory [the financial statements of the pension scheme] should be easy to follow ... [and] if you're just looking at investment performance, there should be enough to indicate ... what the value of the fund at the beginning and at the end of the year is. I think what is missing [is the] liabilities not being shown within the pension scheme accounts ... these accounts are not fit for purpose ... and [if they were] they would be used more.

The trustees of a UK pension scheme have a statutory responsibility to make the annual reports of the pension scheme available to members, however, there is no requirement to automatically distribute them; if a member wishes to see these documents, they need to be proactive and contact the trustees to request a copy. Many of the interviewees in Fox (2010) declared that it was very unusual for the pension scheme to receive a request for a copy of its annual report, as evidenced by one of the auditor interviewees:

> [The members] actually don't ask for the accounts at all. The trustees themselves don't always see the importance of the accounts either. And this is sometimes where we have a real issue because, obviously ... we want to make sure that they do disclose best practice ... we spend a lot of time on these accounts ... And yet the trustees are saying, "Why are you so bothered about this, that and the next thing? Nobody looks at them!"

A Pension Scheme Officer in the same study confirmed that this perception was widely held. He suggested that members may use the pension scheme financial statements "to prop up the tables ... if they even go to the length of that! We don't send many to members. They don't ask for them!"

According to the SORP (PRAG 2007), existing and prospective pension scheme members are deemed to be one of the main users of the annual report of the pension scheme, however, the

interviewees in Fox (2010) suggested that this is not the case in practice. Several of her interviewees suggested that the reason for this apathy was that members of a DB pension scheme find the accounting numbers reported in the financial statements of the sponsoring employer more useful. An actuary interviewee in Fox (2010) explained:

> The pension scheme accounts have very little information about the liabilities ... and if it's a final-salary pension scheme then you only get half the picture ... At least under [FRS 17 and IAS 19] you get an asset figure and a liability figure and therefore you can compare apples with apples. So I would suggest that the information in the company accounts is much more valid to members of final-salary schemes than simply the trustee report and accounts.

An auditor concurred: "What members really want to know is, am I going to get a pension ... I think the members actually tend to look at the corporate accounts and get the FRS17 figures."

Likewise, a finance officer in a sponsoring employer interviewed by Fox (2010) stated:

> Where I think the pension scheme accounts fall down is that it is simply saying here's the pot of money that we've got and it doesn't actually tie into the liabilities which IAS19 ... Now, I think that is quite a deficiency.

Thus, the interviewees suggested that the financial reports of UK pension schemes are not useful to members and consequently they are not requested. Instead, the annual report of the sponsoring employer was considered to be an alternative, and much more useful, source of information.

Conclusions

Thus far, it would appear that UK pension schemes have "a complex web of ownership" (Solomon 2007: 112), which results in multiple governance and accountability relationships. Despite the potential impact that these relationships might have on how pension scheme trustees discharge their fiduciary duties, this area is surprisingly under-researched in comparison to the corporate context (Ammann and Zingg 2008; Evans et al. 2008). As institutional investors, UK pension schemes are dominant in the global financial markets (Useem and Mitchell 2000) and therefore have an important role to play in the governance of the companies in which they invest (Keasey et al. 1997; OECD 2004; Mallin 2007; Solomon 2007; Evans et al. 2008). In this context, a plethora of research exists (see, for example, Pike et al. 1993; Barker 1998; Bell and Jenkinson 2002) and authors such as Short and Keasey (1997) and Solomon (2007) provide excellent summaries of the academic work conducted in this area. However, Epstein (1992: 60) claims that this influence is ironic, given that pension schemes do not "practice what they preach," suggesting that the governance of pension schemes is less than robust. Evans et al. (2008) suggest that there is a gap in academic research relating to pension scheme governance and propose that most of the work that does exist originates from outside the UK. Clark (2008) argues that the UK trust institution has no equivalent in much of continental Europe, and so only some of the existing pension scheme governance research is relevant to the UK.

Evans et al. (2008) provide a useful theoretical discussion of the organizational structures of Anglo-American corporate pension schemes. Conversely, Clark (2000, 2008) concentrates on the specific structures of pension scheme investment management and governance models. Clark (2008) identifies a lack of trustee expertise as being a fundamental problem for pension scheme governance. While he supports the use of codes of practice to evaluate the performance of pension schemes and to improve the cost-efficiency and consistency of their decision-making, he argues that the only real solution to poor pension scheme governance is their transformation into large multi-employer pension schemes. These conclusions are based on similar work by Clark and Urwin (2008), which suggests that the complex network of principals and agents and the inability of beneficiaries to monitor those who manage the pension scheme often impede the effective operation of pension scheme governance mechanisms.

While the majority of the work described in this section is theoretical, discursive and descriptive in nature, other research exists that is arguably more empirically driven and therefore has a more focused approach, concentrating on various component parts of pension scheme governance. For example, the role of trustees has proved a popular governance topic for investigation. Kakabadse et al.

(2003) attempt to clarify the trustee's role and report the results of twenty interviews with a selection of UK-based trustees. These authors conclude that trustees see their role as strategic; they are confident that they make informed decisions and that they believe that they have an appropriate mix of skills. However, Clark et al. (2006) have a contrasting view and question the competence of trustees' investment decision-making in practice, concluding that it varies dramatically from scheme to scheme and that the lack of a common approach has significant implications for pension scheme governance. Alternatively, Cocco and Volpin (2007) concentrate on the role of Employer Nominated Trustees (ENT) and discover evidence to suggest that ENTs act in the interests of the shareholders of the sponsoring employer and not necessarily the pension scheme members/beneficiaries, and that more-leveraged companies, which have a larger proportion of ENTs, make smaller contributions to the pension scheme and higher dividend payments to their shareholders.

Some studies have attempted to associate good pension scheme governance with superior asset performance. For example, Useem and Mitchell (2000) argue that there is a positive relationship between a pension scheme's governance practices and the returns on the pension assets. Likewise, Ammann and Zingg (2008) found that, using a self-designed index as a proxy for the governance of Swiss pension schemes, better governance was associated with improved pension scheme performance. Other studies, however, have opted to investigate the governance of pension schemes within specific contexts. For example, Albrecht and Hingorani (2004) and Impavido (2002) investigate the governance practices that exist in state/local government and public pension funds respectively, whereas Helbronner (2005) and Nöcker (2001) adopt a country-specific perspective.

Some professional research has also been commissioned in this area; PricewaterhouseCoopers (PWC) have administered four questionnaire-based surveys (PricewaterhouseCoopers 2004, 2006, 2008, 2010) the results of which are very similar to the five telephone surveys of pension scheme governance conducted by the PR (Pensions Regulator 2006–9, 2011). The PR uses these surveys as a longitudinal analysis tool and so it is perhaps not surprising that they report similar themes. For example, they document that better governance is associated with the provision of more trustee training, and the existence of adequate risk management processes. Further, bigger schemes are found to be better governed than their smaller sized counterparts.

Yet, despite this work, the governance and accountability mechanisms of UK pension schemes remain opaque; it would appear that they operate in a black box about which very little is known and they are less than transparent (Epstein 1992; Clark 2004; Evans et al. 2008). Consequently, future research could usefully address these issues so that the developments that have been witnessed in corporate governance and accountability research might be replicated in this business context. This issue is significant due to the important role that trustees, and their fiduciary duties, play in the UK economy and the welfare of its population.

References

Accounting Standards Board. 2000. *Financial Reporting Standard (FRS) 17: Retirement Benefits*. London: ASB Publications.

Albrecht, W. and V. Hingorani. 2004. "Effects of Governance Practices and Investment Strategies on State and Local Government Pension Fund Financial Performance," *International Journal of Public Administration* 27 (8–9): 673–700.

Ammann, M. and A. Zingg. 2008. "Performamce and Governance of Swiss Pension Funds," *Journal of Pension Economics and Finance*. www.journals.cambridge.org/action/displayAbstract?aid=2137656.

Asher, A. 2008. "Shortchanged: Conflicted Superstructures," in J. Evans, M. Orszag and J. Piggott (eds.) *Pension Fund Governance*. Cheltenham: Edward Elgar Publishing Ltd.

Barker, R. 1998. "The Market for Information-evidence from Finance Directors, Analysts and Fund Managers," *Accounting and Business Research* 29 (1): 3–20.

Bell, L. and T. Jenkinson. 2002. "New Evidence of the Impact of Dividend Taxation and on the Identity of the Marginal Investor," *The Journal of Finance* LVII (3): 1321–46.

BPP Publishing. 1999. *ACCA Study Text: Professional Paper 13 Financial Reporting Environment*, London: BPP Publishing Limited.

Clark, G. 2000. "The Functional and Spatial Structure of the Investment Management Industry," *Geoforum* 31: 71–86.

2004. "Pension Fund Governance: Expertise and Organizational Form," *Journal of Pension Economics and Finance* 3 (2): 233–53.

2006. "Regulation of Pension Fund Governance," in G. Clark, A. Munnell and M. Orszag (eds.) *Oxford Handbook of Pensions and Retirement Income*. New York: Oxford University Press.

2008. "Pension Fund Governance: Expertise and Organisational Form," in J. Evans, M. Orsag and J. Piggott (eds.) *Pension Fund Governance*. Cheltenham: Edward Elgar Publishing Ltd.

Clark, G. and R. Urwin. 2008. "Best-practice Pension Fund Governance," *Journal of Asset Management* 9 (1): 2–21.

Clark, G., E. Caerlewy-Smith and J. Marshall. 2006. "Pension Fund Trustee Competence: Decision-making in Problems Relevant to Investment Practice," *Journal of Pension Economics and Finance* 5 (1): 91–110.

Cocco, J. and P. Volpin. 2007. "Corporate Governance of Pension Plans: The UK Evidence," *Financial Analysts Journal* 63 (1): 70–83.

Department for Work and Pensions. 2012. www.dwp.gov.uk/policy/pensions-reform.

Epstein, M. 1992. "Pension Funds Should Practice What they Preach," *Business and Society Review* 83: 60–61.

Evans, J., M. Orszag and J. Piggott. 2008. *Pension Fund Governance*. Cheltenham: Edward Elgar Publishing Ltd.

Financial Reporting Council. 2010. *UK Corporate Governance Code*. www.frc.org.uk/corporate/reviewCombined.cfm.

Fox, A. 2010. *An Exploration of the Governance and Accountability of UK Defined Benefit Pension Schemes*. PhD Thesis, University of Dundee.

Gray, R., D. Owen and K. Maunders. 1987. *Corporate Social Reporting: Accounting and Accountability*, Hemel Hempstead: Prentice Hall Europe.

Helbronner, C. 2005. "Pension Plan Governance and Risk Management: A Canadian Perspective," *Pensions* 10 (3): 221–35.

Impavido, G. 2002. *On the Governance of Public Pension Fund Management*, World Bank Policy Research Working Paper No. 2878. www.papers.ssrn.com/sol3/papers.cfm?abstract_id=636241.

Kakabadse, N., A. Kakabadse and A. Kouzmin. 2003. "Pension Fund Trustees: Role and Contribution," *European Management Journal* 21 (3): 376–86.

Keasey, K. and M. Wright. 1993. "Issues in Corporate Accountability and Governance: An Editorial," *Accounting and Business Research* 23 (91A): 291–303.

Keasey, K, S. Thompson and M. Wright. 1997. *Corporate Governance: Economic, Management and Financial Issues*. New York: Oxford University Press.

Laughlin, R. 1990. "A Model of Financial Accountability and the Church of England," *Financial Accountability and Management* 6 (2): 93–115.

Mallin, C. 2007. *Corporate Governance*. New York: Oxford University Press.

McCarthy, D. and A. Neuberger. 2005. "The Pension Protection Fund," *Fiscal Studies* 26 (2): 139–67.

Myners Report. 2001. *Myners Report on Institutional Investment*. London: HM Treasury.

Napier, C. 2009. "The Logic of Pension Accounting," *Accounting and Business Research* 39 (3): 231–49.

National Association of Pension Funds. 2009. "Pension Provision and the Economic Crisis," January.

2010. "A Budget for Pensions," an NAPF submission to HM Treasury on the 2010 Budget, February.

Nöcker, R. 2001. "Pensions Governance: The Control of Occupational Pension Schemes in the UK and Germany," *Journal of Pensions Management* 6 (3): 227–48.

OECD. 2002. *OECD Guideline for Pension Fund Governance*. www.oecd.org/document/54/0,3343,en_2649_37419_2767350_1_1_1_1,00.html.

2004. *Principles of Corporate Governance*. Paris: OECD.

Otley, D. T. 1984. "Management Accounting and Organisation Theory: A Review of their Interrelationship," in *Management Accounting, Organisational Behaviour and Capital Budgeting*. London: Macmillan/ESRC.

Pension Law Review Committee. 1993. *Pension Law Reform: The Report of the Pension Law Review Committee*. London: HMSO.

Pension Protection Fund. 2010. *PFF 7800 Index 30 June 2010*. www.pensionprotectionfund.org.uk/DocumentLibrary/Documents/PPF_7800_July_10.pdf.

Pensions Regulator (2006–9, 2011) *Occupational Pension Scheme Governance*. www.thepensionsregulator.gov.uk/docs/governance-survey-report-2011.pdf.

2006. *Code of Practice 7: Trustees Knowledge and Understanding*. London: Pensions Regulator.

2007a. *The Governance of Work-based Pension Schemes*. Discussion paper. London: Pensions Regulator.

2007b. *How the Regulator will Promote Better Governance of Work-based Pension Schemes: The Regulator's Response*. London: Pensions Regulator.

2007c. *How the regulator will promote better governance of work-based pension schemes: The Regulator's response*. www.thepensionsregulator.gov.uk/doc-library/the-governance-of-work-based-pension-schemes.aspx.

2008a. *Our Corporate Strategy 2008–2012: Next Steps in Risk-based Regulation*. London: Pensions Regulator.

2008b. *Regulatory Guidance: Conflicts of Interest*. London: Pensions Regulator.

2008c. *Regulatory Guidance: Relations with advisers*. www.thepensionsregulator.gov.uk/doc-library/guidance.aspx.

2009a. *Regulatory Guidance: Corporate Transactions*. www.thepensionsregulator.gov.uk/doc-library/guidance.aspx.

PRAG. 2007. *Financial Reports of Pension Schemes*. Statement of Recommended Practice (SORP). London: PRAG.

PricewaterhouseCoopers. 2004, 2006, 2008, 2010. *Are you Managing your Pensions Business?* www.pwc.co.uk/human-resource-services/publications/are-you-managing-your-pensions-business.jhtml.

Pike, R., J. Meerjanssen and L. Chadwick. 1993. "The Appraisal of Ordinary Shares by Investment Analysts in the UK and Germany," *Accounting and Business Research* 23 (92): 489–99.

Scapens, R. W. 1984. "Management Accounting: A Survey Paper," in *Management Accounting, Organisational Behaviour and Capital Budgeting*. London: Macmillan/ ESRC.

Short, H. and K. Keasey. 1997. "Institutional investors and corporate governance in the United Kingdom". In K. Keasey, S. Thompson, and M. Wright, (eds.) *Corporate Governance: Economic, Management and Financial Issues*. New York: Oxford University Press.

Solomon, J. 2007. *Corporate Governance and Accountability*. Chichester: John Wiley & Sons Ltd.

Stiles, P. and B. Taylor. 1993. "Maxwell – the Failure of Corporate Governance," *Corporate Governance: An International Review* 1 (1): 34–45.

Thomas, R. and R. Turner. 2001. *Mirror Group Newspapers plc Investigations under Sections 432(2) and 442 of the Companies Act 1985*. London: Department of Trade and Industry.

Useem, M. and O. Mitchell. 2000. "Holders of the Purse Strings: Governance and Performance of Public Retirement Systems," *Social Science Quarterly* 81 (2): 489–506.

Institutional investment and fiduciary duty in Australia

GORDON NOBLE

CHAPTER 5

Introduction

Australia has one of the largest pension fund systems in the world with $AUD 1.34 trillion in assets as at June 2011. The superannuation system is, however, not a single pool of assets but consists of different segments that have their own features in terms of the way members are recruited and serviced, and investments managed. The system is also divided in the way it is regulated with larger superannuation funds, with total assets of $AUD 810.6 billion, regulated by the Australian Prudential Regulation Authority (APRA) while self-managed superannuation funds, commonly referred to as SMSFs, with $AUD 407.6 billion in assets are regulated by the Australian Taxation Office (ATO). The market for APRA-regulated funds is itself divided between retail funds which held 28 percent of all assets whilst not-for-profits funds' combined assets amount to 35 percent of the total assets. The core difference between retail funds and not-for-profit funds is that retail funds have been established by financial institutions with the objective of delivering an investment return to shareholders from offering superannuation products while not-for-profit funds, as their name suggests, do not have to deliver a return to shareholders.

The structure of Australia's superannuation system

In Australia, superannuation fund members have the ability to select how their funds are invested as well as selecting which institution should invest on their behalf. At the request of a superannuation fund member a superannuation fund must be able to transfer superannuation assets to a newly selected superannuation fund within thirty days.

The impact of choice in the Australian context is that there is significant competition among superannuation funds to recruit and retain superannuation fund members.

The vast majority of Australia's superannuation assets are held in defined contribution schemes where individual members bear investment risk. Defined benefit schemes, while still in existence, are in many cases closed to new members and a relatively small part of the superannuation landscape.

Operating as a separate distinct group within Australia's superannuation system are self-managed superannuation funds (SMSFs), a structure in which the superannuation fund member becomes the trustee of their own assets with responsibility to manage their own investments. SMSFs are required to have less than five members, all of whom are trustees of the fund. SMSFs have emerged as a significant portion of the superannuation system with almost a third of all assets ($AUD 407.6 billion) in the Australian system managed within an SMSF structure. There are no restrictions to prevent Australians setting up their own SMSF. A range of reasons, including taxation benefits and the desire of Australians to exercise control over their own financial decisions, is leading to growth in the SMSF sector with the number of SMSFs growing by 7.2 percent during the 2011 financial year. One of the explanations as to why SMSFs have grown so rapidly may be behavioral. Australia has a strong culture of self-reliance born out of the isolation of early settlers who simply had no choice but to find their own solutions to problems. Australians also have a well-known reputation for distrusting authority, which has created a "do it yourself culture" in many aspects of Australian life. The poor performance of many APRA-regulated superannuation funds during the global financial crisis certainly confirmed the view of many Australians that they could manage their own money better than professional investment managers and is considered one of the explanations as to why SMSFs have continued their rapid growth over the past few years.

The introduction of compulsory superannuation

Whilst Australia's first superannuation fund was set up in 1842 by the Bank of Australasia (now part of ANZ Group) it was with the commencement of the Superannuation Guarantee on July 1, 1992 that Australia differentiated itself from the rest of the world in respect to its retirement incomes policy. At the time of introduction the Superannuation Guarantee required employers whose annual payrolls exceeded $AUD 500,000 to make a contribution of 5 percent of ordinary time earnings into a designated superannuation fund for employees. Smaller businesses were initially required to pay 3 percent of employee wages into superannuation. The level of the Superannuation Guarantee increased to 9 percent by 2002. In 2012, the Australian government passed legislation to increase the Superannuation Guarantee to 12 percent by July 1, 2019.

The Superannuation Guarantee terminology is itself confusing, raising the question as to exactly what is guaranteed. The "guarantee" relates to the requirement under the Superannuation Guarantee Charge Act 1992 that employers that do not make a compliant superannuation contribution for an employee are required to pay a Superannuation Guarantee Charge to the Australian Taxation Office (ATO). The SG Charge consists of the shortfall amount, an interest component and an administration component. In essence the SG Charge represents a fine on an employer that fails to make a compliant superannuation contribution for an employee.

The introduction of the Superannuation Guarantee codified in legislation what had become a national industrial issue. Trade unions in the late 1980s had begun incorporating demands for superannuation into their industrial negotiations. With the election of the Hawke Labor government in 1983 the Australian government established a Prices and Incomes Accord with the Australian Council of Trade Unions (ACTU). The Accord, as it was commonly referred to, provided a mechanism for the Australian government to address the nation's stagflation, with the trade union movement agreeing to wage restraint in return for other trade-offs. In September 1985 the Australian government and the ACTU had agreed that a 3 percent contribution to superannuation would be paid to employees covered by Industrial Awards. In return the ACTU agreed to a wage claim of 2 percent below the prevailing rate of inflation. The Australian Government–ACTU Accord Mark 6, agreed in February 1990 allowed additional superannuation contributions equivalent to 3 percent of ordinary time earnings to be available from May 1, 1991, and no later than May 1, 1993. The increased 3 percent was to be delivered through industrial negotiations, which in reality was a tacit understanding that stronger trade unions had by that point of time become frustrated with the Accord's focus on wage restraint. Importantly for the future development of Australia's superannuation system, the introduction of compulsory superannuation was a deal done without the involvement of employers and opposed by the Liberal and National parties that represented the conservative side of Australian politics.

One of the benefits of the introduction of the Superannuation Guarantee was that it significantly increased the proportion of Australians that received some form of superannuation benefit as part of employment arrangements. Prior to the introduction of award-based superannuation estimates were that only around 40 percent of Australians had some form of superannuation benefit, many of whom were employed in the public sector. The Superannuation Guarantee was introduced at a time of economic recession in Australia. One of the early impacts of the introduction of compulsory superannuation contributions into designated funds was that many employers reviewed their defined benefit pension plans, with many closing altogether, closing to new members or establishing hybrid structures that combined accumulation benefits and defined benefits. By June 2011 defined benefit funds, while significant in absolute terms at $AUD 158.2 billion in assets, represented just over 10 percent of the overall fund in the system of $AUD 1.34 trillion.

Australia's superannuation system's two central features, compulsion and choice, were developed separately. While the federal Labor government introduced compulsory superannuation in the form of the Superannuation Guarantee, it was a Coalition (Conservative) government that introduced legislation in 2004 that gave Australians the right to choose their own superannuation fund. The government's Choice of Superannuation Funds legislation, effective from July 1, 2005, gave employees the right to select their own eligible superannuation fund to receive Superannuation Guarantee (SG) contributions made on their behalf. The legislation covered most employees, although members of defined benefit schemes and employees that were subject to specific enterprise bargaining agreements were exempt. Under Australia's choice of fund rules a member of a superannuation fund can select where future superannuation contributions are to be made, but they also have the right to move their existing superannuation assets between investment choices in the same fund. Investment choices may include broad investment styles such as conservatives, balances or growth as well as the ability to select individual investment managers. Retail superannuation funds have traditionally provided their members with more investment choices than not-for-profit funds. On average retail funds offer an average of 212 investment choices while not-for-profit funds have an average of 12 investment options per fund (Cummings and Ellis 2011). Increased competition within the superannuation industry, which has been heightened as institutions respond to the government's Stronger Super reforms, is leading to convergence. Larger not-for-profit superannuation funds now offer enhanced investment choices – including in some cases the ability to invest directly in shares on the ASX – while retail funds are offering low-cost, no-frills products that meet needs of investors with basic needs that have minimal investment choice. While the dominant parties in Australia's political system each have their own emphasis in terms of changes to the system it is nevertheless the case that the superannuation system is universally supported, both in terms of compulsory superannuation and choice of fund.

Fiduciary duty: the sole purpose test

One of the features of Australia's superannuation system was that in establishing the legislative framework for the Superannuation Guarantee the federal government quite deliberately did not overly restrict the investments of superannuation funds. Speaking at the time of the introduction of the Superannuation Guarantee legislation one Labor MP, Les Scott, stated:

> the Government does not intend to determine the types of investments that funds can be applied to, except where necessary for prudential purposes. Such action, I believe, would restrict the growth potential of the fund and limit access by the general economy to this valuable source of funds, thereby having a detrimental effect on the members' entitlements and the benefits that would normally flow to the economy.[1]

Prior to the introduction of the Superannuation Guarantee, Australia had previously directed the investments of pension funds, a policy that directly led to the formation of the Association of Superannuation Funds of Australia to represent the interests of superannuation funds. In 1960, facing a fiscal credit squeeze the Australian government required that pension funds were required to hold 30 percent of the fund's assets in government securities, of which 20 percent were to be in Commonwealth government securities. The 30/20 rule, as it was known, was finally abolished in 1984, replaced with the ability for superannuation funds to invest in "any manner."

Australia's superannuation system has been established with superannuation benefits of Australians maintained within a trust structure. Under the Superannuation Industry (Supervision) Act 1993 (SIS Act)[2] a superannuation trustee is

[1] Les Scott, Member for Oxley, Appropriation Bill (No. 1) 1991–2, September 10, 1991, Hansard Page: 1049.

[2] The Superannuation Industry (Supervision) Act 1993 or SIS Act as it is commonly referred to provides the legislative framework from Australia's superannuation. In addition to meeting legislative requirements the Australian parliament has also the power to set regulations. Parliament however only has the power to disallow a regulatory instrument. The Australian Prudential Regulation has issued Prudential Practice Guides to outline its expectation on

responsible for formulating an investment strategy that has regard to the whole of the circumstances of the fund. While not restricting the investment universe the Australian government requires super-annuation funds, including SMSFs, to operate according to the Sole Purpose Test with the retirement income objective paramount. Section 62 of the SIS Act requires that a trustee of a regulated super-annuation fund must ensure that a fund is maintained for the core purpose of providing benefits after the member's retirement.[3] The Sole Purpose Test does clarify that certain kinds of investments are regarded as inconsistent with the government's superannuation policy objectives, including lending funds to a member of a superannuation fund or investing in an asset that is not on an "arm's length basis." Specific restrictions are placed on investing in "in-house assets."

As part of the SIS Act legislative framework for superannuation, a superannuation fund trustee is required to ensure that investments are diverse and that the superannuation fund is not exposed to risks from inadequate diversification. The fund must also manage the liquidity of a fund's investments to meet expected cash flow requirements. A superannuation fund's investment strategy must have regard to the risk involved in making, holding and realizing the investments, as well as the likely return from the investments having regards to fund objectives. When monitoring superannuation fund compliance, APRA expects that superannuation trustees will be able to justify and document how all investments made under an investment strategy are consistent with that strategy and the safeguards, if any, that will be used to enable both the objectives of the strategy and the requirements contained in the investment covenant to be met (Australian Prudential Regulation Authority 2006).

In February 2001, APRA provided further clarification on its interpretation of the SIS Act outlining a set of principles in a Superannuation Circular. The principles state that a trustee should exercise

how superannuation trustees should interpret legislation and regulation. This system has recently been superseded with APRA being given Prudential Standard making powers that commenced on July 1, 2013.
[3] Superannuation Industry (Supervision) Act 1993.

care when considering investments to ensure that the provision of retirement benefits for members is the overriding consideration behind the investment decision.

> However, the situation may arise where a properly considered and soundly based investment provides "incidental" advantages to members or other persons which could suggest that the fund is maintained, in whole or part, for an improper purpose (Australian Prudential Regulation Authority 2001).

The principles go on to describe that

> such incidental advantages would not necessarily, in isolation, amount to a breach of the sole purpose test. For example, investment in a well-researched and commercially sound project might incidentally create employment opportunities for members; and it is open to trustees to develop features of their fund which add value to, or differentiate it from, other funds.

The Sole Purpose Test Principles were developed prior to the broader global debate on fiduciary duties and were at that time responding to developments where superannuation funds were investing in projects that in addition to delivering investment returns had an objective of creating employment in industries that were closely aligned to the fund. One example was Cbus, an industry fund for the building and construction sector that had in the 1990s invested in building development at a time of high unemployment in the construction sector. There has been little focus on the concept of "incidental advantage" in the broader debate about fiduciary duties. However in the context of a legislative environment that does not restrict investment, there is no legislative and regulatory restrictions that have for instance prevented the development of traditional forms of ethical investment, so long as investments were made for the purpose of providing retirement benefits. The Sole Purpose Test, with its focus on incidental advantages, may be one explanation as to why Australian superannuation funds were early adopters of the United Nations-backed Principles for Responsible Investment (PRI). A number of not-for-profit superannuation funds were amongst the early signatories to the PRI. The Australian Council of Superannuation

Investors, a not-for-profit industry body that provides superannuation funds with support to engage with corporations around environment, social and governance issues, signed up to the PRI in October 2006. A letter to all ACSI members supporting the PRI provided funds with comfort in terms of their fiduciary duties, with a large number of funds endorsing the PRI in 2007.

Superannuation system investment issues

The way in which Australia's superannuation system has been established and developed over the past twenty years has impacted on the way in which Australian superannuation funds invest.

High allocation to growth assets

One of the features of Australia's superannuation system is the high allocation to growth assets relative to pension systems in other countries. While Australians can select their own superannuation fund and investment choice, where fund members do not make an active choice they are defaulted into superannuation funds nominated either through Australia's industrial award system or to a fund nominated by an employer. Whether or not an individual is defaulted into a fund that is determined through Australia's industrial relations system depends on the occupation of the person. Lower paid occupations are generally governed by industrial awards that determine the pay and conditions of employment for employees. Professional occupations are generally outside Australia's industrial award system and in these cases it is the employer that selects the default superannuation fund for employees that do not elect to make their own selection. Once a contribution has been made by the employer it is allocated to the superannuation fund's default fund that can consist of 75 percent growth assets. There has been a great deal of discussion as to why Australian superannuation funds have disproportionately invested default fund investments in growth assets. Explanations include the demographics of Australia's population and taxation incentives that encourage investments in

Australian equities. One of the explanations is that the competition among funds has led to a concentration on investment returns as the key measure of the performance of a fund. This has been supported by the emergence since choice rules were introduced of commercial ratings agencies that compare the performance of funds.

Speaking in November 2012 at the Association of Superannuation Funds of Australia's (ASFA) annual conference former Prime Minister Paul Keating (considered the original father of the Superannuation Guarantee) believed that a focus on investment returns had its limitations.

> Currently, the system stands at over 100% GDP and will mature nearer to 200% of GDP. It is simply too large in aggregate to consistently return high single or double digit returns. If compound annual returns reflected nominal GDP plus say 1%, the system would be doing well. I am certain expectations as to returns and the search for yield has done two things, managers have adopted a higher risk profile in portfolios and lower returns have soured expectations – encouraging more people to take the initiative and manage their own assets (Keating 2012).

As at December 2011, while total Australian superannuation assets were weighted 50 percent to equities by contrast, the average weighting of OECD country pension assets was 18 percent to equities. According to Keating:

> So, Australia is 2.5 times more heavily weighted into equities and relatively underweight in other asset classes. We are disproportionately weighted into equities – the most volatile and unstable asset class. The question is – how does this weighting work to deliver the key objective of the system? 60% of total superannuation assets are held by investors over the age of 50. A large proportion of these assets should be moving towards less risky, more stable asset classes, protecting capital ahead of the retirement phase (Keating 2012).

The Secretary to the Treasury, Dr. Martin Parkinson, also weighed into the debate at the ASFA 2012 conference, saying:

> I am not necessarily advocating any particular investment pattern, although I do have reservations about excessive reliance on equities. But you are the experts in this field and are best placed to

make those investment decisions, with, as I said, members' interests as the ultimate goal. What members would really like to know is how do you, as trustees; manage the peaks and troughs of the investment market to ensure a fair return for them? As trustees of members' contributions, how are you addressing the demands to develop products that will manage risks over time and that will meet members' expectations of retirement income? How is industry responding to future challenges? (Parkinson 2012)

Parkinson's challenge to the industry, while intuitively simple, may in reality be hard to achieve. There is a history in the superannuation industry of financial products that sought to manage risk that either received little consumer support or suffered due to government regulations. A case in point was the cash management and fixed interest trusts offered by many financial institutions that were frozen to redemptions in the height of the GFC when the Australian government gave Australia's banks a deposit guarantee. While the Australian government protected Australia's banking system, this was not without cost to the institutions offering products outside the banking system.

Liquidity

Choice of fund rules require superannuation funds to be able to transfer superannuation funds of a member to their selected fund within thirty days of the member making a compliant request. Fund members may also request to transfer their assets to a different investment choice within the same fund. The issue of liquidity management became of central focus to APRA following the GFC. While overall most superannuation fund members did not exercise investment choices during the GFC, a number of superannuation funds had a significant portion of members requesting shifts to low risk investment choices, including cash. The continued inflow of superannuation contributions during this time meant that most superannuation funds were able to accommodate investment choice switches without needing to sell assets. Superannuation funds that had high exposures to unlisted infrastructure assets did however come under cash-flow pressure; with a result that Australia's regulatory

authority placed increased emphasis in the aftermath of the GFC on the way in which superannuation funds managed their unlisted assets. The resultant attention by APRA on a small number of superannuation funds contributed to a push for APRA to be given increased prudential powers. APRA's Investment Governance Prudential Standard (SPS530), which became effective on July 1, 2013, requires superannuation funds to formulate and implement a liquidity management plan and undertake comprehensive stress testing of an investment portfolio in a range of stress scenarios.

One of the implications of the focus on liquidity management is that Australian superannuation funds, while not prevented from investing in unlisted or private market assets, have an "illiquidity budget," which is a relatively small portion of an overall fund portfolio. Not-for-profit funds have tended to hold a higher percentage of their unlisted assets in unlisted property whilst retail funds hold higher proportion of investments in private equity. According to APRA research the average not-for-profit fund holds 8.7 percent of assets in unlisted property and 13.2 percent in other assets including infrastructure (Cummings and Ellis 2011). A paper on risk and return of illiquid investments by James Cummings and Katrina Ellis released in November 2011 notes that in the period 2004–10, not-for-profit superannuation funds allocated more of their portfolios to illiquid assets than for-profit superannuation funds and that these investments produced higher risk-adjusted returns. The paper found that not-for-profit funds with higher percentage holdings of illiquid investments and longer average holding periods experience higher risk-adjusted returns. One of the reasons why not-for-profit funds have invested more in infrastructure assets is due to the fact that, prior to the introduction of choice of fund legislation, not-for-profit industry funds had certainty that contributions for employees in their industry sector must be paid into their fund. Restrictions on transferring a fund to another fund meant in practical terms that these funds were closed funds. This provided trustees with greater ability to invest in illiquid assets. Not-for-profit superannuation funds were in fact early innovators in terms of investment allocation. There are a number of examples of this but perhaps the most globally significant has been the role that not-for-profit funds played investing in infrastructure in the early 1990s when state governments privatized electricity assets and established toll roads. Australia's early experience investing in infrastructure, driven by superannuation fund investment, has led to Australian managers including Industry Funds Management, Macquarie, Colonial First State and AMP playing a significant role in the development of infrastructure as a global asset class.

One of the implications of the introduction of choice of fund legislation is that it has restricted the proportion of funds that can be invested in illiquid assets. As the size of the superannuation pool grows, the nominal amount able to be invested in illiquid investments will however continue to grow. At the time the legislation was introduced there was no focus by the government on the impact that the changes would have on the investment universe for superannuation fund trustees.

We are yet to see what impact APRA's focus on liquidity management will have on the allocation by superannuation funds to illiquid assets. One of the likely impacts is that superannuation funds will continue to use their illiquidity budgets to invest in infrastructure but will limit investments in venture capital, which has long lock-in periods. A significant issue is the potential that reduced exposure to illiquid investments has the potential to impact on the overall returns by superannuation funds.

Herding behavior

While Australian super funds are not restricted in their investments it is nevertheless the case that the asset allocation of funds has been similar. The reliance of the early not-for-profit superannuation funds on the one asset consultant may have contributed to herding behavior that became an industry model. This in turn has been exacerbated by the introduction of choice of fund legislation that resulted in superannuation funds competing principally on investment returns. Trustees have become more concerned to deliver returns according to peers than to focus on absolute returns. Private consultants emerged that provided consumers with services to compare the investment performance

of funds, contributing to an overall pressure for funds to deliver out-performance. In the good times, before the GFC, superannuation funds were commonly delivering over 10 percent per annum in returns for their default investment options. As regulations were put in place to provide consumers with better disclosure around all types of investments, superannuation funds were required to issue Product Disclosure Statements that, it can be argued, resulted in further standardization of investment strategies. One of the implications of the pressure to deliver returns was that asset allocations drifted towards growth investments. As the size of assets grew superannuation funds that had begun investing solely in cash developed more sophisticated investment strategies. Fixed interest investments that were once simply invested in capital guaranteed cash products became "enhanced fixed interest" as funds chased returns.

The GFC delivered a shock to many superannuation fund members. Having never experienced negative returns the impact of not just one year, but multiple years of below inflation investment returns was to damage the confidence of superannuation fund members. In the post-GFC environment, the poor performance of APRA-regulated superannuation funds no doubt contributed to the movement of many Australians to set up their own SMSFs. It has also led to a focus on asset allocation, in particular the exposure to growth assets.

Interlinkages with financial system

The GFC in fact highlighted what has been described as the Achilles heel of Australia's financial system – its reliance on global markets to provide wholesale funding to Australia's banks. Ken Henry, former Secretary to the Treasury, stated in March 2012:

> We are a relatively small economy with a large and growing exposure to international financial markets in respect of both assets – principally foreign equities held by our super funds – and liabilities – principally the offshore wholesale borrowings of our banks. In this post-GFC environment, our ability to access global debt capital has a lot more to do with the quality of policy settings and regulatory performance in a lot of other places, especially

the United States and Europe. And, to state the obvious, we don't have much control over US and European economic policy makers (Association of Superannuation Funds of Australia 2012: 9).

According to former CEO of Challenger Limited Dominic Stevens:

> We borrow overseas to fund our current account deficit and in addition we further borrow in offshore markets to fund purchases of offshore equities and, to a lesser extent, offshore fixed income. If you step back from that and think of Australia as an individual, this would appear like a $200–300 billion margin lending exercise. The purpose of this offshore investment is the valid attempt to diversify our holdings of investment assets. However, with a significant current account deficit and challenging global financing markets, this may reduce overall efficiency and add to instability. This reliance of foreign capital to not only fund the excess of investment over savings but, in addition, significant net investment into offshore assets, has helped cause the slow deterioration in the loan-to-deposit ratio of the banking system. In addition, it has also exacerbated the refinancing risk inherent in our banking system as our liabilities are of significantly shorter term than our assets (Association of Superannuation Funds of Australia 2012: 9).

The issue for Australia's superannuation system is that as it grows, it has now become a central part of Australia's financial system. While Australia emerged relatively unscathed from the GFC there is an understanding among policymakers that the structure of the Australian economy and financial system means that the nation remains overly exposed to wholesale securitization markets. Because the Australian banking sector has one of the lowest loan to deposit ratios in the world, if securitized markets were to freeze, the ability of Australian banks to fund loans – and economic activity – is effectively put at risk. The exposure of Australia's financial system to wholesale markets has led to a focus by policymakers on the role that the superannuation system could play to provide stability to the overall financial system. This focus has included discussions on whether Australia's superannuation system can support the development of a local corporate bond market. It is likely that within the next couple of years the Australian

government will conduct a financial system inquiry. The role of the superannuation system will be a core part of such an inquiry. While policymakers are unlikely to tamper with the fundamentals of Australia's superannuation system, it is likely the government will consider how it creates incentives for funds to invest in areas that support domestic economic policies.

While policymakers are concerned at the banking sector's low loan to deposit ratios, SMSFs have emerged as a significant support for Australia's banking system, investing almost a third of all assets directly in bank accounts. The investment decisions of SMSFs are made by individuals. SMSF rules dictate that members of an SMSF must be family members. The most common arrangement is for a husband and wife to operate an SMSF. Most SMSF trustees are not sophisticated investors. This is reflected in the asset allocation behavior of SMSF trustees. In addition to a preference to investing in bank deposits SMSFs also invest almost a third of assets in Australia's listed share market. However less than 1 percent of assets are invested overseas. While SMSFs incur compliance and administration costs there is a clear preference to avoid investment management fees and SMSFs have so far shunned fund management products. The way in which SMSFs invest in the future is likely to be of increased focus for policymakers, particularly as the size of the sector continues to grow.

Current superannuation reforms

One way of thinking about Australia's superannuation is to see it as an evolving project. With the commencement of the Superannuation Guarantee in 1992, the architecture of the superannuation system was in its infancy. The early industry superannuation funds that were established to receive compulsory contributions from employers working in particular industries initially invested principally in cash. It was only as the size of funds grew that more sophisticated investment strategies emerged. As the account balances of individual superannuation fund members have grown so too have the demands from superannuation fund members for customer service, including financial planning advice. The regulatory environment has also evolved including changes to trustee responsibilities including requirements that individual trustees pass a fit and proper test as well as competency and skill criteria.

The superannuation system is today experiencing a new round of legislative and regulatory reform, a process of change that started with the establishment by the Australian government on May 29, 2009, of the Super System Review, which aimed to "comprehensively examine and analyse the governance, efficiency, structure and operation of Australia's superannuation system." The Review, also commonly referred to as the Cooper Review after the Review's chair Jeremy Cooper, had the objective of improving the regulation of the superannuation system while also reducing business costs within the system. The Review's final report was provided to the government on June 30, 2010, and focused on reforms in four areas: MySuper, SuperStream, Governance and SMSFs, under a broad umbrella referred to as a Stronger Super.

While Australians have the ability to select their own investment choice, many superannuation fund members do not actively make an investment decision, with their superannuation contributions going in a fund's selected default fund. Not-for-profit funds hold 45.6 percent in the default investment strategy compared to retail funds at 10.1 percent (Cummings and Ellis 2011). Most often the default fund is invested in a diversified portfolio of assets with between 60 and 70 percent invested in growth assets. The Cooper Review identified that superannuation fund members were in many cases paying for product features, such as a broad range of investment choice and financial planning, which they were not using. In effect it was argued that superannuation fund members that had not made an active investment choice were subsidizing the provision of such services for other members. The Australian government is in the process of introducing a new, low-cost, simple default fund called MySuper.[4] It is likely that the new regime will result in a number of impacts on the way a trustee

manages investments. The Australian government has legislated that a MySuper product must consist of a single diversified investment strategy with a standard set of fees available to all prospective members. MySuper trustees will be required to articulate a targeted rate of return over a ten-year rolling period with a level of investment risk that is appropriate to the MySuper members. It is envisaged that MySuper products may in the end have different levels of risk and return according to the demography of members within the fund. The focus on cost may put pressures on trustees to adopt diversified investment strategies that exclude investments in alternative assets such as hedge funds. In anticipation of the MySuper start date retail sector funds have announced low-cost MySuper products that aggressively compete with not-for-profit funds. One example is ANZ, which has introduced a new product "Smart Choice Super" that will have an investment management fee of 0.50 percent, which will be below the cost of many industry and public sector funds. A simple way for products to reduce costs is to utilize passive investment strategies rather than active management investment strategies. A significant question for the superannuation system is whether the introduction of MySuper, with its focus on cost, will lead trustees to adopt investment strategies that while cost-effective in the short term, may not perform as well in the long term.

The Australian government has also introduced reforms that will increase the responsibilities of trustees of superannuation funds. Australia's trustee system, with the exception of self-managed superannuation funds, is based on principles of equal representation for standard employer sponsored funds. In the case of industry superannuation funds, employee trustees are often nominated directly by trade unions. As part of the Australian government's reforms, the Australian Prudential Regulation Authority has been given powers, from July 1, 2013, to set prudential standards for

---

[4] Details of MySuper, including transition arrangements, are contained in a number of separate Bills: Superannuation Legislation Amendment (MySuper Core Provisions) Bill 2011; Superannuation Legislation (Further MySuper and Transparency Measurers) Bill 2012; Superannuation Legislation Amendment (Service Providers and Other Governance Measurers) Bill 2012.

superannuation trustees. The changes extend and reinforce trust law in areas including investment governance. Prior to being granted prudential standard-making power, APRA's powers derived from both the SIS Act and Superannuation Industry (Supervision) Regulations 1994 (SIS Regulations). APRA also issued various forms of nonbinding guidance material that most superannuation fund trustees adopted. APRA had argued that by being granted prudential standard-making power it would have the power to ensure consistency of practice by setting minimum standards. In the aftermath of the global financial crisis, the increased size and importance of the superannuation sector led the Australian government to conclude that APRA needed more powers than to set guidance, which a trustee could theoretically choose not to implement. APRA has stated that many of the requirements proposed within the prudential standards are already current practice for superannuation fund trustees. As such APRA's Prudential Standards do not change the fundamentals of the system but provide APRA with greater powers to ensure compliance. One of the main impacts is expected to be on smaller superannuation funds that may not have adopted sophisticated practices in areas such as liquidity management and risk management. The increased cost of complying with the prudential standards is likely to lead some trustees to consider merging with other funds in order to build funds that have sufficient scale to be able to cover the increased risk management and compliance costs without significantly impacting member benefits.

Future directions

Celebrating the twentieth anniversary of compulsory superannuation in 2012, Australia's superannuation system is still in its infancy. Not-for-profit superannuation funds have emerged as a significant player in the superannuation product market and it is likely that over the next decade there will be considerable consolidation in the industry as smaller superannuation funds merge. With superannuation contributions increasing from 9 percent to 12 percent over the next six years it can be expected that a small number of large superannuation funds will

emerge with assets between $AUD 50 and $100 billion.

Superannuation fund governance

There has been increased focus in Australia among policymakers; regulators and industry participants on the way superannuation funds are governed. APRA provided clarification on its views on board governance in a Prudential Practice Guide (SPG 520) issued in August 2010 stating that it expects that each trustee board should have a governance policy or code of conduct that identifies the skills and competencies that a trustee board is expected to collectively have in order to effectively carry out its duties. APRA's guidance provides directions to trustees on its expectations on board processes including granular detail such as processes to identify and remedy skills gaps. As part of APRA's newly granted prudential standard-making powers, Prudential Standard SPS 510 Governance sets out minimum foundations for good governance for superannuation funds. The key requirements of this Prudential Standard are that:

- The Board must have a policy on Board renewal and procedures for assessing Board performance;
- a Board Remuneration Committee must be established and have a remuneration policy that aligns remuneration and risk management;
- a Board Audit Committee must be established; and
- a regulated superannuation fund must have a dedicated internal audit function.

While APRA's continued focus on governance is resulting in improved governance practices across the industry, there is continued discussion on the need for future reforms with a particular focus on the role of independent directors. In August 2012 the Financial Services Council (FSC), which predominantly represents retail superannuation funds, released a Draft Standard for Governance of Superannuation Funds. The FSC argues that superannuation funds need to have a majority of independent directors and an independent chairperson. It is also proposing that multiple, competing directorships should be prohibited and that superannuation funds be required to disclose their environmental and social governance risk management policy and proxy voting record disclosure. The Australian Institute of Superannuation Trustees (AIST), which represents not-for-profit industry superannuation funds has issued its own governance framework and is defending the existing status quo, arguing that "all directors should exercise an independence of mind" (Australian Institute for Superannuation Trustees 2012: 13), whether or not they are notionally an independent director. While there are different views around how superannuation fund governance standards should increase, there is consensus across policymakers and industry participants that superannuation funds must raise their governance standards. Jeremy Cooper, who led the government's Superannuation System Review conducted in 2009, commented in October 2012 that it was desirable that there should be more talented business people not directly connected to super funds acting as trustees. "Such people bring the value of their reputations and have the option of resigning if they feel that they are not adding value or are not happy with the way things are going. This reflects the legal notion of the 'disinterested' director."[5]

Cooper went on to argue:

> it is widely accepted that good governance impacts investment returns, possibly as much as one or two percentage points per annum. These issues are therefore not trivial. We are rapidly approaching the point where the leading super funds will control $100 billion each. This led the Panel of the Super Review to question a model that was founded in a $50 million world and to suggest enhancements, including that all APRA-regulated super funds have a majority of non-associated directors unless they were following the equal representation model, in which case it was recommended that not less than one-third be non-associated.[6]

Up until now, Australia's superannuation trustee system has been based on an equal representation model where employer and employee representatives each hold an equal number of board positions. At the time of establishing the

Superannuation Guarantee, the Australian government considered that "[o]ne of the most important ways in which members are able to participate in the management and protection of their retirement savings is through representation on the board of trustees."[7]

The Super System Review questioned whether the equal representation model was still serving the interests of fund members. The Review noted that:

> the employer and employee representatives on many trustee boards are not, in fact, elected by employers or members, but rather are nominated by third party organisations, such as employer associations and trade unions. Current employment and industrial relations practices mean that these organisations do not necessarily represent all employers or all employees. Thus, the democracy that the equal representation policy appears to embed in the governance of superannuation funds is not always present in reality.[8]

Further the Review questioned whether pensioners were being adequately represented and a system of representation based on the place of work. In its conclusions, the Review stated that "the equal representation model appears to impose rigidity into fund governance practices and reduce accountability, without contributing materially to the representation objective on which it was predicated."

While the equal representation model has served superannuation fund members well, one of its weaknesses is the level of skills and experience that trustees possess. As the early not-for-profit superannuation funds that were established to receive compulsory superannuation contributions did not have significant resources they relied on an outsourced model for all their investment decisions. Trustee boards in particular relied on advice from asset consultants on how a superannuation fund should invest. The resulting dominance of a small number of asset consultants in the Australian market may have contributed to herding behavior across the superannuation system. One of the

---

[5] Jeremy Cooper, personal statement, October 1, 2012.
[6] Ibid.

[7] Review into the Governance, Efficiency, Structure and Operation of Australia's Superannuation System, Chapter 2, 4.2, "The Equal Representation Model," June 30, 2010.
[8] Ibid.

potential benefits of reforms that would require a third of a trustee board to be independent is that it would enable boards to increase their investment expertise. The emergence of "disinterested" independent directors, as advocated by Jeremy Cooper, has the potential to give trustee boards the confidence to develop asset allocation strategies that vary from their peers. The importance of addressing peer risk is a core reason why reforms that require having a third of trustee boards as independent directors with investment expertise would be of benefit to the overall performance of the superannuation system.

Investment

As not-for-profit superannuation funds increase in size, a number are actively considering the extent to which they bring investment activities in-house. Whether or not superannuation funds manage their investments in-house or not we are likely to see funds build their in-house investment expertise. This in itself will give superannuation funds the capabilities to do their own research, with less reliance on external asset consultants. One of the potential beneficial impacts of scale by reducing the power of asset consultants could be to reduce herding behavior in the Australian market. It is nevertheless likely that the superannuation system's emphasis on investment returns, which is supported by regulatory requirements, will continue to reward herding behavior.

The building of scale will also lead to a greater focus among policymakers on board governance. A fund that is managing $AUD 100 billion will be required to demonstrate that its trustees have sufficient skills and experience. The implications of professional trustees replacing employer and trade union professionals as the core of the superannuation trustee system are yet to be seen and will in large part depend on the way regulatory changes are made and the quality of professional trustees themselves. With regulators also focusing on investments in unlisted assets due to Australia's choice of fund rules, the ability of superannuation funds to invest in asset classes including venture capital, private equity and infrastructure will be constrained.

Australia has been fortunate in many ways that it established the legislative framework for superannuation without restrictive covenants on where superannuation funds could invest. With a strong foundation of innovation, including early support of infrastructure as an asset class, Australia would seem to be well placed to manage assets for the best long-term interests of superannuation fund members. However a range of factors including herding behavior, high allocation to growth assets and focus on liquidity have meant that Australia's superannuation system is structured to focus on short-term investment outcomes. Future changes, including the introduction of more independent directors, and the increased scale of individual superannuation funds may be beneficial in terms of providing superannuation trustees with the skills and capabilities to steer their own pathway potentially enabling the system to address herding behavior. Broader challenges including the challenge of investing in illiquid assets, the high allocation to growth assets and increased focus on the interlinkages between the superannuation system and the overall financial system will be of continued focus to policymakers with no easy solutions apparent. Overall Australia's combination of choice and compulsion has created a system which is in many ways unique. Over the past twenty years, reform of Australia's superannuation system has been ongoing. The latest round of superannuation reforms continues the evolution of the system, however they are unlikely to be the last changes that will be made.

References

Association of Superannuation Funds of Australia. 2012. *Developing Australia's Fixed Interest Markets*. Sydney: ASFA.

Australian Institute for Superannuation Trustees. 2012. *A Fund Governance Framework for Not-for-Profit Superannuation Funds*, 2nd edition. Melbourne: AIST.

Australian Prudential Regulation Authority. 2001. *The Sole Purpose Test*. Superannuation Circular No. III.A, February.

2006. *Guidance Note and Circulars*. Superannuation Circular No. II.D.1 Managing Investments and Investment Choice, March.

Cummings, J. R. and K. Ellis. 2011. *Risk and Return of Illiquid Investments: A Trade-off for Superannuation Funds Offering Transferable Accounts*. APRA Working Paper, November.

Keating, P. 2012. "New Directions," speech to the ASFA 2012 Conference, Sydney, November 28.

Parkinson, M. 2012. "Future Challenges: Australia's Superannuation System," speech to the ASFA 2012 Conference, Sydney, November 28.

The regulation of institutional investment in Sweden: a role model for the promotion of responsible investment?

JOAKIM SANDBERG, SEBASTIAN SIEGL AND
IAN HAMILTON

Introduction

Over the last half-century or so, the Swedish capital market has increasingly come to be dominated by large-scale institutional investors, such as pension funds, mutual funds, insurance companies and other kinds of financial organizations. Recent estimates suggest that domestic and foreign institutions control more than 85 percent of all outstanding shares on the Stockholm Stock Exchange (Skog 2005; Stattin 2010). This makes the Swedish market among those with the highest concentration of institutional ownership in the world. In this context it is interesting to note that, according to many scholars, Sweden presents a unique regulatory environment for institutional investment; an environment with unparalleled emphasis on responsible investment practices (Richardson 2008; Robins 2006; Statman 2005). Much praise has, for example, been given to the investment mandate of the national pension funds (the AP funds), which obliges them to incorporate ethical and environmental concerns into investment decisions (Hamilton and Eriksson 2011). Sweden also has a comparably well-developed market for retail mutual funds with an ethical or environmental profile, especially in relation to the limited size of the country's total fund market (Eurosif 2012).

This chapter introduces and discusses some main features of the Swedish regulatory environment with regards to institutional investment, with special emphasis on the connection to responsible investment. We start by introducing some of the main legal statutes concerning institutional

investment and compare them with the fiduciary duties imposed on trustees in other countries, such as the UK and the US. Thereafter we discuss the more specific legal framework relevant for mutual funds and pension funds, respectively, and especially discuss their mandate for engaging in responsible investment. Given the centrality of the AP funds, we then present and analyze a case study of how the AP funds developed their understanding of the government directive about taking ethical and environmental concern. Finally, we end with a discussion of to what extent the Swedish regulatory framework should be considered a role model for the promotion of responsible investment in other countries.

Overview of the regulatory environment

Sweden has a *civil law* legal system, which means that legal rules are interpreted or distilled from a consideration of the principles or purposes behind the law's enactment (unlike in a common law system, where the rules are interpreted in light of relevant court decisions). In order to get an overview of the regulatory environment, we studied the most important sources of legislation, including written law, government bills and official government reports from the past two decades.[1] It should be noted that the ensuing discussion of relevant

[1] This section and the next partly build on Siegl's dissertation work.

legislation in no way is intended to be exhaustive and complete. Instead we have chosen to highlight some central statutes that we think are interesting for our present purposes and also indicative of the main tenets of Swedish regulation with regards to institutional investment.

Most financial regulation in Sweden is based on three overriding objectives: (1) to protect or enhance the efficiency of the financial market; (2) to safeguard the public's trust in the same market and its institutions; and (3) to ensure that investors – especially nonprofessional investors – are sufficiently protected from risk.[2] There is no single and unified piece of legislation that covers all aspects of the practices of all institutional investors. Instead, the rules tend to be spread out over different statutes that cover slightly different types of institutions. So, for example, the main statute pertaining to mutual funds is the Investment Funds Act (Lag 2004:46 om investeringsfonder). And the focal legislation for the AP funds is the National Pension Insurance Funds (AP Funds) Act (Lag 2000:192 om allmänna pensionsfonder [AP-fonder]). We will say more about these texts below.

A slightly more general piece of legislation is the Securities Market Act (Lag 2007:528 om värdepappersmarknaden, LVM), which was implemented in November 2007, based on a government bill from the same year.[3] The purpose was to incorporate into Swedish law the Markets in Financial Instruments Directive (MiFID); an EU directive accepted by European ministers in 2004.[4] In line with MiFID, the general objectives of LVM were to harmonize the European financial markets, to secure the public's trust in financial markets and to further enhance customer protection.

LVM, specifically Chapter 8, contains a number of more specific articles that are pertinent for institutional investors. Most importantly, section 1 (of Chapter 8) states that:

A securities institution shall protect the interests of its clients when it provides investment services or

ancillary services to its clients and shall act honestly, fairly and professionally. A securities institution shall also otherwise act in such a manner as to maintain public confidence in the securities market.[5]

Sections 9–11 deal with organizational requirements and state that institutions must establish adequate policies and procedures to ensure stability in operations and full compliance with regulatory demands. Section 21 holds that institutions must take all reasonable steps to identify conflicts of interest between themselves and their clients, as well as between one client and another. Finally, section 28 establishes so-called best execution requirements, according to which securities institutions shall take all reasonable steps to achieve the "best possible result for the client" when executing orders. "Best possible result" is here defined in terms of (among other things) price, fees, size and "any other circumstances material for the client."

In order to put the statutes above into perspective, it may be interesting to compare them to some so-called fiduciary duties imposed on trustees in countries such as the UK and the US.[6] Readers of this volume will notice that there are many apparent similarities. For example, the first part of the opening sentence of LVM Chapter 8 ("A securities institution shall protect the interests of its clients when it provides investment services or ancillary services to [them]") has great affinities to the so-called "duty of loyalty" in the Anglo-American tradition. This duty roughly entails that fiduciaries are to act in the sole interests of the ultimate beneficiaries of the funds, rather than in their own self-interest (Bines and Thel 2004; Pearce and Stevens 2006; Watt 2006). Another article that goes in this direction is the one about clearly identifying conflicts of interest, both between the institution

---

[2] Cf. Prop. 2002–3:150; Prop. 2006–7:115; SOU 2006:50.
[3] Prop. 2006/07:115, "Nya regler för tjänstepensionsinstitut."
[4] Directive 2004/39/EC.

[5] All translations of Swedish law texts in this chapter stem from TransLegal 2009 (a resource that is continually updated when the law is changed). The translations are far from perfect, but we will not quarrel with this here.
[6] It may be noted that some scholars refer to the statutes above as "Swedish fiduciary duties." However, technically speaking, this is incorrect since the term only applies in common law jurisdictions (Freshfields Bruckhaus Deringer 2005).

and its clients and between one client and another (LVM Chapter 8, section 21).

Moreover, the second part of the opening sentence of LVM Chapter 8 (the obligation to "act honestly, fairly and professionally"), as well as other parts of Swedish law, have clear affinities to the so-called "duty of prudence" in the Anglo-American tradition. This duty roughly entails that trustees should be financially competent and exercise due care when managing their funds (Pearce and Stevens 2006; Watt 2006). There may be some very minor differences between Sweden and the US on this point. For example, it has become commonplace in the Anglo-American tradition to regard modern portfolio theory (MPT) as the legal standard for prudence (ibid.). MPT is a theory of finance that stresses the need for portfolio diversification, and holds that asset allocation decisions should be based on the overall risk-return characteristics of the portfolio rather than those of individual securities (see Langbein and Posner 1980). In contrast, Swedish law does not refer to MPT or any other specific theory as a standard of financial professionalism, at least not directly. However, the Swedish legislator similarly stresses the need for well-diversified portfolios, both for mutual funds (Prop. 2002/03:150) and for the AP funds (Prop. 1999/2000:46). Moreover, as we soon will see, the latest amendments to the directives for occupational pension funds explicitly draw inspiration from the Anglo-American duty of prudence.

Coming back to the overriding objectives of Swedish financial regulation in general, it seems fair to say that there are great similarities with many other countries on most aspects. This is hardly surprising since many of the statutes are based on EU directives, as we will see, which in turn often draw inspiration from developments in American law. For example, many of the recent legislative developments in both Europe and the Americas have focused exactly on consumer protection and safeguarding the public's trust in the financial market and its institutions (see Chapter 1 of this volume). However, perhaps the Swedish case is unique in its more specific interpretation of what these objectives entail or, more to the point, to what extent they are compatible with responsible investment practices. We will address this issue more specifically below.

Mutual funds

The focal regulation pertaining to Swedish mutual funds is the Investment Funds Act (Lag 2004:46 om investeringsfonder, LIF). LIF is also an incorporation of EU law; more specifically the Undertakings for Collective Investment in Transferable Securities (UCITS) directives (I, II, III and IV). LIF was last updated in August 2011, based on the latest EU directive (UCITS IV) from 2009.

In line with LVM, a central tenet of LIF is that: "In conjunction with the management of an investment fund, a Swedish management company shall act exclusively in the common interest of the unit holders" (Chapter 4, section 2). In order to ensure this, managers are asked to take all reasonable measures to prevent the unit holders' interest from being negatively affected by conflicts of interest (Chapter 2, section 17b). LIF also echoes LVM's message about conducting one's operations "in an honest, fair and professional manner" (ibid.). The relevant kind of professionalism is taken to involve, first, that the fund has sufficient resources and routines to enable its operations to function well (ibid.). Second, managers of mutual funds are required to "maintain a suitable diversification of investments, taking into consideration the spreading of risk associated with the fund's investment focus pursuant to the fund rules" (Chapter 5, section 1). Finally, LIF contains a number of information requirements: Funds are obliged to give, for example, a clearly declared investment objective, a prospectus including all information necessary for an investor to make an informed judgment, and clear and easy-to-understand information about the risks associated with the fund's investment style (Chapter 4, sections 15–17).

The most interesting of the above features for our present concerns is probably the appeal to "fund rules" ("fondbestämmelser"), which are particular to a given fund (including its investment objective and style). It is well known that, in most jurisdictions around the world, mutual funds enjoy greater autonomy in comparison to, for example, pension funds when it comes to choice of investment objectives and style. As Richardson and Cragg note, "in the retail investment market, mutual funds have much more flexibility in their investment choices and conceivably can cater to any values investors demand including those oppressive to human rights or the environment" (2010: 35). But we think that a pertinent question in the present context is exactly how far this autonomy goes.

Our main interest is, similar to Richardson and Cragg, in so-called responsible investment. This term typically refers to the practice of integrating environmental, social and/or governance considerations (referred to as ESG considerations) in decisions over whether to purchase, retain or realize various investments (Cowton and Sandberg 2012; Freshfields Bruckhaus Deringer 2005).[7] So, for example, an institution may choose to refrain from investing in companies that trade with conflict diamonds (or alcohol, tobacco and firearms), or actively seek out and invest in companies that belong to the cleantech industry, because of the institution's commitment to certain social or environmental values. Interestingly, Sweden has a comparably well-developed market for mutual funds with a responsible investment profile (popularly called "ethical funds" ["etiska fonder"]), especially in relation to the limited size of the total fund market (Eurosif 2012). But a legitimate question is what support such funds enjoy in the official guidelines.

The general principle expressed in LIF (Chapter 4, section 9) is that fund rules must be "reasonable for the holders of units in the collective investment undertaking," and that changes to the fund rules only are permitted if they "do not violate the common interests of the unit holders." While the language here may not be very clear, it is interesting to note that the legislator explicitly mentions responsible investment as an example of the permissibility of certain

nonfinancial fund objectives (Prop. 2002/03:150). The background rationale is roughly that such rules can be acceptable as long as the associated risks are adequately conveyed to the unit holders, in line with Richardson and Cragg's idea above. However, in a preparatory report, it is stressed that this puts an increased disclosure demand on ethical funds: "[Ethical requirements] are not self-evident and cannot automatically be taken to coincide with the common interests of the unit holders. A fund that wishes to [include such requirements] must therefore make a special note of it in the fund rules" (SOU 2002:56: 266, our translation).

Unfortunately, the legislator says nothing more specific about what kinds of risks may be associated with responsible investment practices and, in particular, how these may come into conflict with other statutes that tend to assume strictly financial fund rules. In our view, this makes the current legal situation somewhat unclear. Responsible investment brings the issue of the limits of mutual funds' autonomy to a head because it may lead to sub-par returns – most easily, if institutions establish very strict policies of exclusion (Fabretti and Herzel 2013; Langbein and Posner 1980). This is essentially why some judges and scholars in Anglo-American jurisdictions have argued that responsible investment may be inconsistent with the fiduciary duties of institutional investors (see many other chapters in this volume). Given the many similarities with these jurisdictions, one would have expected the Swedish legislator to say at least something about the obvious conflicts that may arise between ethical requirements and financial requirements such as the need for diversification. For instance, it would at least seem to violate the spirit of both LIF and LVM to knowingly accept sub-par returns for the unit holders in the pursuit of social goals (compare, for example, with the appeal to materiality in LVM's best execution requirements [Chapter 8, section 28]).

To adequately understand how the authorities have reasoned concerning the ethical funds, perhaps one also needs to consider the development of best practice within the industry. In 2004, the Swedish Investment Fund Association (Fondbolagens förening) was asked by the Swedish Consumer Agency (Konsumentverket) to issue

---

[7] In the literature, the term responsible investment is vaguely defined and is also referred to as "socially responsible investment," "sustainable investment" or "ethical investment." Even though the notion is somewhat clouded, and not all scholars agree (Woods and Urwin 2010), it appears that most investors see these various terms as explaining the same mechanism, namely the incorporation of ESG factors into the financial investment decision-making process (see also Sandberg et al. 2009).

some kind of guidelines for so-called ethical funds, so that consumers could know what to expect. Curiously, the designated committee refused to give a more detailed definition of ethical funds, and instead emphasized the overarching need for clear and correct marketing information about such funds' policies to consumers (Etiska nämnden för fondmarknadsföring 2004). This statement seems to go hand in hand with the legislator's hands-off attitude, and again locates the justification of responsible investment practices in adequate and sufficient disclosure.[8] More recently, in 2011 the umbrella organization of the ethical funds themselves – Sweden's Sustainable Investments Forum (Swesif) – launched their "sustainability profiles" framework. This framework lets fund providers present information about their ethical investment policies in a standardized and more accessible way, which is supposed to facilitate easier comparisons between funds by clients.

Swesif's framework may be seen as a voluntary (soft-law) initiative from the industry, which to some extent displaces the need for direct (hard-law) regulation from the government. Most directly, the framework has affinities to the kind of disclosure requirements (although primarily for pension funds) that recently have been introduced in the UK and elsewhere (see Sparkes 2002). In our view, however, similar initiatives do very little in terms of clarifying the more fundamental question of just how far a mutual fund may go with its nonfinancial fund rules (more on this below). Furthermore, it should be noted that Swesif's framework only is voluntary and aspirational; that is, there are no regulatory sanctions associated with it.

Pension funds

The Swedish pension system, much like the pension systems in many other European countries,

involves three main "pillars": public pensions (i.e., a basic pension scheme provided by the state), occupational pensions (i.e., a set of mandatory employer-based pension schemes for most employees) and private pensions (i.e., the full range of optional individual policies open for all) (for overviews of the system, see Berg 2007; Sundén 2006). The regulatory environment for pension funds varies to some degree depending on which of these pillars the fund belongs to. But there are also many similarities.

The regulatory environment of the third pillar is obviously closest to the situation of private mutual funds. The third pillar namely involves pension policies that people choose for themselves on an individual basis; be they, for example, annuities or investments, life insurance or endowment insurance products. It may (once again) seem natural to assume that the underlying funds should be free to "cater to any values investors demand" as long as their investment profile is fully and adequately disclosed, since unsatisfied pension savers simply may opt out and choose a different fund. But we stress (once again) that the legislator says very little about the exact boundaries of this freedom.

Interestingly, recent amendments to the pension system have introduced an element of choice also in the first and second pillars. Most noticeably, since 2001, 2.5 percent of people's pensionable income is placed in an individual account in the so-called premium pension system, which is an independent part of the state-run policy (while 16 percent is transferred into the more traditional income pension system). In the premium system, the pension saver can choose between over 800 mutual and fixed-income funds (spread over more than one hundred investment firms) and the account's balance will thereafter reflect the return on the selected funds. The legislator's objective with this amendment was to make pension savers further involved in the investment decision-making process, and specifically to allow them to set their own risk levels (Sundén 2006). Together with similar amendments elsewhere in the system, this could be said to have introduced further flexibility also in the investment mandates of both public and occupational pension funds.

Swedish occupational pension funds (in the second pillar) are by tradition organized as either

---

[8] The committee's 2009 follow-up guidelines do not offer more concrete advice on this point. Instead it once again stresses the fact that information enabling the unit holder to evaluate if the fund meets his or her requirement on social or environmental issues is key, and therefore the information should be clear and easy to grasp (Etiska nämnden för fondmarknadsföring 2009).

pension trusts (pensionsstiftelser), life insurance enterprises (försäkringsföreningar) or designated pension insurance enterprises (pensionskassor). While many of these previously were tied to individual companies – and mandatory for the employees of those companies – employees may now be free to choose among a limited range of funds (and some of the funds are also available in the third pillar). Pension trusts are regulated by the Safeguarding of Pension Commitments etc. Act (Lag 1967:531 om tryggande av pensionsutfästelse m.m., TrL), whereas life and pension insurance companies are regulated by the Insurance Business Act (Försäkringsrörelselagen 2010:2043, FRL). However, it may be noted that both laws contain roughly similar statements concerning how the funds' assets are to be invested, namely: "in the manner which best serves the beneficiaries of [the pension fund] and also otherwise in a prudent manner."[9]

These similarities in formulations are due to recent changes prompted by an EU directive on "the activities and supervision of institutions for occupational retirement provision" from 2003 (Directive 2003/41/EC). The principal raisons d'être for this directive were guaranteeing efficient investments and ensuring a high level of protection for future pensioners in Europe (the beneficiaries of the pension funds). The directive was implemented into Swedish law in two steps, first in 2006 (SOU 2004:101; Prop. 2004/05:165) and then in 2010 (Prop. 2009/10:246). In our view, what is most striking about these changes is that they explicitly seek to mimic the duty of prudence in the Anglo-American system. As argued in the preparatory report, the Anglo-American framework is advantageous insofar as it is focused on process – rather than outcome – and imposes qualitative rather than quantitative restrictions on the mandate of trustees.[10] Indeed, the report directly cites some formulations of the duty of prudence taken from the OECD and the UK, which then are restated in the subsequent government bill.[11]

Taken together, the occupational pension funds (in the second pillar) manage almost half of the total pension capital in Sweden (Swedish Pensions Agency 2010). However, it is the first pillar (the public pensions) that stands for the largest part of pensioners' income, almost 75 percent (ibid.). This pillar is also the most densely regulated.

As noted above, the Swedish public pension system has two parts: the income pension system is a defined contribution plan, which means that individuals' pension benefits will depend on their contributions as well as the general growth of the economy. In this system, five public pension funds – also called AP funds (allmänna pensionsfonder, AP-fonder) – act as a balancing mechanism; that is, their assets are used to cushion temporary imbalances between contributions and disbursements in the system. These five funds (AP1–4 and AP6) are also known as the "buffer funds."[12] The second part of the system is the premium pension system in which, as noted, individuals are free to choose from a wide range of funds. However, for those that refrain from making an active choice in this system, there is another AP fund (AP7) that functions as the default fund. It is also possible to actively choose AP7, so this fund to some extent competes with retail fund managers. AP7 currently manages about 26 percent of the total fund capital in the premium system, mainly because a considerable amount of pension savers refrain from making an active choice (AP7 2010). Taken together, the AP funds control roughly 25 percent of all listed shares and bonds on the Swedish securities market (Berg 2007).

The main legal statute for the AP funds is the National Pension Insurance Funds (AP Funds) Act (Lag 2000:192 om allmänna pensionsfonder [AP-fonder]). In general, there are many similarities between this statute and, for example, LVM and LIF. For instance, Chapter 3, section 8 contains rules on the avoidance of conflicts of interest, and Chapter 4, section 2 contains rules on adequate risk management. Interestingly, the overriding goal given to AP1–4 is stated in rather concrete terms and without reference to beneficiaries:

---

[9] TrL section 10a; FRL Chapter 6, section 20.
[10] SOU 2004:101: 135–8; see also SOU 2011:68.
[11] Prop. 2004/05:165: 102.

[12] There was previously an AP5, but this fund was removed in the reformed system.

"The First to Fourth AP Funds shall manage fund assets in such a manner so as to achieve the greatest possible return on the income-based retirement pension insurance" (Chapter 4, section 1). With regards to AP7, however, it is said more conventionally that: "The management shall be conducted exclusively for the purpose of promoting the interests of pension savers" (Chapter 5, section 1). One way of interpreting this difference could be that it seems more difficult to identify the exact beneficiaries of AP1–4 – and hence their responsibilities are formulated more as duties to the system in general – whereas AP7 has customers in very much the same way as commercial funds (Hamilton and Eriksson 2011). In practice, however, it is unclear whether this difference has mattered much to the mainstream practices of the funds.

The traditional focus has in both cases been on maximizing portfolio returns. However, in 2001, the five larger AP funds were also given the secondary goal of giving consideration to "ethics and the environment."[13] Given the centrality of this secondary goal for our present concerns, we will here present a case study of how the AP funds came to implement this directive.

A case study of the AP funds

Curiously, the directive is not stated in the AP Funds Act itself. However, in the government bill accompanying the act, it is plainly stated that: "Consideration shall be given to ethics and the environment in investment activities without compromising the overall goal of a high return."[14] This formulation is repeated a couple of times and is seemingly treated as a new requirement on the funds. As far as we can tell, the main justification offered for the directive is an appeal to public confidence; it is said that: "Given their [the AP funds'] role as trustees of public pension assets, the funds must also seek the public's trust."[15]

The practical problem was that the bill contained no further instructions as to how to implement a consideration for ethics and the environment. That is, the government's idea was simply that the AP funds themselves should come up with a plan for interpretation and implementation. In practice, this became the job of the AP funds' management teams (in a broad sense, including CEOs, board members and investment managers). We conducted a series of interviews with the management teams of the five AP funds as well as with outside experts and stakeholders with insights into this process.[16] Our interviews reveal that the directive was a frequently discussed topic among all of the teams during this time, partly since it seemed so open to interpretation. At the same time, it should be said that many of the teams lacked direct expertise and experience concerning – and perhaps also interest in – responsible investment practices, and so they did not always give this issue the highest priority.

A recurring complaint from many team members was that the directive sentence was inconsistent if taken literally. According to financial theory, namely, all nonfinancial restrictions imposed on an investment portfolio will lead to suboptimal returns (they said). So how could there be any room for showing ethical and environmental concern? According to other members, however, the directive could be said to avoid this problem since it talked about "high return" rather than "highest return." In any case, the general consensus among AP fund managers appeared to be that a small cost for ethics and the environment seemed reasonable, but it must not substantially affect their portfolios' risk-return profile.

In the end, the AP funds came to adopt two somewhat different approaches to responsible

of the AP funds. While it is repeated several times throughout the bill that the AP funds are not supposed to have (or be a part of) a political agenda, it is said at one place that: "the funds ought to be able to use their ownership role to contribute to public interest by promoting the kind of ethical and environmental considerations adopted in their investment policies" (ibid., p. 84, our translation).

[16] This section builds on Hamilton's dissertation work. Some of the research has been published previously; see Hamilton and Eriksson (2011). It should be noted that all of the interviews were conducted in 2007–8, and hence may not reflect some later developments.

---

[13] AP6 is exempt from the directive since it only invests in private equity, i.e., small and medium-sized firms that are not listed on the stock exchange (SOU 2008:107: 134).

[14] Prop 1999/2000:46: 76–7, our translation.

[15] Ibid. There is also a brief discussion about the social good that can be achieved through harnessing the financial powers

investment. AP7 was first to act and they chose to develop what we may call a norm-based screening approach. This approach was inspired directly from the so-called ethical funds discussed above, which by tradition have avoided investments in industries such as weapons, tobacco, alcohol and gambling (Bengtsson 2008) – but with some minor adjustments. AP7 believed that excluding entire business sectors would result in too large constraints on their investment portfolio, which could have a negative bearing on their performance. Furthermore, they struggled with the issue of how to justify what kind of companies or industries to avoid – after all, not all Swedish citizens may agree that tobacco and alcohol are immoral products. More importantly, the Swedish state owns companies in many of the most controversial sectors – including tobacco, alcohol and gambling – and it seemed inconsistent for AP7 to adopt an ethical policy that was at odds with the activities of the legislator (AP7 2001).

The solution became to focus only on the (smaller number of) companies that have committed clear violations of either Swedish laws or international treaties signed by the Swedish government (and that preferably have been convicted of such violations in public courts). This includes, for example, corporate responsibility guidelines issued by the United Nations, the ILO and the OECD. Once such a violation is identified (by an external SRI analyst firm), AP7 will sell the company and keep it on its "black list" for five years. The only way for the company to get back in after this period, is through proving that corrective measures are in place regarding its previous violations.

The buffer funds (AP1–4) were in general slower than AP7 in implementing an ethical policy, and in the end they chose a somewhat different path; what we may call an engagement approach. On this approach, problematic companies are identified in the same way as above (and here the buffer funds were in agreement with AP7's work). However, once a violation is identified, instead of selling the shares, the funds will start a dialogue with the company in order to make it change its ways. In essence, the funds try to use their influence as owners of the company in order to make it adopt various ethical and environmental policies. This approach was inspired by the practices of

so-called shareholder activist or advocacy groups in the US (Hebb 2008; O'Rourke 2003).

As far as we can tell, the main justification offered by the buffer fund managers for this approach was that, in their view, directly excluding companies from the portfolio – even to the limited extent favored by AP7 – most likely would have a substantial impact on its risk-return profile, and therefore violate their overriding fiduciary objective.[17] In addition, many of the managers believed that engagement simply is a superior method for influencing underperforming companies with regards to ethics and the environment. As they put it: if you just sell the shares, you achieve nothing.

During the first years, AP1–4 managed their engagement activities separately. In 2007, however, they came together to form "the Ethical Council," which would be a joint forum for their engagement efforts in foreign holdings.[18] The Council consists of representatives from the four buffer funds with the support of a secretary-general and external screening and engagement providers. Besides allowing the four funds to "come together to form one strong voice," the Ethical Council often seeks collaborative support from a coalition of large international institutional investors in its engagement activities. If these activities, either individually or through collaboration, fail to result in a favorable corporate response, the Ethical Council may ultimately recommend its four members to sell the shares of the problematic company.

---

[17] To our knowledge, none of the buffer fund management teams conducted or consulted any more rigorous investigation into the financial dimension of responsible investment. However, in 2004, AP7 conducted an internal inquiry into what returns they could have made (retrospectively) without their portfolio restrictions. The result suggested that their screened fund carried a marginally higher risk than a hypothetical unscreened portfolio, but that there was no significant difference in overall returns (see SOU 2008:107).

[18] It may be noted that the buffer funds do not collaborate with regards to their domestic holdings. This may be due to a feeling that it would interfere too much with their mainstream financial analysis work (which depends to a large extent on having personal relationships with corporate executives). It should be remembered that the funds are separate for a reason, namely in order to compete against each other for highest returns.

Why did they adopt these approaches?

The five larger AP funds were given the same ethics directive by the government, and yet they chose to implement two rather different approaches based on somewhat different interpretations of the directive. Why is this so? We will here discuss two possible background explanations.

One possible explanation concerns the personal expertise of the funds' managers. Rather early on, the AP7 board recruited a CEO with investment management experience of offering ethical mutual funds and who was personally interested in responsible investment. Furthermore, the chairman and vice-chairman of the board both had long experience with and an enduring interest in social responsibility issues. Together, their personal engagement seemed a critical driver behind why AP7 prioritized the government's directive while the initial response of their peers in AP1–4 appeared slower and less committed.

Another possible explanation, which we indeed think is more important, concerns the funds' market situation. As noted above, AP7 operates in the premium pension system in which it to some extent competes with private fund managers over 6.3 million Swedish pension savers' confidence and money. In this competitive race, it is important to build trust and loyalty among your clients. What partly made the norm-based screening approach appealing in this context, say some of AP7's managers that we interviewed, was that it was so simple and straightforward and, therefore, easy to communicate and to understand. Companies involved in transgressions were simply put on a "black list" and avoided until they repented. While an engagement approach perhaps could have been more effective in making companies change, it just seemed more complex and difficult to communicate to the public.

AP1–4, on the other hand, operate in the traditional income pension system, where they only compete among themselves and have no direct contact with or relationship to pension savers. It is likely that this closed market environment put weaker force on the buffer funds to respond quickly to and think proactively about the government's ethics directive. In essence, none of their

beneficiaries are able to opt out of the scheme because they are upset by its behavior. Furthermore, in the absence of an active customer, it seems fair to say that the beliefs and attitudes of financial analysts and investment managers had a stronger influence on the funds' final decision. In contrast with AP7, for example, the buffer funds appear to have taken a more traditional financial view of the threat of having to exclude a large number of firms. And the approach that they finally settled on, the engagement approach, is in many ways similar to the traditional (non-ethical) ownership practices of institutional investors (Hebb 2008).

In retrospect, we believe that AP7's communicative strategy has been successful. Whereas the buffer funds have suffered from bad press on several occasions – when severely mischievous companies (for example, companies involved in tar sand extraction, or mining companies that support oppressive regimes) have been found in their portfolios – AP7 has not had these problems to the same degree. The forming of the Ethical Council may have helped to repair the reputation of AP1–4 to some degree. But it has proven difficult to communicate progress on engagement to the general public, especially while you at the same time have to protect and build trust with the companies you are in a dialogue with.

Role models for responsible investment?

As we noted at the outset, a number of international scholars have held out the Swedish AP funds as role models in terms of responsible investment practices (Richardson 2008; Robins 2006; Statman 2005). But exactly how progressive are the approaches above – especially now, more than ten years after the ethics directive was issued?

Compared with ten years ago, it seems fair to say that the responsible investment community has changed in some ways. One of the more significant developments is the increased emphasis on "ESG integration," or what we may call the integration approach (cf. Aviva Investors 2008; Eurosif 2012). This approach is often said to represent an attempt to make ethical and environmental concerns a more integral part of the standard investment process, including traditional risk analysis and strategic portfolio design. Furthermore, the approach is said to regard ESG issues not only negatively (as possible reputation risks) but also positively (as possible "alpha drivers"). More concretely, on the integration approach, information about companies' social and environmental performance is used alongside – and very much in the same way as – more traditional financial information in decisions over what shares to buy, retain or sell (Derwall et al. 2011).

If the integration approach is the most progressive thing in responsible investment,[19] then it would seem that the AP funds actually are ten years behind. What may have been progressive when they started to work with ESG issues, namely norms-based screening and shareholder engagement, is no longer considered in the same light. Instead, it is increasingly regarded as too heavy-handed (since it divides all companies into good and bad, although most companies have both sides), as well as too external to the core of the investment process (since it focuses exclusively on negative concerns and irrespective of their materiality).

On the other hand, perhaps integration is not the most progressive thing. It should be noted that not all commentators are equally enthusiastic about the integration approach, partly because of its large focus on financial materiality (cf. Richardson and Cragg 2010). In this context, we wish to reiterate the AP fund managers' view that a small cost for ethics and the environment seems reasonable, but that it must not substantially affect their portfolios' risk-return profile. In retrospect, this view actually strikes us as far more progressive than the nowadays-familiar position outlined by the Freshfields report and others (cf. Aviva Investors 2008; Freshfields Bruckhaus Deringer 2005). This position states that ESG considerations may only be taken into account in three very special cases: when they are financially relevant (the materiality

case), when choosing between investments with identical financial qualities (the tie-breaker case) and/or when all beneficiaries share a certain ethical view (the consensus case) (for more on these cases, see Sandberg 2011). Had the AP funds understood their investment mandate in this way, we believe that it is likely that they had devoted even less time and resources on developing a responsible investment agenda.

Conclusions

This chapter has surveyed and discussed the Swedish regulatory environment with regards to institutional investment, with special emphasis on determining whether and how it promotes responsible investment practices. Many previous scholars have argued that Sweden presents a unique regulatory environment with unparalleled emphasis on responsible investment. We have indeed found some support for this view – most importantly, in the explicit mentioning of the permissibility of ethical fund rules for mutual funds, and in the AP funds' mandatory ethics directive. What really stands out in our analysis, however, is how markedly abstract and vague this support is, at least in the official guidelines and regulations. In our view, this makes the current legal situation with regards to responsible investment practices rather unclear. And this lack of clarity indeed makes us hesitant in calling the Swedish case a role model for the promotion of such practices.

In all of the official laws and guidelines for mutual funds, there are only a couple of sentences that deal with responsible investment practices. As already noted, it is promising that the legislator officially condones the use of ethical fund rules as long as the associated risks are adequately conveyed to the unit holders. However, it is unfortunate that nothing more is said about how such rules may come into conflict with the rest of the regulatory framework, which tends to focus strictly on the financial interests of beneficiaries. We have argued that, by and large, the Swedish framework is similar to the Anglo-American tradition with emphasis on fiduciary duties – and this is not strange since most of the latest statutes have

---

[19] The integration approach is seemingly the focal point of the UN Principles for Responsible Investment. For example, Principle 1 says that: "We will incorporate ESG issues into investment analysis" by, among other things, "[asking] investment service providers (such as financial analysts, consultants, brokers, research firms, or rating companies) to integrate ESG factors into evolving research and analysis." See www.unpri.org.

stemmed from efforts to streamline regulations within the EU and elsewhere. Just like in the UK and the US, then, overwhelming emphasis is put on prudence in the financial sense; for example, on providing suitable diversification and having sufficient resources to enable the fund's investment operations to function well. Thus, it is hard to avoid the feeling that it violates the spirit of most statutes to knowingly accept sub-par returns for the unit holders.

An even more progressive feature of the Swedish system is the investment directive of the public pension funds (the AP funds), which obliges them to incorporate ethical and environmental concerns into investment decisions. But we have noted how this directive really originates from a short sentence in a government bill – a sentence which many feel at best is imprecise, at worst inconsistent. In practice, it has been up to the AP funds' management teams themselves to interpret and implement the directive, even though many of them lack experience and expertise in the area. Based on our interviews with the people involved in the process, we submit that the choice of suitable approaches to responsible investment had very little to do with legal statutes or the government's intentions. Instead, salient explanations concern the managers' own personalities as well as the funds' market situation (how much they had to compete for the public's trust and money).

In both cases, then, the official guidelines concerning responsible investment practices are markedly abstract and vague. It is rather clear that the legislator is actively disinterested in discussing the matter further and wants to leave it up to the industry to try things out for itself. Indeed, it may be added that the government has shown little interest in evaluating the AP funds' ethical policies even in retrospect. The law requires the Ministry of Finance to annually evaluate the AP funds, but this request is limited to the financial aspects (Prop. 1999/2000:18). There has only been one more comprehensive follow-up inquiry, in 2008 (SOU 2008:107), but it passed by largely unnoticed. Hence, while the AP funds are officially obliged to show ethical and environmental concern in the management of their assets, it is neither specified in the law how they are to go about doing this, nor are the funds really

evaluated on any such dimensions. In our view, this is not an exemplary way of promoting the use of responsible investment practices among institutional investors.

One could of course argue that the legislator's way of doing it has "worked"; that is, that it has made many Swedish financial institutions become actively engaged in responsible investment thinking. But it is hard to avoid the feeling that this is mainly coincidental and that the legislator could have done more. At the very least, the time may now (some ten years after most of these developments) be ripe for another long look at how laws and official guidelines may strengthen institutional investors' work with responsible investment.

Our most humble suggestion in this context is that a number of regulatory clarifications would be helpful. Most importantly, the legislator could clarify (at least roughly) what level of financial sacrifice is allowed for the sake of ethical or environmental impact for both mutual funds and pension funds. For example, is it going too far to exclude entire business sectors or countries, or does this perhaps depend on the issue at hand, or on the impact that the exclusion has? Furthermore, the legislator may go further in demanding of the funds (both mutual and pension funds) that they clarify their ethical investment policies in terms that are easily comparable and accessible to the general public. While we have noted the existence of some soft-law initiatives in this regard, there is still considerable work to be done until unit holders and pension savers are able to evaluate exactly how responsible their funds are.

Disclaimer

During this *Handbook's* production process, a new government bill was introduced (Prop. 2012/13:155) designed to realize the EU's Alternative Investment Fund Managers (AIFM) Directive (Directive 2011/61/EU). While uncertainties remain concerning the implementation of this bill, its topic is obviously central to institutional investors. It is also clear that it will have more general implications for Swedish financial regulation, including both terminological and substantive effects on LIF and other laws. Unfortunately this means that some of the references to legislation above have or will become obsolete.

References

AP7. 2001. "Sjunde AP-fonden 2001."
2010. "Annual Report 2009."
Aviva Investors. 2008. "Investment Tutor Training Guide: An Introduction to Sustainable and Responsible Investment for Institutional Trustees." www.investmenttutor.com.
Bengtsson, E. 2008. "A History of Scandinavian Socially Responsible Investing," *Journal of Business Ethics* 82: 969–83.
Berg, L. 2007. "Swedish Economic National Report," in R. Påhlsson (ed.) *Yearbook for Nordic Tax Research 2007*. Copenhagen: DJØF Publishing, pp. 191–208.
Bines, H. E. and S. Thel. 2004. *Investment Management Law and Regulation*, 2nd edn. New York: Aspen.
Cowton, C. J. and J. Sandberg. 2012. "Socially Responsible Investment," in R. Chadwick (ed.) *Encyclopedia of Applied Ethics*, 2nd edn, vol. 4. San Diego: Academic Press, pp. 142–51.
Derwall, J., K. Koedjik and J. Ter Horst. 2011. "A Tale of Values-Driven and Profit-Seeking Social Investors," *Journal of Banking & Finance* 35 (8): 2137–47.
Etiska nämnden för fondmarknadsföring. 2004. "Vägledande uttalande avgivet den 19 januari 2004 i ärende 1/03 angående marknadsföringen av etiska fonder."
2009. "Vägledande uttalande avgivet den 5 maj 2009, förtydligat den 8 september 2009, i ärende 4/2008 angående marknadsföring av fonder som riktar in sig på placeringar med särskilda miljömässiga, sociala eller andra liknande hänsyn."
Eurosif. 2012. *European SRI Study*. Paris: Eurosif.
Fabretti, A. and S. Herzel. 2013. "Active Management of Socially Responsible Portfolios," in R. Cressy, D. Cumming and C. Mallin (eds.) *Entrepreneurship, Finance, Governance and Ethics*, Dordrecht: Springer, pp. 213–36.
Freshfields Bruckhaus Deringer. 2005. "A Legal Framework for the Integration of Environmental, Social and Governance Issues into Institutional Investment," report produced for the United Nations Environment Programme Finance Initiative.
Hamilton, I. and J. Eriksson. 2011. "Influence Strategies in Shareholder Engagement: A Case Study of All Swedish National Pension Funds," *Journal of Sustainable Finance & Investment* 1: 44–61.
Hebb, T. 2008. *No Small Change: Pension Funds and Corporate Engagement*. New York: Cornell University Press.
Langbein, J. H. and R. A. Posner. 1980. "Social Investing and the Law of Trusts," *Michigan Law Review* 79 (1): 72–112.
O'Rourke, A. 2003. "A New Politics of Engagement: Shareholder Activism for Corporate Social Responsibility," *Business Strategy and the Environment* 12 (4): 227–39.
Pearce, R. and J. Stevens. 2006. *The Law of Trusts and Equitable Obligations*, 4th edn. New York: Oxford University Press.
Richardson, B. J. 2008. *Socially Responsible Investment Law*. New York: Oxford University Press.
Richardson, B. J. and W. Cragg. 2010. "Being Virtuous and Prosperous: SRI's Conflicting Goals," *Journal of Business Ethics* 92: 21–39.
Robins, N. 2006. "Shaping the Market: Investor Engagement in Public Policy," in R. Sullivan and C. Mackenzie (eds.) *Responsible Investment*, Sheffield: Greenleaf Publishing, pp. 312–21.
Sandberg, J. 2011. "Socially Responsible Investment and Fiduciary Duty: Putting the Freshfields Report into Perspective," *Journal of Business Ethics* 101: 143–62.
Sandberg, J., C. Juravle, T. M. Hedesström and I. Hamilton. 2009. "The Heterogeneity of Socially Responsible Investment," *Journal of Business Ethics* 87 (4): 519–33.
Skog, R. 2005. "A Remarkable Decade: The Awakening of Swedish Institutional Investors," *Studies in International, Financial, Economic and Technology Law* 7: 211–27.
Sparkes, R. 2002. *Socially Responsible Investment: A Global Revolution*. New York: John Wiley & Sons.
Statman, M. 2005. "The Religions of Social Responsibility," *The Journal of Investing* 14 (3): 14–22.

Stattin, D. 2010. "Självreglering av Institutionella Investerares Ägarroll," Uppsala Faculty of Law Working Paper 2010:6.

Sundén, A. 2006. "The Swedish Experience with Pension Reform," *Oxford Review of Economic Policy* 22 (1): 133–48.

Swedish Pensions Agency. 2010. "Orange Report: Annual Report of the Swedish Pension System."

TransLegal. 2009. *Banking, Finance and Securities Legislation: Swedish Law in Translation.* Stockholm: Norstedts Juridik.

Watt, G. 2006. *Trusts and Equity*, 2nd edn. New York: Oxford University Press.

Woods, C. and R. Urwin. 2010. "Putting Sustainable Investing into Practice: A Governance Framework for Pension Funds," *Journal of Business Ethics* 92: 1–19.

The Dutch pension system

RENÉ H. MAATMAN

Introduction

Pensions are a subject of great financial importance. On the micro-level, the pension is a significant factor in people's financial planning. Almost every employee builds up a pension. In most cases it is possible to say that employees work one day a week for their pension. For the employer, the pension is an expensive employment benefit, which can have a decisive impact on companies' balance sheet ratios and financial results. From a macro-economic perspective, the importance of pensions is paramount, especially in the relatively small economy of the Netherlands. The pension sector manages approximately €950 billion (2013) of assets for so-called supplementary pensions in the Netherlands, which are mostly funded through legally compulsory schemes.

People in the Netherlands have high expectations with regard to their ultimate pension, but the fulfillment of those expectations is coming under pressure from factors such as the ageing of the population and unforeseen circumstances arising during the term of the pension contract. Both factors can result in people facing disappointment with regard to their pension. This is referred to as the "gulf in pension expectations." It undermines trust in the financial system and in the economy as a whole, thereby impairing the pension system itself. This requires not only supervision aimed at strengthening the system but also a revision of the system itself.

The pension

The pension can be considered to be a periodic payment that eases the financial burdens of the loss of income associated with the attainment of a certain age, incapacity or death. The pension is an employment benefit. The pension agreement forms part of the employment contract. The Dutch Pensions Act (*Pensioenwet* – Pw) defines the pension agreement as a bipartite contract between the employer and the employee "concerning pensions." The pension agreement is governed by the Netherlands Civil Code, unless the Pw provides otherwise.

On the basis of the Pw, the pension agreement places an obligation on the employer to take measures guaranteeing that the pension will actually accrue to the beneficiary. To this end, the employer must "place" the pension agreement with a pension provider, such as a pension fund. This is known as a "placement obligation."

The aim of such separate pension provision is to protect the employee against the risk that in the event of bankruptcy of the employer the pension assets could go to the employer's creditors instead of being used to pay the pensions of the member(s). This is achieved by effecting a pension provision contract between the employer and the pension provider (Pw, article 23).

The pension provision contract between the employer and the pension provider is of a mixed nature. It incorporates an insurance contract as referred to in title 7.17 of the Netherlands Civil Code (Pw, article 5). As a result of a third-party clause, it also gives rise to a legal relationship between the pension provider, the employee and, if applicable, his partner or dependents (see Maatman 2004: section 2.5). The mutual relationships between these parties are specified in greater detail in the pension scheme, which also contains greater detail than the pension agreement with regard to the pension accrual conditions.

The combination of the pension agreement and the pension provision contract gives rise to a "triangular pension relationship." This can be unraveled into relationships between the employer and the employee, the employer and the pension provider, and the employee and the pension provider (see Lutjens 2013: 156 ff; Lutjens and Kuiper 2008: 79–85).

Types of pension schemes

Pension schemes are traditionally divided into two types: "defined benefit" (DB) schemes, in which the employer and the employee agree on a pension that is related to his salary and length of service, and "defined contribution" (DC) schemes, in which the employer promises a pension contribution, which can be used to acquire a pension.

In the Netherlands, the fulfillment of pension obligations resulting from a DB scheme must be financed in accordance with the funding system. The assets of a pension fund together with the expected income must be sufficient to cover the pension liabilities. In fact, the bulk of the financing comes from investment income. This underlines the importance of good investment management by a pension fund.

Defined benefit

Up until the "pension crisis" of 2002, the Netherlands' "basic pension scheme" (which is compulsory for employees as a whole) was based on a defined benefit in the vast majority of cases. If the defined benefit scheme is to operate as a final salary scheme, the employer agrees to a pension with the employee, which is related to the pensionable salary (the "pension basis"), which the member earns at the end of his career, shortly before his retirement date. Salary increases awarded to the member at the end of his career lead to an increase in the pension liabilities for previous membership years ("back service").

An inherent feature of final salary schemes is the fact that pay rises resulting from inflation or a person's own career automatically affect the level of the pension up to the retirement date. For each "membership year" the member receives a fixed percentage of this pension basis. The idea was that this should preferably result in an old-age pension equivalent to 70 percent of the most recently earned salary, on the basis of forty years of service. The aim of such a final salary scheme has been referred to as "standard of living protection."

Now, in 2013, it is clear that such an attractive pension is no longer in store for this generation of working people. The ageing of the population, combined with the financial crises of the past decade, has shown that we cannot afford such pensions.

If the defined benefit scheme is an "average salary scheme," the member receives each year a fixed percentage of the pensionable salary, which he earns in that year. Under such a scheme the member adds an amount to his pension in every membership year. The total of these amounts is paid from the retirement date. An average salary scheme is therefore also referred to as an accumulation scheme.

In an average salary scheme, salary increases or reductions have no effect on the pension rights, which have been accumulated in previous years; there is no back service. However, it is desirable to protect the rights acquired in each membership year by indexing them on the basis of general rises in salaries and/or prices.

A distinction should be drawn between the indexation of accumulated rights under an average salary scheme (prior to the retirement date) and the indexation of the pension (after the retirement date) under an average salary or final salary scheme. A commitment to full indexation implies the right to a salary index-linked or inflation-proof pension. In most pension schemes, this right is described as a conditional entitlement, to be granted on the basis of a specific decision by the board of the pension fund. The key factor to be considered by the board is whether the pension fund's financial buffers are sufficient to afford the indexation. The buffers are expressed in terms of the pension fund's cover ratio.[1]

---

[1] The cover ratio reflects the relationship between, on the one hand, the assets of a pension fund plus expected income and, on the other, the pension liabilities resulting from the articles of organization and regulations.

Defined contribution

A DC scheme is a pension scheme in which the entitlements are determined by a combination of the contributions, which the employer or the member pays to the pension provider, and the investment results that these contributions generate. A DC scheme results in accumulated capital, which the employee uses on the retirement date to obtain a periodic payment. There is an element of compulsion involved; the employee must use the capital to "purchase" a pension.

DC schemes have increasingly been used as basic pension schemes in the Netherlands, particularly since the financial crises. DC schemes are attractive to employers because they make it possible to control the financing charges associated with a pension scheme. A DC scheme can also be used to offer a customized package of employment conditions. It can offer the employee greater freedom to determine how to finance his retirement. A DC scheme can include a facility whereby members can make "investment choices." The pension fund may offer to invest contributions in accordance with a risk profile selected by the member. This has important consequences for the responsibility of the pension provider and the regulator.[2]

Individualized pension products are also offered to supplement social security benefits, to reduce any pension deficit as a result of the early drawing of a pension or to enable pension to be accrued in respect of particular salary components.

The Pw divides pension agreements into three categories, depending on the nature of the entitlements, which can be derived from the agreement. These are connected with the allocation of actuarial risks (longevity and investment risks) in the contract. According to article 10 of the Pw, the pension agreement can be characterized as a:

a. Defined benefit agreement (longevity and investment risks borne by the pension provider);
b. Capital agreement (longevity risk borne by the employee, investment risk by the pension provider); or
c. Defined contribution agreement (longevity and investment risks borne by the employee, as long as the contribution is not converted into a benefit entitlement).

This three-way allocation does not fully match the traditional distinction between DB and DC. Since 2003, pension schemes have increasingly taken on a mixed form, in the shape of the collective defined contribution scheme (CDC). It is usually an average salary scheme with a fixed contribution obligation on the part of the employer and a conditional right to indexation for the beneficiary. If the pension fund has insufficient resources to meet the conditional entitlements, the amount of the underfunding is allocated to the whole group of members.

Pension financing and investment risk

There are drawbacks to DC schemes. This is because there is no certainty that the accumulated capital will be sufficient to provide a good pension. This must also be "a concern" for the government, since it has a duty to provide assistance for those who are no longer able to provide for themselves as a result of old age, invalidity or the death of the breadwinner.

A defined benefit scheme generally aims to provide a certain percentage of the average or most recently earned salary. That can provide some basis on which to maintain the existing living standard after retirement. That is not the case with a DC scheme: the costs of the pension scheme are predictable, but the result – in terms of purchasing power – is highly uncertain.

In both the DC and DB schemes, the financing charges of the pension scheme can have a major influence on the financial capacity of employers and employees. Pension funds' investment results are playing an increasingly important role in this regard. In a pure DB scheme, shortfalls in the pension fund have to be met largely by the employer; he bears part of the investment risk. Consequently, the employer is uncertain as to the level of the financing liabilities resulting from the pension contract.

---

[2] See Pw, Article 52 and 151.

This situation has been exacerbated by the financial reporting rules in IAS 19.[3] IAS 19 is the standard issued by the International Accounting Standards Committee on employee benefits. It specifies how companies must treat pension liabilities in their financial statements. The aim of IAS 19 is to provide a true and uniform picture of the pension liabilities of companies, regardless of the way in which the pension commitments are implemented. IAS 19 also specifies that, in determining their contribution liability, employers must take account not only of their legal liabilities but also of the obligations, which are *de facto* unavoidable, natural obligations known as "constructive obligations."

A "constructive obligation" describes a situation in which the employer has not wished to commit himself and in which there is no compelling moral obligation within the meaning of article 6:3 of the Netherlands Civil Code. "Constructive obligations" can arise if the employer has held out to his employees the prospect of a certain level of pension. This expectation may *de facto* prevail over the employer's maximum contribution liability that results from the pension commitment:

> Informal practices give rise to a constructive obligation where the enterprise has no realistic alternative but to pay employee benefits. An example of a constructive obligation is where a change in the enterprise's informal practices would cause unacceptable damage to its relationship with employees (IAS 19, paragraph 52).

The application of IAS 19 is particularly onerous for listed companies. A pension fund's investment results rarely match the pension liabilities. Volatility in the financial markets is such that a pension fund would have to contend with an actuarial shortfall or surplus almost every year. If such a shortfall or surplus has to be reflected immediately in the company's balance sheet, it would face an extraordinary profit or loss every year, the size of which will depend on a factor that is scarcely within the company's control: the investment results of its pension fund. This

will be at the expense of the stability of the company's valuation trend, its share and its stock market price.

With requirements relating to solvency and reporting becoming increasingly stringent, employers want to have better control of the liabilities resulting from a pension scheme. Since the financing charges in a DC scheme are known in advance, listed companies prefer pension schemes with a "high DC content." The downside is that the investment risks are transferred to the members – and those risks can be very substantial.

A defined benefit pension product has undeniable advantages. It offers the possibility of obtaining an indexed pension at a price, which is the same for all members. The fact that membership is compulsory by law means that the risk can be spread across generations. This reduces the actuarial and investment risks.

There are also disadvantages. The employers and employees no longer have the power to dispose of the funds set aside for pensions. They must surrender this to the pension fund. Furthermore, the average contribution and the "intergenerational solidarity" are not very attractive to the young generation of members. They incur major risks due to the incompleteness of the pension contract; whether the entitlements are unconditionally vested and enforceable is vaguely defined. This has to do with the very long term and the complex financing relationships, which characterize the pension contract. In the case of a member who accrues pension from the age of twenty-five and dies at the age of eighty, her pension contract has a term of fifty-five years. It is certain at the outset that this contract will have to be "laid on the table" and renegotiated a number of times during the term because unforeseen circumstances will arise.

Pension providers

The Pw defines a pension provider as a pension fund or an insurer. The pension fund may be an industry pension fund or a company pension fund. The employer can decide whether to place the pension contract with a pension fund or with an insurer, unless the "social partners" have stipulated

---

[3] Made compulsory by Regulation (EC) No. 1725/2003 of the European Commission.

compulsory affiliation to an industry pension fund.[4] Many provisions of the Pw apply to both pension funds and insurers.

There are major differences between a pension fund and an insurer as providers of pension schemes. The governance of a pension fund is broadly laid down in pension law, namely the Pw; the governance of an insurer is specified in company law, i.e., Book 2 of the Netherlands Civil Code. There are also different arrangements with regard to financial supervision. This applies in particular to prudential supervision. The prudential regime applying to pension funds is defined in or pursuant to the Pw. Insurers have to comply with very different solvency requirements, which are set out in the Act on Financial Supervision (*Wet op het financieel toezicht*, Wft).[5]

Since the implementation of the Pensions Directive, the employer has also been able to conclude an implementation contract with an Institution for Occupational Retirement Provision (IORP), which is a pension institution with a European passport.[6] An IORP may be established in an EU member state other than the Netherlands.[7] Various European countries have introduced laws allowing the formation of IORPs.

For the purposes of the Pensions Act, an IORP can only qualify as a pension provider if it has its registered office in the Netherlands. A pension fund established under the law of the Netherlands is an IORP. That pension fund can operate across borders under the terms of the Pensions Directive, but its scope to do so is limited by the "domain demarcation." This is a legal requirement, which, according to the government, "is related to the Dutch system of labour relations."[8]

On the basis of this domain demarcation, a pension fund can only work for a specified "solidarity circle." In the case of a company pension fund, that consists of a company or the companies in a group. In the case of an industry pension fund, the solidarity circle comprises employers and employees who belong to the same industry.

Industry pension fund, company pension fund, occupational pension fund

The capital, which serves to guarantee the pension obligations, including the pension contributions, is collected in the pension fund. The pension fund must invest this capital on behalf of the collective membership. The assumption is that the capital sum has been accumulated for a specific purpose; it is a "special purpose fund." Article 1 of the Pw specifies that this special purpose fund can only belong to a legal entity. In practice, most Dutch pension funds opt for the legal form of the foundation.[9]

The Pw distinguishes between industry pension funds and company pension funds. A company pension fund is established for people working in one or more associated companies or institutions. The connection may be a group relationship, or may be based on historical links between the companies or institutions. For example, a company that leaves a group does not necessarily have to terminate its association with the group pension fund.[10]

In an industry pension fund, employers and employees accumulate capital on behalf of people working in a specific industry across a variety of companies or institutions. The concept of an "industry" is not defined in the Pw, nor in the act on obligatory participation in an industry pension fund.[11] Legal history shows that an industry can be deemed to exist in cases where companies or institutions carry out similar activities (Tulfer 1997: nos. 779–80).

Outside the Pw, there is a third "type" of pension fund, the occupational pension fund, which has the

---

[4] Industry Pension Fund (Obligatory Participation) Act 2000 (*Wet verplichte deelneming in bedrijfstakpensioenfondsen 2000*, Wet Bpf 2000).

[5] Parliamentary documents II, 2005/06, 30413, no. 3, p. 8.

[6] See Directive 2003/41/EC and art. 23 para. 1 (b) Pw.

[7] For the sake of brevity, we use the term "EU member state" in this chapter. Strictly speaking, it is a country that is part of the European Economic Area, i.e., the EU member states plus Iceland, Liechtenstein and Norway.

[8] Parliamentary documents II, 2008/9, 31 891, no, 3, p. 2.

[9] As referred to in title 6 of Book 2 of the Dutch Civil Code.

[10] See Tulfer (1997: nos. 773–4).

[11] Wet Bpf 2000.

task of providing a pension scheme for members of the professions. The occupational pension fund is governed by separate provisions in the Act concerning Compulsory Membership of an Occupational Pension Scheme (2005). These special provisions are necessary because a pension scheme for this professional group does not result from an employment contract or an employer/employee relationship. As a result, many concepts used in the Pw do not apply to an occupational pension scheme or the occupational pension fund and are outside the scope of this chapter.

Regardless of the category, a pension fund operates on behalf of a defined group of people. Employers and employees accumulate capital in the pension fund on behalf of at least two members, former members or their dependents. In most cases, people are connected by employment based on an employment contract, but executive directors, supervisory directors, working spouses, standby employees and apprentices can also have a connection. A connection exists with the company if work is carried out for the company within a contractual relationship with the company or in a position provided for in the articles of association. A more precise description of the group of people for whom the pension fund operates must appear in the pension fund's rules and articles of organization.

The distinction between a company pension fund and an industry pension fund is important with regard to the organization of the pension fund. The board of an industry pension fund also has a different composition than that of a company pension fund (Pw, article 99). The composition of the members' council is also governed by different rules (Pw, articles 100, 109, 110). The Industry Pension Fund (Obligatory Participation) Act 2000 (*Wet verplichte deelneming in bedrijfstakpensioenfondsen* 2000, Wet Bpf 2000) applies only to an industry pension fund or employers in a particular industry. This act includes the "compulsory participation," the power of the Minister of Social Affairs and Employment to make participation in a specific industry pension fund obligatory for one or more groups of persons working in an industry. The result is that the employers and employees who belong to the respective group are required to comply with the articles of organization, rules

and resulting decisions of the board of the industry pension fund (Wet Bpf 2000, articles 2 and 3).

The establishment of a pension fund is one of the matters addressed in consultations on conditions of employment between the employer and the employee. If they agree to create a pension scheme, the establishment of the pension fund will follow logically from the consultations on conditions of employment. As a rule, the company pension fund will be established on the initiative of the employer. In an industry pension fund, one or more companies can act as the founder(s).

In the case of industry pension funds, it is also possible that one or more employer and employee organizations will jointly form their own pension fund. The Pw contains no provisions concerning the actual formation and specifies no requirements as to the parties which must be involved in the formation. Article 102 of the Pw nevertheless stipulates that the board of the pension fund must report to the regulator no later than three months after formation. Articles of organization and rules complying with the legal requirements must be submitted within the same period.

Pension fund and stakeholders: standards

Each pension fund has a "circle" of stakeholders, whose asset positions are affected by the financial soundness of the pension fund. That soundness is largely dependent on the way in which the pension scheme is financed, i.e., the extent to which employers and employees are prepared to devote part of their earnings to pensions. However, financial soundness is also affected by the pension fund's own performance. This involves the extent to which the pension fund succeeds in controlling the risks of the scheme (balance sheet management); whether the pension fund is able to achieve an optimum investment return on its assets; and whether it can keep the operating costs at an acceptable level. Costs also depend on factors such as the desired level of service for the fund's stakeholders.

The pension fund's performance in its various areas of responsibility (pension administration, asset management and information provision) must meet certain quality requirements. However, the Pw contains no clear criteria for assessing whether the pension fund and its policymakers have performed "properly." Compliance is determined based on the applicable general principles of law, civil law analogies, case law and literature. There are important pointers from the contract of instruction provided for in Book 7 of the Netherlands Civil Code, the law of legal entities and securities law.[12]

Instruction

The legal relationship between the pension fund and its stakeholders is governed essentially by private law principles relating to: the duty of care on the part of an agent; potential conflicts of interest between the principal and the agent; and the accountability of the agent. Many of the standards, which a pension fund is required to fulfill on the basis of the law of legal entities and securities laws, can be traced back to these principles.

It could be argued that a fiduciary legal relationship exists between the pension fund and the financial stakeholders. This can be traced back to the Roman law concept of *fiducia cum amico*. The separation between the legal entitlement ("ownership") and the economic interest, which is a distinctive feature of a fiduciary legal relationship, also occurs in a pension fund. The pension capital belongs to the pension fund; the economic risk lies with the stakeholders.

In substantive terms, the pension fund has all the major characteristics of an Anglo-American trust. It can therefore be argued with great force that a pension fund operates on the basis of *fiducia cum amico*. It is generally accepted that *fiducia cum amico* should be seen as the Dutch form of the trust. This justifies consulting trust law in order to clarify the legal relationships between the pension fund and its stakeholders. The *fiducia*, the trust and the pension fund reinforce each other; gaps that arise when assessing the position of the pension fund under Dutch law can thus be filled.

The stakeholders entrust the pension capital to the pension fund, in the expectation that it will use the capital in accordance with the mandate given to it. This mandate broadly requires the pension fund to carry out three core tasks: rights administration, asset management and information provision.

Investments – prudent person rule

Article 135 of the Pensions Act specifies that pension funds must implement an investment policy, which accords with the prudent person rule (Pensions Act, article 135, para. 1). The prudent person rule, as a criterion for the prudent management of pension assets, has replaced the previous requirement that a pension fund must invest "soundly." The Dutch legislation operates on the basis that the significance of the prudent person rule does not differ substantially from the "soundness" requirement.[13]

The prudent person rule is derived from the Pensions Directive.[14] Since European law takes precedence over national law, the prudent person rule must be applied in Dutch law in accordance with the intention of the European legislation. If Dutch legislation, regulators or courts depart from this intention, the judgment of the European Court of Justice in Luxembourg may be invoked at the highest instance. Hence the Pensions Directive is the principal source for ascertaining the significance of the prudent person rule.

The Pensions Directive specifies that member states must require pension funds "to invest in accordance with the 'prudent person' rule and in particular in accordance with the following rule." The significance of the prudent person rule is elaborated in the subsequent provisions. First, they set out the loyalty principle (the "solely in the interest rule"), which states that the assets must be invested in the interest of the members and the beneficiaries. If the pension fund encounters conflicts of interest, the interests of the beneficiaries must prevail.

---

[12] See Maatman (2004: Chapters 4–6).

[13] Ibid., para. 7.5.
[14] Directive 2003/41/EC of the European Parliament and the Council on the activities and supervision of institutions for occupational retirement provision of June 3, 2003.

The Pensions Directive then sets out the "total portfolio approach." The assets must be invested in such a manner as to ensure the security, quality, liquidity and profitability of the portfolio as a whole. It follows from this that the risk/return profile of an individual investment is in principle irrelevant; what matters is the impact it has at the level of the portfolio.

The Pensions Directive also emphasizes the importance of diversification. "The assets shall be properly diversified in such a way as to avoid excessive reliance on any particular asset, issuer or group of undertakings and accumulations of risk in the portfolio *as a whole*."[15]

The principle of investment discretion is paramount in the Pensions Directive. Pension funds are permitted to invest in all markets, asset classes and investment instruments. Pension funds must handle this investment freedom professionally and responsibly. To that end the Pensions Directive contains a number of rules to ensure that the pension fund has a clear objective, is professionally managed and is transparent in its investment policy and the implementation of the policy.[16] Hence the pension fund must draw up a "Statement of Investment Policy Principles," a public document explaining *what* the pension fund does and *why*. This fits in with the notion that the prudent person rule demands quality governance of a pension fund.

Although investment discretion is paramount, the Pensions Directive nevertheless opens up the possibility for member states to impose certain investment restrictions on pension funds, "provided that they are prudentially justified" from the perspective of the total assets of the pension fund.[17] However, this power granted to member states must not result in individual "investment decisions" being subject to prior approval *of* or systematic notification *to* a regulator. Nor may member states prohibit pension funds from investing in "risk capital markets."[18]

In summary, the prudent person rule is based on the following pillars:

• professional asset management;
• assets invested in the interest of the beneficiaries;
• assets invested to ensure the security, quality, liquidity and profitability of the portfolio as a whole (i.e., the risk/return profile of the overall portfolio must be constantly geared to the fund's liabilities structure, and the investments must be sufficiently diversified).

Pensions Act

In the Pensions Act, the prudent person rule is followed immediately by the loyalty principle: "the securities are invested in the interest of those with pension claims and entitlements." This is followed by the rule that a pension fund may not invest more than 5 percent of its assets in the contributing company. If that company belongs to a group, the pension fund may invest a maximum of 10 percent in the group. The Pensions Act then specifies that more detailed rules will be specified in or by virtue of an order in council "to guarantee the prudent investment policy." These must not of course breach the prudent person rule, the loyalty rule and the restrictions, which apply to investments in the contributing company. The more detailed rules are included in the Decree on the Financial Assessment Framework for Pension Funds (*Besluit financieel toetsingskader pensioenfondsen* – FTK Decree, 2006).[19]

Those rules are partly the same as the more detailed regulations in the Pensions Directive concerning the prudent person rule.[20] The FTK Decree

---

[15] See Maatman (2004: 240).

[16] See Pensions Directive, articles 7, 9 and 12.

[17] At least that is how I understand the requirement that these regulations "reflect the total range of pension schemes operated by these institutions," see Pensions Directive, Article 18, para. 5.

[18] See Pensions Directive, article 18, para. 4 and 5. "Risk capital markets" were defined in an earlier version of the

Murphy Directive (2001/C 96 E/06) as "markets providing equity financing to a company during its early growth stages." The final Pensions Directive contains no description of this term.

[19] It contains rules relating to the financial assessment framework based on the Pensions Act and the Act concerning Compulsory Membership of an Occupational Pension Scheme (Decree on the Financial Assessment Framework for Pension Funds).

[20] See Directive 2003/41 EC on the activities and supervision of institutions for occupational retirement provision, adopted on June 3, 2003.

leaves pension funds' freedom to invest in markets, asset classes and investment instruments intact as far as possible.[21] Any investment restrictions which result from the FTK Decree are prudential in nature; they concern the pension fund's balance sheet ratios and the solvency requirements formulated by the regulator. The Netherlands Central Bank (DNB) assesses the risk profile of a pension fund's assets. Certain risk-weighting factors apply, depending on the type of asset. These may result in a pension fund with a low cover ratio being forced to withdraw from certain investment categories. The Pensions Directive itself sets out the basis for such a supervisory measure by stating at various places that exceptions to the investment freedom are possible if these are justified from a *prudential* point of view (i.e., with a view to solvency).[22]

Pension fund outsourcing

A pension fund may perform the mandate itself, using personnel employed by the pension fund. This is called a self-administering pension fund. A pension fund may alternatively outsource almost all its tasks. It is of course also possible to outsource part of the (core) tasks. Both types of organization have advantages and disadvantages.

A disadvantage of outsourcing is that it gives rise to outside interests, with agency risks and agency costs. These are not easy to control.[23] However, outsourcing is more the rule than an exception among pension funds. Most pension funds have opted for a model in which all core tasks are assigned to a management organization.

In a self-administering pension fund, the pension assets and the management organization belong to the same legal entity. Up until 2008, the largest Dutch pension funds, ABP and PGGM, were "self-

administering." In 2008, these pension funds transferred their management organizations to separate legal entities and also entered into outsourcing relationships. The demergers were carried out to comply with article 116 of the Pw, which requires pension funds to conduct only activities "relating to pensions and associated work."[24]

The outsourcing relationship between a pension fund and the management organization can be considered a contract of instruction. It is usual for the agent in turn to outsource certain tasks, for example by issuing a mandate to an asset manager. This asset manager can be seen as an agent in relation to the pension provider. During the legislative debate on the Pw, the government considered the inclusion of a provision whereby the regulator could directly investigate and take measures against such agents. Ultimately it decided not to, and article 34 of the Pw takes a line similar to that of the corresponding article in the Wft.

Regulatory provisions

The object of supervision under the Pw is the pension provider. If a pension provider outsources activities, it must ensure that the agent complies with the rules of the Pw that apply to the pension provider. The pension provider therefore remains responsible for ensuring that the agent complies with the rules (Pw, article 3, para. 1). The agent to whom the pension provider outsources tasks is not placed under direct supervision.

According to background in the legislative history memorandum of explanation, the General Administrative Law Act already gives the regulator "supervisory powers" in respect of any party (i.e., including such agents: examples include rights to inspect records, to obtain information and to summon and hear experts) (Parliamentary documents

---

[21] See the notes to the Decree on the Financial Assessment Framework for Pension Funds, Law Gazette 2006, 710, p. 16.

[22] See, for example, Pensions Directive, article 17, para. 3; article 18, para. 5; article 18, para. 5 sub a; article 18, para. 6; as well as points (18), (20), (32), (33) and (36) of the Preamble.

[23] See Broekhuizen (2009); Joosen (2009); Kortmann and Maatman (2005).

[24] ABP and PGGM could only continue their "secondary activities" (including services in the field of insurance, life-course savings and automation) by separating them from the pension fund. ABP then transferred its management organization to APG. PGGM has changed its name to Pensioenfonds Zorg en Welzijn (Pension Fund for the Care and Welfare Sector) and transferred the PGGM name to its management organization.

II, 2005/06, 30413, no. 3, pp. 128–34). Agents established outside the Netherlands do not fall within the scope of such an article (Parliamentary documents II, 2005/06, 30413, no. 3, p. 158).[25]

The Decree on the Implementation of the Pensions Act and the Act concerning Compulsory Membership of an Occupational Pension Scheme (*Besluit uitvoering Pensioenwet* and *Wet verplichte beroepspensioenregeling*) specifies in greater detail what may be outsourced and under what conditions (Law Gazette 2006, 709).[26] The outsourcing contract must specify, among other things, that the regulator can carry out or arrange on-the-spot investigations on the agent's premises.[27] That means that a foreign asset manager can be requested to cooperate. Foreign operators may be uncomfortable with such an obligation. However, they may derive some comfort from the fact that the Decree states that the regulator will only use this power in exceptional cases.[28]

Furthermore, the memorandum of explanation relating to the Pw states that it is not the intention that the agent to whom tasks are outsourced should be placed under the direct supervision of the Netherlands Authority for the Financial Markets (AFM) or the DNB (Parliamentary documents II, 2005/06, 30413, no. 3, p. 158). Moreover, the explanation of the Decree states that the regulator will not, "in principle," consult with the agent to whom the provider has outsourced and will not, "in principle," request any related data or information.[29]

One unresolved question is how these rules will work in a chain of outsourcing relations, for example, if the pension provider outsources to a management organization, which in turn outsources the asset management to a bank, which then outsources a large part of the tasks to a subsidiary or to a joint venture with a third party. Must the relevant legal requirements with regard to outsourcing be passed on through to the last link in the chain? While that is possible, the author cannot see that happening yet, particularly in international relationships.

Regulators – forms of supervision

In the Pw, supervision is carried out by two regulators, the DNB and the AFM. The breakdown of their tasks and responsibilities is outlined in Chapter 7 of the Pw. The DNB and the AFM have entered into a cooperation covenant which sets out the tasks assigned to the DNB and the AFM, how the supervision and its preparation are to be coordinated, what information is exchanged between the DNB and the AFM and what consultation takes place in the event that the use of enforcement methods is considered (Parliamentary documents II, 2005/06, 30413, no. 3, p. 142).[30]

The Pw distinguishes between three forms of supervision, namely prudential supervision, conduct supervision and material supervision (Pw, article 151). The DNB is entrusted with the prudential supervision of pension funds. That involves supervising standards for the financial soundness of pension funds and for the financial stability of the sector as a whole. The DNB establishes whether pension funds are able to meet their financial liabilities and whether there is consistency in terms of the expectations raised, the funding and the conditional bonuses paid (the consistency requirement).

The AFM is responsible for supervising the conduct of pension funds. That includes securities-type conduct and supervision of the information that

[25] The government's view is that according to the Rome Convention of 1980 on contractual obligations the outsourcing contract is governed by the law of the country in which the service provider is established, See Parliamentary documents II, 2005/06, 30413, no. 3, p. 24.

[26] Section 4 of this decree specifies in greater detail which activities are not permitted to be outsourced and which conditions an outsourcing contract must fulfill.

[27] Article 13, para. 2 sub f. of the Decree on the Implementation of the Pensions Act and the Act concerning Compulsory Membership of an Occupational Pension Scheme.

[28] Article 13, para. 3 of the Decree on the Implementation of the Pensions Act and the Act concerning Compulsory Membership of an Occupational Pension Scheme.

[29] Memorandum of explanation on the Decree on the Implementation of the Pensions Act and the Act concerning Compulsory Membership of an Occupational Pension Scheme, Law Gazette 2006, 709.

[30] The existing covenant between the DNB and the AFM dates from March 28, 2013, see www.dnb.nl.

pension funds provide to the beneficiaries.[31] The AFM inspects accessibility, timeliness and accuracy of this information (Parliamentary documents II, 2005/06, 30413, no. 3, p. 143). In addition, the AFM supervises compliance with standards relating to pension products offering investment discretion. With these products, the member can invest the pension contribution in a selection of financial products offered to him by the pension fund. This type of pension product is becoming increasingly important in the Netherlands.

In addition to conduct supervision and prudential supervision, the Pw identified "material supervision." That is a residual category: "supervision of the other standards in the bill." For the government, material supervision concerns rules relating to the employment benefit nature of pensions, which affect the relationship between the employer and the employee, the pension contract, the implementation contract and the pension fund as an institution. Material supervision is also assigned to the DNB.[32]

Prudential supervision – financial assessment framework

Pension funds need to maintain their cover ratios in accordance with the Financial Assessment Framework (*Financieel Toetsingskader*, FTK). The aim of the FTK is to ensure that beneficiaries "can be confident, with a high degree of certainty … that the pension fund can actually pay out the agreed pension" (Parliamentary documents II, 2005/06, 30413, no. 3, p. 83).

Pension funds must value assets and liabilities at fair value.[33] In order to assess the financial position of a pension fund a distinction is drawn between a *minimum* required equity and the required equity that a pension fund must have at its disposal. The required equity cushion is based on the probability of underfunding. The level of required equity is such that, with a certainty of 97.5 percent, it is possible to avoid a situation whereby within one year the value of the pension fund's assets would be less than the required level. In other words, the cover ratio is only allowed to fall below 100 percent once every forty years.[34] The legislation establishes this solvency requirement to sufficiently guarantee fulfillment of the unconditional pension liabilities.[35]

The minimum required equity is constant. Each pension fund must maintain a surplus equity equivalent to 5 percent of the technical provisions, which corresponds to a cover ratio of 105 percent. The 5 percent buffer is intended to absorb unquantified risks. If the pension fund ceases to satisfy this requirement, it must draw up a short-term recovery plan, as a result of which the cover ratio must be returned to a level of at least 105 percent within three years. This period was initially set at one year. However, it drew strong objections, since the recovery options available to a pension fund (increase in contributions, change of investment policy and amendment of the pension scheme) can have drastic macroeconomic consequences in a

---

[31] Beneficiaries are those who can derive (conditional) rights from a pension scheme, including the member, former member and pensioner. See also the definitions of "entitled person" and "pension-entitled person" in Pw, article 1.

[32] See the Decree on the Implementation of the Pensions Act and the Act concerning Compulsory Membership of an Occupational Pension Scheme, Law Gazette 2006, 709. Article 36 of this decree specifies in detail (for each paragraph) what the AFM supervises. DNB supervises compliance with all other rules introduced in or pursuant to the Pw and the Act concerning Compulsory Membership of an Occupational Pension Scheme.

[33] Since 2008, an intense debate unfolded on the appropriate discount rate for pension liabilities. Currently the liabilities are discounted against a risk-free rate based on the interbank swap market. For each liability of the pension fund there is a "dot" on the swap curve that matches exactly the duration of that particular liability. If the discount rate decreases, a pension fund needs more assets today in order to be sure it can generate sufficient investment returns to pay a projected amount of benefits in the future. Since 2008, the risk-free rate has decreased to a historically low level of currently (2013) around 2 percent.

[34] The reliability of this criterion is relative. The expectation is based on a stochastic process in which the parameters are informed by historical values. The extent to which they are representative for the future is uncertain.

[35] See Parliamentary documents II, 2004/05, 28294, no. 11 and Parliamentary documents II, 2005/06, 30413, no. 3, pp. 84–6. Now (2013) it is known that the government was too optimistic.

period of one year. The Lower House was receptive to these arguments and extended the period to three years, other than in exceptional situations (Pw, article 140, para. 3).[36]

According to the FTK, an average pension fund must have a cover ratio of approximately 125 percent; the required equity is 25 percent.[37] The more risks a pension fund incurs in its investments, the higher the equity cushion must be. If the pension fund does not have the required equity, it must draw up a long-term recovery plan that leads to a restoration of the cover ratio within a maximum of fifteen years.[38] The calculation of required equity is based on assumptions concerning actuarial risks, forecasts of wage and price inflation, expected investment income, correlations in the investment results of different investment categories and the impact of specified stress-tests on the pension fund's balance sheet.

Conduct supervision – financial planning

A pension can be seen in a certain sense as a deferred pay scheme. A pension is a lifelong periodic payment after the retirement date. Each employee who has entered into a pension agreement builds up a pension. Salary during employment and pension payments after the retirement date are essential conditions of employment. Just as an employee needs to be able to meet expenses from income, a pensioner needs to be able to rely on pension benefits, which usually consists of old age and supplementary pensions.

Many employees do not confront the question of whether their pension will be a sufficient source of salary replacement until they approach retirement. If they wish to know more about their pension, the pension provider must provide access to up-to-date, intelligible and accurate information. That information must enable the employee to gain an insight into his pension. The employee will then be able to see the pension he is building up for himself and any pension he has arranged for his partner and children in the event of his death.

This information is intended to enable the employee to make decisions with regard to his pension, for example on transfers of accrued benefits from previous employment. Of course, an employee can leave such decisions to an adviser. In both cases, it is important that the employee has access to complete, accurate data, particularly concerning accrued pension and future pension accrual. The introduction of the Pension Register, which provides access to this data via the internet, is an important step in this regard.[39] Once an employee understands the significance of the data, the member can take action, with or without advice, and make "precautionary savings."

The legislation imposes a requirement on the pension provider to, if necessary, timely supply the necessary information in clear, intelligible language (Pw, article 48).[40] According to the legislation, the stakeholder must have good information in order to make financial plans with regard to income for old age or incapacity and/or income for dependents in the event of his death. With that information, he must be able to assess whether the total benefits to which he is entitled, from statutory schemes and supplementary pensions, combined with his own resources, will need to be supplemented, for

---

[36] See Parliamentary documents II, 2005/06, 30413, no. 62, p. 40 and no. 84. The pension crisis of 2008–9 led to the recovery period being extended to five years. See also the letter from Minister Donner of February 20, 2009, available for download at www.szw.nl.

[37] Initially the standard was 130 percent. It was adjusted in response to the recommendation of DNB dated October 3, 2006. See www.dnb.nl. See also Parliamentary documents II, 2006/07, 30413, no. 90. An "average pension fund" invests 50 percent in assets mainly comprising equities and real estate; the duration of its fixed-income investments and liabilities is 5 and 16 respectively. Duration is a measure of interest sensitivity. A duration of 10 means that a 1 percent change in the market interest rate has a tenfold effect on the valuation of the respective fixed-income investments and liabilities.

[38] The system is set out in the Decree of December 18, 2006, containing rules on the financial assessment framework based on the Pensions Act and the Act concerning Compulsory Membership of an Occupational Pension Scheme (Decree on the Financial Assessment Framework for Pension Funds), Law Gazette 710.

[39] See Pw, article 51. This access has been available since January 1, 2011 at www.mijnpensioenoverzicht.nl.

[40] For that purpose, the Uniform Pension Statement (Uniform Pensioen Overzicht) has been developed.

example by joining a voluntary pension scheme or arranging a capital sum insurance. The legislature puts it forcefully: "The general principle … is that the information must enable a member to carry out financial planning" (Law Gazette 2006, decree 709).

The pension, as an employment benefit, must be able to serve as the basis for financial independence in retirement. For most people, the main components of financial planning are their pension, home and mortgage. Both pensions and mortgages involve long-term financial relationships and risks. In both cases, the information that is periodically received also has a substantive purpose. The employee must be able to appreciate the uncertainty of the intended end result of those two relationships.

Conclusions

A pension is an employment benefit whereby an employee accrues an entitlement to deferred pay. The accrual of this entitlement and compliance with pension obligations take place in a tightly regulated triangular relationship. The employee builds up a pension on the basis of a pension agreement between the employee and the employer. The employer enters into an implementation contract with a pension provider, usually a pension fund. This also gives rise to a contractual relationship between the employee and the pension fund. The employee becomes a member of the pension fund and obtains pension entitlements, which are "converted" into pension rights on the retirement date.

The pension fund can be seen as a "sui generis" financial institution. The establishment and operation of the pension fund are governed by the Pw and related legislation. However, the pension fund and the pension are increasingly "exposed" to regular financial law standards based on civil law and as further elaborated in legislation.

Substantial parts of pension funds' activities have been brought directly within the scope of supervision by the AFM. That includes the obligation to provide members with timely, accurate and intelligible information. The DNB is entrusted with prudential supervision of pension funds. Prudential supervision has been substantially tightened due to the solvency problems facing pension funds.

The pension system in the Netherlands, with generally compulsory pension fund membership and compulsory payment of contributions to pension funds, has made the Netherlands a country of savers and investors. However, the members are vulnerable to developments in the financial markets and to the increasing costs of the ageing population. The interests at stake are extremely high, both on the macroeconomic level and in terms of individuals' livelihood. Nevertheless, the Dutch system is still one of the most highly rated and sustainable pension systems in the world.[41] Constant efforts must be devoted to maintaining that position.[42]

References

Ambachtsheer, K. P. 2011. "What is Motivating the New Dutch Pension Accord: 'Solidarity', or Something Else?" *The Ambachtsheer Letter*, July.

2012. "Innovation in Pension Design and Delivery: How Well are Countries Adapting to Changing Times?" *The Ambachtsheer Letter*, April.

2013. "Towards 'Individualized Solidarity' in Pension Design: Why the Dutch Can and Should Lead the Way," *The Ambachtsheer Letter*, August.

Broekhuizen, K. W. H. 2009. "Regulering van belangenconflicten," in D. Busch and C. M. Grundmann-van de Krol (eds.) *Handboek Beleggingsondernemingen*. Deventer: Kluwer, pp. 379–456.

Joosen, E. P. M. 2009. "Uitbesteding van werkzaamheden," in D. Busch and C. M. Grundmann-van de Krol (eds.) *Handboek Beleggingsondernemingen*. Deventer: Kluwer, pp. 457–508.

Kortmann, S. C. J. J. 2009. *Constitutioneel recht*. Deventer: Kluwer.

Kortmann, S. C. J. J. and R. H. Maatman. 2005. "Uitbesteding door Vermogensbeheerders," *Ondernemingsrecht* 311–18.

---

[41] See the Mercer Global Pension Index, www.mercer.nl/articles/global-pension-index.

[42] Since 2010 representatives of employers, employees and the government are engaged in negotiations on the pension contract and changes to the prudential supervision framework (Ambachtsheer 2011, 2012, 2013).

Lutjens, E. 1989. *Pensioenvoorzieningen voor werknemers*. Dissertation, Zwolle.
  (ed.) 2013. *Pensioenwet. Analyse en commentaar*. Deventer: Kluwer.
Lutjens, E. and S. H. Kuiper. 2009. "Pensioenwet en privaatrecht," *NTBR* 76–93.

Maatman, R. H. 2004. *Dutch Pension Funds – Fiduciary Duties and Investing*. Deventer: Kluwer.
Tulfer, P. M. 1997. *Pensioenen, fondsen en verzekeraars*. Deventer: Kluwer.

PART II

Fiduciary duty and the landscape of institutional investment

CHAPTER 8

The philanthropic fiduciary: challenges for nonprofits, foundations and endowments

KEITH L. JOHNSON AND STEPHEN VIEDERMAN

Introduction

Charitable purpose is the primary differentiating factor between nonprofits and their for-profit siblings. Tax-exempt nonprofits are granted special tax status in exchange for pursuing specified public benefits. The underlying rationale is that philanthropic activities will reduce the burdens on government or otherwise provide a social good (Phelan 2010: 12:8). This trade-off between generating a public benefit and receiving an associated tax advantage is the policy basis upon which the nonprofit sector exists.[1]

In order to align the governance of nonprofits with this core policy goal, directors of philanthropic organizations and trustees of charitable trusts are subject to fiduciary standards that serve as guides for their conduct. Those legal obligations are similar to the fiduciary duties of for-profit company directors and trustees of investment trusts. However, nonprofit directors have an additional fiduciary duty, one of obedience to the organization's charitable mission and purpose.[2] That duty

of obedience also engenders an oversight responsibility to prevent drift away from both its charitable mission and the public purpose that underlies the nonprofit's tax exemption.

This chapter explores implications of the nonprofit fiduciary's duty of obedience to charitable mission and purpose in regard to investment activities. It specifically looks at how the duty of obedience plays out at charities that are funded by endowments, particularly where an endowed foundation seeks to maintain its role in perpetuity or has long-term obligations that must be weighed against current spending needs. We approach these issues not from the perspective of advising nonprofit directors on how to meet minimum standards of conduct so as to avoid liability, but rather from the viewpoint of a counselor offering guidance toward fulfilling the fundamental goals that fiduciary duty principles are designed to achieve.

This chapter concludes that philanthropic fiduciaries who oversee investment programs have a legal duty to take an integrated approach toward management of the nonprofit's entire balance sheet – including operations, grant-making and investment activities – to ensure that they operate as seamlessly as possible to serve the organization's charitable mission and purpose.[3] A balanced application of fiduciary responsibility requires

[1] "Charitable exemptions are justified on the basis that the exempt entity confers a public benefit – a benefit that society or the community either may not itself choose or be able to provide, or that supplements and advances the work of other public institutions already supported by tax revenues" (*Bob Jones University* v. *United States* [1983], p. 591).

[2] Throughout this chapter, the words "mission" and "program" refer to the activities undertaken by a charity to fulfill the specific goal(s) to which it is devoted, as are set forth in (or derived from) its organizational documents. The word "purpose" refers to the public benefit(s) specified by law or public policy, which must be provided by a charity in exchange for its tax exemption or other public subsidy.

[3] The governing board or trustees of a nonprofit ultimately bear this responsibility. While some governing bodies delegate specific duties to committees or other subgroups, oversight responsibility for ensuring that both program and investment activities are conducted in accordance with charitable mission and purpose usually cannot be eliminated through delegation.

that directors and trustees avoid treating investment duties as a silo activity that is separated from program implementation of the charity's mission and purpose. Philanthropic investment activities should, to the degree practicable, support and not undermine or be unresponsive to the mission and purpose for which the organization exists. Both fiduciary duty and tax policy direct this holistic approach to integration of investment policy with charitable mission and purpose.

Fiduciaries at endowment funds that have long-term obligations or that exist in perpetuity have an additional challenge. They must impartially balance the need for current income with their duty to preserve assets and generate capital growth for future generations. They have a duty of impartiality, often viewed as part of the fiduciary duty of loyalty, which requires application of different time horizons to investment policy decisions.[4] When the fiduciary duties of obedience and impartiality are combined, philanthropic fiduciaries with long-term obligations are tasked with implementing a holistic approach that impartially balances achieving charitable mission and public purpose for the nonprofit's entire balance sheet over both the short and the long term.

Fiduciary duties of nonprofit directors

There has been extensive debate in the United States recently around the application of divergent trust and for-profit corporate law standards to the governance of nonprofits. Some commentators argue that for-profit corporate standards should be used in determining liability of directors at charitable organizations because the board functions at both are similar (Phelan 2010: 4:9). Others maintain that trust law standards should apply because nonprofits are not subject to the same degree of oversight

that is provided by the shareholders at for-profit corporations and that all nonprofits, regardless of their formal status, have more in common with the goals of charitable trusts than with corporations (Sugin 2007).

While nuances of this debate are outside the scope of this chapter, we think that positioning the question as one of trust law versus corporate law misses the point. Regardless of whether they are organized as trust funds or corporations, nonprofits are subject to similar fiduciary duties of prudence (also referred to as "the duty of care") and loyalty. While there might be variations in how these duties are described across jurisdictions, the duty of prudence essentially mandates that directors become reasonably informed and discharge their duties in good faith and with the care that a person in a like position would reasonably believe appropriate under similar circumstances. The duty of loyalty primarily addresses conflicts of interest and precludes self-dealing with charitable assets (Hazen and Hazen 2012: 356). Under trust law, loyalty (with its related duty of impartiality) also requires that the process of administering assets and investments be structured to accommodate different time horizons and interests associated with the purpose of the trust, as relevant (Hawley et al. 2011: 8; Wakeman et al. 2006: s.17.15).

The duty of obedience is an additional trust law concept that is fundamental to nonprofits, regardless of their trust or corporate form (Sasso 2003: 1530; Sugin 2007: 898). It functions in a way that is similar to the role played by the financial bottom line in the for-profit sector. Nonprofits enjoy a special tax status that requires they have a charitable mission and fulfill a public benefit purpose. Without a commitment to charitable mission and public purpose, a tax-exempt nonprofit cannot exist.

A charitable organization must serve a valid public purpose and must confer a public benefit. According to the Supreme Court, all taxpayers are affected by a governmental grant of tax exemption. The very fact of the exemption means that other taxpayers are indirect and vicarious donors. Charitable exemptions are justified on the basis that the exempt entity confers a public benefit – a benefit that society or the community either may

---

[4] Section 6 of the Uniform Prudent Investor Act frames the duty of impartiality as follows: "If a trust has two or more beneficiaries, the trustee shall act impartially in investing and managing the trust assets, taking into account any differing interests of the beneficiaries." The Commonfund Institute explains: "The trustees of an endowment institution are the guardians of the future against the claims of the present" (Commonfund Institute 2001: 1).

not itself choose or be able to provide, or that supplements and advances the work of other public institutions already supported by tax revenues (Phelan 2010: 12:8, citations omitted).

Board members at charitable organizations are simply not in a position to ignore the fundamental policy trade-off that underlies their special tax status. This is a fundamental reality. For example, even though the duty of obedience is not codified in the New York statutes, the courts have applied it as an inherent nonprofit fiduciary obligation.

It is axiomatic that the Board of Directors is charged with the duty to ensure that the mission of the charitable corporation is carried out. This duty has been referred to as the "duty of obedience." It requires the director of a not-for-profit corporation to "be faithful to the purposes and goals of the organization," since "unlike business corporations, whose ultimate objective is to make money, nonprofit corporations are defined by their specific objectives: perpetuation of particular activities are central to the raison d'être of the organization."[5]

This is not to say that the duty of obedience requires adherence to a narrow or inflexible mission statement. At the insistence of commentators, the courts have begun to allow boards and trustees some flexibility in applying statements of charitable mission, so long as the basic intent for which the charity was created is honored (Sugin 2007: 901–5). The Uniform Prudent Management of Institutional Funds Act (UPMIFA), which has been broadly adopted in the United States, contains provisions that allow court modification of restrictions on investment limits or charitable mission that render management or investment of charitable assets impracticable.[6]

Consistent oversight is also merited in order to avoid inadvertent drift that could result in an organization straying beyond its allowed mission and charitable purposes or otherwise finding itself outside of its authorized scope of operation. This applies to both program and investment responsibilities. Given changes in financial markets and understanding of effects that investment actions can have on society (including the public purpose goals of nonprofits), regular review of the alignment of investment practices with an organization's mission and charitable purpose is warranted.

Role of tax policy in defining nonprofit fiduciary duty

The federal tax code in the United States (as in most countries) sets parameters that effectively define what constitutes an acceptable public purpose that merits receipt of a nonprofit tax exemption.[7] The penalty for a charity's noncompliance with these standards can be loss of the tax exemption (Hazen and Hazen 2012: 366). As a result, tax regulations play a major role in nonprofit governance through the public policy boundaries they set for implementation of the fiduciary duty of obedience.

Tax regulations also demonstrate the importance of investment policy to nonprofit governance and charitable purpose. For example, in the United States, the federal tax code contains provisions that discourage investments that are deemed to be extraneous to charitable purposes by imposing an unrelated business income tax (Internal Revenue

---

[5] *Manhattan Eye, Ear and Throat Hospital* v. *Spitzer*, 186 Misc. 2d 126 (New York, 1999), p. 152.
[6] Section 6 of UPMIFA provides: "The court, upon application of an institution, may modify a restriction contained in a gift instrument regarding the management or investment of an institutional fund if the restriction has become impracticable or wasteful, if it impairs the management or investment of the fund, or if, because of circumstances not anticipated by the donor, a modification of a restriction will further the purposes of the fund. The institution shall notify the [Attorney General] of the application, and the [Attorney General] must be given an opportunity to be

heard. To the extent practicable, any modification must be made in accordance with the donor's probable intention," UPMIFA, www.uniformlaws.org/Act.aspx?title=Prudent Investor Act: s. 6).
[7] For example, section 501 of the Internal Revenue Code and related regulations delineate acceptable public purposes. They include aims such as relief of the poor; advancement of religion, education or science; erection or maintenance of public buildings, monuments or works; lessening the burdens of government; combating juvenile delinquency and community deterioration; eliminating prejudice and discrimination; environmental preservation; defending human civil rights; care for the elderly; and lessening neighborhood tensions.

Code, section 511); levy a tax on "jeopardizing" private foundation investments that are considered too risky or fraught with conflicts of interest, although "program-related" investments made to accomplish the entity's charitable mission are excepted (Internal Revenue Code, section 4944); and assess an excise tax on excess private foundation investment income that is not being expended for program objectives (Internal Revenue Code, section 4940).

These public policies, although contained in tax law, help to frame the governance responsibilities of nonprofit directors and trustees. They also reinforce goals of the fiduciary duty of obedience, mandating a focus on advancement of specified public purposes and demonstrating that investment practices are inextricably tied to implementation of a nonprofit's obligation to serve the public good. As such, tax policies provide a policy mandate for nonprofit fiduciaries to pursue holistic integration of their investment practices with the organization's mission and charitable purpose.

Fiduciary duty in the Uniform Prudent Management of Institutional Funds Act

The UPMIFA, most recently updated by the National Conference of Commissioners on Uniform State Laws in 2006, is intended to govern investment activities of charitable entities organized as corporations. It contains principles that are based on the Uniform Prudent Investor Act (UPIA), which applies to investment of charitable trusts.

The UPMIFA "reflects the fact that standards for managing and investing institutional funds are and should be the same regardless of whether a charitable organization is organized as a trust, a nonprofit corporation, or some other entity" (UPMIFA, Prefatory Note). In fact, the UPMIFA explicitly cites trust law as the definitive source of authority for all nonprofit investment standards.

> Trust law norms already inform managers of nonprofit corporations. The Preamble to UPIA explains: "Although the Uniform Prudent Investor Act by its terms applies to trusts and not to charitable corporations, the standards of the Act can be expected to inform the investment responsibilities

of directors and officers of charitable corporations" (UPMIFA, Comment to Section 3).

In addition, the UPMIFA recognizes importance of obedience to charitable mission and purpose: "UPMIFA requires a charity and those who manage and invest its funds to … develop an investment strategy appropriate for the fund and the charity" (UPMIFA, Prefatory Note). The UPMIFA Drafting Committee explains: "[The] decision maker must consider the charitable purposes of the institution and the purposes of the institutional fund for which decisions are being made. These factors are specific to charitable organizations." The Drafting Committee goes on to confirm that the act is intended to apply to charities the same basic principles that are used in making pension fund investments, as described in the *Restatement of Trusts* (UPMIFA, Comment to s. 3; *Restatement [Third] of Trusts*, s. 379, Comment b).

As a result, examination of trust law principles, particularly how they are being implemented and how they are evolving, is essential to understanding application of fiduciary duty standards at nonprofits.

Fiduciary duty is a dynamic concept

Under trust law, fiduciary duties are neither static nor tied to a single investment theory. They are a flexible set of principles that have been subject to varying interpretations over time. The most recent round of evolution in trust law fiduciary standards occurred during the last half of the twentieth century, as modern portfolio theory replaced explicit lists of permitted trust investments. For example, bonds and real estate had been permitted investments on the legal lists but corporate stock was treated as imprudent.[8] After this transition from a

---

[8] The *Restatement (Third) of Trusts* highlighted five major alterations in prudent investing concepts made with adoption of modern portfolio theory: (1) focusing on the total portfolio, rather than individual investments; (2) defining the fiduciary's central concern as the trade-off between risk and return; (3) removing all categoric restrictions on types of investment; (4) prescribing diversification as integral to prudent investing; and (5) reversing the non-delegation

focus on the prudence of individual investments to a more flexible portfolio-based approach, the following Comment was inserted into the *Restatement (Third) of Trusts*:

> Trust investment law should reflect and accommodate current knowledge and concepts. It should avoid repeating the mistake of freezing its rules against future learning and developments (American Law Institute 1992: section 227 Introduction).

The resulting challenge for fiduciaries at nonprofits is to avoid making this same mistake by unquestioningly adopting investment practices anchored in the economic circumstances and investment approaches of the late twentieth century. Major social and economic changes, as well as advances in knowledge, have occurred over the past couple of decades which compel a current evaluation of whether twentieth-century investment assumptions and practices are still fit for purpose in the context of twenty-first century reality.[9]

This evaluation is particularly relevant to determining whether nonprofit investment practices actually deliver recognized public benefits that are not offset by future costs and risks offloaded to society as a result of those investments. At endowments with perpetual obligations, future costs and risks imposed on society by some investment activities might not be readily evident, especially when the future generations who will bear them are not present to advocate for their interests. Accordingly, investments that are otherwise prudent can generate externalities that work at cross purposes to a nonprofit's mission or charitable purpose, presenting questions about the ongoing legitimacy of a tax exempt entity's license to operate. Seemingly prudent investment strategies also might miss opportunities to foster charitable mission or purpose (i.e., foster positive externalities) when they are developed without a holistic perspective toward

management of the nonprofit's entire balance sheet.[10]

For example, during the first decade of the twenty-first century, a number of reports were issued by nonprofits with missions aimed at addressing climate change that focused only on grant-making program initiatives (Viederman 2008). Opportunities to incorporate climate change considerations into investment policies apparently went unaddressed. However, a holistic application of charitable mission to the entire balance sheet would have encouraged consideration of things such as a climate risk proxy voting guidelines overlay, a company engagement policy on carbon footprint reduction, sponsorship of shareholder resolutions on carbon risk issues, establishment of an investment allocation to companies in the green economy and/or divestment from selected company investments.[11]

Failure to address the investment side of nonprofit balance sheets could result in overlooking proactive investment strategies to achieve charitable mission goals. It could also lead to misalignment of investment practices with mission through financial support of economic activities that undermine grant program goals.

Evolutionary forces shaping the application of fiduciary duties

There are a number of economic, social and knowledge base changes that present significantly altered challenges to nonprofit fiduciaries in fulfilling their

---

rule with respect to investment and management functions (Hawley et al. 2011: 7).

[9] John Kenneth Galbraith noted the difference between accepted beliefs and reality: "It is my conclusion, that reality is more obscured by social and habitual preference or group pecuniary advantage in economics and politics than in any other subject" (Galbraith 2004: ix).

[10] "[Whether] or not a charity's governing board is actively considering either form of socially responsible investment (community development investing or investing primarily for economic gain and secondarily to promote social good or to avoid social harm) board members may have a duty to consider the effect on program of their investment decisions. In order to fulfill their responsibility to see that the corporation meets its charitable purposes, they may have a duty to consider whether their investment decisions will further those charitable purposes, or at least not run counter to them" (McKeown 1997: 77).

[11] The authors do not argue for adoption of a specific approach but contend that fiduciary duty requires knowledgeable consideration and documentation of how the duty of obedience is applied to investment practices.

investment-related responsibilities, especially the duty of obedience. Some of the most important factors are worth highlighting.

Increasing short-termism and value destruction

The average mutual fund holding period for a company's stock has declined from more than five years in 1970 to less than one year (Barton 2011). High frequency trading, which involves holding periods measured in seconds or milliseconds, was estimated to account for 51 percent of trading volume on United States stock exchanges in 2012 and was as high as 61 percent in 2009 (Tabb 2012). Pressure from investors to deliver short-term results has become so strong that nearly 80 percent of corporate chief financial officers report that they would rather sacrifice future company growth in value by reducing current expenditures on research and development than miss Wall Street's quarterly earnings expectations (Graham et al. 2005). The Bank of England found that excessive discounting of long-term investments by 5–10 percent per year has been distorting allocation of capital in the economy (Haldane 2011). After studying short-termism, the Business Roundtable and CFA Institute concluded:

> The obsession with short-term results by investors, asset management firms, and corporate managers collectively leads to the unintended consequences of destroying long-term value, decreasing market efficiency, reducing investment returns, and impeding efforts to strengthen corporate governance (Krehmeyer et al. 2006: 1).

Excessive short-termism is clearly a problem with consequences for nonprofits. For example, short-termism of investors with perpetual or long-term obligations can unwittingly foster reduction of future portfolio growth through pressure on investment managers to deliver quarterly or annual returns, which in turn is transmitted to companies and encourages corporate managers to use available capital to meet quarterly targets rather than for research and development or capital improvements that would generate higher future earnings (Graham et al. 2005; Krehmeyer et al. 2006).

Investment theory assumptions proved to be inadequate

The 2008 financial crisis and its aftermath challenged reliability of prevailing investment and risk models. Many turned out to be inadequate and some even contributed to the crisis. Investors were found to not always act rationally. Many risks proved to be interrelated and produced a cascading contagion throughout the world economy. Investor herding around the same investment strategies magnified risk exposures. Return distributions were found to be asymmetric. Systemic risk was not captured when analyses were based on market-relative benchmarks (Beyhaghi and Hawley 2013; Hawley et al. 2011).

Since many investment portfolios still reflect these discredited assumptions, greater fiduciary and advisor attention to addressing the flaws is merited. One illustration of the hidden risks associated with prevailing finance theory is the systemic divergence from fundamental company value that results from inclusion of a company in a market index (Beyhaghi and Hawley 2013). The consequence of investors herding into passive index funds is distortion in valuation of securities in the index, making them unrepresentative of the market they are supposed to replicate and giving investors a different risk profile than anticipated or recognized.

Market integrity found to matter more than market outperformance

New research shows that 75 percent or more of a typical investment portfolio's returns may be from general exposure to the market rather than from outperformance of market benchmarks (Ibbotson 2010). This makes systemic factors central to investment performance and fiduciary responsibility. Events of the past decade increased awareness that investors are not immune from the state of the economy. Investment success and economic health have a symbiotic relationship. After successive economic crises during the first decade of the twenty-first century, both of which were generated by dysfunctional market practices, the S&P 500 traded below the levels it reached in 2000 for virtually all of the subsequent thirteen years. Market integrity and systemic risks can influence investment success; investment practices can affect market integrity and systemic risks. These connections should not be lost on nonprofits that are chartered to convey public benefits. When acting as investors, fiduciaries have the opportunity to use proxy votes and investment policies to foster market integrity, transparency and accountability.

Environmental, social and governance factors are material

Another growing realization among sophisticated investors is that investment risk and opportunity are not always evident within the four corners of a company's financial statements.

> Analysts are generally well versed in using financial metrics to understand those drivers of corporate value and lend skilled interpretation to what is often highly detailed accounting data. In recent years, however, so-called nonfinancial factors – including environmental, social, and governance (ESG) factors – have figured ever more prominently in the value of corporations (CFA Institute 2008: Introduction).

A recent study by Deutsche Bank found ESG factors to be associated with superior risk-adjusted returns. The study also concluded that companies with high ESG ratings have a lower cost of capital, outperform the market and exhibit better financial performance (DB Climate Change Advisors 2012). Deutsche Bank devoted particular attention to the current sustainability (or ESG) investing approach, which (unlike ethics-based approaches) involves integration of ESG factors into a best in class evaluation of how companies are managed for risk management, financial performance and value creation, especially over the medium and long term.

Use of a forward-looking and broadly risk-adjusted sustainability investment approach, especially with an opportunity-directed component, is fully consistent with a nonprofit's required duty of obedience to charitable public purpose. For example, a nonprofit can use its proxy votes to encourage corporate boards to prioritize environmental, human rights and health and safety

compliance at companies with a history of serious violations. Similarly, a portion of portfolio assets could be allocated to investment in market rate green bonds that provide financing for the transition to alternative energy.

Application of evolving fiduciary duty principles to charitable purposes

Implementation of the fiduciary duty of obedience requires a holistic management approach that integrates investment responsibilities with both charitable mission and public purpose in a way that reflects current knowledge. While program-related investments can be included in this approach, all investment activities should be consistent with a nonprofit's charitable mission and purpose. They should not unnecessarily foster the transfer of corporate costs and risks to society, as that would conflict with the nonprofit trade-off to deliver public benefits in exchange for taxpayer underwriting of nonprofits through tax favored status. The fiduciary duty of obedience to mission and public purpose makes this relevant to all nonprofits that have significant investment responsibilities.[12]

An Association of Charitable Foundations report for British endowed charitable foundations advises that "considering their entire balance sheet through the single lens of their mission may make foundations more successful economic and social agents" (Jenkins 2012: 36). The report counsels that foundations first "reflect on their charitable mission and consider whether there are certain values underpinning it which have implications for the way they use the whole balance sheet in terms of investment as well as expenditure," and second "reflect whether their charitable aims could be served also

---

[12] Regardless of the charitable mission of a nonprofit, the duty of obedience to serve public purposes is relevant to how its investment responsibilities are implemented. For example, whether an endowment has a mission devoted to funding programs on human rights, education, arts and culture, environmental preservation or religious objectives, its investment responsibilities should be exercised in ways that are consistent with (and not destructive of) the public benefit purposes which provide the policy trade-off basis for the very existence of charitable organizations.

by investing in certain ways, either to contribute to systemic change in society or by offering a wider range of options to better serve the beneficiaries" (Jenkins 2012: 37).

For permanent endowments, another challenge relates to balancing current needs with preservation of the trust fund assets in perpetuity. The British Association of Charitable Foundations report cites advice from a former Nuffield Foundation chair.

> Doing the best in terms of investment may not be the same as doing the best for your current beneficiaries, because it is prudent to think ahead for future beneficiaries. This equally means that interpreting the "prudent" thing to do when making investments as simply making the maximum risk-adjusted return almost certainly will not cover all the range of factors foundation trustees need to take into account when considering how best to manage their investments so as to serve future and current beneficiaries[13] (Jenkins 2012: 20).

In regard to use of investment advisors, the British Association of Charitable Foundations report raises a number of issues. First, it notes that investment advisors typically also advise pension funds and have often geared their services toward the different needs of pensions. For instance, pension funds have less flexibility about their liabilities and exist within a regulatory framework designed to ensure their investment strategies are suitable for meeting those liabilities. Preservation of capital is usually a focus for endowments, which do not have the same liability structure and regulatory supervision of investments as pensions (Jenkins 2012: 43).

Second, the report questions endowment use of market benchmarks designed for pension portfolios, as well as use of short-term performance evaluations. It asks whether adoption of a longer-term approach might allow endowments to make more money.

---

[13] While use of the word "beneficiaries" in connection with foundations might not be common in some countries, foundations are required to deliver public benefits as part of the trade-off for their tax favored status. The beneficiaries of these public benefits would typically include both the recipients of program services and the public, whose burdens are lessened by the public benefits that are partially underwritten by them as taxpayers.

The difference in financial objectives between pension funds and foundations intuitively suggests a difference in risk appetites. Do the benchmarks for an endowment properly reflect its unconstrained long-term horizon when compared to the shorter and more cautious approach required of pension funds? (Jenkins 2012: 43).

Third, the report notes that there is often a mismatch between the specific needs of foundations and the services its advisors provide. It cites the need for "improved infrastructure to support foundations in becoming more informed and confident decision-makers and customers" (Jenkins 2012: 47).

> Advice ... often focuses on the asset, whereas trustees will want to think about the whole mission ... There may be a gap in the market for foundations to receive support in determining their whole approach to achieving their mission so that operational policies around investment and expenditure are made within a strategic context rather than separately (Jenkins 2012: 53).

The prescribed remedy is collaboration between foundations, especially smaller ones, to develop peer networks that jointly engage advisors through umbrella bodies on shared issues.

Managing the whole nonprofit balance sheet

In the United States, the F. B. Heron Foundation, whose mission is "helping people and communities help themselves," illustrates how an integrated approach to managing both the program and investment sides of the nonprofit balance sheet can be developed. It has adopted a "foundation as enterprise" approach to investing all of its endowment through an investment strategy that is tied to charitable mission. In addition to making program-related investments, the foundation's investment strategy states that it will seek investments to "nurture economically inclusive enterprises in the 'new' economy" through opportunities to "increase and maintain reliable employment; advance systemic innovations that will help individuals and communities succeed despite changes in the nature of work and a volatile environment; and result in net positive contributions to society's shared capital" including through debt and public and private equity instruments.[14]

The Jessie Smith Noyes Foundation Investment Policy also illustrates the foundation's efforts to "harmonize its grant making values and asset management." The Policy includes the following statement of investment philosophy.

> In concert with the Foundation's mission to promote a sustainable and just social and natural system, we seek to invest our endowment assets in companies that:
> - provide commercial solutions to major social and environmental problems; and/or
> - build corporate culture with concerns for environmental impact, equity and community.
>
> The Foundation will consider:
> - the environmental impact of a business by its use of materials, generation of waste, and the goods it produces or services it provides;
> - issues of corporate governance, including selection of directors, role of independent directors, diversity on the board and executive team, compensation policies, relations with labor unions, employee benefits programs or other demonstrated commitments to the well-being of all individuals involved in an enterprise;
> - a corporation's openness and accountability to all stakeholders, its local job creation, its corporate giving to and active involvement with community organizations, or its other initiatives that provide net benefits to the local economy.[15]

This comes in the context of a growing understanding of ESG materiality. MSCI reports that, after the financial crisis in 2008, company stock prices have exhibited greater sensitivity to significant ESG events than before the crisis, with rapid and persistent stock price movements (MSCI Webinar 2013).[16]

Investors have a number of frameworks and resources available to assist in identifying and evaluating ESG factors at publicly traded companies. For example, the International Integrated Reporting Council is focusing on information relating to management of financial capital, intellectual capital, human capital, social and relationship capital, natural capital and manufactured capital (International Integrated Reporting Council 2013). The World Economic Forum sees core nonfinancial drivers of market value as including human capital (employee engagement, health and safety); customer relations (customer satisfaction, reputation); societal factors (public perception, supply chain management); environmental factors (carbon emissions, waste management); innovation (research and development, intellectual property); and corporate governance (ethics, governance processes and procedures) (World Economic Forum 2011). MSCI identifies ESG risks through examination of macro-trends such as resource scarcity (water stress, limited arable land, other finite resources); demographic shifts (labor shortages, ageing population); climate change (transformation of weather patterns, regulatory responses); and digitalization of data (privacy issues, data security) (MSCI Webinar 2013). For fiduciaries seeking to adopt a more holistic approach to evaluation of investment risks and opportunities, the above analytical tools are among the wide range of available resources.[17]

Conclusions

A unique and fundamental aspect of nonprofit governance and fiduciary responsibility is the duty of obedience to charitable mission and to generation of public benefits. Evolution over the past two decades in the natural, social and economic environment, as well as in understanding of the systemic effects of investment activities, has highlighted previously unrecognized costs, benefits, risks and opportunities that can be associated with investment practices of nonprofit entities and other institutional

---

[14] www.fbheron.org/our-investments.html.

[15] www.noyes.org/taxonomy/term/10.

[16] In drawing this conclusion, MSCI cites market reactions to post-2008 ESG events at British Petroleum, Tokyo Electric Power, Massey Energy, StatOil, Exxon Mobil, ConocoPhillips, Chevron, News Corporation, PG&E, Foxconn and Royal Dutch Shell (MSCI Webinar 2013).

[17] For example, see Krzus (2014) and Urwin (2014) for additional information about the resources available for fiduciaries.

investors. Fundamental fiduciary duty principles are flexible and contemplate periodic adjustments in their application to reflect the dynamic environment in which they must be applied. The challenge to philanthropic fiduciaries is to adopt a holistic approach that integrates investments with nonprofit program goals and the nonprofit's public benefit purpose. The necessary tools and concepts to accomplish this transition are available, but fiduciaries must rise to meet the challenge.[18]

Among other things, the task will require philanthropic fiduciaries to oversee adjustments to investment policies and investment beliefs; modification of advisor, consultant and asset manager selection, contracting and monitoring practices; better alignment of investment time horizons, service provider mandates, risk exposure measurements, performance benchmarks and asset manager compensation with charitable mission and purpose; integration of ESG factors into investment practices; more robust proxy voting and stewardship policies; and revision of nonprofit reporting practices to provide better information on implementation of the fiduciary duty of obedience.[19]

However, alignment of investment activities with charitable mission and purpose also has ramifications for regulators, policymakers and taxing authorities. They have responsibility for ensuring integrity of the nonprofit sector's trade-off between providing a public benefit and receiving a tax preference. An incomplete understanding of how fiduciary responsibility extends to investment activities of nonprofits can not only erode the ability of nonprofits to successfully promote their public purpose, it can also frustrate the fundamental policy basis for the existence of nonprofits, resulting in the generation of unrecognized risks and costs from investment activities that end up being borne in the future by taxpayers.

Public officials should also take a view of philanthropic fiduciary responsibilities that balances short- and long-term needs and reinforces the fiduciary duty of obedience to charitable mission and public purpose. Taxpayers and government, as well as the recipients of nonprofit services, all have a stake in the integration of nonprofit investment and program responsibilities. The challenge is to educate, motivate and empower philanthropic fiduciaries to manage the entire balance sheet of their organizations pursuant to a balanced understanding of fiduciary duty that recognizes impartiality and obedience to both mission and public purpose.

Acknowledgements

The authors would like to thank Lucia Orozco at Reinhart Boerner Van Deuren s.c. for her assistance with research for this chapter.

---

[18] Many issues could be covered in the charity's investment policy. There has been a trend toward requiring that nonprofits develop written investment policies that are tailored to their investment needs. For example, New York added a provision to its Not-for-Profit Corporation Law in 2010 that requires that each institution adopt a written investment policy (New York NCPL, section 552). Many of the organizational changes associated with implementation of an effective sustainable investing program are outlined in the Project Telos Report (Towers Watson 2012).

[19] Selection of service providers and alignment of contract responsibilities with charitable mission and purpose are at the core of the challenge. "[Surely] asset holders have a responsibility to impose discipline upon their service providers! Recognizing the disjunction between their interests and the interests of asset managers, we might imagine that asset holders, acting alone and in concert with one another, might use their market power to set the appropriate terms and conditions for the industry. After all, asset holders have, in theory, an overriding interest in realizing long-term value from their investments, given their planning horizons and the temporal profiles of their liabilities"(Clark 2013: 61).

References

American Law Institute. 1992. "Prudent Investor Rule," *Restatement (Third) of Trusts*.

Barton, D. 2011. "Capitalism for the Long Term," *Harvard Business Review*, March. http://hbr.org/2011/03/capitalism-for-the-long-term/ar/1#.

Beyhaghi, M. and J. P. Hawley. 2013. "Modern Portfolio Theory and Risk Management: Assumptions and Unintended Consequences," *Journal of Sustainable Finance and Investment* 3 (1): 17–37. http://papers.ssrn.com/sol3/papers.cfm?abstract_id=1923774.

CFA Institute. 2008. *Environmental, Social, and Governance Factors at Listed Companies:*

A Manual for Investors, Center for Financial Market Integrity, CFA Institute, July 8. www.cfainstitute.org/about/press/release/Pages/06252008_16419.aspx.

Clark, G. 2013. "The Kay Review on Long-Horizon Investing: A Guide for the Perplexed," *Rotman International Journal of Pension Management* 6 (1): 58.

Commonfund Institute. 2001. *Principles of Endowment Management: The Seven Key Issues Facing Trustees and Financial Officers*. Wilton, CT: Commonfund Institute.

DB Climate Change Advisors. 2012. "Sustainable Investing: Establishing Long-Term Value and Performance," Deutsche Bank Group, June. www.dbcca.com/dbcca/EN/_media/Sustainable_Investing_2012-Exec_Summ.pdf.

Galbraith, J. K. 2004. *The Economics of Innocent Fraud: Truth for Our Time*. Boston, MA: Houghton Mifflin.

Graham, J. R., C. R. Harvey and S. Rajgopal. 2005. "The Economic Implications of Corporate Financial Reporting," *Journal of Accounting and Economics* 40: 3.

Haldane, A. G. 2011. "The Short Long," speech to the 29th Société Universitaire Européene de Recherches Financières Colloquium: New Paradigms in Money and Finance (Brussels) May 11. www.bankofengland.co.uk/publications/Documents/speeches/2011/speech495.pdf

Hawley, J., K. Johnson and E. Waitzer. 2011. "Reclaiming Fiduciary Duty Balance," *Rotman International Journal of Pension Management* 4 (2): 4.

Hazen, T. and L. Hazen. 2012. "Punctilios and Nonprofit Corporate Governance – A Comprehensive Look at Nonprofit Directors' Fiduciary Duties," *University of Pennsylvania Journal of Business Law* 14: 347.

Ibbotson, R. 2010. "The Importance of Asset Allocation," *Financial Analysts Journal* 66 (2): 18.

International Integrated Reporting Council. 2013. *Consultation Draft of the International (IR) Framework: Integrated Reporting*. www.theiirc.org/wp-content/uploads/Consultation-Draft/Consultation-Draft-of-the-InternationalIRFramework.pdf.

Jenkins, R. 2012. *The Governance and Financial Management of Endowed Charitable Foundations*. London: Association of Charitable Foundations. www.acf.org.uk/publicationsandresources/publications/index.aspx?id=&eid=3805.

Krehmeyer, D., M. Orsagh, and K. Schacht. 2006. "Breaking the Short-Term Cycle," CFA Institute and the Business Roundtable Institute for Corporate Ethics. www.cfapubs.org/doi/pdf/10.2469/ccb.v2006.n1.4194.

Krzus, M. 2014. "Reporting and Standards: Tools for Stewardship," Chapter 32, this volume.

McKeown, W. 1997. "Being True to your Mission: Social Investments for Endowments," *Journal of Investing* 6 (4): 78.

MSCI Webinar. 2013. *ESG – Part of the Problem or Part of the Solution?* May 28. www.msci.com/resources/event/webinar/esg_part_of_the_problem_or_part_of_the_solution_for_asset_owners.html.

Phelan, M. 2010. *Nonprofit Organizations: Law and Taxation*. Eagan, MA: Thomson Reuters/West.

Sasso, P. 2003. "Searching for Trust in the Not-for-Profit Boardroom: Looking Beyond the Duty of Obedience to Ensure Accountability," *UCLA Law Review* 50: 1485.

Sugin, L. 2007. "Resisting the Corporatization of Nonprofit Governance: Transforming Obedience into Fidelity," *Fordham Law Review* 76: 893.

Tabb, L. 2012. "Written Testimony to the United States Senate Committee on Banking, Housing, and Urban Affairs," September 20. www.banking.senate.gov/public/index.cfm?FuseAction=Hearings.Home.

Towers Watson. 2012. *We Need a Bigger Boat: Sustainability in Investment*. www.towerswatson.com/en/Press/2012/09/The-rewards-of-investing-sustainably.

Urwin, R. 2014. "Pension Fund Fiduciary Duty and its Impacts on Sustainable Investing," Chapter 21, this volume.

Viederman, S. 2008. "How Grant Makers Can Curb Global Warming," *Chronicle of Philanthropy*, February 7. http://philanthropy.com/article/How-Grant-Makers-Can-Curb/60996/.

Wakeman, A., W. Franklin and M. Ascher. 2006. *Scott and Ascher on Trusts*. New York: Aspen Law & Business.

World Economic Forum. 2011. *Accelerating the Transition towards Sustainable Investing*. www3.weforum.org/docs/WEF_IV_AcceleratingSustainableInvesting_Report_2011.pdf.

Paradigm lost: employment-based defined benefit plans and the current understanding of fiduciary duty

LARRY W. BEEFERMAN

Introduction

This volume is witness to the importance of the meaning and import of "fiduciary duty" for the responsibilities of those who make investment-related decisions on behalf of others – "decision-makers" – especially institutional investors, including pension funds. Focus on the subject is animated by the impact of such decisions on those ostensibly to be benefited by them. However, it has also been spurred by concern about how decision-makers' choices bear upon the behaviors of the enterprises in which they invest and diverse stakeholders in the enterprise and the larger society. Here we largely attend to beneficiaries although we will in some measure address distinct but related concerns of others.

We consider decision-makers for funded employment-based defined benefit plans ("plans") in the United States and the interests they might legitimately seek to advance. Plans promise workers – and sometimes their spousal survivors – a lifetime income starting at retirement – a "pension." We refer to as "members" those who potentially qualify for a pension by virtue of their or their spouse's employment at the enterprise with which the plan is associated. To assure that the promises are kept, workers' and/or employers' contributions to the plan are pooled and invested. Plans, like other retirement schemes, are usually subsidized by tax credits and/or deductions for contributions made and no or lower taxation of investment returns and/or plan payouts after retirement.

Decision-makers' authority is typically framed in terms of "fiduciary duty." It is a term associated with a variety of institutional arrangements but as a historical and legal matter has been closely linked to the law of trusts. Typical dialogue in these terms defines decision-makers' task to be advancing "only members' interests as members" and such interests to be *exclusively* those in their receipt of benefits. The role is correspondingly deemed to permit *only* taking into account financial attributes of investments. This discourse has been married to one about the putative behavior of financial markets, which has reinforced a crabbed understanding of what the role of decision-makers should be.

In this chapter we will contend the following: the trust model is a poor fit for the relationships in which plans are embedded. Those relationships warrant, at minimum, decision-makers considering members' interests as workers at the associated enterprise, which derive from the financial risks of plan investments in other enterprises in general, and arguably the impact of harms that result from the behaviors of specific, sometimes competing enterprises. We express skepticism that these relationships justify taking account of members' interests other than as members or workers. However, it can be justified based on a different line of argument. It concerns the extent to which members (or others) who participate in collective vehicles for investment should retain the voice they would otherwise have with respect to advancement of their interests in the case of their own individual investment decisions. Vindication of a broader range of members' interests might have merit as a matter of social policy rather than as one of advancing those interests for their own sake.

The foregoing points are made within the context of what is deemed to be decision-makers' duty of loyalty. However, we briefly explore the import of what is termed their "duty of care" for the issues explored. In doing so, we assert that the statutory framework that defined that duty was largely devoid of substantive content. The content was supplied by investment theories and practices at best insensitive to the relationships in which plans are grounded. Moreover, those theories and practices embodied problematic claims about the goals that might legitimately be pursued by the enterprises in which plans might invest. These claims stand in tension if not in direct conflict with those of members' interests that decision-makers might appropriately seek to advance. The foregoing suggests a close or intimate connection between how fiduciary duty, with respect to investment in enterprises, and the legitimate goals that might be pursued by those enterprises are understood.

Part I: the duty of loyalty

The trust model: a poor fit for the relationships in which plans are grounded

We start from a broad perspective that we think informs arguments with respect to plans and might, as well, apply to other kinds of retirement schemes (not discussed here). The common starting point is an arrangement for investment by others – "decision-makers" more generally – of monies provided by or on behalf of a person to afford him or her an ostensibly guaranteed lifetime stream of payments. Receipt of this flow of payments is, by definition, of significant interest to people who engage others to advance. The challenge is how to ensure that decision-makers make appropriate choices in pursuing that interest and do so with sufficient care and competence. The two aspects of the tasks are typically put under the rubric of the duties of loyalty and care, respectively.

However, people may want their monies to be invested to achieve other objectives as well, for example, to spur enterprises to treat their workers in certain ways. Among the arrangements through which the single or multiple interest scenarios could play out are ones involving trusts, (defined benefit) plans and insurance companies (as providers of fixed annuities). We refer to trusts separately

from plans because we believe they are not a suitable model for plans.

The matter of trusts arises from the Employee Retirement Income Security Act (ERISA), enacted in 1974, which required that "all assets of an employee benefit plan [must] be held in trust by one or more trustees."[1] Why did legislators prescribe so? ERISA was a novel, extensive federal intervention into the web of relationships among enterprises and their active and former workers. Congress declined to start from scratch, preferring to adapt a pre-existing framework to them. There was a long Anglo-Saxon history of trust law to which Congress could appeal, as well as state law experience with plan assets being held in trusts (Wooten 2009: 15). Moreover, federal tax law had, since the 1920s, incentivized contributions to retirement schemes whose assets were held in trusts.[2] Legislation in 1947 aimed at certain putative abuses in the context of labor relations accorded special status to monies of multi-employer plans held in trust.[3] Yet Congress did concede that the trust model was less than ideal, delegating authority to the US Department of Labor (DOL) to implement it in certain ways and to the federal courts to finally determine the meaning of the skeletal ERISA provisions. Indeed the US House-Senate conference committee's report on the final ERISA bill acknowledged problems with the trust model, stating its "expect[ation] that the courts w[ould] interpret [the prudence requirement discussed below] … (and other fiduciary standards) bearing in mind the special nature and purpose of employee benefit plans" (US Senate Committee on Labor Welfare, Subcommittee on Labor 2000: vol. 3, p. 4569).

There are numerous significant differences between plans and trusts as typically configured. Some were identified by a paper written some years ago, although we go far beyond what the authors propose and advance rather different conclusions (Fischel and Langbein 1988).

First, at the core of trusts is the notion of a "settlor" who *voluntarily and unilaterally* elects to

---

[1] US Code (2012) Title 29, § 1103.
[2] US Code (2012) Title 26, § 401(a).
[3] US Code (2012) Title 29, § 186(c)(5).

donate assets – financial or otherwise – to be managed by another – the "trustee" – for the benefit of third parties, "beneficiaries." But as the cited paper's authors point out, for plans the roles are blurred because plan benefits "are part of a total compensation package *agreed upon* by the employer and employee," that is through collective bargaining or a series of ostensible employer-individual worker contracts (Fischel and Langbein 1988: 1117). The blurring relates not only to what plans specify for benefits, but also what they prescribe for contributions to the plan. Note also that, unlike for the trust, the dual roles may change based on subsequent agreements or understandings, reflecting shifting relationships among the parties.

Second, a settlor prescribes the general goals and specific terms of the trust that are fixed. Subsequently the settlor has no role in the trust's operation (although may voluntarily make additional contributions). By contrast members and the associated enterprise have intimate and ongoing links with one another. The extent to which the plan succeeds in meeting its obligations is closely tied to the financial and other condition of the enterprise. This connection may be strengthened if, as is typical, the enterprise is a guarantor of plan promises. The paper's authors make a somewhat similar point in referring, although mistakenly, to shareholders and employees (and retirees) having conflicting interests as "beneficiaries" of plans. That employers/shareholders may have a great interest in outcomes of investment decisions does not warrant deeming them to be beneficiaries.

Third, a stereotypical trust has a largely individual character. It is established for the benefit of a relative small group of ascertainable people who have no necessary connection with one another, except as defined by the settlor's prescribed allocation of trust income and corpus. By contrast, a plan has a collective character, which is an artifact of the relationships between and among an ostensibly open-ended population of members with one another and the enterprise.

Fourth, the relationship of trust beneficiaries to one another and to the trust is set. A plan has continually changing, and not readily ascertainable members with no necessarily fixed relationship to

the plan, one another or the enterprise. New workers are hired and current workers are fired, quit, become disabled or die. The plan's relationship to unvested workers who leave is severed; for vested workers, it is changed. The relationships with non-workers vary by virtue of marriages, divorces or deaths of spouses. There may be accompanying modifications as to who is obliged to contribute to the plan and how much.

Fifth, a stereotypical trust has a finite life, defined by the lives of the identified or ascertainable beneficiaries for whom it was established. A plan has an arguably indefinite life, identified with the existence of the enterprise that gave rise to it.

Sixth, a stereotypical trust may have so-called income beneficiaries who are entitled to income from the corpus of assets distinct from so-named remaindermen who take the corpus of remaining assets left after income beneficiaries' claims are exhausted. By contrast, a plan has no pure income beneficiaries or remaindermen. Vested members are like income beneficiaries because they have a right to benefit payments. For retirees, the claim has ripened. For vested active or former workers the claims ripen when they satisfy age and service requirements. Vested members are unlike remaindermen because they have no claim on the "corpus" (plan assets) as such, only an implicit claim on plan assets needed to fully pay promised benefits (and perhaps some enterprise assets to back up the guarantee of payment).[4] Further, additional contributions made by or on behalf of active workers – to help ensure that promised benefits are paid – increase the corpus of the plan. Those workers are the opposite of remaindermen.

Finally, benefits are determined by often complex ostensibly agreement-based formulas that reflect members' work histories and that may well change in light of the shifting fortunes of the enterprise and its workers. By contrast, a large

---

[4] "Since a decline in the value of a plan's assets does not alter accrued benefits, members similarly have no entitlement to share in a plan's surplus – even if it is partially attributable to the investment growth of their contributions" (*Hughes Aircraft Co.* v. *Jacobson*, 525 US 43, p. 440).

majority of trusts are hardly likely to reflect such multifaceted arrangements.

Decision-makers can advance members' interests as workers at the associated enterprise: financial impacts of investment in other enterprises

Consider now, by contrast, relationships and interests associated with insurance company marketed fixed annuities. They, like plans, provide an ostensibly guaranteed lifetime retirement income. Premiums, like plan contributions, are pooled for investment purposes. However, in contrast with members, annuity purchasers make one-time, purely individual decisions about ostensibly arm's length transactions, each essentially unrelated to the others. The connections among their subsequent annuity-related decisions are random. Not surprisingly, then, insurance companies have quite different duties from plan decision-makers as to as how monies paid must be invested to honor the promises made. In the US, standards for providers of fixed annuities, set by state law and regulation, have been highly prescriptive and without reference to trusts or trust law. It is perhaps ironic that under ERISA employers who may have and exercise the power to unilaterally close a plan must purchase insurance company annuities matching promised benefits.[5] The employer's (final) fiduciary duty is fulfilled so long is its choice of the insurer is carefully enough made (Pension Benefit Guaranty Corporation 1991).

There are corresponding differences in how trust beneficiaries or annuitants can advance or protect their interests. Beneficiaries have little voice except through *post hoc* legal mechanisms to hold trustees accountable for breach of their duties. The trust is a means for achieving the settlor's goals for disposition of his or her donated assets. The trust vehicle presupposes that beneficiaries either lack the competence to appropriately manage and/or exercise discretion in managing trust assets. Fiduciary law cabins trustees' decision-making power to protect beneficiaries' interests as specified by the settlor.

By contrast, as noted, the roles and interests of plan "settlors" and "beneficiaries" are blurred. That difference grounds members having voice in choosing decision-makers and setting standards for decision-making. By contrast, the one-off, arm's length, individual and narrowly contractual or fee-for-service relationships in which annuities are grounded suggest no basis for annuitant voice. Rather as with trusts, annuitants have resort only to *post hoc*, largely contractual or perhaps statutory remedies.

These issues of voice are connected with the interests that decision-makers are permitted to advance. We suggest two approaches in this regard: one flows directly from the distinctive character of plans; the other derives from what decisions are allowed for plans as collective vehicles in comparison to the ostensibly untrammeled ones that would be the result of individual action. As to the former, we first turn to one of several segments of an ERISA provision with the caption "Prudent man standard of care."[6]

It has two aspects which require a plan fiduciary to act "**solely in the interest of the participants and beneficiaries and ...** *for the exclusive purpose of ... providing benefits to participants and their beneficiaries*; and ... defraying reasonable expenses of administering the plan."[7] We denote the underlined portion as the "to whom" aspect of a duty of loyalty, that is, whose interests must be served: members. The italicized part – termed the "to do what" aspect – specifies that the only interests of members that decision-makers may permissibly seek to advance are those of members in the receipt of benefits. Both requirements make sense. Plans are constituted to serve the interests of members in their receipt of retirement benefits. But, by definition, plans rely on investment returns to pay benefits; hence they presuppose that financial risks will be taken. (The diversification requirement discussed below by its nature acknowledges that fact.) Realization of those risks may require shoring up plan's finances. This frequently leads to higher

---

[5] US Code (2012) Title 29, § 1341 (b)(3(A)(i).

[6] US Code (2012) Title 29, §1104 (a).

[7] US Code (2012) Title 29, §1104 (a)(1)(A)(i) and (ii) (emphasis, italics and underlining added).

plan contributions that, in turn, implicate different interests: most immediately, for shareholders, profits and, for active workers, employment compensation. At the extreme it may result in large financial losses for the enterprise and perhaps bankruptcy and dramatic cuts in wages, benefits or even loss of jobs. Private sector retirees may even lose benefits because available enterprise assets and ERISA-required pension insurance may be inadequate. An ongoing need to attend to such trade-offs is always present.

Several illustrations highlight the point. In one case, New York City teacher pension fund trustees agreed (under specified conditions) to their fund purchasing city bonds in the face of the city's seemingly imminent bankruptcy. The purchase was adjudged to comport with fiduciary duty because it enabled the city to avert bankruptcy and continue to make contributions to the fund. This was deemed "crucial if the fund was to continue to operate for the benefit of all classes of beneficiaries."[8] In other words, it was legitimate and important to shore up the fund by investing in the enterprise which was the ultimate source of contributions to it.

The second case concerns an ERISA provision barring plans from holding enterprise sponsor stock (or real property) representing greater than 10 percent of the fair value of plan assets, a provision justified in the name of enterprises' interests.[9] (A roughly analogous rationale was offered when ERISA, as originally written, permitted defined contribution plans to hold unlimited amounts of enterprise sponsor stock.) A dramatic exception to this limit was allowed by the DOL (among others) in the mid-1990s: the General Motors pension plan was permitted to hold for an extended time company stock with a value upwards of 25 percent of plan assets, in the name of the advancing the company's financial and other objectives (US Department of Labor 1995).

Third, and more generally, in a frank and extensive discussion of the matter, a Nobel laureate financial economist unblushingly makes the case for (corporate executive) decision-makers taking into account the interests of enterprises (although apparently not, in the first instance, those of members as workers) in investment decisions (Merton 2006: 15).[10]

Decision-makers can advance members' interests as workers at the associated enterprise: impacts of investment in other, specific enterprises

These examples suggest at minimum the legitimacy if not the necessity for decision-makers taking account of members' interests as workers at the associated enterprise, which derives generally from the financial risks of plan investments in other enterprises. Different questions are posed when the harm results from the behaviors of other, specific enterprises.

Consider a plan investment in a direct, major competitor of the enterprise that would so enhance its competitiveness as to result in wage and/or benefit cuts or job losses at the enterprise associated with the plan. Should the latter enterprise fail, unvested active workers would be denied the chance to vest; others would lose the chance to enjoy larger pensions (because plans are back-loaded in terms of benefit levels). As noted, even retirees might be at risk. In such circumstances, it is hard to imagine why decision-makers might not be allowed (or perhaps even be required) to take cognizance of these realities in their decisions. Certainly, quantifying the impact and tracing the relevant chain of causality between investment and harm might be difficult. To be sure, reasons of this kind might be a cover for other, more nefarious ones. But all that

---

[8] *Withers* v. *Teachers' Retirement System of City of New York*, 447 F. Supp 1258, affirmed 595 F.2d 1210 (1978), p. 1258.

[9] US Code (2012) Title 29, §1107(a)(2). Note that ERISA, in the name of advancing company interests, overrides trust law conflict-of-interest restrictions, lifting a bar on corporate officers or executives serving as trustees. See US Code (2012) Title 29, §1108 (c)(3).

[10] Note as well a related acknowledgment in the public context, namely the California constitution which, in article 16, section 17(b) provides that "members of the retirement board of a public pension or retirement system shall discharge their duties with respect to the system solely in the interest of, and for the exclusive purposes of providing benefits to, participants and their beneficiaries, minimizing employer contributions thereto, and defraying reasonable expenses of administering the system" (Constitution of California 2013, www.leginfo.ca.gov/const-toc.html).

justifies is a carefully crafted standard applied to particular facts and circumstances not a complete ban on choices of this kind.[11]

Decision-makers can advance members' interests other than as members or workers, including the interests of others

The questions are posed differently should decision-makers act in light of members' interests other than as members or as workers. There is justification for that but the arguments are different because those interests have little link to the roles of members as active and former workers at the associated enterprise.

We start from the premise that people can, with their own funds, make individual investment decisions as they might choose. They are free to advance not only their immediate interests – in, say, retirement benefits – but also their or others' economic, social, environmental, political or other well-being. Challenges are posed when individuals select or are compelled to invest by means of a collective or pooled vehicle.

If a collective vehicle is chosen, then in principle, which interests – financial or otherwise – might permissibly be advanced would be ostensibly a matter of agreement. Of necessity decision-makers can reflect only broadly shared views about the interests to be advanced and how. Those views can be established as a condition for participation in the vehicle when it is offered. Post-entry there could be means by which individuals can exercise voice as to how those views are given expression and others can exit from the vehicle if the meaning given is not acceptable. To be sure, people might well require protection in their relationships with that vehicle as to the inducements to participate, how decision-making is monitored, etc. There are innumerable "socially responsible" mutual funds, which operate along these lines with apparently little suggestion of abuse, gross unfairness, fraud, etc. Indeed, an insurance company might sell

fixed annuities contingent on the premiums being invested in ways consistent with purchasers' specified financial and other interests. Presumably, purchasers would be alerted to and assent to such higher premiums or lower annuity income that might result from nonfinancial factors being taken into account.

If collective vehicles of this sort are or could be legitimate and practicable for individuals, then what is their import for plans? Here there are issues about consent or agreement to plans and what policy concerns might trump them. As for policy, it might be thought that pursuit of non-retirement benefit goals might defeat the purposes of tax subsidies for plans that some claim spur workers to save for retirement and encourage enterprises to establish and perhaps contribute to plans. However, there is relevant literature in the US context that strongly suggests that tax incentives of the sort described actually produce little additional saving overall. But in all events, in the US, Individual Retirement Accounts (IRAs) garner analogous subsidies justified by similar reasons but there are very, very few restrictions as to the choice of investments (US Internal Revenue Service 2012). It could be contended that lower financial yields might result, rendering the subsidy less effective in spurring accumulations for retirement. But, again, the same claim applies to IRAs. Moreover, the empirical literature does not suggest that pursuit of nonfinancial objectives is necessarily harmful and might even be beneficial to returns. Certainly, members must be well enough informed about trade-offs between financial and nonfinancial goals. A similar argument applies to socially responsible mutual funds but seems to have posed no obstacle to their legitimacy and growth. Indeed, a not insubstantial portion of defined contribution plan savings is already invested through such funds (Mercer Investment Consulting and Social Investment Forum 2007). Moreover, nonfinancial considerations might induce some people to participate in or contribute more to plans.

Because US employers have no obligation to offer or agree to plans they might resist, fearful that supposed lower yields from the pursuit of nonfinancial goals could result in shortfalls they would have to remedy. They might contend that their role in establishing (and perhaps contributing to) the

[11] Some might argue that not investing would cause (lack of) diversification-related losses or perhaps that an investment in a competitor might serve as a hedge against failure to compete successfully.

plan warrants their having a voice with respect to permissible plan goals. Although the assertion has merit, arguably it does not square with ERISA's requirement that "the assets of a plan shall never inure to the benefit of any employer and shall be held for the exclusive purposes of providing benefits to participants in the plan and their beneficiaries and defraying reasonable expenses of administering the plan."[12] Moreover, as a conceptual and likely practical matter, employer contributions are part of workers' overall compensation.[13] Also, that employers have a responsibility for plan shortfalls does not necessarily warrant their having a voice with respect to plan goals or operations. Any putative increased costs from pursing nonfinancial goals could be factored into trade-offs as to employees' compensation. In all events, such say as employers might have could be determined by the parties.

Certainly considerations of policy could justify overriding workers' choice (or workers' and their employers' choices). Policy can be crafted in the name of certain members' interests: ERISA was fashioned with a history of abuses in mind (Fischel and Langbein 1988).[14] But that does in itself justify a broader proscription. In all events, ERISA's reference to the exclusive interest of members captures this point. Its deterrents can apply to whatever interests – retirement benefits or otherwise – members want to advance. To be sure, even if there is room for members' voice as to interests to be advanced, giving it practical effect has challenges. Plans are different from SRI mutual funds in which investors are free to make investments and largely free to cash out them out at any time for any reasons. By contrast, members generally are not.[15] This poses problems both at the outset of the plan and on an ongoing basis.

Where there is a union the very existence of the plan and its terms would be set by the collective bargaining agreement. Moreover the union might play an important role in policing its implementation both for its own sake and to inform future changes to it. However, the accumulated assets are those of members as individuals (as beneficial owners). Their status as union members is irrelevant in that respect. Hence insofar as the interests of unions as such and (union) members as individuals are not aligned, the choice of goals might well be reserved to members. Where there is no union, appeal to members' voice would be made directly to them.

That being said, we do not gainsay the challenges with respect to the degree of assent required at the inception of the plan or when new people enter it, and the extent of approval required to make changes in standards. Moreover, there are thorny issues that arise from how already existing investments should be managed insofar as dissenting members being allowed some form of opt out. Nonetheless they are not insuperable or in certain ways entirely novel problems.

Decision-makers can, as a matter of policy, advance interests other than those of members as members or workers, including the interests of others

We have focused so far on members' articulation of their interests to be advanced and the legitimacy, permissibility and necessity of decision-makers pursuing them (only). We have seen that ERISA protects members generally in these terms but as a matter of policy it has been read to do so with respect to a very important but narrow financial interest and bars consideration of others.

---

[12] US Code (2012) Title 29, § 1103(c)(1).

[13] There appears to be little empirical evidence in this regard; it is a practical reality for multi-employer, so-called "Taft-Hartley" or "union" plans: employer contributions are set within the larger context of episodically negotiated overall compensation packages.

[14] "The exclusive benefit rule works well enough against thieves and thugs, but the rule sweeps more broadly, and in the less dramatic setting the rule has proved more problematic" (Fischel and Langbein 1988: 1110). Here the authors refer to union corruption and "looting of union-controlled pension and employee benefit funds." Actually the abuses were also associated with the interests of enterprise employers as such, service providers and even decision-makers themselves.

[15] The only very limited exceptions are those contexts in which non-vested workers, upon leaving employment, may receive such contributions as they may have made plus some modest rate of interest on them and workers, upon retirement, may have the opportunity to receive a lump-sum equivalent of the pension benefits.

But the policy could be different and justified in two kinds of ways. One, offered in the name of member choice allows for the expression and realization of member voice with respect to nonfinancial interests of members, which do not unwarrantedly thwart pursuit of financial ones. However, policy might be grounded on broader societal interests. That is, the establishment or operation of a plan or tax or other governmental financial support for it could be conditioned upon decision-making being in accord with certain parameters. These could be procedural, specifying mechanisms for worker voice in how decisions are made, e.g., decision-makers' reporting on the extent to which they take account of various factors, the reasons for and/or impact of doing or not doing so, etc. Substantive parameters could require decision-makers to accord weight to one or more nonfinancial considerations. These would reflect societal judgments about enterprise behaviors and deem investors' relationship to enterprises as a necessary and important aspect of influencing those behaviors.

To illustrate the point, we note that ERISA requires decision-makers to appropriately exercise the incidents of ownership attached to any investment (US Department of Labor 1988).[16] For publicly traded companies, that means employing shareowner power to choose corporate directors and in limited ways influence the actions of directors and senior executives. Under the current, contested paradigm, directors and executives must single-mindedly pursue profit. In turn, shareholders cannot use their power to oblige the company to attend to nonfinancial outcomes. In that case, this and ERISA's requirement for decision-makers are perfectly aligned. However, suppose decision-makers could be and were authorized by members to act on nonfinancial considerations; then members' desires would be thwarted. The only solace, if any, would be that members (through decision-makers) would be situated in the same ways as other shareowners.

Suppose, however, that corporations were required to consider certain nonfinancial outcomes

grounded in the belief that by doing so they would become more efficient, better improve the lives of those who have stakes in the enterprise, cause less harm to the environment, etc.[17] Indeed, so-called state "constituency" statutes nominally require that corporations take account of the interests of certain specified stakeholders, although so far they seem to have had little practical "bite" (Keay 2010). Even if they did, however, ERISA would bar decision-makers from sacrificing financial to nonfinancial goals and, in turn, from investing in any such corporations. The cumulative impact of that exclusion would be to significantly thwart established policy!

Imagine, instead, that corporations were allowed to consider nonfinancial outcomes. Shareowners other than plans might be free to spur corporations to take up the opportunity, but decision-makers would be barred from doing so. Indeed, decision-makers could arguably be required to contest other shareowners' efforts along those lines. Should those others prevail, decision-makers might be required to sell their shares! Clearly these strictures would operate to thwart public policy and perhaps the wishes of members.

Lastly, posit that worker-owned enterprises loom large. Here, active workers would have personal rights in the management of the enterprise and in the allocation of revenues to wages and salaries and retained profits but property rights only as to a portion of internal capital accounts linked to the enterprise's net asset value (Ellerman 2006). In that case, external investors, including plans, might only have a right to a market-based, interest-like return on monies provided to the enterprise but no say in management decisions. If so, then the universe of investments in other enterprises available to plans would be limited to these debt-like securities. Clearly the financial calculus of risk and reward for investors would be quite different from that under prevailing arrangements, e.g., with largely no scope for equity-associated gains (and in certain respects, losses as well). Under ERISA,

[16] Stating that the fiduciary act of managing plan assets that are shares of corporate stock includes the management of voting rights appurtenant to those shares of stock.

[17] For example, "B corporations" "have a corporate purpose to create a material positive impact on society and the environment" and "are required to consider the impact of their decisions not only on shareholders but also on workers, community, and the environment" (Benefit Corp Information Center 2012).

decision-makers might still be required to pursue only financial objectives but have much more limited ways than currently for doing so. Moreover, their means for influence (in the pursuit of financial or nonfinancial objectives) over the enterprise would derive from the conditions they can set for their provision of funds, remedies for breach of those conditions or failure to pay the debt and such rights as might arise from a bankruptcy of the enterprise.

These examples pose the more general question of what is or should be the relationship between how enterprises are constituted and the goals they may permissibly pursue and how plans are constituted and the objectives they are allowed to achieve.

By definition plans invest in (for-profit) enterprises. (We leave aside lending to nonprofit enterprises and governments.) In turn, by definition, such claims as plans (and other investors) have to the enterprises' profits and against their assets depend upon the plans' relationship as investors to those enterprises to which their investments give rise.

Imagine a plan associated with a worker-owned enterprise of the sort referred to above. Would decision-makers be allowed to invest only in similar worked-owned firms or be required to invest in just conventional ones (grounded in the usual financial considerations) as well? Under ERISA, decision-makers could at best only prefer worker-owned ones to others based on an individual, other-factors-being equal test (US Department of Labor 1994).[18] People would have made an affirmative commitment to (perhaps) establish and work at a particular kind of enterprise, at least in part informed by the notions of worker voice and self-governance it embodies perhaps even notwithstanding any possibility that it might be less "profitable" than conventional ones. Yet they would be

forced to foster other enterprises, which operate quite differently from and in ways that might tend to undermine that model.

In other words the purely financial interest driven ERISA standard strongly reinforces – if it does not in effect mandate – a solely profit driven standard for enterprises. The converse may well be true.

Part II: the duty of care

The discussion above has focused on "duty of loyalty" issues. Here we only highlight certain "duty of care" issues that are not only problematic in and of themselves but also have import for debate regarding the duty of care.

Here, there are two relevant ERISA provisions. One has two aspects, requiring decision-makers to act "<u>with the care, skill, prudence, and diligence under the circumstances then prevailing that</u> *a prudent man acting in a like capacity and familiar with such matters would use in the conduct of an enterprise of a like character and with like aims.*"[19]

With respect to the underlined part we note the following: first, the legislative history for it is quite sparse. The original House bill contained this exact language without an explanation distinguishing among the words "care," "skill," "prudence" and "diligence"; the two original Senate bills included only the word "prudence." Clearly, its location in a larger section labeled "Prudent man standard of care" was circular unless the word "prudence" is distinguished from the other three. A reasonable reading is that the latter relate to the knowledge and tools requisite to the task, hard work and attentiveness to and methodical and thorough consideration of all relevant matters. By contrast, as discussed below, prudence has a different import.

Second, the federal courts largely treat the requirements as process-based: only the decision-making process counts, not investment outcomes, a problematic conclusion.[20]

---

[18] Here the DOL interpreted ERISA's "sole interest" requirement to allow consideration of other than members' financial interest in benefit payments. But any particular investment must be no riskier than competing ones with comparable returns or produce yields not less than other investments with comparable risk. This criterion hardly squares with DOL's view that particular investments must be assessed in relation to the overall portfolio. Moreover, in many cases it is unrealistic or meaningless to make the required one-on-one comparisons.

[19] US Code (2012) Title 29, § 1104(1)(B)j (emphasis, italics, and underlining added).

[20] "As a leading commentator puts it, 'the test of prudence – the Prudent Man rule – is one of conduct, and not a test of

For the italicized part we observe the following: first, and again, legislative history offers little. Second, the standard is a community-based one, but the relevant community is poorly identified. At first blush it would seem to be the community of plans but that is almost circular. Also, a goal of ERISA was to transform prior plan practice. Third, and most importantly, it appears that the (sufficiently) "like" language has been used to justify resort largely to the practices of the asset management industry: concepts, rationales and methodologies largely crafted by or for it in symbiosis with those of academic or other financial economists or other would-be experts in finance and investment. We return to this point below.

Finally, ERISA requires decision-makers to "diversify the investments of the plan so as to minimize the risk of large losses, unless under the circumstances it is clearly prudent not to do so."[21]

Despite judicial emphasis on process, this phrase, which originated in the House, has a substantive feel. It does not absolutely require diversification; rather lack of diversification must be justified. Moreover, diversification is understood in the very narrow sense of minimizing the risk of large losses, which it was thought might result from a portfolio's excessive concentration on a particular kind of investment (US Senate Committee on Labor Welfare, Subcommittee on Labor 2000: vol. 2, p. 3310 and vol. 3, p. 4571). By contrast neither of the original Senate bills referred to diversification.

In essence then, the legislative history offers little beyond a popular nostrum as to what diversification requires.[22]

Thus, it is remarkable that legal, trade and popular literature is replete with assertions that decision-makers must conform to diversification as prescribed by modern portfolio theory (MPT). It is especially so because the DOL, in its first draft regulation (finalized in 1979) explicated the prudence requirement – *essentially with reference to defined benefit plans* – but did not refer to MPT. It did insist that the prudence of any individual investment had to be assessed in relation to the overall investment portfolio, rather than on an individual basis (US Department of Labor 1979). The primary reason it offered for the rule when proposed was that the conflict (in the common law) between income beneficiaries and remaindermen was "presented far differently, if at all, in employee benefit plans" (US Department of Labor 1978). Moreover, the DOL's first explicit reference to MPT was in 1996 and only in an interpretive bulletin relating to defined contribution plans. Even there it concerned only the provision of investment-related information to participants in what the DOL referred to as "participant-directed individual account pension plans" (US Department of Labor 1996).[23] Further, the regulation itself actually made no reference to MPT.

Nonetheless, the "machinery" of MPT, however contested it is otherwise, has been imported into the fiduciary standard with little account of plans' distinctive character. For example, it assumes that individuals maximize portfolio returns in light of their ostensible risk preferences but casts the risk narrowly in terms of the volatility of returns, namely, the standard deviation of returns. This is not apposite with decision-makers' central task: to make choices suitably calculated to the timely and fully satisfaction of benefit payment promises. Decision-makers are situated very differently from MPT's prototypical individual actors: their

---

the result of performance of the investment. The focus of the inquiry is how the fiduciary acted in his selection of the investment, and not whether his investments succeeded or failed'" (*Donovan* v. *Cunningham*, 716 F.2d 1455, 1467 [5th Cir. 1983], cert. denied, 467 US 1251, p. 1467, citation omitted).

[21] US Code (2012) Title 29, §1104 (a)(1)(C).

[22] Senator Russell Long, commenting on the relation between the diversification requirement and restrictions on investments in employer sponsors' stock remarked that "it more or less amounts to putting all one's eggs in one basket" (US Senate Committee on Labor Welfare, Subcommittee on Labor 2000: vol. 2, p. 1849).

[23] According to the DOL, providers to such individuals of information on asset allocation models are not deemed to be a fiduciary if the models or materials provided are consistent not with some version of MPT but rather just broadly stated principles of MPT. Here, the DOL, in connection with the § 2509.96–1 (d)(3)(i), referred to "recognizing the relationship between risk and return, the historic returns of different asset classes, and the importance of diversification" (US Department of Labor 1996: 29587).

risk preferences will vary according to the consequences not only for the plan but also for the enterprises, members as workers, etc. If one credits the ERISA formulation, its principal concern is largely with downside risk. (That is, at first blush, the "risk of large loss" language of ERISA would suggest an analysis of risk in terms of the extent of a possible shortfall and the likelihood of its occurrence.)

Further, the rhetoric and machinery of MPT are closely tied to those of the efficient markets hypothesis (EMH) and, in turn, some version of shareholder "value" or "primacy." However problematic their characterization of how financial markets actually operate they, in any event, understand company "value" solely in financial terms for shareholders/investors, taking little cognizance of all of those who actually constitute enterprises.

In essence, the void left by ERISA was filled institutionally, conceptually and methodologically in these constricted terms. The result has been a discourse littered with innumerable, constantly shifting and frequently complex models – too often loosely tied to systematic learning and meaningful practical experience. It is a discourse that at most resonates with ERISA's language about "care, skill ... and diligence." "Prudence" is another matter.

Prudence is better understood here as practical foresight, wisdom and judgment in light of where plans and their associated enterprises are situated, not only in relation to their ostensibly immediate task but also to others in their industry, sector and the larger society. Conversely, it requires looking beyond decisions' immediate and narrow financial consequences in relation to just the payment of benefits.[24] The practical effect of the ERISA standard confines each plan to its own individual silo, each making decisions within the prescribed narrow compass indifferent to other consequences for their own, let alone other enterprises, and the larger society.

---

[24] Note thirteenth- and fourteenth-century associations of prudence with "'wisdom to see what is virtuous, or what is suitable or profitable,' from O.Fr. prudence (13c.), from L. prudentia 'foresight, sagacity,' contraction of providentia 'foresight'" (Online Etymology, www.etymonline. com).

Conclusions

In this short chapter we have been able to only briefly outline reasoning which supports the contentions listed in the Introduction. We believe that further elaboration would strengthen the case for their being meritorious ones. Here we add only two points. First, we believe that a more thoroughgoing exploration of the nexus among how enterprises are organized (and the values they pursue and the value created and shared), the relationships within which plans are embedded, the nature of decision-makers' duties and the calculus of financial risk and reward that defines the possibilities for keeping pension promises is worth more serious exploration. Second, there has been extensive attention given to "fiduciary duty" as it pertains to defined benefit plans and far too little as it relates to other kinds of retirement schemes. While our discussion has most immediately attended to defined benefit plans we believe that the mode of analysis we have employed may well prove productive with respect to other kinds of schemes though it may yield different understandings of what decision-makers' duties might or should be.

References

Benefit Corp Information Center. 2012. "Quick FAQs." http://benefitcorp.net/quick-faqs.

Ellerman, D. 2006. "Three Themes about Democratic Enterprises: Capital Structure, Education, and Spin-offs," IAFEP Conference, Mondragon. www.ellerman.org/Davids-Stuff/The-Firm/Three%20Themes%20about%20Democratic%20Enterprises.pdf.

Fischel, D. and D. Langbein. 1988. "ERISA'S Fundamental Contradiction: The Exclusive Benefit Rule," *University of Chicago Law Review* 55: 1105–60.

Keay, A. R. 2010. *Moving Towards Stakeholderism? Constituency Statutes, Enlightened Shareholder Value and All That: Much Ado About Little?* University of Leeds, School of Law. http://ssrn.com/abstract=1530990.

Mercer Investment Consulting and Social Investment Forum. 2007. "Defined Contribution Plans and Socially Responsible Investing in the United

States." http://ussif.org/resources/research/
documents/SRIinDCPlans2007.pdf.

Merton, R. C. 2006. "Allocating Shareholder Capital
to Pension Plans," *Journal of Applied Corporate
Finance* 18 (1): 15–24.

Pension Benefit Guaranty Corporation. 1991.
"Opinion Letter 91–4," May 3. www.pbgc.gov/
Documents/91–4.pdf.

US Department of Labor. 1978. "Proposed
Regulation Relating to the Investment of Plan
Assets Under the 'Prudence' Rule," *Federal
Register* 43 (80): 17480–2.

1979. "Rules and Regulations for Fiduciary
Responsibility; Investment of Plan Assets
Under the 'Prudence' Rule," *Federal Register*
44 (124): 37221–5.

1988. "Letter to Helmut Fandl, Chairman of the
Retirement Board of Avon Products, Inc.,"
February 23. www.lens-library.com/info/
dolavon.html.

1994. "Interpretive Bulletin Relating to Written
Statements of Investment Policy, Including
Proxy Voting Policy or Guidelines," *Code of
Federal Regulations*, Title 29. § 2509.94–1.
http://law.justia.com/cfr/title29/29–
9.1.3.1.1.0.16.11.htm.

1995. "General Motors Hourly-Rate Employees'
Pension Plan, Prohibited Transaction
Exemption 95–25," *Federal Register* 60 (50):
140006–12.

1996. "Interpretive Bulletin 96–1, Participant
Investment Education; Final Rule," *Federal
Register*, 61 (113): 29586–90. www.dol.gov/
ebsa/regs/fedreg/final/96_14093.pdf.

US Internal Revenue Service. 2012. "Retirement
Plans FAQs Regarding IRAs." www.irs.gov/
Retirement-Plans/Retirement-Plans-FAQs-
regarding-IRAs#invest.

US Senate Committee on Labor Welfare,
Subcommittee on Labor. 2000. *Legislative
History of the Employee Retirement Security
Act of 1974, Public Law 93–406.*

Wooten, J. 2009. "A Legislative and Political History
of ERISA Preemption, Part 3," *Journal of
Pension Benefits* 15 (3): 15–21.

Economically targeted investing: changing of the guard

CHAPTER 10

TESSA HEBB AND JAYNE ZANGLEIN

Introduction

Economically targeted investing is the consideration of "investments selected for the economic benefits they create apart from their investment return to the employee benefit plan" (US DOL 1994). Often termed collateral or ancillary, these economic benefits include increased affordable housing stock, greater employment opportunities in low- to moderate-income neighborhoods, urban revitalization and clean technologies. US pension regulation, specifically the Employee Retirement Income Security Act (ERISA), allows for economically targeted investments (ETIs) as long as they do not sacrifice risk-adjusted market-rate financial returns to the pension plan. What ERISA's Interpretive Bulletin on ETIs makes clear is the process by which such investment selection can be made.

ETIs have a long history in the US. First used in the 1980s, the Clinton administration codified their applicability for pension fund investment in 1994 through an Interpretive Bulletin of the Department of Labor (US DOL 1994). However, in the final days of the 2008 Bush administration, a new ERISA Interpretive Bulletin on Economically Targeted Investing (ETIs) was issued by the US Department of Labor (US DOL 2008a). This bulletin, together with a similar directive on the Exercise of Shareholder Rights, seemed an odd choice of issues to place front and center on the political agenda, given that the world was deep in the throes of the sub-prime financial crisis.

For several years the US Chamber of Commerce had been asking the Department of Labor (DOL) to clarify its position on pension fund trustees' fiduciary duty with respect to ETIs and shareholder rights. This action was part of ongoing opposition to trade union organizations' encouragement of

active shareholder engagement. The Chamber of Commerce stood firmly against the oversight of management by shareholders. In a series of letters to the DOL they demanded these practices be scrutinized. The Chamber of Commerce accused unions of attempting to "further public policy debates and political activities through proxy resolutions that have no connection to enhancing the cause of the plan's investment in a company."[1]

This chapter asks whether the 2008 ETI Interpretive Bulletin (US DOL 2008a) has chilled this investment strategy by once again raising the question of conflicted fiduciary duty when trustees consider investments that serve broad economic interests, in addition to financial return to the plan. We focus on US pension legislation; particularly the implications of ERISA when pension fund trustees take into consideration ancillary or corollary benefits that may be derived from their investments. While the chapter is US-focused, the DOL Interpretive Bulletin on ETIs has far-reaching consequences. ERISA is one of the few legislative acts that has been interpreted to specify how economic considerations beyond financial return can be made compliant with the fiduciary duties of the pension plan. As such, it serves as precedent both for other US pension plans not governed by ERISA and for other common law jurisdictions around the world.

We ask if the new Interpretive Bulletin on ETIs has had a substantial impact on this activity over the past four years. This chapter examines what has changed under this new ETI Interpretive Bulletin and what has remained the same. We look at the legal ramifications of the bulletin for ERISA-bound fiduciaries and the practical implications for economically targeted investing in the US. We utilize both legal scholarship and qualitative methods,

---

[1] US DOL Advisory Opinion 2007–07a.

particularly a set of semi-structured interviews with key stakeholders and a set of letters both to and from the DOL on the topic of ETIs. We seek to identify how this new Interpretive Bulletin has impacted fiduciary behavior with regard to economically targeted investment. The chapter concludes with an overview of current ETI practice in the US and asks whether the new fiduciary standard in ETI selection created a chill in these investments since 2008.

US Chamber of Commerce lobbies against ETIs

It has long been argued that taking into consideration anything other than maximizing financial return runs counter to trustees' fiduciary duty (Langbein and Posner 1980; Munnell and Sunden 2005). As a result, trustees were (and are) routinely advised against making investments deemed to produce ancillary benefits (Zelinsky 2009). In the face of such bias, the DOL's 1994 ETI Interpretive Bulletin provided a safe harbor for trustees who wished to target their investments, spelling out the process by which such investments could be made. The 1994 ETI Bulletin stated: "The fiduciary standards applicable to ETIs are no different than the standards applicable to plan investments generally. Therefore, if the [ERISA prudence] requirements are met, the selection of an ETI, or the engaging in an investment course of action intended to result in the selection of ETIs, will not violate [ERISA] section 404(a)(1)(A) and (B) and the exclusive purpose requirements of section 403" (US DOL 1994). In effect, the 1994 Interpretive Bulletin provides a tie-breaker mechanism (Sandberg 2011) by which trustees could safely make ETIs, provided the process for such investment selection is adhered to.

Trade union organizations, among other key economic and community stakeholders, encouraged trustees (many of them labor trustees) to take up both ETIs (particularly those that utilize union labor) and shareholder rights as legitimate levers in exercising their role as active asset owners (Fung et al. 2001; Hebb and Beeferman 2010). Environmental, social and governance factors (ESG) are increasingly recognized as critically important for risk

management within pension plan portfolios and therefore well within the fiduciary duties of trustees (Freshfields Bruckhaus Deringer 2005; Keirnan 2009; Viederman 2008). In the period following the global financial crisis of 2008/9 a deeper understanding of the need to take ESG into consideration given the long-term nature of these plans has come to the fore. In addition, ESG factors are increasingly seen as key aspects to ensure broad economic benefit that promotes intergenerational-equity, rather than a narrow-minded focus on short-term financial returns for plan beneficiaries (Hawley et al. 2011).

The dotcom bust of 2001 followed by the financial crisis of 2008 resulted in the loss of trillions of dollars of workers' pensions. Rather than seeing ESG considerations as a failure of fiduciary duty, it was argued that the need to take ESG considerations into account in investment decision-making was in fact a fulfillment of fiduciary duty (Freshfields Bruckhaus Deringer 2005; Richardson 2007, 2008). With the enormous growth of US pension plan assets over the past ten years, rising from $10 trillion in 2001 to almost $18 trillion by 2012 (Investment Company Institute 2012), their influence as major shareowners in our economy has seen increased pressure from external stakeholders, including unions, to take ESG into consideration to ensure our long-term economic health (Hawley and Williams 2007).

In response, the US Chamber of Commerce reacted to this approach with alarm. They claimed that such concerns were being used by organized labor as a means to interfere with ordinary business operations and advance the unions' political agenda.[2] The US Chamber of Commerce began a series of requests for reinterpretation of these rules by the DOL.

In 2007, in response to a letter from the US Chamber of Commerce, the DOL issued an Advisory Opinion on proxy resolutions. The Advisory Opinion, while not altering the DOL's position on this matter in any significant way, clarified whether trustees could financially support proxy battles.

---

[2] Many ETIs have long been associated with "worker friendly" or union requirements in construction, job creation and retention.

The mere fact that plans are shareholders in the corporations in which they invest does not itself provide a rationale for a fiduciary spending plan assets to pursue, support, or oppose a proxy proposal unless the fiduciary has a reasonable expectation that doing so will enhance the value of the plan's investment.[3]

Most ERISA experts felt the Advisory Opinion did not alter the intent of ERISA. Legal scholar Ian Lanoff states "we do not believe that that the new opinion reflects a change in DOL's views regarding proxy voting as expressed in DOL Interpretive Bulletin 94–2" (Lanoff 2008). But it began a series of correspondence between the Chamber of Commerce and the DOL on these issues in which the DOL began to apply a tighter interpretation of ERISA, stating:

> The Department rejects a construction of ERISA that would render the Act's tight limits on the use of plan assets illusory, and that would permit plan fiduciaries to expend ERISA trust assets to promote myriad public policy preferences, and believes that these principles apply with equal force to a plan fiduciary's support or pursuit of a proxy proposal.[4]

Requests for interpretation of ERISA by the Chamber of Commerce didn't stop there. In June of 2008, a letter from Louis Campagna, chief of the Division of Fiduciary Interpretation at the DOL, to David Chavern, executive vice-president and COO of the US Chamber of Commerce opens:

> This is in response to your recent letter requesting guidance on whether fiduciary rules of the Employee Retirement Security Act of 1974 (ERISA) prohibit the use of plan assets to promote union organizing campaigns and union goals in collective bargaining negotiations. Your inquiry was in addition to the issues the Department recently addressed in Advisory Opinion 2007–07 regarding the expenditure of plan assets by plan fiduciaries as shareholders of corporations in support of proxy resolutions (US DOL 2008b).

The letter (discussed in more detail later in the chapter) goes on to reiterate:

The Department has also consistently rejected a construction of ERISA that would render ERISA's tight limits on the use of plan assets illusory and that would permit plan fiduciaries to expend trust assets to promote myriad public policy preferences. Rather the Department has reiterated its view that plan fiduciaries may not increase expenses, sacrifice investment returns, or reduce the security of plan benefits in order to promote collateral goals (US DOL 2008b).

What should be noted in these two letters is the use of the words "tight limits," as it provides a glimpse into the DOL's thinking in the summer of 2008. By October of 2008, the DOL had issued the Interpretive Bulletin on ETIs (US DOL 2008a), which further articulated the "tight limits" that ERISA places on these activities.

> ERISA's fiduciary standards expressed in sections 403 and 404 do not permit fiduciaries to select investments based on factors outside the economic interests of the plan until they have concluded, based on economic factors, that alternative investments are equal. *A less rigid rule* would allow fiduciaries to act on the basis of factors outside the economic interest of the plan in situations where reliance on those factors might compromise or subordinate the interests of plan participants and their beneficiaries. The Department rejects a construction of ERISA that would render the Act's *tight limits* on the use of plan assets illusory, and that would permit plan fiduciaries to expend ERISA trust assets to promote myriad public policy preferences. DOL Interpretive Bulletin on ETIs (US DOL 2008a, emphasis added).

For good measure, five examples of ETIs are detailed in the new ETI Bulletin, of which four are examples of activities that cannot be undertaken. In comparison to the 1994 Bulletin, the process by which trustees can undertake ETIs was tightened and the new Interpretive Bulletin conveys a negative and cautionary tone.

The US Chamber of Commerce was jubilant. On the release of the 2008 Interpretive Bulletins it declared, "The Chamber's research proved that a lot of union pension activism is financially worthless for union pension beneficiaries," and "The Department's new Bulletins make political joyriding on members' pensions against the law" (Chamber of Commerce 2008).

---

[3] US DOL Advisory Opinion 2007–07a.
[4] Ibid.

Historical and political introduction to economically targeted investments in the United States

Economically targeted investing (ETI) is the consideration of "investments selected for the economic benefits they create apart from their investment return to the employee benefit plan."[5] Although pension funds have invested in ETIs since the 1970s, the government has not always been receptive to such investments.

The Employee Retirement Income Security Act (ERISA) and the Internal Revenue Code govern most private US pension funds. ERISA requires fiduciaries to comply with four rules when making a plan investment: the exclusive benefit rule, the prudence rule, the diversification rule and the plan document rule.[6] In addition, the fiduciary cannot engage in self-dealing or certain prohibited transactions.[7]

The exclusive benefit rule requires fiduciaries to act solely in the interests of plan participants and beneficiaries and for the exclusive purpose of providing plan benefits and defraying reasonable expenses of plan administration.[8] In addition, the fiduciary must meet the prudence rule by acting "with the care, skill, prudence, and diligence under the circumstances then prevailing" that a prudent fiduciary familiar with plan investments would use in investing plan assets for a similar employee benefit plan.[9] The fiduciary must diversify plan assets in order to avoid the risk of large losses "unless under the circumstances it is clearly prudent not to do so."[10] Finally, the fiduciary must comply with the plan's governing documents, to the extent that they comply with ERISA.[11]

These rules were originally adopted to prevent the looting of pension funds by trustees and plan administrators and drew on the common law principles of trust law. The DOL struggled to apply these rules to scenarios as vastly different as the overinvestment of pension assets in employer securities,

the embezzlement of plan assets and the use of plan assets to create jobs for union members (Wooten 2004). Trustees viewed pension funds, which have long-term investment horizons of thirty to forty years, as a prime vehicle to finance job-creating investments and influence corporate governance. As trustees of building trades funds began to make construction loans, which created jobs for union members as well as generous returns on the investments, the DOL endeavored to create a rule that permits such investments as long as the pension fund does not sacrifice financial returns for economic returns.

Financial and economic returns

The DOL has never interpreted the exclusive benefit rule to bar ETIs or any other type of investment. The DOL's initial position, adopted in the Carter administration (1977–81), was that although the exclusive benefit rule "does not exclude the provision of incidental benefits to others, the protection of retirement income is, and should continue to be, the overriding social objective governing the investment of plan assets" (Lanoff 1980). This became known as the "all things being equal" test. Under this test, "a fiduciary might choose on the basis of non-economic considerations between two alternatives which in his judgment were economically equally advantageous" (Lanoff 1981). A plan fiduciary cannot consider non-economic factors if

> the investment or investment course of action provide[s] the plan with less return, in comparison to risk involved, than comparable investments or investment courses of action available to the plan; or alternatively, involve[s] greater risk to the security of plan assets than such other investment or investment courses of action offering similar return (US DOL 1981).

Despite this guidance, the DOL aggressively pursued litigation against trustees who engaged in economically targeted investments.

In the 1980s, President Reagan (1981–9) appointed Robert Monks, a long-time corporate governance expert, as the head of the DOL's office of Pension and Welfare Benefit Programs. Monks was the first in a line of republican appointees who understood the role of pension funds as

---

[5] 29 CFR § 2509.08–1.
[6] ERISA § 404(a)(1)(A)–(D).
[7] ERISA § 406.
[8] ERISA § 404(a)(1)(A); IRC § 401(a)(2).
[9] ERISA § 404(a)(1)(B).
[10] ERISA § 404(a)(1)(C).
[11] ERISA § 404(a)(1)(D).

institutional investors and encouraged fiduciaries to make prudent investments that also achieved social objectives (Zanglein 1996). He also encouraged pension funds to take seriously their role as corporate owners by voting on shareholder proposals. Appointees under the senior Bush administration (1989–93) were more conservative, acknowledging that ETIs were permissible as long as return was not sacrificed.

In 1994, near the beginning of the Clinton administration (1993–2001), the DOL issued an interpretive bulletin that provided guidance on ETIs. Interpretive Bulletin 94–1 was short and to the point. It clarified that

> The fiduciary standards applicable to ETIs are no different than the standards applicable to plan investments generally. Therefore, if the [ERISA prudence] requirements are met, the selection of an ETI, or the engaging in an investment course of action intended to result in the selection of ETIs, will not violate [ERISA] section 404(a)(1)(A) and (B) and the exclusive purpose requirements of section 403 (US DOL 1994).

Less than a week later, the DOL issued a second interpretive bulletin clarifying that the "fiduciary obligations of prudence and loyalty to plan participants and beneficiaries require the responsible fiduciary to vote proxies on issues that may affect the value of the plan's investment" (US DOL 1994). Although this second bulletin did not address ETIs, it continued to encourage fiduciaries to consider economic returns as well as financial returns. Not only did the bulletin state that a fiduciary bears the responsibility to vote on shareholder proposals that may impact the value of plan-held stock, it also authorized shareholder activism when the potential returns outweigh the costs of such activism. Interpretive Bulletin 94–2 explained that fiduciaries could meet with corporate officers to discuss "workplace practices" and other "financial and nonfinancial measures of corporate performance" (US DOL 1994). Thus, the DOL recognized that under certain circumstances, it is in the best interests of plan participants and beneficiaries to consider environmental, social and governance (ESG) issues.

In introducing the ETI bulletin, then Secretary of Labor Robert Reich emphasized its significance in an historic perspective in testimony:

> This bulletin comes at a moment when the American economy is in the thick of historic change ... Pension funds – their dollars reaching 900 times to and from the moon – are positioned like no other force in the American economy to raise incomes and spark new jobs ... Economically targeted investments can fortify the foundation of job growth. Investments in the economy's physical foundation – its infrastructure of roads, bridges, highways, airports, and communications networks – can produce high rates of return and enhance the long-term prospect of other portfolio investments (Reich 1994).

Secretary Reich stressed the Clinton administration's support of ETIs as a way to put the US economy back on track. He noted that ETIs differ from social investments, where the investor is willing to sacrifice returns to achieve a social objective. In contrast, ETIs are a "way that pension funds, whose position in the American economy is uniquely powerful, can satisfy their primary responsibility by deploying their assets to lift the entire economy" (Reich 1994). This concept drew on former DOL administrator Robert Monks' classification of pension funds as "universal owners," a phrase that later became the cornerstone of James Hawley and Andrew Williams' book entitled *The Rise of Fiduciary Capitalism* (Hawley and Williams 2000). A universal owner is a "large fiduciary institution which by virtue of its size or asset allocation strategy owns a cross section of publicly traded equity. Such an institution might hold between 1,500 and 4,500 different stocks, in essence owning the economy as a whole" (Hawley and Williams 2001). In essence, the universal owner is the market and its performance is measured "not by the performance of each individual firm it owns, but by the performance of the economy as a whole" (Hawley and Williams 2001).

Although Interpretive Bulletin 94–1 did not state anything new, it was important for several reasons. Pension fund assets had increased enormously, giving them more potential power. Republicans were concerned that the DOL was "encouraging pension funds to invest in ETIs to fill the gap created by reduced government spending," motivated by President Clinton's call for pension funds to increase investments in infrastructure (Zanglein

1996). Soon after Interpretive Bulletin 94–1 was issued, Republicans mounted a campaign against them, dubbing them as "PTIs": Politically Targeted Investments that result in lower pension returns and lower benefits for retirees (Vernuccio 2009). This campaign ignored the long-term and systemic risks of poor governance practices – practices that led, in part, to the Great Recession by rewarding "the quick deal, the short-term gain – without proper consideration of long-term consequences" (Financial Crisis Inquiry Commission 2011). Instead of using their power to encourage investments that over the long term would increase shareholder value, Republicans appeared to be using their political clout to stifle investments at odds with their own personal interests.

During the Clinton administration, pension fund fiduciaries continued to make ETIs. Public funds continued to invest in venture capital funds, with the expectation of creating jobs in their state (Zanglein 1996). In 1997, the American Federation of Labor – Congress of Industrial Organizations (AFL–CIO) Housing Investment Trust boasted assets of $1.67 billion, having funded the construction of more than 50,000 union-built housing units since its inception in 1964. In 1998, the AFL-CIO published a *Union Guide to the High Road*, explaining how unions could invest in ETIs. According to Richard Trumka, then Secretary-Treasurer of the AFL-CIO, "There is no more important strategy for the Labor Movement than harnessing our pension funds and developing capital strategies so we can stop our money from cutting our own throats" (AFL-CIO 1998: 73). The AFL-CIO created the Center for Working Capital[12] to train trustees on ETIs and shareholder activism, and by 2002, pension fund activism had made the cover of *Fortune* magazine, with the heading "Investors of the World Unite!" (Gunther 2002).

Pension funds and corporate governance

With the election of George W. Bush (2001–8), groups continued to lobby for rescission of

Interpretive Bulletins 94–1 and 94–2, but that change was not necessary as long as the Republicans were in control of the White House. As the end of Bush's second term approached, the Chamber of Commerce, among others, pushed the Bush administration to forbid the consideration of social objectives in making pension investments. In 2007, the Chamber of Commerce expressed its concern to the DOL that fiduciaries were improperly using pension fund assets to "further public policy debates and political activities through proxy resolutions that have no connection to enhancing the cause of the plan's investment in a company."[13]

The DOL opined that a pension fund could not sponsor a shareholder proposal requiring corporate directors to disclose their personal political contributions, because it would not enhance the value of the plan-held stock. The DOL concluded:

> In our view, plan fiduciaries risk violating the exclusive purpose rule when they exercise their fiduciary authority in an attempt to further legislative, regulatory, or public policy issues through the proxy process when there is no clear economic benefit to the plan.[14]

Although this advisory opinion does not relate to ETIs, it reflects the DOL's increasingly myopic view that pension funds do not have a voice as universal owners unless the exercise of that voice will financially benefit the plan (see also US DOL Advisory Opinion 2008–05a).

Near the end of Bush's second term (2005–9), at the urging of the US Chamber of Commerce, the DOL issued a second bulletin on ETIs. The purpose of the bulletin was to clarify that fiduciaries should rarely consider non-economic factors when making an investment, but if they did regard these factors as important, then they "should be documented in a manner that demonstrates compliance with ERISA's rigorous fiduciary standards" (US DOL 2008a).

At the same time, the DOL also issued Interpretive Bulletin 08–2 (29 CFR § 2509.08–2), which superseded IB 94–2. The revised bulletin restated the old bulletin but also incorporated the

---

[12] This center was later closed in 2007, however several union-based trustee-training programs have sprung up to take its place in the US.

[13] US DOL Advisory Opinion 2007–07a.
[14] Ibid.

DOL's response in the 2007 and 2008 advisory opinions to the Chamber of Commerce.

Requirements of the Bush administration's Interpretive Bulletin 2008–1

Like the original bulletin, Interpretive Bulletin 2008–1 is grounded in the exclusive benefit rule. The DOL framed the rule slightly differently by quoting ERISA Section 403 (the anti-inurement rule) as the basis for the rule as well as Section 404(a) (the exclusive benefit rule): "[A]ssets of a plan shall never inure to the benefit of any employer and shall be held for the exclusive purposes of providing benefits to participants in the plan and their beneficiaries."[15]

Both bulletins then turn to the prudence regulation for support. This regulation supplements ERISA Section 404(a)(1)(B) by clarifying that a fiduciary will satisfy the prudence rule when making an investment decision if: (1) the fiduciary gives appropriate consideration to relevant factors; (2) and "acts accordingly."[16] In addition, the fiduciary must consider the role of the investment within the investment portfolio with respect to diversification, liquidity, and risk and return characteristics. Finally, both the 1994 and the 2008 bulletins require the fiduciary to compare the expected return on the proposed investment to alternative investments with similar risks. An investment "is not prudent if it would be expected to provide a plan with a lower rate of return than available alternative investments with commensurate degrees of risk or is riskier than alternative available investments with commensurate rates of return."[17]

At this point, the 2008 bulletin differs markedly from the 1994 bulletin although it does not differ significantly from prior DOL statements, in particular the "all things being equal" test. A fiduciary may not make an investment decision based on a non-economic factor (US DOL 2008a). If

several investment alternatives are equal, then the fiduciary can choose the investment that provides the non-economic benefit. The DOL rationalizes this method of choosing among competing investments because ERISA does not specify a means of selection. Because the investments are "economically indistinguishable," the plan is protected (ibid.).

The 2008 bulletin explains that before a fiduciary may apply the "all things being equal" test, the fiduciary must have determined, quantitatively and qualitatively, that "the options are truly equal" (ibid.). It is only after the fiduciary has made this determination that the fiduciary may select an investment because of its non-economic benefits. In other words, the collateral benefits (jobs created or increased contributions to the fund) may not be factored into the calculation. The DOL explains that

> A less rigid rule would allow fiduciaries to act on the basis of factors outside the economic interest of the plan in situations where reliance on those factors might compromise or subordinate the interests of plan participants and their beneficiaries. The Department rejects a construction of ERISA that would render the Act's tight limits on the use of plan assets illusory, and that would permit plan fiduciaries to expend ERISA trust assets to promote myriad public policy preferences (ibid.).

In making the decision, the 2008 bulletin says that the fiduciary must consider the factors described in the prudence regulation, including diversification, liquidity and risk/return characteristics of the investment compared to alternate investments. In addition, the fiduciary must consider "other investments that would fill a similar role in the portfolio with regard to" these factors (ibid.). The DOL concludes that it will be rare that a fiduciary will be able to successfully defend a decision to invest in an ETI unless it has a "written record demonstrating that a contemporaneous economic analysis showed that the investment alternatives were of equal value" (ibid.).

The DOL then provides several examples. The first example is a plan that owns an interest in a limited partnership that is considering investing the plan sponsor's competitor. The fiduciaries may not divest the partnership interest unless they first

---

[15] ERISA Section 403(c)(1).
[16] 29 CFR § 2550–404a-1.
[17] 29 CFR § 2509.08–1; 2509.94–1.

conclude that the replacement investment is equal to or better than the limited partnership investment and would not adversely affect the plan's portfolio, taking into consideration diversification, liquidity, and risk and reward. Such a scenario may occur, for example, where an employer's pension plan owns stock in another corporation, which plans to merge with the employer's largest competitor.

In the second example, a multi-employer plan wants to invest in a construction loan that will fund a large project that is likely to generate jobs for its union members. The trustees must make sure that there are no prohibited transactions, that the return is commensurate with the risk of nonpayment, that the loan's return is greater than or equal to other similar quality construction loans that are available for investments. The trustees decide to make the investment, despite the fact that it has already made several other construction loans in the same geographic area. In doing so, the fiduciaries have violated their fiduciary duty by choosing an investment that will put the plan at risk for lack of diversification.

Third, a fiduciary wants to invest in a bond with a favorable rate of return to finance affordable housing in the local community. The fiduciary cannot make this investment if the size and duration of the bond would place the fund at risk and other bonds are available that would not expose the plan to these risks. The housing bond would not meet the "all things being equal" test.

The final example involves a collective trust that was created to invest in commercial real estate constructed using union labor. The fiduciaries cannot simply eliminate non-union construction projects from the pool of available investments. First, the fiduciaries must "determine that the fund's overall risk and return characteristics are as favorable, or more favorable, to the plans as other available investment alternatives that would play a similar role in their plans' portfolios" (ibid.). The fiduciaries must then compare the union and non-union construction project and determine whether the union project is equal to or better than the non-union project. Fiduciaries should contemporaneously justify this analysis in writing before making the investment. If no union project meets the plan's

financial requirements and is equal to or better than the non-union project, then the trust must invest in the non-union project.

Financial or economic returns?

The DOL has not directly defined the phrase "non-economic factors." Instead, it continues to urge fiduciaries to focus on "financial return." According to the DOL, any other form of return is a "collateral" or non-economic return. Despite being labeled as "non-economic," many of these collateral benefits are, in fact, economic. For example, the DOL has opined that a

> decision to make an investment in CDs of a particular bank may not be influenced by non-economic factors, such as a desire to encourage the bank to take loans to finance re-roofing jobs where the work is being performed by contributing employers unless the CD investment, when judged solely on the basis of its economic value, would be equal to or superior to alternative investments available to the Plan (Pacific Coast Roofers 1999).

Essentially, the DOL is using the phrase "non-economic" as a code word for anything other than the immediate financial return on the investment. In effect, the plan is not to consider the broader economic benefits of the investment to society as a whole or the impact of externalities.

Externalities such as climate change, however, clearly have an impact on the plan's rate of return (Zanglein 2010). Although the DOL has acknowledged this in the following example, it still insists that financial returns are the only appropriate measurement:

> A plan sponsor adopts an investment policy that favors plan investment in companies meeting certain environmental criteria (so-called "green" companies). In carrying out the policy, the plan's fiduciaries may not simply consider investments only in green companies. They must consider all investments that meet the plan's prudent financial criteria. The fiduciaries may apply the investment policy to eliminate a company from consideration only if they appropriately determine that other available investments provide equal or better returns at

the same or lower risks, and would play the same role in the plan's portfolio (US DOL 2008a).

Reactions to Interpretive Bulletin 2008–1

Interpretive Bulletin 2008–1 received mixed reactions. Critics of ETIs praised the bulletin, while others claimed that it added nothing new to the old "all things being equal" test (Zelinsky 2009).

Some commentators believed that the bulletin announced nothing new. Even Bradford Campbell, the Assistant Secretary of Labor described the bulletin as reiterating and clarifying "its long standing view that workers' money must be invested and used solely to provide for retirements, not for political, corporate, or other purposes" (Bureau of National Affairs 2008). Other commentators speculated that the bulletin "makes it tougher for funds investing for the long term to consider environmental, social, and governance issues such as climate change, human capital, and reputation" (*Compliance Week* 2009; Metrick 2011). *Business Week* went even further, reporting that "Socially responsible investing isn't available to private-sector defined benefit plans, whose fiduciaries are prohibited from subordinating the financial interests of plan participants and beneficiaries to other considerations" required by ERISA (Bogoslaw 2010). The AFL-CIO splinter group Change to Win submitted a memo to the Obama Transition Team seeking both bulletins' rescission and the reinstatement of the prior bulletins, because they were solicited by the Chamber of Commerce "and other right-wing groups" (Change to Win 2009). One commentator framed the bulletin as positively as possible, stating that it "provides a legal basis for permitting ETIs when chosen in the context of investment alternatives that would be considered equally valuable when evaluated solely on economic terms" (White 2009). Most took a middle-of-the-road approach.

Ardent critics of ETIs claim that the new bulletin did not go far enough: it should have outlawed ETIs because a "fiduciary cannot serve the exclusive interest of plan participants while simultaneously pursuing benefits for third parties"

(Zelinsky 2009). According to Zelinsky, the DOL's logic in the 2008 Interpretive Bulletin is flawed. The DOL states that "ERISA's plain text does not permit fiduciaries to make investment decisions on the basis of any factor other than the economic interest of the plan" (US DOL 2008a). Having made this statement, the DOL goes on to allow the use of non-economic factors as a tie-breaker when the investment "options are truly equal" (Zelinsky 2009). Zelinsky criticizes the bulletin because it allows plan fiduciaries to consider non-economic factors as a tie-breaker. He argues that there is no reason for a tie-breaker because plans can develop their own tie-breaking rules; even a coin toss would be preferable to this tie-breaking analysis. The bulletin "legitimizes economically targeted investing and thereby encourages the proponents of particular ETIs to pressure plan fiduciaries to declare ties to confer the particular economic benefits such proponents seek" (ibid.). Zelinsky concludes that, "Once the door is opened to concerns other than the welfare of the fiduciary's wards, the door cannot be easily shut" (ibid.).

The Chamber of Commerce, however, was satisfied. In a press release, the Chamber announced that its research had "proved that a lot of union pension activism is financially worthless for union pension beneficiaries … The Department's new Bulletins make political joyriding on members' pensions against the law" (Chamber of Commerce 2008). The Chamber concluded:

> Given the current economic turmoil, the last thing union members need is for pension fund managers to play political roulette with their retirement dollars … This action by the Department of Labor will help prevent the abuse of pension funds to promote political agendas at the expense of beneficiaries and retirees (ibid.).

Ardent proponents of ETIs objected to the bulletin. A 2010 letter to DOL from Jonas Kron on behalf of the Social Investment Forum (SIF) states,

> Since the bulletins were issued almost two years ago, they have been interpreted by corporate management interests as discouraging investors and fiduciaries from being active and responsible shareholders. Political operators such as the US

Chamber of Commerce have used the 2008 bulletins to attack labor unions, stifle corporate governance reform and hobble the ability of fiduciaries to be responsible owners (Kron 2010).

The SIF urged the DOL to reconsider the bulletin, claiming that the bulletin would cause pension fiduciaries to adopt a "do nothing" approach (Social Investment Forum 2008). Moreover, the SIF contended that the DOL's example on "green investment" is not an ETI and by including it as such the DOL was compounding already existing confusion, especially since the US Securities and Exchange Commission regards environmental factors (including climate change) as material in making investment decisions (ibid.). The SIF noted that: "This approach fails to recognize that some criteria that may be viewed as associated with social policy can also present long-term investment risks or opportunities" (ibid.). The SIF also complained that the bulletin consists of

> micro-management in the investment decision-making process [, which] can only create confusion and discourage fiduciaries from doing what the recent financial crisis demands – cast the net wider in terms of long-term risk assessment, because the adequacy of traditional narrow measures of risk have proved to be inadequate (ibid.).

After meeting with the current Assistant Secretary of Labor for the Employee Benefits Security Administration, Phyllis Borzi, the SIF clarified other problems with the bulletins, in particular, the depersonalization of the duty of loyalty by replacing the duty to act solely in the interest of the participants and beneficiaries with a duty to protect the "economic interests of the plan" (US DOL 1994, 2008a; Social Investment Forum 2010). The SIF concluded that, "it is the tone [rather than the substance] of the Bulletin that is clear – fiduciaries, in effect, are discouraged from making these investments" (Social Investment Forum 2010).

Given this history, it appears that Interpretive Bulletin 2008–1 may have been designed to appease the Chamber of Commerce and recast prior advisory opinions in anticipation of a Democrat in the White House. Many observers also believe it was drafted to curtail the AFL-CIO's efforts to employ the enormous power of pensions to influence corporate governance and social policy.

Instead of creating clarity, the ETI bulletin appears to create more confusion. In the face of such confusion have ETIs grown or declined?

Impact of Interpretive Bulletin 2008–1

Current practice

ETIs are generally made in alternative asset classes including real estate, private equity and infrastructure, all areas hit hard by the economic crisis of the past few years. ETIs can also be made in fixed income portfolios and through the use of credit enhancements (guarantees). Two primary areas targeted for both their market-rate financial return and their ancillary benefits are in-state investments with a geographic focus, often invested in by state-based public sector funds, and worker-friendly funds that invest in companies that utilize unionized labor. The later ETIs are often invested in by US Taft-Hartley funds.

There is some disagreement as to how much impact the 2008–1 Interpretive Bulletin has had on economically targeted investing in the US. A 2010 survey conducted by the SIF of financial advisers on their attitudes toward incorporating ESG factors in the investment process provides some evidence that "due to the position of the Department of Labor, at least some private investment advisors will not recommend ESG integration or responsible ownership activities to their clients for retirement plans that are subject to ERISA" (Social Investment Forum 2010).

In contrast, several ETI experts interviewed for this chapter suggested that the 2008–1 Interpretive Bulletin did not have a substantial impact on the industry. "There are not a lot of significant differences; it is a matter of tone. Though tone is important," was the view of one interviewee. "A fiduciary can use subsidiary goals and objectives as a tie-breaker but not as a driver," said another.

"My sense from speaking to a legal expert on ERISA law is that there is no material change in how economically-targeted investments are managed. If anything, the new bulletin spells out more detailed steps to take to ensure compliance ... the bulletin did not reflect a substantive change in the law on this issue," was a view echoed by others.

It could be argued that the 2008 financial crisis had a greater impact on targeted investing than the "tighter" interpretation of ETI rules in the new Interpretive Bulletin. Like most US investments from 2008 to 2010, targeted investment funds, many of which invest in US housing and commercial real estate, declined along with the rest of the market through this period. One interviewee suggests:

> Targeted investing has suffered a reduction in investment capital totals. And, there is no doubt that many of the portfolio companies and projects that were invested in by worker-friendly funds have suffered. There were also significant redemptions in many of the ETI-related housing investment funds.

In 2009 it was estimated that $30 billion was invested in thirteen worker-friendly funds in the United States and Canada (Croft 2010). Of these, four worker-friendly funds alone have assets under management of over $13 billion: AFL-CIO Housing Investment Trust (HIT) AUM $4.56 billion and Building Investment Trust (BIT) AUM $2.39 billion; ULLICO J for Jobs AUM $3.2 billion; and KPS Special Situation Fund AUM $2.7 billion. These funds, with considerable assets under management, have been able to weather the economic downturn of the past few years. Their lengthy track records and benchmark or above-benchmark financial performance provides ample ability for trustees to demonstrate their compliance with ERISA's rules when choosing to invest in these targeted funds. Such funds have the advantage of operating on a national basis, and as a result geographic diversification and in some cases government insurance or guarantees (AFL-CIO HIT and BIT investments are backed by the US government or government-sponsored enterprises) have enabled them to provide relatively safe investments through these turbulent years. As a result, investment in these worker-friendly funds has not been chilled by a "tightening" of the ERISA regulations on ETIs.

Perhaps of even greater impact going forward is the current experience of those funds that have championed economically targeted investing in underserved capital markets (often situated in low to moderate income areas) with a geographic or in-state focus. The California Public Employees Retirement System (the largest pension fund in the US with $240 billion assets under management), is perhaps the best known and strongest advocate of this style of ETIs. In 2007, Hebb and Hagerman estimated that the largest US public sector pension plans invested $12 billion in in-state investments in underserved capital markets (Hagerman 2007). This figure had doubled since 2004 (Hebb et al. 2004). A strong element of that growth could be found in CalPERS' targeted investment program, which had grown to $3 billion by 2008. We have not seen a significant growth in these targeted portfolios over the past few years.

CalPERS currently invests roughly 8 percent of its total portfolio in the State of California ($19 billion) with a target on underserved capital markets; with $1.5 billion in the California Urban Real Estate (CURE) portfolio, $1 billion in the private equity California Initiative and $.5 billion in targeted infrastructure investments (CalPERS 2012a). This number remains more or less unchanged since 2008. Nevertheless, the ancillary benefits generated by this targeted investment program have been significant. CalPERS provide extensive reporting on the ancillary benefits derived from this investment. See *CalPERS for California 2011* on this point (CalPERS 2012a).

However, a recent report to CalPERS' board indicates that the financial returns for the private equity portion of this targeted portfolio have not kept pace with industry benchmarks (CalPERS 2012b). Such a finding may have a much more chilling impact on ETIs (particularly private equity investments in underserved capital markets) going forward, than the rule tightening of Interpretive Bulletin 2008–1.[18]

The future of ETIs

As the US climbs out of the financial crisis, many see increased opportunity for ETIs going forward.

---

[18] It should be noted that benchmarking of private equity and alternative assets in general, whether targeted or not, remains difficult, as they include an array of illiquid assets and varying financial structures that are hard to quantify.

Several experts interviewed for this chapter suggest that ETIs are less siloed than in the past, that the financial crisis presented an opportunity to integrate this investment approach within a broader environmental, social and governance (ESG) frame. If anything, interviews with industry insiders indicate that such approaches have gained strength following the financial crisis. Given the market events of the past decade, there appears to be a deeper understanding of the role played by ETIs and ESG integration as part of a balanced portfolio. Trustees and fund managers are beginning to understand that the long-term economic health of the economy is as important as short-term competitive risk-adjusted returns to their portfolios.

"There has been an uptick in targeted investing; we are seeing more business opportunities post the financial crisis. More attention is being paid to ESG and to alternative investment strategies. There is a greater understanding of the intangible benefits that ESG consideration provides. Modern portfolio theory served institutional investors poorly," said one expert.

Another noted that "this development has the benefit of being perceived as a broader responsible investment development. And it is across numerous asset classes, not traditional ETI classes such as real estate and enterprise investments (venture capital and private equity). The new classes include project finance, infrastructure and energy efficiency." Such new approaches are on a much larger scale than previous ETIs and often are undertaken in partnership with government. As governments are increasingly unable to address all their investment needs, we can expect to see an increase in these new ETIs going forward.

In contrast, ETIs that fail to meet their financial objectives following the 2008 financial crisis have not fared as well.[19] Many of these funds are place-based and designed to fill capital gaps in underserved capital markets, often located in low- to

moderate-income areas. CalPERS is one of the largest investors in this type of ETI.

An August 2012 CalPERS staff report to its Investment Committee alerted the trustees that the targeted private equity portfolio was failing to meet its performance objectives despite its success in achieving ancillary benefits. CalPERS must now grapple with this challenge. In the discussion that followed, CalPERS' trustees indicated that such investment in low- and moderate-income areas might well require greater cooperation between the pension fund and state government in order to achieve its performance goals. They point to recent infrastructure investments made in California as a potential road map for the future (CalPERS 2012b).

This is not a return to the ETIs of the past (see Hebb 2006 on this point) where funds sought out direct government subsidies in order to make such deals. But rather, this approach could usher in a new era of ETIs structured as public/private partnerships that enable private capital to facilitate ancillary community benefits, while securing the financial return required as the primary driver under ERISA.

Responsible investing (RI) is the consideration of environmental, social and governance factors in investment decision-making. Using such extra-financial but important economic factors is becoming increasingly mainstream. The UN-backed Principles for Responsible Investment is a case in point. Currently signatories to this set of RI principles account for approximately $30 trillion of assets under management. In the past, responsible investing has been geared toward large publicly held companies in the public equity portfolios. But increasingly, pension funds are adopting this approach in their alternative assets (such as real estate and private equity) where most ETIs can be found.

The Global Unions, a collective body of trade union organizations around the world, signaled their adoption of this investment approach in 2007. "In particular, the Global Unions urge trustees and institutional investors to embrace this responsible approach to investment decision-making as promoted by initiatives such as the Principles for Responsible Investment" (quoted in Croft 2010: 13).

---

[19] It must be noted that there remains scant research on the performance of ETIs through the 2008 financial crisis, just as there are no aggregate numbers of ETI inflows through this period. Despite the attention the US Chamber of Commerce, DOL, trade unions and social investment organizations have shown on this issue, remarkably little research is available on the topic.

The SIF and its members also place ETIs within the responsible investing framework. "The 2008 Bulletins appear to be seriously out of date and do not accurately reflect widely held understandings of prudent fiduciary conduct, the importance of exercising shareholder rights to manage investment risk, the original meaning of prudence and loyalty expressed in ERISA, and the considerable evidence of the materiality of ESG factors" (Kron 2010).

Establishing targeted investment within the realm of responsible investment, with both its environmental and social considerations, is seen as a welcome opportunity to broaden the appeal of targeted investing going forward. While the 2008 Interpretive Bulletin may well have tightened the rules surrounding ETIs, most do not feel that this change of tone will have a significant impact on the flow of new capital in the future.

Conclusions

This chapter reviews the impact of the 2008 Interpretive Bulletin on economically targeted investment (ETI) in the United States. We find that the US Department of Labor used the interpretive bulletin to convey a "strict" interpretation and a "tightening" of the rules surrounding the making of ETIs by pension funds. However, Interpretive Bulletin 2008–1 has largely been viewed by the industry as a change of tone rather than a change of substance. It is doubtful that the new interpretation has had, in and of itself, a "chilling effect" on ETIs in the US.

For those pension funds and their trustees who practice economically targeted investing, the 2008 financial crisis (that coincidentally began in the same month as the Interpretive Bulletins were released) may well have had a more direct and dramatic impact on targeted investing across the US than IB 2008–1.

ETI funds with large assets under management, long track records and benchmark or above-benchmark performance easily fulfill the strict criteria placed on ETIs by the new DOL Interpretive Bulletin. For these funds, the investment selection process complies with the requirement that risk-adjusted market-rates of return are equal to or better than the next available investment opportunity. As a result, pension fund trustees who choose these investments are well within their fiduciary duty to take into consideration the ancillary benefits derived from the investment. Many of the ETIs with these characteristics are worker-friendly funds invested in companies with unionized workforces. These funds have attracted considerable new investment since 2008 and have not been "chilled" by the new interpretive bulletins.

Increasingly we are seeing ETIs placed in a broader framework of responsible investing, defined as taking environmental, social and governance (ESG) factors into consideration in investment decision-making. Within this framework ETIs are seen as intentionally seeking ESG impacts through targeted investing. ESG itself is gaining traction following the financial crisis, where business as usual and modern portfolio theory were seen as letting investors down. The larger aim of responsible investing offers significant new opportunities and a deeper understanding of the potential for ETIs going forward.

The 2008 Interpretive Bulletins followed a protracted period of lobbying by the US Chamber of Commerce, apparently designed to restrict the role of union members as active owners of today's corporations. The result was a strict interpretation of a tight set of rules that dictate how pension fund trustees can make ETIs. Despite a change of tone, the new ETI Interpretive Bulletins have not had a significant chilling effect on ETIs. Perhaps far more dramatic has been the impact of the 2008 financial crisis. Financial performance of ETIs has always been the driver, a fact reinforced by the new interpretive bulletin, and when financial performance of these funds fails to meet or exceed benchmark objectives, investment in ETIs is curtailed. The challenge for these funds is not in their delivery of ancillary benefits, but as is the case for all investment, in their delivery of financial returns. For most investors, including ERISA fiduciaries, this is how it should be.

Acknowledgements

We would like to acknowledge and thank six anonymous interviewees who provided us with substantial insight into the current practice of ETIs in the US today. We would also like to thank Tom Croft of the Heartland Network for his assistance. We appreciate Keith Johnson's and Jim Hawley's thoughtful comments on an earlier draft of this chapter. All errors and omissions are solely the responsibility of the authors.

References

AFL-CIO. 1998. *Economic Development: A Union Guide to the High Road*. Washington, DC: Human Resource Development Institute, AFL-CIO.

Bogoslaw, D. 2010. "Social Investing Gathers Momentum," *BusinessWeek*, February 4.

Bureau of National Affairs. 2008. "Labor Department Releases Guidance on Shareholder Rights and Investments," *Pension & Benefits Reporter*, October 21.

CalPERS. 2012a. *CalPERS for California 2011, Supporting Economic Opportunity for California*. Sacramento, CA: CalPERS.

2012b. *CalPERS Investment Committee Meeting, Item 08b1–01*, August 13. Sacramento, CA: CalPERS.

Chamber of Commerce. 2008. "Chamber Hails DOL Limitations on Improper Shareholder Activism," press release, October 17.

Change to Win. 2009. "Pension Issues Submitted for Consideration by the Obama Administration." http://otrans.3cdn.net/d59e5f4cdd7f89b728_b7m6bhini.pdf.

Compliance Week. 2009. "Power of Labor (Dept.) May Loom Large in '09," *Compliance Week*, December.

Croft, T. 2010. *Helping Workers Capital Work Harder. Report to Global Unions Committee on Workers Capital*. Pittsburgh, PA: Heartland Network.

Financial Crisis Inquiry Commission. 2011. *The Financial Crisis Inquiry Commission Report*. http://fcic-static.law.stanford.edu/cdn_media/fcic-reports/ fcic_final_report_full.pdf.

Freshfields Bruckhaus Deringer. 2005. *A Legal Frame-work for the Integration of Environmental, Social and Governance Issues into Institutional Investment*. Report produced for the Asset Management Working Group of the UNEP Finance Initiative.

Fung, A., T. Hebb and J. Rogers (eds.). 2001. *Working Capital: The Power of Labor's Pensions*. Ithaca, NY: ILR Press/Cornell University Press.

Gunther, M. 2002. "Investors of the World Unite: It's Up to Institutional Owners to Fix Corporate America, Says Dean of Shareholder Activists," *Fortune*, June 24.

Hagerman, L. 2007. *More Than Profit: Measuring the Social and Green Outcomes of Urban Investment*, Working Paper 07–17. Oxford: School of Geography and the Environment, University of Oxford.

Hawley, J. and A. T. Williams. 2000. *The Rise of Fiduciary Capitalism: How Institutional Investors Can Make Corporate America More Democratic*. Pittsburgh: University of Pennsylvania Press.

2001. "Can Universal Owners Be Socially Responsible Investors?" Conference paper. 7th International Post Keynesian Conference, San Francisco, California, April 2001. Working Papers collection, St. Mary's College of California, CA, USA.

2007. "Universal Owners: Challenges and Opportunities," *Corporate Governance: An International Review* 15 (3): 415–20.

Hawley, J., K. Johnson and E. Waitzer. 2011. "Reclaiming Fiduciary Duty," *Rotman International Journal of Pension Management* 4 (2): 4–16.

Hebb, T. 2006. *CalPERS Case Study A: Private Equity CalPERS California Initiative*, Working Paper 05–15. Oxford: School of Geography and the Environment, University of Oxford. http://urban.ouce.ox.ac.uk/research.php.

Hebb, T. and L. Beeferman. 2010. "US Pension Funds' Labour-Friendly Investments," in M. Hyde and J. Dixon (eds.) *The "Social" in Social Security: Market. State and Associations in Retirement Provision*. Lampeter: Edwin Mellen Press.

Hebb, T., K. Strauss and L. Hagerman. 2004. *US Public Sector Pension Funds and Urban Revitalization: An Overview of Policy and Programs*, Working Paper. Oxford: School of Geography and the Environment, University of Oxford.

Investment Company Institute. 2012. *Investment Company Fact Book*. www.ici.org/pdf/2012_factbook.pdf.

Kiernan, M. 2009. *Investing in a Sustainable World: Why Green is the New Color of Money on Wall Street*. New York: AMACOM.

Kron, J. 2010. "Letter to Phyllis Borzi, DOL from Jonas Kron on behalf of the Social Investment Organization," November 8.

Langbein, J. H. and R. A. Posner. 1980. "Social Investing and the Law of Trusts," *Michigan Law Review* 79 (1): 72–112.

Lanoff, I. D. 1980. "The Social Investment of Private Pension Plan Assets: May It Be Done Lawfully Under ERISA?" *LAB LJ* 31: 387.

   1981. "Letter from Ian D. Lanoff to George Cox," January 16.

   2008. "Memorandum to the Council of Institutional Investors," February 22.

Metrick, C. 2011. "The Line in the Sand: ESG Integration vs. Screening and 'Economically Targeted Investements[sic],'" report, Mercer Inc., February 22. www.mercer.com/articles/1407905.

Munnell, A. H. and A. Sunden. 2005. "Social Investing: Pension Plans Should Just Say 'No'," in J. Entine (ed.), *Pension Fund Politics: The Dangers of Socially Responsible Investing.* Washington, DC: AEI Press.

Pacific Coast Roofers. 1999. "Notice of Proposed Exemption." www.dol.gov/ebsa/regs/fedreg/notices/99022024.htm.

Reich, R. B. 1994. "Testimony of Robert B. Reich Secretary of Labor before the Joint Economic Committee, United States Congress," June 22. www.DOL.gov/oasam/programs/history/reich/congress/062294rr.htm.

Richardson, B. J. 2007. "Do the Fiduciary Duties of Pension Funds Hinder Socially Responsible Investment?" *Banking and Finance Law Review* 22 (2): 145–201.

   2008. *Socially Responsible Investment Law: Regulating the Unseen Polluters.* New York: Oxford University Press.

Sandberg, J. 2011. "Socially Responsible Investment and Fiduciary Duty, Putting the Freshfields Report into Perspective," *Journal of Business Ethics* 101: 143–62.

Social Investment Fund. 2008. "Letter from Lisa Woll and Cheryl Smith to Bradley Campbell," December 18.

   2010. "Domini Social Investments, Walden Asset Management. Letter to Phyllis Borzi," February 17.

US DOL. 1981. Advisory Opinion 81–12.

   1994. Interpretive Bulletin 94–1. Interpretive bulletin relating to the fiduciary standard under ERISA in considering economically targeted investments. 29 CFR § 2509.94–1. 1994.

   2008a. Interpretive Bulletin 08–1. Interpretive bulletin relating to the fiduciary standard under ERISA in considering economically targeted investments. 29 CFR § 2509.08–1. 2008.

   2008b. "Letter from Louis Campagna, Chief, Department of Fiduciary Interpretation, to David Chavern, Executive VP and COO, US Chamber of Commerce."

Viederman, S. 2008. "Fiduciary Duty," in C. Krosinsky and N. Robins (eds.) *Sustainable Investing: The Art of Long-Term Performance.* London: Earthscan.

Vernuccio, V. 2009. "Your Retirement or Our Political Agenda: How Politicized Investment Strategies Threaten Workers' Pensions," *CEI On Point* 160.

White, C. D. 2009. "Recent Developments on Economically Targeted Investments and Proxy Voting," *Pension Plan Investments 2009: Current Perspectives*, April 13.

Wooten, J. A. 2004. *The Employee Retirement Income Security Act of 1974: A Political History.* Berkeley: University of California Press.

Zanglein, J. 1996. "Protecting Retirees While Encouraging Economically Targeted Investments," *Kansas Journal of Law and Public Policy*, Winter.

   2010. *Institutional Investors and Climate Change.* New York: New York University Review of Employee Benefits and Executive Compensation.

Zelinsky, E. 2009. "Interpretive Bulletin 08–1 and Economically Targeted Investing: A Missed Opportunity," *Southern California Law Review*, 82: 11.

Institutional investment in the European Union Emissions Trading Scheme

IVAN DIAZ-RAINEY, ANDREA FINEGAN, GBENGA IBIKUNLE AND DANIEL J. TULLOCH

Introduction

This chapter explores the role of institutional investment in the most high-profile contemporary environmental market – the European Union's Emissions Trading Scheme (EU ETS). Before doing so, it is important to place carbon trading and the EU ETS in its broader historical context in terms of the evolution of institutional investment, fiduciary duty, environmental markets and environmental investment.

Drucker (1991: 106) notes that the establishment of the first modern pension fund in the 1950s heralded a transition in which institutional investors became the "dominant owners and lenders" and represented one of the "most startling power shifts in economic history." This transformation led to the emergence of "fiduciary capitalism," where institutional investors became the largest owners of corporate equity (Hawley and Williams 2000a). Their ever-expanding size and relentless search for "alpha" and diversification benefits have meant that these "universal owners" have diversified long-term investments across asset classes, sectors and geographies (Hawley and Williams 2000a, 2007). Due to these characteristics, universal owners have been aware for some time that their interests are tied to those of the economy and society at large and are therefore unable to avoid externalities, in particular environmental externalities (Hawley and Williams 2000a). The impact of environmental externalities such as pollution, waste or changes in the use of resources can cause institutional

investors to suffer reduced cash flows from investments, increase environmental costs and augment uncertainty in capital markets. Investors with exposure to net losses from portfolios with externalities have an incentive to take action and make investments to hedge the environmental risk (Hawley and Williams 2000b).

In more recent decades, concerns about environmental decay and in particular anthropogenic climate change have led to the development of environmental markets and to the emergence of environmental investment. Environmental investments can be broken down into five major categories: carbon; land use; clean technology; sustainable property; and water (Calvello 2009). Carbon is considered to be a major category, as carbon markets already exist and should "internalize" the cost of emitting greenhouse gases. The internalization of the externality has come through the introduction of "cap-and-trade" environmental markets, most notably the EU ETS. It is important to note, however, the United States' Acid Rain Program, established under the 1990 Clean Air Act, was the first major cap-and-trade environmental market. Its success in tackling sulfur dioxide and nitrogen oxide pollution represented a paradigm shift in environmental policy and paved the way for the more ambitious endeavor of establishing a global market for carbon under the auspices of the Kyoto Protocol.

Further, climate change considerations are increasingly featuring in investment strategies of fund managers. In part, this is driven by legislation,[1] which means that the cost of carbon is incorporated into investment decision-making for the sectors covered by the EU ETS, for example, electricity generation, cement and steel. Climate change is also being considered in sectors that are most affected by climate change events, such as property and infrastructure, which have a longer investment horizon. Against a background of an increasing focus by investors on climate change and the potential impact on investment portfolios, the *Climate Change Scenarios – Implications for Strategic Asset Allocation* (Mercer 2011) report was produced. Mercer compiled the report with the support of institutional investors, the International Finance Corporation and the United Kingdom's Carbon Trust. Climate change is put forward as a systemic risk that needs to be addressed by institutional investors as part of their strategic asset allocation process. The study finds that the impact of climate change may increase portfolio risk by as much as 10 percent for the average asset allocation.[2]

Another indication of the increasing level of institutional interest in climate-related investment is the emergence of related investor networks and collaborations. Such networks include the Institutional Investors Group on Climate Change (IIGCC), with seventy-five European institutional investors covering €7.5 trillion assets; Investor Network on Climate Risk of North America (INCR); Investor Group on Climate Change (IGCC) for Australian and New Zealand investors, covering A$700 billion assets; and the United States-based Council of Institutional Investors, with more than 125 members covering $3 trillion assets. There are also several leading international initiatives, such as the United Nations' Principles for Responsible Investment, with 1,121 institutional investors covering $30 trillion assets, and the Coalition for Environmentally Responsible Economies, with

one hundred institutional investors covering $9.5 trillion assets.

As noted earlier, this chapter explores the role of institutional investment in the most high-profile contemporary environmental market, the EU ETS. It is acknowledged that traditional institutional investors such as endowments, insurance companies and pension funds are relatively small players in the EU ETS (Hill et al. 2008). The discussion here is, therefore, intended to act as a primer for potential institutional investors and identifies the barriers that have discouraged their widespread participation to date. Accordingly, the chapter will address the following questions: how does the EU ETS work? What drives the value of carbon? What potential diversification benefits arise from investing in carbon? How does investing in carbon fit with investors' fiduciary responsibilities? How can institutional investors gain exposure to carbon? What unconventional risks does investing in carbon entail? What is the state of carbon markets post-Kyoto? These questions will be addressed sequentially.

The EU ETS: a brief overview

The Kyoto Protocol came into force in January 2005 and ran until 2012 providing an international emissions trading (IET) mechanism as one of three ways of meeting emissions targets in a cost-effective manner. As a result, the European Union designed the EU ETS, a cap-and-trade IET scheme with a legal requirement for large CO_2-emitting installations to reduce emissions in line with set caps.[3] Installations are issued with permits that allow them to emit CO_2 up to the cap. These permits are called European Union Allowances (EUAs) with one EUA representing one ton of CO_2. The EU ETS currently covers all twenty-seven European Union countries as well as Norway, Liechtenstein and Iceland. Affected companies manage their compliance by selling and purchasing EUAs depending

---

[1] Legislation is still the main driver for inclusion of climate change assessments by investors, for example, emissions trading legislation and subsidies for renewables (Sørensen and Pfeifer 2011).

[2] Two recent papers underscore interest in this area, with Bansal and Ochoa (2011) deriving "temperature Betas" and Griffin et al. (2012) exploring the stock market impact of carbon disclosures by listed companies.

[3] EU Council Directive 2003/87/EC of October 13, 2003, on Establishing a Scheme for Greenhouse Gas Emission Allowance Trading within the Community and Amending Council Directive 96/61/EC.

on how many EUAs they hold relative to their cap (Alberola et al. 2008; Seifert et al. 2008). The EU ETS's main objective is to contribute to the promotion of low-carbon technologies and energy efficiency among major CO_2-emitting companies, thereby reducing CO_2 levels by 8 percent relative to 1990 levels (Christiansen et al. 2005; Benz and Trück 2006, 2009; Mansanet-Bataller et al. 2007; Alberola et al. 2008; Koch 2012).

The other two Kyoto Protocol mechanisms to meet emissions targets are project-based. They are the Clean Development Mechanism (CDM) and Joint Implementation (JI), which produce Certified Emission Reduction units (CERs) and Emission Reduction Units (ERUs) as their emissions certificates.[4] These CERs and ERUs can also be submitted to the EU ETS.[5] Greenhouse gas emissions trading has developed into a multibillion dollar activity, of which the EUAs accounted for 97 percent of the carbon markets in 2011 (Kossoy and Guigon 2012). The carbon markets are one of the largest commodity markets in the world and will grow in importance as more countries implement their own plans to price carbon (Gardiner 2009).

Carbon valuation

Numerous authors have attempted to analyze empirically and theoretically the main determinants of CO_2 price levels. Studies clearly identify three types of price fundamentals: policy and regulatory issues; energy prices; and temperature events. Often the latter two are grouped into market fundamentals relevant to understanding year-by-year changes or underlying market forces (Benz and Trück 2006, 2009; Mansanet-Bataller

---

[4] These projects are emission-reduction projects in developing countries, for example, installation of energy-efficient boilers or electrification of rural areas using solar panels. CDM projects are based in developing countries generating CERs, while JI projects are implemented in countries with an emission reduction target and generate ERUs.

[5] EU Council Directive 2004/101/EC of October 27, 2004, amending Directive 2003/87/EC Establishing a Scheme for Greenhouse Gas Emission Allowance Trading within the Community, in Respect of the Kyoto Protocol's Project Mechanisms.

et al. 2007; Alberola et al. 2008). This section will discuss prior research on all three fundamentals.

Policy and regulatory issues

The first design issue of the EU ETS is that it is separated into three distinct phases, unlike commodity or financial markets: phase I, 2005–7; phase II, 2008–12; and phase III, 2013–20 (Mansanet-Bataller and Pardo 2008b; Daskalakis et al. 2009; Hintermann 2010; Creti et al. 2012; Koch 2012). Between phases I and II there was a prohibition on banking EUAs, meaning that two categories of derivatives now exist: derivatives that are issued and expire in the same phase (intra-phase) and derivatives that mature in the following phase (inter-phase). However, Poland and France were allowed a conditional transfer of EUAs between these two phases (Daskalakis et al. 2009; Hintermann 2010). Because intra-phase derivatives become worthless at the end of each phase, the inter-phase assets are essentially written on an asset that is not tradable during the whole life of the underlying contract (see Daskalakis et al. 2009 and Figure 11.1).

For the phase I (the trial period) and phase II (the Kyoto commitment period), the supply of allowances was capped by the EU ETS through National Allocation Plans (NAPs) (EU Council Directive 2003/87/EC; Christiansen et al. 2005; Mansanet-Bataller et al. 2007; Mansanet-Bataller and Pardo 2008b). The NAPs determine how many allowances were distributed among participating companies affected by EU Council Directive 2003/87/EC, for the current phase as shown in Figure 11.2 (EU Council Directive 2003/87/EC; Alberola et al. 2008). Nonetheless, the carbon market size for EUAs is determined by the number of EUAs each company is willing to trade, and the difference between the expected and real amounts of EUAs in the market drives variations in price levels (Mansanet-Bataller et al. 2007).

This unpredictable market size is exacerbated as the overall European Union target of emission reduction is distributed among member states based on the Burden Sharing Agreement (BSA), in which different targets were set for each member state. Some countries have been set ambitious reduction

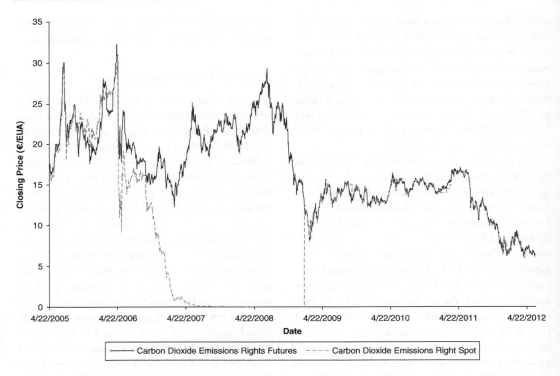

Figure 11.1 Daily close price for carbon dioxide emissions rights futures, and carbon dioxide emission rights spot, in EURs. The data cover the period between April 22, 2005, and June 5, 2012.
Source: Reuters EcoWin Pro data.

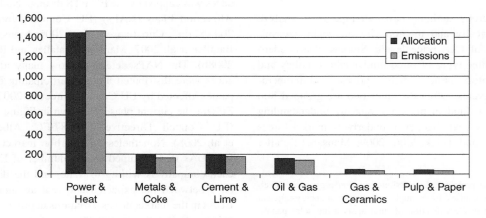

Figure 11.2 Allowance allocations and emissions by sector for 2006.
Source: Adapted from Hintermann (2010). Reprinted with permission from Elsevier.

Table 11.1 Total greenhouse gas emissions (MtCO$_2$e) for base year and 2002; reduction targets for the period 2008–12 according to the EU Burden Sharing Agreement (BSA) for EU-15; and distance to BSA target in 2002.

	Base year (MtCO$_2$e)	2002 (MtCO$_2$e)	Change from base year to 2002 (MtCO$_2$e)	BSA (%)	BSA target (MtCO$_2$e)	Distance to BSA in 2002 (MtCO$_2$e)
Austria	78	85	7	−13	67.9	17.1
Belgium	146.8	150	3.2	−7.5	135.8	14.2
Denmark	69	68	−1	−21.0	54.5	13.5
Finland	76.8	82	5.2	0.0	76.8	5.2
France	564.7	554	−10.7	0.0	564.7	−10.7
Germany	1,253.3	1,016	−237.3	21.0	990.1	25.9
Greece	107	135	28	25.0	133.8	1.3
Ireland	53.7	69	15.6	13.0	60.3	8.7
Italy	508	554	46	−6.5	475.0	79.0
Luxembourg	12.7	11	−1.7	−28.0	9.1	1.9
Netherlands	212.5	214	1.5	−6.0	199.8	14.3
Portugal	57.9	82	24.1	27.0	73.5	8.5
Spain	286.8	400	113.2	15.0	329.8	70.2
Sweden	72.3	70	−2.3	4.0	75.2	−5.2
UK	746	635	−111	−12.5	652.8	17.8
EU−15	4,245.2	4,125	−120.2	−8	3,905.6	219.4

Source: Adapted from Christiansen et al. (2005: 21).

targets, as shown in Table 11.1. Some member states are below their BSA targets and so have the option to either increase emission output or trade EUAs for profit (Benz and Trück 2009). To ensure the carbon market is set on a level playing field, one role of the European Commission is to create scarcity by establishing short positions among participating companies (Christiansen et al. 2005). These companies may be willing to pay higher prices for EUAs to avoid emission penalties.[6]

Finally, Seifert et al. (2008) show that expected emissions may be a realistic way of analyzing spot prices. They find evidence that the publication of participating companies' 2005 emission reports corresponded to a decrease in the EUA price when it was apparent that participating companies were far below expected emission levels. The authors

argue that the time between annual emissions reports is too long, resulting in inefficiencies in expectation-building in the market leading to large spot-price differences.

Energy prices

Christiansen et al. (2005) find that energy prices are the most important drivers of carbon prices due to the ability of power generators to switch between the fuel inputs (see Figure 11.3 and Figure 11.4). This is perhaps not surprising, since a large proportion of the burden of EU ETS falls on the energy sector (see Figure 11.2). Accordingly, the price levels of oil, natural gas and electricity are important determinants of CO$_2$ price levels (Benz and Trück 2006; Mansanet-Bataller et al. 2007; Hintermann 2010). Mansanet-Bataller et al. (2007) show that important energy determinants of CO$_2$ price levels are Brent and natural gas price changes, with coefficients of 23.2 percent and 12.2 percent, respectively.

[6] The penalty for non-compliance was €40 in phase I and €100 in phase II per ton of carbon emitted; allowances for the deficit must be submitted in the following year (Hintermann 2010).

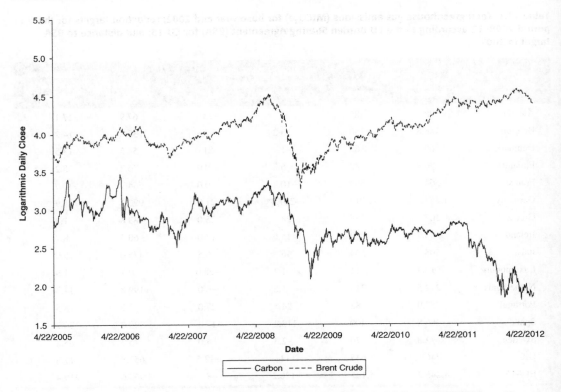

Figure 11.3 Logarithmic daily close price of Carbon Dioxide Emissions Rights ECX CFI Phase II futures and Global Brent Crude futures. The data cover the period between April 22, 2005, and June 8, 2012.
Source: Calculated from Reuters EcoWin Pro data.

Alberola et al. (2008) suggest that the profitability derived from energy production by using specific fuels (coal or natural gas), rather than the cost of the fuel itself, is an important CO_2 price-level fundamental. Alberola et al. (2008) argue that power operators pay close attention to the spark and dark spreads,[7] and the difference between them determines when it is profitable to switch fuel inputs. With the introduction of carbon, these spreads also incorporate EUA costs becoming the "clean" spark and dark spreads. The equilibrium between these spreads represents the carbon price above (below) at which it becomes profitable for

an electric power producer to switch from coal to natural gas (natural gas to coal) (Koch 2012). As long as the carbon price remains below the switching price, coal plants are more profitable than gas plants – even after adjusting for carbon costs. Alberola et al. (2008) support this by finding evidence that natural gas and clean spark spreads positively increase the EUA prices, whereas coal and clean dark spreads negatively affect EUA prices. Alberola et al. (2008) highlight that this result may be because during trial phase I's time series, dark spread prices remained above clean spark spread prices, making coal a more profitable fuel.

Brent oil was not found to be a significant determinant of carbon price; however, it is believed that Brent might affect EUA prices through natural gas prices (Alberola et al. 2008). Mansanet-Bataller et al. (2007) find counterintuitive results that coal,

[7] The spark (dark) spread represents the theoretical profit that a gas- (coal-) fired power plant makes from selling a unit of electricity having purchased the gas (coal) required to produce that electricity.

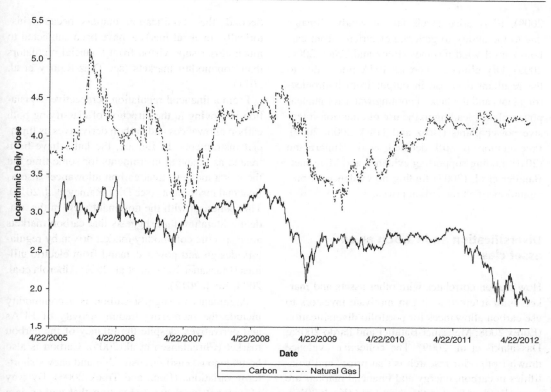

Figure 11.4 Logarithmic daily close price of Carbon Dioxide Emissions Rights ECX CFI Phase II futures and Global Natural Gas futures. The data cover the period between April 22, 2005, and June 8, 2012. Source: Calculated from Reuters EcoWin Pro data.

the most intensive emission source, has no significant effect on CO_2 price levels. This is of interest, as using coal is more profitable per consumed unit than natural gas; however, it is more than twice as emission intensive as natural gas (Christiansen et al. 2005; Benz and Trück 2009; Hintermann 2010). Although there appears to be an indication that there is "cross correlation" between EUA pricing and other assets and commodities in the energy market, the most comprehensive cross-correlation to date appears to be that of Mansanet-Bataller et al. (2007) when using financial instruments. Mansanet-Bataller et al. (2007) find that when using cross-correlation, there were three possible fundamentals that were statistically significant: CO_2 index change (20.2 percent), Brent futures (26.8 percent), and natural gas futures (21.6 percent). Mansanet-Bataller et al. (2007) found no significant cross-correlation for coal futures.

Weather

Numerous studies indicate that weather variables are possible determinants of EUA price levels (Christiansen et al. 2005; Mansanet-Bataller et al. 2007; Benz and Trück 2006, 2009; Hintermann 2010). In contrast, Alberola et al. (2008) find no effect on EUA prices for extremely hot or cold days, contradicting previous literature, leaving the effects of weather and temperature variables a heavily debated topic. With respect to seasonal averages, warmer summers increase the demand for air-conditioning, electricity and the derived demand for coal. Colder winters increase the demand for natural gas and heating fuel. As a result of increasing (decreasing) their output, the power generators will inevitably increase (decrease) their CO_2 emissions and require more EUAs (Christiansen et al. 2005; Alberola et al. 2008; Eurex 2008; Benz and Trück

2009). EUA price levels fall in windy climates due to the ability to generate electricity from carbon-neutral wind turbines (Benz and Trück 2006, 2009). Dry climates increase EUA prices due to the resultant decrease in output from hydroelectric plants and the lack of cooling water for nuclear power plants, leading to the use of emission-intensive power plants (Benz and Trück 2006, 2009). Precipitation is still debated, with Hintermann (2010) finding supporting evidence and Mansanet-Bataller et al. (2007) finding no evidence of precipitation affecting carbon prices.

Diversification and carbon as an asset class

How carbon correlates with other assets and markets is of interest, as it can motivate investors to use carbon allowances for portfolio diversification (Eurex 2008; Mansanet-Bataller and Pardo 2008a; Daskalakis et al. 2009). The collective evidence drawn from prior research is that prices and volatilities in carbon, energy and financial markets are interrelated, at least in the short-term (Koch 2012). The switching costs and equilibrium between clean dark and spark spreads in the power sector immediately connect energy and carbon markets (Alberola et al. 2008; Koch 2012). As noted above, empirical evidence from phase I suggests that commodities such as oil, gas, coal and electricity are important determinants of carbon prices (Mansanet-Bataller et al. 2007; Alberola et al. 2008). Additionally, Koch (2012) finds an increase in correlation for coal and gas in phase II compared with phase I, and Mansanet-Bataller et al. (2007) indicate that extreme weather conditions also influence carbon price. Interestingly, Koch (2012) notes that often correlations between carbon energy markets and carbon financial markets are not stable over time, so unsurprisingly, these correlations are heavily debated.

The issue is also discussed in terms of the question of whether carbon is a commodity or a financial instrument. The question matters on two fronts. The first relates to the potential diversification benefits from investing in carbon in a broader portfolio of assets (this is discussed further below).

Second, the classification matters because historically financial markets have been subjected to much closer supervision from financial regulators than commodity markets (see Diaz-Rainey et al. 2011).

From a financial regulation perspective, legislation is moving in the direction of classifying both carbon allowances and carbon derivatives as financial instruments. In Europe, the latter have been treated as financial instruments for some time but there is a move to treat carbon allowances also as financial instruments (see Diaz-Rainey et al. 2011). This contrasts with the dominant view in the academic literature that suggests that carbon markets are a specific commodity market driven by regulatory design and power demand from electric utilities (Mansanet-Bataller et al. 2007; Alberola et al. 2008; Koch 2012).

Arguments to suggest carbon is a commodity include the increasing trading activity of EUAs and derivatives, despite the infancy of the carbon market (Christiansen et al. 2005). Carbon is also homogenous, easily transferable and shows short-term variations (Benz and Trück 2006). By way of contrast, evidence suggesting that carbon is a financial instrument can be found in the behavior of carbon prices. Daskalakis et al. (2009) find that the logarithmic spot price of phase I EUAs is non-stationary, indicating these assets are not commodities, as commodities for "consumption" exhibit mean-reverting behavior. Daskalakis et al. (2009) also compare weekly phase I EUA futures returns from two markets (Nord pool and the European Climate Exchange [ECX]) against major assets classes, including global equity markets, international interest rates and energy, and found that both series of EUA futures were negatively correlated with equity market returns. Therefore, EUAs can offer portfolio diversification for European equity investors. Eurex (2008) shows that this is indeed the case. By creating a portfolio ratio of 80:20 of the EURO STOXX 50 index and CERs, respectively, it was possible for the portfolio to outperform an all-equity portfolio. In a more formal analysis Mansanet-Bataller and Pardo (2008a) confirm this finding by including carbon in a conventional equity and fixed income portfolio. They note that the inclusion of carbon does extend the efficient frontier of portfolios, however, the weights attributable to carbon are low and diversification benefits were greater during phase I than phase II. The latter is unsurprising in the context of declining carbon prices and associated uncertainties about carbon trading in the future (see Figure 11.1 and discussion of carbon trading post-Kyoto, below).

These limitations notwithstanding, the potential diversification benefits of carbon are underlined by the most comprehensive study on the debate concerning whether carbon is a financial or commodity asset. Medina-Martínez and Pardo (2012: 1) find that the

> majority of the phenomena observed, such as heavy tails, volatility clustering, asymmetric volatility and the presence of a high number of outliers are similar to those observed in both commodity futures and financial assets. However, properties such as negative asymmetry, positive correlation with stocks indexes and higher volatility levels during the trading session, [are] typical of financial assets, … [while] the existence of inflation hedge and positive correlation with bonds, [is] typical of commodity futures.

This leads Medina-Martínez and Pardo (2012) to the conclusion that the EUA is neither a commodity nor a financial instrument; rather, it is a new asset class with distinct characteristics.

Fiduciary and responsible investment considerations

While fiduciary duties are different in different jurisdictions, the key responsibilities of trustees internationally can be summarized as managing funds in the interests of the beneficiaries and exercising prudence when managing funds. This is interpreted by many as profit maximization and then given as a reason for many institutional investors not engaging in responsible investment (Kiernan 2007; Juravle and Lewis 2008; Martin 2009; Richardson 2011). The view that responsible investment is not compatible with investors' fiduciary duties and therefore will have a negative impact on financial returns is unproven. Yet it has prevented many investors from taking environmental, social and governance

(ESG) issues into account in their investment decisions (Renneboog et al. 2008; Sandberg 2011). This is despite there being no evidence that taking environmental factors into account in the pension fund investment process has a negative financial impact (Hoepner et al. 2011).

The discussion around whether investment decisions are allowed to be influenced by socially responsible behavior has been hotly debated since the rise of socially responsible investments (SRI) with a number of high-profile investors. Early pioneers in adopting SRI strategies include the Ontario Municipal Employees' Retirement System, California Public Employees' Retirement System and the Universities Superannuation Scheme in the United Kingdom (Richardson 2007; Sandberg 2011).

In a bid to resolve the debate, the United Nations Environment Programme Finance Initiative (UNEP FI) commissioned a report to look into whether there is a conflict between fiduciary duty and responsible investment. This became known as the Freshfields Report and was entitled *A Legal Framework for the Integration of Environmental, Social and Governance Issues into Institutional Investment* (Freshfields Bruckhaus Deringer 2005). The countries covered were Australia, Canada, France, Germany, Italy, Japan, Spain, the United Kingdom and the United States. The report argued that profit maximization was never an integral part of trustees' fiduciary duties. This assumption stems from an incorrect reading of the 1984 *Cowan* v. *Scargill* court case in the United Kingdom as requiring trustees to "yield the best return for beneficiaries" (Freshfields Bruckhaus Deringer 2005). The Freshfields Report goes on to say that, while the main role of the trustee is to generate a financial benefit for the beneficiaries, this is not at the expense of all other factors. The prudent investor view does not hold with modern portfolio theory, since it requires investments to be looked at in relation to their risk-return profile in the context of the performance of the whole portfolio (Fabozzi et al. 2002; Richardson 2007; Hawley et al. 2011). This would positively encourage investments that are individually risky (for instance, a new renewable technology) but correlate negatively with other portfolio investments (such as those in the oil and gas sector). Accordingly, the Freshfields Report concluded "integrating ESG considerations into an investment analysis so as to more reliably predict financial performance is clearly permissible and is arguably required in all jurisdictions" (Freshfields Bruckhaus Deringer 2005).

There is some debate over whether the Freshfields Report will actually give the trustees the comfort they need to make clear decisions about how to incorporate ESG factors into the investment decision process. Clearly, it allows some ESG criteria to be incorporated some of the time and still be in line with fiduciary duty (Sandberg 2011). Sandberg (2011), however, argues that this level of SRI engagement will not generate the "socially effective" investment strategies required to effect meaningful change through SRI.

The two main routes available to SRI proponents are through shareholder advocacy or managed investments. Shareholder advocacy is the active practice of proposing shareholder resolutions in relation to environmental or social issues. This is a route that has been tried in the United States, although the majority of attempts have been unsuccessful (Haigh and Hazleton 2004). Haigh and Hazleton (2004) find that the effect of these routes was piecemeal. They suggest collaboration between institutional investors who have signed up to SRI principles and government lobbying to price the externalities through legal reform can increase the amount of responsible investment being undertaken by institutional investors.

Legal reform is seen as the only effective method of engaging all investors. It is acknowledged that additional legislation with regard to SRI investment would assist trustees and encourage those who are currently reluctant to move within the current framework. There have been some moves in this direction, for instance, the Canadian province of Manitoba allowing consideration of other factors and the French retirement reserve fund integrating ESG criteria into the investment management mandates (Freshfields Bruckhaus Deringer 2005; Sandberg 2011). Richardson (2009) advocates legal sanctions on financial institutions not meeting restrictive investment criteria or looking at social costs as a means of promoting SRI.

UNEP FI published a follow-up report to the Freshfields Report (UNEP 2009) that acknowledged that steps had been made in increasing responsible investment but suggested further practical steps that needed to be taken to increase the momentum. These suggestions focused on how to incorporate ESG into the investment process through amendments to legal documents, such as the investment mandates and investment management contracts.

In relation to climate change issues, SRI was seen as a means to combat global warming. Increasingly, however, investors are focusing on the business case for SRI by examining risks and opportunities rather than viewing it as a means to enforce rapid change and prevent the potentially catastrophic effects of climate change (Richardson 2009). This makes it difficult to prove the financial case for investment in carbon market instruments unless the social costs for the long term are priced in. The latter will invariably require legislative changes that may have many facets and challenges to implementation (see Richardson 2009; Sandberg 2011).

Gaining exposure to carbon: instruments and markets

Institutional investors have a number of options when it comes to gaining exposure to the carbon markets. The options with specific reference to the EU ETS are, first, through investment in CERs and EUAs and, second, through derivative financial instruments such as futures and options on the underlying CERs and EUAs or swaps on the spread between the two. Third, exposure may be achieved through direct investment in the underlying CDM or JI projects, although given the relatively small size of these projects, the fourth option of investing in carbon funds that invest in the underlying projects and trade in the CERs is a more likely investment route. A fifth option is to invest via a carbon exchange-traded fund (ETF); however, there are only two such funds of any note (the United States-issued iPath Global Carbon ETN and the European-based ETFS Carbon). The relative immaturity of the carbon ETF market belies the development of ETF markets in recent years (Diaz-Rainey and Ibikunle 2012). We discuss the reason for this in the next section. Prior to that, we explore the first four investment options in more detail in the next two subsections.

Trading carbon and carbon financial instruments

The EU ETS remains the largest driver of carbon-based trading; it is estimated that it drove more than 96 percent of the global carbon market in 2010 (Linacre et al. 2011). In 2005, 80 percent of EU ETS trades occurred over-the-counter (OTC); most of these trades meet the widely recognized definition of block trades in the EU ETS. The four emission trading units widely traded in Europe are EUAs, European Union Aviation Allowances (EUAAs), CERs and ERUs (see Daskalakis et al. 2011; Ibikunle and Gregoriou 2011). Most of the trading is undertaken in derivatives of these allowances rather than the allowances themselves, with futures dominating the market, though there is a growing options market (see Kossoy and Guigon 2012).

Over the course of phase I of the EU ETS (2005–7) and during most of phase II (2008–12), there has been a gradual shift away from OTC trading to the point that exchange-based trades accounted for about half of trading in 2011 (see Kossoy and Guigon 2012). This trend is driven by the need to avoid counterparty risks, an issue that has taken on greater significance in derivative markets as a whole in the aftermath of the global financial crisis. The ECX platform is the market leader in EU ETS exchange-based carbon trading, with more than 92 percent market share (Ibikunle et al. 2013). This includes OTC trades registered on the platform in attempts to eliminate counterparty risk. The global dominance of the ECX platform has attracted participants from beyond Europe. In 2009, about 15 percent of trade volume on the platform was from traders domiciled in the United States (see Linacre et al. 2011).

The increasing switch to exchange-based trading mentioned above has consequences for the pricing of permits in the EU ETS, since institutional investors are more likely to trade using block volumes. Ibikunle et al. (2011) analyze approximately €20 billion worth of block trades on the ECX over a forty-month period in phase II. The authors show that buyer- and seller-initiated block trades

significantly impact the price of carbon financial instruments (CFI) on the ECX. Despite this, trading on the ECX has shown a heightened sophistication that is associated with an increase in the number of traders, which, in turn, is reflected in rising volumes and increasing open interest over time (see Ibikunle et al. 2011; Mizrach and Otsubo 2011; Kossoy and Guigon 2012). This increased activity and sophistication has come about despite a low and, in general, declining price of carbon over phases I and II (see Figure 11.1).

Underlining the increased sophistication of trading, Ibikunle et al. (2013) show how traders during the after-hours market employ Exchange for Physical and Exchange for Swap (EFP/EFS) instruments. The use of EFP/EFS trades underlines the level of maturity on the platform. EFP/EFS trades provide a hedging option using ECX EUA futures contracts, in one transaction; that is, the seller of emissions permits assumes the role of the buyer of ECX futures contract and the buyer of the permits, the role of the seller of ECX contracts. The strategy also allows for the substitution of OTC swap positions with corresponding ECX contracts. Further, the authors identify two classes of traders on the platform based on information distribution across the trading day and after-hours trading market. Although there are liquidity induced trades, the after-hours market is dominated by informed traders. This level of trading sophistication is well documented on regular equity platforms and currency markets.

Project-based investment exposure

Institutional investors can get project-related carbon exposure through infrastructure and property investment. Property investment funds with fixed units and life spans usually invest directly in properties or stocks of property firms. Investments are usually low risk, yielding low returns. Empirical evidence points to higher returns for climate-change-based property funds (see Kok et al. 2011), with institutional investors recognizing this opportunity and responding with bespoke funds. For example, APG Asset Management has already founded and is part-financing a performance contracting-focused fund dedicated to energy-efficient

Table 11.2 Carbon investment funds.

Funds	Investment strategy	Year of launch	Size (planned/actual)	Equity investment	CDM (CER)	JI (ERU)	EUA	AAU	Other credits	Trading post-kyoto?
Bunge Emissions Fund	Capital Gains	2006	Not Disclosed	Yes	Yes	Yes	Yes	Yes	Yes	Yes
Carbon Assets Fund	Capital Gains	2006	Not Disclosed	Yes	Yes	Yes	Yes			Yes
Cheyne Carbon Fund Limited	Capital Gains	2005	Not Disclosed	Yes					Yes	Not Disclosed
China Methane Recovery Fund	Capital Gains	2006	€100 million	Yes	Yes					Not Disclosed
Climate Change Capital Carbon Fund II	Capital Gains	2006	€700 million	Yes	Yes	Yes				Yes
Climate Change Capital Carbon Managed Account (C4MA)	Compliance	2006	€100 million	Yes	Yes	Yes				Yes
Climate Change Investment	Capital Gains	2007	€100 million	Yes	Yes	Yes		Yes		
European Carbon Fund	Capital Gains	2005	€143 million	Yes	Yes	Yes				
FE Global Clean Energy Services Fund IV	Capital Gains	2007	$250 million	Yes	Yes	Yes				Not Disclosed
FE Global-Asia Clean Energy Services Fund	Capital Gains	2004	$75 million	Yes	Yes					Not Disclosed
FinE Carbon Fund	Compliance	2007	€30 million		Yes	Yes				
Greenhouse Gas-Credit Aggregation Pool (GG-CAP)	Compliance	2005	$383 million		Yes	Yes				

Fund	Type	Year	Amount								
Grey k Environmental Fund	Capital Gains	2005	$300 million	Yes	Yes	Yes	Yes	Yes	Yes	Yes	Yes
ICECAP Carbon Portfolio (ICP)	Compliance	2004	Not Disclosed		Yes	Yes					
Japan Greenhouse Gas Reduction Fund (JGRF)	Voluntary	2004	$142 million		Yes	Yes					
Merzbach Carbon Finance (MCF)	Capital Gains	2005	$100 million	Yes	Yes	Yes					
Merzbach Carbon Finance Fund (MCFF)	Capital Gains	2007	$50 million	Yes	Yes	Yes					
Natsource Aeolus Onshore & Offshore Funds	Capital Gains	2006	$108 million	Not Disclosed	Yes	Yes	Yes	Yes	Yes	Yes	Not Disclosed
Peony Capital	Capital Gains	2007	€400 million	Yes	Yes						
Sindicatum Carbon & Energy Fund, LP	Capital Gains	2007	€300 million	Yes	Yes	Yes					
Trading Emissions Plc (TEP)	Capital Gains	2005	£100 million	Yes	Yes	Yes					Yes

Source: Cochran and Leguet (2007: 29).

retrofit projects. The Climate Change Capital Property Fund is a similar example of such innovative investment strategies.

Depending on where they are located, industrial projects funded by infrastructure and property funds can generate CERs and ERUs via the CDM and JI mechanisms, respectively. There are specific funds that are designed to achieve this purpose, for instance, Climate Change Capital Carbon funds worth about €800 million. Table 11.2 shows the major private sector carbon investment funds along with their sizes and investment strategies. The majority of fund activities are focused on industrial energy efficiency, destruction of industrial gases and renewable energy. Some funds also invest directly in EU ETS through EUAs; however, most funds are project-focused and accordingly are principally concerned with direct operational returns and profit enhancement from related project allowances (CERs and ERUs).

Unconventional risks from carbon investing

> Institutional investment, including from pension funds, in emissions markets is minimal compared to longer-established commodities markets. This is believed to be due to the emissions market's relative immaturity, its uncertain lifespan, its high volatility and the lack of the same fundamental price drivers which have made many other commodities good portfolio diversifiers for what are usually multi-asset class, long term investors (Hill et al. 2008: 16).

To some extent, the quote above would seem to have been superseded, as the preceding sections of this chapter have established that there are fundamental price drivers and that the EU ETS carbon market is increasingly mature. Accordingly, it would seem on the face of it that "market infancy risk" has been overcome (Hill et al. 2008: 7). Yet institutional investment in carbon markets remains low beyond their participation in the project credit market. This low participation rate is underscored by the small size of ETF carbon funds/funds markets, which contrasts with the large size of the ETF commodities market. Indeed, the growth of the

ETF commodity market has led to concerns about institutional and retail investment flows creating a speculative bubble in commodity prices, which is in sharp contrast to the depressed prices of carbon (see, respectively, Diaz-Rainey et al. 2011; Tang and Xiong 2011; and Figure 11.1).

The continued low participation of institutional investors in EU ETS can be explained by a multitude of factors. Weak fundamentals and an oversupply of credits resulting from the global economic downturn are clearly important (Kossoy and Guigon 2012). Further, and perhaps most prominently, is the uncertainty surrounding carbon-trading post-Kyoto (this is discussed in the next section). As a result of this uncertainty, the pricing of most of the carbon financial instruments traded remains very noisy (see, for example, Ibikunle et al. 2013). This is a reminder that carbon markets are manufactured, and accordingly political risk or "market foundation risk" is still very much present (Hill et al. 2008: 7).

Another set of factors that contribute to the low participation of institutional investors can be termed "market integrity risk" (ibid.). Unfortunately, there have been plenty of examples of such risks in the context of the EU ETS. A price collapse in carbon in 2006 was most likely augmented by the disorderly release of market-sensitive NAPs information by authorities (ibid.). The period between 2008 and 2009 saw unusual trading volumes in EUAs that were associated with a Value Added Tax "carousel" or "missing trader" fraud using EUAs. This is believed to have cost the European Union member states around €5 billion (Daskalakis et al. 2011; Kossoy and Guigon 2012).

Another issue that emerged in recent years is the HFC-23 controversy. This is related to the aforementioned CDM-based projects aimed at the destruction of industrial gases (most prominently HFC-23) to gain CERs. It became apparent that plants that produced HFC-23 were "gaming" the system by timing their production of the gasses so as to gain the maximum amount of CERs. Although not directly related to operation of the EU ETS, the HFC-23 controversy threatened to undermine the price of carbon on the EU ETS through a flood of CERs obtained via HFC-23-related projects. Finally, 2011 witnessed another major market integrity issue in the form of the closing down of EU ETS spot trading in January due to the "cyber" theft of EUAs from national "registries" (Diaz-Rainey et al. 2011). This incident resulted in the theft of a relatively modest €50 million worth of EUAs, but it proved a major embarrassment for the European Union Commission (the driving force behind the EU ETS) and heralded a new regime in terms of how spot carbon markets registries were to operate (see Kossoy and Guigon 2012).

Most of these issues discussed have now been addressed through improved market design, alterations to the rules governing carbon trading and enhanced financial regulation (see Diaz-Rainey et al. 2011; Kossoy and Guigon 2012). However, the fact that they happened in the first place will serve as a sharp reminder to institutional investors that carbon markets face unconventional risks that go beyond "market foundation risk." It is to the latter that we turn next.

Carbon trading post-Kyoto

The agreements of COP 17 provide an opportunity to negotiate a successor to the Kyoto Protocol by 2015 when the parties meet in Paris for COP 21.[8] The expected negotiated treaty will have to come into force by 2020. Recent history suggests, however, it is an opportunity the global community may not take advantage of. The partisan political gridlock in the United States Congress (the world's largest consumer of fossil fuels), the combative stance of India-led developing nations and the seemingly lukewarm stance of China (the world's largest CO_2 emitter)[9] on reaching a credible agreement may all contribute to the loss of this opportunity.

A stable global climate change policy must include the United States in order for it to be effective. In the event that an agreement is reached among negotiators by 2015, the congressional ratification of such a treaty in the United States will require a radical shift in attitude towards climate change amongst the political elite. The re-election of President Obama, which received late impetus from climate change concerns associated with Hurricane Sandy, and further elections in 2014 may make congressional approval of a climate change treaty by 2015 more likely. Further, President Obama has demonstrated an independent streak by pushing his domestic agenda (including climate change policy) through the Environmental Protection Agency and by the use of executive orders. The president's willingness to continue along this path in his second term in office will be critical to easing the uncertainty surrounding a stable global climate policy. Even as the direction of policy at the federal level remains uncertain, some individual states in the United States are taking strong action on climate change through regional market-based carbon-reduction initiatives.[10] This trend is expected to continue post-Kyoto.

However, overall it does not seem likely that the federal government in the United States will be in a position to offer global leadership on emissions trading soon. This leaves Europe and other jurisdictions such as New Zealand, Japan, China, California and Australia in the driving seat on market-based climate change action post-2012. Australia, holding one of the highest per capita emission levels, recently passed its long-awaited legislation for a carbon tax and an economy-wide ETS, which will commence in 2015. The legislation makes the Australian ETS the second largest in the world. By 2015, it is also expected that the Western Climate Initiative (which includes California, Ontario, Quebec, Manitoba and British Columbia) and South Korean schemes will be in operation. There has also been some indication

---

[8] COP 17 refers to the 17th Conference of the Parties to the United Nations Framework Convention on Climate Change (UNFCCC). UNFCCC was the precursor to the Kyoto Protocol.
[9] Since COP 17, China's stance toward carbon trading appears to have improved markedly. A number of provinces and municipalities have announced plans for pilot emissions trading schemes, including Beijing, Shanghai, Guangdong province, Shenzhen and Tianjin (see Kossoy and Guigon 2012).

[10] Note that some states have commenced statewide emission reduction programs, including emissions trading in the United States. An example is the Regional Greenhouse Gas Initiative, an initiative of the Northeast and Mid-Atlantic states.

of a grand alliance of ETS initiatives in the Asia Pacific region to include China, Australia, New Zealand, South Korea, Japan, California and parts of Canada (see Kossoy and Guigon 2012). Japan is still committed to its emissions reduction obligations through implementation of its framework for a market-based emission reduction system, the Basic Act on Global Warming Countermeasures.

Phase III of the EU ETS commencing in 2013 is the next step in the ambitious European plan to combat climate change by using market-based mechanisms. Kossoy and Guigon (2012: 19) note that:

> Phase III of the EU ETS is expected to provide stronger price signals due to a longer trading period (eight years versus five years in Phase II), the annually declining emissions cap, and a substantial increase in the level of auctioning (from less than 4% in Phase II to over 50% in Phase III). Over 1,200 million EUAs are expected to be auctioned every year starting in 2013, compared to less than 100 million EUAs sold in 2011.

Further, the scope of the EU ETS has recently been expanded when the aviation sector was brought into the EU ETS in January 2012. Already, American and Chinese airlines forced to trade in carbon emissions since they fly into the European Union have challenged the power of the European Union to curb their emissions in court. The European Court of Justice, however, has since dismissed the arguments against their inclusion in the scheme (see Kossoy and Guigon 2012).

It is also noteworthy that some of the more active countries with respect to climate change action (for example, New Zealand and Australia) demand commensurate efforts from large emitters such as the United States, India and China before a Kyoto successor can be agreed upon. This demand may still hinder future climate change negotiations and negatively affect the future of global emissions trading. However, since the European Union has already agreed to a post-Kyoto extension for the EU ETS and the European carbon trading platforms continue to mature, the persistent growth of emissions trading is assured for at least another seven years post-2012. The recent agreement reached at COP 17 along with the renewed drive towards the development of regional initiatives should also help. It is important that leading countries in the institutionalization of

cap-and-trade are considering linking their various schemes. In this respect, the recent agreement between the European Union and Australia to link their ETSs sets an important precedent. This raises the specter of a *de facto* global cap-and-trade scheme (rather than one achieved by a grand global political treaty) and will likely drive the adoption of global climate change policies post-Kyoto.

Conclusions

This chapter explored the role of institutional investment in the most high-profile contemporary environmental market – the EU ETS. It did so by addressing sequentially seven questions, namely: (1) How does the EU ETS work? (2) What drives the value of carbon? (3) What potential diversification benefits arise from investing in carbon? (4) How does investing in carbon sit with investors' fiduciary responsibilities? (5) How can institutional investors gain exposure to carbon? (6) What unconventional risks does investing in carbon entail? (7) What is the state of carbon markets post-Kyoto? What will happen to the carbon markets post-2012, once the Kyoto Protocol expires?

From this discussion, it is evident that carbon markets generally and the EU ETS specifically are, from an institutional investing perspective, a paradox. Recent years have seen increased market sophistication (trading efficiency); it is evident that there are potential diversification benefits from investment in carbon and that investing in carbon *can be* consistent with fiduciary duties. Despite this, there is little institutional involvement in the EU ETS due to the unconventional risks that come with investing in carbon allowances and derivatives. In terms of unconventional risks, the VAT carousel fraud and the theft of allowances in 2011 are relatively minor issues when placed against the absence of a clear post-Kyoto agreement.

Despite the absence of a grand global deal for carbon trading post-2012, there are, however, reasons to be optimistic about the future of carbon markets. These reasons include the establishment of new schemes around the world (in particular in China), the ambitious plans for phase III of the EU ETS and the desire to link existing schemes internationally (as evident in the recent deal between the European Union and Australia). This raises the specter of a *de facto* global cap-and-trade scheme rather than one achieved by a grand global political treaty. This is unquestionably a second-best option, and the issue remains of how to encourage more institutional investors to take exposure to carbon. This lack of exposure is not due to an absence of awareness or concern on the part of institutional inventors. This is underscored by the considerable successes in establishing large and influential climate change investor networks (these were discussed in the Introduction to this chapter and included IIGCC, IGCC, INCR and UNPRI).

The progress recorded in establishing large and influential climate change investor networks notwithstanding, the current reality is that long-term direct carbon investment strategies remain largely unpopular among institutional investors as a result of uncertainties surrounding climate change policy. At the moment, climate change policy is not globally stable, transparent and dependable. Pricing of most of the carbon financial instruments traded is very noisy as a result of this level of uncertainty (see, for example, Ibikunle et al. 2013). The Mercer Report, also referred to in the Introduction to this chapter underscores this point (Mercer 2011).

The Mercer-developed TIP[11] framework suggests that the uncertainty surrounding global climate policy is a significant source of portfolio risk for institutional investors; it contributes about 10 percent of the risk profile of investment portfolios. Institutional investors concerned about climate change and acting through some of the large climate change investor networks mentioned above have consistently tried to influence policy in order to fill the so-called "climate investment gap" created as a result of this unpredictability. Their efforts may have contributed to some of the progress made at COP 17 in Durban back in December 2011.

However, if robust growth in climate change-related investing is to continue beyond 2012, more needs to be achieved in order to adequately address the climate investment gap. Legislation incorporating a fiduciary obligation for institutional investors to take into account the social costs of investment as well as private returns would begin to pave the way (Richardson 2009; Sandberg 2011). This may lead to accusations that fiduciary duty is being subverted for social purposes and that any limitations on investable universes will conflict with fiduciary principles (as encapsulated in modern portfolio theory) (see Martin 2009; Richardson 2011). Such an argument misses the point that, although fiduciary duty is grounded on a stable set of principles, its implementation has evolved over time (Hawley et al. 2011). Universal owners and policymakers should, therefore, pursue their long-term economic, social and financial interests by ensuring fiduciary duty is fully aligned with the challenge of anthropogenic climate change.

References

Alberola, E., J. Chevallier and B. Chèze. 2008. "Price Drivers and Structural Breaks in European Carbon Prices 2005–2007," *Energy Policy* 36: 787–97.

Bansal, R. and M. Ochoa. 2011. "Temperature, Aggregate Risk, and Expected Returns," NBER Working Paper No. 17575.

Benz, E. and S. Trück. 2006. "CO_2 Emissions Allowances Trading in Europe – Specifying a New Class of Assets," *Problems and Perspectives in Management* 4 (3): 30–40.

2009. "Modeling the Price Dynamics of CO_2 Emission Allowance," *Energy Economics* 31: 4–15.

Calvello, A. A. 2009. "Taxonomy of Environmental Investments," in A. A. Calvello (ed.) *Environmental Alpha: Institutional Investors and Climate Change*. Hoboken, NJ: John Wiley & Sons, pp. 147–73.

Christiansen, A. C., A. Arvanitakis, K. Tangen and H. Hasselknippe. 2005. "Price Determinants in the EU Emissions Trading Scheme," *Climate Policy* 5 (1): 15–30.

Cochran, I. T. and B. Leguet. 2007. *Carbon Investment Funds: The Influx of Private Capital,*

---

[11] Mercer developed TIP as a framework that can be employed by institutional investors in identifying and managing the risks and opportunities as a result of the emergence of climate change as an investment factor. It considers low-carbon technology (T), physical impacts (I) and climate change related policy (P).

Caisse des Dépôts, Mission Climat, Research Report 12. www.caissedesdepots.fr.

Creti, A., P. Jouvet and V. Mignon. 2012. "Carbon Price Drivers: Phase I Versus Phase II Equilibrium?" *Energy Economics* 34: 327–34.

Daskalakis, G., D. Psychoyios and R. N. Markellos. 2009. "Modeling CO_2 Emissions Allowance Prices and Derivatives: Evidence from the European Trading Scheme," *Journal of Banking & Finance* 33: 1230–41.

Daskalakis, G., G. Ibikunle and I. Diaz-Rainey. 2011. "The CO_2 Trading Market in Europe," in A. Dorsman, M. Karan, Ö. Aslan and W. Westerman (eds.) *Financial Aspects in Energy: The European Perspective*. Amsterdam: Springer.

Diaz-Rainey, I. and G. Ibikunle. 2012. "A Taxonomy of the 'Dark Side' of Financial Innovation: The Cases of High Frequency Trading and Exchange Traded Funds," *International Journal of Entrepreneurship and Innovation Management* 16 (1–2): 51–72.

Diaz-Rainey, I., M. Siems and J. Ashton. 2011. "The Financial Regulation of Energy and Environmental Markets," *Journal of Financial Regulation and Compliance* 19 (4): 355–69.

Drucker, P. F. 1991. "Reckoning with the Pension Fund Revolution," *Harvard Business Review*, March–April: 106–14.

Eurex. 2008. *CO_2 Emissions – A New Asset Class for Institutional Investors*. Eurex Frankfurt AG.

Fabozzi, F. J., F. Gupta and H. M. Markowitz. 2002. "The Legacy of Modern Portfolio Theory," *Journal of Investing* 11 (3): 7–22.

Freshfields Bruckhaus Deringer. 2005. *A Legal Framework for the Integration of Environmental, Social and Governance Issues into Institutional Investment*. www.unepfi.org.

Gardiner, D. C. 2009. "Climate Change Policy: What Investors Need to Know," in A. A. Calvello (ed.) *Environmental Alpha: Institutional Investors and Climate Change*. Hoboken, NJ: John Wiley & Sons, pp. 55–76.

Griffin, P. A., D. H. Lont and Y. Sun. 2012. "The Relevance to Investors of Greenhouse Gas Emission Disclosures," UC Davis Graduate School of Management Research Paper No. 01–11. Available at SSRN.

Haigh, M. and J. Hazleton. 2004. "Financial Markets: A Tool for Social Responsibility?" *Journal of Business Ethics* 52: 69–71.

Hawley, J. and A. T. Williams. 2000a. *The Rise of Fiduciary Capitalism: How Institutional Investors Can Make Corporate America More Democratic*. Philadelphia: University of Pennsylvania Press.

2000b. "The Emergence of Universal Owners: Some Implications of Institutional Equity Ownership," *Challenge* 43: 43–61.

2007. "Universal Owners: Challenges and Opportunities," *Corporate Governance: An International Review* 15: 415–20.

Hawley, J., K. Johnson and E. Waitzer. 2011. "Reclaiming Fiduciary Duty Balance," *Rotman International Journal of Pension Management* 4: 4–17.

Hill, J., T. Jennings and E. Vanezi. 2008. *The Emissions Trading Market: Risks and Challenges*. London: FSA Commodities Group, Financial Services Authority.

Hintermann, B. 2010. "Allowance Price Drivers in the First Phase of the EU ETS," *Journal of Environmental Economics and Management* 59: 43–56.

Hoepner, A. G. F., M. Rezec and K. S. Siegl. 2011. "Does Pension Funds' Fiduciary Duty Prohibit the Integration of Environmental Responsibility Criteria in Investment Processes? A Realistic Prudent Investment Test," working paper. Available at SSRN.

Ibikunle, G. and A. Gregoriou. 2011. "International Emissions Trading: A Survey of Phases of the European Union Emissions Trading Scheme," working paper. Available at SSRN.

Ibikunle, G., A. Gregoriou and N. Pandit. 2011. "Price Impact of Block Trades: New Evidence from Downstairs Trading on the World's Largest Carbon Exchange," working paper. Available at SSRN.

2013. "Price Discovery and Trading after Hours: New Evidence from the World's Largest Carbon Exchange," *International Journal of the Economics of Business* 20 (3): 421–45.

Juravle, C. and A. Lewis. 2008. "Identifying Impediments to SRI in Europe: A Review of the Practitioner and Academic Literature," *Business Ethics: A European Review* 17: 285–310.

Kiernan, M. J. 2007. "Universal Owners and ESG: Leaving Money on the Table?" *Corporate Governance: An International Review* 15: 478–85.

Koch, N. 2012. "Co-movements between Carbon, Energy and Financial Markets, a Multivariate

GARCH Approach," working paper. Available at SSRN.

Kok, N., M. McGraw and J. M. Quigley. 2011. "The Diffusion of Energy Efficiency in Building," *American Economic Review* 101 (3): 77–82.

Kossoy, A. and P. Guigon. 2012. *State and Trends of the Carbon Market 2012*. Washington, DC: World Bank.

Linacre, N., A. Kossoy and P. Ambrosi. 2011. *State and Trends of the Carbon Market 2011*. Washington, DC: World Bank.

Mansanet-Bataller, M. and A. Pardo. 2008a. "CO_2 Prices and Portfolio Management," working paper. Available at SSRN.

2008b. "What You Should Know about Carbon Markets," *Energies* 1: 120–53.

Mansanet-Bataller, M., A. Pardo and E. Valor. 2007. "CO_2 Prices, Energy and Weather," *The Energy Journal* 28 (3): 73–92.

Martin, W. 2009. "Socially Responsible Investing: Is Your Fiduciary Duty at Risk?" *Journal of Business Ethics*, 90: 549–60.

Medina-Martínez, V. and A. Pardo. 2012. "Is the EUA a New Asset Class?" working paper. Available at SSRN.

Mercer. 2011. *Climate Change Scenarios – Implications for Strategic Asset Allocation*. London: Mercer. www.mercer.com/climatechange.

Mizrach, B. and Y. Otsubo. 2011. "The Market Microstructure of the European Climate Exchange," working paper. Available at SSRN.

Renneboog, L., J. T. Horst and C. Zhang. 2008. "Socially Responsible Investments: Institutional Aspects, Performance, and Investor Behavior," *Journal of Banking and Finance* 32: 1723–42.

Richardson, B. J. 2007. "Do the Fiduciary Duties of Pension Funds Hinder Socially Responsible Investment?" *Banking and Finance Law Review* 22: 145–201.

2009. "Climate Finance and Its Governance: Moving to a Low Carbon Economy through Socially Responsible Financing?" *International and Comparative Law Quarterly* 58: 597–626.

2011. "From Fiduciary Duties to Fiduciary Relationships for Socially Responsible Investing: Responding to the Will of Beneficiaries," *Journal of Sustainable Finance & Investment* 1: 5–19.

Sandberg, J. 2011. "Socially Responsible Investment and Fiduciary Duty: Putting the Freshfields Report into Perspective," *Journal of Business Ethics* 101: 143–62.

Seifert, J., M. Uhrig-Homburg and M. Wagner. 2008. "Dynamic Behaviour of CO_2 Spot Prices," *Journal of Environmental Economics and Management* 56: 180–94.

Sørensen, O. B. and S. Pfeifer. 2011. "Climate Change Issues in Fund Investment Practices," *International Social Security Review* 64: 57–71.

Tang, K. and W. Xiong. 2012. "Index Investment and the Financialization of Commodities," *Financial Analysts Journal* 68 (6): 54–74.

UNEP. 2009. *Fiduciary Responsibility: Legal and Practical Aspects of Integrating Environmental, Social and Governance Issues into Institutional Investment*. Geneva: United Nations Environmental Programme Finance Initiative, Asset Management Working Group of the UNEP Finance Initiative. www.unepfi.org/fileadmin/documents/fiduciaryII.pdf.

Have institutional fiduciaries improved securities class actions? A review of the empirical literature on the PSLRA's lead plaintiff provision

MICHAEL PERINO

Introduction

Congress passed the Private Securities Litigation Reform Act of 1995 (PSLRA) to address perceived problems in securities class action litigation.[1] A key feature of the PSLRA was the lead plaintiff provision. Prior to passage of the statute, representative plaintiffs were invariably small shareholders, often with long-term relationships with class counsel (Perino 2008). As a result, these class members typically had insufficient incentives to monitor class counsel, creating the opportunity for attorneys to act in their own best interests rather than the best interests of the class. Inspired by the work of Weiss and Beckerman (1995), Congress created the lead plaintiff position in the hope that institutional investors would volunteer to serve as representative (now dubbed lead) plaintiffs. Weiss and Beckerman argued and Congress expected that because of their larger, often long-term, financial stakes and greater sophistication, institutions

would provide the monitoring necessary to curb the agency costs that had been endemic to securities class actions.

Whether institutions would take up this invitation, however, was an open question. While collective action problems make institutional passivity the norm, investment managers are fiduciaries and as such have a duty to keep "informed of rights and opportunities associated with [their] investments" and to initiate and participate in litigation on behalf of the trust under certain circumstances.[2] Under basic common law principles, the decision to pursue litigation is contingent, in part, on whether the expected gain from litigation will exceed the expected cost. The Employee Retirement Income Security Act (ERISA)[3] imposes a similar duty of care on ERISA trustees, although some commentators have argued that serving as lead plaintiff could itself violate those duties (Martin and Metcalf 2001). To further complicate matters, the decision not to pursue the lead plaintiff position could implicate duty of loyalty issues to the extent that the decision is premised on the investment managers' interests as opposed to those of the beneficiaries.

Weiss and Beckerman and other commentators argue that these crosscutting fiduciary considerations require investment managers, at a minimum, to conduct a careful cost-benefit analysis to determine whether participation as a lead plaintiff in a securities class action is in the best interests of the

---

[1] In the United States, these cases are brought pursuant to a procedural device that allows a court-appointed representative to bring an action on behalf of all investors who share a common claim. Most typically, these cases involve allegations that the defendants induced the members of the class to invest in a particular security by disseminating material false or misleading information about that security. Once the court certifies that a case may proceed as a class action, any judgment in the case will be binding on all class members unless they affirmatively opt out of the class. Any settlement or judgment is distributed to eligible class members pursuant to a court-approved formula. Prior to passage of the PSLRA, the court selected class counsel, which was paid a contingency fee for its services.

[2] *Restatement [Second] of Trusts* § 177.
[3] ERISA is a United States law that sets minimum standards for pension plans offered by private companies.

fund's beneficiaries. In making this decision, institutions could take a narrow focus, in effect making case-by-case determinations of their expected impact. Consistent institutional participation, however, could have broader systemic benefits such as increased average settlements, lower average attorneys' fees, improved corporate governance practices or greater deterrence – matters that might also warrant consideration for an investment manager exercising its fiduciary duty. It is with respect to these systemic effects (as well as the expected impact of participation in an individual case) that fund fiduciaries should consider the growing body of empirical studies generated in the past decade, which have sought to quantify the impact of the lead plaintiff provision. Those studies examine a question that is simple to state but difficult to quantify – has institutional participation as lead plaintiffs under the PSLRA had a beneficial impact in securities class actions? The story that emerges from a review of these studies is of a largely successful statutory innovation that has markedly improved the conduct of these cases.

This chapter proceeds as follows. It first provides a brief sketch of the agency cost problems typically associated with securities class actions and provides an overview of how the lead plaintiff provision was intended to alleviate those concerns. It then discusses the empirical evidence on institutional participation in securities class actions. There is little doubt that passage of the PSLRA spurred institutions to become more active in these cases. Overall, the results of that participation are positive. Existing studies demonstrate that cases with institutional lead plaintiffs settle for more and are subject to a lower rate of dismissal than cases with other kinds of lead plaintiffs, although some questions remain regarding whether these results are driven by institutional self-selection of higher quality cases. One study has shown that institutional participation is correlated with at least some improvements in corporate governance. Institutional lead plaintiffs have had their largest impact on attorneys' fees. Not only is institutional participation correlated with lower fees and greater attorney effort, but there is evidence to suggest that institutions have created an economically significant positive externality – a reduction

in fee awards even in cases without institutional plaintiffs. Institutional participation, however, has not been an unalloyed good. Other studies suggest that institutional investors are subject to their own agency costs, which potentially eliminate some of the beneficial effects associated with their service as lead plaintiffs. Finally, the chapter concludes and suggests directions for additional research.

Securities class actions and the lead plaintiff provision

Agency costs in securities class actions

The debate over the costs and benefits of private enforcement of the federal securities laws is well known. Proponents of private enforcement argue that securities class actions provide a vital supplement to underresourced governmental enforcement authorities that deters wrongdoing and provides compensation to defrauded investors (Seligman 1994). Critics counter that plaintiffs' lawyers typically control securities class actions because they are insufficiently monitored by the relatively unsophisticated individual investors who often serve as representative plaintiffs (Macey and Miller 1991). Due to their small stakes in the outcome of the action, such plaintiffs are rationally apathetic. They do not monitor because they would bear all the costs of doing so, but could expect to collect only a small portion of the gains that might accrue from their efforts.

To further exacerbate this problem, long-term relationships frequently existed between attorneys and individuals (known in some quarters as "professional plaintiffs"), who agreed to buy stock in likely litigation targets and to serve as representative plaintiffs in any ensuing action in exchange for payments from the lawyer (Weiss and Beckerman 1995). While such agreements made sense for plaintiffs' attorneys – who were able to reduce the search costs associated with initiating a case by having a ready stable of plaintiffs – these arrangements made it even more unlikely that the named plaintiff would engage in meaningful monitoring. Indeed, to the extent that the lawyers agree to funnel a percentage of their fee to the representative plaintiff, as several prominent class action lawyers admitted in criminal plea agreements, the representative plaintiff may have an incentive to maximize rather than minimize fees (Perino 2008).[4]

Securities class actions thus represent a classic agency cost problem in which loosely monitored plaintiffs' lawyers have incentives to act opportunistically. Among other problems, insufficient monitoring might lead plaintiffs' attorneys to shirk by settling the case too early and too cheaply where the expected increase in attorneys' fees is less than the costs the attorney would incur in continuing to litigate (Coffee 1987). An insufficiently monitored attorney might also barter a low settlement for an agreement that defendants would not oppose the attorneys' fee request (Macey and Miller 1991). In either case, the attorney may not have incentives to maximize net recovery for the class.

The traditional solution to the inadequacy of plaintiff monitoring is *ex post* judicial review of the settlement and fee request, but critics generally thought that solution was also inadequate (Alexander 1991). The primary litigation mechanism available to provide information to the court, adversarial testing of the proposed settlement and fee, may be largely ineffective because settling defendants have no incentive to challenge the terms and objectors from the class, who are subject to the same rational apathy problems as small stakes representative plaintiffs, are relatively infrequent (Weiss and Beckerman 1995). With respect to fees, there was traditionally no readily ascertainable market rate for the services of plaintiffs' attorneys in class actions and therefore courts' fee determinations were inherently imprecise. Indeed, courts may themselves be subject to significant agency costs because they have incentives to clear their dockets of time consuming and difficult cases and thus may give inadequate scrutiny to proposed settlements or fees (Alexander 1991; Macey and Miller 1991).

Finally, traditional representative plaintiffs and their lawyers had no incentive to consider the long-term health of the defendant company. With no or only a small investment in the company, neither had an incentive to strengthen corporate governance structures at the subject companies as a means for preventing future managerial misconduct. Nor could lawyers expect any greater fee for pushing for governance changes in settlement negotiations. Fee awards in securities class actions are almost always based on a percentage of the negotiated settlement as opposed to the value of other non-monetary benefits achieved for the class.

The PSLRA's lead plaintiff provision

The academic debate over the costs and benefits of securities class actions moved to the political arena in the early 1990s when high technology and accounting firms began to complain that they were disproportionately targeted in these suits (Perino 2003). In response, Congress passed the PSLRA. The lead plaintiff provision is a key feature of the act and represents Congress' primary solution to the monitoring problem.

The provision seeks to encourage institutional investors, which to that point had been largely passive in securities class actions (Grundfest and Perino 1996), to assume primary control over the prosecution of these cases. Modeled on the proposal by Weiss and Beckerman (1995), the provision recognizes that because institutions frequently have the largest claims in class actions and typically recover low percentages of their recognized losses, they may be able to capture enough of the gains from active monitoring to at least partially overcome the collective action problem.[5]

To assist institutions in identifying cases, the PSLRA requires the plaintiff filing the first complaint to publish a notice informing class members of the lawsuit and that they may seek to become lead plaintiff. The court is then required to appoint

---

[4] Plaintiffs' attorneys in securities class actions are invariably paid on a contingency fee basis. They collect nothing if the suit is unsuccessful, but receive a percentage of any recovery they obtain for the class. Although the representative plaintiff is required to negotiate a fee with class counsel, it is the court that ultimately awards the fee, typically when it approves the settlement.

[5] The vast majority of securities class actions that are not dismissed by a court settle. For a variety of reasons, it is often difficult to determine what percentage of actual damages that settlement represents. Settlements, however, are often less than 10 percent of investors' overall market losses (Perino 2012).

the moving party that it determines is most capable of adequately representing the class. The PSLRA presumes that this "most adequate plaintiff" should be the moving party who, among other things, has the largest financial interest in the relief sought by the class. This presumption tends to favor large institutions willing to serve as lead plaintiffs. Once appointed, the lead plaintiff has the power to select a lead counsel for the class, subject to court approval.

Due to their comparative sophistication, the size of their holdings, the fact that they are often long-term investors and their power to select lead counsel, institutional lead plaintiffs could provide significant benefits to the class. Institutions as repeat players may bring a level of expertise to the prosecution of securities class actions that few individual class members could match. The size of their holdings may make monitoring of plaintiffs' attorneys cost-effective and thus may increase attorney effort and reduce the incidence of quick, cheap settlements (Fisch 1997). As large, long-term investors with diverse, often indexed portfolios, institutions may face significant constraints in selling particular securities. They thus may have greater incentives than individual plaintiffs to demand corporate governance changes at defendant firms, which might benefit themselves and other shareholders by reducing the incidence of managerial misconduct in the future.

At the same time, the PSLRA's presumption that the largest investor selects the lead counsel has the potential to create a competitive market among law firms. Under the PSLRA, plaintiffs' lawyers increasingly have incentives to develop longstanding relationships with institutions willing to become active in class litigation because doing so should increase the number of lucrative lead counsel opportunities.[6] Indeed, since passage

of the statute there is evidence of a rise in repeat relationships between the largest law firms and certain institutional investors (Choi and Thompson 2006). Lawyers may thus compete for institutional representation by offering higher quality representation as well as on price. Institutional repeat players, many of which have engaged in substantial arm's length bargaining with prospective counsel or have employed competitive selection procedures, may be able to develop compensation arrangements that reduce both fees and agency costs (Fisch 2002). Institutional investor participation as lead plaintiffs could also positively influence fee setting in cases without institutions. Such an externality might exist if the fee arrangements institutions negotiate influence fee awards in cases without institutional investor participation.

Although institutional monitoring is theoretically beneficial, using institutions as monitors might be ineffective or problematic for a variety of reasons. Institutions might be disinclined to become lead plaintiffs at all because they do not expect to capture enough of the gains their participation creates. Indeed, two studies (Cox and Thomas 2002, 2005) found that a significant number of institutions did not even bother to file claims in settled securities class actions.[7] Institutions are

---

[6] Law firms have used a number of techniques to develop these long-term relationships. Firms have hosted lavish conferences to which they invite institutional managers, have volunteered to monitor institutional portfolios for potential lawsuits and have made campaign contributions in what some have suggested are pay-to-play relationships. The potential impact of pay-to-play is discussed in greater detail below, but all of these techniques raise questions about whether and to what extent institutions are subject to significant agency

costs that may impede their ability to serve as effective monitors for the class. Take, for example, portfolio monitoring arrangements. The potential impact of these agreements is ambiguous and likely highly dependent on the terms of the monitoring arrangement. Employing multiple law firms to monitor an investment portfolio could induce beneficial competition and therefore potentially lower fees. See *Iron Workers Local No. 25 Pension Fund* v. *Credit-Based Asset Servicing and Securitization, LLC*, 616 F. Supp. 2d 461, 466 (SDNY 2009). By contrast, a monitoring agreement that obligated the institution to select a single law firm might have the opposite effect (ibid., pp. 465–6). In many cases, the agreement may not technically obligate the institution to retain the law firm monitoring its portfolio. Nonetheless, where only a single law firm provides this service, it is highly likely that the institution will do so, substantially reducing the possibility of competition for the institution's business. See *United Food & Commer. Workers Union* v. *Chesapeake Energy Corp.*, 281 F.R.D. 641, 649–50 (WD Okla 2012).

[7] In their 2005 study, Cox and Thomas found that in a sample of 118 securities class action settlements, less than 30 percent of institutional investors with provable losses actually filed claims. Without precise trading data from

also subject to their own agency costs. Institutional and individual investors may not be similarly situated with respect to the trading they engaged in or the benefits flowing from any proposed settlement (Chamblee Burch 2011; Webber 2012). Institutions with long-term positions in a company may be willing to trade monetary recoveries for corporate governance changes. These or other conflicts could lead institutions to skew settlements in their favor to the detriment of individual investors. There have been, in addition, pay-to-play allegations involving a number of law firms that reportedly contributed heavily to the campaigns of government officials who control public pension funds and who can therefore influence whether the fund will serve as a lead plaintiff and who it will select as counsel. Public officials might also seek lead plaintiff status for publicity purposes rather than to closely monitor class counsel (Romano 1993). Union-affiliated funds or mutual funds may have substantial conflicts of interest in negotiating with management to settle a securities class action. These agency costs potentially create much the same problem that existed prior to passage of the PSLRA, inadequate monitoring of the attorney by a conflicted representative plaintiff.

Empirical evidence on institutional lead plaintiffs

The frequency of institutional participation in class actions

Passage of the PSLRA is undoubtedly associated with a substantial increase in institutional investor participation in securities class actions, although that increase took a few years to occur. In the immediate aftermath of the act, some institutions viewed participation in securities class actions as a logical

extension of their activism on corporate governance matters (Grundfest and Perino 1996) and began to seek lead plaintiff status. These initial efforts, however, were quite limited. The US Securities and Exchange Commission (SEC) (1997) found that institutions served as lead plaintiffs in only 8 of 105 cases filed in the first year after passage of the PSLRA. That reluctance continued in the ensuing years, with PricewaterhouseCoopers (2005) finding that union and public pension funds served as lead plaintiffs in an average of 4.8 percent of the cases filed in the first three years (1996–8) after passage of the act.

The explanations institutions offered for their continued passivity suggested that the PSLRA did not do enough to overcome existing free-rider problems. Many institutions were uncertain that their participation would yield any tangible benefits and, to the extent that such benefits did exist, they were concerned about whether they would be able to capture a large enough portion of the gains to make participation cost-effective (Grundfest and Perino 1996). Institutions also feared that the costs of participating, including the time and cost of monitoring plaintiffs' attorneys, the possibility that they would be subjected to burdensome discovery,[8] the adverse reactions from company management and the potential for liability to other class members if they were found to have mismanaged the litigation, were too high (Fisch 1997).

Participation by public pension funds has increased steadily over time. Cheng et al. (2010) report statistics for a sample of 1,811 cases filed from 1996 to mid-2005. Overall, institutions appear as lead plaintiffs in 15.7 percent of the sampled cases, with public (5.8 percent) and union pension funds (3.8 percent) the most frequent lead or co-lead plaintiffs. Private institutions, including hedge and mutual funds, appear far less frequently; each type is lead plaintiff in less than 1 percent of cases. Given the low rate of institutional participation in the first years under the PSLRA, these figures represent a substantial increase in institutional participation after 1998. By 2002 public and union

those institutions, it is impossible to know how much money these uncollected claims represent. For some institutions, the amounts left unclaimed were no doubt small; however, for the period 2002–11, securities class action settlements totaled just over $58.5 billion. While we cannot simply extrapolate the Cox and Thomas findings to this later time period, it remains possible that institutional investors collectively forgo what could be substantial recoveries.

[8] Defendants might, for example, make voluminous document requests or subject investment managers to lengthy depositions.

pension fund participation had grown to 27.2 percent of filed cases. The percentage peaked in 2007 at 57 percent. In subsequent years institutions appeared as lead plaintiffs in just under 40 percent of filed cases, a substantially higher rate than before passage of the PSLRA (PricewaterhouseCoopers 2012). In cases where institutions compete with other class members for the lead counsel position, courts show a substantial preference for institutions (Cox and Thomas 2006). In only 11.4 percent of the cases in which individual investors were competing with institutions did the court select individuals as lead plaintiffs.

This increased activism is likely driven in part by changing perceptions of the cost-benefit calculus of becoming lead plaintiff. On the benefits side, in 1998 three public pension funds serving as lead plaintiffs in the *Cendant* litigation obtained a then-record $3.5 billion settlement, which likely suggested to institutions that increased monitoring could yield tangible benefits. Initial institutional experiences as lead plaintiffs also suggested that the costs of institutional participation were not as large as previously anticipated (Cox and Thomas 2006). At the same time, the publicity concerning Enron, WorldCom and other corporate scandals undoubtedly led some institutions to seek a greater role in securities class actions, either as a means of enhancing deterrence or because participation could lead to valuable publicity for the fund's political overseers.

There is thus no doubt that post-PSLRA institutional participation in securities class actions is greater than it was prior to passage of the Act (Choi et al. 2005). The pattern of participation, however, is hardly uniform. Survey evidence suggests that at least some funds appear to consider participation as a lead plaintiff only in those cases in which they have suffered a multimillion dollar loss (Cox and Thomas 2006). That public pension funds rely on such thresholds should not come as a surprise. Monitoring costs are likely relatively insensitive to case size. Because the lead plaintiff provision only partially overcomes the collective action problem, institutions are more likely to serve as lead plaintiffs in cases with larger losses (i.e., a larger stock price drop and longer class periods), larger defendant firms (as measured by market capitalization

or total assets) and greater institutional holdings (Cheng et al. 2010; Cox et al. 2008; Cox and Thomas 2006).[9] Existing research also shows that institutions are more likely to become lead plaintiffs in cases in which the defendant announced an accounting restatement or when the SEC has filed an enforcement action or launched an investigation prior to the filing of the first class action complaint (Cheng et al. 2010; Choi et al. 2005; Cox and Thomas 2006), suggesting that institutions focus on cases that have obvious indicia of merit. These are the cases in which the institution can reasonably expect that the suit is meritorious and that the potential gains from monitoring will exceed the expected costs.[10]

Case outcomes

What, if any, benefits have resulted in the cases where institutions have served, as a lead plaintiff is a separate and more difficult question. Class actions that are not dismissed almost invariably settle and so the most obvious question is whether cases with institutional lead plaintiffs settle for more than cases with other kinds of lead plaintiffs. To answer that question, researchers quickly settled on two measures of settlement size – the total dollar value of the settlement or some measure of settlement size as a proportion of total potential damages. To evaluate the individual influence

[9] This result is consistent with studies of corporate governance activism, which likewise find that institutions tend to target larger firms (Smith 1996).

[10] Institutions' focus on these cases is also likely the result of two provisions in the PSLRA. The act prohibits incentive payments to the lead plaintiff and permits the court to compensate it for costs and expenses directly related to the representation only out of any final judgment or settlement. Any institution considering whether to monitor actively will discount its potential recovery of costs by the probability that it will not prevail in the action. Under these conditions, it is reasonable to expect that risk-averse institutions will only become lead plaintiffs in cases with relatively obvious markers of fraudulent activity. Limiting participation in this manner might be consistent with the managers' fiduciary duties because it limits the downside risk of participation. At the same time, however, it might also limit the benefit of the lead plaintiff provision because these may be the cases where institutional participation can be expected to have the smallest marginal effect on recoveries or fees.

of institutions, researchers then had to account for the myriad other factors that influence settlements. Despite some differences in methodology, the studies almost uniformly find that institutions have had a positive impact on class recoveries.

The first study, by Choi et al. (2005), came roughly a decade after passage of the PSLRA and studied the impact of the lead plaintiff provision by comparing two relatively small samples of pre- and post-PSLRA settlements. Their study design was actually biased against finding a positive impact from institutional activism because they focused on a post-PSLRA time period (1996–2000) when institutions were just beginning to serve as lead plaintiffs. In that early time period, there may simply have been too few cases to find a statistically significant impact even if one existed. Alternatively, institutions just learning how to manage class action lawyers may have developed insufficient expertise to make any difference in outcomes. Nonetheless, the authors found that public pension fund participation was significantly and positively correlated with a dichotomous variable, "high-value outcome case," which they defined as settlements of more than 5 percent of the stakes in the case.

While this result suggested that institutional monitoring was effective, the authors noted that, due in part to their small sample size, they were unable to rule out the possibility that the result was driven by self-selection. Public pension funds may have simply chosen to become involved predominantly in high-profile or easier cases where recoverable damages were higher. If institutions were simply "cherry-picking" the most obvious cases of fraud, then it would be hard to conclude that the lead plaintiff provision worked as Congress intended. The challenge for future studies was thus to increase the sample size and to control for as many variables as possible in an attempt to isolate the impact of institutional participation.

Cox and Thomas (2006) and Cox et al. (2008) relied on a larger dataset and found that institutional lead plaintiffs are positively correlated with settlements, even when controlling for a number of variables correlated with settlement size, including a measure of provable losses, defendant's market capitalization, class period length and the presence

of an SEC enforcement action.[11] The latter study also found variation among institutional types. Both union-affiliated and public pension participation were correlated with settlement size, but the coefficient for the public pension variable was more than twice as large as the coefficient for labor funds, suggesting that public pension funds have a larger effect on settlement size.

These results were consistent with the hypothesis that the lead plaintiff provision had an overall positive impact. By contrast, Cox and Thomas (2006) found that institutional participation was negatively correlated with settlements as a proportion of provable damages, a result that was at odds with the findings of Choi et al. Neither paper, however, controlled for other factors that prior research had shown were correlated with settlement size, such as the presence of certain types of allegations and co-defendants, the presence of certain settlement characteristics, and the presence of certain law firms (Simmons and Ryan 2005). The absence of these controls made it more difficult to conclude that the observed correlation was in fact the product of institutional monitoring and not the product of institutional self-selection.

Cheng et al. (2010) used a large sample and controlled for some of these variables. The study has two significant findings that suggest that institutional participation is correlated with better case outcomes. Compared to cases with individual investors, Cheng et al. found that cases with any kind of institutional investor had a lower likelihood of dismissal. This result is both statistically and economically significant, with institutional participation associated with a 38.2 percent reduction in the probability of dismissal. The authors also find significantly larger settlements in cases with institutional lead plaintiffs. Here, too, the result is economically significant. Overall, the presence of an institutional lead plaintiff is correlated with a

---

[11] The authors find no significant increase in settlement size in post-PSLRA cases and thus call into question whether the reforms the act created were worthwhile. Perino (2012), by contrast, finds a positive correlation between post-PSLRA cases and settlement amounts that is significant at the 10 percent level (probability = 0.062). These disparate findings suggest, at a minimum, that additional research is necessary to evaluate the overall impact of the act on settlements.

58.9 percent increase in settlement size, even when controlling for institutional investor selection of larger cases with greater potential damages. There is, however, some difference across institutional types. Public pension participation is correlated with the greatest increase in settlement size while union and mutual fund participation is only marginally significant.

Perino (2012) employed a large sample of securities class action settlements to determine the impact of institutional investor participation. The sample encompasses time periods of both low and high levels of institutional participation and includes more controls for the case characteristics that have been shown to be correlated with settlement amounts. Although broader in these respects, his study is narrower than some others because he focused on the impact of only one kind of institutional investor, public pension funds. The study found that cases with public pension participation are positively correlated with investor recoveries (measured both in absolute terms and as a proportion of investors' overall market losses), even when controlling for institutional self-selection of larger, more high profile cases. The result with respect to settlements as a proportion of market losses is especially important because it contradicts the results of earlier work by Cox and Thomas (2006), which found that institutional participation was negatively correlated with this measure. That earlier finding, however, must be interpreted with caution given the low explanatory power of the model they employed, which explained only 5 percent of the variation in their sample of 388 settlements. The Perino model, by contrast, explains 61 percent of the variation in his larger sample (n = 668). Combined with the earlier results of Choi et al. (2005), this finding suggests that institutions do in fact recover a higher percentage of the potential damages than other kinds of lead plaintiffs.

To summarize, existing studies have consistently found that institutional participation is correlated with either greater class recoveries or a lower probability of dismissal. To be sure, it remains possible that these studies all fail to control adequately for self-selection effects and that they are all measuring some form of institutional "cherry-picking" of stronger cases. While this possibility cannot be completely discounted, the consistency of the results despite the differences in methodology among the studies and the wide array of control variables the researchers employed suggest that institutional lead plaintiffs have generally had positive impacts on dismissal rates and recoveries. They also suggest something of a hierarchy among institutions, with public pension fund participation being associated with the largest improvements in settlement size.

Corporate governance

As institutional activism through service as a lead plaintiff increased, scattered anecdotal evidence suggested that institutions were negotiating corporate governance changes as part of the settlement package. For example, in one of the first cases with significant institutional investor participation, Cendant Corporation agreed to adopt a stricter definition of board independence, to hold annual election of directors and to change its stock option repricing policies (Green 2011). In a 2008 settlement with UnitedHealth Group involving option backdating, a public pension fund, in addition to obtaining a $925 million recovery, negotiated for "a process for election of a shareowner-nominated director, enhanced standards for director independence," mandated shareholder approval for option re-pricing and enhanced restrictions for option compensation (Webber 2012). Several other cases involve settlements in which the company has agreed to changes in its board structure or compensation practices (Green 2011).

While such changes were commonplace in state derivative lawsuits, they were a relatively novel feature of securities class actions. Some empirical evidence suggests a connection between institutional participation and corporate governance changes even in cases where the changes were not mandated in the settlement. Cheng et al. (2010) find that within three years of filing the lawsuit, defendant firms with institutional lead plaintiffs demonstrate greater levels of board independence than those with individual lead plaintiffs. Board independence increases by about 11 percent over a control sample of non-sued firms and over the sample of class actions with individual lead plaintiffs.

Defendant firms are more likely to adopt such corporate governance changes in the wake of accounting restatements, but even controlling for this variable, the presence of an institutional investor as lead plaintiff remains positive and significant. Institutional investor participation, however, had no observable impact on two other corporate governance measures – the level of audit committee independence or the likelihood that the defendant firm would appoint a lead director. As with settlement size, there is some evidence of differences among institutional types, with public pension funds and private institutions having a significant positive correlation with board independence and union-affiliated funds having no such significant association.

Attorneys' fees and attorney effort

There are several studies that examine fees in securities class actions. Choi et al. (2005) find no significant effect of institutional investor participation on fees, although this result is based on a sample of only seventy-eight post-PSLRA cases taken largely from a time period when institutional participation was in its infancy. Even if such a correlation were found, they point out unobserved characteristics of the cases public pensions select remain a significant problem. If institutions pick only the largest or easiest cases to litigate, then any evidence of lower fees may be a result of the nature of the case rather than the active monitoring of the institutional lead plaintiff.

Using a larger dataset that included more cases from the period of increased institutional activism in litigation, Perino (2012) found that attorneys' fee requests and awards are significantly lower in cases with public pension lead plaintiffs. These reductions are not only statistically significant, but economically significant as well. On average, fee requests are 5.3 percent less and fee awards 3.4 percent less than in cases without public pension funds. The average fee award in the sample was 26.6 percent. That means that average fee awards in cases with public pension fund lead plaintiffs were 12.8 percent lower than in cases with other kinds of lead plaintiffs. There is also evidence that courts show greater deference to the fees negotiated by public pension funds. Eisenberg et al. (2009) find that, all else equal, courts award a greater percentage of the requested fees in cases with public pension lead plaintiffs than cases with other lead plaintiff types.

As with settlement amounts, there is evidence that institutional investors are not monolithic when it comes to their ability to bargain for lower fees. Choi (2011) breaks institutional investors into two categories: (1) institutions that sought lead plaintiff status in less than five cases; and (2) institutions that sought lead plaintiff status in five or more cases. While the coefficients for both were negative, it was only significant for the frequent lead plaintiff movants.[12] On average, frequent institutional movants were correlated with a 3.3 percent reduction in fee requests. In other words, on average fee requests in those cases were 12.4 percent below the average fee request of 26.6 percent observed in the sample. Choi et al. (2011) find no statistically significant correlation between union-affiliated funds and attorneys' fees. They also find that larger institutions negotiate for lower fees, a finding that makes great intuitive sense. Larger institutions will tend to have the largest financial interest in a particular case, making it more likely that they will be selected as lead plaintiffs and giving them greater bargaining leverage with potential law firms eager to capture the role as lead counsel.

These findings on decreased fees become even more intriguing in light of the available data on the relationship between attorney effort and institutional participation. Choi (2011) found some evidence that attorneys work more hours in cases with institutional lead plaintiffs than in other securities class actions. In one specification of his model, which controlled for case strength, attorney hours in cases with institutional lead plaintiffs were 40 percent higher than in cases with other kinds of lead plaintiffs. That result is consistent with unpublished work by Perino (2006), which found that attorney effort (measured by docket entries in the case) was significantly higher in cases with public

---

[12] The lack of significance for the infrequent institutional investor variable may be the result of the small sample size (n = 127) Choi employed compared to the Perino (2012) study (n = 698).

pension fund lead plaintiffs even when control-ling for variables associated with case complexity. Taken together, these studies of fees and attorney effort suggest that institutional investors are able to significantly reduce the agency costs traditionally associated with securities class actions.

The available empirical evidence also suggests that institutional investor participation has broader beneficial effects that extend beyond the particu-lar cases in which they are involved. Perino (2012) provides evidence of a substantial positive external-ity associated with institutional activism in securi-ties class actions. As public pension fund activism became more widespread, fee awards in cases without public pension lead plaintiffs declined significantly as well, suggesting that the fees insti-tutions negotiated influenced fee setting more generally. Here too the decline was economically significant; in cases without public pension lead plaintiffs that were settled after 2002, fee awards dropped on average 2.2 percent. In their analysis of fee awards, Eisenberg et al. (2009) included fixed effects for the year in which fees were awarded. Starting in 1998 and for each year thereafter the coefficients were negative and significant, indicat-ing that fee awards in these years were lower than the reference year for the study, 1991. The emer-gence of this correlation in 1998 coincides with the increased participation of institutions as lead plaintiffs, lending additional support to the hypoth-esis that institutions have contributed to a secular decline in fee awards. Together, these findings sug-gest that public pension funds act as more effective monitors of class counsel than traditional repre-sentative plaintiffs, that the lead plaintiff provision has reduced the transactions costs associated with securities class actions and thus that the lead plain-tiff provision has largely been successful.

Despite these benefits, public pensions are still agents subject to their own agency costs. By far, the largest concerns involve pay-to-play. Are law firms making campaign contributions to increase the likelihood of being selected as lead counsel for the fund and, if so, what if any impact does this practice have on attorneys' fees? Webber (2010) provides some evidence that pay-to-play may not be widespread and that it may have little influence over counsel selection. In particular, he finds that

political control over pension funds is negatively correlated with lead plaintiff appointments while beneficiary control of fund boards and the degree of the pension fund's underfunding are positively cor-related with such appointments. From these data, Webber concludes that beneficiary board members, not politicians, drive pension fund pursuit of lead plaintiff appointments and that their motivation for doing so involves the financial soundness of the fund. The more underfunding at the pension fund, the more likely the fund is to pursue lead plaintiff appointments. Webber's study, however, is indi-rect – without looking at actual campaign contribu-tions (which he does not do) it is difficult to draw firm conclusions on the role contributions play in the selection of counsel. Johnson-Skinner (2009), by contrast, provides summary statistics demon-strating that law firms in fact appear to contribute to the campaigns of officials who select them as lead counsel. The study found law firm contributions in 55 percent of the cases in the dataset involving funds controlled by state level officials (forty-one or seventy-four cases).

A more recent study by Choi et al. (2011) evalu-ates the impact of these campaign contributions and concludes that they make public pension funds far less effective monitors of law firms. They find that the state pension funds whose officials received the largest campaign contributions negotiated fees that were statistically indistinguishable from the fees negotiated by individual lead plaintiffs. In other words, pay-to-play appeared to eliminate all of the beneficial effects on attorneys' fee awards. Similarly, if the pension fund tended to rely on a sin-gle law firm that made campaign contributions, fees were significantly higher, suggesting that the fund provided little effective monitoring. Pay-to-play, however, did not appear to recreate all of the prob-lems Congress sought to redress when it passed the PSLRA. Campaign contributions were, for example, uncorrelated with pension funds bringing weak, low-value claims. Still, these findings suggest that courts should take seriously pay-to-play allegations and should require disclosure of contributions and assess whether those contributions render the fund inadequate to serve as lead plaintiff. Alternatively, in the presence of such contributions, courts should more vigorously monitor any fee request.

Conclusions

The empirical evidence on the PSLRA's lead plaintiff provision suggests that courts should continue their preference for institutional over individual plaintiffs in securities class actions. On average, cases with institutional plaintiffs are dismissed less, settle for more and have lower fees than cases with other kinds of lead plaintiffs.

While the existing research answers many important questions about the effectiveness of institutional investors as lead plaintiffs, some significant questions remain. For example, courts tend to treat all institutions uniformly when it comes to appointing lead plaintiffs, an unsurprising result given that the PSLRA draws no distinctions among institutional types. The evidence collected to date, however, suggests that all institutions are not created equal – public pension funds appear to be associated with better case outcomes than other institutional investors. Additional research should analyze whether there is a real difference between institutional types or whether these results are driven by the comparative size of institutional claims in the litigation. If real differences exist, courts should consider this evidence in deciding among institutions competing to serve as lead plaintiff.

Given the substantial evidence that institution participation is correlated with reduced fees, additional research should examine the extent to which courts defer to the fee arrangements institutions negotiate. With respect to the pay-to-play problem, additional research should try to evaluate the impact of the practice on recoveries. Current research shows that campaign contributions have a deleterious effect on the ability of the funds to monitor fees effectively. If a similar effect is observed for settlement amounts, then courts or Congress should consider a range of reforms, including disclosure of campaign contributions. Such information would appear to be relevant in connection with lead plaintiff appointments, settlement approval and fee awards.

Scholars have likewise raised concerns about whether other institutional conflicts – their use of derivatives trading strategies and their alleged willingness to trade corporate governance reforms for increased settlement dollars – make institutions inadequate plaintiffs when it comes to representing the interests of individual investors. Unfortunately, these perceived conflicts are speculative – no empirical research has been done to evaluate whether individual investors in fact fare worse in cases with institutional lead plaintiffs. The aggregate data on enhanced recoveries and lower fees in institutional investor cases certainly suggests otherwise, but additional research might evaluate whether, for example, monetary recoveries are lower in cases where institutions negotiate corporate governance reforms. Careful analysis of settlement agreements might also reveal whether allowed damages are skewed in favor of institutional claims. Without such data there appears to be little reason to ignore the PSLRA's statutory scheme of appointing the investor with the largest financial interest in favor of appointing mixed groups of individual and institutional investors, as these scholars advocate.

After passage of the PSLRA, some institutions pursued a strategy of opting out of class actions to pursue individual actions. Anecdotal evidence suggests that institutions might be able to obtain higher returns than they would get in a class action, but it is also possible that opt-out actions benefit attorneys who may have lost a bid to win the lead counsel role. Additional research should analyze the effectiveness of this strategy. Research should also evaluate other avenues for institutional investor participation in securities class actions. In several cases, for example, institutions have objected to proposed settlements, most often to attorneys' fee requests.[13] Studies should assess whether such objections represent an effective, low-cost strategy for institutional activism in securities litigation.

---

[13] Under relevant procedural rules in the United States, when a court is asked to approve a final settlement of a class action, affected class members may submit their objections to any of the settlement's terms, including the proposed attorneys' fee. These objections have met with mixed results. Compare *In re Cardinal Health, Inc. Sec. Litig.*, 550 F. Supp. 2d 751 (SD Ohio 2008) (reducing requested fee from 24 percent to 18 percent based in part on objections lodged by institutional investors) with *In re Adelphia Communs. Corp. Sec. & Derivative Litig.*, 2006 US Dist. LEXIS 84621 (SDNY November 16, 2006) (declining to reduce fee request despite institutional investor objection).

Finally, institutions' participation in securities class actions has led to increased involvement by institutions in cases brought under state law involving mergers and acquisitions or corporate governance matters. Unpublished work by Webber (2011) finds results that parallel those of federal securities class actions. Since Delaware adopted a presumption in favor of selecting institutional lead plaintiffs, their participation in these cases has been substantial, with institutions now appearing in 41 percent of filed cases. As in securities class actions, institutions tend to focus on higher quality cases. Specifically, institutions tend to serve as lead plaintiffs in cases involving lower merger premiums or other unfavorable deal terms. There is also evidence of substantial variation among institutional types both in terms of case selection and outcomes. Public pension funds, for example, tend to serve as lead plaintiffs in cases involving controlling shareholder transactions. The study finds, however, that only public pension fund participation is significantly correlated with improved share prices for target shareholders. However, more work is necessary to confirm these results and to examine institutional litigation in non-transactional contexts.

The findings cited in this chapter should help to inform fiduciaries when considering their obligations in regard to participation in securities litigation. In the end, fiduciaries must weigh the costs and benefits to their beneficiaries of the various options available for pursuing legal claims.

References

Alexander, J. C. 1991. "Do the Merits Matter? A Study of Settlements in Securities Class Actions," *Stanford Law Review* 43: 497–598.

Black, B. S. 1990. "Shareholder Passivity Reexamined," *Michigan Law Review* 89: 520–608.

Chamblee Burch, E. 2011. "Optimal Lead Plaintiffs," *Vanderbilt Law Review* 64: 1109–92.

Cheng, C. S. A, H. H. Huang, Y. Li and G. Lobo. 2010. "Institutional Monitoring through Shareholder Litigation," *Journal of Financial Economics* 95: 356–83.

Choi, S. J. 2011. "Motions for Lead Plaintiff in Securities Class Actions," *Journal of Legal Studies* 40: 205–44.

Choi, S. J. and R. Thompson. 2006. "Securities Litigation and Its Lawyers: Changes during the First Decade after the PSLRA," *Columbia Law Review* 106: 1489–1533.

Choi, S. J., J. E. Fisch and A. C. Pritchard. 2005. "Do Institutions Matter? The Impact of the Lead Plaintiff Provision of the Private Securities Litigation Reform Act," *Washington University Law Quarterly* 83: 869–905.

Choi, S. J., D. T. Johnson-Skinner and A. C. Pritchard. 2011. "The Price of Pay to Play in Securities Class Actions," *Journal of Empirical Legal Studies* 8: 650–81.

Coffee, J. C., Jr. 1987. "The Regulation of Entrepreneurial Litigation: Balancing Fairness and Efficiency in the Large Class Action," *University of Chicago Law Review* 54: 877–937.

Cox, J. D. and R. S. Thomas. 2002. "Leaving Money on the Table: Do Institutional Investors Fail to File Claims in Securities Class Actions?" *Washington University Law Quarterly* 80: 855–88.

2005. "Letting Billions Slip Through Your Fingers: Empirical Evidence and Legal Implications of the Failure of Financial Institutions to Participate in Securities Class Action Settlements," *Stanford Law Review* 58: 411–54.

2006. "Does the Lead Plaintiff Matter? An Empirical Analysis of Lead Plaintiffs in Securities Class Actions," *Columbia Law Review* 106: 1587–640.

Cox, J. D., R. S. Thomas and L. Bai. 2008. "There Are Plaintiffs and … There Are Plaintiffs: An Empirical Analysis of Securities Class Action Settlements," *Vanderbilt Law Review* 61: 355–86.

Eisenberg, T., G. P. Miller and M. A. Perino. 2009. "A New Look at Judicial Impact: Attorneys' Fees in Securities Class Actions after *Goldberger* v. *Integrated Resources, Inc.,*" *Washington University Journal of Law and Policy* 29: 5–35.

Fisch, J. E. 1997. "Class Action Reform: Lessons from Securities Litigation," *Arizona Law Review* 39: 533–59.

2002. "Lawyers on the Auction Block," *Columbia Law Review* 102: 650–728.

Green, L. 2011. *Governance Reforms through Securities Class Actions*. ISS Monograph.

Grundfest, J. A. and M. A. Perino. 1996. "The Pentium Papers: A Case Study of Collective Institutional Investor Activism in Litigation," *Arizona Law Review* 38: 559–626.

Johnson-Skinner, D. T. 2009. "Paying to Play in Securities Class Actions: A Look at Lawyers' Campaign Contributions," *New York University Law Review* 84: 1725–55.

Macey, J. R. and G. P. Miller. 1991. "The Plaintiffs' Attorney's Role in Class Action and Derivative Litigation: Economic Analysis and Recommendations for Reform," *University of Chicago Law Review* 58: 1–118.

Martin, C. C. and M. H. Metcalf. 2001. "The Fiduciary Duties of Institutional Investors in Securities Litigation," *Business Lawyer* 56: 1381–416.

Perino, M. A. 2003. "Did the Private Securities Litigation Reform Act Work?" *University of Illinois Law Review* 913–77.

  2006. "Markets and Monitors: The Impact of Competition and Experience on Attorneys' Fees in Securities Class Actions," St. John's Legal Studies Research Paper No. 06–0034.

  2008. "The Milberg Weiss Prosecution: No Harm, No Foul?" 11 *Briefly ...*, American Enterprise Institute Monograph.

  2012. "Institutional Activism through Litigation: An Empirical Analysis of Public Pension Fund Participation in Securities Class Actions," *Journal of Empirical Legal Studies* 9: 368–92.

PricewaterhouseCoopers. 2005. *2005 Securities Litigation Study*.

  2012. *The Ever-changing Landscape of Litigation Comes Full Circle: 2011 Securities Litigation Study*.

Romano, R. 1993. "Public Pension Fund Activism in Corporate Governance Reconsidered," *Columbia Law Review* 93: 795–853.

Securities and Exchange Commission. 1997. *Report to the President and Congress on the First Year of Practice under the Private Securities Litigation Reform Act of 1995*.

Seligman, J. 1994. "The Merits Do Matter: A Comment on Professor Grundfest's 'Disimplying Private Rights of Action under the Federal Securities Laws: The Commission's Authority'," *Harvard Law Review* 108: 438–57.

Simmons, L. E. and E. M. Ryan. 2005. *Post-Reform Act Securities Settlements*. Cornerstone Research.

Smith, M. P. 1996. "Shareholder Activism by Institutional Investors: Evidence from CalPERS," *Journal of Finance* 51: 227–52.

Webber, D. H. 2010. "Is 'Pay-to-Play' Driving Public Pension Fund Activism in Securities Litigation?" *Boston University Law Review* 90: 2032–81.

  2011. "Private Policing of Mergers and Acquisitions: An Empirical Assessment of Institutional Lead Plaintiffs in Transactional Class and Derivative Actions," working paper, Boston University.

  2012. "The Plight of the Individual Investor in Securities Class Actions," *Northwestern Law Review* 106: 157–224.

Weiss, E. J. and J. S. Beckerman. 1995. "Let the Money Do the Monitoring: How Institutional Investors Can Reduce Agency Costs in Securities Class Actions," *Yale Law Journal* 104: 2053–127.

The future of fiduciary obligation for institutional investors

CLAIRE MOLINARI

Introduction

The context of this chapter is one of change. The world of institutional investment has been undergoing some fundamental structural shifts for a number of years, and many of these have direct implications for the future of fiduciary obligation.

The defined benefit pension fund, once the mainstay of institutional investment funds, is quickly being replaced by the defined contribution scheme.[1] This transfers the risk of poor investment performance from corporate and state employers to individual beneficiaries. At the same time, pension fund trustees, the traditional bearers of fiduciary obligation, are now rarely the key players in investment decision-making. Virtually all asset owners[2] have delegated day-to-day investment decision-making to asset managers and strategic planning to investment consultants, and whether these agents are bound by fiduciary obligation is often unclear. Finally, trust-based pension funds are increasingly giving way to contract-based schemes operated by large insurance companies. These are governed by the law of contracts, under which fiduciary obligation does not exist.

Fiduciary obligation is at once more important for beneficiaries (who now bear the risks of investment failure), and less clearly allocated. This chapter considers the future of fiduciary obligation in the UK in this altered investment world, drawing on other common law jurisdictions for comparison. It explores the rise of the defined benefit pension scheme, the significance of the shift from trust-based to contractual funds and the duties of trustees' agents along the investment chain. By the end of the chapter, it becomes clear that the space for fiduciary obligation in the institutional investment world is shrinking at a time when beneficiaries may need it the most.

To be clear, this chapter identifies the broader structural issues affecting the overall roll of fiduciary obligation within institutional investment in the future rather than commenting on its effectiveness as a mechanism for encouraging more sensible investment or for protecting beneficiary interests. While the closing remarks of this chapter mention a number of ways in which the protection of beneficiary interests might be strengthened, a more detailed examination is beyond its scope.

Background

In medieval England, a branch of law known as equity arose to provide justice when the existing law could not. Equity's most enduring innovation, the trust, developed as a means to protect the property of those who could not legally manage it themselves.[3] The trust is imbued with the quality its name implies: a great deal of personal trust was placed in the trustee, who held the legal title to property on behalf of the beneficiary. The equity courts held that trustees were under a fiduciary obligation to manage trust property loyally and prudently on behalf of the beneficiary.

---

[1] In the UK, for example, private sector defined contribution pension schemes are expected to have more than 16 million active members by 2020, whereas defined benefit pension fund members will decline to under 1 million (Carrera et al. 2012).

[2] In this chapter, "asset owner" refers to the pension fund trustees who represent a fund's ultimate owners, the beneficiaries.

[3] Early trust beneficiaries were often landed minors who could not manage their property until they came of age.

When the first legal cases about trustee fiduciary obligation were decided in the eighteenth century, the investment decisions made by trustees were not particularly complex. There was a limited range of asset classes available for investment, complex derivative financial products had not yet been invented and businesses themselves were generally smaller and simpler. This is not to say that mistakes were not made; the legislative list approach was introduced in response to trustees' misplaced zeal for the South Sea Company, which turned into the South Sea Bubble in 1720 and lost a fortune in beneficiary money (Langbein 1996). As a result, the UK parliament limited trustees' scope for error by limiting them to a short list of investable asset classes. This lasted well into the twentieth century, when the Trustee Act 2000 finally gave trustees the freedom to invest across all asset classes. A legislative similar path was followed in the US (see Langbein 1996).

By the second half of the twentieth century, investing had begun to change significantly. Modern portfolio theory, described by Markowitz (1952, 1959), dictated that investors should minimize risks by investing across a range of asset classes and industries. At the same time, the institutional investment industry matured significantly. Until the 1930s, care for the elderly was seen as a responsibility of the family and, to a lesser extent, the community. As the welfare state developed, a new ethos began to emerge. By the post-war period, employers (either the state or companies) provided pension funds to most employees in the developed world (see Clark 2000). With the growth in pension funds came a large industry dedicated to the management of these assets. Anderson (2006) states that the entire US asset management industry held about a total of $1 billion assets under management in 1940, compared to around $17.4 trillion in pension assets in 2010 (CityUK 2011). The UK has followed a similar trajectory of growth, with around $2.9 trillion assets in 2010.

The structure of these investment funds remained largely trust-based, with a board of trustees acting as agents of the ultimate asset owners (the beneficiaries). However, their investment responsibilities had grown significantly more complex. Owing to the influence of modern portfolio theory, the trustees were now responsible for investing in a much broader range of asset classes than had previously been required.[4] Trustees had become responsible for burgeoning funds for which complex day-to-day investment decisions were required. Institutional investment funds had outgrown the traditional, trustee-led management structures that had governed trust funds since medieval times.

The rapid development of the investment management industry has occurred out of pace with the incremental evolution of trust law through the court systems. As Langbein (2007) notes, "common law processes of incrementalism were no more suitable for today's trust law than for the regulation of nuclear power plants." Instead, legislation was needed to create a step-change in regulatory standards for institutional investment funds. Today, trustees of pension funds are rarely responsible for making day-to-day investment decisions. Laws now require them to appoint and monitor appropriate asset managers, and to produce a Statement of Investment Principles. Asset owners typically rely on investment consultants to provide strategic advice on the running of the pension funds.

In *Our Mutual Friend*, first published in 1865, Charles Dickens (2008: 226) describes a trustee as "an oilcake-fed style of business-gentlemen with mooney spectacles." Trustees may still be mostly grey-headed men in their twilight years (see Clark et al. 2006), but the investment world around them has changed. As trustees retreat into the sidelines of institutional investment, will fiduciary obligations fade with them?

I have argued elsewhere that pension fund trustees' fiduciary obligation is able to adapt to new contexts (Woods 2011). The question in this chapter is whether pension funds are moving beyond the realms of fiduciary obligation altogether.

---

[4] In the US, both ERISA (29 USC § 1104(a)) and UPIA (comment to § 5) include the "modern prudent investor rule," which requires fiduciaries to ensure prudent investment across a whole portfolio in the best interests of beneficiaries and for the purposes of the fund. In the UK, the Occupational Pension Schemes (Investment) Regulations (2005) (cl. 2(2)(a)) require pension fund assets to be adequately diversified.

The shift from defined benefit to defined contribution pension funds

On June 1, 2012, General Motors Corporation announced a plan to remove pension liabilities from its balance sheet by offering employees an opportunity to buy their pensions as a lump sum, and by handing management of the funds to Prudential Financial (Seetharaman and Klayman 2012). The move was a final chapter in the company's troubled history of recent years; the pension liabilities had contributed to the company's bankruptcy and government bailout in 2008 (McCrum 2011). Although it came as no surprise, it marked the end of an era. "Defined benefit" (DB) pension funds were once a mainstay of workers in unionized industries and in the public sector. The DB pension fund sponsor, usually the employer (either a company or the state) promised each pension fund member a predefined amount of money upon retirement as part of the employment contract. If the pension fund was insufficient to meet the amount promised to members, the pension fund sponsor was obliged to reach into its own pockets to fill the gap.

Times have changed. It has become apparent over the past decade that neither companies nor governments on either side of the Atlantic can afford to pay the generous pension fund benefits once promised to all employees. In the US, at the end of 2011, there was a gap of around 25 percent between assets and liabilities across state and local government DB pension funds (Munnell et al. 2012a). US corporate pension funds face a similar shortfall (McCrum and Bullock 2012). Recent changes to the Governmental Accounting Standards Board accounting rules could widen this gap.[5] In the UK, corporate DB pension funds are also increasingly underfunded (Cohen 2012). In 2011, Shell was the last FTSE company to shut

its final salary pension scheme to new members (Cohen 2012). The UK's set of public DB pension funds, the Local Government Pension Scheme, has also suffered a significant funding deficit since the financial crisis (Redgrave 2011).

Clark and Monk (2007) argue that there are three central causes of the "crisis" in DB pension funds. First, funds have failed to account for increased longevity, which increases pension liabilities. Second, inflation risk is salient for firms that index pension fund obligations (they note that this is chiefly a UK problem, as US DB pension funds tend not to be indexed). Third, DB pension funds have been unable to accurately predict the effects of wage inflation and regulatory change.

The demise of DB pension funds could not come at a less convenient time: at present, the baby boom generation is reaching retirement while the working population is in decline in most developed countries. Something must replace the social security gap that widens as DB pension funds disappear. Increasingly, the gap is filled by "defined contribution" (DC) pension funds. In the UK, there were around 8 million active members of DB funds in 1967, compared to only 1.6 million in 2011 (Carrera et al. 2012). In DC pension funds, employers typically contribute a determined amount at regular intervals. The performance of the DC pension fund determines the amount that the employee will receive upon retirement. As such, it is the beneficiary (employee) who bears the risk that the fund will underperform his or her expectations.

The shift from DB to DC pension funds has two main implications. First, beneficiaries are increasingly expected to guide their own pension outcomes. The language of autonomy and responsibility pervades much of the literature on defined contribution plans. For example, an introductory paragraph on the Royal Mail pension website states, "to help to provide you with a secure retirement, you need to consider ways of building for your future."[6] Along these lines, Clark and Urwin (2011: 39) argue that "[i]n liberal democracies, there is a presumption in favour of individual

---

[5] Or at least it would increase the appearance of the gap. The new accounting rules require plans to report annual assets and liabilities, rather than "smoothing" these across the past five years as currently happens. In 2010, the application of the new rules would have led to a funding level of 57 percent rather than 76 percent (Munnell et al. 2012b). The rules were approved on June 25, 2012 (Governmental Accounting Standards Board 2012).

[6] See www.zurich.co.uk/royalmaildcplan/home/introduction.htm.

autonomy such that it is the responsibility of the participant to be an effective decision-maker consistent with his or her long-term interests."

But beneficiaries are not all up to the task. In fact, the extent to which the average DC pension fund member is equipped to make informed decisions about investment strategy is questionable. Many individuals are poor financial decision-makers, lacking financial understanding and being subject to behavioral biases in their choices (Akerlof and Shiller 2009; Clark et al. 2006; Kahneman and Tversky 1976). More often than not, moreover, they are not financial decision-makers at all: many DC pension fund providers do not offer beneficiaries a choice of funds, or offer a very limited choice. Of those that do, the vast majority of beneficiaries do not opt out of the default fund (Byrne et al. 2007). Despite the trappings of modern society, a member of a DC pension fund is not so far from the vulnerable beneficiary of Dickens' stories.

Second, as DC pension funds become the norm, beneficiaries will increasingly bear the risks of investment failure. As a result, the conduct of various actors along the investment chain (trustees, asset managers and investment consultants) will have a more material effect on beneficiaries' financial situations. Ensuring that beneficiary interests are protected becomes more important. In the future, the form of protection available to beneficiaries will depend on the structure of each pension fund: while fiduciary obligation remains the obvious source of beneficiary protection in a trust-based pension fund, contract-based pension funds operate outside of the law of trusts and fiduciary obligation.

The obligations of asset managers and investment consultants

Fiduciary obligation in the investment world has always been associated with trustees. Case law and legislation clearly depicts the fiduciary obligations of trustees: trustees must manage trust funds loyally and prudently in the best interests of beneficiaries. In addition, they must treat beneficiaries within the fund impartially. Trustees' duties and powers are set out in the trust deed, but generally

include setting the broad investment strategy of the pension fund, and maintaining a statement of investment principles that governs "decisions about investments for the purposes of the scheme," including the kinds of investments to be held, the level of risk taken and the expected return on investments (in the UK, see Pensions Act 1995, s. 35). This is true across all common law jurisdictions (see UNEP FI 2005). The precise implications of these duties are sometimes subject to debate (see, for example, Richardson 2008; Woods 2011 in the context of sustainable investing). Nonetheless, the obligations, whatever the exact nature of their content, clearly apply to trustees.

The status of other players in the investment chain differs between jurisdictions. US legislation explicitly states that asset managers and investment consultants are fiduciaries. The US Employee Retirement Income Security Act (1974) states that anyone who exercises "any discretionary authority" or control over a pension plan's assets is a fiduciary.[7] As asset managers exercise discretion over the manner in which assets are invested, they are bound by fiduciary obligations in the US. US investment consultants are also considered fiduciaries under the Investment Advisors Act (1940).[8]

In the UK, as in the US, many trustees delegate day-to-day investment decision-making to asset managers (this is possible under section 34 of the Pensions Act 1995). In practice, asset managers have a large impact on the interests of beneficiaries: the management of the investment fund makes all the difference to the benefits available to beneficiaries. Similarly, trustees often appoint investment consultants to provide strategic investment advice and to help choose asset managers. While investment consultants do not directly manage trust funds, they nonetheless exert a significant influence over the way those funds are directed.

Despite their centrality to the modern institutional investment purpose, the obligations of UK asset managers and investment consultants are less

---

[7] 29 USC I(A) § 1002 (21)(A).
[8] While the term "fiduciary" is not used explicitly in the act, the Supreme Court has found that a fiduciary obligation is implied: *SEC* v. *Capital Gains Research Bureau*, 375 US 180 (1963).

clear. Neither case law nor legislation explicitly states that these agents owe fiduciary obligations to beneficiaries (FairPensions 2011). As such, it is worth returning to first principles in order to gain a better idea of whether a court might find that such fiduciary obligations exist in the future.

Traditionally, the law of trusts recognized a range of set relationships as "fiduciary." These vary somewhat between jurisdictions, but tend to include the relationships of trustee and beneficiary, principle and agent, doctor and patient and parent and child (for a distinction between jurisdictions, see Hudson 2009: 617–19).[9] Fiduciary obligations are presumed to apply in these situations. According to the Law Commission (1992, at 27), "it would appear that each of the relationships is of such importance and of such a nature that it needs protection by the imposition of fiduciary status." The asset manager-beneficiary and investment consultant-beneficiary relationships do not fall within one of these traditional categories.

Courts will also sometimes recognize a fiduciary relationship arising from particular factual circumstances. In this context, Finn (1977: 201) argues, a fiduciary is "simply, someone who undertakes to act for or on behalf of another in some particular matter or matters." Few commentators would apply fiduciary obligation as liberally as Finn. Nonetheless, courts have been willing to set out principles by which they would recognize fiduciary obligation. The Canadian and Australian courts have been the principle developers of this jurisprudence. In the Canadian case of *Frame* v. *Smith*,[10] Justice Wilson identified three general characteristics of relationships which courts were willing to recognize as fiduciary (p. 99):

(1) The fiduciary has scope for the exercise of some discretion or power.
(2) The fiduciary can unilaterally exercise that power or discretion so as to affect the beneficiary's legal or practical interests.

(3) The beneficiary is peculiarly vulnerable to or at the mercy of the fiduciary holding the discretion or power.

Both the Canadian Supreme Court and Australian High Court have applied a test along these lines to business relationships, with varying results. In *Hospital Products* v. *United States Surgical Corporation*, the Australian High Court found that the relationship between two contracting parties was not fiduciary in nature. The Court expressed reluctance to find that fiduciary obligations exist between two commercial parties interacting at arm's length. By contrast, in *LAC Minerals Ltd* v. *International Corona Resources Ltd.*,[11] the Canadian Supreme Court found that a fiduciary relationship existed between two mining companies.

The significance of these cases for this chapter is that courts have been willing to recognize the existence of a fiduciary relationship in new situations, provided certain facts can be established. As institutional investment processes have become more complex, many of the investment decisions that have the greatest impact on beneficiaries are made not by trustees, but by asset managers and investment consultants. Given their discretion over the deployment of pension fund assets, the impact this discretion can have on beneficiary interests, and the practical inability of individual beneficiaries to influence or oversee investment processes, it seems reasonable to imagine that a UK court would be willing to recognize a fiduciary relationship between these agents and beneficiaries in certain circumstances.

Whether or not an obligation is fiduciary can have significant implications for the remedies available for its breach. While the law of equitable remedies is a complex and unsettled area (Martin 2005), several general observations can be made. Whereas at common law, the normal remedy for loss is damages, equity provides a much greater range of remedies. Beneficiaries who suffer a loss as a result of breach of fiduciary obligation are entitled to reclaim the loss that they have suffered. English

---

[9] Hudson (2009: 617) states that only four strict fiduciary relationship categories exist in England and Wales: trustee/beneficiary, company directors, partners *inter se* and principal and agent.
[10] *Frame* v. *Smith*, 42 DLR (4th) 81 (1987).

[11] *LAC Minerals Ltd* v. *International Corona Resources Ltd.*, 61 DLR (4th) 14 (1988).

courts[12] were traditionally generous in compensating those who suffered as a result of breach of fiduciary obligation (Hudson 2009). Fiduciaries were held strictly liable for "all unauthorised gains made by the fiduciaries deriving, however obliquely, from their fiduciary duty" (Hudson 2009: 620). Under English law, a beneficiary's "loss" may include circumstances where the profits of the trust fund are smaller than they would have been had the fiduciary acted prudently.[13] By contrast, the remedy for breach of contract involves putting the injured party into the position he or she would have been in had the breach not occurred.

The rise of contract-based pension schemes

The most significant change for the future of fiduciary obligation is the rise of contract-based pension schemes. Recent years have seen a marked increase in the relative number of contract-based pension schemes. In the UK, for example, there are currently approximately 3.2 million trust-based pension funds (including both DC and DB), and about 3 million contract-based schemes (all of which are DC) (Pensions Regulator 2011). This change has significant implications for the relevance of fiduciary obligation in the future.

There are a number of practical differences between contract-based and trust-based pension schemes. Although contract-based schemes are established with a trust-deed in the UK, these schemes do not have trustees in the traditional sense (Pensions Regulator 2007). The provider of contract-based pension schemes is usually an insurance company. The companies that provide contract-based pension schemes do not owe fiduciary obligations to members. Instead, the relationship between members and providers is governed by the terms of the contract between them. If a member of a contract-based pension scheme wished to take

the provider to court for failure to act in his best interests, he or she would have to point to a relevant contractual clause.

The Financial Ombudsman Service will hear complaints that cannot be resolved by the parties themselves (Pensions Regulator 2007). Although contract-based pension scheme providers are not subject to the same requirements of prudence or skill, care and diligence as trustees, they must be authorized by the FSA to establish and operate the scheme (Pensions Regulator 2007).

As the employer is normally not a party to the contract, it owes no duty to the pension fund member with respect to the pension fund. However, the Pensions Regulator (2007: 43) argues that, as the employer is usually the conduit through which pension contributions are made "it retains an interest in the efficient running of the scheme." Neither the employer nor trustees formally represent the interests of beneficiaries in contract-based pension schemes.

More fundamentally, trust law and contact law are guided by very different principles. The principles that underlie trust law derive from conscience-oriented equity. Among the commonly recognized equitable maxims are these (see for example Bray 2012):

- Equity regards done what ought to been done.
- Equity will not suffer a wrong to be without a remedy.
- Equity delights to do justice and not by halves.
- Equity imputes an intent to fulfill an obligation.

These imply intent by the court to go out of its way to help those it sees as suffering an injustice. Indeed, equity developed as a means for courts to find just outcomes in situations where existing law had no remedy. As noted in the section above, the area of fiduciary obligation, in particular, is premised on protecting the interests of vulnerable parties when others make decisions on their behalf. Thus those beneficiaries who are members of a trust-based pension fund are afforded a high level of legal protection, with courts predisposed to protect their interests.

By contrast, contract law as a general rule assumes that parties to a contract begin on equal footing. The law of contract is underlined by the

---

[12] See for example *Boardman* v. *Phipps*, 2 AC 46 (1967) (concerning a solicitor owing fiduciary obligations to his clients, who were trustees).

[13] *Nestlé* v. *National Westminster Bank plc*, 1 WLR 1260 (1993).

idea that commercial certainty is best achieved by courts refraining from intervening in arm's length agreements between people. Writing about the "sparing, if not niggardly" remedies often associated with contract law, Linzer (1981: 111) argues that contract law "has emphasized an approach that excludes considerations of morality and is said to advance the objective of economic efficiency."

When discussing contract-based pension schemes, the Kay Review (Kay 2012: 66) argued, "*caveat emptor* is not a concept compatible with an equity investment chain based on trust and stewardship." The implication here is that the principle of *caveat emptor*, or buyer beware, would apply within contract-based schemes. This principle, originating in property law, was designed to prevent the law from having to intervene in situations where a complainant had merely made a poor decision or failed to do adequate research before entering into an agreement to purchase something. If this principle were held to apply to pension-fund contracts, it could place beneficiaries in a weak position vis-à-vis providers. For many years, however, in the UK (and to an extent in the US), courts have become less stringent in applying the principle (Keeton 1936: 14–16):

> When Lord Cairns stated in *Peek* v. *Gurney* that there was no duty to disclose facts, however morally censurable their non-disclosure may be, he was stating the law as shaped by an individualistic philosophy based upon freedom of contract. It was not concerned with morals. In the present stage of the law, the decisions show a drawing away from this idea, and there can be seen an attempt by many courts to reach a just result in so far as possible.

In particular, courts have been less willing to apply the principle of *caveat emptor* in situations where the buyer is an individual and the seller a company. Arguably regulation by the FSA and the Pensions Regulator will provide further protection of the interests of contract-based pension scheme beneficiaries in their dealings with providers. While the concern about the influence of *caveat emptor* in contract-based pension schemes appears to be somewhat overstated given legal developments last century, the law of contract is nonetheless underpinned by a very different philosophy than that of equity.

What will happen to pension scheme members whose interests are not represented by trustees? On the one hand, members may become more actively interested in their scheme, thinking more carefully about its investment strategy and performance. They might even try to bargain more with the pension scheme provider. This rosy scenario seems unlikely, for several reasons. First, many members of contract-based pension schemes are subject to auto-enrolment, meaning that the employer provides only one pension scheme option; members do not have a say in the specifics of the scheme. Second, contract-based pension fund providers have greater bargaining power than their customers. They have greater information, expertise and resources. While competition does exist in the market for contract-based pension scheme provision, there is a high level of inertia once members have signed up to a particular scheme due to the costs involved in switching and to the behavioral bias toward inertia found in consumers more generally. Third, as noted above, where several choices of scheme are offered, pension fund members tend overwhelmingly not to opt out of the default option (Byrne et al. 2007).

It is more likely that contract-based pension scheme members will be more vulnerable to pension fund underperformance than their peers in trust-based pension funds. While pension fund members have always borne a risk of poor investment *outcomes*, contract-based scheme members will be more vulnerable to poor investment *processes*, because the providers are not bound by the same fiduciary requirements.

Trustees' fiduciary obligations go beyond merely setting the investment strategy. They may also be required to engage with companies; to act as stewards. This is something that will fade as contract-based pension schemes replace trust-based funds.

Conclusions

In the UK, the role of fiduciary obligation in pension fund investment is being diminished from two fronts. Over the past fifty years, institutional investment has become significantly more complex. As a result, the day-to-day investment decisions that have the largest impact on returns to beneficiaries are made almost exclusively by asset managers, whose professional experience places them in a better position than trustees for this type of decision-making. Similarly, the major strategic decisions are often made by investment consultants. In the UK, unlike the US, neither of these groups of the agents is bound by any explicit fiduciary obligation.

For contract-based pension schemes, fiduciary obligation is cut out of the investment chain completely. Fiduciary obligation exists in equity, not contract law. Fundamentally, the two branches of law are underpinned by very different principles: whereas equity has since its inception been concerned with coming to the aid of those who were unable to find relief in existing law, contract is premised on the equal position of bargaining parties, and generally aims to promote commercial efficiency. If the trend toward contract-based schemes continues, fiduciary obligation may become obsolete.

Much has changed since the time of Dickens' trustees. Picture a trust fund in the mid-nineteenth century. The beneficiary is rather defenseless and, whether by will or by circumstance, unable to contribute to the investment decisions happening around her. The trustee may not be the most astute financial decision-maker, but he is bound by stringent fiduciary obligation to act in the best interests of his beneficiary. If nothing else, the trustee is expected to be a strong advocate for the interests of the beneficiary.

Compare this to a future pension scheme. It is defined contribution and contract-based. Its members, ill-equipped for financial decision-making, bear the risk of poor investment performance. No mooney-spectacled gentleman trustee guards the interests of beneficiaries; they have a contractual relationship with their pension fund provider. Fiduciary obligation does not apply to the scheme providers. Instead, any obligations on behalf of the provider are outlined in the contract.

In a world where trustees are fading from relevance, fiduciary obligation is applied to a declining proportion of investment decision-makers and beneficiaries bear the risks of investment failure, how can the interests of beneficiaries best be protected? There are several options. The first is for regulatory

bodies such as the Pensions Regulator and the Financial Services Authority to expand their remit, and enter the wake left behind fiduciary obligation. This seems the most likely approach. Whether regulation can fully replace a famously flexible and beneficiary-centric set of obligations is, however, questionable. A second possibility is the extension of fiduciary obligation by the courts. Although courts have been willing to establish the existence of fiduciary obligation in new types of relationships in the past, this is by no means certain. If it did occur, it would arguably lead to a piecemeal application of standards of conduct throughout the investment industry. Finally, legislatures could decide to follow the US route, and enact legislation conferring fiduciary responsibility on providers of pension investment services, regardless of their legal providence and role along the investment chain.

Above all, it seems that fiduciary obligation has limited a limited future within the pension fund industry. It will continue to apply where it does currently, but future pension schemes are likely to increasingly be built outside the legal realms of fiduciary obligation. Pension scheme members of the future can expect a less paternalistic type of protection, and will be expected to be self-sufficient in advancing their own interests. Given the demonstrated weaknesses in beneficiary investment participation, to place the hopes of future beneficiary protection in the hands of beneficiaries themselves is to invite disappointment. Governments should bear in mind that the financial security of a whole society is at stake.

References

Akerlof, G. A. and R. J. Shiller. 2009. *Animal Spirits: How Human Psychology Drives the Economy, and Why it Matters for Global Capitalism.* Princeton University Press.

Anderson, S. 2006. *Investment Management and Mismanagement: History, Findings and Analysis.* New York: Springer.

Bray, J. 2012. *A Student's Guide to Equity and Trusts.* Cambridge University Press.

Byrne, A., K. Dowd, D. P. Blake and A. J. G. Cairns. 2007. "Default Funds in UK Defined-Contribution Pension Plans," *Financial Analysts Journal* 63: 40–51.

Carrera, L., C. Curry and N. Cleal. 2012. *Changing Landscape of Pension Schemes in the Private Sector in the UK*. London: Pensions Policy Institute.

CityUK. 2011. *Fund Management*. London: CityUK.

Clark, G. L. 2000. *Pension Fund Capitalism*. Oxford University Press.

Clark, G. L. and A. H. B. Monk. 2007. "The 'Crisis' in Defined Benefit Corporate Pension Liabilities Part II: Current Solutions and Future Prospects," *Pensions* 12: 68–81.

Clark, G. L. and R. Urwin. 2011. "DC Pension Fund Best-practice Design and Governance," *Benefits Quarterly* Fourth Quarter: 36–49.

Clark, G. L., E. Caerlewy-Smith and J. C. Marshall. 2006. "Pension Fund Trustee Competence: Decision-making in Problems Relevant to Investment Practice," *Journal of Pension and Economic Finance* 5: 91–110.

Cohen, N. 2012. "Record Deficit for Pension Funds in Red," *Financial Times*, January 10.

Dickens, C. 2008. *Our Mutual Friend*. Australia: Accessible Publishing Systems Pty Ltd.

FairPensions. 2011. *Protecting Our Best Interests: Rediscovering Fiduciary Obligation*. London: FairPensions.

Finn, P. D. 1977. *Fiduciary Obligations*. Sydney: Law Book Company.

Governmental Accounting Standards Board. 2012. "GASB Improves Pension Accounting and Financial Reporting Standards," press release 25 June.

Hudson, A. 2009. *Equity and Trusts*. London: Taylor and Francis.

Kahneman, D. and A. Tversky. 1979. "Prospect Theory: An Analysis of Decision Under Risk," *Econometrica* 47: 263–91.

Kay, J. 2012. *The Kay Review of UK Equity Markets and Long-Term Decision-Making: Final Report July 2012*. London: HM Government.

Keeton, W. P. 1936. "Fraud – Concealment and Non-disclosure," *Texas Law Review* 15: 1–40.

Langbein, J. H. 1996. "The Uniform Prudent Investor Act and the Future of Trust Investing," *Iowa Law Review* 81: 641–69.

2007. "Why Did Trust Law Become Statute Law in the United States?" *Alabama Law Review* 58: 1069–82.

Law Commission, 1992. "Fiduciary Duties and Regulatory Rules." Consultation Paper No 124.

Linzer, P. 1981. "On the Amorality of Contract Remedies – Efficiency, Equity and the Second Restatement," *Columbia Law Review* 81: 111–39.

Markowitz, H. M. 1952. "Portfolio Selection," *Journal of Finance* 7: 77–91.

1959. *Portfolio Selection: Efficient Diversification of Investments*. New York: Wiley.

Martin, J. E. 2005. *Hanbury and Martin: Modern Equity*, 17th edn. London: Thomson, Sweet and Maxwell.

McCrum, D. 2011. "Gap in US Pension Plans Hits $388 bn," *Financial Times*, September 5.

McCrum, D. and N. Bullock. 2012. "Funding Gap Doubles for US Corporate Pensions," *Financial Times*, January 2.

Munnell, A. H., J.-P. Aubry, J. Hurwitz, M. Medenica and L. Quinby. 2012a. "The Funding of State and Local Pensions: 2011–2015," *State and Local Pension Plans* 24: 1–14.

Munnell, A. H., J.-P. Aubry, J. Hurwitz and L. Quinby. 2012b. "How Would GASB Proposals Affect State and Local Pension Reporting?" Working Paper 2012–17, Center for Retirement Research at Boston College.

Pensions Regulator. 2007. *The Governance of Work-based Pension Schemes*. London: Pensions Regulator.

2011. *Enabling Good Member Outcomes in Work-based Pension Provision*. London: Pensions Regulator.

Redgrave, J. 2011. "Full Extent of LGPS Fund Value Fall Revealed," *Pensions Week*, May 9.

Richardson, B. R. 2008. *Socially Responsible Investment Law: Regulating the Unseen Polluters*. Oxford University Press.

Seetharaman, D. and B. Klayman. 2012. "GM to Cut about One-Fourth of US Pension Liability," *Reuters.com*, June 1.

United Nations Environment Programme Finance Initiative. 2005. *Fiduciary Responsibility: A Legal Framework for the Integration of Environmental, Social and Governance Issues into Institutional Investment*. Geneva: United Nations.

Woods, C. 2011. "Funding Climate Change: How Pension Fund Fiduciary Duty Masks Trustee Inertia and Short-termism," in J. Hawley, S. Kamath and A. T. Williams (eds.) *Corporate Governance Failures: The Role of Institutional Investors in the Global Financial Crisis*. Philadelphia: University of Pennsylvania Press, pp. 242–78.

PART III

Challenging conventional wisdom on fiduciary duty

CHAPTER
14

Is the search for excessive alpha a breach of fiduciary duty?

AARON BERNSTEIN AND JAMES P. HAWLEY

Introduction

Events of the past decade have challenged the efficient market hypothesis and the use of modern portfolio theory that is at its core as the basis for prudent investment and risk management practices. Accordingly, such questioning may – and we argue should – impact the legal framework governing pension fiduciaries. For example, it is now broadly accepted that most funds' returns come from general exposure to the market (beta) rather than seeking market benchmark outperformance strategies (alpha) (Ibbotson 2010).[1] This makes systemic market factors more critical to fiduciary responsibility. It also raises the question of whether large, highly diversified institutional "universal owners" should even attempt to employ alpha-seeking investment, or active management, as a major part of their portfolio (Hawley and Williams 2000). We argue that it is questionable at best and perhaps bad investment strategy at worst to devote significant resources to seeking above-market returns. Indeed, we suggest it raises questions about consistency with fiduciary obligations, since achieving alpha means besting the average return, which is a mathematical impossibility for the average investor. Additionally, alpha-seeking, if linked to leverage and/or use of derivatives, may contribute to systemic risk as well.[2]

Our argument is as follows: alpha, or active management, has been, among both practitioners and academics, used in two quite different ways. In much but not all academic theory it is defined as above-market (risk-adjusted) returns (RAR) within an asset class (e.g., equity, real estate). This typically involves active trading (that is, stock picking/asset picking and cross asset investments of various types) rather than indexation. Yet it has also been widely used to mean seeking above-average return across asset classes. That is, typically using various alternative, sometimes leveraged investments (e.g., private equity, hedge funds, commodities) to increase portfolio-wide returns. Indeed, since the financial crisis this has been a pronounced trend for many defined benefit plans, as we discuss below.

Complicating this dual meaning is the fact that institutional investors' alpha investments are often in various forms of hybrid ("alternative") investment through hedge funds and private equity vehicles.[3] Both of these may use various forms of derivatives and/or leverage to attempt to achieve "alpha." In so doing, there is an often extremely complex mix of investments across various asset classes, which raises the possibility that they are negating alpha within one asset class in order to achieve it in another. For example, if a private equity investment destroys (over time) the value of a previously held equity, it could hurt the overall portfolio's value.

Additionally, asset classes are far from neat, self-contained categories as in the previous example where a private equity or hedge fund investment in a takeover situation directly impacts equity investments held in a universal owner's portfolio. (A universal owner is a large, diversified intuitional

---

[1] While this concept is widely embraced by academics and market professionals, there remains a significant gap in practice. We suspect that many pension trustees would be hard pressed to explain the difference between alpha and beta in this context and that most continue to assess their managers in relation to benchmarks. See also Beyhaghi and Hawley (2013).

[2] We do not explore this element in this chapter. See Beyhaghi and Hawley (2013).

[3] CalPERs, for example, suggests that not all "excess return" is "alpha, it may be due to leverage, out of benchmark and factor exposure." They claim they want to seek only "true alpha" (Baggesen et al. 2012).

owner that owns a representative cross section of much of the "entire" economy; thereby internalizing some proportion of externalities[4] produced by the companies it owns.) The situation can be similar with debt or a hedge fund (which is highly leveraged) acting as a private equity investor or vice versa. Thus, even in relatively simple cases there may well be externality impacts on other investments within the same portfolio. To our knowledge such externality effects are typically not considered and accounted for in risk assessment or in calculating the interactive effects with a portfolio. We will use alpha in this chapter to mean active management. When "alpha" is used differently we will make note of this.

This confusion about the meaning of "alpha" is exemplified, especially in the pre-crisis decade (up to 2007), in the popularity of so-called portable alpha (PA). PA mostly makes use of leverage, shorting and derivatives strategies. "Alpha"-seeking in the case of PA is defined as assumed non-correlated assets (of any kind) that will, on a risk-adjusted basis, outperform a given benchmarked portfolio (across asset classes). It may be achieved by using active management techniques of all sorts, and be measured against a passive beta (market) index. The difference between PA and "traditional" hedge funds is in the eye of the beholder. PA is to be distinguished from alpha-seeking through active management (stock picking) by its use of leverage, shorting and derivatives of various types (Advisor Perspectives 2007). Callin and Jones (2009) make clear that what the various definitions of PA have in common is leverage and diversification "as a means to increase the return per unit of risk ... two of the key concepts that underlie modern portfolio theory."

Even apart from these considerations, there is the more straightforward problem of risk and net

costs for most institutional investors. As we discuss below, net costs over time eliminate most alpha gains and typically result in a net loss for the average institutional investor (French 2008).

Additionally, implementation of alpha strategies using hedge funds and/or private equity (or when hedged internally within an institution) may well contribute to systemic risk, especially when similar strategies are adopted by numerous large investors acting in unison in response to similar market forces. In this case systemic risk is due to herding, with many or most players taking parallel and similar actions in the market. Thus, such alpha-seeking may contribute to destroying value across an entire portfolio, which could partially or even entirely offset any net gains that may be achieved under even the most optimistic assumptions and conditions. One example can be found in the periodic bubbles that erupt in stock markets. Investors all chase rapidly rising stocks long past levels that can be justified by economic fundamentals, leading to the inevitable collapse that destroys value across the market.

Alpha: definitions and practices

Although the term alpha has only become widespread in recent years, for decades investors have embraced the practice of active management, or stock-picking strategies intended to beat market averages after factoring in risk. The concept came under serious assault in the 1960s when economists such as Eugene Fama and Paul Samuelson introduced the efficient-market hypothesis. It holds that, in markets with full and free information flows, prices constantly adjust to new data. As a result, it is extremely difficult to achieve investment returns in excess of market averages, on a risk-adjusted basis over time. These insights spawned generations of index funds whose aim is to match market returns rather than best them. French's argument cited above (2008) is very much in this vein.

However, the efficient market idea has not stopped the proliferation of alpha-seeking investment strategies, which are offered by asset managers and mutual funds across virtually every asset class. This is due, at least in part, to the fact

---

[4] An externality is a positive or negative effect on a third party not directly involved in the economic activity between a hypothetical producer and buyer of that product for which there is an explicit or implicit contract. Externalities are of two types: pecuniary and non-pecuniary. The former has a direct monetary cost (e.g., pollution of a river's impact on downstream users), while the latter has a real, but non-monetary cost (e.g., the cost to the long-term growth of an economy using child labor (therefore undereducating its labor force).

(as compared to the idea) that markets are either not efficient, or are weakly efficient, allowing for alpha-seeking. Indeed, with a weak or non-existent efficient market, some investors will achieve alpha. The key point is that is the average institutional investor will not and especially will not over time: for every average winner there will be an equal set of losers. We elaborate this dynamic below.

The basic idea of alpha is relatively straightforward: how much can a fund outperform a relative benchmark, such as a market index, theoretically on a risk-adjusted basis *but often in practice not risk-adjusted* (Evans 2006: 14).[5] Typically it is defined as a fund's excess return over a given market benchmark after factoring in the fund's beta, or its risk relative to the benchmark's risk (Lo 2007).

Advocates of alpha rely on the same basic argument, explicitly or otherwise: while it may be difficult to outperform allegedly efficient markets over the longer term, it has been done, as real markets are often less than efficient. Managers routinely cite data to back up their claim, arguing that their particular approach – a technical model, theoretical insights, better than average information, etc. – gives them an edge over the market. Berkshire Hathaway's Warren Buffet is often held up as an example of an investor who has outperformed over decades, which offers anecdotal but compelling evidence that markets can be beat with the right approach. Yet by citing outliers to support what is allegedly possible this argument ignores the very fact that they *are* outliers. (Indeed, Buffet's investment style is in some part based on long-term, strategic buyouts of entire firms, a type of private equity or merchant bank approach. It is not stock-picking. We return to this point below.)

Regardless of whether and how an individual fund manager can generate alpha, the question that remains is whether fiduciaries of large institutional investors can or should devote significant portions of their portfolios to active management. Lost in the debate is the compelling fact that, in any given market, the average return is composed of the aggregate returns of all investors holding positions in it. For a defined period such as a year, investor performance falls into three groups. Some will have no net (after expense) gain or loss. Others will have enjoyed above-average gains – i.e., alpha – either by strategy or luck. The third group includes all that came through with net losses. The market average is the average of all investors' performance; it is a relative measure.[6] By definition, the total alpha achieved by the second group must be offset by an equal amount of below-average returns by the third group. That, of course, is how an average is defined, as the average of all gains and losses. It is therefore a zero-sum game, since any alpha enjoyed by one investor is offset by an equal loss of other investors. Because the average investor cannot outperform the average investor, the average investor cannot achieve alpha.

The conclusion is even worse once active management costs are factored in. As French argues, after aggregate costs, "active investors [seeking 'alpha'] are playing a negative sum game" (French 2008: 1538).[7] The findings from French (and others, see below) are of special significance to large universal owners, as their portfolio typically encompasses many elements of various externalities of all types (so-called "social costs" of economic behavior). One such cost is the cost society bears, the extra costs expended, to beat the market, as French argues. While neither he, nor to our knowledge others, have attempted to estimate

---

[5] Alpha is typically calculated against a benchmark, such as the S&P 500, on a risk-adjusted basis. Yet benchmarking returns against an artificial group of investments raises the question of whether this is tied to the beneficiaries' interests and goals, as fiduciary law requires an explicit evaluation of how practices are linked to beneficiaries. It does so because alpha (however defined) is based on increasing challenged theoretical constructs, modern portfolio theory in particular.

[6] This does not imply that there cannot be absolute gains, which are spread across the universe of all investors. In this sense, it can be (costs excluded) a nonzero-sum game. This is another way of stating the beta of the market reflects (over time) the real state of the economy.

[7] It should be clear that markets need active investors in order to facilitate price discovery: a market composed of only passive investors is not a market. The question of whether (and if so, where) there is a tipping point is beyond the scope of this chapter. French estimates the "social cost" of price discovery/active investing between 1980 and 2006 in the US was 0.67 percent of the value of the NYSE, Amex and NASDAQ (French 2008: 1538). Put differently, assuming a 6.7 percent real return in this period, price discovery was about 10 percent of the market's current value.

or measure the costs to universal owners, some of these costs logically must be incorporated in their portfolios, as typically such large investors use multiple "styles" of investment. These costs are in addition to whatever fees they will pay for their own active investment as such.

All investors cannot be above average

Is it rational for a pension fund fiduciary to assume he or she is above average, and if so, why? This poses a difficult challenge for the fiduciary investor that has been largely ignored. A reasonable interpretation of the prudent investor rule would hold that fiduciaries should assume that their investment strategies are likely to produce average results in a world in which everyone has access to the same information. The exception is unless they have specifically determined there is compelling evidence to the contrary of the particular skills they bring to the task. While many asset managers will claim this, we emphasize "compelling evidence," which would exclude, for example, several quarters or even more of above-average "abnormal" risk-adjusted returns. Of course, any particular investor can outperform the average. But most investors have the option of adopting alpha strategies offered by managers, and a majority of them actually adopt one or more of them. Yet in doing so, each assumes they can outperform a majority of other investors with similar strategies, even though that is a mathematical impossibility for investors as a whole. *Prima facie*, this would seem to be an imprudent investment assumption. By definition, average investors cannot achieve alpha over long time periods, as we discuss below. Thus, is it reasonable to make investment decisions on the assumption that they can?

This perspective casts a new light on how a fiduciary should approach active management. From the standpoint of the average investor, alpha-seeking may not make sense as a strategy adopted for a majority of its portfolio. Instead, it is a gamble that that one investor can find a strategy that many other investors have not found or used properly. Such risk-taking might make sense for perhaps 5 or 10 percent of a fund's assets that could be invested in speculative ventures without incurring significant damage if they fail. But it would seem imprudent to devote significantly more, to say nothing of the majority of a fund's assets, to a strategy doomed to fail for the average investor.

Yet that is exactly what fiduciaries have done in recent decades. More than 69 percent of the domestic equity investments of defined-benefit US pension funds of all sizes are devoted to active management, with the residual invested in passive indices, according to a study by Bauer et al. (2010). They also found 56 percent active management among US defined-contribution funds. They note that these results likely underestimate total active management, because "the passively managed investments could include 'enhanced' index funds and could potentially further profit from stock lending programs (however, we lack more precise information on this)" (ibid.).

These findings exclude non-equity investments of the kind often used by alpha-seekers using alternative strategies. Other data show significant asset allocation here as well. For example, the largest US public pension funds (those with assets over $5 billion) have an average of nearly 27 percent of their portfolios devoted just to alternative investments, such as private-equity and hedge funds, while the ten largest have 21 percent in alternative investments (Corkery 2013).

The zero-sum/negative sum nature of alpha can too often be obscured by the short-term nature of most investing. Indeed, for those not achieving alpha in a given time period, alpha is a negative sum game after fees. Many investors outperform the market average in any given year. But very few do so every year.[8] As a result, a majority of investors can achieve alpha at some point, prompting asset owners and managers alike to believe that they could do so more consistently if they just chose the correct alpha strategy. So the response to a string of losing years is not to recognize that alpha is a zero-sum game, but to change alpha strategies. Even those that should be long-term investors such as public pension funds and other retirement

[8] There is a large literature on active manager's historic failure to beat market averages. One recent summary of findings applied to mutual funds is Petajisto (2013).

vehicles (e.g., 401(k)s in the US) often embrace this logic. Despite their multi-decade stewardship obligations, funds still face tremendous pressure to meet annual, if not quarterly, investment targets. Alpha strategies are seen as a key element in doing so, particularly when market averages turn sharply negative as they did in 2008; or when equity markets stagnate, as they did from 2001 to 2008. This prompts funds to devote an even larger share of assets to alpha-seeking (see, for example, O'Hara 2005).

A small case in point: information and first-mover effects for ESG

ESG is the shorthand for environmental, social and governance factors that are or may be material to a firm's value in the future. Often called "extra-financial" factors they are, more accurately, "not yet recognized as financial" by "markets." Aside from the average investor problem discussed above, there is an important point regarding information and knowledge, which is raised by the efficient market hypothesis. This theory in its various forms (e.g., weak or strong) posits that while access to relevant information may for a (brief) moment enable above-market gains, such gains will be temporary as they will be arbitraged away, typically very rapidly. Yet these formulations typically ignore that it is not "information" as such that enables this form of temporary alpha, but rather how the information is understood, that is, how it becomes knowledge and then "accepted knowledge." When there is widely accepted knowledge, it becomes part of market price.

An example is provided by one study that suggests ESG factors were alpha factors in the 1990s, but by the early twenty-first century the market as a whole recognized and incorporated ESG analysis into valuation, thereby eliminating its above-market "alpha" value. Borgers et al. (2012) conclude:

[There is] moderate evidence that errors in investors' expectations explain abnormal returns on ES(G) portfolios in the 90s, [although the] evidence is not pervasive across all dimensions of stakeholder relations. [Additionally, the] evidence of association between information and abnormal

returns, and earnings announcement returns, if any, has decreased over time.

That is to say, once alpha information became "common market knowledge" it was priced into the market valuation; which reverted to the mean.

There is nothing surprising in this development. Since markets are in fact less than efficient, either arbitrageurs or those recognizing mispricing (environmental and social in this case) due to lack of knowledge (but not information) will seek and find temporary gains. There are first-mover effects. But once those effects are offset, a tipping point is reached so that the gains decrease and eventually revert to the mean, at which point seeking alpha again becomes a zero (or potentially negative) sum game since environmental and social knowledge routinely becomes incorporated into price.

The search for alpha, whether in the ESG example above or in the more complex (and risky) portable alpha varieties, poses a basic problem: as more and more funds seek alpha using similar strategies there tends to be reversion to the mean, at which point if the correlation is high enough what is achieved is beta, but at higher levels of both cost and risk. It becomes perverse once first-mover effects cease.

Active and activist investors and the 'alpha' search

An important exception to our argument involves so-called, but sometimes misnamed, "alpha"-seeking strategies aimed at altering a specific company's business strategy, structure or behavior. Investors such as corporate governance and private equity funds typically attempt to achieve "alpha" by increasing a firm's profits and hence its market value through various forms of engagement with, or in the case of private equity, possible takeover of, the firm. They often are referred to as activist investors because they attempt to actively intervene in or engage with a company's governance to reshape its competitive position. Governance funds often engage a company's board and/or management to persuade them to adopt a new approach intended to boost performance. They might buy a significant ownership position as part of the engagement. Private equity funds go a step further and purchase the entire company, then change management or the strategy in an attempt to lift its performance. Short of taking the company private, however, all investors share gains (or losses), they are free-riders, meaning that this is not truly "alpha," but rather a means to enhance beta.[9] Yet even if a company is taken private, typically it (or part of it) is returned to the market *within five years*, although there is significant variation, ranging between 3.9 and 4.9 years during 2006 to 2011. This is what could be called delayed beta enhancement if indeed value is increased, which is far from always the case (Prequin 2011).

Thus, there is a world of difference between active investors and activist ones, despite the linguistic similarity of the terms. The former are called active because they buy and sell specific stocks that they believe will perform best. They may also engage in complex trading strategies involving hedging and leverage. They are defined in opposition to passive investors who do not engage in active trading. Instead, they either purchase all stocks in a given market and hold them for longer periods, or buy select companies and hold them long term. (Exchange-traded index funds have muddied the waters somewhat by allowing investors to actively trade holdings in entire markets.)

From the perspective of activist investing, active investors actually should be considered to be acting passively. They trade based on how they believe a company will perform, without attempting to intervene in how it is run. Active investors stand outside the company and passively accept the business strategy pursued by management and the board. They achieve their alpha aims if the stocks they choose or if the strategies they select outperform their benchmarks, but they make no effort to influence the company's potential to do so.[10]

Activist investors, by contrast, attempt to alter a company's course in the hopes that doing so will improve its performance. They use various forms of engagement, including corporate governance, to effect corporate change. Of course, such efforts may fail. Activists may not persuade management and the board to change course. Or the new strategy they advocate may not succeed. But activists are not making passive bets that a particular choice of stocks will outperform the market average; they are attempting to reshape a company to improve its performance. In doing so they may achieve increased value using fundamentally different tactics than an active investor. But this is not alpha, which entails beating the market. Rather activist investing, if successful, lifts the market as a whole, albeit incrementally. If a company's shares would have gained 10 percent in a given year and intervention by an activist lifts that to 15 percent, the market average is that much larger than it would have been.

As a result, seeking misnamed "alpha" through activist investing does not pose the fundamental challenge to fiduciaries that active (stock-picking and a host of hedging strategies) investing does. Because activists can achieve alpha in a way that also lifts the market average as a whole, they are not attempting something that cannot be done by the average investor. At least in principle it is possible to improve the performance of every company, so theoretically any or perhaps even every investor could engage in activist misnamed "alpha"-seeking. Such improvement also may be beneficial beyond the target firm in that it can have demonstrations effects over time, creating value at other companies as well.

Of course, activist investing is restricted to a relatively small share of any investor's portfolio. Even the largest funds can only attempt to change a handful of companies, and investing too much in individual stocks remains riskier than holding

---

[9] See Dimson et al. (2012), wherein it is argued that the two most salient "alpha-seeking" engagement issues have been governance and climate change. Yet as engagement involved tiny, albeit powerful, groups of activist investors, "alpha" was shared by the whole market (a point the authors do not make). That is it was not alpha but increased beta. See also Gilson and Gordon (2013).

[10] A caveat is that to the degree that a company's management receives and acts on market signals (e.g., shorting its stock; significant price declines) "acting passively" can and has affected business strategy and behavior.

indices. Still, activism as part of a diversified port-folio can stand up to a robust interpretation of fidu-ciary duty in ways that active investing cannot.

For example, one closely studied activist port-folio bears out this analysis. In 1999, the California Public Employees' Retirement System (CalPERS) initiated what it calls a Focus List. Over the sub-sequent eleven years, CalPERS targeted a total of 169 companies whose shares lagged relevant indi-ces due to perceived corporate governance prob-lems. The fund then engaged with management to seek governance improvements. Overall, "the average engaged company produced excess returns of 17.08% above the Russell 1000 index," accord-ing to an external review done for CalPERS by Wilshire associates last year (CalPERS 2012: 5). Of course, those gains accrued to all other inves-tors owning shares of these companies.

Costs and risks

Let us consider in more detail some of the costs and risks focused on two of the alpha-seeking strategies discussed above: "simple" stock-picking and cross asset allocation, hedging and trading. Utilizing a database of most (but not all) of the largest US, Canadian and a few European pen-sion (defined benefit) funds, Andonov et al. (2012) reported that in the period under study (2000–10) fully 80 percent of the funds had 80 percent of their assets in active mandates. From these investments they report that there was an "alpha" (not their term) of 25 basis points (that is, 0.25 percent). But after costs are included there was a net loss due primarily to the necessity to rebalance the port-folio across asset classes. Had those investments been entirely in passive categories the costs would have been 5.67 basis points compared to the actual costs of 45.22 basis points for the active mandates (Andonov et al. 2012: 5).[11] Between 2000 and 2010 pension fund investment costs rose from 31 basis

points to 55 basis points due to the growth of alter-native investments allocations. By 2010 alternative asset allocation among those pension funds studies was about 16 percent of total assets. The study con-cludes that: "Our results thus suggest that pension funds, and especially the larger funds, would have done better if they invested in passive mandates without frequent rebalancing across asset classes" (Andonov et al. 2012: 25).

In general, externally managed defined benefit plans with active mandates have higher costs than internally managed ones. Of particular interest is that smaller funds outperform larger ones in active management, although most of them are externally managed. This is likely, the study concludes, due to smaller funds' greater nimbleness and a greater concentration in small cap equity. Yet the average size of the smaller funds was only $4.2 billion. Bauer et al. (2010) note that, "[t]he sheer size of the largest fund might make active management more complicated."[12] They provide two possible explanations for this apparently odd discrepancy. In the case of small cap investments, managers' skill may play a role that cannot happen with larger cap investments, in which larger funds, due to their very size, tend to concentrate. Additionally, the authors find that smaller funds are somewhat more liquid than larger funds enabling greater and more successful use of tactical asset allocation.

While there is some evidence, as briefly dis-cussed above, that small and more liquid defined benefit pension funds can generate alpha, large funds (in one study, "large" being those over $10 billion in assets) have huge problems "beating the market." The majority of funds in defined benefit plans are held in large plans, although there are far more small plans (Andonov et al. 2012: 5). When expenses and risk adjustment are taken into account (not just benchmark comparisons, which is typic-ally often how performance is measured) one study concludes, similarly to French's 2008 study cited above, that "pension funds benefit from simultan-eously investing in multiple asset classes, but would do better (after costs and on average) if they would

---

[11] The authors also note that funds that used internal manag-ers had a 5.4 basis points lower costs than funds that used external managers, due to a combination of lower internal costs and high agency costs for external managers (Andonov et al. 2012: 21).

[12] Small funds are in their great majority actively man-aged, while larger funds have greater allocation in passive mandates.

have invested exclusively in passive mandates without frequent rebalancing across asset classes" (Andonov et al. 2012: 6). The study concludes that large pension funds would have been better off had they invested in passive mandates rather than in frequent rebalancing across asset classes in a vain attempt to beat the market (ibid.: 25).[13]

Why have large institutional investors opted to invest so much of their portfolios in some form of alpha-seeking despite all the evidence about its risk and low probability of success? There are multiple factors at play. Perhaps the most basic may be that over the decades an entire industry of asset managers has developed, which exists solely to sell them such products. When alpha services are marketed by the vast majority of professional managers in every global market, it is difficult for asset owners to maintain that the entire approach should be confined to a small portion of their portfolio devoted to speculative investment.

This environment also has bred a culture in which alpha has become central to the careers of in-house professionals at asset owners. With every fund attempting to beat the market, it has become the norm to tie compensation and career advancement to market-beating metrics. What is typically overlooked in this competition is what should be the underlying metric and lodestone, the purpose of the fund, of the fiduciary duty of loyalty to the beneficiary.

The problem has been exacerbated at many US public pension funds by the politics that affect the use of their assets – something over which the professional managers typically have little or no control or even input. For several decades, stakeholders such as politicians, unions and retiree groups have often urged funds to spend assets during bull markets. When stock markets jump by double digits, benefits are raised and tax contributions to the funds are lowered, suspended or kept below inflation. Then the inevitable bear market hits and the funds find themselves in deficit. At that point their

officials face tremendous pressure to make their assumed rates of return in order to meet the pension promise and/or to avoid hiving off the burden to tax payers. Adopting or maintaining a passive investment strategy when markets are flat or negative is politically very challenging and sometimes untenable.

One example where many of these factors may have come into play is at CalPERS. It pursued "alpha" aggressively during the US housing market boom of the 2000s, lifting the share of its assets invested in real estate from 5 percent in 2005 to 9.2 percent in 2008 (Ang and Kjaer 2012).[14]

CalPERS incurred heavy losses when the housing market collapsed, which were compounded by other alpha-seeking practices that failed along with the stock market as well, such as stock lending. The resulting liquidity crisis forced the fund to sell equities at the bottom of the market to meet its obligations. Equities shrank from 60 percent of CalPERS' portfolio in 2007 to 44 percent in 2009, causing it to miss some of the market rebound, which started early that year (Jacobius 2012; Mendel 2010; Whelan and Karmin 2012).

Conclusions

Our conclusion is that the excessive emphasis on achieving alpha, in particular by means of active stock picking and the use of various forms of leveraged investment vehicles, that characterizes much of institutional investment today is incompatible with a clear understanding of fiduciary duty. Because alpha represents a goal unachievable by a majority of investors, those with fiduciary duties should pursue it with a prudently small portion of their portfolios. Other forms of what is sometimes referred to as alpha-seeking, such as direct investment in infrastructure projects, either managed in-house with the proper expertise or contracted to third-party management, is not in fact alpha-seeking at all, but rather an entirely different form of investment that may produce returns above equity market returns. For example, the Canadian Ontario

[13] The authors note that when alpha was achieved it was due to strategic asset allocation and market timing (tactical asset allocation) rather than from either security selection (stock picking) or identifying "superior active managers for given asset classes" (Andonov et al. 2012: 18). See Andonov et al. (2012: 20) for risk adjustment discussion.

[14] Large funds are defined at those with assets over $5 billion.

Municipal Employees Retirement System's long-term goal is to have 47 percent of its assets in private market investment. A focus on asset class investment represents an important and interesting alternative to the "standard model" based on modern portfolio theory and its derivatives (Falconer 2013). The principle underlying this type of approach is that it is possible to target capital, balancing public and private markets (under the control and definition of a fiduciary), in effect making the investment institution look something like a merchant bank. This type of investment focuses on long-term, intergenerational return, clearly directed to the interests and goals of beneficiaries and retirement investors.

Widespread adoption of a conservative posture toward alpha would drastically reduce the amount of active management in the US and other markets. But it would by no means eliminate it. Fiduciaries would still pursue alpha on a smaller scale. In addition, there are many non-fiduciary asset owners for whom alpha-seeking can make good sense, such as those with shorter-term horizons and those willing to accept large risk. Alpha-seeking plays an important role in providing price discovery and liquidity that would not be threatened by a market in which passive investment became the norm rather than the exception. But it should not serve to confuse those institutional investors charged with securing the retirement benefits and investments of individuals to whom there is a strict and clear-cut fiduciary duty.

Acknowledgements

We wish to thank Keith Johnson and Ed Waitzer for their criticisms and suggestions.

References

Advisor Perspectives. 2007. "The Alpha-Beta Chowder: Understanding Portfolio Risk and Return." www.advisorperspectives.com/pdf/newsltr21–2.pdf.

Andonov, A., R. Bauer and M. Cremers. 2012. "Can Large Pension Funds Beat the Market?" September. http://papers.ssrn.com/sol3/papers.cfm?abstract_id=1885536.

Ang, A. and K. Kjaer. 2012. "Investing for the Long Run," January 5. http://papers.ssrn.com/sol3/papers.cfm?abstract_id=1976310.

Baggesen, E., D. Bienvenue and J. Cole. 2012. "Global Equity Education Workshop," September 10. www.calpers.ca.gov/eid-docs/about/board-cal-agenda/agendas/invest/201209/workshop-item01–01.pdf.

Bauer, R. M. M. J., K. J. Martijn Cremers and R. G. P. Frehen. 2010. "Pension Fund Performance and Costs: Small is Beautiful," April 29. http://papers.ssrn.com/sol3/papers.cfm?abstract_id=965388.

Beyhaghi, M. and J. P. Hawley. 2013. "Modern Portfolio Theory and Risk Management: Assumptions and Unintended Consequences," *Journal of Sustainable Finance and Investment* 3(1): 17–37.

Borgers, A., J. Derwall, K. Koedijk and J. Ter Horst. 2012. "On Errors in Expectations and Learning," presentation at BSI Gamma Conference, "The Future of Socially Responsible Investment," Zurich, February 1. www.corporateengagement.com/files/publication/ECCE%20Presention%20on%20ESG%20and%20Learning.pdf.

Callin, S. and S. Jones. 2009. "The Future of Portable Alpha." www.indexuniverse.com/publications/journalofindexes/joi-articles/6044-the-future-of-portable-alpha.html.

CalPERS. 2012. "Investment Committee Agenda: Global Corporate Governance Update." www.calpers.ca.gov/eip-docs/about/board-cal-agenda/agendas/invest/201211/item09a-03.pdf.

Corkery, M. 2013. "Pensions Bet Big With Private Equity," *Wall Street Journal*, January 24.

Dimson, E., O. Karakaş and X. Li. 2012. "Active Ownership," September 30. http://ssrn.com/abstract=2154724.

Evans, R. B. 2006. "Does Alpha Really Matter? Evidence from Mutual Fund Incubation, Termination and Manager Change," June 15. www.darden.virginia.edu/web/uploadedFiles/Darden/Faculty_Research/Directory/Full_time/do_mf_risk_adjust.pdf.

Falconer, K. 2013. "OMERS Private Equity Drives Pension Fund's Returns," PEHub Canada. www.pehub.com/187917/omers-private-equity-drives-pension-funds-returns.

French, K. R. 2008. "Presidential Address: The Costs of Active Investing," *The Journal of Finance* LXIII (4): 1537–73.

Gilson, R. J. and J. N. Gordon. 2013. "The Agency Costs of Agency Capitalism: Activist Investors and the Revaluation of Governance Rights," January 29. http://papers.ssrn.com/sol3/papers.cfm?abstract_id=2206391.

Hawley, J. P. and A. T. Williams. 2000. *The Rise of Fiduciary Capitalism*. Philadelphia: University of Pennsylvania Press.

Ibbotson, R. 2010. "The Importance of Asset Allocation," *Financial Analysts Journal* 66: 18.

Jacobius, A. 2012. "How CalPERS' Strategy Backfired," *Pensions and Investments*, December 28. www.pionline.com/article/20091228/PRINTSUB/312289983.

Lo, A. W. 2007. "Where Do Alphas Come From? A New Measure of the Value of Active Investment Management," May 8. http://papers.ssrn.com/sol3/papers.cfm?abstract_id=985127.

Mendel, E. 2010. "How CalPERS Bet Big on Real Estate and Lost." http://calpensions.com/2010/04/30/how-calpers-bet-big-on-real-estate-and-lost.

O'Hara, N. 2005. "Portable Alpha: A Case Study," *Futures Industry*. www.futuresindustry.org/downloads/fimag/septoct/sept-oct_portalpha.pdf.

Petajisto, A. 2013. "Active Share and Mutual Fund Performance," January 15. http://papers.ssrn.com/sol3/papers.cfm?abstract_id=1685942.

Prequin. 2011. "Average Holding Period for Buyouts and Public to Private Deals Exited since 2006." www.preqin.com/blog/101/4103/holding-periods-for-buyouts.

Whelan, R. and C. Karmin. 2012. "CalPERS Downsizes Housing Portfolio," *The Wall Street Journal*, January 28. http://online.wsj.com/article/SB1000142405297020373530457716727356706994.html.

CHAPTER 15

Fiduciary duty and sin stocks: is vice really nice?

ANDREAS G. F. HOEPNER AND STEFAN ZEUME

Introduction

Based on a conservative interpretation of fiduciary duty, pension funds are considered to arrive at investment decisions purely based on the financial performance of the underlying assets. Hence, whatever the real world implications of the asset, trustees following this view are legally obliged to invest as long as the expected returns in financial markets are abnormally high (Entine 2005; Munnel and Sundén 2005; Rounds 2005). Practically, this means that they have to speculate with soft commodities and thereby potentially drive basic food prices so high that the poorest on this planet can barely afford two meals a day. More paradoxically, a pension fund representing health care workers is legally obliged to invest substantially in alcohol, tobacco or gambling companies, so called "sin stocks," should they be associated with an abnormally high return. Even the Freshfields Report, a rather liberal interpretation of the constraints that fiduciary duty imposes on pension funds aiming to consider social criteria in their decision-making, can hardly be interpreted as recommendation to ignore financially well-performing stocks on moral grounds. Its most liberal conclusion is that social criteria may be considered by pension funds if they do no financial harm, which effectively prohibits underweighting or excluding well-performing sin stocks (Freshfields Bruckhaus Deringer 2005).[1]

Hence, the question is, can undesirable assets such as soft commodities or sin stocks reasonably be expected to experience an abnormally good financial performance? While we are not aware of such evidence for soft commodities, there is a very prominent academic study finding portfolios of sin stocks to have a superior financial performance: Hong and Kacperczyk (2009). This study has been discussed in various mainstream media sources such as *Financial Times*, *Forbes*, Reuters or the *Wall Street Journal*. As a result, pension funds are in a dilemma: many stakeholders – although not necessarily all members – put pension funds under considerable pressure to act with a social consciousness, while the mainstream media celebrates sin stocks for their financial performance and hence fiduciary duty obliges them to invest in these over-proportionally.

While this dilemma appears tragic, it is not necessary definitive, as Hong and Kacperczyk (2009) – as well as all other studies documenting a strong financial performance of sin stocks – analyzed hypothetical investment portfolios created by the researchers instead of actual investment funds specializing in sin stocks (see, for example, Salaber 2009; Statman and Glushkov 2009; Lobe and Walkshäusl 2011). This means that the researchers enjoyed the benefit of hindsight in their security selection, which real world investment managers do not. While this research method is completely legitimate and, in fact, we employ it frequently ourselves, it is important to remember that it can only highlight investment opportunities. Whether real world investment managers are able to capitalize on these opportunities, however, is a separate question. This separate question is the crucial one for pension funds. If the managers specializing in sin stocks can outperform, pension funds face a big dilemma. If the managers, however, cannot outperform, then pension funds do not need to worry about their fiduciary duty to appreciate sin stocks.

[1] The only exception from this reasoning is a clear consensus among all beneficiaries that would allow to exclude or underweight well performing sin stocks. Such a clear consensus, however, is practically hard to achieve and potentially even harder to defend in court (Freshfields Bruckhaus Deringer 2005).

The first indication that a real world capitalization on the sin stock effect found by academics is harder than one might think is implied by the simple number of sin mutual funds worldwide: in other words, there are more academic studies finding an effect than fund managers aiming to exploit it, which is puzzling. It raises the question why some of the academics did not aim to set up a sin investment fund themselves, if they believed strongly in their findings, as Hong and Kacperczyk communicated via various media sources. In any case, it seems rather important from a pension fund perspective to undertake a rigorous and robust analysis of this one sin stocks focused investment fund, called the "Vice Fund."

To date, only one published analysis of the Vice Fund exists, which found the Vice Fund to significantly outperform its conventional benchmark (Chong et al. 2006). However, Chong et al. (2006) estimate the Vice Fund's financial performance only over three years and neither control for its investment style nor its exposure to the excess legal risk of tobacco stocks. Hence, a sophisticated analysis of the Vice Fund's financial attractiveness is clearly needed to inform pension funds.

We pursue this in-depth analysis and thereby aim to contribute to the academic literature as well as the professional responsible investment debate. We find Chong et al.'s (2006) result to be an artifact of their simplistic approach. Once we double their sample period, control for small stock exposure or control for exposure to tobacco stocks' excess legal risk, the Vice Fund does not significantly outperform its conventional benchmark anymore. This finding is robust to the inclusion of further (time varying) Carhart (1997) control variables and a variation in the market benchmark.

Interestingly, we observe the Vice Fund's asset selection and market timing skills not to be financially appealing. Even worse, we find the Vice Fund's managers to possess significantly value-destructing directional trading and crisis management skills. Consequently, the existing vice investment product can currently not be recommended from a financial perspective and does not seem to impose a sin stock-driven fiduciary duty dilemma on pension funds.

We organize our analysis as follows. The second section analyzes the existing literature. The third and fourth sections describe our data sample and research methods, respectively. We provide sufficient technical detail to allow replication but emphasize the rationales of our research methods to offer an intuitive understanding to the non-technical reader. Sections five and six discuss the results of our main analyses and robustness tests, respectively, before section seven concludes.

Literature review

Hong and Kacperczyk (2009) find sin stocks to generate significantly positive abnormal monthly returns against comparable non-sinful stocks. Their finding is based on equal weighted portfolios of 193 sinful North American and European alcohol, defense, gambling and tobacco stocks over the period from 1965 to 2006 and is robust to a selection of control factors and sensitivity analyses. While Hong and Kacperczyk find tobacco stocks' (excess) litigation risk to explain their findings somewhat, they consider the primary theoretical explanation of their results to be (especially institutional) investor negligence of sin stocks as a result of social norms. This negligence depresses sin stocks' share price, which can fairly be expected to lead *ceteris paribus* to an abnormally high dividend yield.

However, Hong and Kacperczyk's results do not imply that existing more responsible investment approaches are necessarily, on average, financially less attractive than sin investment for three reasons. First, generating value-weighted portfolios of 158 alcohol, tobacco and gambling stocks from eighteen European countries over a period of more than twenty-five years, Salaber (2009) finds sin portfolios to result in significantly positive abnormal returns against non-sin stocks in countries with a high litigation risk and excise taxation on tobacco but not in low risk and excise taxation countries. Her excise taxation results appear particularly strong, as they are robust to controls for litigation risk and religious beliefs about sin. This implies that investors require an excess return from (at least) tobacco sin stocks for their excess legal, especially taxation related, risk which is simply not yet incorporated in abnormal return estimation procedures such as the Fama and French (1993) or Carhart (1997) model employed by Salaber (2009) or Hong and Kacperczyk (2009), respectively. As Salaber's (2009) results sufficiently explain the significantly positive abnormal returns of tobacco stocks as reward for excess risk, potential tobacco portfolios are unlikely more attractive from a financial return for risk perspective than existing conventional or responsible funds. However, her results do not substantially explain the significantly positive abnormal returns of alcohol and gambling stocks documented by Hong and Kacperczyk (2009) as well as Luck and Tigrani (1994).

Second, besides legal risk, the significantly positive abnormal returns of sin portfolios appear to be substantially driven by equal weighting rather than value weighting a portfolio's assets. Analyzing up to 3,000 US companies over more than fifteen years, Statman and Glushkov (2009) closely replicate Hong and Kacperczyk's (2009) finding, as they observe equal weighted portfolios of alcohol, defense, firearms, gambling, nuclear and tobacco companies to generate significantly positive abnormal returns against non-sin stocks in most of their estimation specifications. However, value weighting their portfolios leads all significant results to vanish. In similar settings, Galema et al. (2009) and Lobe and Walkshäusl (2011) find value-weighted sin stock portfolios to experience no significantly positive abnormal returns against the market benchmark, whereas at least Lobe and Walkshäusl's equal weighted portfolios which include gambling stocks outperform the market benchmark. These results imply that an abnormally strong performance of overweighted small stocks and a lower performance of underweighted large cap stocks might drive their results instead of the sin characteristics. While Hong and Kacperczyk control for a small cap or large cap tilt of their portfolios economy wide, they do not control for a small cap tilt specifically among sin stocks despite Statman and Glushkov's results, which clearly imply that small cap sin stocks and equal weighted portfolios perform unusually and unjustifiably well. A small cap instead of sin driven result would be quite conceivable, since the general tendency of small stocks to outperform large

stocks is well documented (e.g., Banz 1981; Fama and French 1993). Nevertheless, Salaber (2009) finds value weighted sin portfolios to result in significantly positive abnormal returns. Hence, equal weighting inflates significantly positive abnormal returns to sin stocks, but cannot, on its own, fully explain their existence in all studies.

The third reason that Hong and Kacperczyk's (2009) and similar findings do not imply that existing more responsible investment products are necessarily, on average, financially inferior to sin investment, derives from the fact that their findings are based on potential rather than existing sin investment products. Potential responsible investment products have also been found to deliver significantly positive abnormal returns (Derwall et al. 2005; Kempf and Osthoff 2007; Edmans 2011; Dimson et al. 2012). But the average existing responsible investment fund or index failed to release this potential (Bauer et al. 2005; Kreander et al. 2005; Scholtens 2007; Schröder 2007). Our comparison of previous analyses of potential sin investment products unveiled drivers of sin stock performance. However, we can only test if pension funds' fiduciary duty puts them into a sin stock dilemma by studying the only existing sin investment product: USA MUTUALS' Vice Fund.

The Vice Fund was launched end of August 2002 as a non-diversified fund. It disapproves social criteria by concentrating its commitment to 80 percent equity investment predominantly on US alcohol, aerospace, defense, gambling and tobacco stocks.[2] It remains the only sin investment product, since the publicly announced plan of a UK broker to launch a British equivalent failed due to a lack of interest from the comparatively more socially concerned British investors (Aguilera et al. 2006; McAuley 2007). To date, the only published study of the Vice Fund's financial performance has been undertaken by Chong et al. (2006). These authors find the Vice Fund to deliver a positive abnormal return at the 5 percent significance level over the period from September 16, 2002, to September 16, 2005, in contrast to their selected responsible benchmark, the Domini

---

[2] More information on the Vice Fund can be found on its website www.ViceFund.com/.

Social Equity Fund, which they estimate to generate an insignificantly negative abnormal return. Estimating abnormal returns using Jensen's (1968) model and hence ignoring common controls included in the current "state of art" models (Fama and French 1993; Carhart 1997), Chong et al. (2006) display sufficient confidence in their results to title their publication "To Sin or Not to Sin? Now that's the Question." Our skepticism is supported by a recent working paper of Areal et al. (2010), however, which did not find the Vice Fund to significantly outperform. Hence, a more sophisticated analysis of the Vice Fund's financial attractiveness seems strongly needed to clarify the situation and inform pension funds regarding their possible dilemma. We pursue such a sophisticated, in-depth analysis of the Vice Fund's financial performance in three steps.

First, we estimate the Vice Fund's abnormal return using the current "state of art" estimation models developed by Fama and French (1993) and Carhart (1997). As vice investment appears favored by equal weighting portfolios, especially the control for the possibly superior returns of potentially more risky small cap stocks incorporated in these two models might reduce or eliminate the significance of the Vice Fund's positive abnormal return identified by Chong et al. (2006). While Hong and Kacperczyk (2009) propose two theoretical reasons (negligence of sin stocks by social norm driven investors, litigation risk of tobacco stocks) for vice investments to deliver positive abnormal returns, we are not aware of anyone suggesting theoretical rationales resulting in negative abnormal returns of the Vice Fund. As of now, we could theoretically explain an insignificant abnormal return of the Vice Fund only with a lack of statistical power in our estimation procedure. However, we argue that Hong and Kacperczyk's argument of the negligence of sin stocks by investors' commitment to social norms can not only be reasoned to result in positive but also in negative abnormal returns of vice stocks. Specifically, we suggest that an increase in the degree of investor negligence of sin stock would, *ceteris paribus*, lead to lower investor demand for sin shares and hence to a reduction of sin stocks' share price. This loss in market valuation might

well outweigh the abnormally high dividend yields of sin stocks. Such an increase appears to be taking place currently given the strong growth of (institutional) responsible investment (Friedman and Miles 2001; Hoepner and McMillan 2009). In summary, we consider any abnormal return of the Vice Fund to be approximately a net effect of legal risk, superior dividend yield due to negligence of vice stocks and changes in the degree of vice stock negligence and related investor demand.

Second, we extend Jensen's (1968), Fama and French's (1993) and Carhart's (1997) model to appropriately incorporate the legal, especially taxation related, risk which sufficiently explains tobacco stocks' significantly positive abnormal return in Salaber's (2009) study. This analysis allows us to infer whether the Vice Fund is financially more attractive than the average existing conventional or responsible investment product after adjusting for its excess legal risk. An insignificant abnormal return would indicate that the Vice Fund does not possess exploitable portfolio management skills resulting from the joint effect of the fund's strategy, the fund managers' asset selection and the fund managers' asset management skill. However, it would not necessarily mean that the Vice Fund's managers might not offer outstanding asset management (e.g., market timing) skills, which are not observed of the average responsible or conventional fund manager (Bollen and Busse 2001; Schröder 2004; Kreander et al. 2005). Vice investors could utilize such outstanding asset management skills to generate a significant positive abnormal return by hedging the funds' asset selection and letting their vice investment performance (nearly) exclusively be determined by the fund managers' asset management skills.[3]

---

[3] As a fund's portfolio management performance is driven by the fund's strategy (FS) as well as the fund managers' asset selection (AS) and asset management (AM) skill, investors might theoretically consider five alternative strategies to separately invest in these drivers instead of purely investing in AM and hedging FS and AS. These alternative strategies would *hedge* (Alternative 1) FS and AM, (A2) AS and AM, (A3) FS, (A4) AM and (A5) AS. However, hedging fund managers' asset management skills (e.g., market timing) separately from their asset selection skills is virtually

Third, we consequently test the Vice Fund managers' asset management skills. We separately incorporate the following four asset management skill tests in our abnormal return estimation models: (1) Henriksson and Merton's (1981) market timing skill test, (2) Pfleiderer and Bhattacharya's (1983)[4] market-timing skill test, (3) Hoepner and Zeume's (2009) directional trading skill test and (4) Hoepner and Zeume's crisis management skill test. The Vice Fund's managers might display superior asset management skills, as USA MUTUALS subcontracts two hedge fund managers as subadvisors, which appear to have led the Vice Fund to take a few short positions, and (at least top) hedge fund managers are found to display superior skills

(Kosowski et al. 2006). However, while responsible funds receive overproportional investor loyalty in return for their restricted investment focus, the Vice Fund restricts its investment focus in a way (Bollen 2007) which appears to create the additional burden of underproportional investor interest (McAuley 2007). Why should fund managers, who can attract inflows with their outstanding skills, be interested in launching such a problematic niche fund? From an incentive perspective, we therefore suggest the Vice Fund to be launched by managers with a comparatively low confidence in their skills, who aimed to generate a unique selling proposition for their investment product by being the first mover into a niche market.

Data sample

We aim to ensure highest possible comparability between our analysis and Chong et al.'s (2006) investigation. Therefore, we select the same equity index and responsible fund as benchmarks of the Vice Fund, which are the S&P 500 Composite Index (S&P500) and the Domini Social Equity Fund (DSEF), respectively. However, the DSEF differs considerably in terms of size and age from the Vice Fund. Hence, we select three additional benchmark funds, two conventional and one responsible, which match the Vice Fund as closely as possible with respect to inception date, home base and net asset base (as of January 2003).[5] Our chosen responsible fund is the Calvert Social Investment Equity I (CSIE). The conventional funds are American Funds Fundamental Investments (AFFI) and the Morgan Stanley Value Fund (MSVF). Hence, we compare the Vice Fund with two responsible and two conventional funds.

However, we cannot claim the results of our four benchmark funds to be in any way as reliable as the findings of large empirical studies on responsible or conventional funds' financial performance and we do not aim to replicate these analyses (see, for example, Bauer et al. 2005; Kosowski et al. 2006).

---

impossible at reasonable transaction costs, which rules out A1 and A4. An alternative strategy A2 would basically hedge the fund manager altogether and represent a vice index fund or a vice index. Such investment products currently do not exist, but with respect to potential index like products, responsible investment does not appear less promising than vice investment (Derwall et al. 2005; Kempf and Osthoff 2007; Edmans 2011; Statman and Glushkov 2009; Hong and Kacperczyk 2009). Furthermore, investors could consider only hedging the Vice Fund's strategy and investing in its fund managers' asset selection and asset management skills (A3). However, in unspectacular results available upon request, which are not reported here for brevity, we find the Vice Fund's managers to add no significantly abnormal return to its underlying sin industry base. Finally, it would be beneficial for investors who assume the Vice Fund managers to possess an outstanding asset management skill to hedge only the Vice Fund's managers' asset selection (A5) instead of the manager and strategy based asset selection as discussed in the text, if the Vice Fund's strategy would be abnormally attractive. However, our discussion of A2 does not indicate this condition and hence A5 does not appear abnormally attractive either.

[4] The two-factor market-timing skill estimation model developed by Pfleiderer and Bhattacharya (1983) is more commonly known as the Treynor and Mazuy (1966) model. However, Treynor and Mazuy's original one-factor model has substantially different statistical characteristics than Pfleiderer and Bhattacharya's two-factor extension of it. As the former does not linearly control for the equity market benchmark in estimating a portfolio's exposure to a quadratic function of the equity market benchmark, we prefer to label the model by the names of its actual developers rather than the authors, who initially suggested the intuition of relating a portfolio's performance to a quadratic function of its equity market benchmark. Subsequently to Pfleiderer and Bhattacharya's (1983) technical report, the model was first published in Admati et al. (1986).

[5] We use Market Watch's fund finder as of March 2009 and the Social Investment Forum's Socially Responsible Mutual Fund charts as of July 2009 for the matching process.

Therefore, we intend our comparison of the Vice Fund's financial performance with its benchmark funds to represent a sensitivity analysis controlling for potential impacts of our fund matching characteristics. For our main comparison of the Vice Fund's financial attractiveness with the average responsible and conventional funds' equivalent, we use our estimations of the Vice Fund's financial performance and compare them with the numerous previous empirical estimations of responsible and conventional funds' financial performance.

We employ the same daily sample period as Chong et al. (September 16, 2002–September 16, 2005) as well as an about 100 percent extended sample period (September 16, 2002–September 16, 2008) to investigate the robustness of their findings. The use of daily instead of less frequent data is especially beneficial in the analysis of fund managers' asset management skills, as it allows us to capture the dynamics of the managers' daily decision-making as well as of more strategic choices (Goetzmann et al. 2000; Bollen and Busse 2001). We retrieve return data for the five funds, the S&P500 and our risk-free asset[6] from Datastream. The fund returns are net of annual management fees, fund and index returns are inclusive of all distributions and all returns are denoted in US dollars.

Research methods

Jensen, Fama–French and Carhart models

Jensen (1968) pioneered the assessment of mutual funds' financial performance based on the Capital Asset Pricing Model (CAPM), which assumes stock returns to be entirely driven by their degree of systematic exposure to the overall equity market (Sharpe 1964; Lintner 1965; Mossin 1966). He suggests that a mutual fund's financial performance is well approximated as the fund's systematic return component which cannot be explained by the overall equity market's return variation. This systematic return component, commonly known as Jensen alpha, is precisely defined by equation (1), in which it is denoted α_p,

[6] We use the investment yield of the four weeks US Treasury bill as risk-free asset return.

$$r_{p,t} = \alpha_p + \beta_{1,p} r_{m,t} + \varepsilon_{p,t} \qquad (1)$$

whereas $r_{p,t}$ and $r_{m,t}$ denote the continuously compounded return of fund p and the equity market m in excess of the continuously compounded return of the risk-free asset at time t, respectively.[7] The coefficient $\beta_{1,p}$ can be interpreted as a fund's systematic risk of being exposed to the equity market's return variation during the sample period. $\varepsilon_{p,t}$ is a random disturbance term. It captures the part of a fund's return variation, which the ordinary least squares regression does not consider to be either systematically related to the equity market's return variation or the fund itself. Neither Chong et al. (2006) nor Shank et al. (2005) estimate the Vice Fund's financial performance with a more complex model than this four decades old one.

However, evidence was presented in the 1980s that small cap stocks (e.g., Banz 1981) and so-called value stocks with a high book value to market value ratio (e.g., Rosenberg et al. 1985) achieved significantly higher Jensen alphas than their counterparts. Consequently, Fama and French (1993) extend Jensen's (1968) model by two independent variables, SMB_t and HML_t, which control for a fund's over- or underproportional exposure to small and value stocks, respectively. Precisely, the Fama–French (1993) model is defined as shown in equation (2),

$$r_{p,t} = \alpha_p + \beta_{1,p} r_{m,t} + \beta_{2,p} SMB_t + \beta_{3,p} HML_t + \varepsilon_{p,t} \qquad (2)$$

where SMB_t and HML_t represent the continuously compounded return of a long/short investment strategy, which invests in small cap and value stocks financed by short selling large cap and growth stocks, respectively.[8] A fund's overproportional small stock and value stock exposure is respectively indicated by positive $\beta_{2,p}$ and $\beta_{3,p}$ coefficients and vice versa. α_p represents a fund's

[7] We transform the investment yield of the four weeks US Treasury bill stated as arithmetically calculated per annum return in a daily risk-free return in a two-step process. First, we arithmetically transform the annual figure in a 28-day return using 365.25 days per year. Second, we geometrically transform the 28-day return in a daily risk-free return.
[8] For a precise description of the construction of the SMB_t and $HMLt$ variable, see Fama and French (1993).

systematic return component, which cannot be explained by equation (2)'s independent variables. $\varepsilon_{p,t}$ is a random disturbance term, which captures all of a fund's return variation that cannot be systematically related to the regression equation's independent variables or its constant.

One month after Fama and French published their model, Jegadeesh and Titman (1993) publicized evidence that portfolios with superior previous one to four quarter returns tend to outperform their counterparts over the following one to four quarters. Consequently, Carhart (1997) extends Fama and French's (1993) model by an independent variable, MOM_t, which controls for a fund's over- or underproportional exposure to past winning or losing stocks. The Carhart (1997) model can be defined as in equation (3),

$$r_{p,t} = \alpha_p + \beta_{1,p} r_{m,t} + \beta_{2,p} SMB_t + \beta_{3,p} HML_t + \beta_{4,p} MOM_t + \varepsilon_{p,t} \qquad (3)$$

where MOM_t represents the continuously compounded return of a long/short investment strategy, which finances an investment in past winning by short-selling past losing stocks. A positive $\beta_{4,p}$ indicates a fund's overproportional exposure to past winning stocks and vice versa. We retrieve daily data on the simple returns of the SMB_t, HML_t, and MOM_t investment strategy from Kenneth French's Data Library.[9]

Legal risk-adjusted models

To develop an abnormal return estimation model that adjusts for the especially taxation related legal risk, which Salaber (2009) finds to sufficiently explain tobacco stocks' significantly positive abnormal excess returns, we add an independent variable to the previous models. To develop this variable, we utilize the return variation of the value-weighted US tobacco industry cleared from any impact of our market benchmark as well as over- or underproportional exposure to small, value and previously winning stocks. We label this variable TLR_t and consider it to

be predominantly driven by tobacco stocks' legal risk given Salaber's (2009) convincingly robust results.[10]

Following Hong and Kacperczyk (2009), we define the US tobacco industry as all US stocks in Fama and French's (1997) industry group 5, which covers stocks with the standard industry classification (SIC) codes 2080–5. Data on value weighted US tobacco industry returns is retrieved from Kenneth French's Data Library. To generate TLR_t, we employ an unwanted impact-clearing method inspired by Elton et al.'s (1993) orthogonalization technique. Specifically, we regress the continuously compounded tobacco industry returns as substitute for fund p on the independent variables of our Carhart (1997) model and define TLR_t as the sum of the disturbance term $\varepsilon_{p,t}$ and the systematic constant return component α_p at time t. Eventually, we add our TLR_t variable to the previously introduced models. Equation (4) illustrates this legal risk adjustment for the example of the Carhart model,

$$r_{p,t} = \alpha_p + \beta_{1,p} r_{m,t} + \beta_{2,p} SMB_t + \beta_{3,p} HML_t + \beta_{4,p} MOM_t + \beta_{5,p} TLR_t + \varepsilon_{p,t} \qquad (4)$$

in which a positive $\beta_{5,p}$ coefficient indicates a fund p's exposure to the legal, especially taxation related, risk of tobacco stocks and vice versa.

Asset management skill tests

Despite us adding our asset management skill tests to all previously discussed models, we illustrate them only in relation to the CAPM model for simplicity. Hence, our baseline asset management skill estimation model is the simple two-factor model displayed in equation (5),

$$r_{p,t} = \alpha_p + \beta_{1,p} r_{m,t} + \gamma_{s,p} AMS_{s,t} + \varepsilon_{p,t} \qquad (5)$$

where $AMS_{s,t}$ is the independent variable, which measures the fund's exposure to the asset management skill s and a positive $\gamma_{s,p}$ coefficient suggests a positive asset management skill and vice versa. We investigate three asset management

---

[9] Kenneth French's Data Library is available from http://mba.tuck.dartmouth.edu/pages/faculty/ken.french/data_library.html. It also offers a precise description of the construction of the three investment strategies.

[10] However, as we cannot empirically reject the hypothesis that any other factor than legal risk has more than an inconsequential impact on TLR's return variation, we interpret the results from our legal risk-adjusted abnormal return estimation models with some care.

skills – market-timing, directional trading and crisis management – using four tests.

Market-timing skill tests. Fund managers' market-timing skill refers to their ability to predict the general direction of the equity market movement in the near future. If fund managers possess this ability, they can deviate upwards or downwards from their target systematic risk exposure to the equity market in expectation of an overproportionally or underproportionally performing equity market, respectively. This behavior would allow them to earn an excess return in strong market states and to experience overproportional loss protection in bear markets. The currently common tests for fund managers' market-timing ability have been developed by Henriksson and Merton (1981) as well as Pfleiderer and Bhattacharya (1983).

Henriksson and Merton's (1981) model substitutes $AMS_{s,t}$ in equation (5) against a time series variable, which comprises any observation in the sample period that displays the equity market benchmark's return to trail the risk-free return and is zero otherwise. Hence, their model estimates, if fund managers are able to significantly reduce their mean equity market exposure during periods with, on average, detrimental effects from holding stocks. Technically, Henriksson and Merton realize this test by setting $AMS_{s,t}$ equal to $I_{p,t}r_{m,t}$, whereby $r_{m,t}$ is the continuously compounded return of the equity market in excess of the continuously compounded return of the risk-free asset at time t and $I_{p,t}$ is a dummy variable that takes the value -1 for $r_{m,t} < 0$ and the value of zero otherwise.

Pfleiderer and Bhattacharya (1983) build their model on Treynor and Mazuy's (1966) assumption that fund managers with market-timing ability can fairly be expected to increasingly expose their portfolios to strengthening equity markets. Consequently, Treynor and Mazuy consider extra returns resulting purely from fund managers' timing activities to rise concavely with the equity market's return. To estimate the existence of such extra returns, Pfleiderer and Bhattacharya (1983) substitute $AMS_{s,t}$ in equation (5) against $r_{m,t}^2$, which represents the squared continuously compounded market excess return.[11]

Directional trading skill test. Fund managers' directional trading skill refers to their ability to predict asset price directions as well as asset entry and exit points in the near future. Fund managers realize gains from this ability by entering assets before a move in the predicted direction, which sufficiently exceed the transaction costs of the directional trade, and exiting assets after this move has been completed.[12] If fund managers possess such a directional trading skill, then they can fairly be expected to earn more extra return based on it during observation intervals, in which the equity market displays stronger abnormal movement. Based on this intuition, Hoepner and Zeume (2009) developed a simple directional trading skill test. In case of daily return analysis, it estimates fund managers' ability to utilize the daily market return range in excess of the expected market return range given the respective day's eventual return for profitable directional trading activities.

Precisely, Hoepner and Zeume set $AMS_{s,t}$ in equation (5) to equal $((r\max_{m,t} - r\min_{m,t}) - \beta_{MaxMin} |r_{m,t}|)$, where $|r_{m,t}|$ is the absolute value of the continuously compounded excess return of the equity market at time t. $(r\max_{m,t} - r\min_{m,t})$ is the difference between the maximal and minimal continuously compounded return, which the market benchmark would have achieved on a trading day, if it had closed at its highest and lowest value, respectively. β_{MaxMin} is the coefficient of a single factor regression of $(r\max_{m,t} - r\min_{m,t})$ on $|r_{m,t}|$ over the sample period.

Crisis management skill test. In the first decade of the twenty-first century alone, equity markets have experienced two substantial bear markets credited to the burst of the dotcom bubble and the

---

company size, we expect to control for any consequential source of possible artificial timing skills of pure stock portfolios, which Jagannathan and Korajczak (1986) find in a CAPM regression of portfolios with different company size exposures especially for sample periods in the first half of the twentieth century. Nevertheless, we also pursue a robustness test, in which we control for the Vice Fund's full industry exposure, to investigate if sin industry stocks have any supportive or detrimental effects on fund managers' market-timing skills.

[12] In case fund managers would already hold an asset, whose direction they predict, they would increase or decrease their exposure instead of entering the asset long or short and proceed with the directional trade equivalently.

---

[11] By adding our market timing skill tests to our multifactor models, which all control for a portfolio's exposure to

global credit crunch. Consequently, equity and balanced fund managers' skill to manage an equity market crisis is becoming increasingly important. Especially drawdowns are dangerous for mutual funds. These drawdowns are periods of consecutive observations of equity market losses that can result in a large accumulated loss until the next observation of an equity market gain (e.g., Eling and Schuhmacher 2007). During these periods, mutual funds are experiencing a substantial risk of running in major liquidity problems resulting from a combination of losses and withdrawals. Hence, the ability of fund managers to mitigate losses during such drawdowns represents a crucial crisis management skill, which Hoepner and Zeume (2009) approximate with a simple test. Their test substitutes $AMS_{s,t}$ in equation (5) against $DD_{m,t}$, which represents the accumulate drawdown of the equity market at time t. This accumulated drawdown is defined as zero for each observation with a positive market return in excess of the risk-free return. For any other observation, the accumulated drawdown is defined as the absolute value of accumulated continuously compounded equity market excess return since the last observation defined as zero.

Discussion of results

Summary statistics

The descriptive statistics presented in Table 15.1 display the strength of the Vice Fund with respect to raw returns. Over both, the three- and the six-year sample periods, the Vice Fund achieves a higher mean daily return than the equity market benchmark and all four benchmark funds. Despite being deliberately undiversified, the Vice Fund's standard deviation and minimum return are also quite competitive.[13] However, in relation to the sin industries, which the Vice Fund targets, its mean daily return appears to be rather average. Among the sin industries, the tobacco industry clearly

achieves the highest mean daily return over the longer sample period. This is in line with Hong and Kacperczyk's (2009) theoretical suggestion that tobacco stocks experience considerably more excess legal risk than other sin stocks.

In summary, the descriptive statistics indicate that the Vice Fund might have achieved significantly positive abnormal excess returns against the market benchmark over both sample periods as found by Chong et al. (2006). However, the substantially overproportional returns to value and especially small cap stocks over both sample periods could well lead such abnormal returns to represent an artifact of the Vice Fund's exposure to these stocks instead of a sign of superior financial attractiveness resulting from the vice label of the fund.

Abnormal returns estimated with Jensen, Fama–French and Carhart models

Despite employing the same three-year sample period as Chong et al. (2006) and the same market benchmark, our Jensen (1968) model surprisingly finds the Vice Fund to generate significantly positive abnormal returns against the market benchmark only at the 10 percent significance level (p-value of 0.0896), while Chong et al. (2006) report a 5 percent significant result (p-value of 0.494). However, we find a nearly identical result as Chong et al. (p-value of 0.491), if we omit to adjust our Vice Fund and market benchmark return data for distributions. Hence, we are led to believe that the significance level of Chong et al.'s findings is partially explained by an inappropriate adjustment for distributions in their Yahoo Finance data. Nevertheless, our Jensen (1968) model estimates the Vice Fund to deliver a significantly positive abnormal return against the market benchmark over the three-year sample period in contrast to three of our four benchmark funds as shown in Table 15.2.

Table 15.2 reports fund performance as measured by the Jensen alpha using a one-factor model adjusting for systemic risk (equation 1), a two-factor model additionally adjusting for size effects, a three-factor model additionally controlling for book-to-market effects (equation 2) and a four-factor model additionally adjusting for Momentum

---

[13] This observation should be interpreted with care, however, since the hedge fund managers subadvising the Vice Fund appear to have led it to hold a few short positions, which consequently reduce its variation.

Table 15.1 Summary statistics: this table summarizes key statistics for the sample funds, the market proxy, size, book-to-market and momentum portfolios, and sector portfolios used in our analysis. All summary statistics are based on daily data.

	Mean	SD	Min	Max
PANEL A: Chong Period (September 16, 2002–September 16, 2005)				
Mutual Funds				
Vice Fund	0.0676%	0.83%	–2.94%	2.77%
Domini Social Equity Fund	0.0470%	0.99%	–3.70%	4.71%
Calvert Social Investmt. Equ.	0.0434%	0.98%	–3.45%	3.97%
American Funds Fundamental	0.0587%	0.82%	–3.00%	3.65%
Morgan Stanley Value Fund	0.0595%	1.01%	–4.19%	5.05%
Market				
S&P 500	0.0506%	0.97%	–3.59%	4.63%
SMB	0.0279%	0.51%	–2.01%	1.34%
HML	0.0217%	0.37%	–2.10%	1.13%
MOM	–0.0139%	0.67%	–3.82%	2.60%
Sectors				
Tobacco	0.0804%	1.73%	–14.36%	9.45%
Alcohol	–0.0021%	0.97%	–7.27%	3.90%
Guns/Defense	–0.0020%	1.41%	–10.86%	6.62%
Gambling	0.0938%	1.34%	–6.04%	4.38%
Aerospace	0.0843%	1.35%	–6.24%	5.02%
PANEL B: Extended Sample Period (September 16, 2002–September 16, 2008)				
Mutual Funds				
Vice Fund	0.0375%	0.87%	–4.06%	3.90%
Domini Social Equity Fund	0.0196%	1.00%	–4.45%	4.71%
Calvert Social Investmt. Equ.	0.0216%	0.98%	–4.63%	4.00%
American Funds Fundamental	0.0293%	0.89%	–4.95%	3.65%
Morgan Stanley Value Fund	0.0223%	1.05%	–11.84%	5.05%
Market				
S&P 500	0.0279%	0.98%	–4.83%	4.63%
SMB	0.0159%	0.49%	–2.01%	1.60%
HML	0.0175%	0.41%	–2.39%	3.23%
MOM	0.0109%	0.81%	–6.00%	3.62%
Sectors				
Tobacco	0.0654%	1.44%	–14.36%	9.45%
Alcohol	0.0209%	0.87%	–7.27%	3.90%
Guns/Defense	0.0364%	1.30%	–10.86%	6.62%
Gambling	0.0266%	1.55%	–9.46%	6.97%
Aerospace	0.0528%	1.28%	–6.24%	5.02%

Table 15.2 Fund performance according to the Jensen, Fama–French and Carhart models. This table reports fund performance as measured by the Jensen alpha using a one-factor model adjusting for systemic risk (equation 1), a two-factor model additionally adjusting for size effects, a three-factor model additionally controlling for book-to-market effects (equation 2), and a four-factor model additionally adjusting for Momentum effects (equation 3). †, *, ** and *** attached to a t-statistics (t-stats) indicate whether a coefficient (coef.) is significantly different from zero (alpha, SMB, HML, MOM) or one (beta) at the 10%, 5%, 1%, and 0.1% level, respectively. Standard errors and coefficient covariances are made heteroscedasticity and autocorrelation consistent based on the approach of Newey and West (1987).

	Jensen alpha		Beta		SMB		HML		MOM	
	coef.	t-stats	coef.	t-stats	coef.	t-stats	coef.	t-stats	coef.	t-stats
PANEL A: Chong et al. period (September 16, 2002–September 16, 2005)										
Vice Fund										
Jensen	0.0308	1.70 †	0.7024	−10.48 ***						
Jensen + and Size	0.0220	1.30	0.6994	−13.50 ***	0.3210	9.85 ***				
Fama and French	0.0164	0.97	0.7233	−13.10 ***	0.3340	9.96 ***	0.1905	3.37 ***		
Carhart	0.0206	1.23	0.7344	−12.66 ***	0.2833	6.92 ***	0.1121	1.62	0.1141	2.48 *
Domini Social Equ. Fd.										
Jensen	−0.0040	−0.73	1.0067	0.98						
Jensen + Size	−0.0048	−0.90	1.0064	0.95	0.0321	3.36 ***				
Fama and French	−0.0009	−0.18	0.9895	−1.55	0.0228	2.20 *	−0.1345	−7.07 ***		
Carhart	−0.0018	−0.36	0.9871	−1.93 †	0.0336	2.94 **	−0.1178	−5.82 ***	−0.0243	−2.23 *
Calvert Social Investmt Equ.										
CAPM	−0.0064	−0.86	0.9822	−1.31						
CAPM + Size	−0.0102	−1.36	0.9809	−1.69 †	0.1393	8.43 ***				
Fama and French	−0.0061	−0.83	0.9633	−3.30 ***	0.1296	8.04 ***	−0.1407	−5.28 ***		
Carhart	−0.0071	−0.97	0.9606	−3.62 ***	0.1418	7.21 ***	−0.1218	−4.23 ***	−0.0275	−1.47 **
American Funds										
Jensen	0.0174	1.77 †	0.7994	−20.31 ***						
Jensen + Size	0.0155	1.60	0.7987	−21.43	0.0709	3.88 ***				

Table 15.2 (*cont.*)

	Jensen alpha		Beta		SMB		HML		MOM	
	coef.	t-stats	coef.	t-stats	coef.	t-stats	coef.	t-stats	coef.	t-stats
Fama and French	0.0046	0.58	0.8448	−15.65	0.0961	6.20 ***	0.3679	13.61 ***		
Carhart	0.0029	0.36	0.8401	−16.18	0.1176	6.98 ***	0.4011	13.45 ***	−0.0483	−2.99 **
Morgan Stanley Val. I										
Jensen	0.0091	0.87	0.9948	−0.23						
Jensen + Size	0.0106	1.01	0.9953	−0.21	−0.0572	−2.56 *				
Fama and French	0.0040	0.40	1.0236	1.04	−0.0418	−2.01 *	0.2258	6.80 ***		
Carhart	−0.0016	−0.17	1.0088	0.44	0.0255	1.14	0.3298	10.74 ***	−0.1513	−8.02 ***
PANEL B: Extended sample period (September 16, 2002–September 16, 2008)										
Vice Fund										
Jensen	0.0155	1.19	0.7253	−12.59 ***						
Jensen + Size	0.0114	0.92	0.7145	−15.50	0.2707	8.81 ***				
Fama and French	0.0113	0.90	0.7146	−15.38	0.2711	8.53 ***	0.0056	0.10		
Carhart	0.0094	0.75	0.7366	−14.45	0.2546	8.05 ***	0.0395	0.70	0.0978	3.42 ***
Domini Social Equ. Fd.										
Jensen	−0.0082	−1.52	0.9969	−0.50						
Jensen + Size	−0.0088	−1.64	0.9953	−0.74	0.0384	2.93 **				
Fama and French	−0.0080	−1.48	0.9946	−0.86	0.0353	2.70 **	−0.0421	−1.53		
Carhart	−0.0070	−1.34	0.9831	−2.22 *	0.059	3.09 **	−0.0598	−2.54 *	−0.0511	−3.48 ***
Calvert Social Investmt Equ.										
CAPM	−0.0051	−0.69	0.9455	−4.61 ***						
CAPM + Size	−0.0069	−0.94	0.9409	−5.36 ***	0.1146	6.27 ***				

Fama and French	-0.0030	-0.45	0.9373	-6.38***	0.0096	6.38***	0.2007	-10.19***	
Carhart	-0.0033	-0.48	0.9405	-6.65***	0.0972	5.22***	-0.1956	-9.75***	0.0145
American Funds									
Jensen	0.0050	0.55	0.8280	-16.17***					
Jensen + Size	0.0044	0.48	0.8262	-16.88	0.0447	2.14*			
Fama and French	0.0034	0.38	0.8272	-15.90	0.0486	2.02*	0.0522	0.85	
Carhart	0.0001	0001	0.8657	-13.37***	0.0197	1.08	0.1115	3.70***	0.1713
Morgan Stanley Val. I									
Jensen	-0.0052	-0.46	0.9800	-1.11					
Jensen + Size	-0.0050	-0.43	0.9806	-1.10	-0.0158	-0.63			
Fama and French	-0.0101	-0.91	0.9855	-0.78	0.0042	0.17	0.2696	7.41***	
Carhart	-0.0067	-0.63	0.9451	-3.22**	0.0346	1.58	0.2074	8.13***	-0.1799

Carhart (American Funds)	10.31***
Carhart (top group)	1.20
Carhart (Morgan Stanley Val. I)	-14.92***

effects (equation 3). †, *, **, and *** attached to a t-statistics (t-stats) indicate whether a coefficient (coef.) is significantly different from zero (alpha, SMB, HML, MOM) or one (beta) at the 10 percent, 5 percent, 1 percent and 0.1 percent level, respectively. Standard errors and coefficient covariances are made heteroscedasticity and autocorrelation consistent based on the approach of Newey and West (1987).

However, if we extend our sample period by three years, the significance of the Vice Fund's abnormal return vanishes and we cannot reject the hypothesis anymore that the return differential between the Vice Fund and the market benchmark is zero. Even more, we only need to add a control to the return differential between small and large stocks to the Jensen model and the significance of the Vice Fund's positive abnormal return over the shorter sample period also vanishes, since it has a very strong overproportional exposure to small stocks. The strength of this overproportional exposure is highlighted by a comparison of the Vice Fund with its benchmark funds. Despite three of the four benchmark funds being also significantly overexposed to small stocks, their sensitivity to small stocks' differential return characteristics is in both sample periods at most a half of the Vice Fund's sensitivity. In combination with our observation from our analysis of previous studies that small vice stocks are the predominant driver of vice stock portfolios' performance, this finding suggests vice stock return characteristics to be to a substantial degree small stock return characteristics.

Extending our analysis to Fama and French's (1993) and Carhart's (1997) model, we find the Vice Fund to be somewhat exposed to previously winning stocks but have no clear favor for value or growth stocks. As all four benchmark funds, it fails to deliver significantly abnormal returns against the market benchmark over both sample periods for any abnormal return estimation model but Jensen's (1968).

Abnormal returns estimated with legal risk-adjusted models

Adjusting our previous abnormal return estimation models for the especially taxation related excess legal risk of tobacco stocks, we observe the Vice Fund to have, unsurprisingly, a highly significant exposure to tobacco stocks' excess legal risk. However, this exposure is not even half as strong as the Vice Fund's exposure to small stocks' differential return characteristics. This, again, implies the very high relevance of small stock returns for the Vice Fund's performance. Nevertheless, even before an adjustment for small stocks' differential return, adjusting for tobacco stocks' excess legal risk is in itself more than sufficient to explain the significance of the Vice Fund's positive abnormal excess returns over the three-year period as shown in Table 15.3. Consequently, none of our legal risk-adjusted models over both sample periods indicates a significant positive abnormal return of the Vice Fund.

Furthermore, our most robust estimation, the legal risk-adjusted Carhart (1997) model over the longer sample period, displays the weakest abnormal return estimation for the Vice Fund (t-stat of 0.32). Hence, after controlling for common return drivers and tobacco stocks' excess legal risk, our results suggest that the financial performance differential between the Vice Fund and the market benchmark is most likely inconsequential. Consequently, we consider Chong et al.'s (2006) finding of the Vice Fund's 5 percent significant abnormal return to be a result of four artifacts instead of an authentic indication of the Vice Fund's financial attractiveness. These four artifacts are the apparent lack of distributions in Chong et al.'s Yahoo Finance return data, their omission to control for the return differential between small and large stocks as well as for the excess legal risk of tobacco stocks, and their unique, short sample period.

Asset management skills

Although we do not find the Vice Fund itself to be financially more attractive than the market benchmark, an asset selection hedged investment in the Vice Fund might still be abnormally attractive for investors if the Vice Fund's managers possess superior asset management skills in contrast to the average responsible or conventional fund manager (e.g., Bollen and Busse 2001; Kreander et al. 2005). However, our results presented in Table 15.4 show

Table 15.3 Legal risk-adjusted fund performance measurement. This table reports fund performance adjusted for tobacco stocks' excess legal risk estimated in line with equation (4). The legal risk-adjusting independent variable (LR) represents the returns to the tobacco industry cleared from all impacts of all stock return drivers incorporated in Carhart's model. †, *, ** and *** attached to a t-statistics (t-stats) indicate whether a coefficient (coef.) is significantly different from zero (alpha, LR, SMB, HML, MOM) or one (beta) at the 10%, 5%, 1% and 0.1% level, respectively. Standard errors and coefficient covariances are made heteroscedasticity and autocorrelation consistent based on the approach of Newey and West (1984).

	Jensen alpha		Beta		Legal risk (LR)		SMB		HML		MOM	
	coef.	t-stats	coef.	t-stats	coef	t-stats	coef.	t-stats	coef.	t-stats	coef.	t-stats
PANEL A: Chong et al. period (September 16, 2002–September 16, 2005)												
Vice Fund												
Jensen	0.0308	1.70†	0.7024	−10.48 ***								
Jensen + Legal Risk (LR)	0.0251	1.48	0.7024	−10.39 ***	0.1077	8.52 ***						
Jensen + LR + Size	0.0163	1.04	0.6994	−13.25 ***	0.1077	8.85 ***	0.3210	10.88 ***				
Fama and French + LR	0.0107	0.68	0.7233	−12.54 ***	0.1077	9.10 ***	0.3340	10.86 ***	0.1905	3.96 ***		
Carhart + LR	0.0148	0.97	0.7344	−12.27 ***	0.1077	9.84 ***	0.2833	8.45 ***	0.1121	1.98*	0.1141	3.10**
PANEL B: Extended sample period (September 16, 2002–September 16, 2008)												
Vice Fund												
Jensen	0.0155	1.19	0.7253	−12.59 ***								
Jensen + Legal Risk (LR)	0.0099	0.80	0.7253	−12.81 ***	0.1147	9.74 ***						
Jensen + LR + Size	0.0058	0.50	0.7145	−15.84 ***	0.1147	10.33 ***	0.2707	9.10***				
Fama and French + LR	0.0057	0.48	0.7146	−15.75 ***	0.1147	10.34 ***	0.2711	8.78 ***	0.0056	0.11		
Carhart + LR	0.0039	0.32	0.7366	−14.93 ***	0.1147	10.95 ***	0.2546	8.43 ***	0.0395	0.73	0.0978	3.66 ***

the complete opposite. Adding our asset management skill test variables to the Jensen (1968) model, we find the Vice Fund's managers to experience a significant inability in all three asset management skill types – market-timing, directional trading and crisis management – over at least one sample period.

However, the Vice Fund's at most 5 percent significant market mistiming ability vanishes once we control for the differential return between previously winning and losing stocks as well as the Vice Fund's exposure to tobacco stocks' excess legal risk. In contrast, the Vice Fund managers' negative crisis management skill during our more crisis-prone, extended sample period is more robust. After adding all our previously used controls to our asset management skill estimation model, it is still significant at the 5 percent level. Even worse, the Vice Fund managers' directional trading inability is at least 5 percent or 1 percent significant over the three- or six-year sample period in any of our specifications of Hoepner and Zeume's (2009) test presented in Table 15.4, respectively. Hence, even after controlling for the Vice Fund's exposure to Carhart's control variables and tobacco stocks' excess legal risk, our results indicate that the Vice Fund managers' inability to pursue directional trades with sin stocks significantly reduces investor value.[14] In other words, investors who did not pursue any directional trades and simply invested in the market benchmark would have achieved a better result from directional trading and saved on the fees charged by the Vice Fund for their asset management (in)competence.[15]

In summary, our results are clearly consistent with the hypotheses (1) that the return differential between the Vice Fund and the equity market benchmark is zero and (2) that the Vice Fund possesses no or negative asset management skills. Thus, we conclude that the financial attractiveness of the Vice Fund and thereby all existing vice investment products is likely indifferent from the market average. Similarly, it is also likely indifferent from the result of the vast majority of studies on the financial attractiveness of the existing responsible investment products (e.g., Statman 2000; Bauer et al. 2005; Kreander et al. 2005; Derwall 2007; Schröder 2007). Our results are therefore supportive of an inductively built theory that existing responsible investment products, on average, do not forgo financial performance opportunity compared with alternatives.

Robustness tests

We pursue four robustness tests.[16] First, while we choose the S&P 500 as equity market benchmark to give our results the highest possible comparability with Chong et al.'s (2006) findings, the Vice Fund's currently chosen benchmark is the Russell 1000. Hence, it is possible that some of the results, especially the ones related to asset management skills, are an artifact of our smaller market benchmark. Consequently, we re-estimate all regression specifications presented in Tables 15.2–15.4 using the Russell 1000 instead of the S&P 500 as equity market benchmark. We find the significance levels of the Vice Fund's abnormal return estimated in Tables 15.2 and 15.3 to remain unchanged. Only the best benchmark fund (AMMI) improves, as it offers a 5 percent significant positive abnormal return also in Table 15.2's two-factor model. With the bigger benchmark, the asset management skill estimations presented in Table 15.4 become slightly weaker for all five funds. However, the Vice Fund still displays an at least 5 percent significant negative directional trading skill in any specification over both sample periods.

---

[14] As discussed in a note to the research aims section, we do not consider the significantly positive abnormal alphas resulting from the significantly negative asset management coefficients in Table 15.4 to be virtually exploitable for investors, as this would require near perfect knowledge of the Vice Fund managers' asset management transactions, which is extremely unlikely available at sufficiently low transaction costs.

[15] In contrast to the Vice Fund, we find our four benchmarks funds' asset management skills to be more mixed. One fund displays some significantly positive and another fund some significantly negative asset management skills, while the third and fourth fund experience on balance inconsequential asset management skills. We do not report these results here for brevity, but they are available upon request.

[16] Results of all sensitivity analyses or robustness tests not reported here are available upon request.

Table 15.4 Vice Fund managers' asset management skills. This table displays our estimations of the Vice Fund managers' asset management skills. We employ the market-timing ability tests of Pfleiderer and Bhattacharya (1983) as well as of Henriksson and Merton (1981) and the directional timing and crisis management skill tests of Hoepner and Zeume (2009). We illustrate the application of these tests for the example of the Jensen (1968) model as underlying the abnormal return estimation model in equation (5). Their application to the other four models (defined in equations 2–4) displayed in this table is equivalent. †, *, **, and *** attached to a t-statistics (t-stats) indicate whether a coefficient (coef.) is significantly different from zero (alpha, Asset Management, SMB, HML, MOM, LR) or one (beta) at the 10%, 5%, 1% and 0.1% level, respectively. Standard errors and coefficient covariances are made heteroscedasticity and autocorrelation consistent based on the approach of Newey and West (1987). The equivalent results for the three responsible funds are available upon request.

	Jensen alpha		Beta		Asset Management		SMB		HML		MOM		Legal Risk (LR)	
	coef.	t-stats	coef.	t-stats	coef.	t-stats	coef.	t-stats	coef.	t-stats	coef.	t-stats	coef.	t-stats
PANEL A: Chong et al. period (September 16, 2002–September 16, 2005)														
Pfleiderer and Bhattacharya's Market Timing Test														
Jensen	0.0598	2.94 **	0.7127	−11.47 ***	−3.1278	−2.20 *								
Jensen + Size	0.0415	2.28 *	0.7063	−14.46 ***	−2.0736	−1.86 †	0.3118	10.12 ***						
Fama and French	0.0324	1.72 †	0.7274	−14.06 ***	−1.6642	−1.43	0.3259	10.37 ***	0.1797	3.26 **				
Carhart	0.0366	2.01 *	0.7386	−13.29 ***	−1.6653	−1.51	0.2752	7.13 ***	0.1013	1.51	0.1141	2.48 *		
Carhart + Legal Risk	0.0234	1.39	0.7366	−12.64 ***	−0.8921	−0.66	0.2790	8.53 ***	0.1063	1.95 †	0.1141	3.10 **	0.1069	9.40 ***
Henriksson and Merton's Market Timing Test														
Jensen	0.0833	2.90 **	0.6343	−7.09 ***	−0.1463	−2.03 *								
Jensen + Size	0.0604	2.50 *	0.6497	−8.58 ***	−0.1068	−1.83 †	0.3157	10.01 ***						
Fama and French	0.0446	1.80 †	0.6858	−7.87 ***	−0.0775	−1.35	0.3294	10.17 ***	0.1795	3.25 **				
Carhart	0.0505	2.07 *	0.6949	−8.01 ***	−0.0820	−1.46	0.2780	7.02 ***	0.0997	1.48	0.1151	2.51 *		
Carhart + Legal Risk	0.0329	1.41	0.7105	−7.29 ***	−0.0496	−0.81	0.2801	8.46 ***	0.1046	1.90 †	0.1147	3.11 **	0.1072	9.57 ***
Hoepner and Zeume's Directional Trading Test														
Jensen	0.1336	4.11 ***	0.6710	−10.53 ***	−0.0844	−3.24 **								
Jensen + Size	0.1144	3.84 ***	0.6712	−13.38 ***	−0.0758	−3.18 **	0.3174	9.87 ***						

Table 15.4 (cont.)

	Jensen alpha		Beta		Asset Management		SMB		HML		MOM		Legal Risk (LR)	
	coef.	t-stats	coef.	t-stats	coef.	t-stats	coef.	t-stats	coef.	t-stats	coef.	t-stats	coef.	t-stats
Fama and French	0.0884	2.94 **	0.6986	−13.30 ***	−0.0585	−2.54 *	0.3296	9.97 ***	0.1672	3.07 **				
Carhart	0.0921	3.16 **	0.7099	−13.22 ***	−0.0581	−2.66 **	0.7099−1	7.00 ***	0.0891	1.35	0.1138	2.54 *		
Carhart + Legal Risk	0.0741	2.92 **	0.7141	−12.46 ***	−0.0481	−2.45 *	0.2798	8.54 ***	0.11	1.76 †	0.1138	3.15 **	0.1070	9.87 ***
Hoepner and Zeume's Crisis Management Test														
Jensen	0.0603	2.63 **	0.6674	−9.29 ***	−0.0517	−1.61								
Jensen + Size	0.0391	1.80 †	0.6792	−10.51 ***	−0.0298	−0.99	0.3172	9.74 ***						
Fama and French	0.0251	1.10	0.7126	−9.29 ***	−0.0148	−0.47	0.3318	9.84 ***	0.1857	3.22 **				
Carhart	0.0317	1.36	0.7209	−9.42 ***	−0.0190	−0.60	0.2801	6.69 ***	0.1053	1.47	0.1150	2.49 *		
Carhart + Legal Risk	0.0283	1.41	0.7181	−9.24 ***	−0.0230	−0.77	0.2794	g 22 ***	0.1038	1.81 †	0.1153	3.12 **	0.1079	9.87 ***

PANEL B: Extended sample period (September 16, 2002–September 16, 2008)

	Jensen alpha		Beta		Asset Management		SMB		HML		MOM		Legal Risk (LR)	
	coef.	t-stats	coef.	t-stats	coef.	t-stats	coef.	t-stats	coef.	t-stats	coef.	t-stats	coef.	t-stats
Pfleiderer and Bhattacharya's Market Timing Test														
Jensen	0.0298	1.87 †	0.7251	−12.65 ***	−1.4905	−1.18								
Jensen + Size	0.0250	1.77 †	0.7143	−15.50 ***	−1.4075	−1.42	0.2700	8.96 ***						
Fama and French	0.0251	1.80 †	0.7143	−15.33 ***	−1.4142	−1.48	0.2698	8.73 ***	−0.0027	−0.05				
Carhart	0.0193	1.39	0.7357	−14.34 ***	−1.0077	−1.10	0.2542	8.16 ***	0.0326	0.58	0.0950	3.32 ***		
Carhart + Legal Risk	0.0097	0.75	0.7361	−14.79 ***	−0.5978	−0.64	0.2544	8.49 ***	0.0354	0.67	0.11431	3.63 ***	0.1143	10.65 ***
Henriksson and Merton's Market Timing Test														
Jensen	0.0489	2.41 *	0.6774	−8.59 ***	−0.0943	−1.79 †								
Jensen + Size	0.0451	2.55 *	0.6662	−10.66 ***	−0.0951	−2.14 *	0.2708	8.97 ***						

Fama and French	0.0453	2.57 *	0.6660	−0.0953	−2.18 *	0.2707	8.71 ***	−0.0025	−0.05			
Carhart	0.0350	1.99 *	0.6994	−0.0715	−1.68 †	0.2549	8.14 ***	0.0322	0.57	0.0943	3.29 **	
Carhart + Legal Risk	0.0220	1.30	0.7102	−0.0507	−1.18	0.2548	8.48 ***	0.0343	0.64	0.0953	3.57 ***	0.1141	10.68 ***

Hoepner and Zeume's Directional Trading Test

Jensen	0.1023	3.87 ***	0.7052	−0.0724	−3.32 ***							
Jensen + Size	0.0986	3.76 ***	0.6943	−0.0727	−3.34 ***	0.2709	8.91 ***					
Fama and French	0.0986	3.71 ***	0.6943	−0.0727	−3.33 ***	0.2709	8.65 ***	−0.0001	0.00			
Carhart	0.0884	3.20 **	0.7173	−0.0657	−2.87 **	0.2551	83.27 **	0.0329	0.60	0.0938	3.27 **	
Carhart + Legal Risk	0.0804	3.02 **	0.7179	−0.0637	−2.83 **	0.2551	8.47 ***	0.0331	0.63	0.0939	3.49 ***	0.1144	10.94 ***

Hoepner and Zeume's Crisis Management Test

Jensen	0.0501	3.17 **	0.6819	−0.0625	−2.78 **							
Jensen + Size	0.0438	2.84 **	0.6739	−0.0585	−2.70 **	0.2689	8.92 ***					
Fama and French	0.0437	2.78 **	0.6740	−0.0584	−2.68 **	0.2691	8.65 ***	0.0023	0.04			
Carhart	0.0340	1.74 *	0.7047	−0.0441	−2.01 *	0.2541	3.17 **	0.0350	0.62	0.0921	3.17 **	
Carhart + Legal Risk	0.0274	1.86 †	0.7061	−0.0422	418.48 *	0.2541	8.48 ***	0.0352	0.66	0.0924	3.42 ***	0.1145	11.00 ***

Table 15.5 Robustness of asset management skills. This table displays our estimates of the robustness of the Vice Fund managers' negative Directional Trading and Crisis Management skills to the inclusion of pure vice industry returns in our asset management skill estimation models. The baseline model is overtaken from Table is 4 and generated equivalent to equation (5). It comprises the Carhart factors, the pure tobacco industry returns, which we consider to be predominantly driven by tobacco stocks' excess legal risk given Salaber's (2009) results, as well as the asset management test variable. To generate the pure industry returns, which we add stepwise to our model, we regress the respective industry's continuously compounded return in excess of the risk-free rate on the model, to which its pure effect is to be added. The sum of the intercept and the residuals of this regression represent our pure industry return. †, *, ** and *** attached to a t-statistics (t-stats) indicate whether a coefficient (coef.) is significantly different from zero (alpha, Asset Management, SMB, HML, MOM, LR) or one (beta) at the 10 percent, 5 percent, 1 percent and 0.1 percent level, respectively. Standard errors and coefficient covariances are made heteroscedasticity and autocorrelation consistent based on the approach of Newey and West (1987).

	Jensen alpha		Beta		Asset Management		SMB		HML		MOM		Tobacco (T)		Alcohol (A)		Defense (D)		Gambling (G)		Aero	
	coef.	t-stats	coef.	t-stats	coef.	t-stats	coef.	t-stats	coef.	t-stats	coef.	t-stats	coef.	t-stats	coef.	t-stats	coef.	t-stats	coef.	t-stats	coef.	t-stats
PANEL A: Chong et al. period (September 16, 2002–September 16,2005)																						
Hoepner and Zeume's Directional Trading Test																						
Carhart + T	0.07	2.92 **	0.71	−12.46 ***	−0.05	−2.45 *	0.28	8.54 ***	0.09	1.76 †	0.11	3.15 **	0.11	9.87 ***								
Carhart + T +A	0.07	2.67 **	0.72	−13.41 ***	−0.04	−2.22 *	0.28	8.82 ***	0.10	1.73 †	0.11	3.33 ***	0.11	11.17 ***	0.10	4.80 ***						
Carhart + T +A + D	0.06	2.31 *	0.72	−14.79 ***	−0.03	−1.81 †	0.28	9.72 ***	0.10	2.17 *	0.11	4.38 ***	0.11	11.25 ***	0.10	5.27 ***	0.09	7.57 ***				
Carhart + T +A + D + G0	0.02	0.66	0.51	−27.25 ***	0.00	−0.21	0.30	12.85 ***	−0.05	−1.21	0.06	2.33 *	0.11	12.97 ***	0.10	6.54 ***	0.09	8.28 ***	0.24	20.67 ***		
Carhart + T +A + D + G + Aero	0.01	0.50	0.51	−26.66 ***	0.00	−0.07	0.30	12.79 ***	−0.04 **	−1.20	0.06	2.28 *	0.11	12.20 ***	0.10	6.45 ***	0.09	8.32 ***	0.24	20.48 ***	0.04	2.57 *
Hoepner and Zeume's Crisis Management Test																						
Carhart + T	0.03	1.41	0.72	−9.24 ***	−0.02	−0.77	0.28	8.22 ***	0.10	1.81 †	0.12	3.12 **	0.11	9.87 ***								
Carhart + T +A	0.03	1.46	0.72	−9.74 ***	−0.02	−0.80	0.28	8.51 ***	0.10	1.72 †	0.12	3.30 ***	0.11	11.18	0.10	5.02 ***						

Model																						
Carhart + T + A + D	0.03	1.67 †	0.72	−10.81 ***	−0.02	−0.85	0.28	9.44 ***	0.10 *	2.15 *	0.12	4.44 ***	0.11	11.21 ***	0.10	5.46 ***	0.09	7.65 ***				
Carhart + T + A + D + G	0.02	0.98	0.50	−19.02 ***	−0.01	−0.39	0.30	12.74 ***	−0.05 ***	−1.30	0.06	2.36 **	0.11	12.88 ***	0.10	6.48 ***	0.09	8.34 ***	0.24	20.77 ***		
Carhart + T + A + D + O + Aero	0.01	0.87	0.50	−18.83 ***	−0.01	−0.30	0.30	12.71 ***	−0.05 **	−0.30	0.06	2.30 *	0.11	12.11 ***	0.10	6.36 ***	0.09	8.38 ***	0.24	20.50 ***	0.04	2.58 **

PANEL B: Extended sample period (September 16, 2002–September 16, 2008)

Hoepner and Zeume's Directional Trading Test

Model																						
Carhart + T	0.08	3.02 **	0.72	−13.93 ***	−0.06	−2.83 **	0.26	0.94 ***	0.03 *	0.63	0.09	3.49 ***	0.11	10.94 ***								
Carhart + T + A	0.08	2.96 **	0.72	−14.49 ***	−0.06	−2.80 **	0.26	8.57 ***	0.03 *	0.65	0.09	3.70 ***	0.11	12.23 ***	0.09	4.83 ***						
Carhart + T + A + D	0.07	2.72 **	0.72	−15.29 ***	−0.06	−2.65 **	0.26	9.05 ***	0.03 *	0.70	0.09	4.12 ***	0.11	12.27 ***	0.09	5.29 ***	0.10	9.00 ***				
Carhart + T + A + D + G	0.03	1.32	0.50	−27.15 ***	−0.02	−1.03	0.30	13.29 ***	−0.01 *	−0.33	0.02	1.15	0.11	15.05 ***	0.09	6.06 ***	0.10	11.56 ***	0.24	19.36 ***		
Carhart + T + A + D + G + Aero	0.02	0.87	0.50	−29.57 ***	−0.01	−0.66	0.36	13.60 ***	−0.01 **	−0.36	0.02	1.23	0.11	13.64 ***	0.09	6.07 ***	0.10	11.24 ***	0.24	20.60 ***	0.10	6.14 ***

Hoepner and Zeume's Crisis Management Test

Model																		
Carhart + T	0.03	1.86 †	0.71	−11.87 ***	−0.04	−1.98 *	0.25	8.48 ***	0.04 *	0.66	0.09	3.42 ***	0.11	11.00 ***				
Carhart + T + A	0.03	1.82 †	0.71	−12.16 ***	−0.04	−1.96 *	0.25	8.59 ***	0.04 *	0.68	0.09	3.62 ***	0.11	12.30 ***	0.09	4.86 ***		
Carhart + T + A + D	0.02	1.64	0.71	−12.78 ***	−0.04	−1.85 †	0.25	9.07 ***	0.04 *	0.73	0.09	4.07 ***	0.11	12.32 ***	0.09	5.33 ***	0.10	9.14 ***

Table 15.5 (cont.)

	Jensen alpha		Beta		Asset Management		SMB		HML		MOM		Tobacco (T)		Alcohol (A)		Defense (D)		Gambling (G)		Aero	
	coef.	t-stats	coef.	t-stats	coef.	t-stats	coef.	t-stats	coef.	t-stats	coef.	t-stats	coef.	t-stats	coef.	t-stats	coef.	t-stats	coef.	t-stats	coef.	t-stats
Carhart + T + A + D + G	0.02	1.45	0.49	−24.10***	−0.02	−1.23	0.30	13.33***	−0.01	−0.34	0.02	1.05	0.11	15.06***	0.09	6.10***	0.10	11.66***	0.24	19.26***		
Carhart + T + A + D + G + Aero	0.01	0.98	0.50	−25.58***	−0.01	−0.80	0.30	13.64***	−0.01	−0.37	0.02	1.16	0.11	13.65***	0.09	6.11***	0.10	11.39***	0.24	20.55***	0.10	6.07***

Second, Ferson and Schadt (1996) find that allowing a fund's exposure to market risk or other factors to vary over time according to lagged public information improves abnormal return estimations. Hence, we re-estimate our Jensen (1968) and Carhart (1997) model based regression specifications displayed in Tables 15.2–15.4 and allow fund exposures to vary over time with the lagged macroeconomic variables used in Renneboog et al.'s (2008) analysis of responsible funds. Our results remain qualitatively unchanged.[17]

Third, although it appears unlikely given our finding of a comparatively weak financial performance of the Vice Fund, it is possible that the Vice Fund's managers possess significantly positive asset selection skills. If they were able to pick the best performing sin stocks and abandoned their unsuccessful asset management activities, investors could profit from an industry class hedged investment in the Vice Fund. We test this possibility by estimating if the Vice Fund managers deliver a significantly positive abnormal return in comparison with their fund strategy's sin industry base.[18] Our robustness test shows that the Vice Fund managers do not possess significantly positive asset selection skills.

Fourth, idiosyncratic behavior of vice industry stocks might hamper the managers' directional trading or crisis management abilities. However, such a finding would not excuse the Vice Fund's managers, since the Vice Fund currently holds a few short positions and hence its managers could just short sell instead of investing in vice stocks, which hamper their directional trading or crisis management ability. Nevertheless, it would (somewhat) explain the Vice Fund's significantly negative directional trading and crisis management skills.

To identify possible effects of sin stocks on fund managers' directional trading or crisis management skills, we stepwise extend our six-factor asset management test regression based on our legal risk-adjusted Carhart model to a ten-factor model. The four stepwise added factors are the continuously compounded return of the alcohol, defense, gambling and aerospace industries in excess of the risk-free return cleared from any impact of the independent variables of the model, to which it is added, using Elton et al.'s (1993) orthogonalization approach.[19]

Our results displayed in Table 15.5 show that some sin stocks, indeed, have detrimental effects on fund managers' directional trading and crisis management skills. The Vice Fund's significant negative directional trading ability over both sample periods and its significantly negative crisis management skills over the longer sample period are robust to alcohol stocks and relatively robust to defense stocks as additional controls. However, once we control our model for gambling stocks, the negative significance vanishes in all cases. Our additional incorporation of aerospace stocks eventually leads the t-stats of all negative asset management skill coefficients to drop below one. Hence, we find the Vice Fund's managers to have a tendency towards poor directional trading and crisis management skills. These inabilities, however, become significant asset management weaknesses only through the Vice Fund's overproportional

---

[17] Since the results of our one- and four-factor model-based regression specifications are qualitatively unchanged, we expect the same relationship to hold for our two- and three-factor model-based regression specifications.

[18] To cover the full industry base, we regress the continuously compounded return of the Vice Fund in excess of the risk-free rate on the respective excess returns of the tobacco, alcohol, defense, gambling and aerospace industries, whereby the excess return of any latter industry is cleared from the impact of any former industry following the orthogonalization approach of Elton et al. (1993).

[19] We obtain most daily return data for the relevant industries from Kenneth French's Data Library. In line with Hong and Kacperczyk (2009), we define the alcohol and defense industries as Fama and French's (1997) industry groups 4 (Beer & Liquor) and 26 (Guns/Defense), respectively. We approximate the aerospace industry, which Hong and Kacperczyk (2009) do not investigate, as Fama and French's (1997) industry groups 24 (Aero/Aircraft). With respect to the gambling industry, for which no Fama and French industry group exists, we again follow Hong and Kacperczyk's (2009) approach. Specifically, we use their list of thirty-five gambling stocks existent in 2003, which we were kindly provided by Marcin Kacperczyk, and compose a value-weighted index of the distribution including stock returns of thirty-two gambling stocks, which we retrieved from Datastream. We drop BlackHawk Gaming and Leucadia National, as we cannot retrieve data for them as of April 2009. Hilton Hotels is excluded, as we consider it to be predominantly a hotel rather than a gambling business.

exposure to long investments in gambling and aerospace stocks.

Nevertheless, we can conclude that the Vice Fund managers' crisis management and daily directional trading skills are significantly value-destructing, since the managers could have short sold more gambling and aerospace stocks. This practice would have turned these stocks from directional trading and crisis management hampering equities into stocks, which support these asset management skills. In summary, active investment in the existing vice investment products cannot be recommended from a financial perspective.

Conclusions

Several recent studies led by Hong and Kacperczyk (2009) document that companies in industries perceived as sinful – so called sin stocks (i.e., alcohol, tobacco, gambling) – deliver a significant and positive abnormal stock market performance. This potentially attractive characteristic makes these sin stocks a relevant investment opportunity for pension funds. In fact, following a rather conservative interpretation of pension funds' fiduciary duty, one might argue that pension funds have to invest overproportionally in sin stocks due to their seemingly superior returns to act in the best financial interest of their beneficiaries. This best financial interest, however, is unlikely the best interest of the beneficiary from a wider well-being perspective as, for instance, investments in tobacco companies are unlikely supportive of public health and hence beneficiaries' life expectancy.

Before one dives into this legal paradoxon it is worth considering the practicalities of investing in these so called sin stocks, as the academic studies documenting their preferential characteristics used nearly exclusively hypothetical portfolios and not actual investment funds. In fact, only one sin stock-based investment fund exists to the best of our knowledge, the Vice Fund. In this chapter, we pursue the first in-depth analysis of the financial attractiveness of the Vice Fund, which penalizes, rather than rewards, responsible corporations. Despite the financial potential of the Vice Fund's underlying sin stocks that has recently been indicated, we find the

Vice Fund's abnormal return to be statistically indistinguishable from zero. Interestingly, the Vice Fund managers possess significantly value-destructing directional trading and crisis management skills. Consequently, we cannot see any practical reason why pension funds would have to invest overproportionally in sin stocks, as their actually realized investment performance is no better than ordinary. Our finding is not necessarily inconsistent with Hong and Kacperczyk (2009), as they regressed equal weighted sin stocks against a value-weighted market benchmark and economy-wide investment style controls, which means that their significant positive alphas could have resulted from a clever portfolio weighting instead of any sin characteristics (i.e., the overproportionally weighted small sin stocks could have outperformed the underproportionally weighted large sin stocks).

Acknowledgements

We are very grateful to Hampus Adamsson, Christoph Biehl, Jimmy Chen, Alan Goodacre, Michael Rezec, John Wilson and seminar participants at the SDMC 2009 and the BAFA 2011 conferences for constructive comments. We are indebted to Marcin Kacperczyk, Julie Salaber and Paul Pfleiderer for clarification on their work as well as to Kenneth French and Marcin Kacperczyk for provision of benchmark factors and a vicious stock list, respectively. Any remaining errors or omissions are the sole responsibility of the authors. The views in this chapter are not necessarily shared by the Principles for Responsible Investment. Authors are listed alphabetically.

References

Admati, A. R., S. Bhattacharya, P. Pfleiderer and S.A. Ross. 1986. "On Timing and Selectivity," *Journal of Finance* 41: 715–30.

Aguilera, R. V., C. A. Williams, J. M. Conley and D. E. Rupp. 2006. "Corporate Governance and Social Responsibility: A Comparative Analysis of the UK and the US," *Corporate Governance: An International Review* 14: 147–58.

Areal, N., M. C. Cortez and F. Silva. 2010. "Investing in Mutual Funds: Does it Pay to be

a Sinner or a Saint?" working paper. http://
fsinsight.org/docs/download/research-paper-
investing-in-mutual-funds.pdf.

Banz, R. W. 1981. "The Relationship between
Return and Market Value of Common
Stocks," *Journal of Financial Economics*
9: 3–18.

Bauer, R., K. G. Koedijk and R. Otten. 2005.
"International Evidence on Ethical Mutual Fund
Performance and Investment Style," *Journal of
Banking & Finance* 29: 1751–67.

Bollen, N. P. B. 2007. "Mutual Fund Attributes and
Investor Behavior," *Journal of Financial and
Quantitative Analysis* 42: 683–708.

Bollen, N. P. B. and J. A. Busse. 2001. "On the
Timing Ability of Mutual Fund Managers,"
Journal of Finance 56: 1075–94.

Carhart, M. M. 1997. "On Persistence in Mutual Fund
Performance," *Journal of Finance* 52: 57–82.

Chong, J., M. Her and G. M. Phillips. 2006. "To
Sin or Not to Sin? Now that's the Question,"
Journal of Asset Management 6: 406–17.

Derwall, J. 2007. *The Economic Virtues of SRI and
CSR*. Rotterdam: Erasmus Research Institute of
Management.

Derwall, J., N. Guenster, R. Bauer and K. G.
Koedijk. 2005. "The Eco-Efficiency Premium
Puzzle," *Financial Analysts Journal* 61: 51–63.

Dimson, E., O. Karakaş and X. Li. 2012. "Active
Ownership," working paper, London Business
School.

Edmans, A. 2011. "Does the Stock Market Fully
Value Intangibles? Employee Satisfaction and
Equity Prices," *Journal of Financial Economics*
101: 621–40.

Eling, M. and F. Schuhmacher. 2007. "Does the
Choice of Performance Measure Influence
the Evaluation of Hedge Funds?" *Journal of
Banking & Finance* 31: 2632–47.

Elton, E. J., M. J. Gruber, S. Das and M. Hlavka.
1993. "Efficiency with Costly Information: A
Reinterpretation of Evidence from Managed
Portfolios," *Review of Financial Studies*
6: 1–22.

Entine, J. 2005. "The Politization of Public Investment,"
in J. Entine (ed.) *Pension Fund Politics: The
Dangers of Socially Responsible Investing*.
Washington, DC: The AEI Press, pp. 1–12.

Fama, E. F. and K. R. French. 1993. "Common Risk
Factors in the Returns on Stocks and Bonds,"
Journal of Financial Economics 33: 3–53.

1997. "Industry Cost of Equity," *Journal of
Financial Economics* 43: 153–93.

Ferson, W. and R. Schadt. 1996. "Measuring Fund
Strategy and Performance in Changing Economic
Conditions," *Journal of Finance* 51: 425–61.

Freshfields Bruckhaus Deringer. 2005. *A
Legal Framework for the Integration of
Environmental, Social and Governance
Issues into Institutional Investment*. London:
Freshfields Bruckhaus Deringer.

Friedman, A. L. and S. Miles. 2001. "Socially
Responsible Investment and Corporate Social
and Environmental Reporting in the UK: An
Exploratory Study," *British Accounting Review*
33: 523–48.

Galema, R., A. Plantinga and B. Scholtens. 2009.
"Diversification of Socially Responsible
Investment Portfolios: Testing for Mean-
Variance Spanning." http://papers.ssrn.com/
sol3/papers.cfm?abstract_id=1086560#.

Goetzmann, W. N., J. Ingersoll and Z. Ivkovic. 2000.
"Monthly Measurement of Daily Timers,"
Journal of Financial and Quantitative Analysis
35: 257–90.

Henriksson, R. D. and R. C. Merton. 1981. "On
Market Timing and Investment Performance. II:
Statistical Procedures for Evaluating Forecasting
Skills," *Journal of Business* 54: 513–33.

Hoepner, A. G. F. and D. G. McMillan. 2009.
"Research on 'Responsible Investment': An
Influential Literature Analysis Comprising a
Rating, Characterisation, Categorisation and
Investigation." http://papers.ssrn.com/sol3/
papers.cfm?abstract_id=1454793.

Hoepner, A. G. F. and S. Zeume. 2009. "Do Mutual
Fund Managers Have Asset Management
Skills? Evidence from New Measures
on Crisis Management and Directional
Trading." http://papers.ssrn.com/sol3/papers.
cfm?abstract_id=1470497.

Hong, H. and M. Kacperczyk. 2009. "The Price of
Sin: The Effects of Social Norms on Markets,"
Journal of Financial Economics 93: 15–36.

Jagannathan, R. and R. A. Korajczak. 1986. "Assessing
the Market Timing Performance of Managed
Portfolios," *Journal of Business* 59: 217–35.

Jegadeesh, N. and S. Titman. 1993. "Returns
to Buying Winners and Selling Losers:
Implications for Stock Market Efficiency,"
Journal of Finance 48: 65–91.

Jensen, M. C. 1968. "The Performance of Mutual
Funds in the Period 1945–1964," *Journal of
Finance* 23: 389–416.

Kempf, A. and P. Osthoff. 2007. "The Effect
of Socially Responsible Investing on

Portfolio Performance," *European Financial Management* 13: 908–22.

Kosowski, R., A. Timmermann, R. Wermers and H. White. 2006. "Can Mutual Fund 'Stars' Really Pick Stocks: New Evidence From a Bootstrap Analysis," *Journal of Finance* 61: 2551–95.

Kreander, N., R. H. Gray, D. M. Power and C. D. Sinclair. 2005. "Evaluating the Performance of Ethical and Non-ethical Funds: A Matched Pair Analysis," *Journal of Business Finance & Accounting* 32: 1465–93.

Lintner, J. 1965. "The Valuation of Risk Assets and the Selection of Risky Investments in Stock Portfolios and Capital Budgets," *Review of Economics and Statistics* 47: 13–37.

Lobe, S. and C. Walkshäusl. 2011. "Vice vs. Virtue Investing Around the World." http://papers.ssrn.com/sol3/papers.cfm?abstract_id=1089827.

Luck, C. and Tigrani, V. 1994. "Ethical Investing and the Returns to Sinful Industries." www.barra.com/research/BarraPub/sinful-n.aspx.

McAuley, T. 2007. "The Morality Play." www.cfo.com/article.cfm/9944819/c_10004388.

Mossin, J. 1966. "Equilibrium in a Capital Asset Market," *Econometrica* 34: 768–83.

Munnel, A. H. and A. Sundén. 2005. "Social Investing: Pension Plans Should Just Say 'No'," in J. Entine (ed.) *Pension Fund Politics: The Dangers of Socially Responsible Investing.* Washington, DC: The AEI Press, pp. 13–55.

Newey, W. K. and K. D. West. 1987. "A Simple, Positive Semi-Definite, Heteroskedasticity and Autocorrelation Consistent Covariance Matrix," *Econometrica* 55: 703–8.

Pfleiderer, P. and S. Bhattacharya. 1983. "A Note on Performance Evaluation," Technical Report no. 714, Graduate School of Business, Stanford University.

Renneboog, L., J. Ter Horst and C. Zhang. 2008. "The Price of Ethics and Stakeholder Governance: The Performance of Socially Responsible Mutual Funds," *Journal of Corporate Finance* 14: 302–22.

Rosenberg, B., K. Reid and R. Lanstein. 1985. "Persuasive Evidence of Market Inefficiency," *Journal of Portfolio Management* 11: 9–16.

Rounds, C. E., Jr. 2005. "Why Social Investing Threatens Public Pension Funds, Charitable Trusts, and the Social Security Trust Fund," in J. Entine (ed.) *Pension Fund Politics. The Dangers of Socially Responsible Investing.* Washington, DC: The AEI Press, pp. 56–80.

Salaber, J. M. 2009. "The Determinants of Sin Stock Returns: Evidence on the European Market," working paper, Paris-Dauphine University.

Scholtens, B. 2007. "Financial and Social Performance of Socially Responsible Investments in the Netherlands," *Corporate Governance: An International Review* 15: 1090–105.

Schröder, M. 2004. "The Performance of Socially Responsible Investments: Investment Funds and Indices," *Financial Markets and Portfolio Management* 18: 122–42.

2007. "Is there a Difference? The Performance Characteristics of SRI Equity Indices," *Journal of Business Finance & Accounting* 34: 331–48.

Shank, T. M., D. K. Manullang and R. P. Hill. 2005. "Is it Better to be Naughty or Nice?" *Journal of Investing* 14: 82–7.

Sharpe, W. F. 1964. "Capital Asset Prices: A Theory of Market Equilibrium under Conditions of Risk," *Journal of Finance* 19: 425–42.

Statman, M. 2000. "Socially Responsible Mutual Funds," *Financial Analysts Journal* 56: 30–9.

Statman, M. and D. Glushkov. 2009. "The Wages of Social Responsibility," *Financial Analysts Journal* 65: 33–46.

Treynor, J. L. and K. K. Mazuy. 1966. "Can Mutual Funds Outguess the Market?" *Harvard Business Review* 44: 131–6.

Whose risk counts?

RAJ THAMOTHERAM AND AIDAN WARD

In the expectations market the goal is to make a trade in which you have the upper hand, no matter what the impact is on the other party.

Roger Martin (2011: 32)

Of all imaginary organisms – dragons, gods, sea monsters ... – economic man is the dullest.

Gregory Bateson (1987: 175)

This makes investors focus on returns without paying sufficient regard to the risks that are being taken to achieve these returns. Rarely do funds make their principal focus risk-adjusted return.

(Towers Watson 2012: 13)

Introduction

The title of this chapter points to a deep unease the authors have about the workings of the investment industry. In an industry where the size of one's "risk appetite" is a marker of one's virility, where the biggest brains are drawn to interpreting the subtleties of the movements of markets, the dominant belief is that it is right that outsized financial rewards should go to those who deliver alpha (and clients). Our hypothesis is that, in this context, some simple and common sense truths about risk are ignored.

Here are some generalizations about the investment industry. In an industry where herd behavior is prevalent, the exceptions validate these norms.

A. The industry's narrative, what it says about itself, is that it spreads risk to make the investment space safer and more stable for everyone. In practice, however, it creates risk. What is more, it offloads risk from those with the best understanding and the most power to act onto those with less understanding and less capacity to act. It is fundamentally asymmetric and this is worsening (Hawley et al. 2011).

B. The industry claims to be full of high-powered specialists who create sophisticated mathematical models to meet client needs in every circumstance. In practice the industry tends towards herd behavior and a monoculture of offerings on risk. These offerings are heavily marketed to clients who don't want to be seen to be different. These same clients are then blamed for not asking for what they need. Reliance on these experts is the reason why fiduciary responsibility exists, while the experts take advantage of fiduciary loopholes to avoid taking on the responsibility for which they are being retained.

C. The industry is organized around fostering an image of playing a vital role in establishing a market price for risk and a market estimation of levels of risk on which much regulation is based, without however accepting the implied fiduciary duty: power without responsibility. In practice the dominant risk model, VaR, is known to misallocate resources seriously, and of course it neglects the risks created by the industry and much the same can be said for other risk processes.

These and other realities result in a situation which we term "asymmetric financial risk." In the field of warfare when combatants are of completely unequal strength and sophistication, we get asymmetric warfare: long drawn-out, highly destructive "insurgencies" that can undermine a country or a region from within. Our hypothesis is that asymmetric financial risk is a much bigger hazard to the well-being of many more people than asymmetric warfare. It destroys wealth and investment and it destroys the economic and wider ecosystem.

To be specific, a pension fund has a mission: to deliver investment returns that underpin the retirement well-being of its members. This is primarily a financial mission, but the fund cannot lose sight of the fact that its members live in a real environment with real social and political systems that are affected by investment. What we do in this chapter is to highlight the investment industry practices that put that fund mission at risk, in order that we can then focus on things the industry can and should do for its clients.

The fiduciary duty of service providers sits alongside this fund mission. The notion of fiduciary duty necessarily includes customer loyalty. What matters to the customer is the effect of service outcomes on the fund mission. While it is common, almost universal, to draw very narrow boundaries around the nature of the outcomes to be measured, the customer has their own perception of the effects of service actions. The customer will perceive a failure of loyalty if they feel disadvantaged in either absolute or relative terms in mission delivery (Hawley et al. 2011).

Investment managers want to be seen as competing to deliver investment returns to their clients, alpha. At the level of the investment industry there are many problems with this stance, indeed it is increasingly common to hear senior investment managers say, generally in private, that they have become locked in to their own game. To summarize these problems with alpha:[1]

A. It is inherently zero-sum: if one investment manager really beats the trend, by definition someone else is below trend. A pension fund that has multiple managers is thus vulnerable to cancelling out any performance gains. And taking clients as a whole they cannot become better off by trying to buy alpha "performance."

B. Inherently short-term in its derivation and its reporting, and becoming more so, competition for alpha thus tends to promote short-term

decisions, earnings management and damage to the underlying beta on which everyone depends. Arguably beta has declined markedly over the past twenty-five years (Stout 2012).

C. Any focus on headline figures drives activity, which in investment terms is churn. Churn generally benefits the investment industry disproportionately compared with its clients. Investment analysts, managers and consultants need to be seen to be active when the evidence from Berkshire Hathaway and others is that reduced churn is a good strategy for outperformance.

In the quotes at the start of this chapter are three angles on what we are examining here. Roger Martin, Dean of Rotman Business School, insists that markets have become markets in expectation and are fundamentally about gambling on sentiment not about investment at all, a fact confirmed by McKinsey & Co. who document how "intrinsic investors" are now down to about 20 percent of the market (Palter et al. 2008). Martin sees gamblers playing the alpha game: knowing they can only win by someone else losing. And Gregory Bateson with his penetrating cybernetic insights thinks that by putting economic man into our equations we lose all imagination. It is therefore unsurprising to find leading investment consultants, Towers Watson, conclude that the investors – as a matter of routine – do not do what they imply they do, namely make investment decisions on the basis of risk-adjusted returns.

Risks created by the investment industry

The investment industry is huge, it channels vast amounts of finance and wields enormous influence. As a senior adviser to President Clinton has said, "I used to think if there was reincarnation, I wanted to come back as the president or the pope or a .400 baseball hitter. But now I want to come back as the bond market. You can intimidate everybody" (Carville 1993).

Just looking at this picture structurally or systemically it is inconceivable that all this influence does not create some risks of its own and the recognition that asset managers may soon be

---

[1] Alpha is a risk-adjusted measure of the so-called active return on an investment. It is the return in excess of the compensation for the risk borne. Cf. beta, which measures the part of the asset's statistical variance that cannot be removed by the diversification provided by the portfolio of many risky assets, because of the correlation of its returns with the returns of the other assets that are in the portfolio. Beta can be estimated for individual companies using regression analysis against a stock market index (Wikipedia).

categorized as "SIFIs" (systemically important financial institutions) is proof of this. Neither should it be a surprise that any risks that are created are not the subject of extensive research by the industry itself or its supportive think-tanks and academics: this would be to expose its soft underbelly. As a simple illustration, using Google Scholar, we found "Volatility" gave 1,130,000 results, while "Endogenous risk" only 3,500 results.[2] The significance of this mismatch between research focus and importance will become clear below.

The first set of risks created by the industry is termed endogenous risk. Well-respected but yet contrarian mainstream thinkers talk openly about this risk and analyze its effect on market assumptions. They see themselves as forward-looking professionals correcting the tools of the trade so that they still work.

The second set of risks that the industry creates we call iatrogenic risks because they are a direct result of what the industry sells, including but not limited to its risk management approach. As yet, even the most contrarian of mainstream specialists have not incorporated this agenda. By chasing headline alpha to succeed vis-à-vis clients, we contend that the industry creates several risks to beta. As denialism fades, we expect that what we call iatrogenic risks will increasingly become included in endogenous risks.

Given the numerous examples of how fundamental aspects of risk are mismanaged – and space constraints mean we can only mention a few – there is a very solid case for saying that "asymmetric financial risk" is a bigger hazard to well being for more people than "asymmetric warfare."[3] One implication is that we need a "war on dysfunctional financial behavior" and this should be rapidly escalated and the key battlefield on which to fight is risk. Interestingly the CFA Institute and forward-thinking academics have highlighted the importance of "dysfunctional financial behavior" but have chosen to focus on the errors of the masses, ignoring the thinking of the so-called "1 percent" (Freedland 2012).

Endogenous risk

The financial industry is widely known for operating as a monoculture – its actors do compete but within a narrow band of similar behaviors and endogenous risk comes as a combination of the size of the finance industry and the coordinated signals it sends (and does not send).

For example, only one US bank has faced a "no vote" on executive pay – and even that just scraped through at 55 percent.[4] The banking industry says pay is not an issue and investors duly follow their lead (Treanor 2013a). Put simply, bank executives are being rewarded for taking risks that put society and pension fund members at levels of risk which the executives have immunity against. Indeed, the banks are "too big to fail" meaning there is a very high chance that governments will nationalize unexpected debts. Bank pay may not be an issue to investment managers – who themselves have rewards which are difficult to justify in real world terms (Treanor 2013b) – but it is a huge issue to their clients, whose tax money and jobs are put on the line.

Endogenous risk is an effect of the numbers that the industry chases, and so it has a reflexive effect on those numbers. A good example of this is leverage about which Woody Brock is appropriately damning:

> a proof of why excess leverage is bad for society: It is a non-market "externality" because it dramatically increases the riskiness of wealth growth over time, while failing to deliver any corresponding gain in aggregate societal wealth itself. That is to say, excess leverage creates an "inefficiency" since it generates more pain – but no more gain.
>
> This is a deep observation that constitutes a paradox within the very foundations of modern financial theory: The irrationally high levels of leverage justified by the Efficient Market Theory via its dramatic underestimation of risk becomes the source of Economic Inefficiency in the precise and revolutionary sense first proposed by Kenneth Arrow in 1953: a misallocation of risk itself. [Recall the reason why the EMT necessarily underestimates risk: It implies zero endogenous risk] (Brock 2008).

---

[2] Search done on March 16, 2013, thanks to Kazutaka Kuroda.
[3] www.rand.org/topics/asymmetric-warfare.html.

[4] Citi.

And the principle of reflexivity, that some things cannot be known in advance because they are the outcomes of the very decision processes being considered, has been well articulated by George Soros:

> To understand the uncertainties associated with reflexivity, we need to probe a little further. If the cognitive function operated in isolation without any interference from the manipulative function it could produce knowledge. Knowledge is represented by true statements. A statement is true if it corresponds to the facts – that is what the correspondence theory of truth tells us. But if there is interference from the manipulative function, the facts no longer serve as an independent criterion by which the truth of a statement can be judged because the correspondence may have been brought about by the statement changing the facts (Soros 2009).

There are also crucial questions about the game itself. The narrative that the industry promotes to regulators and clients is that financial instruments are designed to stabilize the market. In a major paper in *Nature*, Andy Haldane – the well-respected Bank of England strategist – reported a model for whether derivatives stabilize or destabilize a market. The model shows that, while derivatives correspond to real world assets that may need to be hedged in some way, they have a stabilizing effect. When there are more derivatives being traded than are required for fundamental hedging they have a destabilizing effect. What is intuitively obvious has now got empirical backing from a leading figure in the debate (Haldane and May 2011). The challenge is to convert these contrarian insights into action by the mainstream and to stimulate much more of this kind of challenging applied research.

MIT's Andrew Lo, in considering what the latest financial crisis can tell us, is perhaps the most blunt:

> "When you have large amounts of assets being thrown around, you're going to create instabilities," he said, adding: "If everybody goes to the left side of the boat one day, and everybody runs to the right side of the boat the next, you're going to see that kind of unusual period of volatility."[5]

[5] Interview in *Pensions and Investments* on July 13, 2009. www.pionline.com/article/20090713/PRINT/307139990.

Then he goes on to say, quoting Lowenstein with approval, that the risk created is highly asymmetric and is exported onto people who are supposed to be end-beneficiaries:

> Intriguingly, he considers the crisis a natural consequence of a financial system that, rather than extracting Marxist super-profits from society, extracted risk from its investments and dumped it on those members of society least able to handle it (Lo 2012: 171).

Endogenous risk is often caused by too much money chasing too few productive investments. This is a "tragedy of the commons" that makes the commonly heard argument that we do not have the resources to invest in sustainability even more bizarre! Three likely effects are a bubble in prices, unwise investments by corporations in the market and earnings management to make sure the music does not stop playing. In summary, endogenous risk is created by the operation of professionals in the market and is highly asymmetric in its effects on the various participants.

Iatrogenic risk

An iatrogenic illness is an illness caused by medication or a physician. By analogy iatrogenic risk is risk caused by the investment industry itself relating to the real world of the end-beneficiary, a world that investment intermediaries, especially the richest and most senior decision-makers isolate themselves from. In a nutshell the financial return from investment of, for example, a pension fund may fail to compensate for the costs imposed by environmental and social degradation owing to the said investments.

The instability caused directly by investors causes the destruction of value for investors and in the target corporation. However, it generally creates profitable work for the investment industry supply chain. Notice, however, that any mechanism to reduce volatility of this nature would need to be implemented by the investment industry itself, i.e., the people who have little personal interest in doing so.

The line the industry sells to regulators and clients is that financial instruments are designed to stabilize the investment environment and protect clients. It is clear that this is a damaging half-truth. When is a derivative not a derivative? When it becomes purely speculative. But who is best placed to determine when financial instruments have stopped working in the clients' interests? The industry itself! The existing situation verges on a financial protection racket: the industry works by keeping the level of mugging high, encouraging the best customers – sovereign wealth funds, ultra high net worth individuals, endowments – to believe they can do better than "muppets." The net result is more need for its products.

Here are two case studies that show how iatrogenic risk happens in practice.

Example 1: Why are long-term investors going for a stranded asset – coal?

On a ten-year view, investing in coal-fired power is simply an irrational way to try to make money. When reality hits, governments will move into a wartime footing to stop the slide to a world which is 4–6 degrees warmer, as even the International Energy Authority now warns is likely.[6] Any discounted cash flow model should therefore either insert significant cost increases, collapse the revenue forecast, increase the Weighted Average Cost of Capital (WACC) or include a significant Capital Expenditure (CAPEX) uplift.[7]

In addition, owners of companies should be very actively engaging with board and senior management on the core CAPEX decisions. But this kind of action is outside the comfort zone of even many environmental, social and governance (ESG)/corporate governance analysts, even when their employers have signed up to the UN Principles of Responsible Investment. And it really shouldn't be! The UK's largest coal-fired power station, Drax, confirmed last year that it intends to move to predominantly biomass.[8]

Example 2: Putting the bee back into beta

What is the price of a bee? And more generally, where does the extinction of bee populations – and with bees much of agriculture as we know it – fit into discounted cash flow and other investment/risk decision-making tools? The simple answer is that they don't.

To summarize, the scientific case that one class of pesticides, neonicotinoids, are particularly dangerous to bees is now very clear (Maxim and van der Sluijs 2013). Bayer and Syngenta are among the biggest producers of these chemicals and have also played leading roles in the powerful industry push back against regulatory action. Already too late, the industry has persuaded some supportive governments to back further delay

(Jolly 2013). Like the gorilla in experiments about the importance of selection attention, the role of investors is very important but hidden.[9] Investors incentivize corporate management to worry (much) more about shareholder returns than helping to cause a form of ecocide that could be economically disastrous for asset owners and their members. In addition, investors show no real stewardship activity to counterbalance the effect of company management who use shareholder money to lobby for what is not in the real interests of the end-beneficiaries. Thus it is not surprising that we can only find one fund manager that has been explicit about engaging on this issue.[10]

---

[6] www.businessspectator.com.au/article/2012/6/12/smart-energy/iea-we%E2%80%99re-track-6-degree-warming.
[7] Personal communication, Benjamin McCarron, April 2, 2013.

[8] www.draxpower.com/biomass/cofiring_plans.
[9] www.youtube.com/watch?v=vJG698U2Mvo.
[10] http://co-operativeassetmanagement.co.uk/downloads/TCAM-Responsible-Investment-Annual-Review-09–10.pdf.

Systematically undervaluing beta risks is nothing new. Insiders know well that about 80 percent of the ability of a fund to meet its liabilities comes from the beta, the market return, but that 80 percent of the resources are funneled into chasing alpha, which is often illusory or not cost-effective when real costs (including trading activity and knock-on impact) are considered.

But undermining ESG beta is probably the much bigger issue. As Jeremy Grantham has said about climate change "we should not unnecessarily ruin a pleasant and currently very serviceable planet just to maximize the short-term profits of energy companies and others" (Grantham 2012). Of course, he could also have been talking about bees, bribery and corruption or indeed any of the other market-critical ingredients, which professional investors tend to think of as "saving the world" activities that, at best, require tokenistic or compliance-style attention.

One cannot blame fund managers for this failure to do what end-beneficiaries need. It is not, in general, what they were asked to do. It is not how they are monitored, rewarded (or sacked). And it is not what their professional training equips them to do.

Some argue that this gap in services can be filled by new market players, engagement overlay providers (EOPs). But as far as the authors are aware, only one EOP has been active on the issue of bees, demonstrating how major societal risks can fall between the cracks. EOPs are today as much about managing defensive "CYA" risk for the client as anything else: the good ones offer action-packed reports at regular intervals. With clients expressing a broad range of competing demands – child labor, genetically modified organisms (GMOs), water scarcity, etc. – and especially given the resources EOPs have (clients typically pay less than 1 basis point), they are completely overstretched.

There are, of course, ways around this. Members of pension funds are not in competition with each other for a better quality of life. If one pension fund led on action to protect bees, supported by an EOP, members of all other funds benefit. And that would free other funds to lead on other critical issues and problem companies. This calls for a much more collaborative, strategic and joined-up approach to stewardship.[11] As John Kay has said, stewardship is today the primary role of investors – to make sure CAPEX is well deployed and at an absolute minimum, to ensure it is not harming the interests of society as defined in scientific, economic and shared legal ways (Kay 2012).

To summarize, we have a class of risk that tends to undermine the investment industry's own theories and assumptions – endogenous risk – and a class of risk that undermines the wider context that the beneficiaries and the enterprises that generate beta depend upon – iatrogenic risk. The way these risks fall is highly asymmetric: it is the professional advisors who benefit from the way risk is defined and the supposed beneficiaries that end up carrying the bulk of the risk.

Industry record of risk management services

Taking our cue from Gregory Bateson again, we now consider the track record of the investment industry in managing risk for its clients. First, it is important to understand that there is little way for clients to assess the degree to which their risks have been managed independently of the industry and its risk models. The industry sells the description of the problem, for instance volatility, and the solution to that problem with little process for client verification, not least about fundamental assumptions (for example, is volatility the key risk for long-horizon investors?). The potential for conflict of interest in such a situation is huge, and regulation is also largely captured by the industry.

Bateson's point is that if the communication, between asset owner and investment manager for instance, is on the basis of the numbers and not about the complex real world situation of the client, then what will follow is the management of the numbers, not of the real world risks. Meadows makes the same point when numbers come bottom of her list of powerful places to intervene in a system, the least effective (Meadows 1999). For an investment manager to add value in risk management, they must both understand the underlying

---

[11]   http://intranet.unpri.org/?p=411.

situation facing the real client (i.e., the end-ben-eficiaries, not the technical specialist who might be intermediating on their behalf) and want to do something to ameliorate these risks.

Second, some risks are modeled and others are not and nowhere are the costs of this selective approach clearer than value at risk (VaR), the dominant industry model. To quote Woody Brock: "the theory underlying VAR completely side steps the endogenous risk story and with it the very kinds of risk that recently brought down the world financial system" (Brock 2012: 147). In addition, VaR, models often weight exposure to the other risks in a way that is known to misallocate resources. VaR, is so widespread, and indeed embedded in regulation, that it amounts to a monoculture within the industry. Taking the metaphor from agriculture, monocultures have two key attributes: they often destroy their supporting ecosystem and they are brittle and subject to sudden and widespread failure.

Third, there is a substantial misallocation of resources when it comes to risk versus returns. Towers Watson estimates that a typical fund spends "usually above 50 basis points for external portfolio management and under five basis points for the fund's asset allocation and risk management activities" (Towers Watson 2012).

It is not surprising, therefore, that risk professionals who seek to do their job well struggle to be heard and eventually, to retain their positions,[12] often being forced to resort to whistleblowing (Neville 2012). Nor is it surprising that others simply dumb down and do what their peers and sponsors find acceptable. There has been longstanding concern that the chairs and members of audit committees have failed to provide informed and independent oversight. It is not that these problems are unknown, rather it is the complacency of the insiders and their advisers that is the issue. Back in 2007 a business-friendly briefing made the rather naively optimistic statement that: "The days of boards and committees packed with friends of the CEO have passed, replaced by questioning, engaged directors with an extensive

workload" (Tapestry Network 2007). Auditors are also increasingly recognized, by insiders, to have failed to do what they could have (Chambers 2012).

So what then is real risk management?

If we return to our pension fund and its mission: in what ways is that mission at risk and what sort of risk management has a serious impact on those risks? This is the upstream question that does not get asked and is the foundation of our chapter title, whose risk counts?

There are two key determining factors in deciding whether risk management is real:

A. Is it concerned with events and factors in the real economy?
B. Does it recognize that different players have different interests?

Real risk management – from the perspective of long-horizon, well-diversified investors – drives beta, the underlying real return on productive investment, by limiting the negative impact of real economy events. The best way to understand the intentions of the different players is to understand their actions, and the outcomes that flow from those actions, as distinct from listening to their stated purposes.

Suppose there is a food scandal in which commodity trading is seen to be causing widespread starvation as many NGOs, Oxfam included, have argued could happen. An asset manager in this scenario would have to demonstrate that their investment strategy was having at least a neutral, and ideally a positive effect on the management of the risk fundamentals and that they were supporting collaborative risk management for the situation. We doubt that there is any commodity trader globally that could do this today.

The basic framework for actually managing risk comprises:

• **The situation that can go wrong.** The risk itself, which comprises lack of time, lack of information and lack of control. Anything that does not affect these fundamentals, either directly or indirectly, is not risk management. Note that the fundamentals can generally be traded off against each other. Insurance is not risk management until it can be shown to deal with significant aspects of mission risk itself.

- **Who is involved and who cares.** The stakeholders for that risk, who has skin in the game, with dimensions of power over the risk situation, closeness to the risk and interest in the risk. When horsemeat is found in burgers, whose business might be damaged, who do they need to deal with to limit that business damage, and in the end who cares whether they suffer or not. It is commonly the case that the person with the most power to intervene has no interest in doing so, and the people who most want to intervene to prevent a disaster have no power. Risk management has to realign these mismatches if it is to be effective.
- **How they frame it, who gets blamed by default.** The perspective stakeholders take on the risk with dimensions of vision about the context, trust in the other stakeholders and work or effort applied. If a quant believes they can deliver an enhanced return while diversifying against risk without dealing with the actual risk to actual enterprises, they are going to be hard to align with the fundamentals. The focus needs to move from investing in models and static assets to investing in dynamic enterprises in a networked world.

In the investment industry the stakeholding for risk is singularly fragmented, with different people in the supply chain looking to profit from handling the risk to their own advantage and often to the detriment of their customers' interest. Mapping who the stakeholders are and what their perspective is on a given risk scenario could not be more important or more revealing.

The industry has been amazingly successful at getting end-"beneficiaries" to accept wholeheartedly risk models that suit the providers and not the clients. So much so that the end-beneficiaries, or at least their agents, drive the use of these models. A good example is the widespread use of relative return benchmarks that are generally based on capital weighted indices that have been heavily criticized (Hu 2006). When we asked one of the major providers of these cap weighted indices if there were plans to review their response was:

No ... we have a full range of cap-weighted indices. We also have ESG indices. Customers are free to choose. So it isn't a matter of changing the indices; rather it is a matter of customer choice. Someone interested in changing the use of cap-weighted indices may want to focus on the customers and their choices.[13]

Another example is how companies in the UK were sold complex hedging products to protect their income from currency fluctuation but ended up making payments to the providers in changed circumstances that were so large that they bankrupted many companies (FSA 2012). It is simply implausible to maintain that the providers concerned were trying to help companies manage currency risk.

Given the lack of alignment of interests between members of the supply chain (i.e., the inherent tendency to take advantage of others when there is the opportunity to do so) then the management of stakeholding itself is important. The way forward calls for a trusted inner circle of stakeholders who share full information so that they can actually assist each other in managing the underlying risks, and an outer circle who are not trusted fully and have to be managed by understanding how they will act to further their own interests. It may or may not be possible to use their services wisely. Others are less sanguine that such conflicts of interest can be managed: Yale's David Swensen maintains that conflicts of interests are the core of how the financial industry operates. The idea that the industry delivers value, and then, as an afterthought, can be tasked to manage conflicts better, is an illusion.

It is important to note these misalignments need not be ill-intentioned or consciously exploitative in intent. Robert Shiller, in his book *Finance and the Good Society* (Shiller 2012) devotes a whole section to explaining that most people were insured for losses from the Gulf oil spill and that if everyone had been fully insured, the event would be nothing to get too excited about. Which shows that even the best of mainstream behavioral economists – of which he is clearly one – can take positions that

---

[13] Personal email communication, Anonymous, February 27, 2012.

an end-beneficiary living in the Gulf would not be able to relate to. In this case it probably reflects the mindset that environment is a second-order issue, at best externalities that can be cleaned up. This separation of "value" and "risk" in managing the effects of environmental damage from industrial operations goes a long way to explain why we are failing to deal with climate change risk. Many key decision-makers today do not see the environment as the context from which economic value is generated. As Harvard's Clay Christensen has shown, the obsessive focus on greater efficiency is killing real wealth generating innovation (Niesen 2012). It is also making us more fragile: ever-leaner supply chains and production methods mean that no slack is built into the system. Fragile systems break rather than bend: damage is maximized and the impact of risks is much greater than it would otherwise be. Driving efficiencies can easily be the direct opposite or enemy of effective risk management and value creation (Lietaer et al. 2010).

Does anyone have good information about real risk?

When our pension fund manager goes looking for information about the real mission risk his fund faces, he finds that what the industry calls risk management, basically managing the numbers, thoroughly obscures the information he needs. Imagine that he had doubts about BP's safety record before the Gulf oil spill: where should he have gone for hard information?

Before we get to risk, let's consider the basics of company performance:

- The expectations market is tied to the real economy in a way that thoroughly obscures underlying performance (Martin 2011).
- Even within companies, real information about performance is obscured by:
  - Misattribution of meaning to data.
  - Multiple pressures to meet expectations and targets.
  - Rapidly changing context.

Risk to that obscured performance is doubly difficult to understand. Of course the illusion that "risk professionals" understand actual company

performance is important to their ability to avoid fiduciary responsibilities.

What we are challenging here is the view that the underlying risk to investment in a corporation is already largely factored in to the price of those investments by the market. Sometimes the crowd wisdom of the market is superior to the insights that executives have into their own business situation. Sometimes the chicanery of executives outwits the markets (and everyone else). But these are both speculative views and the fundamentals are more prosaic and much messier.

Let's consider food price volatility. There will be no doubt about the prices of food that people cannot afford to pay, including some beneficiaries to whom duties of loyalty are owed. But the factors and risks that lead to those prices will immediately be the subject of intense speculation themselves. There will be witch-hunts. This pressure makes real risk management more important, to relieve the distress of both the starving who are not getting the food they need and the producers struggling to grow and distribute it. We know that the market rhetoric of higher prices bringing increased production is not the answer because it was the market that produced the volatility that made the underlying problems urgent.

As soon as we move away from proxy measures taken from aspects of markets, we find solid information very hard to come by. At a recent presentation on ESG issues, a specialist fielded a question about the error bars on a figure on his screen and he said they always reported the exact figure.[14] The idea that there can be precise numbers on these ESG data points is plainly absurd. To perform risk management that affects the fundamentals in a positive way real information is needed. Even mainstream auditors are beginning to understand this as the recent "confidence accounting" movement shows.[15] And the challenges are even greater with regards to ESG data, which has a far shorter history and is generally not audited. Put simply, risk information is real only when it helps align stakeholders in collaborative risk management.

[14] Bloomberg, November 19, 2012.
[15] www.zyen.com/index.php/knowledge?Content= confidence%20accounting.

Conversely, it is a sign of how little real risk management is performed that there is no widespread perception that the data is inadequate.

We have already referred to BP's problems in the Gulf – what management at some level knew but did not address and what investors did not know, both of which interfered with good financial risk management decisions. The data about BP's safety record was available before the accident but only if you asked searching questions and went beneath the surface reporting (Thamotheram and Le Floc'h, 2011). To understand the issues for instance analysts probably had to reckon with regulatory capture. The risks BP was running were absolutely not factored into the share price or its volatility, because in practice the cover-up was extensive and successful. To be clear, cover-up does not mean conspiracy: almost all useful information is hidden and distorted by the very processes that generate it. It has been said that "spreading the risk" actually means those who understand the risk dumping it on those who do not – in the case of BP, it was not that analysts did not know that BP was cutting costs, but rather analysts considered this cost cutting to be a reason to buy (Shefrin and Cervellati 2011).

Managers and investors want to believe that bias and obfuscation in their information is a trivial problem but it is not. Clearly taking a risk that is tolerably understood is different in kind from taking one that is not understood. And taking a risk where there may be systematic misinformation is something else again. This is an oblique reason for the rise of statistical methods of "dealing with" investment risk. Systemic risk concerns the circular patterns of causation that allow risks that people suppose are separate and manageable to sweep away swathes of productive capacity, and they, by definition, cannot be factored in to statistical methods because they are highly non-linear.

Moreover, actually playing risk as an investment theme is a growing trend, but it is questionable whether analysts appreciate how contrived the numbers can be. A finance director of a Mental Health Trust explained to one of us that UK Treasury regulation now meant that new builds could only happen under the Public Finance Initiative Scheme which means making projections over thirty years. In his opinion anyone who thought they could predict the need for mental health accommodation in five years' time was a candidate to become an inmate. However, he needed to demonstrate that risk was exported to the private sector by the proposed scheme so using an accepted risk model from an approved consultancy company, he adjusted the input to give the required result. Creating non-financial risk numbers to meet the requirements of important stakeholders (in this case, HM Treasury) is a likely consequence of box-ticking engagement by these important stakeholders. But what is the chance that the quantification and management of those risks remain meaningful when they are part of a process of this nature?

A good example is the number of major mergers and acquisitions where the acquired company is not what it seemed to be. Indeed most research indicates that M&A activity has an overall success rate of about 50 percent although analysts are routinely positive about the vast majority. In these cases neither the share price nor the due diligence process appears good enough to discover the real investment risk. In contrast, it is well known that insiders (staff and key suppliers/customers) can often sense when a company is being groomed by its management to be sold, smoothing the earnings figures and ignoring maintenance and investment needs.

These realistic evaluations are not a prophecy of doom. Rather, they are intended to underpin the value of asking skeptical questions well upstream of where analysts and clients usually begin. In practice it is necessary to question whether the risk models and tools being used are tending to reveal or tending to hide the critical information. And then it is necessary to ask the question of this chapter: whose risks are they? Who is impacted by significant risks and who is in a position to manage them? How much "risk management" actually exacerbates the risk to investors?

If, as we believe to be the case, today's risk management is largely illusory or frankly harmful, then the answer is to shift to a substantially more basic approach to investment – a proper partnership between investors and executives that depends on growing the fundamental economic base. Not only can there be a long-term focus on strategic risks (which still regularly destroy even the largest companies) but the information that allows proper management and proper investment can be cleaned up along the way. The fiduciary duty of impartiality implies an obligation to provide capital gains and an impartially secure standard of retirement and manage risks which extends fifty-plus years into the future, for younger beneficiaries. To be short-term in decision-making is at the very least to privilege older beneficiaries above younger ones.

To move forward, given all the difficulties and lack of confidence that we have discussed, it is always worth taking an anthropological and systems view. If we discount all the intentions and rationalizations, and focus on what is being delivered to whom, what does that tell us about what is actually going on?

Whose risk counts? What we can tell based on what has happened

In a classic book from the 1930s Fred Schwed asks *Where Are the Customers' Yachts?* He is pointing to a pattern where brokers get rich consistently while their customers do not always do so. Stafford Beer coined the acronym POSIWID – the purpose of a system is what it does – to draw attention to the disparity between what people say about a system and what the behavior of a system is in practice. If the investment industry consistently allows its firms and professionals to become wealthy when the experience of the end-beneficiaries is more mixed then we are entitled to say that, systemically, that is its purpose.

If we are indeed entering a period of low growth, then it will be less easy to hide the systemic facts of the situation. Even at a level of contractual engagement, if a retail owner of a pension scheme is charged 1.5 percent of his fund value for administration of the fund and if the growth of the fund is less than 1.5 percent, that does not look like a service worth paying for. Although the detailed causes behind such a situation need careful examination, such examination is likely to result in a view that the way in which investment risk is shared between the parties is inequitable. That a situation has grown up where such questions have not been forcibly asked has much to do with the period of inflation from which we are emerging (taking inflation to mean various asset bubbles as well

as inflation *stricto sensu*) and the "cognitive capture" that is closely associated.[16]

Again from a systemic perspective, many asset owners are looking for reliable long-term returns to match their liabilities. Finding such returns is a matter of understanding which parts of which economies is producing sustainable economic value. What is destructive of long-term value are the asset bubbles that produce exaggerated returns followed by losses. The investment industry is obviously central to the operation of such bubbles: they are founded on its judgments and behaviors. Indeed it seems highly likely that these bubbles are one of the main mechanisms by which assets are transferred from asset owners to so-called service providers. Yet it need not be this way: what if investment firms were engaged in counter-cyclic activity to protect their clients' assets?

From the end-beneficiary perspective, a house price bubble could well be a disaster financially and otherwise. Like the wrong sort of snow, there can be the wrong sort of (apparent) wealth. Yet that end-beneficiary's pension fund could be invested in the bubble both directly and via firms making outsized profits. One of the effects of a house price bubble is to effect huge transfers of wealth between generations, from the young to the old. Transfers that would never be countenanced politically take place as side-effects of political policies and are driven by investment behavior. As Michael Sandel has argued, there are some places where the intrusion of market values and market behavior is undesirable and should be resisted and reversed (Sandel 2012).

It is important to note that the investment industry is far more than a passive bystander in this process. In the US, for example, weak regulation has made American pension funds "the world's biggest risk-takers" as a result of not lowering their liability discount rates in response to low interest rates (as happens routinely with European, Canadian and Australian funds). As an aside, US funds have also made least progress on mainstreaming ESG and doing stewardship because of concerns that this activity may be "anti-fiduciary!" The main

---

[16] The phrase was introduced by Willem Buiter, now chief economist at Citigroup, to describe how Wall Street had influenced regulators. See http://willembuiter.com/chicago.pdf.

beneficiaries of this lax regulatory regime are fund managers who are able to continue to push "high alpha" investment products and investment consultants who can advise on which manager to select. Of course, trustees and executives of asset owners are colluding with these indefensible assumptions because it would be politically disruptive in the short-term to face reality. But the end result is that risk is transferred to ordinary US citizens (as has happened in many European countries, Cyprus most recently) while risky investment behaviors – including bubbles – are encouraged.

Once we accept that the investment industry has a much wider, more complex and more questionable impact on the real world than simply generating alpha, then the genie is out of the bottle. Can we really be content with rhetoric saying that investment returns are being maximized when it is easy to show that the potential for future returns is, by those same actions, being deeply damaged? Can we really be content talking about underpinning the financial future of pensioners and other investors when those same actions are increasing costs for those same people and degrading their quality of life in a myriad of ways, not to mention undermining the prospects for their children?

Using the POSIWID framework and based on widely observed outcomes, the purpose of the investment system today can be summarized by the following points:

A. To increase volatility and thus trading opportunities, even though most clients need long-term and stable returns.

B. To favor short-term predictability and performance at the expense of future returns and resilience.

C. To make advisers and intermediaries rich, regardless of what happens to end-beneficiaries.

D. To outsource risks to the environment, future generations and the poor (e.g., GFC saw a bailout of the rich, climate change will see a bailout of insurance companies who, like auto companies, have failed to respond in a timely or responsible manner). This is certainly the case when such outsourcing is legal (or can be made so by political influence) but also often the case where illegal activity has a favorable

cost-benefit ratio (i.e., where likely fines are much less than likely profits).

Actions that can be taken now

Albert Einstein's famous dictum – "It's not answers that changed the world, it's questions!" – is relevant here. Given the cognitive capture of even progressive players in the system, we have sought to focus this chapter on asking provocative and hopefully some novel questions, relating to alignment of the industry with fundamental fiduciary responsibilities to end-user beneficiary interests.

There are so many things wrong with the investment industry as it stands that the need is for those who are concerned, and especially asset owners and their direct agents, to engage much more vigorously than has happened to date about how they can intervene for maximum positive impact. There is no "one size fits all" list so here are some examples that we consider could cause the system to do less harm and ideally to support thriving sustainable economies and societies:

1. **Build relationships capable of carrying real, complex information about the real economy and its ESG ecosystem.**
   Knowing where the key gaps in awareness are and who can bridge those gaps is critical. In a world of too many reports and too many numbers, simple truths get lost because it is not in the interests of the powerful that they get heard. Ensuring a good whistleblowing system is in place is a powerful fail-safe system.[17] More proactively, there are already private networks[18] of people with expertise but lower conflicts of interests/higher integrity than normal who carry some of these simple truths and who are skilled at "positive deviant leadership."[19] Fund managers who want to be a bigger part

---

[17] www.ted.com/talks/margaret_heffernan_dare_to_disagree.html.
[18] See, for example, 300 Club, Capital Institute, Long Finance, Network for Sustainable Financial Markets, Preventable Surprises.
[19] www.iedp.com/magazine/2012issue7/index.html?pageNumber=14.

of the solution could usefully plug into these networks. Boosting the diversity of risk thinking by having industry professionals to interact more with informed but contrarian voices from other communities (NGOs, academics) can happen within companies (e.g., Aviva RI advisory group) or could happen at a sector level (e.g., the proposed UK Investor Stewardship Forum could proactively engage non-investors).[20]

2. **Do possibilistic thinking about potential "preventable surprises"[21] and use it to assess industry readiness.**

Form an "outside VaR," club. Look at systemic effects that tend to align bad news like the "investment sinkhole" phenomenon (Tverberg 2013). Agree on monitoring of early warning signals. Get agreement with regulators to post official notice of triggers and signals.

3. **Develop independent models to allow clients to understand the value of services.**

What is the likely net impact on mission risk of services paid for by a fund? Where is there real value? Where is value destroyed? Where is the price disproportionate to the benefit? Where do accidents happen? Which providers share risk in any meaningful way?

4. **Set up a survey/polling service to understand which pension fund members are sensitive to what is affected by investment externalities.**

Use on a per-fund or per-country basis. A shoot-yourself-in-the-foot index. Report on the service website incidents where fund members' interests have been damaged and encourage people to report issues.

5. **Special interest mutual clubs to ensure professionally managed real economy risk management on particular issues with a shared risk/reward model for members.**

For instance a stranded assets mutual would create incentives to discover methods to assess the risk of assets being stranded and would mean that there was no financial interest in trying to rescue assets first.

[20] www.efinancialnews.com/story/2013–03–06/questions-loom-over-kay-investor-forum.
[21] http://preventablesurprises.com.

Conclusions

Cynically one has to say that the first thing any manager learns, and must learn in order to survive, is to sell the importance and success of what he does. It is not surprising at all that there are convincing stories about efficient capital allocation and risk-spreading and packaging of investment opportunity so that it is accessible. Alongside these stories, it is important to see also that the purpose of a system is what it does: the effects and outcomes of the investment industry as a whole do not map well onto these stories. There are also systemic stories that put forward theories of why the industry cannot achieve its stated intentions, stories about conflicting interests, investment theories that don't work, and a lack of interest in the real world activities that generate the underlying returns on which the whole industry depends. Clients need to perform stakeholder analysis to understand their risk to mission and build this into the core of how they manage their suppliers in the investment industry. This is what fiduciary relationships require.

The financial sector as a whole has a credibility problem, and the investment industry needs to do more than keep telling stories that were credible in the past. Continuing to sell services into a captive market is not enough. The focus of fiduciary duty is to ensure services are fit for purpose – from the viewpoint of beneficiaries. By focusing on risk two key questions emerge:

1. How well is risk to the value of customer assets handled when we look at fundamentals and when we look at who benefits from risk? If we take a risk to mission perspective on customer assets, whose risk counts? Does the delivery of service to customers in this respect come first, or essentially last?

2. How well is risk to the continued production of value by the underlying investment targets being handled and what is the contribution of the investment industry to success and failure? What is the effect of so-called risk management at the level of portfolio management on the ability of productive enterprises to manage their real risk? Do investment managers and corporate executives collaborate to produce good returns?

The industry, including in-house professionals, need to understand the actual long-term effects of the industry if they are to continue to provide a service to a new breed of informed clients.

It has been said many times that finance is the last major sector not to understand that everything affects everything else and that we are all in this together. In terms of specific systemic damage the industry needs to take immediate steps to address the most damaging side-effects of its work:

A. Decrease the risk and volatility the industry creates.
B. Decrease the harm the investment industry does to the real economy through negative externalities.
C. Boost significantly the resources spent on risk (as opposed to performance) and within risk, on beta (as opposed to alpha).

References

Andonov, A., R. Bauer and M. Cremers. 2012. "Pension Fund Asset Allocation and Liability Discount Rates: Camouflage and Reckless Risk Taking by US Public Plans?" http://papers.ssrn.com/sol3/papers.cfm?abstract_id=2214890#%23.

Bateson, G. and M. C. Bateson. 1987. *Angels Fear*. London: Macmillan.

Brock, W. 2008. "Five Delectable Examples of 'Stein's Law'," *InvestorsInsight.com*.

2012. *American Gridlock: Why the Right and Left Are Both Wrong*. New York: John Wiley & Sons.

Carville, J. 1993. "February 25." *Wall Street Journal*, February 23: A1.

Chambers, A. 2012. "Is Audit Failing the Global Capital Markets?" *International Journal of Disclosure and Governance* 10: 195–212.

Freedland, C. 2012. *Plutocrats: The Rise of the Super-Rich and the Fall of Everyone Else*. Harmondsworth: Penguin.

FSA. 2012. "Interest Rate Hedging Products," FSA Update.

Grantham, J. 2012. "On the Road to Zero Growth," *GMO Quarterly Letter*, November.

Haldane, A. and R. May. 2011. "Systemic Risk in Banking Eco-systems," *Nature* 469: 351–5.

Hawley, J., K. Johnson and E. Waitzer. 2011. "Reclaiming Fiduciary Duty," *Rotman International Journal of Pension Management*, Fall.

Hu, J. 2006. "Cap-Weighted Portfolios Are Sub-optimal Portfolios," *Journal of Investment Management* 4 (3): 1–10.

Jolly, D. 2013. "No Decision on Bee-Harming Pesticides in Europe," *New York Times*, March 15.

Kay, J. 2012. "Finance Needs Stewards, Not Toll Collectors," *Financial Times*, July 22.

Lietaer, B., R. Ulanowicz, S. Goerner and N. McLaren. 2010. "Is Our Monetary Structure a Systemic Cause? Evidence and Remedies from Nature," *Journal of Futures Studies*, April.

Lo, A. 2012. "Reading about the Financial Crisis: A Twenty-One-Book Review," *Journal of Economic Literature* 50 (1): 151–78.

Martin, R. 2011. *Fixing the Game*. Cambridge, MA: Harvard Business Review Press.

Maxim, L. and J. van der Sluijs. 2013. "Seed-dressing Insecticides and Honey Bees," *Late Lessons from Early Warnings: Science, Precaution, Innovation*, European Environment Agency, January.

Meadows, D. 1999. *Leverage Points: Places to Intervene in a System*. Hartland, VT: The Sustainability Institute.

Neville, S. 2012. "Hero or Pariah? A Whistle-blower's Dilemma," *Guardian*, November 22.

Niesen, M. 2012. "Clay Christensen: Our Obsession With Efficiency Is Killing Innovation," *Business Insider*, December 12.

Palter, R. N., W. Rehm and J. Shih. 2008. "Communicating with the Right Investors," *McKinsey & Co.* 27.

Sandel, M. 2012. *What Money Can't Buy: The Moral Limits of Markets*. London: Allen Lane.

Shefrin, H. and E. Cervellati. 2011. "BP's Failure to Debias: Underscoring the Importance of Behavioral Corporate Finance", SCU Leavey School of Business Research Paper No. 11–05, March. http://papers.ssrn.com/sol3/papers.cfm?abstract_id=1769213" \l "%23.

Shiller, R. J. 2012. *Finance and the Good Society*. Princeton University Press.

Soros, G. 2009. "Soros: General Theory of Reflexivity," *Financial Times*, October 26.

Stout, L. 2012. *The Shareholder Value Myth*. San Francisco: Berrett-Koehler.

Tapestry Network. 2007. "Four Lessons for Audit Committees from High-profile Accounting Scandals," *Tapestry Network*, April 6.

Thamotheram, R. and M. Le Floc'h. 2011. "The BP Crisis as a 'Preventable Surprise': Lessons for Institutional Investors," *Rotman International Journal of Pension Management* 5 (1): 68–76.

Treanor, J. 2013a. "Standard Chartered Refuses To Claw Back Bonuses After American Fines," *Guardian*, March 28.

2013b. "Standard Life Pays Executives £12 Million," *Guardian*, April 2.

Towers Watson. 2012. "Risk Management Revisited: The Wrong Type of Snow." www.towerwatson.com/en/Insights/IC-Types/Survey-Research-Results/2012/03/Risk-management-revisted-The-Wrong-Type-of-Snow.

Tverberg, G. 2013. "Our Investment Sinkhole Problem," *Our Finite World*. http://ourfiniteworld.com/2013/02/08/our-investment-sinkhole-problem.

Sustainability, financial markets and systemic risk

DIETER GRAMLICH

Introduction

Financial markets serve as a fiduciary for individuals and institutions. Their key strength is to act as an intermediary "able to link and enable people" (Remer 2011: 193). While providing services on the asset and liability side, financial institutions – particularly banks and funds – assume responsibility for their customers (deposit taking, financing) and the environment (capital allocation) as a whole. Fiduciary duties of financial institutions are discussed from the institutions' commitment to ethical (social responsibility) and/or legal (financial regulation) obligations. Even more important, from a business point of view financial institutions depend on confidence as a "license to operate." Confidence itself is considered as being closely related to "loyalty" (balance) and "care" (prudence) as two standards of fiduciary behavior (Hawley and Williams 2002: 285, Martin 2009: 550). Therefore, serving as a financial fiduciary is closely linked to an environment of stability and continuity – here referred to as sustainability – both on the side of single institutions (micro) and the system as a whole (macro).

In this chapter, the issue of systemic stability and continuity as a prerequisite for fiduciary services on financial markets is emphasized. The characteristics of sustainability on financial markets as a macro condition for micro fiduciary services are examined. However, referring to sustainability as a concept of equilibrium in the long term, today's financial markets appear to be mostly incompatible with sustainability. The increasing volatility of prices on financial markets ("boom and bust"), growing imbalances between the financial system and the real economy ("bubbles") and, in general, the exhibition of a behavior on financial markets highly assumed to be critical (speculation, manipulation, materialism) are all reflexes to an absence

of fiduciary responsibility and expose the financial system to existential risk. This has incentivized massive criticism regarding the functional mechanisms of modern financial markets (Lietaer et al. 2012). In an unstable and discontinuous environment, single institutions cannot comply with their fiduciary duties.

It should not be ignored that the financial system previously contributed to a period of unprecedented growth and innovation thereby largely fostering economic welfare. It may therefore be too simplistic to solely blame the markets for some kind of egoism and exaggeration. The question is rather what factors drive the system's balance and ability to foster sustainable development and fiduciary duties or, vice versa, what are the conditions that make a financial system turn from one of sustainability to unsustainability and expose it to systemic risk. Sustainability in finance, here first interpreted as stability in financial markets, in this perspective refers to the ambivalence of financial systems and explores the necessary conditions for systemic stability.

Sustainability and stability

Since the inception of the most recent crisis,[1] research into causes and consequences has grown

---

[1] The most recent crisis started in 2007 with the breakdown of the US housing market and subsequent default risks of banks as a consequence of excessive lending to doubtful customers (sub-prime crisis). In an environment of increasing distrust on financial markets the sub-prime crisis turned into a global banking and liquidity crisis. A further stage of the crisis highlights the indebtedness of governments and adds new financial constraints due to the enormous bailout programs of countries worldwide, particularly in Europe and the US.

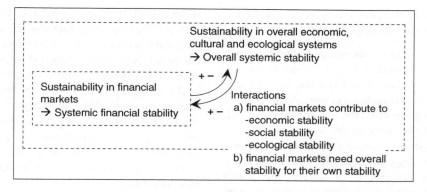

Figure 17.1 Systemic financial and overall systemic stability – integration and interaction. This figure illustrates the basic connectivity between finance and sustainability as a driver of fiduciary responsibility ("loyalty" and "care" as elements). First, sustainability in finance is to be perceived both as stability of financial markets and as an indispensable component of overall systemic sustainability (integration). Second, this connectivity comprises a series of incentives and feedbacks between the systems (interaction) with either stabilizing or destabilizing effects.

exponentially. Existing work mostly focuses on the economic dimension of the crisis, exploring particularly the drivers for risks in banking systems and market related conditions for stability. However, this research should be extended for several reasons. Centering on financial markets as a "self-referential" system neglects to address the fact that the financial crisis has impacted human life in many negative ways. It has to be considered that financial markets are embedded into a much broader context and both impact and depend on a more general concept of stability in the overall cultural and natural context (see Figure 17.1). In particular, this comprises confidence in political and economic systems, the maintenance of social security and conservation of the environment with respect to climatic conditions and finite resources.

This perspective emphasizes the fiduciary role of the financial system to support sustainability in the overall system in two ways (active variable): it enables overall sustainability via its own systemic financial stability and it provides additional positive stimulus for sustainability in the surrounding environment. In addition, these linkages have to be looked at from an inverse point of view: stability or instability in finance is thus an indirect and somehow lagging variable of the overall conditions in the surrounding spheres (passive variable).

Finally, there is a degree of interaction and feedback in these relationships: while financial stability fosters overall stability, favorable conditions from the environmental systems may in turn support future financial stability (e.g., financing projects to reduce greenhouse emissions feeds back in terms of lesser credit defaults from environmental risk). Vice versa, instability of financial markets may destabilize surrounding systems resulting in further negative feedbacks on financial markets themselves (e.g., money needed for the bailout of banks cannot be invested in social security with further effects on consumption and production).

Research on the interaction between financial markets, fiduciary responsibility and (overall) sustainability is only beginning to evolve (Lietaer et al. [2012: 9] refer to a "missing link"). While first contributions were mainly concerned with products and processes on financial markets to foster sustainability in societal and natural systems (Hesse 2007; Jeucken 2001, 2005), more recent work centers on ethical and cultural foundations for financial stability as a prerequisite for overall sustainability (Schlag and Mercado 2012; Sun et al. 2011; Weber and Remer 2011). In the following, this study provides an overview of the main directions in assessing the interaction between sustainability, financial markets and systemic risk as the drivers of fiduciary duties of intermediaries. The contents are developed in three steps:

- In the first step ("Concepts of sustainability and systemic financial risk"), the concepts of sustainability in finance and systemic risk and their relationship are analyzed in more detail. From an extended perspective, the notion of systemic risk does not only refer to risk in financial markets alone (systemic financial risk) but to risks in society and ecology in general (overall systemic risk).
- Second ("The absence of sustainability within financial markets"), in order to explore the conditions for sustainability or, reciprocally, the causes of missing sustainability (systemic risk) on financial markets and the overall system, the experiences from research on financial crises are assessed. This analysis provides first economic and technical explanations for crises and further an investigation of drivers related to the nature of complex systems and to behavioral characteristics of modern economies.
- Third ("Implementing sustainability on financial markets"), based on the analysis of requirements for sustainability and systemic stability, suggestions for further developing sustainability in finance – and the connected fiduciary services – are addressed.

Concepts of sustainability and systemic financial risk

Following the findings of the World Commission on Environment and Development (1987: part I.3, no. 27), that development should "meet the needs of the present without compromising the ability of future generations to meet their own needs"; the term sustainability basically refers to continuity as a time dimension. Ensuring stable and frictionless developments in a world that can be described as a multifaceted and interdependent system[2] further implies that the different subsystems and elements of the overall system and their connectivity are respected. For the most part, economy, society and the environment are considered to be essential subsystems (thereby integrating also technology and law) and it is necessary to ask how economic value can be achieved in a "socially and environmentally sustainable framework" (Becchetti 2012: 50). This is closely related to the concept of "triple bottom line investments" (Elkington 1999)[3] as a set of objectives for value creation. Sustainability therefore comprises the dimensions of stability over time and balance across (sub-) systems and may be conceived as a concept of equilibrium spanning time and space.

Relating to sustainability, financial markets and systemic risk addresses the following:

- First, the issue of stability in financial systems; and
- second, how financial markets interact with overall sustainability in economy, society and environment (see Figure 17.2).

The first perspective addresses the importance that stability has for the fiduciary functions exercised from a monetary system and basically asks how systemic financial crises – in the sense of financial unsustainability – can be avoided. The second perspective refers to the more comprehensive perception of overall systemic risk including relevant systems in addition to financial markets and their connectivity (Camdessus 2012: 112).

Financial markets comprise products, players and prices for the management of liquidity, return and risk (Berger et al. 2010; UNCTAD 2009: 11–18). The main actors are banks, investment houses and finance companies as suppliers of financial products and services to private households, industrial companies and governments on the demand side. As financial products and services mostly involve confidence in the future ability to settle transactions, they are widely dependent on credibility and highly susceptible to expectations. Total global financial assets at the end of 2011 are estimated at €169,000 billion (McKinsey & Co. 2012: 6). At the end of 2011, the gross financial assets of private households worldwide amounted to €103,000

---

[2] System theory is particularly suited to describe elements and interactions in a complex framework and to foster connected thinking; see Meadows (2008) and Vester (2002).

[3] The triple bottom line comprises economic, social and ecological dimensions (people, planet, profit) for measuring success in real economy and finance.

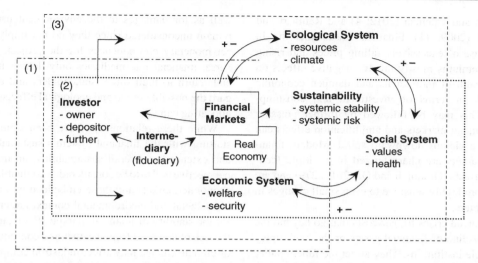

Figure 17.2 Framework for sustainability and systemic stability/systemic risk – institutional perspective. The figure illustrates the connectivity between finance and sustainability from an institutional point of view. The systemic context can be looked at from a purely economic perspective (1), an integration of economic and social issues (2) and an overall integration of economic, social and ecological issues (3). The investors may operate directly on financial markets or via intermediaries (fiduciaries) who in turn have indirect responsibility for systemic sustainability and also depend on it.

billion (world gross domestic product for 2011 was about €53,800 billion); 30 percent were held at insurance companies and pension funds, 33 percent at banks and 35 percent invested directly into securities (Allianz SE 2012: 2, 7).

Varying assumptions regarding future developments, high-speed transactions and global connectivity determine the dynamics on financial markets. A basic volatility is therefore persistent in the monetary system and may be considered as a natural instability or ongoing process of adjustments (arbitrage). This makes it difficult to define unsustainability in a precise way, e.g., in the sense of excess volatility or financial crisis. Further problems in evaluating the system's contribution to sustainability and risk arise, for example:

- The transformation of size, duration and (default) risk means that financial intermediaries naturally assume some part of risk by themselves in order to provide protection to their clients.
- While derivatives are mostly assumed to provide for systemic financial risk, they are an indispensable tool for easily transferring risk within markets. Particularly, commodity derivatives have originally been developed to hedge against the risks faced by farmers, but are criticized today for their speculative use in the food market.[4]
- While financial globalization is assumed to contribute to output and growth, it has also increased the risk of contagion among countries and losses from crises.[5]

Approaches to capture unsustainability in financial markets therefore have to refer to the extent of volatility or deviation in a financial system and on the net effects caused (relative assessment of systemic risk) instead of blaming principally the use of certain products and processes. This explains, for example, why different definitions and thresholds for determining financial crises exist. Overviews of financial turmoil with a different notion of crises are given by De Bandt et al. (2010: 635–42),

[4] Claessens et al. (2011: iii, xiv) relate this to the need for regulators having better access to trading data.
[5] Cline (2010: 26) calculates the net profit arising from financial openness to 0.35 percent of GDP.

Laeven and Valencia (2012: 4) and Reinhart and Rogoff (2009: 11). Financial unsustainability in the sense of excessively falling prices and rising risk premiums mostly involve negative effects on the wealth of individuals and dampen economic activity in terms of investment and consumption. This may be followed by further pressure on financial markets and amplification effects can create a vicious downward spiral. Modern financial markets are characterized by multiple feedback effects (Gramlich and Oet 2011: 279) and are therefore highly sensitive to even small changes in parameters.

Financial crises trigger costs that go beyond the pure decline of financial assets or the bankruptcy of single institutions. They affect the functionality of the financial system itself creating further distortions in the real economy (Basel Committee 2011: 1; Kroszner et al. 2007). As far as the financial crisis of 2007–10 is concerned, the output losses cumulated over the four years are estimated at 25 percent of the Gross Domestic Product (GDP) of exposed countries.[6] From a microeconomic perspective, losses from bonds and stocks as a consequence of financial unsustainability affect the investor's wealth and his economic flexibility. Considering the fact that financial assets in many cases are part of pension plans and provision for future charges, excess losses are closely related to social insecurity and to a loss of individual freedom.

Where this considers the monetary system as a direct cause for overall instability, imperfect monetary markets are to be perceived as being indirectly responsible for unstable societal and environmental systems through their role of allocating capital. As a financial intermediary, banks and other financial institutions make decisions on what type of project or debtor money from depositors is further invested. Those decisions are based on evaluations of risk and return, mostly in the sense of default risk and risk premium of the counterparty. Further effects from the funded projects such as socially critical consequences for health and social life as well as for damages to the environment usually remain unconsidered since they do not imply direct monetary consequences for the project. Vice versa, financial intermediaries only deliver financial return to their direct stakeholders and disregard the possible social and ecological effects from allocating capital.

While these relationships have been examined starting with the financial system's sustainability and extended to overall sustainability, an inverse perspective is also to be considered. Sustainable real economic markets and those embedded into a stable societal and environmental context are crucial for the stability of financial markets. For example, the risk of damages from weather as a consequence of climate change may affect industrial companies and therefore raise individual credit default risk. Furthermore, if climate risks are insured, the costs for insurers directly apply to financial markets. The main framework for the impact of climate changes on the real economy and on financial markets is provided by the Stern reports (Stern 2006, 2009). These reports conclude that, while maintaining the present manner of production ("business as usual"), the net effect from economic growth and costs relating to climate change will be negative. Otherwise, investments to alleviate the negative effects caused by climate change may achieve overall positive results and provide new business opportunities on financial markets.[7]

Interactions between ecological issues and their direct and indirect (via the real economy) implications for financial institutions are still to develop in a systematic way (Whalley and Yuan 2009). The discussion includes the integration of environmental effects into credit rating systems (sustainability rating) and new products for the management of ecological risks from a micro perspective. It extends to further effects from natural disasters via the insurance sector and credit default derivatives for the systemic risk on financial markets. Rising

---

[6] In addition to output losses direct fiscal costs have also to be considered. In 2010, the world GDP was US$63 trillion, US$12.2 trillion for the Eurozone and US$14.6 trillion for the US.

[7] The investigation of Furrer et al. (2009) on the involvement of 114 major global banks in climate related business such as climate loans, advisory services and asset allocation showed that 48.2 percent of banks were "hesitators" and only 5.3 percent were "forerunners" concluding that "banks have only just started to factor climate change issues in" (Furrer et al. 2009: 23).

materialism as a social phenomenon emphasizes monetary perception also between individuals and financial institutions. From an overall perspective, sustainability and financial markets are related in an existential and reciprocal way. In order to examine how sustainability can be achieved on financial markets, the next step is to explore the causes for the lack of sustainability as observed through past financial crises.

The absence of sustainability within financial markets

Economic perspective

Investigating the history of financial turmoil, Reinhart and Rogoff (2009: 154) find forty-eight systemic banking crises since the year 1800.[8] On average there is a crisis every four years. This raises concern whether crises (as opposed to the fiduciary duty of financial intermediaries) are naturally inherent to financial markets and to be accepted as the price for growth and innovation in finance. Yet, an important observation is that the amplitude of crises has increased and that consequences from a more extreme instability may severely affect and even trigger the collapse of economies and societies worldwide (cycles in financial and real markets are examined in Borio 2012 and Drehmann et al. 2012). The most recent financial crisis has received particular attention for its strength and duration. Arguments put forward to explain the ongoing crisis[9] are similar for other financial crises.

Most analyses center on purely economic and technical terms as explanation (see Table 17.1).

---

[8] Laeven and Valencia (2012: 8) determine thirteen international banking crises since 1970. Further to systemic banking crises, multiple (sovereign) debt crises and currency crises have to be considered.

[9] Hannoun (2010: 2) mentions that while for the recent crisis there is "still no consensus on its root causes," reckless behavior, poor market discipline and the failure of risk management systems are among the primary causes. Ahrend and Goujard (2011: 5) see external imbalances of countries of particular interest, while in general there is "no clear consensus in the literature regarding the main causal factors of financial crises."

Excessive credit expansion mainly into the mortgage business (Borio 2012: 2–3), supported by lax risk standards and securitization as a technique to separate risks from the underlying business, created an imbalance between financial assets and the real economy (technical economic aspects are overviewed from Basel Committee 2011: 1–10; Cline 2010: 238–40, 279–99). As a consequence from the oversupply of real estate (and rising interest rates to slow down credit), house prices went down, creating a vicious circle of asset losses, decrease in collateral, default risk and need for liquidity. Similar mechanisms can be observed for further crises, for example, related to the housing markets of Iceland, Spain and Sweden (Peachey 2011 summarizes financial disasters worldwide). Similarly, the high indebtedness of governments, particularly in the countries of the European Monetary Union, can at least partly be attributed to deficits in the risk management and lack of foresight of financial institutions that engaged themselves in excess lending to already highly indebted countries.

The building-up of bubbles was partly enhanced by missing evidence of the systemic, market-wide effects from aggregate lending. Both individual institutions and supervision did not possess the instruments to be sufficiently aware of the build-up of bubbles and high systemic connectivity or ignored the signs. The concept of financial supervision was based on the regulation of single institutions (microprudential approach) and did not focus sufficiently on the build-up of system-wide risk concentrations (macroprudential approach). Further, competition among institutions and the specific set of incentives within institutions caused system-wide and long-term consequences of the business to have been neglected. Variable income based on the volume of products sold and participation in the profits made both employees and managers look on their personal benefits, but not on those of their customers and the system itself. Compensation structures rewarded short-term return, not long-term value creation. In an asymmetric remuneration framework, managers benefited from gains in the first and profitable phase of unsustainable business, but did not compensate for losses in the second phase.

Table 17.1 Causes of unsustainability (systemic risk) in financial markets.

Economic-technical Perspective	
De Bandt et al. 2010	- accumulation of imbalances (credit booms) - contagion via "real" and "informational" channels - amplification of shocks through endogenously emerging risks
Ahrend and Goujard 2011	- skew in liabilities towards short-term debt - vulnerability from past crises - international bank balance-sheet contagion (third countries)
Claessens et al. 2011	- high concentration and connectedness in the financial markets - traditional financial system indicators obscured risks - weaknesses in crisis management and resolution
Extended Perspective	
Helbing 2010	- complex and hard to control financial systems - instability is beneficial to some interest groups - herding as the product of information feedback and psychology
Donaldson 2012	- rewarding short and suffering long - normalization of questionable behavior - hypernorms instead of precise (microsocial) ethics
Griffiths of Fforestfach 2012	- economic: imbalances, complex structures - ethical: questionable business, lax standards - spiritual: materialistic culture, belief in markets

In addition to critical incentives and lack of overview, specific products and processes are criticized for their negative impact. Particularly, it is argued that securitization while separating and selling risks from the underlying credit business interrupts the underlying lender-borrower relationship (Cline 2010: 284–8; Gorton 2010: 20–3, 83–107). As a first consequence, the assessment of risks is transferred from the first lender to further investors or to rating agencies that have no direct financial connection with the borrower. The evaluation and management of risks gets more complicated (Claessens et al. 2011: 6) and even provides opportunities for moral hazard.[10] As a further consequence the process of "slicing" risks, restructuring them within a portfolio and selling them worldwide created an opaque market. Institutions set up special purpose vehicles mostly abroad and off the institutes' balance sheet while at the time providing liquidity facilities. This ultimately resulted in institutions themselves losing transparency about their own engagement. Overall, the business became too complex and no longer manageable. The transition from a high gain to a low gain system failed.[11]

Extended perspective

While the majority of crisis explanations focus on economic and technical issues, few authors analyze meta causes of the crisis pointing to conceptual and ethical deficits in financial markets (Lietaer et al. 2012; Schlag and Mercato 2012). Basically, the combined negative effects from innovations in global risk transfer and incentives related to profit and growth feed criticisms of a purely economic driven and highly self-regulated system. Capitalism as an organizational framework of modern economic systems is itself challenged (Shahrokhi 2011). This refers first to the inherent mechanism where prices and competition are supposed to regulate systemic balance almost automatically ("invisible hand").

---

[10] Moral hazard in this case means that the original lender may reduce its own risk standards when planning to sell the risky asset further on.

[11] See Shaw (2010). A high gain system is concerned with the immediacy of living (livability, live for the moment), while a low gain system is concerned with the wider effects of actions (sustainability, long term).

However, the prices of financial assets and interest rates cannot exercise their coordination function in an opaque environment and when they are easily manipulated. The breakdown of this mechanism as made evident by the recent financial crisis is therefore interpreted that the economy was "slapped in the face by the invisible hand" (Gorton 2010: 13).[12]

Another characteristic of financial markets jeopardizing stability is their strong dependence on expectations and sensitivity to changing sentiments:

- Particularly, most prices on financial markets are based on calculating present values from estimated future cash flows (Berd 2011: 68; Bessis 2010: 118, 143–7). However, in dynamic markets the prediction of cash flows is difficult and false predictions in line with volatile discount rates largely impact present values.[13] The volatility of discounting rates is basically explained from the credit spread (Berd 2011: 74–8) and that is supposed to be highly susceptible to emotional aspects of exuberance and fear (Che and Kapadia 2012; Chen et al. 2009).[14]
- The impact of implicitly volatile present values is further augmented by the fact that accounting systems refer more and more to present value calculation in the sense of "fair value" obtained from markets or internal models. In addition to the extended use of volatile information it has to be considered that new information affects a broader fraction of the market (Ryan 2009 discusses the effects from fair value accounting on financial markets).
- This consequence is related to the increasing importance of public ratings: Rating up- or downgrades announced from major agencies are accessible by the whole market instantaneously. The high speed dissemination of abruptly changing information in line with subsequent transaction orders that are very often automatically driven provides additional explanation for the dynamics inherent in today's financial systems.

While these aspects question the principles of a price-driven financial system and therefore the conceptual design of modern economic systems, an even more fundamental aspect refers to the value created from the system itself. Luhmann (1998) qualifies the economic system as "self-referential and autopoietic" in the sense that it is limited to the (monetary) effects and valuation principles accepted within the system, but does not account for the implications of financial decisions outside the system's borders. Similarly, Becchetti (2012: 48) and Donati (2012: 61–4) address a three-sided problem caused from self-referential economic decisions when pointing to the consequences of financial profit-driven decisions on global poverty, environment and general well-being. Poverty generally refers to the inequality in income associated with decisions where one party benefits to the detriment of another (e.g., while speculating on default risk). Environmental effects are disregarded insofar as in the present they do not cause any financial burden, and general well-being reminds us that human welfare cannot be based on "financialization" (Donati 2012: 62) alone. However, a financial system that is self-referential refrains from impacts outside the border of monetary areas and principles, and not taking into account long-term effects is contrary to sustainability.

An unsustainable financial system is characterized by critical impacts and missing support for sustainability in surrounding areas. Analogous to a financial institution's role as an intermediary between offer and demand in monetary markets, the system as a whole has to be perceived as an intermediary between financial investors and social and ecological systems. In this sense, financial markets have to respect the social and ecological responsibility of capital. Systemic responsibility and intermediation is, for example, executed while directly financing projects or institutions of social and ecological relevance. This includes borrowing to sovereign debtors such as communities and

---

[12] Reinhart and Rogoff (2009: 15, 20) refer to the recent crisis as "The This-Time-Is-Different Syndrome" arguing that the assumption of benefits from globalization, technology and superior financial system failed.

[13] Gorton (2010: 22) refers to "information-sensitive asset classes."

[14] Che and Kapadia (2012: 2) regress credit spreads upon the options volatility index VIX as a "fear index."

countries or financing infrastructure projects with a high environmental impact as, for example, the production of alternative energy and investments within the Carbon Disclosure Project (Bopp 2010: 275–6).

An even more important indirect effect arises from the allocation of capital to businesses and individuals, thereby affecting production technologies and consumer behavior. Subsequent consequences in the production sector are related to resources attributed to and used within companies and further the handling of substances from production that affect biodiversity and climate. Financing companies means also to accept their labor policy, whereby high pressure and low safety standards mostly imply an economic benefit for the company but a social burden for the workforce. Excessive credits to individuals as a result of persistently and excessively incentivizing their consumption may over-accent materialism as an objective of individuals and may also exceed their ability to meet their credit obligations.

Whereas unsustainable capital allocation may involve some benefits in the short term – losses in society and ecology without any direct financial relevance are disregarded and also cause damages in the distant future – today's decisions necessarily imply future feedbacks. It is evident that future imbalances are caused by presently incomplete financial decisions or, in other words, future crises by today's financial unsustainability. In this sense, the fundamental or long-term causes for financial crises must be looked at from a much more comprehensive perspective. For example, global poverty and imbalances in nations' wealth as the basic drivers for international financial crises are addressed (Köhler 2009). The sub-prime crisis from mortgage lending in the US may be traced back to a failed US social policy: in order to provide material safety (Gorton 2010: 66) in a system almost without public social security, the mortgage business was supported to provide homes for low-income US citizens. However, this support was exaggerated and led to the disastrous consequences for the US housing market.

As a result, the explanation of financial crises cannot be limited to unsustainable structures on the financial markets themselves. Unsustainable aspects such as asymmetric incentives, excessive growth in line with individual profit maximization and complexity of financial markets are some reasons but not the only ones. In addition, unstable financial behavior affects social and ecological systems with resulting imbalances feeding back to the financial system with a timely delay. Remedies to the systemic crisis have to be evaluated in this expanded context.

Implementing sustainability on financial markets

Suggestions from a financial markets perspective

As a consequence of the extended analysis of causes for unsustainability in finance, suggestions for implementing sustainability as a support for systemic stability and fiduciary responsibility of financial intermediaries have to be assessed in a more comprehensive framework. Directions for more sustainability comprise the following:

- Economically and technically driven reforms of financial markets:
  - Reforms of financial supervision and systemic resilience.
  - Market-driven transformation towards sustainability.
- Culture-based reforms:
  - Ethical principles.
  - Individual consciousness.

From an economic and technical perspective, financial resilience is a function of stability policy and market discipline (Hannoun 2010: 2). Regulatory reforms as an element of stability policy are crucial since supervision tends to avoid market imperfections resulting from critical individual behavior. As a public corrective to market imperfections they center on individual critical behavior ("laissez-faire") and failed market principles. Regulators operate from an aggregate market-wide perspective enabling them to oversee policies from a systemic point of view (macroprudential approach).

The Basel III framework[15] derives from experiences of the recent financial crisis and addresses weaknesses in the existing financial regulation. Strengthening the institutions' resilience against increased default and liquidity risk (see Table 17.2) basically points in the right direction. However, the recommendations are in line with former reforms and enforce existing regulation, but do not really provide any new directions. As has to be perceived from past regimes of regulation, in most cases the regulated institutions found ways to circumvent their obligations. Particularly, the reform concentrates on banks, whereas further institutions such as finance companies, private equity companies and hedge funds are not included (the shadow banking system). As a consequence, financial transactions may be transferred to the shadow banking system and within this largely non-regulated sector create even more systemic instability (regulatory arbitrage).

The basic design for current regulatory principles is relating the extent of risk assumed from an institution to its risk capital. It impacts risk-taking as a cause for bank losses insofar as financial institutions have to assess from the very beginning what risk is inherent to the institution's business and accordingly adjust the amount of risk assumed. The identification of risk can be based on a standardized measure[16] or individually assessed on the basis of internal risk models. As far as standardized measures are concerned, the corresponding percentages are taken from past experiences where aspects of unsustainability have not yet played a major role. It may also be concluded that up to now aspects of sustainability have not been very much considered in internal models or included in the risk assessments of major rating agencies. Sustainability ratings and, similar, indexes for the inclusion of social and ecological responsible companies as a basis for investments are still to be evolved (Gabriel 2005; Statman 2006). As a consequence, the relation between banks' lending decisions and their effects on society and ecology are not sufficiently respected, and therefore, in the mid and long term, risks from an unsustainable social and ecological environment may further affect the financial system.

Finally, the Basel III rules refer almost exclusively to the banks and bank management. They do not take into account that decisions within banks are largely driven by expectations of their stakeholders and that large shareholders may exercise significant power on the managers. They may reclaim large dividends in the near future thereby incentivizing managers to take large risks, whereas the negative mid-term consequences for shareholders can simply be avoided by just selling their shares.

Although not at the center of reforms, it may further be critically asked if today's organization of financial markets fosters stability (Gorton 2010: 23; Gramlich and Oet 2011). The evolution of financial markets is characterized by globalization, securitization and acceleration making, on the one hand, markets grow and profitable, while increasing volatility and risks from contagion on the other. Particularly, the dynamic pattern within the markets has changed. Where on average there are higher oscillations of prices and spreads, the potential of losses in extreme scenarios has also increased.[17] The concept of expected and unexpected loss (Bessis 2010: 214–16), usually applied to individual transactions, may also be applied to the market as a whole: financial markets dynamics have to be assessed both in the context of average fluctuations and fluctuations in extreme cases, where extreme cases are more and more close to the collapse of the entire system. In order to reduce the likelihood of extreme losses, Lietaer et al. (2012: 79) claim that financial markets have to be organized as a trade-off between efficiency and resilience. Concepts to avoid incubation and spillover effects with extreme consequences include the build-up of firewalls, use of negative feedbacks, enhancement of idiosyncratic risks and

---

[15] The Basel III suggestions for a revised financial regulation are a response to the most recent crisis (Basel Committee 2011). They comprise decisions made from worldwide supervisors and are coordinated from the Bank for International Settlements (BIS) in Basel.

[16] Depending on the type of debtors different percentages representing the exposure at default are predefined.

[17] Taleb (2008) refers to a higher probability of the occurrence of "black swans."

Table 17.2 Directions towards sustainability (stability) in financial markets.

Economic-technical Perspective	
Basel Committee 2011	- higher risk coverage and quality of risk capital - liquid and stable resources to enhance liquidity profile - contain systemic risk from procyclicality and connectivity
UNCTAD 2011	- break the spiral of falling asset prices and falling demand - comprehensive re-regulation to intervene for speculation - need for global cooperation and global regulation
IMF 2012	- bank restructuring to strengthen capital and risk sharing - centralized coordination of policy and supervision - firewalls to arrest contagion
Extended Perspective	
Köhler 2009	- new regulation on monetary markets (Bretton Woods II) - actions against poverty and climate change - ethics of a global community and global solidarity
Camdessus 2012	- incentives and sanctions in order to strengthen regulation - new forms of collaboration based on subsidiary and solidarity - strong sense of social and political responsibility of men
Lietaer et al. 2012	- monetary ecosystem with diversity of issuing institutions - complementary financial and non-financial incentives - organizational pattern of robustness and transparency

ring-fencing (Bank of England 2011; Oet et al. 2012).

These concepts seem promising and fragile at the same time. For example, negative feedbacks associated with the use of anticyclical capital buffers assume that this capital is available in stress phases and has not been previously used for expanding risky business. Building idiosyncratic positions assumes low connectivity between an individual transaction and the rest of the market. However, in a globally interdependent world and in high speed information processes there is little possibility for standalone business and high diversification effects. Enabling idiosyncratic business therefore builds on a more fragmented financial world, for example, realized by a higher focus on national or regional markets.

In addition to redesigning the conceptual pattern of financial markets and its conduciveness to sustainability, further suggestions are concerned with the adaptation of specific products, processes and structures:

- In the context of securitization there is an abstract or indirect relationship between the owners of the securitized assets and the underlying borrower

(Shaw 2010: 485–6). This puts the management of securities and security prices in the center of financial considerations, but not the management of the basic lender-borrower relationship. The interaction is no longer individual with many possibilities for personal experiences and respect but it is abstract and neglecting social considerations. The lack of experience and concern for the lender may involve a further decrease of the risk quality and even support moral hazard (e.g., speculation on decreasing credit quality).

- In social banking (Remer 2011), microfinance as an organizational framework with a group of alternating borrowers that both assist and control each other is suggested as an alternative to traditional lending. In addition to effects on the stability of the financial relationship via collective responsibility, microfinance displays direct social benefits as no collateral is assumed and credits are accepted to borrowers with low credit standing.

- Arguing that the emphasis on prices and profits is too short oriented, it is further assumed that incentives related to an interest-free and social conform business – such as Islamic banking, for example – may be an alternative (Trabelsi 2011).

However, as evidenced in some places (such as Dubai), Islamic countries are not free from financial crises and interest is not really absent but calculated differently. Karwowski (2010) concludes that Islamic banking may prove as similarly unstable as Western banking systems.

Sustainable products and processes may be promoted in a profit-based financial system while focusing on estimated economic advantages ("business case for sustainability," Holliday et al. 2002). In the context of recent crises, more and more investors are becoming aware of the social and ecological dimension of financial markets and consequently of their own responsibility for allocating capital in a sustainable manner (Remer 2011: 153). Further awareness for sustainability arises from concerns that money invested in non-sustainable companies and countries is affected by social and ecological risks specifically affecting those companies. Vice versa, sustainable companies may benefit from additional opportunities. Financial markets respond to this by developing products linked to the sustainability of companies and countries.

Extended perspective

It may critically be asked if economically and regulatory motivated incentives for sustainability are sufficient to achieve overall systemic stability. As can be observed from history, regulatory reforms are only able to prevent unsustainability for a short time and markets quickly adjust to new opportunities not covered by law (since regulation often lags behind events, Donaldson [2012: 5] argues that "it is only ethics that can save us"). Concerning the business case for sustainability as a market-driven remedy, this largely depends on public awareness and understanding. However, as financial markets recover from the crisis, public awareness of sustainability on financial markets may decrease, as does the demand for sustainable products. Generally, the potential for business cases for sustainability may be limited and not be enough to achieve comprehensive systemic stability. Therefore, a more extended consciousness of the relationship between sustainability and risk

is necessary to guide sustainable actions and further, personal commitment to sustainability must be grounded more on an ethical than an economic motivation.

New consciousness of sustainability of financial markets recognizes the need for companies to operate in a sound environment. In the concept of economic rationality (Becchetti 2012), intact social and ecological structures are existential for economic success. No institution may survive in the long run if surrounding systems are weak and even collapse. The principal notion of economic rationality applied to sustainability is therefore linking future survival to present care. In addition, future competitiveness and performance is enhanced by today's sustainability. Where in the short run there are higher costs from implementing sustainability, these are offset in the long run by a more stable environment and a higher motivation among the workforce. Further to an economic perspective, value creation has to be perceived in a more comprehensive way integrating the social and ecological dimensions of economic production. Therefore, the concept of "sustainable value" (Figge and Hahn 2008) is relevant in pointing out how companies' means of production differs from the market standard.

The concept of economic rationality can be extended to further principles guiding financial markets and economies in general. Particularly the concept of permanent growth and even exponential growth conflicts with a context of finite resources (Lietaer et al. 2012). On financial markets, interest paid on invested money is basically driven by the rate of growth. In economic systems adjusted to a given capacity of naturally and technically reproducible resources, growth rates tend towards zero and return on capital has to be interpreted in a different way.

A way to overcome the limits to monetary growth and to account for the multiple effects generated from invested money is interpreting return and value creation in a much more comprehensive manner. In a systemic perspective, the effects from money allocated have also to be assessed in terms of the implications for systemic stability and the contribution to social and ecological valuable projects. In addition to monetary return directly delivered to individual stakeholders (e.g., owners and depositors), the systemic usefulness of money invested has to be considered as a concept of extended value creation, here the concept of sustainable value, with further implications: instruments for the assessment of sustainable value creation, notably sustainability rating systems, have to be designed.[18] The awareness of creating sustainable value has to be developed both for managers inside financial institutions and for further external stakeholders.

Sustainability as a concept of equilibrium across time and systems is based on individual consciousness of relevant (sub-) systems, their connectivity and evolution (systemic paradigm). The more financial decisions from investors and managers are taken with awareness of interrelationships, the more sustainable they are. Vice versa, the more limited and short-term oriented decisions are, the more they tend to be unsustainable. Risks from isolating decisions from the decisions' context increase as markets become complex and more dynamic. However, it has also to be noted that even when the financial institutions and stakeholders refer to sustainable policies from a micro perspective, this may not guarantee sustainability in the overall market. In addition to sustainable micro approaches, a system-wide sustainability perspective is needed:

- If too many institutions and investors adopt strategies in the sustainability domain, the risk of bubbles within sustainability may increase (e.g., too many projects on alternate energy).
- Investments in similar areas of sustainability may increase concentration in the portfolios of financial institutions.

In order to approach the multiplicity of financial markets and their connectivity with the social and ecological system, appropriate models are needed.

In a more complex and dynamic environment, a new class of models specifically has to account for the impact of financial decisions on further systems. These models are basically to be developed in the spirit of system theory allowing the assessment of multiplicity and connectivity in a dynamic environment. Traditional economic models that are often based on narrow assumptions, linear equations and past observations[19] will lose their impact. Instead, the new class of models for sustainability includes besides formal functionality also elements of randomness and simulation (Szyszka 2011: 211). Approaches from econophysics that transfer experiences from biological systems into economic markets (Haldane and May 2011; Strogatz 2001) and form system dynamics as a modeling specifically developed for feedbacks in connected systems point in this direction (Helbing 2010; Radzicki 2011).

Closely related to systemic thinking is the perception and handling of risk in modern societies. Usually there is a psychological bias to reduce or even to neglect possible negative outcomes from economic decisions, particularly if the negative outcome may be subject to delay in manifestation, has no direct personal consequences or, simply, if the positive outcome is strongly desired (Donaldson [2012: 6] refers to the "normalization of questionable behavior," Helbing [2010: 12] to "over-confidence"). In financial models, the positive and negative outcomes from decisions are mostly displayed as distributions of a stochastic variable. Hereby risk is assessed as the maximal loss within a confidence level or below a threshold (Bessis 2010: 215). Losses beyond are not further taken into consideration. As a consequence, the remaining (residual) risk that may include extreme losses is not adequately assessed ("black swans"). This may partly be explained by the assumption that even extreme risks do not imply any existential damage or can simply be repaired.

Finally, new consciousness and new thinking are grounded on the consideration of a higher impact of ethical rules for business.[20] Higher

---

[18] Given the complexity of an overall sustainable value, first approaches address selected social and ecological effects from financial investments. For example, the project of French banks investigating how much bank credits are linked to financing carbon dioxide and the Swiss bank Julius Bär enabling the neutrality of carbon dioxide in a portfolio are first steps in this direction. See Utopies and Les Amis de la Terre (2010).

[19] This is also expressed as the "assumption of stationarity."

[20] Donaldson (2012: 5) comments that "the ethical story is at least as important as the regulatory one."

awareness of the financial and economic systems' dependence on societal and ecological conditions relates to a lower self-reference of the monetary system. Instead of behaving autonomously, both a social responsibility (Griffiths of Fforestfach 2012: 140) and an ecological responsibility of capital is to be respected. Sustainable financial markets, particularly the safety of deposits and stability of money have to be conceived as public common good (Camdessus 2012: 111, 114) impacting multiple dimensions of human life. The behavior of agents on financial markets is therefore not only a function of individual benefit from short-term and long-term economic rationality but further dependent on a more fundamental ethical responsibility. To implement this responsibility, joint efforts from education, research, political and cultural organizations are necessary.[21] The central challenge to this extent is to overcome the individual perception and appreciation of materialism as the dominant principle on financial markets up to now.[22]

Conclusions

Sustainability has been conceived to be conducive to the fiduciary duties of financial intermediaries. As a concept of continuity and equilibrium it is almost equivalent to loyalty and care as two dimensions of fiduciary responsibility. Sustainability in the macro system of financial markets ("financial equilibrium") is a prerequisite for the fiduciary function of institutions at the micro level. In a further interpretation, sustainability is seen as an organizational pattern that is conducive both to stability in the financial and the surrounding systems, notably the social and ecological environment ("general equilibrium").

The relationships between financial markets, sustainability and risk (instability) as parameters

of fiduciary responsibility in finance are multiple. In addition to direct (stability on financial markets) and indirect (financial markets as allocation of sustainability) relationships, two further basic patterns have been considered.

- Usually, financial institutions and financial regulators are seen as dominant players on financial markets and are therefore primarily in charge of stability. This disregards the fact that managers and regulators do not act on their own but are dependent on the objectives of investors and depositors on financial markets. This emphasizes both the importance and the responsibility of private investors for sustainability in finance ("sustainability market discipline").
- Whereas many analyses center on products and processes as drivers of sustainability and stability, this study also emphasizes systemic structures in financial markets and the role of ethics as further conditions for stability. Basically, modern financial and cultural systems have become complex and dynamic. This has also increased systemic fragility and specific macroprudential policies have to be designed to maintain stability from an aggregate point of view (thereby avoiding also bubbles and risk concentrations that may arise from excessive investments in sustainable finance).

Finally, as a generally underlying principle, products and processes of financial markets should refer to a broader ethical context. The impact of stability comes here from the fact that, in addition to monetary return, the respect of the social and ecological values affected by financial decisions enables more balanced solutions and reduces the consequences of future negative feedbacks associated with today's unbalanced decisions. In total, the interaction of sustainability, financial markets and systemic stability can be related to three major organizational dimensions:

- an economic-technical dimension focusing on specific products and processes;
- a systemic dimension respecting the fragility of complex and high-speed systems;

[21] A major example for incentives from cultural organizations is "Caritas in veritate" from Benedict XVI. See Donati (2012: 76–9).
[22] See also Donati (2012: 74) as a setting of the "After-Modern Society."

- and finally the dimension of ethics and consciousness as the basis for human behavior in general.[23]

Given the multiple ways to implement sustainability and the creation of sustainable value on financial markets, the concept of sustainability in finance is not only to be conceived as an adaptation of the existing system. Instead, it may be assessed as a new pattern of dynamic and structure, a paradigm of sustainability. Although desired, the transformation may be difficult to achieve via rapidly changing the system. To avoid unsustainability in the transformation process, smaller steps seem to offer a promising way forward.

It is questionable if overall sustainability and fiduciary responsibility may fully be achieved by only referring to the economic advantages resulting from sustainability (business case for sustainability). Instead, in a broader context, a more ethically driven creation and evaluation of financial goods and processes are necessary. From this perspective, sustainability on financial markets is essentially a function of consciousness and responsibility of individuals and society. The way towards greater sustainability and stability in finance may therefore be perceived as a trade-off between traditional short-term, individual and material advantages on the one hand and the new long-term, systemic and ethical value creation on the other.

References

Ahrend, R. and A. Goujard. 2011. *Drivers of Systemic Banking Crises*. Paris: OECD Economics Department Working Paper, No. 902.

Allianz SE. 2012. *Global Financial Assets of Private Households*. Munich: Allianz Global.

Bank of England. 2011. "Instruments of Macroprudential Policy," discussion paper, Bank of England and Financial Services Authority, London.

Basel Committee on Banking Supervision. 2011. *Basel III: A Global Regulatory Framework for More Resilient Banks and Banking Systems*. Basel: Bank for International Settlements.

Becchetti, L. 2012. "Why Do We Need Social Banking?" in O. Weber and S. Remer (eds.) *Social Banks and the Future of Sustainable Finance*. Abingdon-on-Thames: Routledge, pp. 48–70.

Berd, A. M. 2011. "A Guide to Modelling Credit Term Structures," in A. Lipton and A. Rennie (eds.) *The Oxford Handbook of Credit Derivatives*. Oxford University Press, pp. 66–122.

Berger, A. N., P. Molyneux and J. O. S. Wilson (eds.). 2010. *The Oxford Handbook of Banking*. Oxford University Press.

Bessis, J. 2010. *Risk Management in Banking*, 3rd edn. Chichester: John Wiley & Sons.

Bopp, R. E. 2010. "Die Finanzwirtschaft – Anmerkungen zum Risiko- und Ertragsmanagement von Finanzdienstleistern," in M. S. Aßländer and A. Löhr (eds.) *Corporate Social Responsibility in der Wirtschaftskrise*. Munich and Mering: Rainer-Hampp-Verlag, pp. 267–81.

Borio, C. 2012. "The Financial Cycle and Macroeconomics: What Have We Learned?" Working Paper No. 395, Bank for International Settlements, Basel.

Camdessus, M. 2012. "From a 'Culture of Greed' to a Culture of Common Good," in M. Schlag and J. A. Mercado (eds.) *Free Markets and the Culture of Common Good*. Dordrecht: Springer, pp. 111–19.

Che, X. and N. Kapadia. 2012. "Understanding the Role of VIX in Explaining Movements in Credit Spreads," working paper, University of Massachusetts, Amherst.

Chen, L., P. Collin-Dufresne and R. S. Goldstein. 2009. "On the Relation Between the Credit Spread Puzzle and the Equity Premium Puzzle," *Review of Financial Studies* 22 (9): 3367–409.

Claessens, S., C., Pazarbasioglu, L. Laeven, M. Dobler, F. Valencia, O. Nedelescu and K. Seal. 2011. "Crisis Management and Resolution: Early Lessons from the Financial Crisis," IMF – International Monetary Fund Staff Discussion Note, Washington, March 9.

Cline, W. R. 2010. *Financial Globalization, Economic Growth, and the Crisis of 2007–09*. Washington: Versa Press.

---

[23] Basically, this may be referred to as transferring the pillars of the Basel framework to sustainability in finance: pillar one relates products and processes to sustainable return and risk, pillar two refers to the systemic dimension of sustainability and pillar three emphasizes sustainable market discipline.

De Bandt, O., P. Hartmann and J. L. Peydró. 2010. "Systemic Risk in Banking: An Update," in A. N. Berger, P. Molyneux and J. O. S. Wilson (eds.). *The Oxford Handbook of Banking*. Oxford University Press, pp. 633–72.

Donaldson, T. 2012. "Three Ethical Roots of the Economic Crisis," *Journal of Business Ethics* 106 (1): 5–8.

Donati, P. 2012. "Beyond the Market/State Binary Code: The Common Good as a Relational Good," in M. Schlag and J. A. Mercado (eds.) *Free Markets and the Culture of Common Good*. Dordrecht: Springer, pp. 61–81.

Drehmann, M., C. Borio and K. Tsatsaronis. 2012. "Characterising the Financial Cycle: Don't Lose Sight of the Medium Term," Working Paper No. 380, Bank for International Settlements, Basel.

Elkington, J. 1999. *Cannibals with Forks: Triple Bottom Line of 21st Century Business*. Mankato: Capstone Publishers.

Figge, F. and T. Hahn. 2008. "Sustainable Investment Analysis with the Sustainable Value Approach – A Plea and a Methodology to Overcome the Instrumental Bias in Socially Responsible Investment Research," *Progress in Industrial Ecology* 5 (3): 255–72.

Furrer, B., V. Hoffmann and M. Swoboda. 2009. *Banking & Climate Change: Opportunities and Risks*. Zürich: SAM Group.

Gabriel, K. 2005. *Nachhaltigkeitsindices – Indices of Sustainability*. Frankfurt am Main: Iko – Verlag für Interkulturelle Kommunikation.

Gorton, G. B. 2010. *Slapped by the Invisible Hand*. Oxford University Press.

Gramlich, D. and M. Oet. 2011. "The Structural Fragility of Financial Systems: Analysis and Modeling Implications for Early Warning Systems," *The Journal of Risk Finance* 12 (4): 270–90.

Griffiths of Fforestfach, Lord B. 2012. "Ethical Dimensions of Finance," in M. Schlag and J. A. Mercado (eds.) *Free Markets and the Culture of Common Good*. Dordrecht: Springer, pp. 139–52.

Haldane, A. G. and R. M. May. 2011. "Systemic Risk in Banking Ecosystems," *Nature* 469: 351–5.

Hannoun, H. 2010. "Towards A Global Financial Stability Framework," *Bank for International Settlements Management Speeches*, 45th SEACEN Governors' Conference, Siem Reap Province, Cambodia, February 26–7.

Hawley, J. P. and A. T. Williams. 2002. "The Universal Owner's Role in Sustainable Economic Development," *Corporate Environmental Strategy* 9 (3): 284–91.

Helbing, D. 2010. *Systemic Risks in Society and Economics*. Lausanne: International Risk Governance Council.

Hesse, A. 2007. *Sustainable Development Management – Politik- und Geschäftsfeld-Strategien für Banken*. Münster: SD-M Sustainable Development Management.

Holliday, C. O., S. Schmidheiny and P. Watts. 2002. *Walking the Talk – The Business Case for Sustainability*. Sheffield: Greenleaf Publishing.

IMF. 2012. *Global Financial Stability Report. The Quest for Lasting Stability*. Washington: International Monetary Fund.

Jeucken, M. 2001. *Sustainable Finance and Banking: The Financial Sector and the Future of the Planet*. London: Earthscan.
  2005. *Sustainability in Finance: Banking on the Planet*. Delft: Eburon Publishers.

Karwowski, E. 2010. "Bringing Islamic Banking into the Mainstream is not an Alternative to Conventional Finance," *Journal of Financial Transformation* 30: 155–61.

Köhler, H. 2009. *Die Glaubwürdigkeit der Freiheit*. Berliner Rede of German President Horst Köhler, Bulletin of the German Government No. 37–1, Berlin, March 24.

Kroszner, R. S., L. Laeven and D. Klingebiel. 2007. "Banking Crises, Financial Dependence, and Growth," *Journal of Financial Economics* 84 (1): 187–228.

Laeven, L. and F. Valencia. 2012. "Systemic Banking Crises Database: An Update," IMF Working Paper 12/163, Washington.

Lietaer, B., C. Arnsperger, S. Goerner and S. Brunnhuber. 2012. *Money and Sustainability – The Missing Link*. Axminster: Triarchy Press.

Luhmann, N. 1998. *Die Wissenschaft der Gesellschaft*, 3rd edn. Frankfurt: Suhrkamp.

Martin, W. 2009. "Socially Responsible Investing: Is Your Fiduciary Duty at Risk?" *Journal of Business Ethics* 90 (4): 549–60.

McKinsey & Co. 2012. *The Hunt for Elusive Growth: Asset Management in 2012*. June.

Meadows, D. 2008. *Thinking in Systems*. White River Junction: Chelsea Green Publishing.

Oet, M. V., S. J. Ong and D. Gramlich. 2012. *Policy Applications of a Systemic Risk Early Warning*

System. Mimeo, Federal Reserve Bank of Cleveland.

Peachey, A. N. 2011. *Great Financial Disasters of Our Time*, 3rd edn. Berlin: Wissenschafts-Verlag.

Radzicki, M. 2011. "System Dynamics and Its Contribution to Economics and Economic Modeling," in R. A. Meyers (ed.) *Complex Systems in Finance and Econometrics*. New York: Springer, pp. 727–38.

Reinhart, C. M. and K. S. Rogoff. 2009. *This Time is Different – Eight Centuries of Financial Folly*. Princeton University Press.

Remer, S. 2011. "Social Banking at the Crossroads," in O. Weber and S. Remer (eds.) *Social Banks and the Future of Sustainable Finance*, Abingdon-on-Thames: Routledge, pp. 136–95.

Ryan, S. G. 2009. "Fair Value Accounting – Policy Issues Raised by the Credit Crunch," in V. V. Acharya and M. Richardson (eds.) *Restoring Financial Stability: How to Repair a Failed System*. Hoboken: Wiley, pp. 215–28.

Schlag, M. and J. A. Mercado (eds.). 2012. "Ethical Dimensions of Finance," in M. Schlag and J. A. Mercado (eds.) *Free Markets and the Culture of Common Good*. Dordrecht: Springer, pp. 139–52.

Shahrokhi, M. 2011. "The Global Financial Crises of 2007–2010 and the Future of Capitalism," *Global Finance Journal* 22 (3): 193–210.

Shaw, D. R. 2010. "Sustainability and Livability in the 2007 Banking Crisis: A Failed Transition to a Low Gain System," *Systems Research and Behavioral Science*, 27 (5): 480–95.

Statman, M. 2006. "Socially Responsible Indexes," *The Journal of Portfolio Management* 32 (3): 100–9.

Stern, N. 2006. *Stern Review on the Economics of Climate Change*. London: HM Treasury.

2009. *Deciding our Future in Copenhagen: Will the World Rise to the Challenge of Climate Change?* Policy brief, London.

Strogatz, S. H. 2001. "Exploring Complex Networks," *Nature* 410: 268–76.

Sun, W., C. Louche and R. Pérez (eds.). 2011. *Finance and Sustainability: Towards a New Paradigm? A Post-Crisis Agenda*. Bingley: Emerald.

Szyszka, A. 2011. "The Genesis of the 2008 Global Financial Crisis and Challenges to the Neoclassical Paradigm of Finance," *Global Finance Journal* 22 (3): 211–16.

Taleb, N. N. 2008. *The Black Swan: The Impact of the Highly Improbable*. London: Penguin.

Trabelsi, M. A. 2011. "The Impact of the Financial Crisis on the Global Economy: Can the Islamic Financial System Help?" *The Journal of Risk Finance* 12 (1): 15–25.

UNCTAD. 2009. *Global Economic Crisis: Systemic Failures and Multilateral Remedies*. New York and Geneva: United Nations.

Utopies and Les Amis de la Terre. 2010. *L'Empreinte Carbone des Banques Françaises – Résultats Commentés*. Paris: Utopies and Les Amis de la Terre.

Vester, F. 2002. *Unsere Welt – ein vernetztes System*, 11th edn. Munich: Deutscher Taschenbuch Verlag.

Weber, O. and S. Remer (eds.). 2011. *Social Banks and the Future of Sustainable Finance*. Abington-on-Thames: Routledge.

Whalley, J. and Y. Yuan. 2009. "Global Financial Structure and Climate Change," *Journal of Financial Transformation* 25: 161–8.

World Commission on Environment and Development. 1987. *Our Common Future. Report of the World Commission on Environment and Development (Brundtland Report)*. Oslo: World Commission on Environment and Development.

Uncertain times, plural rationalities and the pension fiduciary

LIAW HUANG, DAVID INGRAM, THOMAS TERRY AND
MICHAEL THOMPSON

[E]ven as the Federal Reserve continues prudent planning for the ultimate withdrawal of extraordinary monetary policy accommodation, we also recognize that the economic outlook remains unusually uncertain.

Ben S. Bernanke, chairman of the Federal
Reserve, July 21, 2010

Introduction

Modern portfolio theory is no longer quite the safe harbor for fiduciaries making investment decisions that it once was (Hawley et al. 2011). One reason for this is the prolonged uncertainty in the financial markets that was mentioned by chairman Bernanke in 2010 and which still seems to be with us two years (at the time of writing) down the line. In such an environment, the pension fiduciary faces both the external pressures stemming from a prolonged uncertain investment outlook, and the internal pressures stemming from employers and participants reacting to economic uncertainty and voicing their concerns related to the investment of pension assets. Fiduciaries have a duty to balance the interests of their different participant groups, and understanding the perspectives of those beneficiaries is critical to successful implementation of fiduciary obligations (Hawley et al. 2011; Berry and Scanlan 2014). From a practical perspective, unrecognized stakeholder expectations can pose risks to follow-through on implementation of investment strategies.

How should the pension fiduciary act when the expected correlations among asset classes fail to materialize? How should the pension fiduciary interpret the apparently mixed signals from plan sponsors whose reactions to the sudden exposure to significant unfunded liabilities range all the way from derisking (by shifting more plan assets into fixed income investments) to seeking higher expected returns (by increasing the plan's exposure to hedge funds and private equities)? What is the framework for making asset allocation decisions in such an environment?

If uncertainty can persist for several years, then perhaps fiduciaries need to have a strategy for uncertainty. A strategy, moreover, that is based upon a theory that admits the existence of an uncertain phase to the economy. Such a theory exists, but not in the investment literature. It has been developed over the past thirty or so years in anthropology and applied, not to financial risk, but to environmental and technological risk. Now known as the theory of plural rationality,[1] the ideas were first articulated by Mary Douglas in the 1970s (Douglas 1972, 1978).

Plural rationality posits four states to the world, one of which abounds with uncertainty stemming from forces relentlessly pressuring the world to change state. This is not the reassuring environment that is envisaged by modern portfolio theory, in which the market always knows the correct price changes needed to bring things back into equilibrium. It is, however, indicative of what we have

---

[1] Sometimes called "cultural theory" and sometimes "neo-Durkheimian institutional theory." The latter, unfortunately, is too much of a mouthful, while the former risks conveying the impression that it is culture that is doing the explaining.

experienced in our economies over the past fifteen years.

The pension fiduciary who recognizes the possibilities that emerge from plural rationality theory will be able to use that perspective to form strategies that can be more effective more of the time. He will also have a different and possibly more productive insight into the motivations of the various other stakeholders who are often tugging him in opposite directions.

This chapter first examines decision-making by the fiduciaries of US private pension plans through the lens of the plural rationality theory from anthropology. Next, a brief overview of the plural rationality theory is given. The process by which fiduciaries find themselves balancing different stakeholder perspectives is described as being "clumsy" in this anthropological theory. Awareness of this process can facilitate avoidance of surprises. Looking back at the 2008 financial crises, different responses from pension fiduciaries and pension stakeholders are seen to conform to the expectations of plural rationality theory. Finally, the chapter looks ahead to a future filled with uncertainty, and summarizes fiduciary decision-making in the context of this theory.

US private pensions: roles and responsibilities of the stakeholders

The Employee Retirement Income Security Act (ERISA) of 1974 sets forth the framework in which private sector defined benefit pension plans in the United States operate. Central to the well-functioning of the United States defined benefit pension system is the role of pension fiduciaries, who must act solely in the interest of pension plan participants and beneficiaries, and balance the interest of other stakeholders in the pension system. Other stakeholders include the employers, who are the main source of pension funding, the participants, whose pension benefits are paid from plan assets, and the government, who oversees the pension system and provides some level of pension insurance through the Pension Benefit Guaranty Corporation (PBGC). These stakeholders may have conflicting interests, and exhibit tendencies towards different attitudes about risk.

The employer. The employer sponsors the pension plan in the context of its business purpose and makes initial and ongoing decisions that, together, fulfill what is commonly referred to as the settlor function. The employer will tend to think of risk and risk-taking as a necessary part of doing business and as an essential prerequisite for fulfilling the return expectations demanded by shareholders. In addition, employers often feel that they can use the expertise of their firm to successfully manage their risks.

The participants. The participants are the employees and beneficiaries of the pension plan, consisting of current retirees (annuitants currently receiving benefits) and future retirees (those entitled to benefits at a later time and who may continue to accrue benefits as active employees in the interim). For current retirees receiving fixed income for life, their interest is in benefit security and the maintenance of their fixed pension's purchasing power in the face of inflation. Therefore, they may find any risk to that security unacceptable. On the other hand, future retirees can have varied perspectives on risk. Some future retirees may be very interested in maximizing the growth of future benefit accruals and so are willing to accept some risk to achieve that growth. Other future retirees may lack the confidence that management's, the plan fiduciaries' or their own risk-taking will result in a viable retirement income stream for them.

The government. The United States government often pursues social policy through the use of tax incentives. ERISA was enacted in 1974 to establish general rules (for example, minimum standards of funding, participation and vesting) for tax-qualified private pensions, and to provide some level of insurance for those pensions through the PBGC. The government is interested in the long-term sustainability and well-functioning of the private pension system and the PBGC, and in keeping the systemic risks under control through its rules and compliance systems for private pensions.

The fiduciaries. The fiduciaries have authority and control over the management and administration of the pension plan and are responsible for the investment of its assets. In this capacity, their interest is to ensure the proper administration of the pension plan in accordance with applicable rules and regulations, control the risks of the pension plan for plan participants, and avoid conflicts of interest and unnecessary expenses. Fiduciaries place heavy emphasis on governance, process and control. With respect to the investment of plan assets, an investment committee usually serves as the pension plan fiduciary, and is responsible for asset allocation decisions, diversification requirements, performance measurements and periodic reporting.

The various stakeholders of the US private pension system are compelled to make decisions and take actions in order to fulfill their responsibilities. Inevitably, these decisions are influenced by how they perceive the world. The theory of plural rationality offers four such worldviews. We will briefly look at these four and then discuss how fiduciaries might work with the stakeholders having these worldviews.

Plural rationality

Social anthropologists look to understand and explain the underlying logic of social behaviors. And some of them – they have been dubbed "the new Durkheimians" – argue, first, that the ways in which people organize their social relations match the ways in which they perceive the world, second, that there is just a small number (four) of viable ways in which relationships can be organized and, third, that the states of the world can be categorized into a small number of choices that match up with the ways in which they are perceived. These propositions – propositions that stand in marked contrast to both rational choice theory (which holds that we are all rational in the same utility-maximizing way) and post-structuralism (which holds that we are all incomparably different) forms the basis for the theory of plural rationality. And these insights, as we will show, can be applied to the world of the pension fiduciary.

If people can see the world in four different ways then it is plausible to suggest that the world, at times and in places, can actually be each of those

ways. Otherwise those views that were never supported would have quickly died out. This does indeed seem to be the case, because three of these "states of the world" have their parallels in the economic literature, while the fourth – the state of uncertainty invoked by Ben Bernanke – is the one that is still missing from that literature.

Nature benign (captured by the icon of a ball in a basin; see Table 18.1) is the environment where the invisible hand does exactly what Adam Smith said that it would: steadily increasing the wealth of the whole by ensuring that individuals do well only when others also benefit. In economics, this state would be called a boom time.

Nature ephemeral (captured by the icon of a ball on an upturned basin; see Table 18.1) is almost the exact opposite of the nature benign state. Here the world is a truly perilous place. With disaster lurking in almost any action, that famous hand is not so much invisible as absent. Economists call this state a recession or depression.

Nature perverse/tolerant (captured by the icon of a ball in a trough between two peaks; see Table 18.1) is congenial to those who urge "everything in moderation," in that it lies somewhere between the extremes of the first two. Neither fully safe nor completely dangerous, it enables those who can determine where the safe limits are to prosper and to add to the wealth of the whole. But, unlike in nature benign, things can no longer be left entirely to the market; there have to be controls to prevent reckless actors venturing into the danger zone and impoverishing us all. The most recent example of this state is the great moderation. Economists, we suggest, would call this state moderate.

Nature capricious (captured by the icon of a ball on a flat and featureless surface; see Table 18.1) is the state that features uncertainty. This is a world where nature operates with neither rhyme nor reason. Nothing is predictable, results cannot be reliably replicated, and learning, it soon becomes apparent, is impossible. While this environment has clearly predominated in many parts of the economy for most of the period following the worst of the recession, economists have no name for it and hence no clear strategy to recommend.

Forms of social solidarity are nowadays defined as *the various ways in which we bind ourselves to*

Table 18.1 Plural rationality states.

Plural rationality state		Traditional economic theory
Nature benign		Boom time
Nature ephemeral		Recession or depression
Nature perverse/tolerant		Moderate
Nature capricious		(Uncertainty – theory is non-existent)

one another and, in so doing, define our relationship with nature and they, along with their distinctive perceptions as to how the world is and people are, are set out in Figure 18.1. We will explain these four forms in just a moment – they are called individualism, egalitarianism, hierarchy and fatalism – but the icons that capture these various "contradictory certainties" already give us some indication of how those who are binding themselves in these different ways are likely to behave in relation to investments and financial risks.

- Upholders of individualism are the optimists – we can dub them maximizers – who see the world moving towards equilibrium and, in the process, delivering ever-increasing prosperity (nature benign).
- Upholders of egalitarianism are conservators, striving to preserve what capital they have: the obvious strategy, given that they see the world as headed for total collapse if its delicate balance is not maintained at all times (nature ephemeral).
- Upholders of hierarchy are managers; they see the potential for prosperity, but only if the risks are clearly identified and carefully controlled (nature perverse/tolerant).

- Upholders of fatalism are pragmatists; facing a future that they see as inherently unpredictable, they back away from all forms of strategic behavior and concentrate on finding short-term ways of coping: keeping their heads down, ensuring all their eggs are not in the same basket and so on (nature capricious).

Pension plan stakeholders are likely to be distributed among all these solidarities, and this means that fiduciaries, if they are to be successful, will need to understand these contending "anchorages," and to then find constructive ways of reacting to them. So we now need to explain our theory in a little more detail, before applying it to the fiduciary in order to help us understand all the complex dynamics in which he or she is caught up.

The bare bones of the theory

Structured disagreement, theorists of plural rationality suggest, is a perennial characteristic of debates concerning the state of the world and concerning what, if anything, needs to be done about it. Climate change is a topical and glaring example,

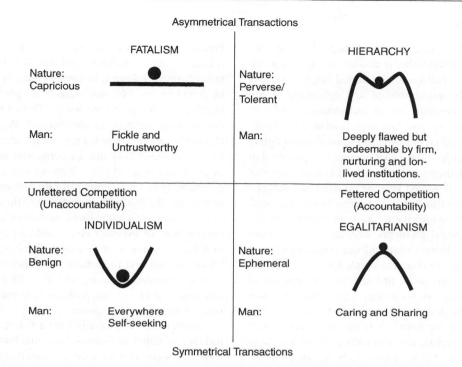

Asymmetrical Transactions

Figure 18.1 The theory of plural rationality: the four forms of social solidarity and their associated premises (or myths of nature).

and so too is the apportioning of blame for the credit crunch, along with the vexing question of what, if anything, needs to be done to prevent that sort of thing happening again.

Such disagreements are "structured" in the sense that people espousing each position are all the time defining themselves not only by their own ideas but also in contradistinction to the others. What results, when people act upon these contradictory positions, is a self-organizing system that continually reinforces the various premises – these various convictions as to how the world is and people are – that those who are doing the disagreeing are arguing from (these sets of convictions are summarized in the four quadrants in Figure 18.1).

Individualism

For upholders of the individualist solidarity, nature is benign and forgiving – able to recover from any exploitation (hence the icon – the myth

of nature – with its ball that, no matter how profoundly disturbed, always returns to stability) – and man is inherently self-seeking and atomistic (like the "island" that, John Donne argued, "no man is"). Trial and error, in self-organizing ego-focused networks (markets), is the way to go, with Adam Smith's invisible hand ensuring that people only do well when others also benefit. Individualist actors, in consequence, trust others until given reason not to and then retaliate in kind (the winning "tit for tat" strategy in the iterated Prisoner's Dilemma game [Rapoport 1985]). They see it as only fair that (as in the joint stock company) those who put most in get most out. Managing institutions that work "with the grain of the market" (getting rid of environmentally harmful subsidies, for instance) are what are needed.

This is the voice that calls for deregulation, for the freedom to innovate and take risks, and for the internalization of environmental costs so as to "get the prices right."

Egalitarianism

Nature, for those who bind themselves into the egalitarian solidarity, is almost the exact opposite (hence the ball on the up-turned basin) – fragile, intricately interconnected and ephemeral – and man is essentially caring and sharing (until corrupted by coercive and inegalitarian institutions: markets and hierarchies). We must all tread lightly on the earth, and it is not enough that people start off equal; they must end up equal as well – equality of result. Trust and leveling go hand-in-hand, and institutions that distribute unequally are distrusted. Voluntary simplicity is the only solution to our environmental problems, with the "precautionary principle" being strictly enforced on those who are tempted not to share the simple life.

This is the voice that defines the opposite of development as hospitality, that scorns the idea of "trickle down" and instead seeks to target "the poorest of the poor." It is the voice that argues for zero-growth, and that calls urgently for major shifts in our behavior so as to bring our profligate consumption down within the limits that have been set by Mother Nature.

Hierarchy

The world, in the hierarchical solidarity, is controllable. Nature is stable until pushed beyond discoverable limits (hence the two humps), and man is malleable: deeply flawed but redeemable by firm, long-lasting and trustworthy institutions (as in the headmasterly "Give me the boy and I will give you the man"). Fair distribution is by rank and station or, in the modern context, by need (with the level of need being determined by an expert and dispassionate authority). Environmental management requires certified experts (to determine the precise locations of nature's limits) and statutory regulation (to ensure that all economic activity is then kept within those limits). This is the voice that talks of "global stewardship," that readily invokes the fallacy of composition (that what is rational for the parts – belt-tightening during a recession, say – may be disastrous for the whole) and that insists that global problems (such as climate change) demand global solutions.

Fatalism

Fatalist actors expect to find neither rhyme nor reason in nature, and know that man is fickle and untrustworthy. Fairness, in consequence, is not to be found in this life, and there is no possibility of effecting change for the better. "Defect first" – the winning strategy in the one-off Prisoner's Dilemma – makes sense here, given the unreliability of communication and the permanent absence of prior acts of good faith. With no way of ever getting in sync with nature (push the ball this way or that and the feedback is everywhere the same), or of building trust with others, the fatalist's world (unlike those of the other three solidarities) is one in which learning is impossible. "Why bother?" Diversification and the careful avoidance of concentrated investments, along with the willful underinvestment of a large cash position, is therefore the rational management response.

Fatalist actors don't really have a voice; if they had they wouldn't be fatalistic! Nevertheless, since time and money that are spent on something about which nothing can be done is time and money wasted, there is some wisdom here that should not be ignored.

These four solidarities, in varying strengths and patterns of pair-wise alliance, have been found in many places: in debates over water engineering in South Asia (Gyawali 2001); in international forums where delegates struggle to do something about climate change (Thompson et al. 1998; Verweij 2006); in the different ways international regimes cope with transboundary risks such as water pollution (Verweij 2000) and municipalities go about the business of transport planning (Hendriks 1994); in the various ways households set about making ends meet (Dake and Thompson 1999); in the different diagnoses of the pensions crisis in countries with ageing populations (Ney 2009); and in the different panaceas that are variously championed and rejected by theorists of public administration (Hood 1998), to mention but a few. And our aim in this chapter is to add one more application to this list: financial risk of pension plans that is the responsibility of the fiduciary. But, before we do that, we should quickly explain the two axes (in

Figure 18.1) that generate these four forms of solidarity.

Hierarchies institute status differences: asymmetrical transactions (as in Boston where, it is said, "Lowells speak only to Cabots and Cabots speak only to God"). And hierarchies, by requiring forms of behavior appropriate to those of differing rank and station (accountability), set all sorts of limits on competition. Markets – the transactional arrangements that accompany individualism – do the diametrical opposite; they institute equality of opportunity (symmetrical transactions, as in "you scratch my back and I'll scratch yours") and promote competition (unaccountability, as in "if I don't do it someone else will").

The other two permutations – symmetrical transactions with accountability (egalitarianism) and asymmetrical transactions without accountability (fatalism) have tended to be ignored by social science in general and by policy science in particular. Economists, for instance, have long spoken of "market incentives" versus "social sanctions," while many a pundit, in the wake of the credit crunch, has invoked a destruction-dealing pendulum swinging between "light touch" and "heavy hand" regulation. Such dualistic schemes therefore lack the "requisite variety," in that they fail to capture the full repertoire of strategies; this shortcoming, as it is played out in the field of financial risk, is something that we are seeking to remedy in this chapter.

Social solidarities among pension plan stakeholders

There are many examples of these four solidarities among a pension plan's stakeholders as they think about investments and financial risks:

- Examples of the individualist solidarity: employers investing to maximize profits for their shareholders; future retirees believing the financial market will provide good returns that will position themselves for growth in retirement benefits.
- Examples of the hierarchical solidarity: employers concerned about the environment, societal

well-being or social justice and thus are willing to modify their normal corporate behavior so as to better address these concerns; governments that permit employers to offer retirement plans that meet their business need but within predefined limits.
- Example of the egalitarian solidarity: current retirees who want to protect their pension benefits against all risks.
- Example of the fatalist solidarity: employees who view retirement as a distant future concern for which they show little interest in advance planning; fiduciaries who see future investment returns as unpredictable.

The stakeholders individually can have any of the four risk attitudes, and in some cases an entire group of stakeholders can have a risk attitude that is different from what would be expected based upon their role. This arises when recent experiences result in a major surprise. We saw such shifts occurring during the dotcom bubble, when the standard for the proportion of pension assets that were invested in equities shifted upwards even in the case of the most conservative/egalitarian stakeholders. It also happens when experience changes the situation for the pension drastically. A plan that has just experienced a very large loss, and finds itself suddenly in an underfunded position, might trigger a bout of high conservatism or a rush of very aggressive investing from an investment committee. How, then can a fiduciary respond to all this plurality? To answer this question we need to go back to the theory and look at its normative implications.

In all these examples we have just listed – water engineering, climate change and so on – we find that each solidarity, in creating a context that is shaped by its distinctive premises, generates a storyline that inevitably contradicts those that are generated by the other solidarities (Thompson and Rayner 1998; Douglas et al. 2003; Ney 2009). While none of the underlying myths is false – the world, at times and in places, can be all these ways (boom, recession, moderate and uncertain) – each of the storylines that they generate makes coherent sense only because of what it leaves out that

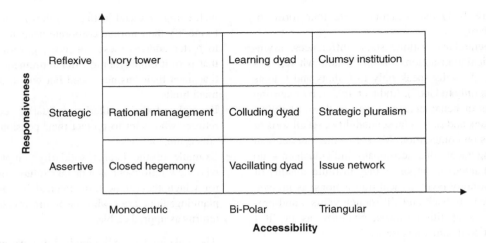

Figure 18.2 A handy tool for moving towards clumsiness (Source: Ney 2009: 198). [Properly speaking, of course, this should be a 4×4 diagram, but the fact that the fatalist solidarity tends not to have a voice provides a justification for simplifying it to 3×3.]

the others, in different ways, include. In consequence, since each is distilling certain elements of experience and wisdom that are missed by the others, and since each is providing a clear expression of the way in which a significant portion of the populace feels we should live with one another and with nature, it is important that they all be taken some sort of account of in the policy process. That, in essence, is the case for what is called clumsiness, clumsiness being the state of affairs in which each of the solidarities is able to make its voice heard and is then responsive to the others (Verweij and Thompson 2011; Verweij 2011). Something similar, therefore, should hold for fiduciary duty; the challenge is to work out precisely what it is!

Clumsiness is a tongue-in-cheek label, of course, in that it is questioning the "elegance" that is achieved by choosing just one of the storylines – just one definition of problem-and-solution – and dismissing the rest: the orthodox "decision-making under uncertainty," with its single definition of the problem, its purportedly clear separation of facts and values, its imposition of a single metric (dollars, lives saved, etc.) and its pursuit of optimization. "Decision-making under contradictory certainties," however, is quite different; indeed it has much in common with Robert Dahl's (1989)

theory of pluralist democracy, with its two dimensions – accessibility and responsiveness – and its focus on discourse, argumentation and the constructive engagement of all those discordant voices that, in the orthodox approach, are whittled down to just one.

That democratic insight then suggests that if, for example, a firm is carrying out a scenario-planning exercise, it will need to ensure that all the storylines are fully developed into scenarios – visions of the future – that are then engaged with one another: something that is not easily achieved if some of those voices have already been drowned out. The climate change scenarios developed by the Intergovernmental Panel on Climate Change, for instance, have been shown to all be elaborations of the hierarchical storyline (Janssen 1996). And Shell's scenarios – Shell is famous for its pioneering of scenario-planning – have consistently missed out the egalitarian storyline (Elkington and Trisoglio 1996).

So making yourself (or, rather, your organization) clumsy is never going to be easy, even when you are trying to be clumsy. Figure 18.2 is a handy tool for checking how well you are doing in this difficult task of "getting to clumsy," in that it shows all the possible steps and pathways by which the transition from closed hegemony (one voice drowning out all the others) to clumsy institution (all the voices heard and responded to) can be effected. Interestingly, political scientists already had names for all the "provinces" in this scheme; it is just that there was no real understanding of how they were related to one another – no map of the various steps and pathways – until this theory of plural rationality came along (all this is set out in Ney 2009).

So it begins to look as though what we need for our fiduciary duty purposes is, first, the full four-fold complement of states of the world and their appropriate strategies and, second, an institutional design that will ensure that each of the four "voices" that these plural rationalities generate can enjoy both access and responsiveness.

So do pension fiduciaries try to be clumsy about risk?

Pension fiduciaries necessarily need to be clumsy about risk. In contrast to defined contribution plans, where each participant makes his or her investment decision based on his or her own circumstances and perception of risks, pension fiduciaries need to make investment decisions on behalf of all plan participants. Furthermore, they realize that the benefit security desired by plan participants is closely tied to the employer's ability to fund the pension plan. Therefore the resulting investment decisions are often a compromise that, while not optimal with respect to any one stakeholder, is sensitive to all their diverse needs, and stays within the regulatory requirements.

Consider, for example, the increasingly common situation whereby an employer contributes company stock into its pension trust. Once contributed, the fiduciary takes over and must decide whether to hold the contributed shares as a trust investment or trade the shares for cash or other securities. The stakeholders may have different perspectives on this: the employer may intend that the trust hold onto the shares, while the participants – particularly the retirees – may prefer liquidation of the shares so as to provide better diversification. And, the government, in part protecting its insurance program administered by the PBGC, may wish to limit the exposure to a single issue and so will insist on adherence to the 10 percent statutory limit on employer securities. Here, the fiduciary is necessarily engaged with finding a clumsy solution, which may look like the precise solution advocated, by a specific stakeholder perspective, or it may be an entirely different solution such as the systematic selling of the shares over time.

The insights from plural rationality theory suggest that fiduciaries should examine the worldview from which the decisions are made and understand their limitations. In particular, consider two additional storylines that are commonly missed:

- The fatalistic view that the financial market volatility will continue and its outcomes are unpredictable, and the egalitarian view of a total collapse. Under these two scenarios how would the stakeholders be impacted and what are the responsibilities of the pension fiduciaries?

- If pension fiduciaries only look at the world from the individualistic or hierarchical perspective in the context of modern portfolio theory, they may feel comfortable with their decisions only if the actual world stays within the limits of their expected outcomes. If the actual world unfolds differently, they may be unprepared to handle the consequences. For instance, in recent years the increased correlation of all asset classes in a declining market makes diversification less effective in mitigating risks. Pension fiduciaries who understand the "total collapse scenario" under the ephemeral view of nature will be less surprised.

- Given the same set of circumstances, decisions made based on the risk attitudes of just one group of stakeholders will often be different from decisions made by another group of stakeholders with different risk attitudes.

- Different stakeholders will react very differently from one another when the actual results of decisions and actions are known. This point is expanded in the following section describing surprise.

- Given these perceptual divergences, perhaps the fiduciaries should intentionally aim to be clumsier: perhaps they should consciously look for responsible solutions that are acceptable for most stakeholders realizing that perfect solutions probably do not exist. Certainly in other applications of plural rationality, these considerations can lead to better and more robust solutions (e.g., Verweij and Thompson 2011).

Plural rationality thus begins to lead towards a conscious strategy for fiduciaries: a strategy that gives names and concepts to choices that they have been tasked to make. In other words, plural rationality gives fiduciaries a framework for formulating a strategy for uncertainty: a strategy that, as we will now try to show, will lessen the likelihood of their being surprised.

Clumsiness and surprise avoidance

The central hypothesis in the theory of plural rationality is that the way we are caught up in the process of social life (in hierarchically structured relations, in ego-focused networks, in egalitarian enclaves, and so on) supplies us with our convictions as to how the world is (stable within limits, able to take anything we throw at it, everywhere fragile, and so on). Mother Nature, however, cannot always comply. In these non-compliant circumstances there will be a persistent, and very likely growing, mismatch between what some stakeholders expect to happen and what actually happens. In contrast to those situations where the world happens to be the way we are insisting it is (think of Alan Greenspan and his forty years of being served so well by his "self-interest ideology") our behavior is penalized rather than rewarded (by, in Alan Greenspan's case, a "once-in-a-century credit tsunami"). This means that, sooner or later, as Frank Sinatra was always telling us, something's gotta give.

What it is that gives, and how, depends of course on the particular mismatch – on just how the world actually is and on just how we happen to be insisting it is – and this means that surprises, when they come, can come in a total of twelve different ways (Figure 18.3).

- Conservators, secure in the knowledge that nature is ephemeral, do not expect to see others

prosper and, when some do – in the normal or boom environments – they are surprised and begin to doubt their fundamental pessimism.
- Conversely, maximizers never expect to see a partial or total collapse with the whole world running into difficulty, and so are surprised when – in the bust and moderate environments – it does.
- Pragmatists, expecting a world (nature capricious) in which learning is not possible, but finding themselves in one of the three worlds in which it is, will be slow to pick up on all the recurrent regularities that are being thrown up around them. And when they do begin to pick up those regularities – when they begin to learn (in one or other of the three possible ways of learning that this typology gives us) – then, inevitably, they will find themselves being eased away from the fatalist myth of nature and being brought under the thrall of one of the others.
- If we are hierarchists, like most pension fiduciaries, we expect a world (nature perverse/tolerant) in which there is a clear boundary between equilibrium and disequilibrium. But if the world we occupy is irregular and unpredictable, as the uncertain environment of the past several years has been, then try as we may (and we will!) we will not be able to obtain the crucial information that we need if we are to act rationally (i.e., in a way that will uphold the particular patterns of relationships – hierarchy – that we have bound ourselves into). Our information costs, as we put our strategy of certainty-creation to work, will shoot off to infinity, and our resources (which we have defined as limited but expandable within the positive-sum portion of our world) will drain away into a plugless sink. The hierarchical strategy, of course, will probably lead us to switch resources to some other area of information needs, but if the world is everywhere flat we will just be switching them from one plugless sink to another. Eventually, as we learn that learning is not possible, we will find ourselves abandoned by the hierarchical myth of nature and embraced by the fatalist myth: nature capricious.

And so it goes, each in its distinctively surprising way, for each of the various possible mismatches.

	UNCERTAIN	 RECESSION	 BOOM	 MODERATE
 PRAGMATIST (Fatalism)	ALIGNED No surprises	Expected windfalls don't happen	Unexpected runs of good luck	Unexpected runs of good and bad luck
 CONSERVATOR (Egalitarian)	Caution does not work	ALIGNED No surprises	Others prosper (especially individualistic strategists)	Others prosper (especially hierarchical strategists)
 MAXIMIZER (Individualism)	Skill is not rewarded	Total collapse (when none was expected)	ALIGNED No surprises	Partial collapse
 MANAGER (Hierarchy)	Unpredictability	Total collapse (when only partial was expected)	Competition	ALIGNED No surprises

Figure 18.3 A typology of surprises. Each row shows the observations, which are surprises in three out of four alternatives, for one of the four beliefs.

In keeping with anthropological usage, these beliefs about the world – the myths of nature (each captured by a ball-in-landscape "econ") – are not falsehoods. Rather, they are the minimal representations of reality that must be ascribed to these various strategists if they are to be seen as rational. Hence our theory's name. We mention all this so as to make clear that, with its wide range of areas of application and its bold interdisciplinarity, this is really a systems theory that happens to have originated in anthropology. So perhaps – strange-looking though it might seem – it is exactly what we need if we are to get to grips, first, with the systemic risks that, as all the pundits have been pointing out, were completely ignored in the run-up to the credit crunch, and, second, with the uncertain state that has gone unrecognized in economics but which we have now been stuck in for nigh on five years.

So our typology not only tells us how the various surprises differ; it tells us just how nice or nasty they are likely to be. To discover that you win life's lottery more often than you expected you would (row I, column III) is to be quite pleasantly surprised; to experience total system collapse (rows III and IV, column II) is to be rather unpleasantly surprised. So we can give a positive or negative value to each of the surprises. Our typology is then transformed into what game theorists call a "pay-off matrix."

When we apply the concept of surprise and the associated pay-off matrix to pension stakeholders, we should recognize that the pay-off matrix can be asymmetric; that is, there may be limitations on the rewards one can receive from a good surprise (i.e., limited upside), but one may need to bear all the consequences of a bad surprise (i.e., no limit on the downside). For instance, when a pension plan is overfunded, there are limitations under United States pension law on the employer's scope to access the surplus; the employer, however, is responsible for funding any shortfall. In consequence, therefore, a healthy employer with a fully funded pension plan cannot fully realize the benefits of a positive surprise. On the other hand, a financially distressed (i.e., bankrupt) employer can transfer the unfunded pension obligation to the PBGC who then insures the private pensions. This is commonly referred to as the "PBGC put." In this situation, the PBGC will share with the employer the impact of negative surprises, but the employer can reap the full benefit of positive surprises. Fiduciaries, therefore, in addition to gaining an understanding of the nature and variety of risk attitudes, benefit from this clarification of the asymmetric impact of surprises on different stakeholders when formulating responses to the actual world.

Response to economic events since 2007

The financial and economic events since 2007 have had a profound effect on pension plan sponsor and fiduciary decision-making. The following analysis applies the theory of plural rationality to the responses of the pension plan sponsors and fiduciaries to the economic events since 2007.

What has emerged from the prolonged market uncertainty, the breakdown of expected relationships among asset classes, and a persistent fear of an unexpected "black swan" event are two distinct views on defined benefit pension plans:

- defined benefit pension is a non-core business to be divested, and;
- defined benefit pension is an ongoing risk to be managed.

With the first view, the pursuit of pension plan "derisking" strategies is the hottest trend in pension plan management. With the second view, pension plan sponsors are recommitting to their pension plans (and their proper management) as essential elements of their human resource endeavors.

The theory of plural rationality offers us insight into these disparate plan sponsor and fiduciary behaviors. This general sense of uneasiness and uncertainty is indicative of the view that the world is moving in unpredictable ways – making sensible forecasts and risk controls difficult. This is consistent with a shift from the nature benign (or individualist) worldview to the nature capricious (or fatalist) worldview. Similar to a fatalistic investment manager keeping large cash positions (i.e., keeping assets risk-free), the increasingly fatalistic plan sponsors and fiduciaries will look to take all risks out of the pension plan (hence "derisking") with an eye toward plan termination.

Defined benefit pensions – a non-core business to be divested

Broadly speaking, derisking strategies can involve changes in plan design, changes in investment strategies and/or shifting plan obligations to others.

- **Plan design changes** include making the defined benefit plan more defined contribution-like (i.e., by shifting risks from the employer to employees), closing the defined benefit plan to new participants or freezing defined benefit plan benefit accruals for current participants.
- **Investment changes** stem from using surplus or surplus volatility as a benchmark for setting asset allocation targets, and include increasing the allocation to liability-hedging assets and various other means of more actively managing interest rate risk.
- **Shifting plan benefit obligations to others** includes cashing out employees and/or retirees in pay status, or shifting obligations to an insurance company through an annuity purchase arrangement.

Plan design changes and *shifting benefit obligations to others* are both settlor functions and so are the responsibilities of the plan sponsor. *Investment changes* are the responsibility of the fiduciary, obviously with input from the sponsor.

As an example of a comprehensive derisking strategy, consider the "glide path" strategy for underfunded plans used by some plan sponsors and fiduciaries to manage the pension plan toward plan termination, and to deal with unwelcome surprises over a medium-term time horizon. The glide path strategy will often involve elements of all three of the derisking categories listed above. The plan is closed to new participants and benefit accruals are frozen for existing participants. The fiduciaries set in place a dynamic asset allocation strategy in which an ever-greater percentage of plan assets are invested in fixed income securities as the funded status improves over time. Those fixed income securities are managed to hedge the plan liabilities. The intent is that, when the pension plan becomes fully funded, the sponsor has a fully derisked plan that can then be fully annuitized – thus completing the "glide path" toward termination. From plural rationality's perspective, the "glide path" is a systematic and disciplined way to reduce surprises, as the asset allocation decision is put on autopilot.

Furthermore, a properly conceived derisking strategy often involves an increasingly fatalistic plan sponsor, divesting itself from the defined benefit pension business, working with the plan fiduciaries and other stakeholders to manage the pension plan in a way that is highly collaborative and, therefore, can only be described as being clumsy. As depicted here, "glide paths" tend not to be considered optimal strategies; rather, they are introduced as a means of achieving the goal of plan termination in a disciplined manner, over a finite time period, and within acceptable levels of risk.

Defined benefit pensions – an ongoing risk to be managed

Some plan sponsors may see uncertainty not as fundamentally unpredictable (i.e., not the fatalists' view of uncertainty), but as random variations that occur in the midst of the economy seeking to reach a new equilibrium (i.e., an "expected" uncertainty).

Accordingly, they may believe that the risks associated with defined benefit pension plans can be effectively managed and the consequences of bad surprises can be mitigated. For these plan sponsors, plan termination does not emerge as a logical next step.

Such plan sponsors and fiduciaries will maintain an individualistic or hierarchical worldview that posits an infinite time horizon for their ongoing pension plans and a belief that the economy will always perform well over the long term. They will invest in assets that are traditionally expected to earn higher returns over the long term.

The investment decisions of many public pension plans (state and local government pension plans) in the United States suggest an orientation toward either the individualistic or the hierarchical perspective. Comparing the asset allocation from 2007 to 2011 for public pension plans, the fixed income allocation has not changed much, from 25 percent in 2007 to 24 percent in 2011, while the allocation to alternatives (real estate, private equity, hedge funds and commodities) has increased from 12 percent in 2007 to 20 percent in 2011 (Pollard 2012). By increasing the allocation to alternatives, the plan fiduciary gives up liquidity in exchange for higher returns and further diversification. It is believed that over the long term there will be mean reversion for asset prices and the economy will reach a new equilibrium, a typical premise of an individualist or hierarchical worldview. It is important to note that the stakeholders of public pension plans consist of taxpayers, state and local legislators, and employee unions. The process by which decisions regarding pension plans are reached can be very different from private companies, and not all stakeholders may agree with the course of actions taken. Thus, the collaborative (clumsy) process ensues, with an outcome that appears to embrace or default into an optimistic outlook on the future, dominated by a strong desire to see the pension assets grow. The continued investment in equities and alternatives is in stark contrast with plan sponsors that pursue a derisking strategy, but the plural rationality theory can provide an alternative framework to understand and analyze pension issues.

Conclusions

So here we stand, perhaps at or near the end of an unusually long uncertain period in the economy. Such an extended uncertain period is creating many converts to the pragmatist (fatalist) point of view and approach to risk – keeping commitments small and short-termed with a large cash cushion. Sooner or later, out of the chaos will emerge a string of either favorable or unfavorable circumstances. The best strategy for the plan at that time will vary accordingly, either abrupt expansion or contraction. But the pension fiduciary also needs to be aware that the plan stakeholders will likely be looking at the same potential future and seeing it totally differently. Some will cling tightly to their functional solidarities and others will be slow to move away from the expectations they have formed in the long uncertain times. Fiduciaries can now see this debate through the lens of plural rationality theory and recognize that, rather than seeking to win over all of the plan stakeholders to the one "correct" view of the future, they need to work for a collaborative, clumsy course of action. And, moreover, that such a resolution is likely to be good for the plan over the long run.

Now, in the light of this brief exposition of plural rationality, the pension fiduciary will see that these disagreements over strategy are never going to go away. With that dynamic plurality accepted and mapped, he or she will be able to face the surprises and their fiduciary risks with a little less agitation, a bit more clumsiness, and some diminution of the more unpleasant of those surprises.

References

Berry, C. and C. Scanlan. 2014. "The Voice of the Beneficiary," Chapter 26, this volume.

Dahl, R. A. 1989. *Democracy and its Critics*. New Haven, CT: Yale University Press.

Dake, K. and M. Thompson. 1999. "Making Ends Meet, in the Household and on the Planet," *GeoJournal* 47 (3): 417–24.

Douglas, M. 1972. "Environments at Risk," in J. Benthall (ed.) *Ecology: The Shaping Enquiry*. London: Longman, pp. 129–45.

1978. "Cultural Bias," Occasional Paper No. 35, Royal Anthropological Institute: London. Reprinted in M. Douglas (1982) *In the Active Voice*. London: Routledge and Kegan Paul.

Douglas, M., M. Thompson and M. Verweij. 2003. "Is Time Running Out? The Case of Global Warming," *Daedalus*, Spring: 98–107.

Elkington, J. and A. Trisoglio. 1996. "Developing Realistic Scenarios for the Environment: Lessons from Brent Spar," *Long Range Planning* 29 (6): 762–69.

Gyawali, D. 2001. *Water in Nepal*. Kathmandu, Nepal: Himal Books. (International edition published by Zed Books, London, as *Rivers, Technology and Society*, 2003.)

Hawley, J., K. Johnson and E. Waitzer. 2011. "Reclaiming Fiduciary Duty Balance," *Rotman International Journal of Pension Management* 4 (2): 4–16.

Hendriks, F. 1994. "Cars and Culture in Munich and Birmingham: The Case for Cultural Pluralism," In D. J. Coyle and R. J. Ellis (eds.) *Politics, Policy and Culture*. Boulder, CO: West View Press.

Hood, C. 1998. *The Art of the State: Culture, Rhetoric and Public Management*. Oxford: Clarendon Press.

Janssen, M. 1996. *Meeting Targets: Tools To Support Integrated Assessment Modelling of Global Change*. Den Haag: CIP-Gegevens Koningklijke Bibliotheck.

Ney, S. 2009. *Resolving Messy Policy Problems*. London: Earthscan.

Pollard, T. 2012. "Public Pension Funding Ratios Still Tumbling," *Pensions & Investments*, October 1.

Rapoport, A. 1985. "Uses of Experimental Games," in M. Grauer, M. Thompson and A. Wierzbicki (eds.) *Plural Rationality and Interactive Decision Processes*. Berlin: Springer-Verlag.

Thompson, M. and S. Rayner. 1998. "Risk and Governance Part 1: The Discourses of Climate Change," *Government and Opposition* 33 (2): 139–66.

Thompson, M., S. Rayner and S. Ney. 1998. "Risk and Governance Part 2: Policy in a Complex and Plurally Perceived World," *Government and Opposition* 33 (3): 330–54.

Verweij, M. 2000. *Trans-Boundary Environmental Problems and Cultural Theory: The Protection of the Rhine and the Great Lakes*. Basingstoke: Palgrave-Macmillan.

2006. "Is the Kyoto Protocol Merely Irrelevant, or Positively Harmful, for the Efforts to Curb Climate Change?" in M. Verweij and M. Thompson (eds.). *Clumsy Solutions for a Complex World*. Basingstoke: Palgrave-Macmillan.

2011. *Clumsy Solutions for a Wicked World*. Basingstoke: Palgrave-Macmillan.

Verweij, M. and M. Thompson. 2011. *Clumsy Solutions for a Complex World*, revised edn. Basingstoke: Palgrave-Macmillan.

Emotional finance and the fiduciary responsibility of asset managers

ARMAN ESHRAGHI AND RICHARD TAFFLER

Introduction

Recent events in the capital markets and the continuing high-profile cases of investment fraud have led to increasing questioning of whether asset managers necessarily act always in the best interests of their clients. A fresh look at the roles of investment professionals and the nature of their investment processes is thus called for. In this chapter, we draw on insights from emotional finance to help us better understand and analyze the behavior of such fiduciaries. Emotional finance is a new area of finance that seeks to understand financial market behavior and investment processes by formally recognizing the role unconscious emotional needs and fantasies play in all investment activity (see, for example, Taffler and Tuckett 2010; Tuckett 2011; Tuckett and Taffler 2012).

All investments have the potential to generate high levels of excitement and anxiety. Using the language of psychoanalysis, investments can become phantastic objects, a term we will carefully define in the next section. Emotional finance helps us better understand how investors in general, and fiduciary investors in particular, can be swayed in their investment decisions by feelings of which they are consciously aware, and specially by those unconscious needs, drives and fears not directly accessible to conscious thought. What does this mean for the clients of investment funds as well as the investment industry more generally? From the perspective of responsible ownership, we argue that all investors, and fiduciaries in particular, have a social, ethical and legal responsibility to explicitly acknowledge the key role emotions, both conscious and unconscious, play in their investment decision-making.[1]

In illustrating why, how and through which mechanisms fiduciary investors can be negatively influenced by their underlying unconscious fantasies, we draw on evidence from the recent hedge fund "bubble" (e.g., Eshraghi and Taffler 2012) together with an examination of the fund management industry more broadly (e.g., Tuckett and Taffler 2012). From a psychoanalytic perspective, both regulated and unregulated investment vehicles can be viewed, by their investment beneficiaries and managers alike, as unconscious wish-fulfilling objects. This can lead to problematic investment decisions and, as we have seen in the case of the recent financial crisis, ultimately even financial market instability. In particular, investing in non-conventional funds or markets employing novel investment strategies is more likely to be prone to such unconscious fantasies. This is due to the "excitement" associated with their "specialness" and the mystique often associated with their fiduciaries, all of which can negatively affect the long-term interests of investors in such vehicles.

This chapter is organized as follows. In section two, we provide a brief introduction to the new paradigm of emotional finance. Section three provides extensive evidence suggesting how emotions can drive the behavior of hedge fund managers and investors in their funds. In section four, we make a similar argument concerning more traditional asset management vehicles such as mutual funds and pension funds. Finally, section five brings together our discussion of hedge funds as largely unregulated investment vehicles and more traditional regulated investment vehicles from a fiduciary perspective, and suggests a number of policy implications for asset managers and regulators.

---

[1] For a critical study of the contemporary debate on ethics in finance see, for example, Boatright (2008, 2010).

Emotional finance: a brief overview

Traditional finance, derived from neoclassical economic theory, assumes investors are rational and competent. Behavioral finance, borrowing largely from cognitive psychology, explores investing as a special class of decision-making under uncertainty and highlights serious judgmental biases. Emotional finance is a new area in finance and is at an early stage of its development as a coherent discipline. It provides a better understanding of financial market behavior and investment processes by formally recognizing the role unconscious emotions play in all investment activity. Both traditional and behavioral finance perspectives can provide important insights into the workings of financial markets and investor behavior. However, they do not, and cannot, directly acknowledge the key role unconscious psychic processes play in all human activity – the realm of emotional finance in understanding investor decision-making.

Emotional finance draws on the psychoanalytic understanding of the human mind and the dynamic states of mind explained originally in the works of Sigmund Freud and later psychoanalytic thinkers such as Melanie Klein and Wilfred Bion. As Taffler and Tuckett (2010: 4) explain, emotional finance explores "how a highly complex, opaque, unpredictable, and competitive market environment inevitably leads to investors being caught up emotionally in a major way." This emotional entanglement includes, among other elements, the stress and anxiety generated by unfavorable investment outcomes, and the joy and euphoria associated with favorable investment outcomes. To understand these subtle processes, we use the psychoanalytic term "phantasy" for describing the unconscious emotions that underpin all investment activity.[2]

The concept of phantasy derives mostly from the writings of Freud and Klein. Freud (1911: 343) defines phantasy as a "wish-fulfilling activity that can arise when an instinctual wish is frustrated."

Klein (1975: 290) regards phantasy as more central and argues that phantasies are not only the constituents of dreams but of all forms of thought and activity. She suggests the whole of an individual's psychic life is dominated by phantasies originating from the earliest stages of emotional development: "Infantile feelings and phantasies leave, as it were, their imprints on the mind, imprints that do not fade away but get stored up, remain active, and exert a continuous and powerful influence on the emotional and intellectual life of the individual." We argue that all investments have the potential to become "phantastic" in the minds of market participants, i.e., phantastic objects.

The term "object" in psychoanalysis refers to a mental image of something or someone in the real world, i.e., objective reality. As the object points to the image rather than the actual thing or person, multiple versions of the same object can exist in the minds of different individuals. The phantastic object is thus defined as "a mental representation of something or someone, which in an imagined scene fulfills the protagonist's deepest desires to have exactly what she wants exactly when she wants it," (Tuckett and Taffler 2008: 89). Hence, when discussing phantastic objects, the term "phantasy" suggests the potential of the object for transformation into an exceptionally exciting and desirable mental image. The thrill, and sometimes euphoria, associated with a successful investment may be explained by the unconscious role the phantastic object plays, be it a winning stock, a top-performing mutual fund or a celebrated hedge fund (and its billionaire manager).

Individuals are more susceptible to the phantastic object when a particular sense of reality dominates their thinking. According to Klein (1975), people make decisions in one of the two basic oscillating states of mind, the integrated state of mind and the divided state of mind. In the integrated state, we see others and ourselves more or less as we are, both good and bad. In the divided state of mind, the psychic pain of dealing with undesirable reality is avoided by mentally splitting off the good from the bad.[3] The unconscious search for the phantastic

---

[2] Psychoanalysts conventionally distinguish *phantasy* (with a "ph") as in unconscious fantasy from the vernacular term "fantasy" in the sense of reverie or daydreaming, which is in the realm of conscious awareness.

[3] In formal psychoanalysis literature, these states are known as the depressive (D) state and the paranoid-schizoid (PS) state, respectively. An integrated state involves "giving up

object triumphs over "realistic" judgments when a divided state of mind dominates. In such settings, investments can be transformed in the minds of investors into vehicles that promise, much like Aladdin's lamp, to fulfill their masters' deepest unconscious desires, i.e., their "stuff of dreams."[4] For example, during dotcom mania, firms experienced an immediate increase of around 60 percent in their stock price by simply adding a dotcom suffix to their names (Cooper et al. 2001). In fact, as Taffler and Tuckett (2005) explain, dotcom mania is a rich case study of how unconscious fantasies can dominate realistic enterprise valuations.

Importantly, once an investor comes to "believe" that a particular investment can earn exceptional returns, he or she is likely to repress any doubts associated with investing in it. Hence, in the investor's unconscious search for a phantastic object, the investment vehicle's stated purpose may well be ignored. When the excitement of investing in the phantastic object takes over, the normal capacity to judge risk breaks down, unless sufficiently large losses literally wake the investor up from his reverie. Information processing takes on a different purpose when a phantastic object is unconsciously believed to exist. The phantastic object "appears to offer the opportunity to break the rules of usual life and so turn 'normal' reality on its head" (Tuckett and Taffler 2008: 89), which creates the impression that what was previously considered impossible can, in fact, happen after all.

In such settings, market participants essentially become a "basic-assumption group" that

unconsciously colludes in supporting the same strong belief in the phantastic object.[5] Individuals in a basic-assumption group do not think for themselves; they rather operate in a particular sense of reality, a divided state of mind, which blocks any attempt to think clearly and independently. By collectively engaging in groupthink (Janis 1982), basic-assumption group members adopt unconscious defenses against anxiety, and collectively push away anything that might spoil the "party." Their activities, which look chaotic at first, are given "a certain cohesion if it is assumed that they spring from basic assumptions common to the entire group" (Bion 1952: 146).

When reality finally intrudes, investors feel cheated, and the once dominant feeling of desire for the phantastic object changes to anger and blame. In such settings, blame is often intertwined with a hatred of reality, which can result in objective external reality not being appropriately acknowledged. When investors in a divided state of mind are eventually let down, this is inevitably associated with the avoidance of feelings of guilt and shame, and the wish to learn from the experience, which would be the appropriate emotional response in an integrated state of mind. As Kirsner (1990: 53) explains, "it takes a major shock to make us give up illusion – and then, unhappily, only for a while. Mostly people come back to their old preconceptions very quickly – precisely because they have such a strong psychic, if not financial, investment in maintaining the situation as they would like it to be."

the feeling that one is all-powerful and all-knowing ... feeling a certain amount of regret about the consequences of past actions, and a potential anticipatory feeling of depressive anxiety or guilt when contemplating potentially repeating past actions which led to failure or suffering" while in a divided state, "all such feelings are evaded by evacuating them from awareness" (Tuckett and Taffler 2008: 89).
[4] The "stuff of dreams" refers to Prospero's famous lines in Shakespeare's *Tempest*, "such stuff as dreams are made on," which in modern usage means an idealized scenario or situation that can be only fantasized or wished for. This strong desire for the phantastic object is often intertwined with an inevitable sense of omnipotence. As Westlund (1986: 67) explains, Prospero selfishly refers in his famous epilogue only to himself, using the first-person pronoun fifteen times in no more than twenty lines, and subsequently asks for applause and pardon, again only for himself.

Emotions and unregulated fiduciary investments: the case of hedge funds

Emotions drive investors, whether individual or institutional, in many different ways. In essence, investments are synonymous with uncertainty, which, in turn, is always associated with anxiety. Thus, investing generates high levels of stress and

[5] Bion (1952) contrasts the basic-assumption group with the "work group" whose members cooperate in the performance of a task, are clear about their purpose and act in a rational and constructive manner.

anxiety. Also, as we explained in the previous section, investments can easily turn into phantastic objects in the minds of investors, being viewed, unconsciously, as wish-fulfilling objects capable of generating high levels of excitement and euphoria.

What makes hedge funds an interesting asset class and a prime case study in emotional finance is their versatility as investment vehicles, as well as how they can be perceived in the minds of investors. Hedge fund assets under management grew at the rate of 25 percent per annum from 1990 to June 2008, peaking at almost $2 trillion. The hedge fund industry then consisted of no fewer than 10,000 hedge funds and funds of hedge funds (HFR Industry Report 2009). In the following six months, assets under management collapsed by almost a third following negative investment returns, associated investor withdrawals and fund closures.[6] Eshraghi and Taffler (2012) explain the rise and fall in hedge fund assets under management by addressing, among other factors, the unconscious needs and beliefs of investors in such funds, their managers and the financial media and gossip writers among others. High-profile hedge funds were transformed, in investor phantasy, into objects of excitement and desire, and were associated with unrealistic expectations and wishful thinking. Specifically, they came to assume a very different meaning in investors' unconscious reality to their stated "non-phantastic" aim of providing investment returns less correlated with more traditional asset classes.

During the hedge fund "bubble" and before it burst, the excitement of investing in what hedge funds represented became divorced from the anxiety associated with the potential consequences of taking excessive investment risk. Against this backdrop of collective euphoria, all such doubts were dismissed or rationalized away. However, any such euphoric state is likely to be unsustainable, leading to widespread denial, anger, blame and panic

when reality ultimately intrudes. The rapid growth and then dramatic collapse of hedge fund assets under management followed a trajectory common to most asset-pricing bubbles (Kindleberger and Aliber 2011: 26–33). This is because of the financial innovations that many hedge funds claim to represent, the potential opaqueness of their investment strategies, the implicit promise of wealth, their often exclusive nature and, finally, the way many of their managers and returns are reported on in the financial media.

Alternative investments such as hedge funds are viewed, on the one hand, as promising higher returns through the often sophisticated and wide range of investment strategies and asset classes available to them, including flexibility in short-selling, and using leverage and derivatives. This implicit promise of wealth can become a key driver of investor fascination with them. On the other hand, the asymmetry (skewness) and fat tails in hedge fund return distributions can further enhance their appeal to investors and lead them to "expect a more thrilling investment ride" (Gregoriou 2006: 139). Finally, hedge funds' exclusivity also contributes to their magical appeal. Being accredited to invest in a high-profile hedge fund represents membership of an exclusive, elite society of rich and sophisticated individuals (see, for example, Lowenstein 2000: 24; Farrell 2002).

Not only are wealthy individual investors in hedge funds but also hedge fund managers themselves prone to investment phantasy. "Star" managers, particularly when portrayed in exaggerated and unrealistic ways, can become represented in the minds of market participants as investment gods or gurus, i.e., phantastic objects, further disconnecting investors from their underlying anxiety about the possibility of loss. The language used to describe hedge funds and their managers in the media implies their assumed power and mystique. Phrases such as "masters of the new universe," "this generation's robber barons" and "Delphic oracles of finance" are only a few examples out of many (Anderson and Creswell 2007; Niederhoffer 1998). Another interesting example is the singular names they bear, such as Dragonback, Eclectica, Richland, Matador, Maverick, Helios (the ancient Greek god of the Sun), Farallon (radioactive

---

[6] Total assets invested in the hedge fund industry had, however, recovered to $2.2 trillion by the end of September 2012 although returns suffered from increased volatility (HFR Industry Report 2012). This high level of volatility in hedge fund assets under management provides further evidence for our core argument.

islands), Cerberus (three-headed mythological creature) and Appaloosa (a horse breed known for its distinctive physical characteristics) among others. The media portrayal of hedge funds and their managers in this spirit not only adds to the mystique associated with such investment vehicles, but also serves to enhance the hubristic self-perceptions of their managers.

Finally, we wish to emphasize that traditional hedging and other non-correlated strategies are a necessary part of an investment portfolio from a fiduciary perspective (see, for example, Ruce 2012). In addition, although hedge funds are largely unregulated investment vehicles, their managers still are in a fiduciary relationship with their clients. As the *Restatement (Third) of Trusts*, prudent investor rule (§227) observes, "the trustee is under a duty to the beneficiaries to invest and manage the funds of the trust as a prudent investor would, in light of the purposes, terms, distribution requirements, and other circumstances of the trust."[7]

Emotions and regulated fiduciary investments

In contrast to alternative investment vehicles such as hedge funds that are largely unregulated, more traditional investment vehicles such as mutual funds and pension funds have to observe formal financial regulation. However, their managers and investors are similarly prone to unconscious fantasies. It is, therefore, equally important to consider the nature of the fiduciary roles and responsibilities of this group of asset managers from an emotional finance perspective.[8]

Tuckett and Taffler (2012) conduct interviews with more than fifty prominent fund managers around the world, most of them managing regulated

investment funds. Based on a detailed analysis of these interviews and specifically the stories told by their respondents, the authors describe how fund managers essentially enter into ambivalent emotional relationships with the assets they buy, sell and hold. The interviews show clearly how emotion-laden fund management activity is. Fund managers form these relationships, whether consciously or not, with "objects" that they hope will produce gain but that can also easily let them down and, in any case, often take time to play out. Therefore, during the investment process, the feelings of fund managers often oscillate between excitement and anxiety.

Much of fund management activity is driven by a range of emotions, which are mostly unconscious and thus completely hidden from market participants (Tuckett and Taffler 2012). One can perhaps begin to understand the nature of these emotions by letting them "come to surface" as feelings, for example in the natural environment of a semi-structured interview. Using a simple content-analysis approach that counts the occurrences of emotion-laden keywords in the said interviews, one observes that fund management can be viewed in terms of *pleasure* versus *unpleasure* (Taffler and Tuckett 2010: 96). That is to say, keywords belonging to each category are used almost equally in the interviews, i.e., feelings of trust (113), hope (102), excitement (32) and love (90) are pitted against feelings of worry (199), disappointment (80), fear (62) and hate (26).[9] In other words, we find directly illustrated the oscillating feelings of excitement and fear referred to earlier. Reinforcing this point, that anxiety is *the* key emotion experienced by fund managers, was demonstrated, paradoxically, by the almost complete absence of the word itself (only three voluntary mentions) during the complete set of interviews.

Importantly, the traditional non-phantastic role of a regulated fund manager is often neglected in investor phantasy. Since fund managers have to constantly outperform their competition/market,

---

[7] The full text of the prudent investor rule is accessible, *inter alia*, on the website of American Law Institute at www.ali. org.

[8] Mutual funds are a prime example of regulated investment funds that supervise substantial assets under management globally. Total worldwide assets invested in mutual funds reached almost $24 trillion in 2011 (ICI Factbook 2012) and is continuing to rise.

[9] Figures inside brackets report the number of times the indicated word (or its related forms) was mentioned in the complete set of fifty interview transcripts excluding the interviewer remarks.

they are faced with an important psychological dilemma in doing their daily jobs: they have to reconcile the conscious or unconscious awareness that they cannot control the performance of their investments with the fact that they have to "believe" or "pretend" they do. In other words, fund managers have to believe they can find and invest in phantastic objects with which they (and implicitly *only* they) can have special relationships, and that they, themselves, can be phantastic and outperform on a consistent basis in competition with other fund managers, on which basis their funds are advertised and sold to investors. Hence, fund managers have to cope with the high levels of anxiety associated with this paradox. In addition to all this, they must observe, or appear to do so, many rules and regulations that often have little to do with the subtle complexities of their fiduciary roles.

The fund management industry needs to acknowledge that it unhelpfully requires its foot soldiers always to be phantastic. Fund managers' clients also expect them to do the impossible on a consistent basis. How do fund managers cope with their own anxieties and those of their clients in such circumstances, particularly when their investments are underperforming? Jameson (2000) and Eshraghi and Taffler (2013) describe how fund managers use commentaries in annual reports to tell investment stories to their clients, and to themselves, in an attempt to both make sense of their investment outcomes and to persuade their clients that their investments are properly managed even if they have underperformed. In this way, fund managers not only provide the utilitarian benefits of skilled investment decision-making by diversifying within and across different markets, as often explained in conventional finance, they also provide their clients with certain expressive benefits including feelings of status by association, patriotism, social responsibility and fairness (Statman 2004), and more fundamentally, we emphasize, feeling of excitement by proxy, i.e., partaking in the investment phantasy through the medium of their fiduciaries.

All market participants need to acknowledge that emotions can also significantly affect the quality of decisions made by fund managers. Where the risks to decision process quality and the influence

of emotional biases can be recognized, failure to do so would appear to raise questions about self-serving conduct by these fiduciaries. This behavior would also be inconsistent with the fiduciary duties of prudence, loyalty and care as described in the prudent investor rule as well as in the CFA Code of Ethics and Standards of Professional Conduct.[10] In fact, resistance to coming to grips with these influences could (or should) be viewed as rooted in the self-interests of investment managers, consultants and advisors that put their unwillingness to address their unconscious needs and phantasies above the interests of beneficiaries.

Conclusions

As we have seen, investing arouses strong emotions. On one level, investment is always associated with excitement (Taffler and Tuckett 2010), and the search for excitement is a universal human activity. Investments as phantastic objects can therefore become a source of emotional attachment for all investors. Even prudent and sophisticated investors can be susceptible to the unconscious lure of phantastic objects and dependency basic-assumption groups, as, for example, the long list of victims in the Madoff fraud demonstrates.

Therefore, there is a need for all investors to be protected against their and their fiduciaries' unconscious search for phantastic objects. The *caveat emptor* philosophy whereby investors are deemed responsible for the consequences of investing in certain funds, even if not appropriate for them, is highly problematic.[11] What is needed instead is

---

[10] Specifically, Principle III.A observes: "Members and Candidates have a duty of loyalty to their clients and must act with reasonable care and exercise prudent judgment. Members and Candidates must act for the benefit of their clients and place their clients' interests before their employer's or their own interests."

[11] The defense of *caveat emptor* is often used by investment banks in justifying their activities. For example, in the securities fraud case brought by the SEC against Goldman Sachs in connection with a synthetic collateralized debt obligation (CDO) product they structured and marketed to investors known as Abacus 2007-AC1, which led to a $550 million fine, the bank argued that the investors who bought its CDOs were "among the most sophisticated mortgage investors in

the establishment of "suitability regulations" that correlate investor suitability with appropriate risk exposure by implementing suitability standards (Kaal 2009). Well-enforced suitability regulations, in this spirit, would serve to protect investors from themselves and others. Even compulsory disclosure of investment risk in a transparent manner is insufficient. What is needed is the economic equivalent of "mandatory immunization" to prevent the carelessness of some investors from infecting all others (Statman 2009).

Why should financial regulators be concerned about unconscious emotions? Since all investors are at least partially influenced by their own or others' emotions, "financial regulation will always have some degree or level of emotional impact, such as reduced anxiety or decision-making stress, and increased fear or exuberance" (Huang 2003: 24). We echo Huang's view that if a desired rationale of investment regulation is to promote investor confidence in the integrity of securities markets, then regulators need to recognize and explicitly acknowledge the role of unconscious fantasies in permeating all investment activity. We argue for a new attempt to understand and integrate the role of emotions in financial regulations concerning investment products and markets.

Regulators should also bear in mind that fundamentally, wealth is not a suitable proxy for investors' knowledge, sophistication and understanding of underlying investment risk. Promoters of investment funds need to have a reasonable expectation that their prospective purchasers, or their advisers, properly understand the operational and financial risks associated with their often complex investment vehicles, and that these products are suitable for them, i.e., meet general investor suitability requirements. This argument follows similar rules promulgated by the Financial Industry Regulation

Authority (FINRA) governing its members' dealings with their clients as well as the Principle of Fair Representation outlined in the CFA Code of Ethics.[12] It is equally important to point out that regulators are, in theory, susceptible to the same range of phantasies as investors and investment fund promoters (Eshraghi and Taffler 2012) and are easily seduced by the self-serving but seemingly plausible arguments of the industry they seek to regulate. The SEC's inability to detect the Madoff fraud is a prime example in this regard.[13]

Fiduciary investors are particularly susceptible to moral hazard. As a case in point, JP Morgan recently paid more than $150 million to settle charges because of failing to tell its investors that a prominent fund, which heavily influenced its selection of mortgage securities, would financially profit from their failure (Garcia 2011).[14] As for hedge funds, studies suggest that their managers have the ability and, in principle, the incentive, to overvalue their portfolios and avoid reporting losses to attract and retain investors (Bollen and Pool 2009).[15] In such environments of information asymmetry, commitment to appropriate levels of transparency is essential, and likely to be profitable both for investment funds and their investors.

---

[12] Specifically, Principle I.C states "CFA Members and Candidates must not knowingly make any misrepresentations relating to investment analysis, recommendations, actions, or other professional activities."

[13] Langevoort (2009) describes how journalists and authors searched for popular sense-making narratives to explain this inability, and thereby resorted to simple hero-villain characterizations while failing to capture the more complex underlying reality.

[14] Similar examples abound in the banking industry, such as the recent Libor scandal involving such banks as RBS, Barclays and UBS. For example, UBS paid $1.5 billion in fines when faced with allegations it had tried to manipulate the benchmark interest rate, while Citi, Deutsche Bank and HSBC all made settlements over mortgage-related fraud in the middle of the financial crisis (Bart et al. 2012).

[15] Hedge fund managers also have the incentive to routinely revise their previous returns history thereby altering their performance record (Patton et al. 2011). By studying a comprehensive sample of due diligence reports, Brown et al. (2012) show hedge funds frequently misrepresent past legal and regulatory problems. However, the costs of commissioning such reports are prohibitive for smaller investors.

the world" and thus they owed them no duty of care (Ford and Jones 2010). The reality, however, was different. For example, although "IKD [a German bank which was one of the main purchasers of the Abacus CDO] had an army of PhD types to look at CDO deals and analyse them … Wall Street knew that they didn't get it. When you saw them turn up at conferences there was always a pack of bankers following them" (ibid.).

The roles and responsibilities of the media deserve proper attention in our view. Journalists need to avoid being carried away by the excitement-generating potential of certain investment vehicles, and this must be embedded in the commonly accepted principles of responsible reporting. Given the well-documented impact of media coverage on investment fund flows (see, for example, Ozik and Sadka 2010; Solomon et al. 2012), the importance of the financial media following appropriate ethical reporting practices cannot be emphasized enough. Financial and public media need to contain, rather than spread, the excitement associated with innovative financial products, and the individuals behind them. This argument applies not only to hedge funds, but to all asset classes and financial markets.

In addition, investors should take a fresh look at the ethics of investing in highly innovative products and, in doing so, fiduciary investors must lead *par excellence*. This renewed commitment fits in well with the underlying spirit of corporate governance, often defined as the "set of legal, cultural, and institutional arrangements that determine what publicly traded corporations can do, who controls them, how that control is exercised, and how the risks and returns from the activities they undertake are allocated" (Blair 1995: 3). Along similar lines, we believe the United Nation's Principles for Responsible Investment should include, perhaps under Principle One, an advisory clause on seeking to understand and moderate, to the extent possible, the key role of both conscious and unconscious emotions in making investment decisions.[16]

Finally, we need to emphasize that the transformation of investment vehicles into phantastic objects can happen across the board. Risks posed by phantastic objects can go beyond financial markets since

all technological innovations, whether of a financial nature or not, can become phantastic as they run the risk of "temporarily exceeding our ability to use those technologies wisely" (Lo 2008: 2). As for fiduciary investments, the prudent investor rule §227 observes that trust law should "reflect and accommodate current knowledge and concepts [and] avoid repeating the mistake of freezing its rules against future learning and developments." Naturally, as our understanding of emotional finance develops, we should expect fiduciaries and court to begin applying these new concepts.

References

Anderson, J. and J. Creswell. 2007. "Hedge Fund Managers Leading in Race for Riches," *New York Times*, April 23.

Bart, K., T. Miles and A. Viswanatha. 2012. "UBS Traders Charged, Bank Fined $1.5 Billion in Libor Scandal," *Reuters*, December 19.

Bion, W. R. 1952. "Group Dynamics: A Re-View," *International Journal of Psychoanalysis* 33: 235–47.

1961. *Experiences in Groups*. New York: Basic Books.

Blair, M. M. 1995. *Ownership and Control: Rethinking Corporate Governance for the Twenty-first Century*. Washington, DC: The Brookings Institution.

Boatright, J. 2008. *Ethics in Finance*, 2nd edn. Oxford: Blackwell.

2010. *Finance Ethics: Critical Issues in Theory and Practice*. Oxford: Wiley.

Bollen, N. P. B. and V. K. Pool. 2009. "Do Hedge Fund Managers Misreport Returns? Evidence from the Pooled Distribution," *Journal of Finance* 64 (5): 2257–88.

Brown, S. J., W. N. Goetzmann, B. Liang and C. Schwartz. 2012. "Trust and Delegation," *Journal of Financial Economics* 103 (2): 224–34.

Cooper, M. J., O. Dimitrov and P. R. Rau. 2001. "A Rose.com by Any Other Name," *Journal of Finance* 56 (6): 2371–88.

Eshraghi, A. and R. Taffler. 2012. "Hedge Funds and Unconscious Fantasy," *Accounting, Auditing and Accountability Journal* 25 (8): 1244–65.

2013. "Fund Manager Self-belief, Sensemaking and Storytelling," working paper.

---

[16] The six Principles include: (1) incorporation of environmental, social and governance (ESG) issues into investment analysis and decision-making processes; (2) incorporation of ESG issues into ownership policies and practices; (3) seeking appropriate disclosure on ESG issues by the entities invested in; (4) promoting acceptance and implementation of the Principles within the investment industry; (5) working together to enhance effectiveness in implementing the Principles; and (6) reporting on activities and progress towards implementing the Principles. The list can be accessed at www.unpri.org.

Farrell, C. 2002. "Before You Jump into a Hedge Fund," *Business Week*, May 17.

Ford, J. and S. Jones. 2010. "A Tricky Pick," *Financial Times*, June 10.

Freud, S. 1911. "Formulations Regarding the Two Principles of Mental Functioning," *The Standard Edition of The Complete Psychological Works of Sigmund Freud*, Vol. 12, London: Hogarth.

Garcia, C. 2011. "JPM to pay $153m to Settle Magnetar-related Charges," *Financial Times*, June 21.

Gregoriou, G. 2006. *Funds of Hedge Funds: Performance, Assessment, Diversification, and Statistical Properties*. Oxford: Butterworth-Heinemann.

HFR Industry Report. 2009 and 2012. *Hedge Fund Research*. www.hedgefundresearch.com.

Huang, P. H. 2003. "Trust, Guilt, and Securities Regulation," *University of Pennsylvania Law Review* 151 (3): 1059–95.

ICI Factbook. 2012. Investment Company Institute. www.icifactbook.org.

Jameson, D. A. 2000. "Telling the Investment Story: A Narrative Analysis of Shareholder Reports," *Journal of Business Communication* 37 (1): 7–38.

Janis, I. L. 1982. *Groupthink*, 2nd edn. Boston, MA: Houghton Mifflin.

Kaal, W. 2009. "Hedge Fund Valuation: Retailization, Regulation and Investor Suitability," *28th Annual Review Banking & Financial Law*, 581.

Kindleberger, C. P. and R. Z. Aliber. 2011. *Manias, Panics, and Crashes*, 6th edn. New York: Palgrave Macmillan.

Kirsner, D. 1990. "Illusion and the Stock Market Crash: Some Psychoanalytic Aspects," *Free Associations* 1T: 31–59.

Klein, M. 1975. *Love, Guilt and Reparation, and Other Works: 1921–1945*. London: Karnac Books.

Langevoort, D. C. 2009. "The SEC and the Madoff Scandal: Three Narratives in Search of a Story," *Mich. St. L. Rev.*, 899–914.

Lo, A. 2008. *Statement before the US House Committee on Oversight and Government Reform*, November 13.

Lowenstein, R. 2000. *When Genius Failed: The Rise and Fall of Long-Term Capital Management*. New York: Random House.

Niederhoffer, V. 1998. *The Education of a Speculator*. New York: John Wiley and Sons.

Ozik, G. and R. Sadka. 2010. "Does Recognition Explain the Media-Coverage Discount? Contrary Evidence from Hedge Funds." http://ssrn.com/abstract=1563703.

Patton, A. J., T. Ramadorai and M. Streatfield. 2011. "The Reliability of Voluntary Disclosures: Evidence from Hedge Funds." http://ssrn.com/abstract=1934543.

Ruce, P. J. 2012. "The Trustee and the Prudent Investor: The Emerging Acceptance of Alternative Investments as the New Fiduciary Standard," *South Texas Law Review* 53 (4): 653–94.

Solomon, D. H., E. F. Soltes and D. Sosyura. 2012. "Winners in the Spotlight: Media Coverage of Fund Holdings as a Driver of Flows." http://ssrn.com/abstract=1934978.

Statman, M. 2004. "What do Investors Want?" *Journal of Portfolio Management* 30 (5): 153–61.

2009. "Regulating Financial Markets: Protecting Us from Ourselves and Others," *Financial Analysts Journal* 65 (3): 22–31.

Taffler, R. J. and D. Tuckett. 2005. "A Psychoanalytic Interpretation of Dot.com Stock Valuations." http://ssrn.com/abstract=676635.

2010. "Emotional Finance: The Role of the Unconscious in Financial Decisions," in K. H. Baker and J. R. Nofsinger (eds.) *Behavioral Finance*. New York: John Wiley & Sons, pp. 95–112.

Tuckett, D. 2011. *Minding the Markets: An Emotional Finance View of Financial Instability*. New York: Palgrave Macmillan.

Tuckett, D. and R. J. Taffler. 2008. "Phantastic Objects and the Financial Market's Sense of Reality: A Psychoanalytic Contribution to the Understanding of Stock Market Instability," *International Journal of Psychoanalysis* 89 (2): 389–412.

2012. "Fund Management: An Emotional Finance Perspective," CFA Foundation.

Westlund, J. 1986. "Omnipotence and Reparation in Prospero's Epilogue," in L. Layton and B. Schapiro (eds.) *Narcissism and the Text: Studies in Literature and the Psychology of Self*. New York University Press.

PART IV

Towards a broader interpretation of fiduciary duty

Fiduciary duty and the search for a shared conception of sustainable investment

GORDON L. CLARK

Introduction

The trust is a means of conserving and transferring assets to nominated beneficiaries (Langbein 1997). Regulating the behavior of trustees, the principle of fiduciary duty governs the relationship between trustees and beneficiaries (Thomas and Hudson 2004: s. 1.56). In some jurisdictions, it also enables intermediaries to represent the interests of beneficiaries, providing the former with authority to invest on behalf of the latter. There are a variety of definitions of fiduciary duty ranging from the abstract through to the domain-specific. Atiyah (1995: 255) observed that a fiduciary relationship binds trustees to beneficiaries such that "the person in the fiduciary position is under a duty not to abuse that position, and this duty involves the duty to disclose all material facts." Stapleton (1996: 13) noted, in relation to company directors and senior executives, being a fiduciary also involves "honesty and loyalty, and a duty of care and skill." Langbein (2007: 1075) observed the "core fiduciary principle … is the duty of impartiality"; a rule conceived and policed so as to regulate conflicts of interest.

The chapter begins with the historical significance of fiduciary duty (see also Hawley and Williams 2001). This allows us to understand fiduciary duty in relation to functionally efficacious common law norms and conventions. Whereas some might suggest that fiduciary duty evolved as the standard of behavior because of its effectiveness in maximizing social welfare, it is important to acknowledge the idealism about past communities of practice, which is embedded in such claims. This is illustrated by a rereading of two landmark cases that effectively defined the nature and scope of fiduciary duty, relevant to investment management. I suggest that whatever its ideal conception, it has proven insufficient as the golden rule governing the trust institution. Government policies designed to define and regulate the governance of the trust institution represent attempts to solve problems evident in the practice of investment.

Whereas explanations of common law doctrine typically refer to community norms and conventions, the very idea of commonly shared norms and conventions has been undercut by moral pluralism and contestation over basic values (Clark 1985). Indeed, so pervasive is dispute over the nature and scope of fiduciary duty that it is tempting to reread the doctrine so as to pull apart idealism about the past. As indicated below, the evidence suggests that community norms and conventions have been suborned by powerful interests that use the rhetoric of fiduciary duty to advance their own causes. Just as Alan Greenspan's idealism about the social value of rational self-interest was brought asunder by the global financial crisis, it would seem that the moral imperatives of individual reputation and community standing are not effective in sustaining the authority of fiduciary duty (compare Braithwaite 1989). These norms have wilted in the face of contests for control over the investment management process.

Notice, I am not optimistic about the value of government regulation "standing-in" for fiduciary duty. Realist conceptions of the formation and passage of statute provide many lessons not least of which is the realization that "solutions" may be partial and partisan – statute may be a constraint on innovation as rules and regulations designed to solve past problems stifle attempts to meet the future (Roe 2006). The challenge is to bring together the interests of the various stakeholders in investment management so as to reconceptualize the practice of investment in ways that advance sustainable investment (Woods and Urwin 2010). This may seem to be a form of idealism by the back door. What is remarkable, however, is the variety of attempts to do just that by the various interests and parties embedded in the industry. In conclusion, I remind the reader that UK governments over the past thirty years have repeatedly confronted the question of the social value of investment only to duck the issue.

Rereading *Harvard College* v. *Amory*

The classic case defining fiduciary duty relevant to investment management is *Harvard College* v. *Amory*.[1] The College and Massachusetts General Hospital (MGH) sued a trustee seeking restitution of losses sustained in an investment fund established by a wealthy businessman for his surviving widow. In his will, the businessman had provided capital for investment on behalf of his widow and, upon her death, the disbursement of the assets of that fund to the two institutions. The two trustees identified by the businessman as executors of his will and trustees of the fund were provided

> the sum of $50,000 in trust nevertheless to loan the same upon ample and sufficient security, or to invest the same in safe and productive stock, either in the public funds, bank shares or other stock, according to their best judgement and discretion, hereby in joining on them particular care and attention in the choice of funds, and in the punctual collection of the dividends, interest and profits thereof, and authorising them to sell out, reinvest and change said loans and stocks from time to time, as the safety and interest of said trust fund may in their judgement require.

The businessman's will and the intentions of the executors and trustees (as one) to invest according to the mandate (above) were not contested by either institution in the court of probate. Having invested in the stock of manufacturing companies, matching previous investment decisions of the deceased,

[1] 26 Mass. (9 Pick.) 446 (1830).

the trust incurred losses on those investments such that when the surviving trustee came to retire the two institutions sought restitution of those losses from the trustee. As the Massachusetts Supreme Court rehearsed the facts of the case, assessed the responsibilities of trustees and the virtues of different types of investments reference was made throughout to English common law. In that regard, Justice Putnam (p. 22) observed:

> [A]ll that can be required of a trustee to invest, is, that he shall conduct himself faithfully and exercise sound discretion. He is to observe how men of prudence, discretion and intelligence manage their own affairs, not in regard to speculation, but in regard to the permanent disposition of the funds, considering the probable income, as well as the probable safety of the capital to be invested.

Friedman (1964: 554) noted that this definition of prudent behavior "has been so often quoted, cited, and repeated, that the eye is apt to pass over it without noticing the precision of its phrasing." Friedman explained its conceptualization by reference to Boston society of the time, including its strong family commitments, the rise of a mercantile aristocracy and the common use of trustee institutions to manage investments. So "men of prudence" was not some abstract, dislocated reference point but local people, including businessmen. Equally important, and resonating with late twentieth century investment strategy and the management of risk and returns, the court emphasized that investment is all about probabilities (risk) rather than certainties.

The court also noted that the testator was a "man of extraordinary forecast and discretion" and that his wealth was not an accident, but the result of "calculation and reflection." Equally, the court made considerable play of the fact that the executors and trustees were, in fact, family members, being (respectively) the brother and cousin of his wife (the surviving widow). There was no reason to doubt the competence of the testator, there was no reason to doubt the motives of the trustees, nor was there reason to doubt their judgment given the norms and conventions governing the behavior of similarly located individuals. Considering the investment strategy conceived by the trustees, the court argued that the investments made were consistent with local experience and were not like lotteries and games of chance. There were reasonable grounds to invest in manufacturing companies considering the risks associated with options such as public funds.

This opinion is rightly lauded for its scope and significance for common law jurisdictions around the world. Nonetheless, it should be noted, as many commentators have noted, that it was not determinate of US standard practice. Hawley et al. (2011) observe that nearly forty years later the court returned to the more constrained English standard, including a general prohibition against investments in traded company stocks and securities. This held for the majority of states through to at least the 1930s; state lists of permitted investment instruments were only abandoned in the 1940s after their costs became widely acknowledged. It took publication of the American Law Institute's *Restatement (Third) of Trusts* in 1992, which included reference to the use of modern portfolio theory, for US standards of fiduciary duty to return to the expansive conception of trustee responsibility enunciated in *Harvard College* v. *Amory* (conceptualized as the prudent investor rule; see Langbein and Posner 1976).

If surprising when considered in the light of the development of the financial services industry over the second half of the twentieth century, more surprising is the comment made by Aalberts and Poon (1996: 39) to the effect that it was possible to distinguish between private trusts and estates and pension funds. Noting fiduciaries of pension funds are subject to the prudent man rule, they also suggested that pension fiduciaries are different because they "do not have to contend with the conflict between income beneficiaries and remaindermen, but benefit from a constant influx of contributions, and realize favorable tax treatment." This comment suggests considerable ignorance of the realities of defined benefit pension plans. In any event, through the passage of the Employee Retirement Income Security Act,[2] the federal government determined that "a fiduciary shall discharge his duties ... With the care, skill, prudence, and diligence under the

circumstances, then prevailing that a prudent man acting in a like capacity and familiar with such matters would use in the conduct of an enterprise of a like character and with like aims."

The relevant community of practice was not Boston or a state jurisdiction but rather a similarly placed *individual* with the same set of goals and objectives and consequent responsibilities (see also Schanzenbach and Sitkoff 2007). The geographical extent of this community of practice was, effectively, the United States (and the jurisdiction of federal district courts). Note, however, in ERISA the expansive definition of fiduciary duty was conditional on the "exclusive purpose" of a pension fund fiduciary, "reasonable expenses," the diversification of plan investments "so as to minimise the risk of large losses," limits on the ownership of overseas assets, and the representation of other parties' interests "adverse to the interests of the plan or the interests of its participants or beneficiaries." These conditions made explicit expectations of the court in *Harvard College*, which, according to Friedman (1964), were apparent in the conservative culture of Boston in the early nineteenth century. Passage of ERISA in 1974 was premised upon the belief that the (state-by-state) community of practice was not robust enough to impose discipline upon those who would violate beneficiaries' interests.

Rereading *Cowan* v. *Scargill*

Decided in April 1984, *Cowan* v. *Scargill*[3] was precipitated by the newly elected president of the National Union of Mineworkers (NUM) joining the trustee board of the Mineworkers Pension Scheme. At the time, there was widespread debate about the causes and consequences of the UK's poor economic performance over the previous decade (Peston 1980). Further, with a Conservative prime minister committed to altering the balance between labor unions and management and promoting denationalization and deregulation in industry and the financial sector, this case can be read as one step towards open hostilities between the union and national government. It is normally

---

[2] Pub.L. 93–406, 88 Stat. 829 Sept. 2, 1974.

[3] Ch. 270 (1985).

read as the definitive judicial decision effectively outlawing the consideration of "moral and social matters" in pension fund investment decision-making (Freshfields Bruckhaus Deringer 2005). It is the standard reference point when considering socially responsible investment, including response to climate change (see Thornton 2008 on related cases).

Joining the trustee board of the fund, Scargill brought to the table an agreed policy of the NUM conference that the fund not invest in oil stocks (deemed a competing industry with coal), and that the fund withdraw from overseas investments. This policy was clarified by the plaintiffs to be a claim on the fund's Investment Strategy and Business Plan 1982 to the effect that "(1) there is to be no increase in the percentage of overseas investment; and (2) overseas investment already made is to be withdrawn at the most opportune time; and (3) the committee adopts a proposal within the business plan of not investing in energies which are in direct competition with coal." Justifying this policy, Scargill repeatedly argued it would be in the best interests of beneficiaries *and* he contended that the union had obtained a legal opinion to the effect that this policy would be consistent with fiduciary duty. Megarry discounted the first claim by clarifying the nature of pension funds and dismissed the second noting "Mr Scargill's assertions of such support are simply untrue."

Observing that retired miners, their widows and children were dependent upon the pension fund for their well-being, Judge Megarry suggested that any distinction between the majority of beneficiaries and the beneficiaries of private trusts could not be sustained. Drawing upon two US federal court decisions concerning the responsibilities of pension fund trustees, the judge concluded that whatever the structure and organization of the pension institution, these decisions had "reaffirmed the duty of undivided loyalty to the beneficiaries the trustee owes" based on a commitment to "the best interests of the beneficiaries." Arguing that these cases were "soundly based on equitable principles, which are common to England," he concluded, "Pension funds are in general governed by the ordinary law of trusts." Referencing nineteenth-century English common law, Megarry stated "the standard

required of a trustee in exercising his powers of investment is that he must 'take such care as an ordinary prudent man would if he were minded to make an investment for the benefit of other people for whom he felt morally bound to provide.'"

Importantly, Megarry did not discount the notion that there may be "a strong case" for legislation regulating pension fund investment overseas and at home, but this was the responsibility of government, not trustees. Further, in relation to investment in South Africa, the judge noted that, while trustees are barred from making investment decisions based upon "social or political reasons," they could reasonably consider issues related to the "political stability in South Africa and the long-term financial soundness of its economy." Just as importantly, Megarry recognized that there may be some issues of such significance for the overwhelming majority of beneficiaries that it is reasonable to suppose that the relevant fund could "receive less by reason of the exclusion of some of the possibly more profitable forms of investment." He also said, however, "the present case is not one of this rare type of cases." See Berry (2011) and Richardson (2011) for related commentary.

Scargill sought to overturn the structure and management of the pension fund in the interests of the union's political objectives. Using the 5+5 membership of the board (five employer and five union representatives), and the fact that it was based on consensus without the prospect of a casting vote, Scargill sought to hold the board hostage to the union's policy. Disputing the division of responsibilities between the board and the Joint Investment Subcommittee, wherein the latter composed of investment experts and fund investment staff managed the investment process and the former ratified the fund's overarching Investment Strategy, Scargill sought to impose NUM policy. Disputing the minutes of meetings, Scargill sought to dominate the fund's decision-making process. Disputing the interpretation of fiduciary duty, Scargill invoked a legal opinion justifying his stance while refusing to provide the opinion to the board. Scargill also claimed pension funds were different from private trusts and, as such, common law norms and conventions did not apply.

Setting aside Scargill's attempt to control the fund, the court returned to the common law *and* to American precedent classifying beneficiaries in a manner consistent with the common law while invoking US federal court decisions relevant to the issues of substance considered in this case. In this respect, the "community of practice" invoked to sustain Megarry's opinion was found in legal formalism rather than similarly positioned fiduciaries bound together by shared norms and conventions with regard to investment practice. Vital for his opinion was the desirability of risk management through stock diversification established in the UK Trustee Investments Act of 1961.[4] Equally important, however, was the sense in which the responsibility of trustees was conceived in terms of the individual trustee or prudent *man* as opposed to the community. Subtly, Megarry's opinion discounted community norms and conventions precisely because of the union's attempt to define, in political terms, the meaning of customary practice.

Trust law and statute

Rereading important cases from the past while making connections, backwards and forwards, between jurisdictions with regard to developments in English common law allows us to see aspects otherwise submerged in standard interpretations of these cases. Stripping cases of their detail is, of course, the way legal positivists produce rules for behavior that apply across relevant cases rather than simply to specific cases (Coleman 2001: 77). So, it is not surprising that the details of these cases have been submerged so as to leave general rules about trustee obligation and fiduciary duty. In this section I emphasize neglected aspects of these cases, which deserve closer attention. From these neglected elements, we can discern the clues that unlock the puzzle as to why fiduciary duty has been marginalized and why the regulation of fund governance has assumed such significance.

Take, for example, the issue of trustee commitment; alliances and relationships that extend beyond their obligations with respect to beneficiaries' well-

being. In *Harvard College* this issue was resolved in two ways that reinforced one another. On the trustee side of the equation, they were deemed to have a strong moral commitment to the welfare of the testator's beneficiary by virtue of their familial relationship with the beneficiary. As well, third parties to that relationship were kept at arm's length; their interests were treated as "residual" and excluded from consideration in the investment process until the interests of the beneficiary were exhausted. By contrast, trustees in *Donovan* v. *Mazzola*[5] and in *Cowan* had rather remote relationships to the vast majority of beneficiaries. In both cases, trustees may have had familial relationships with some beneficiaries: but it seems likely that any such relationships were swamped by other kinds of relationships based upon the notional interests of the unions or organizations to which they belonged. In other words, the rule of fiduciary duty was required to stand in place of moral or emotional commitment to beneficiaries' interests.

In the *Harvard College* case, the interests of third parties to the primary relationship were kept at bay by being designated "residual" claimants. By contrast, in *Donovan* trustees were inveigled to frame and implement investment strategy so as to benefit third-party interests. In *Cowan*, the union's political interests were claimed to have equal standing with beneficiaries' interests in the sense that the latter would be served by the former. As for Robert Maxwell, his companies' interests were served by suborning the Mirror Group's pension schemes' assets. Whereas trustees were responsible in each instance for realizing beneficiaries' welfare, one way or another they were willing to treat those interests as fungible in relation to other claims on their decision-making. At one level, it is entirely plausible that investment strategy can be framed in ways that meet subsidiary objectives (as suggested by Megarry when referring to the long-term risks of investing in South Africa). Nonetheless, fiduciary duty requires an explicit ordering of goals and objectives such that the first priority dominates any other goals and objectives.

An intriguing aspect of *Harvard College* concerned the recipe for fiduciary duty provided by

---

[4] Trustee Investments Act 1961 (c. 62).

[5] 716 F2d 1226 (1976).

community norms and conventions. By virtue of the particular culture of Boston in the early nineteenth century, these norms and conventions were apparently easily codified in common law. By contrast, it would seem that the idealized "community of practice," which sustains fiduciary duty, is all too easily subsumed by "local" commitments and relationships. In judgment, the courts on both sides of the Atlantic have reached for statute to set the record straight: in *Donovan*, the federal appeals court referred to ERISA (1974) whereas in *Cowan* the court referred to the UK statute (1961) on the diversification of risk in investment management. Either statute was invoked as an expression of community norms and conventions or statute was invoked because the substantive issues involved in pension fund investment are more complex than private trusts or because it was not possible to identify relevant and accepted norms and conventions. One way or another, modern society cannot deliver on the promise of the common law.

In *Harvard College*, the two trustees were apparently joined in a common mission to realize the testator's wishes. By virtue of their intimate relationship to the beneficiary as well as their social standing in the community, it seems that common agreement was easily realized. But notice, in *Cowan* any sense of a common mission was disturbed by the union's interests prompting Megarry to explicitly locate fiduciary duty with the individual rather than the group or collective. His reading of fiduciary duty isolates the individual from the community precisely because the community may make competing demands on his or her loyalties. Two implications follow. First, by his account in acting together trustees should begin from their own legal responsibilities and must join together to set commonly agreed objectives. Second, realizing those objectives is a matter of negotiating agreement in circumstances where it may be difficult to be precise about what constitutes beneficiaries' interests separate from those of the sponsors.

Even well-intentioned trustees may be uncertain about their legal responsibilities if, as the common law would suppose, the appropriate reference point is the community of practice. Where there are competing interpretations of community norms and conventions, uncertainty about their legal

responsibilities may make negotiating agreement with other trustees problematic. It is not surprising individual trustees gravitate to what appear to be, if only momentarily, authoritative interpretations of both their responsibilities and the proper way forward for trustees as a collective. At the same time, recognizing the possibility of contravening norms and conventions, trustees uncertain about their legal responsibilities and the interests of others may gravitate to recipes for decision-making that have the virtue of judicial respectability. Instead of looking forward and being part of a process whereby community norms and conventions adapt to a changing environment, trustees may seek refuge in the past where certainty prevails, albeit at the cost of reinforcing convention (contra expectations regarding the potential of the common law; see Calabresi 1982).

Statute, governance and fiduciary duty

The Myners inquiry (2001) was charged with the responsibility of identifying the barriers to innovation in pension fund investment (compared to US funds). Focusing upon the constitution and governance of UK pension funds, Myners concluded that the typical pension fund trustee lacked the necessary skills and resources to be an effective investment decision-maker. Further, he concluded that UK pension funds were far too conventional in terms of their investment strategies, congregating around accepted benchmarks of performance rather than focusing upon asset allocation decisions consistent with funds' liabilities. Myners was especially critical of the benchmarking phenomenon, implying that it was a rather naïve conception of investment management considering the risks associated with effectively unmanaged liabilities. These arguments gathered force in part by virtue of the 2001 implosion of the TMT financial bubble in the aftermath of 9/11 (see also Shiller 2002).

Assuming trustees act on behalf of beneficiaries, Myners doubted whether they had the appropriate levels of "prudence, discretion and intelligence" given the risks and uncertainties associated with investment management (quoting and paraphrasing *Harvard College*). Myners also sought to shift the reference "community of practice" from UK trustees to best practice found in a number of large US pension funds, industry experts and the frontiers of investment management. He suggested that UK norms and conventions reinforced complacency while adding unjustified costs to the investment management process. Furthermore, in relation to the responsibilities that go with the control of large pools of financial assets in the modern economy, Myners contended that trustees had failed to sustain their commitment to shareholder value. He argued that corporate engagement should be seen as an element in an expanded conception of trustee fiduciary duty (formally recognized in 2010 by the UK Financial Reporting Council's voluntary Stewardship Code).

If debate about the Myners Report ignored private equity, his critique of trustees' qualifications prompted government legislation in 2004 designed to promote trustee knowledge and understanding and set codes of practice relevant to the governance of pension institutions. Establishing the Pensions Regulator (TPR), the Labour government joined expectations about improving trustee knowledge and understanding with statutory recognition of beneficiary representation on trustee boards. Furthermore, by promulgating codes of practice aimed at promoting best practice pension fund governance, the government through TPR used the mantra of "comply or explain" to encourage funds to be more systematic about "managing" the governance of their procedures and decision-making processes. At the same time, the government resisted the temptation to rewrite the definition of fiduciary duty in a manner consistent with the relevant US standard as detailed in ERISA Section 404 (1974), which refers to "a prudent man acting in a like capacity and familiar with such matters" in "an enterprise of a like character and with like aims."

The first codes introduced in April 2005 referred to the duties of sponsors, fund executives and trustees as regards notifying the regulator of breaches in the law and a related duty to provide timely notification to the regulator of possible problems associated with pension funding that could result in a call upon the Pension Protection Fund (PPF). At one level, the regulator has used codes of practice to substantiate the interpretation and effective implementation of fiduciary duty as the principle underpinning the governance of pension funds. It has done so because the norms and conventions associated with the "community of practice" have been shown to be either ineffective given the responsibilities and significance of UK pension plans for retirement income or, worse, subject to dispute.

Further, responding to past cases where trustees were effectively "captured" by other interests, the appointment of member-nominated trustees to represent beneficiaries introduced the possibility of governance and decision-making being systematically undermined by gross differences in trustee competence and skills. Anticipating the possibility that the average trustee would not be able to give effect to fiduciary duties, codes of practice have been introduced to compensate for this possibility. As suggested elsewhere, there is a significant tension between representation and expertise (Clark 2007).

Importantly, the codes of practice are related to the regulator's statutory responsibility to oversee the funding of defined benefit pensions and in particular the obligations on sponsors to make good on pension promises. Notice, however, the regulator is, in effect, a mediator between trustees and sponsors; as the regulator has a responsibility to sustain pension funding in relation to the PPF, it does so in a way that seeks to dampen trustee demands on sponsors that would otherwise precipitate a claim on the PPF's assets and benefit guarantees. So, for example, through the recent global financial crisis the regulator encouraged trustees to develop extended "recovery plans" so as to provide for scheme funding based, in part, upon assessment of the notional "long-term" financial strength of the sponsor. In this respect, negotiations between trustees and scheme sponsors have typically involved agreeing on investment strategies and expected rates of return targets. In this sense, fiduciary duty is contingent upon the particular circumstances of sponsors *and* negotiation with the sponsor about its capacity to *incrementally* fund current and expected shortfalls.

Whereas fiduciary duty is commonly understood to govern the relationship between trustees and beneficiaries, the effect of statute has been to introduce into that relationship two other parties: the government through TPR and the PPF and the employer as scheme sponsor. If the regulator represents the public interest in workplace pensions, it also represents the government interest in limiting calls upon the PPF. At the same time, given the challenging market conditions facing many private pension schemes sponsors, trustees' claims on scheme sponsors have been deemed by the regulator to be conditional rather than absolute. In effect, the regulator is risk-averse in a political sense but may impose on trustees a level of risk-taking that is antithetical to the best interests of beneficiaries in the full-funding of their pension schemes.

Innovation and investment

Advocates of fiduciary duty believe that it provides an adaptive, non-governmental mechanism for innovation in investment management. Based upon independent, expert judgment in the context of "communities of practice" capable of vetting new ideas against collective experience, the common law would seem to have many of the attributes Surowiecki (2004) suggested is characteristic of the "wisdom of crowds." As such, it need not share with government bureaucracies the inertia typical of centralized, administrative institutions that rely upon rules and regulations to affect private behavior. By contrast, it is supposed that the doctrine of fiduciary duty codifies practice disciplined by shared norms and conventions in ways that promote the evolution of private behavior consistent with social welfare. For La Porta et al. (1998) it is the bedrock of financial innovation and development, distinguishing the histories of Anglo-American economies from the various continental European traditions. Reliance upon fiduciary duty is one reason why Anglo-American countries tend not to use administrative rules for asset allocation (as illustrated by OECD 2011).

However, governments have used statute to buttress the authority of fiduciary duty. In effect, governments have filled in the gaps left by contestation over community practice so as to realize promised pension benefits and their security. For example, the US federal government has used ERISA to clarify

and define the standards of expertise and experience deemed consistent with fiduciary duty. In this respect, statute has emphasized expertise over common sense denying the "wisdom of crowds." In the UK, government has sought to affect the application of expertise through promulgating "comply or explain" codes of practice, thereby attempting to balance the need for competence with a commitment to representation. In the UK, the government has also sought to affect standards of trustee knowledge and understanding as well as the principles and procedures of fund governance so as to sustain effective investment management.

In a similar manner, governments have used legislation to establish the significance of investment principles including portfolio diversification and, at the limit, modern portfolio theory (MPT). It is apparent that, if left to the common law, MPT would have remained at the margins of community norms and customs in many jurisdictions. This has a number of lessons for those advocating a genuine commitment to long-term investment, including intergenerational equity and sustainable investment (see also Woods 2011). In the first instance, it is apparent that advocates of MPT struggled for recognition in the face of the inertia associated with community norms and conventions. In the second instance, its advocates waged a long-running campaign for recognition based upon a combination of theoretical insight and innovation and the formulation of practical recipes for investment management. In the third instance, its advocates were successful because they effectively commandeered public and private institutions of standard-setting.

It seems likely that governments will be enlisted to formalize the principles of long-term investment in rules and regulations consistent with authoritative interpretations of fiduciary duty. But it also seems likely that academics and the investment community will need to take responsibility for substantiating the theory of long-term investment and formulating practical recipes for investment management. This project is, no doubt, very ambitious. Even so, in the aftermath of the global financial crisis and widespread disenchantment with the principles and practices of what Merton and Bodie (2005) referred to as the "neoclassical" theory of financial markets, there is a ready-made audience for conceptual innovation. As such, there appear to be a number of strategies being used to prompt conceptual innovation relevant to long-term investment. These are noted below, paying regard to the diversity of strategies as well as their various sponsors.

Best practice case studies: often sponsored by leading consulting companies, and based on collaboration with experts inside and outside of the industry, these projects tend to focus on pension fund governance (see Clark and Urwin 2008). Here, the goal has been to set the agenda with respect to informal or formal codes of practice (in effect, anticipating government policy and regulation). Considering that government typically does not have the resources to undertake the detailed research necessary to identify best practice, and considering that trustees themselves are not knowledgeable about the nature and scope of pension fund governance around the world, these projects have been effective in strengthening the resources available for investment decision-making. These studies take as given conventional definitions of fiduciary duty and the statutory obligations of trustees but articulate new ways of conceptualizing the investment management process.

Clubs of research and practice: sponsored by a diverse range of institutions, bringing together relatively small groups of investors around a particular issue or theme, these clubs seek to translate research in the practice of investment management. A particularly successful instance was the recent Mercer Report on climate change and long-term investment. There, like-minded investment institutions underwrote the costs of research on the probable nature and scope of climate change through to 2050 and its implications for investment management. Rather than framing the problem as an environment, social and governance (ESG) issue, it was framed as an issue of investment value over a series of time horizons going forward through to 2050. A similar type of study, this time aimed at establishing investment protocols, was led by Towers Watson via their Telos project.

Multilateral and international standard-setters: whether sponsored by the accounting professions or by other independent, professional bodies, standard-setting has become a crowded field of endeavor. Based upon research and their own communities of practice, these institutions have sought to establish principles and practices relevant to even the most difficult issues and thereby stimulate forward-looking decision-making. Importantly, in this world standard-setting is a collaborative project among private agents sometimes (but not always) given status by government and international organizations. If epitomized by the International Accounting Standards Board, other entities have also entered the field including the United Nations through the Principles of Responsible Investment (UN PRI) and the OECD. These organizations claim legitimacy and authority if not the coercive powers of a regulatory agency.

Academic research in the media spotlight: if often-times also sponsored by large investment houses and consulting groups, academic research has also played a role in clarifying the issues as regards to the cost-effectiveness of investment management. There is a veritable industry in disciplines as diverse as finance, economic geography and sociology focused upon the structure and performance of the investment management industry (Clark and Monk 2013). Often-times obscure in terms of the nature of problems tackled and the results produced, some media groups have played crucial roles in translating this research into bite-sized chunks relevant to the industry as a whole as well as its decision-makers. The *Financial Times* has been particularly effective in bridging these two very different worlds.

Crises and their post-mortems: the Asian financial crisis of 1997, the implosion of Long-Term Capital Management, the bursting of the TMT bubble, and global financial crisis and the euro crisis have been important for clarifying industry-wide expectations as to the nature of market behavior and prospects for the future. Not only is there a vibrant market for accounts of the events leading up to these crises, systematic accounts of institutional failure and the documentation of perverse and self-defeating behavior, these stories play a crucial role in organizing industry and government responses to their immediate consequences and long-term implications.

Government inquiries and reports: if largely backwards-looking in impulse, and about allocating blame especially if the government sponsor seeks to find fault with previous governments' policies, these events can provide contemporaneous strategies of community-building, a stage for setting the agenda for the future. While neither the Wilson Report of 1980 nor the Myners Report of 2001 made a substantial difference to the problem posed, they did articulate the issues for at least the following decade. The same fate appears likely for the Kay Report (HM Government 2012a) on UK equity markets and long-term investment. Its explicit reference to "asset owners' long term objectives" and the UK Stewardship Code provided an opportunity for a reconceptualization of the logic of fiduciary duty which the coalition government explicitly denied in its response to the report (see Clark 2013 for a critical review).

These are just six mechanisms for organizing and institutionalizing communities of practice. Some are more formal than others and some have greater innovative potential than others if judged against the unresolved issues made apparent by recent financial crises. One obvious issue associated with the inherited norms and conventions of investment management is the cost of short-term market trading; notwithstanding the widespread adoption by institutional investors of strategic asset allocation, many of their service providers churn their assets under management seeking to meet quarter-to-quarter benchmark targets. At one level, this is a problem of governance – setting incentives consistent with long-term investment goals and objectives. At another level, however, it is an issue of breaking with convention via strategic use of the contracts that govern service contracts across the entire industry.

Conclusions

The virtue of the common law was found in its permissive framework for private action. Based upon "communities of practice" it was supposed to be an adaptive "regulatory" mechanism consistent with the promotion of social welfare. In fact, the argument presented in this chapter suggests that the common law doctrine of fiduciary duty is an historical anachronism without firm foundations in the

contemporary world. If there were "communities of practice" with the authority to set and maintain norms and conventions, this does not seem to be a plausible characterization of the second half of the twentieth century or the first decade of the twenty-first century. Indeed, the evidence suggests that "communities of practice" are more likely associated with the subversion of beneficiaries' interests than with social welfare.

Recognizing the problems associated with the common conceptions of fiduciary duty, statute has been used to provide comprehensive frameworks for social problems (Posner 1990: 252). Statutes are thought more appropriate to the complex world of modern economies, overlapping interests and economic processes, and the never-ending quest for power and influence over the factors that affect economic growth. They are, as well, blueprints or solutions to problems that go well beyond the immediate interests of private agents. But, notwithstanding the optimism associated with the passage of legislation and the establishment of regulatory agencies in the second half of the twentieth century, it is arguable that statute is as much defensive and reactive as it is forward-looking. So, for example, the passage of legislation in the UK designed to protect workplace pensions over the past twenty years can be read as reactions to apparent problems of pension fund governance.

Basically, legislation was deemed necessary because the golden rule of fiduciary duty was obviously inadequate as the instrument for "regulating" pension fund decision-making. In this chapter, I suggested that this is because "communities of practice" have lost their legitimacy and authority. Equally, it is arguable that statute was necessary because pension funds are actually financial institutions not just decision frameworks, embodying interests and claims for representation that transcend simpleminded recipes for decision-making. This point was illustrated by reference to the nature and effects of the codes of practice introduced by the UK Pensions Regulator. Whereas fiduciary duty would have it that beneficiary interest is the cornerstone of decision-making, through statute the UK government has sought to "balance" the interests of beneficiaries with the interests of the government, the employer and society at large through best practice models of pension fund governance.

The Myners Report was highly critical of UK pension fund trustee skills and expertise, and derided inherited norms and conventions that govern the investment decision-making process. For Myners, the issue was about the lack of pension fund investment at the frontiers of economic innovation. Curiously, however, the government sidestepped the issue relying upon the common law principle of fiduciary duty to set the framework for asset allocation and investment management. Here, as in other Anglo-American countries, government was unwilling to set priorities for pension fund investment, enumerate permitted investments or use a quantitative formula for asset allocation. In a similar manner, the Cameron government sidestepped the core findings of the Kay Report as regards the necessity of clarifying the scope of fiduciary duty in relation to long-term investing (HM Government 2012b).

Paradoxically, the promotion of innovation in long-term investment relies heavily upon a social commitment to the common law principle of fiduciary duty and its associated "communities of practice" otherwise rejected by government in its regulation of pension fund governance. Worse, perhaps, is the fact that the interpretation of fiduciary duty has been captured by interests largely antagonistic to innovation in investment management. In so many ways, fiduciary duty has been so denuded by government regulation that what is left is a rhetorical gesture on behalf of those that stand to benefit by the status quo. At best, fiduciary duty remains as a case specific mechanism for restitution in circumstances where government policy, regulation and its guarantee institutions are either not relevant or unable to deal with the issue. At worst, fiduciary duty remains as a trump card for those that would wish to protect their own interests in the face of obvious demands for profound change in the nature of investment practice.

References

Aalberts, R. J. and P. S. Poon. 1996. "The New Prudent Investor Rule and the Modern Portfolio Theory: A New Direction for Fiduciaries," *American Business Law Journal* 34: 39–71.

Atiyah, P. S. 1995. *An Introduction to the Law of Contract*. Oxford University Press.

Berry, C. 2011. *Protecting our Best Interests: Rediscovering Fiduciary Obligation*. London: Fair Pensions.

Braithwaite, J. 1989. *Crime, Shame, and Reintegration*. Cambridge University Press.

Calabresi, G. 1982. *A Common Law for the Age of Statutes*. Cambridge, MA: Harvard University Press.

Clark, G. L. 1985. *Judges and the Cities: Interpreting Local Autonomy*. University of Chicago Press.

2007. "Expertise and Representation in Financial Institutions: UK Legislation on Pension Fund Governance and US Regulation of the Mutual Fund Industry," *Contemporary Social Science* 2: 1–23.

2013. "The Kay Review on Long-Horizon Investing: A Guide for the Perplexed." *Rotman International Journal of Pension Management* 6 (1): 58–63.

Clark, G. L. and A. H. B. Monk. 2013. "The Scope of Financial Institutions: In-sourcing, Outsourcing, and Off-shoring," *Journal of Economic Geography* 13 (2): 278–98.

Clark, G. L. and R. Urwin. 2008. "Best-practice Investment Management," *Journal of Asset Management* 9 (1): 2–21.

Coleman, J. 2001. *The Practice of Principle: In Defence of a Pragmatic Approach to Legal Theory*. Oxford University Press.

Freshfields Bruckhaus Deringer. 2005. *A Legal Framework for the Integration of Environmental, Social and Governance Issues into Institutional Investment*. London.

Friedman, L. M. 1964. "The Dynastic Trust," *Yale Law Journal* 73: 547–92.

Hawley, J. P. and A. T. Williams. 2001. *The Rise of Fiduciary Capitalism: How Institutional Investors Can Make America More Democratic*. Philadelphia: University of Pennsylvania Press.

Hawley, J. P., K. Johnson, and E. Waitzer. 2011. "Reclaiming Fiduciary Duty Balance," *Rotman International Journal of Pension Management* 4 (2): 4–16.

HM Government. 1980. *Committee to Review the Functioning of Financial Institutions: Report.* [Wilson Report]. Cmnd. 7937. London: HMSO.

2012a. *The Kay Review of UK Equity Markets and Long-Term Decision-making*. London: Department of Business, Innovation & Skills.

2012b. *Ensuring Equity Markets Support Long-Term Growth: The Government Response to the Kay Review*. London: Department of Business, Innovation & Skills.

La Porta, R., F. Lopez-de-Silanes, A. Shleifer and R. Vishny. 1998. "Law and Finance," *Journal of Political Economy* 106: 1113–55.

Langbein, J. H. 1997. "The Secret Life of the Trust: The Trust as an Instrument of Commerce," *Yale Law Journal* 107: 165–89.

2007. "Why Did Trust Law Become Statute Law in the United States?" *University of Alabama Law Review* 58: 1069–82.

Langbein, J. H. and R. A. Posner. 1976. "The Revolution in Trust Investment Law," *American Bar Association Journal* 62: 887–91.

Merton, R. and Z. Bodie. 2005. "The Design of Financial Systems: Towards a Synthesis of Function and Structure," *Journal of Investment Management* 3: 1–23.

Myners Report. 2001. *Institutional Investment in the United Kingdom: A Review*. London: HM Treasury.

Organisation for Economic Co-operation and Development. 2011. *Survey of Investment Regulation of Pension Funds*. Paris: OECD.

Peston, M. 1980. "The Wilson Report," *Political Quarterly* 51: 481–4.

Posner, R. A. 1990. *The Problems of Jurisprudence*. Cambridge, MA: Harvard University Press.

Richardson, B. J. 2011. "From Fiduciary *Duties* to Fiduciary *Relationships* for Socially Responsible Investing: Responding to the Will of Beneficiaries," *Journal of Sustainable Finance & Investment* 1 (1): 5–19.

Roe, M. J. 2006. "Legal Origins, Politics, and Stock Markets," *Harvard Law Review* 120: 460–527.

Schanzenbach, M. and R. H. Sitkoff. 2007. "Did Reform of Prudent Trust Investment Laws Change Trust Portfolio Allocation?" *Journal of Law and Economics* 50: 681–711.

Shiller, R. J. 2000. *Irrational Exuberance*. Princeton University Press.

2002. "Bubbles, Human Judgement, and Expert Opinion," *Financial Analysts Journal* 58 (3): 18–26.

Stapleton. G. P. 1996. *Institutional Shareholders and Corporate Governance*. Oxford University Press.

Surowiecki, J. 2004. *The Wisdom of Crowds*. New York: Random House.

Thomas, G. and A. Hudson. 2004. *The Law of Trusts*. Oxford University Press.

Thornton, R. 2008. "Ethical Investments: A Case of Disjoined Thinking," *Cambridge Law Journal* 67: 396–422.

Woods, C. 2011. *Intergenerational Equity and Sustainable Investment*. DPhil Thesis: University of Oxford.

Woods, C. and R. Urwin. 2010. "Putting Sustainable Investing into Practice," *Journal of Business Ethics* 92: 1–19.

CHAPTER 21

Pension fund fiduciary duty and its impacts on sustainable investing

ROGER URWIN

Introduction

This chapter considers the evolving application of fiduciary duty to pension funds and how this affects funds' investment exposures to sustainability generally and environment, social and governance (ESG) factors more specifically. We focus principally on European and US pension funds. Fiduciary duty in the UK has developed through common law origins to exert particular influences on pension fund practices. A similar background applies to US pension funds that have been particularly influenced by the ERISA legislation of 1974. The pension funds from continental Europe have a different legal context from the UK and the US but share many of the same principles. While unique national circumstances and legal contexts dictate certain pension fund differences, the concepts underlying fiduciary duty taken from the UK and the US have broad similarities in all countries where agents invest institutional funds on behalf of others.

The core issues of fiduciary duty are that those who manage investments on behalf of others are bound by a number of fiduciary obligations (Woods and Urwin 2010). There are four principal forms of this obligation:

- **Loyalty:** putting the interests of beneficiaries first when determining the investment strategy and avoiding conflicts of interest.
- **Prudence:** investing to the standard of a prudent expert.
- **Diversification:** diversify according to the principles of accepted investment theory.
- **Impartiality:** avoid favoring the interests of a particular beneficiary or class of beneficiaries over others.

The form of these obligations presents two particular challenges for pension funds. The first is that their interpretation will not be black and white. Expert opinion differs on their correct application. This nuanced context tends to lead funds to use current peer practice as the dominant paradigm. The argument applied is that it is prudent to follow one's peers although this carries certain systemic risk for a reflexive system like investment (Hawley et al. 2011). There are significant dangers from herding and pro-cyclicality creating market volatility as a result of feedback to the markets from such "prudent" behaviors (Haldane and Davies 2011).

The second issue is that appropriate interpretation of the principles of fiduciary duty should change as investment principles; theory, practice and circumstances evolve. So it is reasonable to anticipate some changing context to fiduciary duty. No strict interpretation of fiduciary duty would be expected to fix the concept in time.

These two points present an innate challenge for the new circumstances involved with the field of sustainable investing. Our suggestion for a working definition of sustainable investing is an investment approach that is efficient in the long term (in terms of returns per unit risk) and intergenerationally fair (future generations of stakeholders are not penalized by current generations) (Urwin 2009). There is new context for fiduciary duty to incorporate in such a framework. However, the current fiduciary duty paradigm based on prior investment practice cannot be easily adapted to this new context (Richardson 2008).

This chapter describes three interpretations of fiduciary duty arising from this changing context: a narrow version that takes its lead from current practice and so omits any ESG policy or practice; and two alternative wider versions that lead to the inclusion of ESG policy and practice. Both of these interpretations appear consistent with fiduciary duty and with good practice.

Terminology around sustainable investing

The overlapping concepts and terminology in the area of sustainable investing are confusing. "Socially responsible investment" and "ethical investment" were early concepts generally associated with the promotion of certain social or ethical values. Such approaches had limited applicability to pension funds because they involved potential conflicts with fiduciary duty.

More recently, "responsible investment" has appeared and has won mainstream support in pension funds by being first and foremost financially oriented. It also has an ancillary goal associated with producing environmental, social and governance benefits but couched in "business-case" terms.

While this approach is seen by some as controversial, responsible investing defined this way has become an accepted model. The UN-sponsored Principles of Responsible Investment (PRI) provide a widely used description of responsible investing through a combination of integration of ESG issues and exercising ownership responsibilities over investee companies. PRI specifically has been adopted by many leading pension funds and there are network benefits at work between signatories – for example knowledge-sharing and active ownership practices (PRI 2011).

The model for "sustainable investing" adds to the content of responsible investment as defined above. The additions are twofold: an orientation to efficient long-term financial outcomes consistent with a fund's long-term mission; and a goal of producing intergenerational fairness in future outcomes in which future stakeholders are treated equivalently to current stakeholders.

This more expansive idea behind sustainable investing needs the support of certain investment principles and investment beliefs to be justifiable and actionable. The beliefs-based rationale is crucial to the effectiveness and resilience of any sustainable investing strategy to provide the framework for future decision-making. While the rationales behind responsible investing and sustainable investing appear to differ, reconciliation of the concepts is possible. In particular, responsible investing principles may be upheld using the support of a well-founded, beliefs-based sustainable investing strategy.

Long-termism and intergenerational equity

Pension funds exist to carry wealth from one generation to the next. Ideally they will do so in an economically efficient way as measured over appropriately long time horizons (reflecting prudence) and in a way that promotes intergenerational equity (to deal with the duty of impartiality and loyalty).

The problems of short-termism in institutional investment have had considerable attention. A combination of the behavioral biases, pressures on pension fund boards to demonstrate their successful stewardship and agency issues appear to produce a chain of behaviors that are destructive to value (Krehmeyer et al. 2006).

The norms of current practice place heavy emphasis on investing relative to fund benchmarks defined in terms of peer practice and measured in the short term. Other evidence of short-termism is present in high portfolio turnover, the use of short-term incentives and the limited preparedness to consider longer-range issues particularly where uncertainty is involved (Hawley et al. 2011).

The limited attention to intergenerational equity is also a governance deficit (Urwin 2009). It is characterized by placing more emphasis on the current generation of beneficiaries at the expense of future generations. This reflects the cognitive error of overvaluing current performance with associated undervaluation of performance at more distant horizons (Haldane 2010).

These fiduciary principles of long-termism and intergenerational equity can be captured in a sustainable investing approach. However, it is reasonable to suggest that normal practice in pension fund investing rarely takes much account of either principle. This can be attributed to the complex nature of these principles and the concept of sustainability. It is widely evident how industry participants have all sorts of problems with the word "sustainable."

One further point needs to be considered.

The acid test of long-termism is the following: does investing explicitly over a longer-term horizon (which we might take as ten years and longer) do better than investing over successive short-term horizons (taken as a quarter) by adjusting the strategy each quarter as new information arises for the next quarter? There is a strong conjecture that optimizing the long-term strategy in an integrated way and holistic way is a more efficient strategy (higher return per unit risk) than optimizing the long-term strategy through the sum of the short-terms. This was demonstrated in a significant research project undertaken during 2012 by Towers Watson and a large group of asset owners and asset managers – the Telos Project (Towers Watson 2012).

The Telos Project on sustainable investing

This research was undertaken in collaboration with outside academics at Oxford University drawn from multiple disciplines including climate change, resource scarcity and demography. It addressed the challenges in the sustainable investing field with consideration of asset allocation, risks and investment mandates but interpreted through a fiduciary duty lens.

The first key conclusion was that asset owners and asset managers around the world were struggling with what it means to be a sustainable investor. That struggle was twofold: thinking long-term when short-term considerations come first, and considering nonfinancial factors when all that seems to count are financial factors. The research observed how asset owner governance is creaking under financial pressure arising from weak solvency and the challenges introduced by complexity. Reasons for this difficulty were accentuated by pension funds' current interpretations of fiduciary duty that seem to impede the broadening of the investment mandate (adopting some stakeholder responsibilities) and were not helpful in the lengthening of investment horizons. The research highlighted the tendency for pension fiduciaries to interpret fiduciary duty conservatively due to a legacy of case law interpretation, commentary and accepted practice dating from the 1980s. Encouragingly, however, more recent legal guidance and commentary provided support for the view that fiduciary duty supports consideration of longer-term and wider stakeholder issues (Woods 2011).

The second key point was how the task for asset owners and managers of meeting their performance goals is set to get more difficult given the significant transformational change occurring in world economies, politics and capital markets. This argues that strategies needed to be adapted to the deleveraging cycle, underpowered economic growth, resource scarcity and ageing demographics to reach their performance potential. This requires advanced planning to secure good results for current and future generations of stakeholders through investment strategy being tuned for the present and the anticipated future. This is an expansion of current thinking, factoring in future changes to operating conditions and prices. It also supports investors in considering the longer-term externalities created by their investments recognizing that many of these will develop into internalized costs over various investment horizons. Understanding these factors is important for both long-term efficiency and intergenerational equity. Studies commissioned by PRI and UNEP FI suggest that the environmental externalities of current corporations could be priced as costing an annual $2.15 trillion in 2008, representing just under 7 percent of revenues and over 50 percent of earnings (PRI and UNEP FI 2011).

At a time when the investment world is changing so radically, it is unrealistic to expect acceptable results from dealing with the future on a year-by-year basis, taking a narrow view of macro risk factors. To be successful, investors will need to incorporate longer time horizons and adapt to anticipate the structural changes coming from these economic ESG factors, particularly those related to the principal externalities.

The way this can be accomplished is by creating an operating framework driven by pure long-term finance, but incorporating some regard for short-term and nonfinancial factors such as externalities. It also requires structuring the debate around values and beliefs. It will no doubt also involve certain changes to mandates, reducing the impact of the oppressive regime of judging managers quarterly on outperformance of benchmarks.

The application of values and beliefs

A key governance best practice conclusion is that investment decisions are best developed if there is particular attention paid to the values and investment beliefs of the board and the expression of decision-making policies (explicit guidance on how to deal with certain events and contingencies) and norms (guidelines on how to deal with certain contingencies that are written in flexible terms or not committed to writing) (Clark and Urwin 2008).

Values in this framework are convictions about what matters to the fund's fiduciaries and its stakeholders, often expressed as views about desirable behaviors and outcomes for the fund captured in a mission statement. Research has shown a positive link between better performance and pension funds with clear beliefs about asset pricing and risk diversification (Koedijk and Slager 2009).

Beliefs are working assumptions about the investment world that underlie investment practices and decisions that, when developed and shared, help make goal-setting and decision-making more effective. The most helpful beliefs accurately describe future outcomes, get organization-wide traction and are actionable.

Values and investment beliefs are challenging but rewarding concepts. First, they are subjective and require considerable thought. That said, the thinking process in itself appears to produce much value. Second, the values and beliefs may differ across the members of a fiduciary board, but for effective practice it is critical to develop shared values and beliefs requiring a measure of negotiated settlement. Third, the process of codifying values and beliefs involves considering something inherently abstract (or "soft") and codifying it in a clear and more tangible form (or "hard"). Fourth, using values and beliefs in practice requires some discipline but the reward is more coherent and logical decisions. This is why the link between values and beliefs, and policies and norms is critical.

In particular well thought through values provide the foundations to clarity of mission, one of the critical determinants of strong governance practice (Clark and Urwin 2008). The use of beliefs has particular relevance to the effective use of agents, which is so significant in the pension fund field (ibid.). The risks pension funds incur from agency issues are the consequence of widespread misalignments of interests and exacerbated by asymmetries in knowledge and influence. Clear beliefs with associated actions can improve the framework for managing agency interests to the benefit of the fund rather than to the benefit of the agent. It is worth noting that the duties of agents are in certain jurisdictions made stronger than those of contract law and may even resemble a fiduciary test of requiring the agent to pursue actions with the sole interest of the fund in mind. Whatever the legal position, there is a natural conflict between the goals and interests of agents and those of the ultimate beneficiaries to whom fiduciary duties are owed, which has implications for mission design and governance practices under the duties of loyalty and impartiality.

The choices of "mission"

The critical questions for fiduciaries to consider are their view on three values:

- What time horizon is appropriate for considering the mission and the fiduciary duties of loyalty and prudence implied?
- What level of wider responsibility should fiduciaries assume for the entities that they own (recognizing the spectrum from none, through "do no harm" to fuller responsibility for ownership externalities)?
- What place is there, if any, for assuming any additional nonfinancial goals in respect of ownership exposures to externalities and the ESG areas (recognizing that this could be positioned with a weighting, presumably small, alongside the pure financial factors)?

The missions adopted by pension funds can be divided into three main types reflecting responses to these points. These are described below.

Traditional mission – the exclusive objective is financial

The traditional mission of trustees has finance as the sole and exclusive objective. It is generally expressed in terms of meeting liabilities within affordability parameters. The objective of the mission is exclusively financial leaving no ancillary objective. So we might consider it narrower than the others we debate below. This type of mission is overwhelmingly dominant among pension funds currently and understandably so. The only issue is whether its lack of explicit consideration of a number of sustainability factors – long-term investment efficiency, intergenerational equity and longer-term stakeholder interests – represents an opportunity cost. The question is whether a wider mission would achieve more.

Sustainable business-case mission – the exclusive objective is financial, but nonfinancial outcomes are considered

Additional to the traditional mission is the incorporation of additional goals, which express a wider and longer-term view of responsibilities, arising from ownership but couched in business-case terms. The framing of the mission is again exclusively financial but nonfinancial goals and outcomes are incorporated under the condition that they do not compromise the finance-first approach. Under this wider, more sustainable mission, goals can be concentrated on long-term financial outcomes with attention to intergenerational fairness. This mission aligns particularly well with asset owners that are PRI signatories. There are certain challenges in putting this mission into practice, the biggest issue being the development of beliefs that make the thesis coherent.

Wider sustainable mission – the financial objectives are dominant alongside ancillary nonfinancial objectives

This mission explicitly combines financial with broader nonfinancial goals. The framing is with finance dominant. The inclusion of nonfinancial goals is explicit, but for fiduciary duty reasons the financial impacts involved with this goal and approach need carefully defined and controlled downside limits. The mission therefore accepts the thesis that the fund performance could be adversely affected by the nonfinancial goal but places strict limits on the potential size of this impact. This framework allows the impact of nonfinancial exposures to be sized, targeted and measured in financial terms.

This mission is adopted by a number of European funds in the public sector with explicit mandates for responsible practice from the state. There are obvious challenges in putting this into practice, the biggest issue being how to balance the two goals and weight the limits to performance impact.

Beliefs on sustainability

While statements of mission should reflect clear values, investment strategies should reflect clear investment beliefs. Investment is essentially about making judgments and decisions in the present, typically with reference to the past, to cope with or exploit an uncertain future. Investors do this by using their underlying beliefs about how the world works. The quality of those underlying beliefs is a major determinant of success in investment and was highlighted by Clark and Urwin (2008) as a key attribute of well-governed funds.

The sustainability beliefs involve a fund's fiduciaries considering some finely balanced issues:

- Are ESG factors likely to have small but not insignificant performance impact over the short term and significant over the medium term? Or are these impacts insignificant?
- Are funds better off in performance and risk terms if they understand externalities? Or does it not matter?
- Are ESG factors sufficiently considered by managers within normal mandates and benchmarks without drawing attention to them? Or are they not?
- Are big funds investing in perpetuity, often referred to as "universal owners" (Hawley and Williams 2007), in a position to use their size

Table 21.1 Potential investment beliefs supporting sustainable investing.

Source of risk/return	Related investment belief
ESG issues	ESG issues influence financial returns and risk over the long term, and should form a part of all investment analysis and decision-making.
Active ownership	The execution of ownership rights can positively influence the performance and risk of investments over time.
Engaged ownership	The active use of engagement with investee companies can enhance the financial performance of an investment over time and/ or reduce exposure to risks.
Contracts with asset managers	Contracts and fees for the fund's asset managers can be designed to align their long-term interests with those of the fund.
Oversight of delegated responsibilities	Appropriate oversight of asset managers' integration of ESG issues into investment analysis can improve its effectiveness.
Benefits of activities outweigh the costs	The performance and other benefits of the activities envisaged for integrated ESG and active/engaged ownership outweigh their costs over the beneficiaries' time horizons.
Targeted investment in sustainability mandates	Investment in assets with exposure to ESG factors can produce higher than mainstream risk-adjusted returns from both beta and alpha.
Long-term investment in sustainable mandates	Longer-term risks of climate change and resource degradation can be offset by investment in environmental opportunities and clean technology.
Exploitation of long-term mandate	Certain asset classes/opportunities can be selectively exploited by the fund given the comparative advantage it has in its long-term mandate.
Preservation of intergenerational equity	To address the mission from the perspective of both present and future beneficiaries and other stakeholders, the fund's strategy should be an inter-temporal plan highlighting the funding goals and risk bearing of the various stakeholders.

Table 21.2 Comparison of conventional and sustainable (SI) pension fund investment strategies (adapted from Woods and Urwin 2010).

Traditional investment strategy	Investment focus based on short-term benchmarks/time horizons. High degree of delegation of ownership interests to managers.
Integrated sustainable strategy	ESG issues integrated into investment decision-making and analysis including active ownership. Managers given specific instructions with respect to ESG integration and the exercise of ownership interests. Performance benchmarks and therefore investment focus based on longer-term time horizons.
Targeted sustainable strategy	Integrated sustainable strategy components, plus: Investment in environmentally targeted opportunities, such as climate bonds and clean technology ventures, alternative energy and energy efficiency; water and other scarce natural resources; waste and resource management; environmental services. Investment in other themes with social impact such as microfinance, health care themes, inequality.

and influence and long-term sustainable orientation as a performance edge through active ownership and strategy?

- Do such funds' decisions influence the future state of the economy and society? And if so, how?

The discussion on beliefs can be profoundly challenging in the ESG area. The strategies and mandates associated with ESG and sustainability can also be complex. Examples of sustainability strategies and the beliefs supporting them are shown in Tables 21.1 and 21.2.

Table 21.3 The sustainable investing matrix.

Strategy/Mission			
Targeted sustainable strategy - includes ESG thematic mandates			Current minority practice
Integrated sustainable strategy - integrated ESG and active ownership		PRI signatory practice	
Traditional investment strategy - ESG and ownership unspecified	Current majority practice		
	Traditional mission - Goals exclusively financial - Pure finance driven; nonfinancial factors not considered - Benchmark and monitor short-term versus other funds	Sustainable business-case mission - Goals exclusively financial but nonfinancial factors considered - Consideration of nonfinancial factors which have no *ex ante* downside impact on financial outcomes - Benchmark and monitor relative to longer-term mission	Sustainable wider mission - Goals predominantly financial but nonfinancial goals included - Nonfinancial factors have measurable but limited *ex ante* downside impact on financial outcomes - Benchmark and monitor relative to longer-term mission

The sustainability matrix

By far the biggest challenge in the sustainability area is straightening out values and beliefs.

The matrix representation in Table 21.3 is a tool to illustrate this challenge. Values lie horizontally across the chart and differentiate the investment mission and goals of a fund. Investment beliefs differentiate the investment strategy moving up the chart. As outlined earlier, traditional thinking in mission has been narrow. Funds have clustered predominantly in the bottom left box.

But many funds have been prompted to consider the merits of a more forward-thinking mission. When fiduciaries are asked to assign a weight to financial goals in their mission they say that it is dominate, but not on any terms. An obvious issue is concerned with contravening the principle of "do no harm" in investment, which could carry considerable reputational risks as well as investment

risks. Such thinking carries a fund one notch to the right; and correspondingly such funds often recognize the risks and the opportunities in ESG areas and find reason to go one further notch up the matrix. This leads to the middle box where most PRI signatories are positioned.

A few funds have taken their mission position one further notch to the right reflecting a more conscious stance with the ESG agenda but remaining with a finance first mission; and including an assignment of assets to mandates that are specifically targeted at sustainability taking them one notch higher. This leads to the top right box where a few leading public funds in Europe are positioned.

This matrix has been at the center of the sustainability debate for a number of asset owners in which the discussions have led to funds moving away from the bottom left. The asset owners with the most enthusiasm for such a change have been the universal owners (Urwin 2011).

Suitable frameworks for sustainable investing

While the dominant process in the allocation to integrated ESG is considering mandates on a case-by-case basis, this cannot be used in the case of the targeted mandates involving concentrated investing in environmentally targeted areas such as clean technology where a different approach is required.

Traditional approaches to asset allocation employ various optimization methods (Markowitz 1951; Litterman 2003). The common characteristic of all these processes is identifying through analytic and Monte Carlo processes a number of specific asset allocations, strategies and mandates that are optimal or close to optimal in having higher expected return per unit of risk.

Applying this approach to sustainable strategies seems inherently problematic. The robustness of the assumption setting can be challenged, given the relatively limited amount of empirical data on which to base it. However, some quantitative support can be employed with respect to risk control.

The critical point is to give an influential position to downside risk relative to benchmark. This measure of "tracking error risk" can be seen as a form of regret risk and can also be used to demonstrate that the impact of these sustainability mandates will not "significantly" impact overall results. This discipline provides some control over the sustainability of the mandate and the resilience of the asset owner to prematurely judged decisions through periods of underperformance.

The overall philosophy behind this framework is:

- using qualitative beliefs to support the merits of the expected returns from the mandate or strategy;
- using quantitative beliefs where they are statistically valid – in the downside underperformance risk of this mandate or strategy, on its own, and more importantly how it affects the overall fund;
- the allocation should be positioned by assessing the resilience of the fiduciary through various performance cycles (where "resilience" in this context is the capacity of the fiduciaries to ride out periodic performance issues);
- the allocation should reflect conviction – higher convictions in the beliefs underling the strategy would allow the threshold – the strategy norm – to be set a higher point; stronger governance would do the same; so would the degree of conviction coming from the mission statement.

How is the practice of fiduciary duty likely to develop?

We observed earlier on that fiduciary duty is not a stationary concept. How might its interpretation develop over time?

The more obvious path occurs through incremental change in the absence of a significant catalyst. This suggests a period in which ESG integration, engagement and longer investment horizons become embedded as a standard way of operating. The steady adoption of the PRI by mainstream investors suggests that the investment community is becoming more positive about forms of sustainable and responsible investment and it is plausible to expect a continuation of this trend. What remains to be seen, however, is the pace of change.

Possible catalysts to accelerate change are new legislation and the impacts of litigation. One scenario involves statutory changes to the concept of fiduciary obligation in order to clarify that fiduciaries can or should consider the financial impact of various environmental, social and corporate governance factors associated with a particular investment and the exercise of ownership interests. Legislative change or collective industry-based initiatives could spread the cost of stewardship amongst investors and reduce the free-rider problem.

Legislative changes to the content of fiduciary obligations have occurred in the past and could happen again (Woods 2011). Legislative clarification of fiduciary obligation has been canvassed in both the UK and the US. In the UK, the UK Law Commission is undertaking such a review during 2014 and FairPensions (now ShareAction) has drafted a proposed legislative provision in order to overcome confusion over the legal status of sustainable investing. The provision is modeled on S.172 of the Companies Act 2006, which permits directors to incorporate longer-term considerations and wider stakeholder interests in their strategy.

Academic studies have advocated legislative change or permissive safe harbors as a means to overcome the uncertainty about the status of sustainable investment vis-à-vis fiduciary obligation (see Richardson 2008; Woods and Urwin 2010; Woods 2011). However, a number of factors make this set of scenarios less likely in the near future given the legislative traction and politics needed for such a change.

Finally, litigation could act as a catalyst for the development of fiduciary obligation but it is hard to predict quite how this situation might develop.

Conclusions

Current investment practice, with its focus on short-term performance against financial benchmarks, can be seen to have shortcomings on the broader requirements of three of the fiduciary obligations (loyalty, prudence and impartiality). This argues for extension of the focus towards the long term with some consideration of nonfinancial factors. This version can be presented as more consistent with the exercise of fiduciary obligations (Urwin 2009).

Sustainable investing continues to suffer from four obstructions; the newness of investment thinking and practice that, in a conservative industry, takes a while to become mainstream; the stringent requirements for "pure finance" support for the strategies, which is a reflection of the narrow and doubtful interpretation of fiduciary duty; the lack of accepted process to its adoption, given limited empirical data; and the structure of the industry with the heavy influence of agency issues.

In the author's view, there are sustainable investing models and practices that are financially superior to traditional investment models. These have the direct support of a strong financial case and the collateral support of certain critical benefits delivered to wider stakeholders and ultimately to society.

We outline the need for a clear framework for proceeding with sustainable investing strategies using two critical disciplines: investment beliefs and downside risk control relative to the mainstream market and peer practices.

We highlight the significance of the monitoring process, which, in addition to informing future iterations of the process, must be expanded to include some reporting on outcomes from the nonfinancial mission in addition to the core financial measures. We foresee considerable work ahead in the industry to sharpen the tools necessary to support this nonfinancial reporting and accounting.

Looking ahead, there are likely to be a number of new factors affecting the sustainable investing field including:

- the leadership and influence of world class pension funds;
- the influence of PRI and other industry collaborations to converge and enhance strong practice in the area;
- measurement and benchmarking support;
- stronger board governance – boards have limited experience with sustainability issues;
- governments – their influence on markets and institutional funds through policy.

The most likely scenario is that sustainable investing will take a steadily increasing profile in the institutional funds area. This will likely arise from the dual reasons of addressing risk and exploiting opportunities given the transformational changes of economic adversity; environmental and social change and the growing significance of externalities; and adverse demography that lie ahead. Greater understanding and conviction around interpretations of fiduciary duties is likely to play a more constructive role in this change in the future than has been the case in the past.

References

Clark, G. L. and R. Urwin. 2008. "Best-Practice Investment Management," *Journal of Asset Management* 9 (1): 2–21.

Haldane, A. G. 2010. *Patience and Finance*. Oxford: China Business Forum, Bank of England.

Haldane, A. G. and R. Davies. 2011. *The Short Long*, Proceedings of the 29th Societe Universitaire Europeene de Recherches Financieres Colloquium, May.

Hawley, J. P. and A. T. Williams. 2007. "Universal Owners: Challenges and Opportunities," *Corporate Governance* 15 (3): 415–20.

Hawley, J. P., K. L. Johnson and E. J. Waitzer. 2011. "Reclaiming Fiduciary Duty Balance," *Rotman International Journal of Pension Management* 4 (2): 4.

Koedijk, K. C. G. and A. Slager. 2009. "Do Institutional Investors have Sensible Beliefs?" *Rotman International Journal of Pension Management* 2 (1): 12–19.

Krehmeyer, D., M. Orsagh and K. N. Schacht. 2006. *Breaking the Short-term Cycle.* Charlottesville, VA: CFA Institute and the Business Roundtable Institute for Corporate Ethics.

Litterman, B. 2003. *Modern Investment Management: An Equilibrium Approach.* New York: John Wiley & Sons.

Markowitz, H. 1951. *Portfolio Selection.* Oxford: Blackwell.

PRI. 2011. *Annual Report of the PRI Initiative.* Geneva: UNEPFI and UN Global Compact.

PRI and UNEP FI. 2011. *Universal Ownership: Why Environmental Externalities Matter to Institutional Investors.* www.unpri.org/files/6728_ES_report_environmental_externalities.pdf.

Richardson, B. 2008. *Socially Responsible Investment Law.* Oxford University Press.

Towers Watson. 2012. *We Need a Bigger Boat: Sustainability in Investment.* www.towerswatson.com/en/Insights/IC-Types/Survey-Research-Results/2012/09/Sustainable-investing-we-need-a-bigger-boat.

Urwin, R. 2009. *Sustainable Investing Practice: Models for Institutional Investors.* Ottawa: PRI Academic Conference.

2011. "Pension Funds as Universal Owners: Opportunity Calls and Leadership Beckons," *Rotman International Journal of Pension Management* 4 (1): 26–33.

Woods, C. 2011. "Funding Climate Change: How Pension Fund Fiduciary Duty Masks Trustee Inertia and Short-termism," in J. P. Hawley, S. J. Kamath and A. T. Williams (eds.) *Corporate Governance Failures: The Role of Institutional Investors in the Global Financial Crisis.* Pittsburgh: University of Pennsylvania Press.

Woods, C. and R. Urwin. 2010. "Putting Sustainable Investing into Practice: A Governance Framework for Pension Funds," *Journal of Business Ethics* 92: 1–19.

Reason, rationality and fiduciary duty

STEVE LYDENBERG

Introduction

The concept of fiduciary duty sits at the confluence of two powerful streams of Western intellectual thought, the legal and the economic: the legal because fiduciaries are managing the assets of others whose interests the law seeks to protect; the economic because fiduciaries assume the role of investors in the marketplace in managing these assets.

These legal and economic traditions pull fiduciaries in different and sometimes conflicting directions because their standards of appropriate behavior differ. Lawyers often use the standard of "reasonable" behavior, while economists frequently presuppose that people act "rationally." Reasonable behavior, which finds notable expression in tort law, supposes that one takes into account the effect of one's actions on others. The reasonable is by extension concerned with the protection or enhancement of a common good. Rational behavior, which is axiomatic to many neoclassical economists, is essentially self-interested and seeks to identify the most efficient means of achieving one's personal ends. The rational is primarily concerned with the attainment of private goals.

This chapter argues that since the last decades of the twentieth century the discipline of modern finance, under the influence of modern portfolio theory, has directed fiduciaries to act rationally – that is, in the sole economic interests of their funds – downplaying the effects of their investments on others. This approach has de-emphasized a previous interpretation of fiduciary duty that drew on a conception of prudence characterized by wisdom, discretion and intelligence – one that accounted to a greater degree for the relationship between one's investments and their effects on others in the world. As increasing numbers of institutional investors have adopted the self-interested, rational approach,

some of its limitations have become apparent. In particular, the rational fiduciary is not inclined to assess the objective well-being of beneficiaries, to recognize underlying sources of investment reward in the real economy or to allocate benefits impartially between current and future generations.

One indication of the current discomfort among institutional investors with an exclusively rational approach is the growing interest in socially responsible investment. This practice inclines fiduciaries to manage their funds in ways that are reasonable as well as rational – that is to say, that take into account the interests of others as embodied in the real world and the economy, as well as themselves as embodied in their funds.

Reason and rationality can work in a complementary way to make investment long-term in its perspective and beneficial to society and the economy, as well as to specific portfolios. Determining how to achieve this challenging goal is part of the obligation of fiduciaries as they seek to realize the full potential of the investment assets entrusted to their care.

Reasonable investment and fiduciary duty

Distinction between reason and rationality

Although the terms reason and rationality can be used interchangeably, this chapter draws on distinctions made by twentieth-century thinkers such as John Rawls, Amartya Sen and Jon Elster. This distinction is helpful in understanding two differing approaches to fiduciary duty.

Rawls, for example, points out that we often make a common sense distinction between the concepts of reason and rationality when we make remarks such as "Their proposal was perfectly rational given their strong bargaining position, but it was nevertheless highly unreasonable, even outrageous" (Rawls 1991: 48).[1]

This distinction between the two terms is useful. Persons act reasonably when "they are ready to propose principles and standards as fair terms of cooperation and to abide with them willingly, given the assurance that others will likewise do so" (ibid.: 49). In other words, reasonable persons understand that there are certain principles and standards that they agree to respect with regard to others when making decisions and choosing actions. As a reasonable person, one understands one's decisions and actions *with reference to others* in society. This conception of reason, familiar in tort law, is associated with certain traditions of moral philosophy and bound up with the concepts of fairness, justice and the public good.

Although rational persons act as if "every interest is an interest of a self," that doesn't mean that "self" needs to be narrowly defined (ibid.: 51). One's self-interest can encompass that of one's family, a community to which one belongs or one's nation. One's self-interest does not depend, however, on a broadly shared idea of mutually agreed upon standards and principles. Rational behavior is based on the efficient achievement of one's self-interested goals *without reference to others*. This conception of rationality is associated with utilitarian philosophies and bound up with concepts of efficiency, maximization of usefulness and private welfare.

Arguing similarly, Elster (2009: 2) asserts that "The idea of reason is intimately connected to that of the common good" and Sen (2009: 53) has observed that "the reasonable is public in a way the rational is not."

It is this distinction between reasonable behavior – a publicly oriented process that takes into account the opinions and expectations of others – and rational behavior – a self-interested, efficient maximization of personal interests – that is used in this discussion of the duties of fiduciaries.

The reasonable, the rational and trends in interpretation of fiduciary duties

The reasonable man is a standard frequently invoked in law, particularly tort law.

Black's Dictionary of Law defines a reasonable person as:

> A hypothetical person used as a legal standard, esp. to determine whether someone acted with negligence: specif., a person who exercises the degree of attention, knowledge, intelligence, and judgment *that society requires of its members for the protection of their own and others' interests* (emphasis added).

Reasonableness here is defined in terms of the interests of oneself in relationship to society's interests and the interests of others in that society. Note also that according to this definition, society requires that individuals employ, among other things, "judgment" in order to understand what society requires. Legal scholars have variously interpreted the means through which a reasonable person exercises judgment, but the core concept is that judicious reflection upon the interests and rights of others is essential to reasonable behavior in society.[2]

The courts and regulators have applied the language of reasonableness to financial matters and fiduciary issues in various cases over the years. For example, in the seminal ruling on the duties of fiduciaries in the 1830 case *Harvard College* v. *Amory*,[3] the courts instructed trustees "to observe how men of prudence, discretion and intelligence manage their own affairs, not in regard to speculation, but in regard to the permanent disposition of their funds, considering the probable income, as well as the probable safety of the capital to be invested."

Trustees are instructed to understand the nature of prudence and discretion by observing the prudent behavior of *others*, not by pursuing their own interests. Distinguishing speculation, which runs contrary to the fiduciary duty of care, from "the permanent disposition" of funds – that is, something akin to what we would call today long-term investments or preservation of capital – requires

---

[1] See also Scanlon (1998: 192) on the common sense distinction between reasonable and rational behavior.

[2] For an overview of these interpretations of how reasonable standards can be derived, see Solum (2009).

[3] 9 Pick. (26 Mass.) 446 (1830).

fiduciaries to "observe how men of prudence, discretion and intelligence manage their own affairs."

The courts and financial regulators have continued to invoke the reasonable investor and reasonableness in investment as a standard for the financial community. For example, the Securities and Exchange Commission *Staff Accounting Bulletin 99* on materiality asserts that "A matter is 'material' if there is a substantial likelihood that *a reasonable person* would consider it important"[4] (Securities and Exchange Commission 1999, emphasis added). Similarly, in its 2010 interpretive guidance on what information corporations should disclose to investors on the materiality of climate change to their operations, the Commission noted that "Information is material if there is a substantial likelihood that a *reasonable i*nvestor would consider it important in deciding how to vote or make an investment decision" (Securities and Exchange Commission 2010, emphasis added). In doing so it relied upon a similar definition of materiality and the reasonable investor set forth by the US Supreme Court in the case *TSC Industries* v. *Northway, Inc.*[5]

Whether the SEC and Supreme Court were explicitly drawing a distinction between a reasonable and a rational investor is not entirely clear, but it is clear that from a legal perspective the standard of reasonableness in investment is an acceptable norm.

In practice, during much of the twentieth century, the emphasis on prudence, diligence and intelligence as part of the duty of care led to what today would be viewed conservative investment practices. As Jay Youngdahl reminds us, as late as 1959,

> The Second Restatements of Trust mandated that the following were improper investments:
> The (1) purchase of securities for purposes of speculation, for example, purchase of shares of stock on margin or purchase of bonds selling at a great discount because of uncertainty where they will be paid on discount because of uncertainty

whether "they will be paid on maturity"; (2) purchase of securities in new and untried enterprises; (3) employment of trust property in the carrying on of trade or business; (4) purchase of land or other things for resale (*Restatement (Second) of Trusts*, Section 227, Comment f. (1959) as cited in Youngdahl 2010).

During the latter half of the twentieth century, a number of factors contributed to a new definition of what in practice the duties of care and loyalty meant for fiduciaries, a definition that implied a more rational and less reasonable approach.

The fundamental changes that swept through the investment community included the globalization of financial markets, advances in information technology and innovations in investment products. These developments were accompanied by the emergence of new theories of risk control, diversification, derivative pricing and the efficient pricing of securities by markets, which were collectively gathered together under the banner of modern portfolio theory (MPT).[6]

MPT directed fiduciaries toward a rational, rather than a reasonable, approach to investment. Academic economists, rather than legal scholars or financial professionals, laid the groundwork for MPT. Economists applied mathematical models to the investment process and came to substitute risk control at a portfolio level for caution in individual security selection as the philosophical basis for prudent investment. The net effect of this revolution was to substitute judgment-free decisions based on portfolio characteristics for judgment-driven assessments of the prospects and impacts of specific investment decisions.

Youngdahl (2010) notes: "It wasn't until 1992 that the American Law Institute came out with its Third Restatement of the Law of Trusts that formally permitted fiduciaries to authorize a more diversified – and more risky – portfolio." The *Restatement (Third) of Trusts* articulated a "prudent *investor* standard" as opposed to the prudent man rule, in which the prudent fiduciary was directed to follow the dictates of MPT, which was described by one legal expert as "consistent themes

---

[4] Securities and Exchange Commission Staff Accounting Bulletin 99 – Materiality, 17 CFR Part 212. August 13, 1999. Available at www.sec.gov/interps/account/sab99.htm.
[5] 426 US 438 (1976).

[6] See Bernstein (2005, 2007) for extended discussions of the origins and evolutions of modern portfolio theory.

of legitimate financial theories" based on "principles upon which general agreement exits." These changes were intended "to liberate expert trustees to pursue challenging, rewarding, non-traditional strategies when appropriate to a particular trust" in the course of which, in contrast to past practice, "no investments are generally impermissible" (Halbach 1991–2: 1154, 1155, 1184).

The second driving factor in this revolutionary change related to the growing influence of fiduciaries. The last half of the twentieth century and first decade of the twenty-first century saw dramatic growth in pension funds' assets and their role in the global economy. By 2008, the cumulative value of pension fund assets alone had grown to $22 trillion (Clark and Urwin 2010: 63). So-called sovereign wealth funds had, as of September 2011, some $4.7 trillion in assets under management.[7] In addition fiduciaries oversaw the management of the substantial investment assets of mutual funds, bank trust departments and insurance companies.

With this growing financial power and the responsibility for the best interests of huge numbers of beneficiaries came an increasing recognition of the seriousness of fiduciaries' potential for abuse or mismanagement of the funds under their control, as well as their potential to contribute positively to the economy. Starting in the 1970s, the possibility that fiduciaries of these funds might use them for their personal benefit became apparent. For example, in the 1960s and 1970s, the Teamsters Central States Pension Fund in the United States became notoriously involved in series of scandals involving corruption and self-dealing (see Williams Walsh 2004). At the same time, others called attention to the potential for investments from pension funds and other institutional investors to help promote general economic growth (see, for example, Rifkin and Barber 1978).

This concern about the appropriate conduct of trustees extended beyond narrowly defined self-dealing and corruption to the influence of politicians and others on pension-fund trustees. Academics, consultants and various others criticized the influence of politicians on the use of pension fund assets without due consideration

to financial returns. Typically "political" meant local investments that supported community economic development but failed to product market-rate returns. By extension, however, it was also applied to any consideration of societal effects other than portfolio-level returns. Critics, for example, raised concerns about pension fund investments in a local automobile manufacturing plant that later moved out of state, as well as about divesting from companies that were deriving profits from operations under the apartheid legal system in South Africa (see, for example, Romano 1993).

Both corrupt self-dealing and local, political and "social" investments were seen as a violation of fiduciary duty not because they were self-interested, but because they had misidentified the "self" that they should have been serving. Fiduciaries should be self-interested, but that self-interest should be defined solely as returns to the portfolio.

This version of the rational approach to investment solved two problems. First, it opened the door to the exploding world of investment opportunities that, according to MPT, could theoretically be added to portfolios without increasing their overall risk or speculative nature. Second, it eliminated from the investment process self-interest in the form of all personal or politically related considerations by fiduciaries or others, and substituted self-interest defined solely as related to the financial returns of the portfolio.

This approach effectively crowded out the remnants of the reason-based, legal thinking that empowered fiduciaries to define prudence in terms of "others" and society as a whole – that is to say, consideration of the role of their investments in the lives of their beneficiaries and world in which they live. Those advocating this dominance of the rational may not have intended to eliminate all consideration of beneficiaries' lives from fiduciary considerations, but that was in fact the net effect of this approach.

This shift away from conception of the fiduciary based on the legal tradition of reasonable behavior capable of judgment is reflected in the shift in plain text interpretation of ERISA provided by the Department of Labor. In 1994 in its Interpretive

---

[7] www.swfinstitute.org/fund-rankings.

Bulletin relating to investing in economically targeted investments, it stated that:

> The Department has construed the requirements that a fiduciary act solely *in the interest of, and for the exclusive purpose of providing benefits to, participants and beneficiaries* as prohibiting a fiduciary from subordinating the *interests of participants and beneficiaries in their retirement income to unrelated objectives.*[8]

Then in 2008 the Department of Labor revised this language to read:

> [F]iduciaries may never subordinate the *economic interests of the plan* to unrelated objectives, and may not select investments on the basis of any factor outside the *economic interest of the plan* except in very limited circumstances.[9]

This revision shifted the interpretation of ERISA with regard to fiduciaries' duty from safeguarding those objectives that related to retirees' retirement income to safeguarding the economic interest of the plan. In doing so, it effectively steered fiduciaries away from considerations of what they might reasonably judge to be the interests of the beneficiaries when it comes to the usefulness of their incomes in achieving a satisfactory retirement. Instead, it directed fiduciaries to narrow considerations of the economic performance to the plan. The two are not synonymous, as will be discussed in greater detail below. The important point here is that considerations of beneficiaries' sources and uses of retirement income involve a far broader range of concerns than does consideration of the financial performance of a fund.

This narrowing of focus may have addressed various agency problems that fiduciaries were perceived at that time to have faced. However, as an increasing number of fiduciaries followed the call to adopt the precepts of MPT, its policies and practices created a set of problems and concerns of their own. Most important, once widely adopted these investment practices appear to have

had a destabilizing effect on financial systems – as demonstrated by the major booms, busts and financial crises that began in the first years of the twenty-first century – and have shown themselves incapable of considering or dealing with the implications of their investments for the sustainability of the environment and the stability of society.

Current state of reasonable investment

This tension between the concern for others and the concern for self places fiduciaries in an uncomfortable position in which the old definition of investment prudence (e.g., hold only high-quality bonds) has long since vanished and the new definition (e.g., pursue aggressive portfolio-level risk management) no longer provides a viable sense of security. Fiduciaries cannot reasonably ignore the instability in today's financial markets and its effects on their beneficiaries, not to mention on the economy. Nor can they reasonably neglect to ask how their investment decisions relate to these problems and the increasing weakness of the very governments upon which their beneficiaries' retirement security in large part depends.

As these weaknesses in the systematic application of MPT have become increasingly apparent, a number of institutional investors have started to explore ways in which reasonable approaches to investment – that is, those that take into account the effects of their investments in the real world – can supplement their current practices.

These approaches fall into three categories: a universal owner approach, a sustainable or responsible investment approach and a broad-based-norms approach. The universal owner approach argues that the portfolios of the largest institutional investors are of such size that they "own the economy" and that their mandate to safeguard their assets is effectively a mandate to safeguard the economy.

The universal owner theory was first proposed by Robert Monks and Nell Minnow and later elaborated by James Hawley and Andrew Williams. The implication of this approach is that attention to portfolio-level returns alone is inadequate and that

---

[8] Department of Labor, Interpretive Bulletin §2509.94–1 (29 CFR 2509.94–1), emphasis added.
[9] Advisory Opinion No. 2007–07A (December 21, 2007) and Advisory Opinion No. 2008–05A (June 27, 2008), emphasis added.

"universal" considerations of economic well-being are in fact synonymous with the well-being of their beneficiaries.

> [U]niversal owners are uniquely positioned to develop and pursue a potentially virtuous efficiency cycle of minimizing negative externalities [on the economy] and encouraging positive ones by the firms in their portfolios ... Universal owners need to begin a process of extending the definition of prudential fiduciary duty to include attention to the universal aspects of their portfolios (Hawley and Williams 2000: xvii).

This approach embodies the intuitively reasonable position that investments overall won't do well unless the economy does well. This contrasts with the somewhat paradoxical position that rational investors can find themselves taking when asserting that an investment strategy was a "success" because, although the overall market was down 20 percent, their portfolio was "only" down 18 percent.

The sustainable or responsible investment approach has been adopted by fiduciaries at numerous mutual funds, religious organizations, foundations and sovereign wealth funds since the 1980s. What distinguishes this approach from that of the universal investor is its emphasis on the impacts of investments on the well-being of society broadly construed, rather than on the economy. It makes these considerations because, as Rawls (1991: 49) observes, "Reasonable people take into account the consequences of their actions on others' well-being."

Prior to the early 1970s, a number of religious investors defined harmful investments as those in "sin stocks" – alcohol, gambling, tobacco and, in certain cases, military contracting. This approach was typified by John Wesley, founder of the Methodists, who believed one should "Gain all you can, without hurting either yourself or your neighbor, in soul or body."[10]

Starting in the 1970s in the United States, responsible investors extended their concerns to matters of environmental sustainability, peace and justice, and civil rights. As early as 1972, the authors of *The Ethical Investor*, one of the

first in-depth studies of the theoretical underpinnings of social investment, took the position that investors had an inherent obligation to consider the potential social harm caused by their investments – and asserted the practical reasonableness of such considerations.

> Although the notion of social injury is imprecise, and although many hard cases will be encountered in applying it [to investments], we think that it is a helpful designation and that cases can be decided on the basis of it. In the law, many notions (such as negligence in the law of torts or consideration in the law of contracts) are equally vague but have received content from repeated decision-making over time (Simon et al. 1972: 18, 21).

In the 1990s the concept of sustainability began to drive the investment policies and practices of an increasing number of responsible investors, including institutional investors, in Europe. These investors were influenced in part by the 1987 publication of the Brundtland Report, which highlighted and defined the concept of sustainability and by the 1997 ratification of the Kyoto Protocol on climate change. Developments such as these led to the emergence of so-called "green" funds less concerned with avoidance and more concerned with identification of specific positive sectors or activities linked to the environment, such as renewable energy and clean technologies (Louche and Lydenberg 2010: 398).

This trend toward positive social and environmental opportunities has continued into the first decade of the twenty-first century with the emergence of "impact" investing, with its emphasis on small-scale investments with high environmental and social impact (Thornley et al. 2010: 7).

Some argue that these sustainable or responsible investment practices fill a self-interested, rational role – i.e., that it "doesn't pay" in the long run to harm others and does pay to consider positive environmental and social impacts. Sustainable and responsible practices should ultimately help portfolio performance in the long run because doing harm hurts companies' reputations, incurs legal liabilities, undercuts employee and customer loyalty, and proves short-sighted and, conversely, positives enhance customer loyalty, attract quality employees and help ensure long-term viability.

---

[10] http://new.gbgm-umc.org/umhistory/wesley/sermons/50.

Whether there is actually a financial benefit or cost to the performance of sustainable and responsible investment practices has been the subject of academic debate since the 1980s. Many of these studies have found no statistically significant differences in financial performance between portfolios that take social and environmental factors into account and those that do not. For example, Kurtz and DiBartolomeo (2011) found that, after adjusting for risk factors, a longstanding US social investment index produced positive returns statistically indistinguishable from the similarly maintained Standard and Poor's 500 Index over an eighteen-year period.[11]

Responsible investors, however, can be seen as having motivations beyond financial self-interest and as being driven by deeper values: the inherent duties that come with substantial assets in a world where assets are unevenly distributed. As Amartya Sen argues, with the accumulation of assets comes an unequal allocation of power that requires action that is not motivated by yet further gain for those who have the disproportionate access to that power.

> Mutual benefit, based on symmetry and reciprocity, is not the only foundation for thinking about reasonable behavior towards others. Having effective power and the obligations that can follow unidirectionally from it can also be an important basis for impartial reasoning, going well beyond the motivation of mutual benefits (Sen 2009: 207).

For investors in possession of this "effective power," these obligations might include not profiting from investments complicit with genocide or environmental injustice. Or, more positively, they might involve choosing investments that help those lacking access to capital, to information technologies in developing countries, or to vaccines to stop the spread of communicable disease in underserved regions.

Broad-based norms and standards can serve as important, objective guidelines for institutional investors wishing to avoid the appearance that their decisions derive from merely personal ethics or local political pressures. These investors can seek out the broadest, most widely recognized norms and standards to guide their policies – for example, the Nuclear Non-Proliferation Treaty or the United Nations' Universal Declaration of Human Rights.

Sen has described such broadly accepted norms as the result of "reasoning that we can reflectively *sustain*" (ibid.: 194, emphasis in original) or what he also refers to as "public" reasoning. Here sustainable means reasoning that derives from and can stand up to the scrutiny of others. The broader the definition of the "others" that have been involved, the more likely the decision is to be free from the personal or political biases of the fiduciaries themselves.

In keeping with this approach, SNS Asset Management, for example, employs a number of social and environmental principles in its fundamental investment policies. SNS explains that

> The[se] fundamental principles are derived from international treaties, guidelines or codes. They are not based on subjective preferences, but on broadly-accepted values in the global civilization that are set down internationally in authoritative documents.[12]

Implications for reasonable fiduciaries

The demands of rationality serve a useful function in directing fiduciaries' attention to the maximization of portfolio-level returns and their obligation to keep their decisions free from personal conflicts of interest and local political pressures. Reasonable decision-making by fiduciaries offers a number of additional strengths that the rational approach lacks. A reasonable fiduciary can understand how investments:

- make beneficiaries objectively better off;
- create value that allows each fund to benefit along with others;
- can be impartial with respect to future generations.

---

[11] See also http://sristudies.org for a comprehensive listing of academic studies on the relationship between socially responsible investment and financial performance.

[12] www.snsam.nl/index.asp?NID=7622.

The reasonable fiduciary, objectivity and benefits

Fiduciaries should care if their beneficiaries are objectively well off – not simply happy – in the same sense that doctors should care whether their patients are objectively healthy, not simply "feeling good." Patients may assert that smoking or drinking excessively makes them "feel good," but a doctor has an obligation to determine if these activities are making them objectively unhealthy.

To measure benefit solely in terms of financial returns is to make an essentially subjective measurement. It makes you feel good to know you have money in the bank, but you don't know if that money makes you better off without looking to the objective circumstances in your life. Fiduciaries whose *sole* goal is the economic interest of the plan cannot by definition seek to establish objective benefit with reference to the outside world. This is in keeping with what Jon Elster (2009: 28) terms "the radically subjective nature of the notion of rationality."

Specifically, rational fiduciaries are not, and essentially cannot be, concerned with whether, during the past quarter or year, their beneficiaries' funds have lost ground to price increases or can purchase the same quality health care or higher education that they did a year ago; whether the environment in which their beneficiaries live is more or less healthy; whether the streets they walk on at night are more or less secure; whether their beneficiaries' potential for secure retirement income from contributions by their employer or government has increased or decreased; or whether the financial markets upon which their beneficiaries depend for the growth of their retirement assets have become more or less honest and stable. Purely rational fiduciaries cannot know whether investments with a positive relative financial performance provide a positive benefit to current or future beneficiaries without reference to the outside world.

Among the connections between their investments and the real world that a reasonable fiduciary might consider are the cost of health care; the state of the environment; the state of financial markets and the economy; the financial strength of local and national governments; and the prospects for security at home and peace abroad.

Beneficiaries being objectively better off does not require that they be happy about fiduciaries' assessment of that objective state. Indeed, beneficiaries may not care whether the cost of health care is rising exponentially; the physical environment is deteriorating or urban streets are becoming unsafe; the government or corporation for which they are working and on which they depend for retirement benefits is becoming financially unsound; or future generations inherit a livable world. Fiduciaries have no way of knowing if what will make beneficiaries objectively better off will also make them subjectively "happy."

What reasonable fiduciaries can determine is what, in their best judgment, the objective state of their beneficiaries and the world in which they live is and whether their investment decisions on the whole are contributing positively to that state. Their reasonable judgment is an objective one, not a subjective one.

The reasonable fiduciary and the creation of value

Reasonable fiduciaries focus on ways in which their investments can positively impact the whole – including the social, environmental and economic systems upon which they depend for prosperity and survival – while increasing their funds' return. In doing so, they effectively create value for the beneficiaries of all funds, rather than simply benefitting their own at others' expense. And they expect that other reasonable fiduciaries will act similarly, creating value in, not extracting value from, the system upon which all depend. By contrast, rational fiduciaries who are focused exclusively on their funds' economic interests are likely to fail to fully comprehend these longer-term, sustainable sources of value and seek short-term, unsustainable benefits – typically at the expense of others.

Reasonable investors are not engaged in a philanthropic activity, but rather participate in a world where investors make decisions that create reciprocal benefits among peers. As Rawls puts it:

Reasonable persons ... are not moved by the general good as such but desire for its own sake a social world in which they, as free and equal, can cooperate with others on terms all can accept. They insist that reciprocity should hold within that world so that *each benefits along with others* (Rawls 1991: 50, emphasis added).

By contrast, if fiduciaries define the sole economic interest of their plans as beating the market – that is, outperforming their peers – they are likely to behave as if the market is a zero-sum game. To outperform one's peers it is only rational to identify and take advantage of their mistakes. According to the precepts of MPT, one of the techniques for doing so is knowing the historical value of a company and avoiding the irrational overpricing or underpricing of its securities; or knowing more than one's peers about the value of a company through better research. Those adopting these active investment techniques effectively presuppose that a limited number of highly sophisticated investors can consistently take advantage of less sophisticated investors' mistakes. In Paul Samuelson's words, these techniques work only for "the happy few."

[M]odern day bourses display what I like to call Limited Micro Efficiency. So long as a minute minority of investors, possessed of considerable assets, can seek gain by trading against willful uniformed bettors, the Limited Efficiency of Markets will be empirically observable. The temporary appearance of aberrant price profiles coaxes action from alert traders who act gleefully to wipe out the aberration (in Bernstein 2007: 40).

Those from whom these rational institutional investors and "alert traders" extract excess returns in this zero-sum game may be the beneficiaries of less-sophisticated funds or even unsophisticated individuals who are their own beneficiaries. The net effect to the overall world of beneficiaries is redistribution of wealth, but with no necessary net gain to the system as a whole.

The other rational approach to this zero-sum investment game is passive, or index, investing. If you believe that your investment decisions cannot ultimately generate returns above those provided by the market, then it becomes rational to "buy the market" and cut your costs. Keeping fees and transaction costs as low as possible is at least guaranteed to help portfolio performance, whatever that may turn out to be.

Indexers buy and sell at today's market prices. They make no judgment as to whether that price reflects underlying value – whether a stock or the whole market is overpriced or underpriced. They don't have to pay for high-priced stock analysts. They don't research the investments they are making. They place blind faith in the markets to serve the economy well and to give them the best possible returns.

Counterintuitively, this widely adopted buy-and-hold approach increases the short-termism of the markets. Simon Zadek accurately describes the situation when he asserts, "When pension funds say they are long-term investors, what they mean is that they have rolling investments in largely indexed linked funds. To speak accurately this makes them *perpetual investors* making short-term investments, forever."[13]

As increasing numbers of passive index investors enter the markets they encourage a blind "herding" behavior that exacerbates the bubbles and bursts created by the speculators who are increasingly left to set prices in the markets. In addition, indexers deprive corporate managers of intelligent feedback from the capital markets through the price mechanism, thus undercutting one of the primary purposes of financial markets: to allocate funds efficiently through informed and intelligent choices.

In his book *A Call for Judgment*, Amar Bhidé points out that while it is possible to scale up manufacturing operations of, say, a computer from a few thousand units to hundreds of thousands without sacrificing quality and thereby gain efficiencies of scale, the same exercise is far more problematic for finance. Sound financial decisions depend on the sound analysis and judgment of individual situations and the development of personal relationships, and those cannot be easily scaled up. As he puts it, "Relying on case-by-case judgment does have drawbacks: It is labor intensive and slow. But mechanized decision-making is

---

[13] Simon Zadek, Presentation at World Economic Forum, 2005 (emphasis in original).

rarely a good alternative when the choices involve willful humans" (Bhidé 2010: 44).

Both reasonable and rational fiduciaries understand that a primary source of wealth associated with their funds derives from the underlying strength of the economic and financial systems within which they operate. Rational fiduciaries ignore the impacts of their investments on these systems. Reasonable fiduciaries seek to understand how their investments can impact them positively or negatively. In doing so, reasonable investors are willing to accept what Rawls (1991: 50) calls "the burden of judgments and ... their consequences." That is to say, when more than mere price considerations become part of the investment process, investors are forced to ask questions about whether their investments have a net positive effect on the economy (including society and the environment) and the financial system as a whole – and to accept the responsibility for their potential to make positive contributions and create general value available to all.

It may be rational to put considerations of the financial performance of one's fund ahead of considerations of the integrity of the financial markets and the public good, but it is not reasonable.

The reasonable fiduciary, sustainability and future generations

Part of the fiduciary's duty of loyalty is a duty of impartiality, including impartial consideration of benefits for future generations. This duty of impartiality and its relationship to questions of sustainability has been relatively neglected until recently. As one legal scholar described the situation "[T]he nature and implications of the duty [of impartiality] have been left vaguely defined and infrequently explained." Consequently, the American Law Institute devoted considerable attention to this question in its 1992 *Restatement (Third) of Trusts*, addressing issues such as the differing needs of beneficiaries for income and tax benefits and the like, "[i]n addition to the obvious competition between present and future interests" (Halbach 1991–2: 1171).

This competition between present and future generations is particularly relevant for pension

funds, sovereign wealth funds and other funds with long time horizons. The US Supreme Court has made its relevance for pension funds clear in its *Varity* v. *Howe* (1996) ruling where it held that "the common law of trusts [made applicable to ERISA §§404, 409] recognizes the need to preserve assets to satisfy future, as well as present, claims and requires a trustee to take impartial account of the interest of all beneficiaries" (Hawley et al. 2011: 13).

In a 2011 article, Hawley et al. stressed the importance of this concept of intergenerational impartiality for fiduciaries.

> Fiduciaries must ensure that their decision-making processes balance allocation of capital between near-term needs and future wealth creation and consider the potential transfer of risks between participant generations. Intergenerational wealth maximization requires active consideration of a range of factors beyond narrow financial criteria (ibid.: 8).

Rational fiduciaries narrowly focused on current price and calculable risk can find this task difficult because they are constantly driven toward short-term anonymous investment decision-making that helps them "beat the market" today but offers little hope of serving the interests of future generations.

Because it involves intergenerational equity, the duty of impartiality compels responsible investors to confront questions of sustainability and sustainable development, which was defined in the Report of the 1987 Brundtland Commission, *Our Common Future,* as "development that meets the needs of the present without compromising the ability of future generations to meet their own needs" (WCED 1987).

To address intergenerational equity, fiduciaries must go beyond today's price and yesterday's returns if they are to manage assets with an eye toward impartiality across generations. Reason can help in this task because it is naturally disposed to considerations of the future. Indeed, Elster (2009: 8) asserts that "[r]eason requires impartiality about the future." The tool that reason places in the fiduciary's hands that allows for impartial consideration of the future is the ability to cope with matters of irreducible uncertainty.

In his *Treatise on Probability* Keynes distinguishes among three types of risk: precisely calculable risks or probabilities (e.g., casino odds); risks that are only calculable in relative terms (e.g., the likelihood of rain tomorrow); and irreducible uncertainties (e.g., the price of oil ten years from now). Rational investors have developed risk control models that can cope with the first and, to a certain extent, the second type of probability in investment. But they ignore the third.

How do reasonable investors cope with the irreducibly uncertain aspects of the future? Keynes's answer is that they fall back on convention. "[F]aced with varying degrees of uncertainty, it is rational to fall back on conventions, stories, rules of thumb, habits, traditions in forming our expectations and deciding how to act" (Skidelsky 2010: 87). In other words, forms of what could be called common sense are a reasonable approach to investment in the face of uncertainty. Common sense may not be able to predict the uncertain future – no one can do that – but it is as reasonable an approach as possible.

If reasonable behavior in the face of irreducible uncertainty on the part of investors means falling back on convention, that of governments is in Keynes' view of a related sort. While uncertainties cannot be eliminated, their range can be reduced and it is government's role to do so. "If ... there is bound to be irreducible uncertainty in financial operations, the state has an additional role, which is to protect the economy as a whole against the consequences of uncertainty" (ibid.: 174). That is to say, government needs to acknowledge uncertainties, account for them, and to minimize their sway as prudently as possible. As Robert Skidelsky observes, "Prudence in the face of the unknown is the key to Keynes's philosophy of statesmanship" (ibid.: 158). In many senses, sovereign wealth funds and public pension funds are fiscal agents of national and local governments. Their fiduciaries share these governments' broad interest in protecting future as well as present beneficiaries against "irreducible uncertainty in financial operations" and wish "to protect the economy as a whole against the consequences of uncertainty."

As Hawley points out, the pursuit of intergenerational equity "requires active consideration of a range of factors beyond narrow financial criteria." These include nonfinancial criteria related to the sustainability of society and the environment and the stability of the financial markets, in addition to those more narrowly related to today's market price and calculable risks.

A reasonable fiduciary might, for example, conclude that the issues of global warming and human rights are likely to be with us for generations to come, as are concerns about the nonproliferation of nuclear weapons; the elimination of communicable childhood diseases; access to high-quality, low-cost health care and a healthy environment; and access to communications technologies that can facilitate education, commerce and entertainment.

To understand how investments can be used to reduce the realm of uncertainty about issues such as these specifically or more generally about what kind of world will make future generations objectively well-off may be a challenging task, but it is one on which reasonable persons engaged in open and impartial public reasoning can surely make progress.

Conclusions: need for both reason and rationality

This chapter has concentrated on the limits of rationality and the virtues of reason to dramatize the point that the tools of rational behavior in finance have been so extensively elaborated in recent decades as to effectively crowd out those of reason and common sense. This is not to say that the two are diametrically opposed or that reason should supersede or replace rationality in investment. In fact, the two not only can coexist but need to complement each other in practice.

Philosophers dealing with the relative roles of reason and rationality in society recognize their necessarily complementary nature. As Rawls puts it:

> [W]ithin the idea of fair cooperation the reasonable and the rational are complementary ideas ... As complementary ideas, neither the reasonable nor the rational can stand without the other. Merely reasonable agents have no ends of their own they wanted to advance by fair cooperation;

merely rational agents lack a sense of justice and fail to recognize the independent validity of the claims of others (Rawls 1991: 52).

Or, as the economic anthropologist Stephen Gudeman argues, "the economy is built around the dialectical relation of two value realms, mutuality and trade, and contains a tension between two ways of making material life – for the self and for others" (Gudeman 2008: 14).

For financial fiduciaries this view implies that they must remain fully aware of the self-interested needs of their beneficiaries, including the returns of their portfolios. At the same time they must remain equally aware of the effect of their decisions on others – that is, on the world that their beneficiaries occupy – and of their ability to influence that world positively or negatively.

It is not surprising that fiduciaries would feel uncomfortable serving these two demanding masters. Their task as fiduciaries would be vastly simpler if all they had to do was to look out for the "economic interests of the plan," leaving to blind faith considerations of how that narrowly conceived self-interest might promote stable financial markets, a sound economy and a sustainable environment. Ultimately, however, reasonable fiduciaries cannot avoid the responsibility for understanding how their decisions can maximize the positive impacts and minimize the negative impacts of their investments.

Serving these two masters may involve extra costs, take extra effort and leave the door open to free-riders. As challenging as these additional concerns may be, they can be dealt with through a combination of best practice, education, regulation and cultural change. They are concerns that political will and collective action can overcome.

We have reached a point in the financial world where the exclusive focus on rational behavior in finance has been extended beyond the limits of its usefulness. The hyperactive search for yet more self-interested investments has begun to destabilize finance, harm social structures and neglect much-needed opportunities to build sustainability and durability into our world. The idea that reasonable fiduciaries cannot impartially and objectively use their investments to achieve positive ends leaves their potential to serve their beneficiaries

substantially unrealized. As Sen (2009: 194) rightly observes, "The insistence … on defining rationality simply as intelligent promotion of personal self-interest sells human reasoning extremely short."

It is time for fiduciaries to return reason – with its insistence on the outward-looking acknowledgment of one's duties to others and the importance of the sustainability for future generations – to its rightful place alongside self-interested rationality. It is time for fiduciaries to listen to the calls of the likes of Ed Waitzer (2009: 5) when he insists that,

> The time has come for trustees and investment managers to assume a broader and more active leadership role in financial markets and beyond. Why? Because their failure to look ahead and outward, given the increasingly obvious impacts on investment over the long term, may well constitute a failure of duties owed to those who entrust their savings with them.

Acknowledgements

A longer version of this chapter is being published in *Journal of Business Ethics*. Reprinted with kind permission from Springer Science+Business Media. The author thanks Joakim Sandberg for helpful comments.

References

Bernstein, P. L. 2005. *Capital Ideas: The Improbable Origins of Modern Wall Street*. Hoboken, NJ: John Wiley & Sons.
  2007. *Capital Ideas Evolving*. Hoboken, NJ: John Wiley & Sons.
Bhidé, A. 2010. *A Call for Judgment: Sensible Finance for a Dynamic Economy*. Oxford University Press.
Clark, G. L. and R. Urwin. 2010. "Innovative Models of Pension Fund Governance in the Context of the Global Financial Crisis," *Pensions: An International Journal* 15 (1): 62–77.
Elster, J. 2009. *Reason and Rationality*. Princeton University Press.
Gudeman, S. 2008. *Economy's Tension: The Dialectics of Community and Market*. New York: Berghahn Books.

Halbach, E. C. 1991–2. "Trust Investment Law in the Third Restatement," *Iowa Law Review* 77: 1151–85.

Hawley, J. P. and A. T. Williams. 2000. *The Rise of Fiduciary Capitalism: How Institutional Investors Can Make Corporate America More Democratic.* Philadelphia: University of Pennsylvania Press.

Hawley, J. P., K. Johnson and E. Waitzer. 2011. "Reclaiming Fiduciary Duty Balance," *Rotman International Journal of Pension Management* 4 (2): 4–16.

Kurtz, L. and D. DiBartolomeo. 2011. "The Long-Term Performance of a Social Investment Universe," *The Journal of Investing* 20 (3): 95–102.

Louche, C. and S. Lydenberg. 2010. "Responsible Investing," in J. R. Boatright (ed.) *Finance Ethics: Critical Issues in Theory and Practice.* Hoboken, NJ: John Wiley & Sons.

Rawls, J. 1991. *Political Liberalism.* Cambridge, MA: Harvard University Press.

Rifkin, J. and R. Barber. 1978. *The North Will Rise Again: Pensions, Politics, and Power in the 1980s.* Boston: Beacon Press.

Romano, R. 1993. "Public Pension Fund Activism in Corporate Governance Reconsidered," *Columbia Law Review* 93 (4): 795–853.

Scanlon, T. M. 1998. *What We Owe to Each Other.* Cambridge, MA: Harvard University Press.

Securities and Exchange Commission. 1999. *Staff Accounting Bulletin 99 – Materiality.* 17 CFR Part 212. August 13. www.sec.gov/interps/account/sab99.htm.

2010. *Commission Guidance Regarding Disclosure Related to Climate Change*, Release Nos. 33–9106; 34–61469; FR-82. www.sec.gov/rules/interp/2010/33–9106.pdf.

Sen, A. 2009. *The Idea of Justice.* Cambridge, MA: Harvard University Press.

Simon, J. G., C. W. Powers and J. P. Gunnemann. 1972. *The Ethical Investor: Universities and Corporate Responsibility.* New Haven, CT: Yale University Press.

Skidelsky, R. 2010. *Keynes: The Return of the Master.* New York: Public Affairs.

Solum, L. B. 2009. "Legal Theory Lexicon: The Reasonable Person," *Legal Theory Blog*, April 6. http://lsolum.typepad.com/legaltheory/2009/04/legal-theory-lexicon-the-reasonable-person.html.

Thornley, B., D. Wood, K. Grace and S. Sullivant. 2010. *Impact Investing: A Framework for Policy Design and Analysis.* Cambridge, MA: Initiative for Responsible Investment.

Youngdahl, J. 2010. "Fiduciary Duty: Challenges to the Traditional View," presented at the Program for Advanced Trustees Studies, Harvard Law School, Cambridge, MA, July 28.

Waitzer, E. 2009. "Defeating Short-Termism: Why Pension Funds Must Lead," *Rotman International Journal of Pension Management* 2 (2): 4–8.

WCED. 1987. *Our Common Future, Report of the World Commission on Environment and Development.* Published as Annex to General Assembly document A/42/427, Development and International Co-operation: Environment, August 2.

Williams Walsh, M. 2004. "Teamsters Find Pensions at Risk," *New York Times*, November 15.

Socially responsible investment and the conceptual limits of fiduciary duty

JOAKIM SANDBERG

Introduction

Socially responsible investment (SRI) can be defined as the practice of integrating putatively social, ethical and/or environmental considerations into one's financial investment process. Whereas conventional or mainstream investment focuses solely upon financial risk and return, SRI also includes social or environmental goals or constraints in decisions over whether to, for example, acquire, hold or dispose of a particular investment. This practice has received increased attention over the last couple of decades (Eurosif 2010; Social Investment Forum 2010). However, the factor that many commentators think will determine whether it can grow further in the future is whether SRI is a viable form of investment for large-scale institutional investors like pension funds (Kiernan 2002; Sparkes and Cowton 2004).

Pension funds are basically enormous pools of money, invested in a wide array of shares and bonds on the stock market with the ultimate aim of providing retirement income for future pensioners. These funds have become the dominant players on the world's financial markets over the past fifty years or so. For instance, global pension assets are estimated to be worth some $24 trillion (IFSL 2009). Quite obviously, if a lot of pension funds could be persuaded to invest according to social and environmental guidelines, the SRI movement could become an important force for corporate social responsibility worldwide. But in what manner or for what reason could they be persuaded to do so – that is, how could one justify pension funds' engagement in SRI?

This chapter seeks to answer this question by addressing a more specific politico-legal problem, namely that arising from pension funds' so-called fiduciary duties. Put briefly, the problem originates from the fact that pension funds manage money that ultimately belongs to someone else – to present and future retirement pensioners – and by law they have certain obligations towards these underlying owners. Among other things, the law states that they are required to manage their funds in the best (financial) interest of the beneficiaries and to do so without attending to personal biases. A vast amount of pension fund trustees around the world interpret this legislation as precluding them from doing anything else than seeking maximum returns on investments, which generally is considered to rule out SRI. In a survey among American pension fund trustees, for example, as many as 45 percent indicated that considerations of fiduciary duty were their main reason for not engaging more actively in SRI (Hess 2007). But is this negative view really correct?

In the recent debate among both academics and practitioners, one could say that two kinds of "solutions" have been presented to open up for SRI. (1) Some suggest that the view above simply is incorrect; that is, that already the current legislation allows pension funds to engage in SRI. There are two versions of this idea. According to one, it is simply a mistake to think that SRI is incompatible with the duty of seeking maximum returns. According to the other, the mistake is rather in equating fiduciary duty with the duty of seeking maximum returns. (There will be much more on both of these views below.) (2) Others argue that the current legislation indeed precludes SRI. However, what we need is simply some reinterpretation of fiduciary duty that puts stronger emphasis on the social and environmental dimensions. That is, fiduciary duty should "really" be understood in a slightly different manner, and we then need our politicians to update the relevant legal framework.

I will here take a pessimistic stance and argue that none of these "solutions" will work. That is, fiduciary duty cannot be reconciled with SRI; at least not for a sufficiently wide set of social and environmental issues. If we still want our pension funds to engage more actively in SRI, then, we must seek justification for this elsewhere – perhaps in what I call independent social or environmental obligations (more on this at the end of the chapter). It should be noted that my main concern is not with legal matters or how the current legislation should be "correctly" interpreted (a project of legal clarification). Rather, I will address the more theoretical issue of how far the *concept* of fiduciary duty can be "stretched" to accommodate for SRI (a project of conceptual clarification). By carefully going through a range of variations in how the fiduciary duties of pension funds can (philosophically) be understood, I hope to provide an evaluation of the contemporary debate that is independent of squabbles about existing law.

The chapter proceeds as follows: I start with exploring the limits of the traditional view that equates fiduciary duty with a duty to seek maximum returns. Thereafter, I move through increasingly revisionary territory: The third section explores slightly alternative interpretations of this view, whereas the fourth section discusses the view that trustees may take beneficiaries' ethical opinions into account. I then discuss the idea that beneficiaries' interests should be understood more broadly as their welfare interests. Finally I discuss the idea that the group of beneficiaries as such should be expanded to include further stakeholders. After having gone through these interpretations, I briefly elaborate on my own positive suggestion about independent social and environmental obligations. The chapter closes with a brief summary.

The traditional view

"Fiduciary" comes from a Latin verb meaning "to trust" and, hence, "fiduciary duties" is the common term for the duties which trustees – e.g., pension funds – have towards their beneficiaries – e.g., present and future retirement pensioners. It should be noted from the start that the extent to which these duties are legally defined, how they are legally defined and then how they are understood in practice and what specific requirements they impose on pension funds varies to some extent between jurisdictions and circumstance (as witnessed by many other chapters in this volume). It is therefore difficult to be specific about the exact formulations or codifications of these duties in contemporary law. As a rough and general background to our present discussion, however, we may say that fiduciary duty generally consists in two tenets (Watt 2006; Whitfield 2005): first, an idea about adequate aims; namely that trustees are to manage their funds in the interests of the ultimate beneficiaries and not in their own self-interest. This is sometimes called the "duty of loyalty," and may be stated more generally as the duty to act in accordance with the purpose of the underlying trust arrangement. Second, an idea about adequate means; namely that trustees are to exercise due care and prudence when managing their funds. This is sometimes referred to as the "prudent man rule" and is typically taken to imply that trustees should, for example, seek adequate information before making investment decisions and carefully weigh the expected risk and return of possible investments.

The two tenets roughly combine into the idea that trustees are to act prudently in the interest of their beneficiaries. But now, what would a prudent man do with a chunk of money to invest? Perhaps it is not so strange that the received view equates fiduciary duty with an obligation to seek maximum risk-adjusted returns on investments. According to the classic and oft-cited commentary of the Chicago law professors Langbein and Posner (1980: 98), for instance: "The duty of prudent investing … reinforces the duty of loyalty in forbidding the trustee to invest for any other object than the highest return consistent with the preferred level of portfolio risk." Furthermore, this is then thought to forbid trustees from taking various nonfinancial considerations into account in their investment decisions. As Langbein and Posner (1980: 98) put it, "both the duty of loyalty and the prudent man rule would be violated if a fiduciary were to make an ... investment decision based on other objectives, such as to promote [job security or social welfare]."

Proponents of the SRI movement have long sought to challenge Langbein and Posner's conclusion in various ways. Judging from recent discussions, it seems fair to say that attempts at justifications embedded directly in the traditional interpretation of fiduciary duty have stirred up the most enthusiasm. Justifications of this type are central in the influential "Freshfields Report"; a legal report promoted by the Finance Initiative of the United Nations Environment Programme (Freshfields Bruckhaus Deringer 2005). While the report roughly confirms the traditional equation of fiduciary duty with a duty to seek maximum returns, its originality lies in a series of arguments supposed to show that this does not rule out SRI. Indeed, according to the report's main argument, integrating social or environmental concerns is *obligatory* when such concerns are financially relevant; that is, when a given company's social or environmental performance reasonably can be expected to have an impact on its financial performance or valuation. The authors contend:

> In our view, decision-makers are required to have regard (at some level) to ESG considerations in every decision they make. This is because there is a body of credible evidence demonstrating that such considerations often have a role to play in the proper analysis of investment value. As such they cannot be ignored, because doing so may result in investments being given an inappropriate value (ibid.: 10–11).

The Freshfields Report has been called "the single most effective document for promoting the integration of environmental, social and governance (ESG) issues into institutional investment" (UNEP FI 2009: 13). And most of the recent praise has focused on the argument above, even though the report covers a lot of ground (see Sandberg 2011). But how far does this argument really extend pension funds' possibility to engage in SRI?

The financial relevance of social and environmental considerations has been the subject of a great amount of academic studies over the past couple of decades. In a recent meta-analysis, probably the most ambitious one to date, Margolis et al.

(2007) compared a total of 192 statements in as many as 167 previous studies on the link between what they call corporate social performance (CSP) and corporate financial performance (CFP). The result of their analysis is that the overall link seems "positive but small" (ibid.: 2). However, what is most interesting in the present context is the spread or, perhaps one may say, the fragility of results unveiled by the analysis. A clear majority (58 percent) of the studies actually found no statistically significant relationship between CSP and CFP, whereas 27 percent found a positive relationship and 2 percent a negative relationship (ibid.: 21).

The authors suggest that the variation to some extent can be explained by differences in how CSP and CFP were defined in the studies, and perhaps also by differences in research methodology. Indeed, in a more detailed analysis of the results, they found that some aspects of CSP seemed more strongly correlated with CFP than others (ibid.: 17–21). However, they hesitate to draw any general conclusions even on these aspects. In the end, the authors suggest that "[t]he variation in results across types and measures of CSP may itself be the most important signal to emerge from the 35 years of research on the connection between CSP and CFP" (ibid.: 24).

This meta-analysis undermines the suggestion that there is clear evidence for saying that social and environmental considerations always – or even most often – have financial relevance, at least on the level of individual companies and investments. But if this is correct, it seems that the above argument from the Freshfields Report does not extend pension funds' possibility for engaging in SRI very far. Whereas they may be allowed to act on *some* social or environmental considerations under *some* circumstances, that is, they have no legal justification for continuously doing so as a matter of principle. And taking a step back from the empirical enquiries, I suggest that the fragility of the results should come as no surprise from a theoretical point of view. We are talking about certain *non*financial considerations after all, and whether companies choose to engage on social or ethical dimensions is supposed to be motivated, at least to some extent, by directly social or ethical reasons quite apart from their motivation to seek maximum profits.

Intuitively, then, the relationship between social and environmental factors and financial performance could be a contingent one at best.

Reinterpreting the traditional view

The traditional understanding of fiduciary duty holds that pension fund trustees should maximize the risk-adjusted returns on investments or, more generally, provide financial benefits for their beneficiaries. But precisely what does this mean? In order to avoid the troubling results above, a first thing that SRI proponents can do is to reinterpret the traditional view only slightly. It may be noted that the Freshfields Report is silent on the issue of over what *timeframe* social and environmental considerations may be financially relevant, and it also seemingly focuses on the level of *individual* companies or investments. Here there are at least two possible alternative interpretations of fiduciary duty.

First, SRI proponents may suggest that pension funds should be more interested in profitability over the long term, and perhaps the connection between CSP and CFP gets stronger with time. This is indeed a fairly common hypothesis among SRI proponents. According to Sethi (2005: 103), for example, the fiduciary duties of pension fund trustees require them to base investment decisions on "a careful assessment of long-term risks and benefits of investments." On this note, it is argued that the term "nonfinancial" considerations is misguided: "The long-term implications of SRI are anything but non-financial" (ibid.: 100). Most importantly, "companies conducting their operations in a socially responsible manner should be viewed as comparatively better and relatively safer long-term investment choices" (ibid.: 101).

Additionally or alternatively, SRI proponents may argue that pension funds should be concerned with the overall profitability of their *portfolios*, and perhaps the link between CSP and CFP is stronger on a more general level in the economy. This hypothesis is becoming increasingly popular and is sometimes called the "universal owner thesis," as put forward by Hawley and Williams (2000). According to their thesis, pension funds typically invest in a very large sample of companies across different industries and places and, therefore, the returns on their portfolios will depend on "the overall health of the economy." Now, while individual companies often may be able to avoid bearing the full costs of their poor social or environmental performance – that is, the costs are "externalized" and CSP is decoupled from CFP locally – it is argued that these costs will be borne by other companies in the economy. Hawley and Williams conclude: "a universal owner that really wants to maximize the shareholder value of its portfolio would need to develop public policy-like positions and monitor regulatory developments and legislation on a number of key issues to the economy as a whole" (ibid.: 170). In other words, pension funds are more likely to maximize portfolio returns if they take social and environmental considerations into account.

I contend that both of the suggestions above are interesting and deserve further attention from both investors and scholars. But do they really ground an extended possibility on the part of pension funds to engage in SRI? Unfortunately, even proponents of the SRI movement must accept that there is no solid empirical evidence in support of them at the present stage; and so they are best described as optimistic hypotheses. For example, it may be noted that many of the studies included in Margolis et al.'s (2007) meta-analysis above concern exactly the long-term correlation between CSP and CFP, and yet the analysis showed no stable results. Similarly none of the summaries published by the UNEP Finance Initiative itself show that there always – or even most often – is a connection between CSP and CFP over the long term (see Sandberg 2011).

Whether there is a connection between the social and financial performance of very large investment portfolios is difficult to test empirically and, to my knowledge, no solid evidence has yet to be presented either way. However, there would at least seem to be anecdotal evidence *against* the universal owner thesis. Many influential scholars have noted the existence of severe externalities also on the societal (or indeed global) level related to issues such as global poverty and climate change (Pogge 2008; Stern 2007). According to these scholars, it is exactly the fact that so few companies (and, for that matter, governments) have been ready to bear the cost for these things that has created a need for action on the part of international charities and non-governmental organizations.

The considerations above suggest that while SRI proponents may *want* there to be a connection between CSP and CFP, simply wanting something to be the case does not make it so. This point may seem trivial enough, but it highlights a more fundamental problem with all attempts at justifying SRI from an appeal to financial relevance. Arguably, part of the reasoning behind the SRI movement is exactly that SRI *as such* could be a force for penalizing poor social or environmental performance – that is, that pension funds should be able to *create* a link between CSP and CFP (see Haigh and Hazelton 2004; Rivoli 2003). However, if SRI only can be justified by reference to the prior existence of such a link, then obviously we have a problem. Or at least, I suggest, the SRI of pension funds could only be reactive and never truly proactive on this view.

The ethical opinions of beneficiaries

If it is not possible to justify SRI by an appeal to financial relevance, the obvious alternative may seem to be to rethink the exclusive focus on beneficiaries' *financial* interests. We are here leaving the traditional understanding of fiduciary duty behind us but, as we soon will see, many SRI proponents indeed question this understanding. For example, Peter Kinder, president of the largest SRI analyst firm in the US, suggests that "[t]he principle of the beneficiaries' 'best interests' is not restricted to financial benefit. Having regard to ESG issues is about more than financial performance: it is about asking business to move away from prioritizing profit over all else" (Freshfields Bruckhaus Deringer 2005: 28).

A first issue on this new path is precisely what nonfinancial interests trustees should aim at instead. Judging from the last point above, the most straightforward idea may be that trustees should take their beneficiaries' *ethical* "interests" or opinions into account – that is, beneficiaries' direct views on what companies are socially and environmentally sustainable. After all, SRI is exactly

investment directed by social and environmental concerns. This is indeed the main suggestion in the extensive legal commentary on SRI by Richardson (2007, 2008, 2011). Richardson rather straightforwardly suggests that:

> The duty of loyalty has been interpreted as requiring the trustees to demonstrate that the decision is motivated only by the financial interests of the beneficiary. […] However, a "benefit" is not necessarily confined to a financial benefit. If beneficiaries share a moral objection to a particular form of investment, it could be construed as for their benefit if the trust avoided that investment, possibly even at the cost of a lower financial return (Richardson 2007: 158–9).

Interestingly, this particular quote is talking about existing law – that is, it is suggested that already the current legislation permits trustees to take their beneficiaries' ethical views into account. A similar position is taken by the Freshfields Report, which notes that "[c]ourts in the UK have recognised that … the concept of beneficiaries' 'best interests' under a general pension trust may extend beyond their financial interests to include their 'views on moral and social matters.' In a similar way, US law permits investments to be excluded where the beneficiaries so consent" (Freshfields Bruckhaus Deringer 2005: 12). But we must now ask our perennial question: exactly how far does this provision extend pension funds' possibility to engage in SRI?

The obvious problem with the line of reasoning above, I submit, is that different beneficiaries have different ethical opinions – that is, that you get different "values" or "views on social matters" depending on what beneficiaries you ask. According to the Freshfields Report, the straightforward rule in this context is that trustees only are allowed to exclude investments for ethical reasons when they have reason to believe that *all* beneficiaries consent to doing so – "[a] decision-maker who chooses to exclude an investment or category of investments on this basis will need to be able to point to a consensus amongst the beneficiaries in support of the exclusion" (ibid.). The reason for this is that trustees are required to treat beneficiaries even-handedly, and to not take sides between different groups (this is sometimes called the duty of impartiality, see Richardson 2011). But what are really the odds of there being many social or environmental issues on which trustees would be able to point to a consensus among all of their beneficiaries; that is, among both present and future pensioners, and also their dependents?

Proponents of the SRI movement may here try a number of counterargument strategies. They may first try to downplay the problem and suggest that the possibility of finding a consensus really depends on the particular ethical issue at hand. Richardson (2007: 166) at one point, curiously, suggests that the consensus problem is exaggerated: "While disagreements will most likely permeate traditional ethical or religious issues, such as alcohol or gambling," he writes, "substantial agreement in other areas may readily arise. For instance, members of a pension fund probably rarely favour deliberate environmental degradation or human rights' violation." I agree that there may be some interesting differences between different ethical issues in this way, but in the end it is hard to avoid finding this comment naïve. Even though many pension fund members may think that environmental degradation is ethically problematic to some extent, they will disagree about precisely how unethical it is and what their pension fund should do about it – most importantly, to what extent it is adequate to sacrifice financial returns in order to avoid supporting it (see my empirical research in Chapter 27 of this volume). As far as the concrete ethical choices facing pension trustees are concerned, then, the lack of consensus on social and environmental issues among beneficiaries is a very real problem.

A second kind of counterargument strategy could be to suggest ways of getting around the problem. For example, after acknowledging that it often may be practically impossible to determine what beneficiaries want, the Freshfields Report unexpectedly suggests that trustees may use certain well-established social conventions as a kind of proxy for the ethical opinions of beneficiaries. This may be understood as a suggestion of how trustees can work around the consensus problem.

> Whilst there is little guidance directly on point, it can … be argued that even in the absence of …

express consensus, there will be a class of investments that a decision-maker is entitled to avoid on the grounds that their ESG characteristics are likely to make them so repugnant to beneficiaries that they should not be invested in, regardless of the financial return that they are expected to bring. It is not possible to define the parameters of this class, but it might include investments that are linked to clear breaches of widely recognised norms, such as conventions on the elimination of child labour (Freshfields Bruckhaus Deringer 2005: 12).

I can see the point of this suggestion, but once again I am not convinced that it solves much in the present context. It is true that there are some fairly robust social conventions on some of the issues raised by the SRI movement; for example, international treaties on environmental protection and labor standards signed by a majority of nations. But there is simply a vast range of important ethical issues where there are no clear social conventions or international political treaties (Sandberg 2011). Furthermore, it remains unclear how this suggestion is supposed to square with the original appeal to a consensus among beneficiaries. Even though at least some social conventions (such as national laws and international treaties) are the result of democratic processes, for example, this should in no way be taken to mean that everyone agrees with them.

Interestingly, Richardson acknowledges the greater complexity of the consensus problem in a later paper (Richardson 2011). But here he offers a different way to get around the problem. His suggestion now is that legislative improvements aimed at making beneficiaries more directly involved in their pension funds' decision-making processes may lead to increased consensus on many issues. This is so because "theories of ethical and democratic deliberation suggest that social values can evolve among participants through appropriately structured forums for reasoned discussion" (ibid.: 10). Strengthening the voice of beneficiaries themselves in fund governance thus "provides a concrete way of conveying their views and enabling trustees to make investment decisions legitimated by the imprimatur of the democratic process [– and i]t could even provide a framework for ethical deliberation to guide SRI" (ibid.: 14). I will not quarrel with this suggestion here, except to say that perhaps not all naïvety has been washed away. Presumably, not all ethical disagreements are dissolved by simply sitting down and talking it out.

The arguments above all try to mitigate the consensus problem. But a final strategy for SRI proponents in this context could be to simply accept it and embrace its implications. The idea here would roughly be that beneficiaries should be able to choose the ethical direction of their pension fund themselves, and perhaps we also need an expanded market of funds with different ethical outlooks. (There is already an element of choice in some pension fund arrangements, but this suggestion would go even further in that direction.) Many individuals may be enthusiastic about such a proposal, and it can also be a chance for pension funds to try to reach new client groups. I cannot discuss all aspects of this proposal in the present context since that would take us too far off topic. However, I think it suffices to say that the vision we are getting into really is quite different from the vision of SRI proponents. If beneficiaries could choose the ethical direction of their pension fund entirely on their own, it seems likely that the majority would choose non-SRI funds; that is, they would choose funds that give little or no attention to ethical considerations. Judging from what investment vehicles individuals choose in other contexts, at least, it seems safe to say that egoism often crowds out ethics.

The welfare interests of beneficiaries

The considerations above indicate that appealing directly to the ethical opinions of beneficiaries is unlikely to work. But perhaps there are other ways of appealing to the nonfinancial interests of beneficiaries? In the literature, at least one other interpretation of fiduciary duty along these lines can be found; namely the suggestion that pension fund trustees should act in ways that promote the interests of beneficiaries in a "broader" sense, which includes their welfare interests or their quality of life.

This interpretation has been defended by Joly (2002: 294), who argues that fiduciary duty needs to be reformed to require institutional investors to attend to the "broader welfare interests of their principals." Indeed he suggests that it is both "reasonable and prudent to accept some degree of sacrifice in financial performance in exchange for better health and quality of life." The underlying justification is formulated as follows:

> In the case of long-term savings and pension funds, the interests of owners could, without too much imagination, be understood to include their social and environmental interests in addition to their purely financial interests, insofar as the purpose of money is instrumental rather than an end in itself and if and when the process of creation of wealth is contradictory to the eventual enjoyment of such wealth. This point of view is captured by two rather commonsensical rhetorical questions: what good is money if it causes harm to its owners? What good are competitive returns in collective investment instruments like … pension annuities if the underlying companies do things that significantly deteriorate public health or degrade the quality of life of the public? (ibid.)

It seems possible to read Joly's argument in at least three different ways. On one reading, the point is simply that focusing only on beneficiaries' financial interests is too simplistic since they also have other kinds of interests including social and environmental ones. On another reading, the point is also that these interests may be more important to them than enjoying sizeable retirement benefits (see also Chapter 22 in this volume). On a third reading, the point is that their properly *enjoying* sizeable retirement benefits actually *requires* the fulfillment of some of their social or environmental interests (because what good are financial benefits if beneficiaries are unable to breathe?).

We now need to ask whether the present interpretation of fiduciary duty can be a full vindication of the idea that pension funds should engage in SRI. Unfortunately there are a number of problems. First of all, there is the familiar kind of problem stemming from the heterogeneity of beneficiaries; that is, that different beneficiaries are likely to have different welfare interests and it is difficult to see how trustees should prioritize between them. More importantly, I believe that there also is a limit to how much it is plausible to include in beneficiaries' "social and environmental interests." I will try to explain.

Consider first issues where the primary reason for action is of a deontological nature; I believe that discrimination is such an issue. Many SRI agents refrain from investing in, or choose to engage in progressive dialogue with companies that discriminate against women or minorities in their employment practices (see Domini 2001; Sparkes 2002). But what is the point of doing this? I contend that the point simply is to counteract practices that are morally wrong or unjust and that this has little to do with anyone's welfare interests. It is of course possible to argue that non-discrimination is in the interests of women and minorities and, since these groups also will become pensioners in the future, it may be in the interest of at least some pension funds' beneficiaries. But is not the latter connection far-fetched?

If the example above is unconvincing, consider instead issues that primarily concern third parties' interests. As the Freshfields Report suggests, there is a fairly broad societal consensus in Western countries that child labor is morally repugnant. Hence, many SRI agents refrain from investing in, or choose to engage in progressive dialogue with, companies that are suspected of using child labor (ibid.). But in whose interests is this done? It seems that the natural reply here concerns the affected children (mainly living in the developing world), rather than the beneficiaries of some Western pension fund. These beneficiaries may of course care about the children that are affected. It is also possible that at least some of the children will move to the West and end up as beneficiaries of a pension fund. But once again, are not these connections to beneficiaries far-fetched?

The examples above indicate a limit in how far the present interpretation of fiduciary duty is able to justify SRI. To put this point bluntly, it is unlikely that doing the right thing always will be in the interests of a given pension fund's members – even if these are more or less the entire population of a Western country, and even on a broader conception of welfare interests.

Expanding the group of beneficiaries

The final kind of reinterpretation that we will discuss here is one that tries to recast the group of relevant beneficiaries so as to justify pension funds' engagement in SRI in this way. I just said that it seems far-fetched to try to connect all social and environmental problems to the members of a given pension fund. But one may thus wonder whether it is possible to find a different way of delimiting the relevant beneficiaries.

This idea is certainly not as prominent as the previous ones, but some authors in the recent literature indeed suggest that trustees' fiduciary duties extend to people beyond their beneficiaries. For example, according to Viederman (2008: 192): "Fiduciaries must also consider the social and environmental consequences for the investors, the beneficiaries and society at large. We are all universal owners, as shareowners and stakeholders." A similar formulation can be found in Richardson's work, although not fully distinguishable from the suggestion discussed above.

> In reframing financial institutions, a potential model for reform would be to expand fiduciary obligations beyond the investors they serve to a broader stakeholder community. This would require a redefinition of the law of fiduciary responsibility to require fiduciaries to promote the interests of an expanded concept of beneficiary with broader social interests for sustainability (Richardson 2008: 540).

I suggest that SRI proponents that are keen on expanding the group of beneficiaries should take note of the concept of stakeholders invoked above. Speaking in terms of obligations to stakeholders is often a neat way of codifying more elusive social and environmental obligations. In the contemporary business ethics literature, for instance, a growing number of scholars support what has become known as the stakeholder theory of the firm, which holds that corporations have ethical obligations not only to their shareholders but also to consumers, employees, suppliers and local communities. The stakeholder concept is typically defined very broadly in this literature; for example as "any group or individual that can affect or be affected by the realization of an organization's purpose" (Freeman et al. 2010: 26). Equipped with this concept, SRI proponents could argue in an analogue manner that pension fund trustees have responsibilities also towards destitute children in the developing world, because these are people that (at least potentially) are affected by the funds' actions.

I am tentatively positive towards this way of expanding the group of people towards which pension funds have obligations. But I believe that an important question is whether it makes sense to think of these as *fiduciary* obligations. My plain suggestion is that it does not. In order for someone to be a beneficiary in the standard sense, it would seem necessary not only that they "can be affected" by a given pension fund's activities indirectly, but that they have a more direct connection to the aims for which the pension fund was set up or for which contributions were paid into it. Perhaps destitute children in developing countries are important stakeholders whose needs really should be considered, but I suggest that it just seems far-fetched to include them among the beneficiaries or members of our pension funds.

To put this in other words: my ultimate contention is that the suggestions above have taken us too far outside the normal realm of the concepts of both beneficiary and fiduciary duty. I have tried to show this by putting them in the end of a long line of possible (re-)interpretations of fiduciary duty, starting with the traditional ones and moving my way into increasingly revisionary territory. To the extent that it still is politically desirable to give pension funds obligations towards an expanded group of stakeholders, I suggest that a more promising path forward – rather than taking the route via fiduciary duty – is to talk about independent social and environmental obligations. Before leaving, let me say a bit more about this alternative.

Independent social and environmental obligations

As I intend the term, a pension fund has *independent* social and environmental obligations if it is required to take into account certain social and environmental aspects of the activities of corporations *irrespective* of whether this is in its beneficiaries' interest. We may say that these social and environmental obligations are owed to society and the environment *directly*, then, rather than to the (possible) fact that beneficiaries happen to care about or depend upon these things. Or, what is essentially the same, the reason for why pension funds should engage in SRI has to do with social and environmental considerations *as such*, and not with the interests of the funds' beneficiaries. For example, the reason why they should interact with companies on child labor (if they indeed should do so) is not that child labor hurts beneficiaries, but instead that it is morally repugnant and wrong.

As should be obvious from this brief characterization, independent social and environmental obligations may or may not coincide with fiduciary duties under the various interpretations discussed above. At some times and on some issues, the two may complement each other, whereas they most probably will come into conflict at other times and on other issues. I do not at this point wish to say anything more substantial about how these things should be weighed against each other in concrete legislation; that is, whether independent social and environmental obligations should be allowed to (always or sometimes) trump fiduciary obligations, or the other way around. I may simply warn that the former run a great risk of becoming toothless and pointless if they are not given sufficient priority – for example if social and environmental efforts are not allowed to cost anything at all (for more on this, see Sandberg 2011).

Many details remain to be filled in before my suggestion is practically usable. Some central issues are, for example, exactly what social and environmental aspects are relevant, what specific investment strategies are most suitable to handle these issues, and to what precise extent profits may be sacrificed. However, many of these details have to be filled in irrespective of the chosen justification. I must in the end acknowledge that what I am proposing simply is a better *structure* for justifying pension funds' engagement in SRI. The important point is that SRI needs a justification that fits its nature better than the legal construct of fiduciary duty.

Conclusions

A critical issue for the future growth of socially responsible investment (SRI) is to what extent institutional investors such as pension funds can be persuaded to engage in it. In this chapter, I have considered various attempts at justifying such engagement stemming from a range of possible (re-)interpretations of the fiduciary duties of pension fund trustees towards their beneficiaries. Previous commentators on these issues, in academia and elsewhere, have suggested that fiduciary duties either already mandate SRI for pension funds (because many social and environmental aspects are financially relevant, or because beneficiaries generally care about these issues); or it is suggested that they at least can be made to do so rather easily (through reinterpretations that focus more on the long term or on the general welfare interests of beneficiaries). In contrast with this, however, I have found that none of the considered interpretations is able to justify engagement on social and environmental issues across the board. Indeed, to some extent the problem seems rooted in the very concept of fiduciary duty, which ties pension funds to the interests (financial or otherwise) of a rather limited group of people (the beneficiaries), which often lacks direct connection to the ethical issues at hand.

My results should not be taken to mean that pension funds' engagement in SRI is unjustified or unjustifiable more generally. Towards the end of the chapter I suggested that a more promising way forward could be through what I call independent social or environmental obligations. Many details remain to be filled in concerning this suggestion, but I at least hope that it provides a better structure for the political support of SRI. The important point is that SRI needs a justification which fits its nature better than the legal construct of fiduciary duty.

Acknowledgements

This chapter is an abridged and revised version of the article "(Re-)Interpreting Fiduciary Duty to Justify Socially Responsible Investment for Pension Funds?" *Corporate Governance: An International Review* 21 (5): 436–46. Reprinted with permission from John Wiley & Sons.

The author gratefully acknowledges financial support from the Swedish Foundation for Strategic Environmental Research (Mistra) through the Sustainable Investment Research Platform (SIRP).

References

Domini, A. L. 2001. *Socially Responsible Investing: Making a Difference and Making Money.* Chicago: Dearborn Trade.

Eurosif. 2010. *European SRI Study*. Paris: Eurosif.

Freeman, R. E., J. S. Harrison, A. C. Wicks, B. L. Parmar and S. de Colle. 2010. *Stakeholder Theory: The State of the Art*. Cambridge University Press.

Freshfields Bruckhaus Deringer. 2005. *A Legal Framework for the Integration of Environmental, Social and Governance Issues into Institutional Investment*. Report produced for UNEP FI.

Haigh, M. and J. Hazelton. 2004. "Financial Markets: A Tool for Social Responsibility?" *Journal of Business Ethics* 52: 59–71.

Hawley, J. P. and A. T. Williams. 2000. *The Rise of Fiduciary Capitalism*. Philadelphia: University of Pennsylvania Press.

Hess, D. 2007. "Public Pensions and the Promise of Shareholder Activism for the Next Frontier of Corporate Governance," working paper, Ross School of Business, University of Michigan.

International Financial Services London (IFSL). 2009. *Fund Management 2009*. London: IFSL.

Joly, C. 2002. "The Greening of Financial Markets," in *Finance for Sustainable Development*. New York: United Nations.

Kiernan, M. 2002. "SRI: From the Margins to the Mainstream," in P. Camejo (ed.) *The SRI Advantage*. Gabriola Island, BC: New Society Publishers.

Langbein, J. H. and R. A. Posner. 1980. "Social Investing and the Law of Trusts," *Michigan Law Review* 79 (1): 72–112.

Margolis, J. D., H. A. Elfenbein and J. P. Walsh. 2007. "Does it Pay to be Good?" working paper, Harvard Business School.

Pogge, T. 2008. *World Poverty and Human Rights*, 2nd edn. Cambridge: Polity Press.

Richardson, B. J. 2007. "Do the Fiduciary Duties of Pension Funds Hinder Socially Responsible Investment?" *Banking and Finance Law Review* 22 (2): 145–201.

   2008. *Socially Responsible Investment Law*. New York: Oxford University Press.

   2011. "From Fiduciary Duties to Fiduciary Relationships for Socially Responsible Investment," *Journal of Sustainable Finance & Investment* 1: 5–19.

Rivoli, P. 2003. "Making a Difference or Making a Statement? Finance Research and Socially Responsible Investment," *Business Ethics Quarterly* 13 (3): 271–87.

Sandberg, J. 2011. "Socially Responsible Investment and Fiduciary Duty: Putting the Freshfields Report into Perspective," *Journal of Business Ethics* 101 (1): 143–62.

Sethi, S. P. 2005. "Investing in Socially Responsible Companies is a Must for Public Pension Funds," *Journal of Business Ethics* 56: 99–129.

Social Investment Forum. 2010. *Report on Socially Responsible Investing Trends in the United States*. Washington, DC: SIF.

Sparkes, R. 2002. *Socially Responsible Investment: A Global Revolution*. New York: John Wiley & Sons.

Sparkes, R. and C. J. Cowton. 2004. "The Maturing of Socially Responsible Investment: A Review of the Developing Link with Corporate Social Responsibility," *Journal of Business Ethics* 52 (1): 45–57.

Stern, N. 2007. *The Economics of Climate Change: The Stern Review*. Cambridge University Press.

United Nations Environment Programme Finance Initiative (UNEP FI). 2009. *Fiduciary Responsibility: Legal and Practical Aspects of Integrating Environmental, Social and Governance Issues into Institutional Investment*. Geneva: UNEP FI.

Viederman, S. 2008. "Fiduciary Duty," in C. Krosinsky and N. Robins (eds.) *Sustainable Investing: The Art of Long-Term Performance*. London: Earthscan.

Watt, G. 2006. *Trusts and Equity*, 2nd edn. New York: Oxford University Press.

Whitfield, J. 2005. "Trustees' Investment Duties," in C. Scanlan (ed.) *Socially Responsible Investment: A Guide for Pension Schemes and Charities*. London: Key Haven.

Fiduciary duty at the intersection of business and society

REBECCA K. DARR

Introduction

Like a Rorschach drawing, views about the "business and society perspective" on the fiduciary duty of institutional investors appear to be in the eye of the beholder. Since the Aspen Institute is known for its transformative dialogues through the convening of strange bedfellows, the author sought to mirror how the Aspen Institute works, selectively crowd-sourcing a quilt of views. In so doing, the author interviewed sixteen people with deep experience in the capital markets, including "insiders" who live the day-to-day of what it means to be a fiduciary and who reside in Asia, Europe and North America. The resulting interviews illuminated a range of perspectives, which seem to demonstrate that broader societal expectations of institutional investors around the world are increasing, although at different speeds – and these societal expectations may not yet be construed as legal duty.

When asked to reflect on what the subject of this book chapter means to them or their organizations, most experts began by deconstructing the component parts – "business and society" and "fiduciary duty." A few experts sought to broaden the frame in which the question was asked and argued that understanding must begin first with context, a context understood philosophically or pragmatically. In this chapter, we will present the highlights of what was shared by the interviewees and:

(1) consider how one's framing significantly affects the response;
(2) see how a "business and society perspective" can be implemented practically by institutional investors; and finally
(3) note where there may be room for change and where there are open questions.

Definitions

For an investor to take into account a "business and society perspective" meant different things to the experts, but generally they described a concept beyond an immediate financial return, including responsible investing, corporate responsibility as applied to portfolio companies, social/environmental sustainability, environmental, social and governance (ESG) factors and a concern for the externalities produced by most forms of capitalism.

As for the meaning of "fiduciary duty," most believed that there is a narrow definition of such duty that does not vary by fund size: a financial fiduciary acts in the beneficiaries' interests. For most institutional investors, this practically means maximizing the risk-adjusted returns for a portfolio over a predefined timeframe. For others, such as state or national pension funds, the mandate may be the maximization of returns plus a commitment to invest locally a percentage of the portfolio. However, the author was reminded by several experts that the basis of fiduciary duty, at least in common law countries, is trust law; thus duty is whatever a trustor outlines as the trustees' duties plus any prevailing national regulations. A smaller portion of experts believed that a broader definition of "fiduciary duty" was possible especially if one considers the extent to which the trustee is acting on behalf of the beneficiaries' interests and the timeframe in which these interests are considered. Finally, one expert on governance in Korea stated that the concept of fiduciary duty of institutional investors was still a foreign one in his country, let alone the implementation of a "business and society perspective" on such a duty.

Context

Reminded by several experts that legal duties do not exist in a vacuum, the author asked interviewees to consider what fiduciary duty means in the broader environment in which investment decisions are made. Opinions of interviewees diverged on a multitude of dimensions and some of that ground would be covered here, starting first with the pragmatic.

Mindy Lubber, president of the US-based environmental NGO Ceres, provided one perspective on the pragmatic context in which investors operate:

> Institutional investors, like other investors and companies, have a license to operate. They, then, need to look at risk and opportunity as part of what they do, whether it is described as fiduciary duty or not. I believe all capital market institutions have a duty to look at risk in a broad way including climate change, supply chain, reputation, safety. Institutional investors are invested in a lot and therefore have an obligation to look at the "true value of the investment," which needs to be broader than the narrow definition of risk versus return and alpha. Some investors are looking at "true value." Some aren't.

Damon Silvers, director of policy and special counsel of the AFL-CIO, the Labor Federation of fifty-five US unions, shared another view on the pragmatic context in which fiduciary duty plays out:

> There isn't a broad versus narrow interpretation [of fiduciary duty] at all. Under US law, there's a single doctrine ... What is most important is what happens next: how these duties are understood in the world. So the question [of a business and society perspective on fiduciary duty] is not a legal question, but rather an empirical one.

Klaus Leisinger, chairman of the Novartis Foundation for Sustainable Development, reminds us that different mental filters influence how an individual considers institutional investor duties from a business and society perspective. He noted:

> Human beings perceive the world around them through a filter made up of personal preferences, value judgments, worldviews and "lessons learned" from past experience ... [C]onclusions derived from social science and political analysis depend to a large extent on personal values, worldviews (for example, about the "right" thing to do), and axiomatic assumptions (for example, on the legitimacy of market mechanisms versus a "rights-based" approach). Such judgments are not only a theoretical academic matter – they very practically influence an individual's viewpoint about whose interests should be pursued with what priority – and who should pay for it in what kind of a timeframe.

Therefore, the answers to "what is business?" and "how does it and should it interact with society?" change dramatically depending on one's mental filters. For example, said Leisinger, "someone who assumes that the *business of business* is *business* ... will define the role of a business enterprise structurally different than someone who sees a business enterprise as an 'organ of society'" (Friedman 1962: 133). Further, he adds, "If one understands profits as sustained proceeds from corporate activities pursued in a responsible way, one is likely to work on the assumption that sustained earnings can only be realized if and when a company uses its resources in a socially responsible, environmentally sustainable and politically acceptable way."

Timeframe

As the author's work at the Aspen Institute is largely focused on capital markets' short-termism, she was not surprised that timeframe came up repeatedly, unsolicited, in interviews for this book chapter. Timeframe becomes critical to the fulfillment of one's fiduciary duty if one's definition involves "maximizing the risk-adjusted returns for a portfolio over a predefined timeframe." For the end beneficiaries who hope to receive a payout for a future retirement or other long-term goals and for the companies that aim to have patient, long-term investors, time horizons are also important. Yet the author was surprised by the ways in which the question of timeframe inserted itself into understanding the "business and society perspective" of the fiduciary duty of institutional investors.

The time horizon and liabilities of an institutional investor should dominate buy and sell decisions, such as valuation calculations (how far your spreadsheet models go out), as well as the degree to which an investor decides to engage with a company or sector. For an institutional investor with long-term liabilities, Dan Feldman, associate professor of public management at City University of New York, believes that

> Fiduciaries of [such] funds with permanent responsibilities to beneficiaries should see themselves as very long-term investors, perhaps "perpetual" investors. They should, therefore, be wary of companies that may be pursuing short-term gains at the expense of their long-term prospects and open to [investing in] companies that show outstanding long-term prospects.

If beat the market and exploit externalities over the long haul is the implicit or explicit modus operandi of an institutional investor, then this very strategy should be called into question by trustees. Silvers of the AFL-CIO remarked that "most investors cannot systematically beat the market, nor can you in the long run exploit externalities."

He added that one implication of the inability to neither systematically beat the market nor take advantage of externalities over the long haul for long-term oriented institutional investors is that it provides a justification for collective action; he continued:

> About fifty percent of investors [in listed companies in the US], right now, do have a horizon longer than one year. Those longer-term holders need to organize if they want to counterbalance the noise from the short-term holders. After all, if the long-term holders are looking to the market to solve problems, it will likely end badly for [the long-term investor], as the short-term traders, because they are transacting and setting market prices, may dominate the attention of management.

Another implication, according to Silvers, is that "diversified long-term global[1] investors are generally not in the position to lay off externalities on others: they really have to think and act in their investment behavior in the interest of the global economy and society."

Further, if trustees or managers are measuring an investment portfolio solely by short-term indicators, the fund may be missing the forest for the trees, and thereby neglecting to fulfill its fiduciary duties. As Mark J. P. Anson, chief investment officer at Acadia Investment Management, a new Bass Family Office, described:

> You might think that maximizing profits would not be incompatible with maximizing value, but they can be. Profits/returns are a much more short-term principle – quarterly or annual profit measures are examined. In contrast, maximization of value requires a much longer time horizon – it can be several years. Value maximization takes into account not only profits and returns, but the long-term sustainability issues that are beneficial to the long-term viability of an economic society: employment growth, the environment, improved welfare and labor productivity, etc.

If a company has no major investors pushing the management team to pursue success over the long haul, the natural, human bias of the company's board and management is to focus on short-term execution. Chancellor Leo E. Strine, Jr. of the Delaware Court of Chancery commented:

> If the electorate [the investor] acts as patient capitalists, this provides companies with more time to act on thoughtful business plans, the chance to make deeper investments, et cetera – all of which can be in the interest of both the business and society. You get decreased acts of social irresponsibility when no one is pushing a company to act in the gray areas of legal but risky behavior. But, you get the opposite if investors are too short-term sighted and exert pressure for immediate results. In reaction to markets that rewarded hinky behavior[2] that generated high GAAP profits,[3] WorldCom distorted the capital allocation of

---

[1] Even if an investor is not obviously global, Silvers notes that the proportion of assets and income derived from the domestic country alone is much lower than it used to be.

[2] Hinky is not a commonly used word in English. Oxford defines it as "dishonest or suspect," but it can also mean "suspicious" or "something that is wrong or out of place."

[3] GAAP (generally accepted accounting principles) refers to the accounting standards that are followed in the US, Australia, and some other countries. "GAAP profits" is shorthand for measures of accounting profits, based on choices made using GAAP. Implicit in Strine's remark is

its entire industry by its actions.[4] It had financial analysts asking other companies in the industry why they weren't following WorldCom's lead. And today, a further consequence of a company not following the "wise example of a WorldCom" could mean the effective firing of its board of directors [through the no-confidence vote allowed in the US].

As a long-term investor, the level of analysis that is conducted before and while holding an investment in a company needs to go beyond the company, looking at broader social and environmental challenges, while a short-term trader can get away with understanding the interesting and temporary trends that face a company, an industry or an economy. Dr. Daniel Summerfield, co-head of Responsible Investment for Universities Superannuation Scheme Ltd., shared an overview of their investment process, noting that "we look at the company, sector, and market-wide issues … We are involved in lots of projects that consider industry issues twenty years out. It's not necessarily just about how long we will hold a company."

Fund size and other characteristics of an institutional investor

Experts were asked to reflect on the following question: "With respect to 'a business and society perspective,' does the fiduciary duty of an institutional investor change depending on the size of the investment fund (that is, do large and small funds have the same responsibilities with respect to societal concerns)?" The general consensus of the experts interviewed was that fiduciary duty is the same for institutional investors with identical mandates but differing sizes; however, an institutional investor's ability to act with greater attention

that accounting performance measures, which are by definition backward-looking, are not necessarily good predictors of future company value, or even current value.

[4] Some of the top executives at WorldCom, the second largest US-based telecommunications company in the early 2000s, were found to have manipulated WorldCom's accounting in order for it to appear stronger than it was and to support its story of high growth potential (and hence, a higher stock price).

to a business and society perspective does, can and perhaps should differ with size.

Experts provided similar responses to the first part of the question: "Does fiduciary duty change with fund size?" For example, Anson of Acadia Investment Management remarked:

> Fiduciary duty should not vary with size … I think a better way to frame the issue is that those pension or endowment funds that have greater resources might be expected to take a leadership role in sustainability issues, but it should not be their sole responsibility … activist or sustainable objectives within a pension fund require time, resources, and human capital. A larger pension fund might have more resources to address these issues compared to a smaller pension fund, but the larger fund's access to more resources should not place a higher fiduciary duty standard upon the pension fund.

David C. Mills, trustee and chair of the Investment Committee, Casey Family Programs Foundation and retired former executive director, State of Wisconsin Investment Board, and Silvers of the AFL-CIO agreed that the legal duty of a fund's trustees does not change with fund size.

Similarly, experts provided consistent responses to "Do responsibilities toward society change with fund size?" For example:

- "All fiduciaries of funds with the same purpose have the same [fiduciary] duty. However, larger funds generally have more resources and greater potential for influence. Pension funds typically have a longer-term financial purpose, which requires a 'societal lens' consistent with the generation of long-term value. Charitable trusts and foundations may have other purposes, which can and should, inform the fiduciary duty of their trustees" (Colin Melvin, CEO of Hermes Equity Ownership Services Ltd.).
- "I think the larger funds do recognize they have a greater responsibility. They are able to build a case to engage in certain ways and make certain investments, plus they have in-house experts to address issues" (Simon C. Y. Wong, partner at Governance for Owners and adjunct professor of law at Northwestern University School of Law).
- "A large fund has greater possibilities, perhaps even responsibilities, to act on systematic issues

that need to be addressed in order to provide beneficiaries and society with a resilient pension system" (Eva Halvarsson, CEO of Swedish public pension fund, AP2).

The business and society perspective and mitigating portfolio risk

When capital market and governance experts discuss fiduciary duty, the management of portfolio risk is often brought up early in the conversation. Therefore, a keen understanding of risk is important for fiduciaries and a key differentiator among trustees appears to be what type of risks are considered, to what depth and over what timeframe.

Some experts tend to look at risks more narrowly: to them, it is about avoiding an investment in a company that faces significant chance of political, legal or reputational risks leading to value destruction over the time horizon in which the investor expects to hold. For example:

- "A fiduciary must consider reputational and political risk when considering investments. On that basis, for example, New York State's Common Retirement Fund divested holdings in certain companies doing business in Iran and Sudan, in the financial interest of the Fund's beneficiaries" (Feldman, City University of New York).

- "We do not distinguish between domestic and international investments in the exercise of our fiduciary duty. However, there is little question that there is even more opportunity in some less developed emerging and frontier markets for 'bad actor' companies to conduct themselves in ways detrimental to the broader interest of a good business environment and society, hence increasing risk" (Mills, Casey Family Programs Foundation).

On the other hand, some capital market experts believe there are a number of important, material risks that go beyond legal, political and reputational risk. For example, Silvers observed:

> Fiduciary duty IS about everything. What companies don't see is that their risk calculations may not be the same as the diversified long-term global investor. For example, climate change may

not be the most important business risk/material risk to Company X. However, for the CalPERS of the world who are invested in Company X, but [who] are dependent on the overall health of the global economy to meet their returns objectives, climate change may be the most important issue. Hence institutional investors may try to put pressure on companies in their portfolio when they are concerned about a particular issue's impact on their whole portfolio … Yet in the end, the global long-term diversified investor may be the one left holding the bag on any particular externality, and so investors in this category need a wider view on societal risks.

How concern for society is demonstrated by institutional investors

Experts were asked to consider: "As a practical matter, how might an institutional investor demonstrate concern for 'business and society?' Through voting? Activism? Monitoring? Other? What might be the best or most effective methods, practices, and other behaviors that demonstrate such a concern?" All of the above and more was the response of most experts.

Melvin of Hermes EOS Ltd. described the range of activities by which an institutional investor may demonstrate concern for society, "through voting and engagement with companies (good 'stewardship') and participating in the development of public policy and best practices relevant to the markets in which they invest." Mr. Mills added:

> A fiduciary who concludes that there is a material risk of any company being a "bad actor" can reasonably decide to use any of the [engagement] tools noted above – along with divestment – to demonstrate their concern. Such action would be based upon a determination that the long-term reputational and legal risk to the company has the potential to negatively affect its ability to produce the risk-adjusted returns envisioned.

Eva Halvarsson, CEO of the Swedish public pension fund AP2, elaborated:

> Voting, monitoring ESG issues, and engaging with corporations on sustainability issues are all valid methods to raise concerns … We vote both Swedish and foreign stocks. In our engagements

with corporations, we have learned that face-to-face meetings are important in order to build trust and get results. It is, of course, important to bring knowledge/insights to the discussion in order to have a constructive dialogue ... companies welcome dialogues with their shareholders, and we are not seldom invited to companies to discuss ESG issues.

Concern for business and society at the level of a company: the buy-sell decision

Institutional investors engage with a company throughout the life of the investment with that company. Once the investment is sold, engagements ends and most believe that there is no more responsibility. The decision of what sectors to buy into, what factors are considered as part of due diligence, as well as the amount and type of investment can all serve to exercise concern for society.

Factors that come into play when deciding whether to invest in a company originate from both sides of the proposed transaction, as articulated by Mills, trustee of Casey Family Services Foundation:

> The most appropriate point for consideration of the potential impact of an investment is at the point of investment. Potential reputational risks may raise questions about the likelihood of [the portfolio] earning the expected risk-adjusted return. Or, in the alternative, the purposes of the trust may suggest that such an investment, given the foreseeable consequences, would be inappropriate. Finally, if the investment would appear contrary to values set forth by the grantor in the trust document, consideration of the impact may be appropriate. In each instance, one still adheres to the tenets of fiduciary duty, which require a single master.

The decision to invest in a company can also serve as an important signaling device as elucidated by Leisinger with the Novartis Foundation:

> Institutional investors usually have a long-term view on their investments – they should support companies that feel accountable to a wider constituency than the financial one. Companies that not only avoid scandals and legal wrongdoings, but are perceived to strive for legitimacy in their (global) business activities and be "part of the

solution" of the "big" problems, are likely to attract funds fed by investors who are not interested in the "fast buck" but in a reliable and secure allocation of capital with proceeds that may grow slower but steadily.

To understand the risks and potential rewards of a company, the due-diligence and ongoing reviews must take into consideration a variety of factors. Halvarsson shared how AP2 approaches this multi-factorial risk and reward analysis for the assets they hold directly:

> According to our model, we shall consider ESG issues if these have a material impact on the financial performance. If a "green" investment is equally attractive financially as a "normal" investment, we may consider it. An investment in green bonds versus investment in government bonds is an example of investments that can be seen as equal from a financial point of view. Therefore, the Second AP Fund has invested in green bonds issued by the World Bank and the European Investment Bank that will finance a number of environmental projects.

Even the size and concentration of an institutional investor's holdings have implications for the wider society. After all, an institutional investor with a very large portfolio and a small staff can be spread rather thin, leaving its staff little time to help improve companies in its portfolio or to serve as a stable yet informed source of capital. A May 2012 White Paper by the Henry Jackson Initiative for Inclusive Capitalism therefore recommends that:

> the pension funds, insurance companies, mutual funds, and sovereign wealth funds that together hold $65 trillion, or roughly 35 percent, of the world's financial assets, should create long-term investment portfolios consisting of larger shares of a smaller number of companies (and should reward their asset managers on the basis of their long-term performance too!).

On the other end of the investment life cycle, an investor may choose to divest in a company if risks continue to remain unmitigated or if the business model is no longer viable. Noted one asset manager: "The decision to sell is a drastic measure that we take if needed. Usually it's because we view the business model as broken."

Concern for business and society at the level of a company: between buy and sell

Most experts in North America and Europe who were interviewed as part of this chapter agreed that fulfilling one's fiduciary duty is more than just exercising due diligence at the point of investment or divestment. As one expert succinctly stated, "Throughout the investment period, the fiduciary continues to have the obligation to carefully monitor an investment to ensure it meets the initial investment premise (for risk-adjusted return) and maintains consistency with the purposes as set forth by the trust."

Mills noted that an institutional investor must decide how much involvement is right:

> A fiduciary must fulfill their obligation to evaluate an investment on risk-adjusted return and consistency with the trust's purpose, but then may select the alternative it believes serves to also further the broader interests of business and society. Having done so, it is reasonable to use the tools of proxy voting, activism and monitoring to ensure that the company continues to promote that broader purpose. But with each such potential action comes a requirement to re-evaluate whether the new action or activism continues to promote achievement of the expected risk-adjusted return.

Anson believes there is a set of minimum activities that an institutional investor should conduct in order to fulfill their duties and consider societal needs. He explained that

> at minimum, institutional investors should demonstrate their concern through the voting of their proxies. To the extent that an institutional investor employs an outside proxy voting service, the institutional investor should communicate to that outside firm what its concerns are and provide directions to vote their proxies consistent with those objectives. Activism requires time, human capital, and resources. As a result, many institutional investors do not have the resources to engage in activism. However, an institutional investor can establish its directions/objectives on sustainability issues and communicate these to its proxy voting service, outside asset managers that it hires, and consultants it employs.

While this advice may be followed in North America, informed voting as a minimum form of engagement and demonstration of concern for society is not universally practiced. An expert on Korean markets, Dr. Sea-Jin Chang, provost's chair professor of business administration at the National University of Singapore, offered that:

> There are some barriers to engagement by institutional investors in Asia: for example, intervening in portfolio companies by voting is not yet socially acceptable. There is a discussion among [Korean] policy makers whether or not pension funds should exercise their voting rights. Some raise objections on the ground that it might lead to too much government intervention. Furthermore, the pension funds and other institutional investors do not have much incentive and will to do so. For example, it can be a tall order to challenge big business groups like Samsung. If the institutional investors do not like what a company is doing, they will then sell out, like transient investors.

If an institutional investor chooses to go beyond the minimum, Lubber with Ceres described some of the proactive ways that institutional investors can engage with companies in their portfolio, addressing fundamental questions such as: how are the companies being managed; how are they integrating issues of environmental (and social) sustainability into value; and how they are addressing sustainability at the board level. Ceres in 2011 led a coalition of investors to send a letter to Russell 1000 companies;[5] the letter described what a well-managed company should be looking at and urged the CEOs "to encourage your management team and Board of Directors to address sustainability issues across your organization, which can enhance long-term company and shareholder value."

Institutional investors are distinguishing themselves by the degree of obligation to the companies in their portfolio. Those investors who commit to be mutually invested are beginning to describe themselves as stewards and not just investors.[6]

---

[5] The Russell 1000 refers to the 1,000 largest companies, by market capitalization, traded on US equity exchanges.

[6] For example, TIAA-CREF, the US-based institutional investor that invests on behalf of 3.7 million individuals in academia, medicine and the like, stated: "As providers of capital, long-term investors have among the most to lose

Dr. Summerfield with the UK-based institutional investor USS added:

> As a defined benefit and open scheme, operating as an in-house fund manager and asset owner, USS' long-term and universal investor perspective distinguishes us from many other institutional investors. We take seriously our role as a long-term owner and stewards of companies and other assets, and devote substantial resources to oversee and monitor the management of those assets. We believe shareholder engagement and active oversight of our assets is vital for ensuring we deliver long-term and sustainable value for our beneficiaries. Therefore, our ownership responsibility extends globally and to all asset classes in which we invest.

From the formal to the more informal and the unusual engagement

Institutional investors can demonstrate their concern for society and simultaneously help improve a company or industry through more informal means of engagement. Nick Moakes, head of public markets for the Wellcome Trust, shared a number of engagement methods practiced by his organization: "On the informal side [of engagement with portfolio companies], we have done an exchange of personnel with companies directly held in our portfolio. For example, we sent one of our investment team to Australia to work on a six-week project on the environmental impacts of investment projects for a portfolio company; the portfolio company sent someone here who learned more about how we analyze investment opportunities." Other forms of informal engagement by the Wellcome Trust include their chief investment officer being invited to sit on a portfolio company's sustainability committee and Wellcome Trust science people being invited to meet with the R&D groups of several

if markets deteriorate and asset prices fall. Therefore, it is critical that such investors use their influence and leverage to promote good corporate governance and effectively functioning markets. This makes good economic sense in terms of our mission and is part of our job as fiduciaries representing our clients. Our participants and clients expect us to be stewards of their savings and to help provide for their financial security" (TIAA-CREF Institute 2010: 2).

portfolio companies. Remarked Mr. Moakes, "As we become more familiar with the companies in our portfolio, they become more open and these types of informal sharing of expertise occur. We are providing feedback as a long-term investor."

As part of being a responsible investor, an institution could choose to be more transparent about their holdings, providing a clear signal to companies that they have investors with a long-term bias and may be a potential ally. This communication could be private but there also mechanisms for sharing more publicly where not otherwise mandated by law. Many operating companies are frustrated by the fact that they do not know who holds the majority of their shares, unless a major position is taken and the company is listed in a country with mandated disclosures at certain levels of holding. Knowing who is trading in their shares would help management separate out noise and algorithmic trading from trading that occurs as an evaluation of the current or future performance of the company. While not a duty, one institutional investor based in the UK concluded our interview with the following statement: "I believe it is very important for companies to know who owns them. We publish our direct holdings on Bloomberg and update them quarterly. Generally, we try to approach companies and let them know we are here as long-term investors and want to be viewed as constructive engagers." Voluntarily publishing their positions is an act of transparency that signals this institutional investor's attitude toward engagement with their portfolio companies: a desire for open, honest communication.

Concern for business and society: at an industry and macro level

A common theme was shared by interviewees about larger institutional investors: while fiduciary duty may not mandate engagement, it behooves investors who are invested in much of the market to be concerned with addressing industry, national and/or global issues that have a bearing on the future of companies in their portfolio. Under these circumstances, cooperative action made eminent sense to most.

Dr. Summerfield with USS Ltd. remarked,

As a large pension fund manager investing at a global level and across multiple asset classes, we aim to prioritize our activities to maximize the impact of our engagements, utilizing the limited resources we have available. This entails:

- First, asking ourselves, 'Does an issue impact a large proportion of our portfolio?' If so, we might address it.
- Second, collaborating with other investors at a global level, on both company and market-wide issues.
- Third, emphasizing quality over quantity of engagement: our preference is to undertake deep dives and intense engagement with select-ive engagement candidates, when appropriate, rather than attempt to engage with every com-pany in our portfolio.

Dr. Summerfield continued,

As a long-term investor, we look at company, sec-tor, and market-wide issues. For example, we are always likely to have an exposure to the pharma-ceuticals sector. So we will ask ourselves, 'What issues is the sector likely to face going forward and what opportunities and risks present themselves to long-term investors?' We are involved in several projects that consider similar issues of importance to long-term investors with exposure to many sec-tors, markets and companies.

Ms. Halvarsson of AP2 picked up on this point and shared the following:

From a long-term global asset owner perspective we take part in discussions to influence regula-tory/legislative bodies on, for example, corporate governance issues through ICGN and advocating a global framework (price) on carbon through IIGCC. We also engage with our local university to support sustainability issues in the curriculums at the Business School. Finally, we think it is important to take part in public debate on issues that are important for us and long-term value cre-ation, for example board diversity.

The US-based NGO Ceres, originator of the Global Reporting Initiative, has engaged with investors for a number of years and has several prominent institutional investors on its board of directors. Ms. Lubber described some of its more recent activities involved in addressing the macro

environment in which companies operate: "For example, investors went to see the SEC to ask for more information on environmental risks for disclosures. Investors, like companies, need the right kind of information." Along the same vein she noted, "Investors have been pushing the stock exchanges to reflect on their expectations of listed companies. Ceres is now talking with several North American exchanges, and investors are helping us in this process."

Dilemmas in the world of investment

During the course of conversations, a number of topics were raised that are not specific to the busi-ness and society perspective on the fiduciary duty of institutional investors but rather more broadly address how value is being created by companies and investors, for whom, and in what timeframe.

Mr. Anson posed this question on the context in which investors operate: "How do we turn an economic society around from a short-term focus on profits and returns to long-term value creation? This is the most difficult issue with which we have to wrangle." He then defined the solution space,

I don't have a perfect answer to this dilemma. It will have to come from a combination of new directions in education – training the next gener-ation of MBAs and CFAs to consider these issues; potential regulation which is often a sledge ham-mer rather than a finer tool; and the courage of corporate CEOs to provide some leadership in long-term value creation.

According to Dr. Lynn A. Stout, Distinguished Professor of Corporate and Business Law at Cornell Law School[7] and advisory board mem-ber of the Aspen Institute's Business and Society Program:

There are several different ways in which share-holder value thinking can create an investor Tragedy of the Commons and prove a bad strat-egy for investors collectively ... Long-term

[7] Professor Stout was interviewed for this chapter but had a forthcoming book on related topics and was kind enough to share a manuscript; quote taken from her original manu-script. But also see Stout (2012).

shareholders fear corporate myopia. Short-term shareholders embrace it – and many powerful shareholders today are short-term shareholders … When long-term and short-term investors' interests diverge, shareholder value thinking poses the same risks as fishing with dynamite. Some individuals may reap immediate and dramatic returns. But over time and as a whole, investors and the economy lose.

Reinterpreting duty to reinforce "basic" role of the institutional investor

While these first two dilemmas are not easily addressed, the role of the long-term institutional investor was identified as an area that is ripe for examination and improvement. A belief was expressed by several respondents, including Strine and Melvin, that the current set of institutional investors are not uniformly acting in the interest of their own beneficiaries, a clear repudiation of fiduciary duty. Therefore, before fiduciary duty is expanded or more responsibilities are placed on institutional investors, there should be rules and other mechanisms put into place to better ensure that the current set of duties are upheld. Melvin noted:

> Trust law already describes a duty for pension fund trustees to look after the financial interests of the pension fund's beneficiaries. However, this is almost universally interpreted in a short-term way, leading to actions such as stock-lending and supporting excessive transactions through "supplier control" … The UK and US governments could issue guidance on the interpretation of fiduciary duty making clear that this should be considered from a longer-term perspective, leading to less value lost through excessive transactions and more gained through good stewardship.

In a similar vein, Strine remarked:

> Let's ensure we have a notion of fiduciary duty that says if you, as an institution, take the money of long-term oriented investors and those investors need you to act long term, then your institution needs to act in a different way that attends to this long-term responsibility. Hence, your due diligence of companies is less about takeover defenses and more about the business itself: does

it have a viable business plan? Is it reporting consistently with integrity? … To leap over this core duty to beneficiaries to something more expansive (that is, a larger business and society perspective) seems unrealistic, at best.

Conclusions

During a March 2012 Aspen Institute roundtable focused on reconsidering shareholder primacy and corporate purpose, a participating academic from a prominent university posed a challenge to the room, in stating: "Corporations are a social construct. So if society is not happy with that construct, let's change it." The author is sure this same professor would speak similarly of the duties of institutional investors: if we, as members of society and beneficiaries of institutional investors, are not happy with the fiduciary duties, in theory or as practiced, let us reconsider them.

In the re-examination of the social contract, one expert cautioned us to be careful to not impose an ambiguous and not-clearly-linked-to-economic-performance minority view on the majority. With this cautionary note firmly in mind, Dr. Bradley Googins, professor of organizational studies at Boston College's Carroll School of Management and executive director emeritus of the Boston College Center for Corporate Citizenship, offered up thoughts with which this chapter shall conclude:

> We are clearly in a major transformational stage in the global economy and around the social contract. Although we are probably too close to the upheavals that are swilling around us, change is definitely in the air. Taken together, the Arab Spring, Occupy Wall Street, the growing awareness within the American political electorate of hedge funds and capitalism on trial, all are serving to peck away at the status quo and attempting to create a new awareness and dialogue that can lead to change … This provides a long overdue and welcome development to introduce new thinking and new mechanisms for institutional investors to consider and adopt a more sustainable business and society perspective than they have in the past. The social and environmental issues are becoming more critical to business success and a variety of forces from

transparency and the calls for increased accountability, along with growing expectations of society on business, powerful NGO and movements around sustainability, human rights, etc., all will be potent allies in changing the calculus and the agenda for institutional investors. What has not appeared yet is a more potent leadership, a better use of social technology, and convincing new models and pathways for corporations to reflect these new realties. But all of the current unrest points to a world of opportunities for creating new measures of success and standards for evaluating success.

References

Friedman, M. 1962. *Capitalism and Freedom*, Fortieth Anniversary Edition. The University of Chicago Press.

Stout, L. 2012. *The Shareholder Value Myth: How Putting Shareholders First Harms Investors, Corporations, and the Public*. San Francisco, CA: Berrett-Koehler.

TIAA-CREF Institute. 2010. *Responsible Investing and Corporate Governance*. New York: TIAA-CREF.

Challenging conventional wisdom: the role of investment tools, investment beliefs and industry conventions in changing our interpretation of fiduciary duty

DANYELLE GUYATT

Introduction

This chapter explores the link between investment tools, investment beliefs and industry conventions to the interpretation of fiduciary duty. There is no hard rule about what is, or is not, in the best interest of beneficiaries and as such, it will always come down to judgment. It is interesting to see over recent years the beliefs that underpin investment decisions being challenged and evolving to support a long-term investment horizon and the integration of environmental, social and governance (ESG) factors into decision-making. This chapter argues that a combination of new tools, evolving beliefs and industry conventions are integral to supporting a wider interpretation of fiduciary duty. While some challenges remain in applying new tools and moving from beliefs into action, the building blocks are in place for change to be meaningful and sustained.

Current investment theory and the interpretation of fiduciary duty

Trustees have a fiduciary duty, or legal responsibility, to act in the best interests of their beneficiaries. "Acting in the best interest" is about ensuring that beneficiaries' interests are protected and enhanced by the trust. If beneficiaries believe that their best interests have not been protected or enhanced,

trustees can be sued for a breach of fiduciary duty and potentially held liable. Many trustees in pension funds and charities don't have specialist investment knowledge and there is generally no legal requirement for them to do so in most countries. For example, in the UK there is only the requirement that they "obtain proper advice" (Myners Review 2001: 5). As a result, most trustees rely heavily on external advice from investment consultants and internal investment executives who advise on strategy and manager selection.

This is where the prudent person rule becomes important. Without listing the details of all the laws that apply within each country, for the purposes of this chapter we only need be concerned with the goal of the regulations – that is, they are there to ensure that institutional assets are managed prudently and in a manner that is in the best interest of its beneficiaries. An article published by the OECD set out the following definition of the prudent person rule:

> A fiduciary must discharge his or her duties with the care, skill, prudence and diligence that a prudent person acting in a like capacity would use in the conduct of an enterprise of like character and aims (Galer 2002).

Trustees are heavily dependent on the advice and expertise of external agents, be it the in-house investment executive, investment consultants or professional fund managers. The delegation of investment decision-making introduces a myriad of potential agency issues and inefficiencies as the agents can often be better informed and have a tendency to act in their own interests in maximization of profit rather than acting in the best interest of pension fund beneficiaries over the long term (Ambachtsheer 2007). As a result, a large part of a trustee's role becomes one of monitoring agent behavior to ensure that the agents acting on their behalf behave in a prudent way.

The prudent person rule suggests that the investment process must be coherent and justifiable and that the institution has investment principles that are transparent, robust and testable. Galer (2002) highlighted that the prudent person rule is less about a set of definitive rules and outcomes and more about behavior and processes. As a result, a set of norms has evolved in the industry to promote prudent behavior.

One is the duty to monitor, which relates to the way in which trustees monitor professional investment managers when they have been appointed to manage a portion of a pension fund's assets. The second relates to the principle of diversification, which posits that risk can be reduced through diversification across different asset classes and investments. The principle of diversification has evolved as a well-entrenched industry norm, but it also has the potential to distort the interpretation of fiduciary duty, investment decision-making and consequently investment outcomes for pension fund members.

We have reached the crux of the issue concerning this chapter – the industry's interpretation and notion of appropriate investment processes is heavily dependent and guided by existing theory that arguably goes beyond the original intention or capacity of those theories. When theory is being inadvertently misused or its continuing validity goes unchallenged then the tools that underpin decisions by fiduciaries may no longer be in the beneficiaries' best interest. Let's take a look at one of the dominant theories related to diversification to see what this means in practice and specifically why it might be acting as a blockage to ESG being considered as part of fiduciary duty; namely mean-variance analysis.

Mean-variance analysis remains the dominant paradigm

Within the institutional investment industry, the legal definition of "best interest" of beneficiaries has widely come to be interpreted as meaning that it is in their best financial interest, which inadvertently means maximizing portfolio return for a given level of risk with the ultimate aim to provide them with a secure retirement future. Indeed, the influence of modern portfolio theory and the framework for measuring and managing risk through diversification is the dominant paradigm that institutional investors rely on. This chapter explores how the application of this theory through mean-variance analysis might be impacting on our understanding of fiduciary duty.

Markowitz (1952) developed a mean-variance optimization framework that has come to be referred to as modern portfolio theory. As Figure 25.1 illustrates, the construction of an efficient portfolio with minimum variance shows the potential gains to be made from having a diversified portfolio, whereby assets could be combined optimally to reduce portfolio risk for a given level of return when the asset/security returns are negatively correlated (or at the very least are not perfectly correlated). This is most commonly represented in the form of an efficient frontier, where the most efficient portfolio along the frontier is the mix of securities that produces the minimum standard deviation for the maximum level of expected portfolio return (point A in Figure 25.1).

One of the implications stemming from this theory is that the benefits of diversification are said to increase, as more assets with low or uncorrelated returns are included in the portfolio. In reality, it is very difficult to find securities whose returns are uncorrelated or perfectly negatively correlated hence it tends to come down to seeking low correlation between assets. The lure of diversification and the associated aim to achieve efficient portfolio construction has encouraged the appeal and wide adoption of indexes/benchmarks among institutional investors as a proxy for a global diversified equity portfolio. The industry relies heavily on the principle of diversification and it is fair to say that

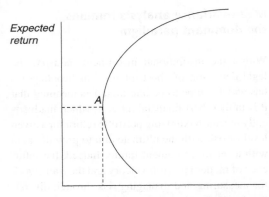

Figure 25.1 Efficient frontier with uncorrelated security returns.
Reproduced from Markowitz (1952)

it has become such conventional practice that its validity is no longer challenged or questioned. It is, by implication, embedded into the way trustees and their agents interpret fiduciary duty – to put it simply, maximizing diversification within and across assets that have been less than perfectly correlated in the past in the belief that this will persist and hence be in beneficiaries' best interest in the future.

There is an overreliance on historical relationships

One problem with mean-variance analysis is that it does not provide a robust means by which decision-makers can construct reliable expectations about the future performance of investments. Markowitz himself noted that the mean-variance model is only concerned with the process of optimization and it is assumed that investors behave optimally when forming their judgments and valuations during the first stage of investment, as indicated by the following statement:

> The process of selecting a portfolio may be divided into two stages. The first stage starts with observation and experience and ends with beliefs about the future performances of available securities. The second stage starts with the relevant beliefs

about future performance and ends with the choice of portfolio (Markowitz 1952: 77).

The mean-variance model of optimization does not claim to address issues related to the valuation process or formation of expectations, but rather is concerned with the process of constructing an optimal portfolio for a given set of assets. The logical observation that follows is that, in the absence of a robust process of valuation and expectation formation, the construction of an "optimal" portfolio is effectively meaningless and unhelpful.

This leads to the question of how expectations about future portfolio returns are formed in practice by fiduciaries and their investment committees. In a mean-variance framework, historical returns, variance and covariance between assets are the starting point for discussion. There may then be some assumptions tweaked depending on the investment committee's view about key variables such as economic growth, inflation and interest rates. This assessment is typically undertaken with a long-term horizon, at least five years, but is updated on an annual or biannual basis.

There may also be some stress testing or event risks to examine portfolio impacts, which mainly evolve around repeating past events or periods of market turbulence.

Forward-looking analysis of future risks or events that may not have occurred before might take place as part of this process, but it is typically not given much weight as tail risks fall too much into the "unknowable/guess-work" realm and take committees out of their comfort zone. As a result, the industry overemphasizes the likelihood of the past repeating itself to the detriment of spending more time in looking for where future risks might come from and how to best protect against these risks. This is a problem because, as the recent credit crisis showed and the evidence increasingly suggests, the viability of diversification through a mean-variance lens is strongly undermined by tail risk events and it does not provide downside protection in times of extreme market stress (Ibragimov and Walden 2007; Amenc and Martinelli 2011).

With the odd few exceptions, the industry standard among institutional investors does not really stretch itself too far from this approach. Most investors will openly admit that they see the mean-variance framework as being rather limited and hence do not implement it blindly, but at the end of the day the portfolio structure (in terms of strategic asset allocation) is heavily influenced by the assumptions used and the suggested portfolio weights that result in the context of a fund's liabilities. These observations are not intended to suggest that mean-variance analysis should be abandoned, but it serves to highlight the shortcomings with overemphasizing portfolio diversification at the expense of investing time/resources to improve the formulation of expectations that underpins it.

The paradigm does not allow for ESG factors

Another challenge to the heavy reliance on the theory of diversification through a mean-variance lens is that there is little room for ESG issues to be truly accepted as an integral part of the portfolio construction process. It is more likely to move down the priority scale of fiduciaries or be treated as secondary to other factors that are considered to be "core" investment drivers of return, volatility and correlations.

The fact that hundreds of institutional investors around the world now have a responsible investment (RI) policy and are signatories to initiatives such as the Principles for Responsible Investment (PRI) presents the industry with somewhat of a challenge. If so many investors are pledging to integrate ESG and behave as long-term investors through collaborative initiatives and their own investment policies, how can they reconcile achieving that goal with the somewhat narrow and backward-looking interpretation of fiduciary duty as described here? Furthermore, knowing what we know about the limits of mean-variance analysis and its failings in times of market stress, as the credit crisis has painfully shown, the logical conclusion is that the current approach can no longer be construed as being in the best interests of beneficiaries. Change is inevitable.

One part of the solution is to look for improvements in the tools that the industry relies on, so that there is more forward-looking analysis and a wider definition of risk. Investment committees need to think more broadly, beyond historical events and statistical analysis, to embrace an approach to portfolio management that is truly forward-looking and one where numerous future possibilities have been explored in detail through a rigorous and engaged process amongst the decision-makers.

A factor risk framework could go some of the way to allowing ESG to be considered a core part of investment risk provided it is developed in a way that emphasizes qualitative inputs as being just as important as quantitative outcomes. The other part of the answer lies in widening the interpretation of fiduciary duty and indeed I would argue this is underway; first, through embedding ESG into investment beliefs and second, by continually evolving and challenging the industry's conventional approach to investment management. We will now take a look at these issues.

The role of new investment tools

Factor risk analysis is less a theory than a set of tools that allow investors to think about diversification and portfolio risk in a wider, more dynamic way. In its purest form, thinking about portfolio risk in terms of factor risks means that the decision-making framework is not divided up along asset class lines but by "sources of risk." The asset classes are thought of in terms of how they will be impacted by those sources of risk, with the ultimate goal to achieve diversification across risk factors.

Importantly, this approach necessitates the engagement of fiduciaries and their investment committees for it to be effective. It is not a question of one black box replacing another. The potential value of factor risk analysis is that it would encourage investment committees to engage in meaningful conversations about the different sources of risk that might impact on the portfolio's value. There are quantitative outputs that result from the analysis, as all decisions will need some numerical evaluation. But it requires greater time spent on the formulation of expectations and discussion around the assumptions in a multidimensional way compared to the standard mean-variance approach.

The risk factors can be defined in many ways, but would typically fall into categories of fundamental risks (e.g., macroeconomic variables), market risks (volatility and liquidity) and asset specific risks (regulation, demographic shift, technological change, which vary by asset class). Thinking about portfolio management in terms of the potential source of future investment risks that rely less on historical relationships is a relatively new approach for institutional investors; hence I will provide a few additional observations on how a factor risk framework can be used.

Building portfolio resilience through risk factors

First, diversification across different sources of risk can help to ensure that a portfolio is resilient to a number of different potential factors that might impact on future performance and is not overly exposed to each one. The objective is not to maximize exposure to one factor or minimize to another, but rather to have an asset mix that is broadly dispersed across the sources of risk.

Second, a high sensitivity to a source of risk does not necessarily indicate that it will be negative (or positive) for investments. For example, listed equity has a high sensitivity to the economic cycle but this relationship can be either positive or negative depending on the different stages of the economic cycle. Likewise, assets that are highly sensitive to regulatory or political change, such as real estate and infrastructure, may benefit from favorable policies or suffer from unfavorable ones.

Judgment and qualitative discussions improve understanding of risk

Finally, interpreting the direction of the potential risk (whether it will be positive or negative) requires an element of judgment and discussion about the changing investment conditions. As mentioned earlier, this is one of the primary benefits of integrating factor risk analysis into investment discussions, as it encourages fiduciaries to step back from quantitative model results and ask questions to test their thinking. This might be in the form of stress testing for the impact of extreme situations, tail risk events or combined qualitative and quantitative scenario analysis.

A factor risk framework is also helpful in considering how intangible factors might impact on a portfolio's asset mix, since the sources of risk might not always come through financial variables that traditional portfolio optimization models rely on (Mercer 2011). Moreover, there is not always the historical data available on risks such as climate change, corporate governance or health and labor standards – since in these instances it will be more about looking into the future and less about modeling the past. The framework can place as much emphasis on qualitative discussions around the assumptions and how to interpret the quantitative outputs. It can be designed to encourage discussion among fiduciaries, lending itself to a wider interpretation of risk and ultimately a more engaged process in formulating expectations.

Forward-looking and holistic thinking required

To sum up, factor risk analysis is a tool that could support the interpretation of fiduciary duty to be widened in a way that will encourage fiduciaries to take a more forward-looking and holistic approach to thinking about risk beyond historic volatility and correlations. The prudent person rule and mean-variance framework are not redundant, but rather than being boxed into an increasingly narrow corner of interpreting what this means in practice, the application of a more forward-looking and qualitative approach that recognizes the limitations of model outcomes will ultimately improve the decision-making process that trustees utilize in the management of pension fund beneficiaries' savings.

This is only one example of a new approach to thinking about risk that goes beyond conventional wisdom, and there are many more innovations around asset-liability matching and hedging instruments that could be better utilized in the finance industry (Amenc and Martinelli 2011). But to support a transition in interpreting fiduciary duty that incorporates ESG analysis in a meaningful way, as well as new tools such as these, we would also need to see a continued evolution in investment beliefs and industry norms.

The role of investment beliefs

Investment beliefs are an important part of an institutional investor's framework for decision-making. Each trustee board will formulate and agree on a set of beliefs that help to guide their decisions. The beliefs are usually developed together with a chief investment officer of a fund, if one exists, the board of trustees and their external advisors. The beliefs do not change much over time, they are designed to withstand short-term trends and help to protect the decision-makers against themselves, i.e., not to deviate from their core beliefs when making investment decisions on behalf of beneficiaries. An investment policy will include the investment beliefs and the policy is usually reviewed and ratified on an annual basis. Depending on the country in question, the relevant regulator will be aware of a fund's investment policy and investment beliefs.

When a trustee board approves and signs up to initiatives such as the International Corporate Governance Network, the UN PRI or any initiative that sets out to widen the focus of the fund and pursue ESG-related issues then in many cases, although not all, the board will also embed ESG into their investment beliefs statement. The extent of this will vary, and sometimes it may be a very high level statement that doesn't really say much. But the trend for best practice is moving in that direction. And funds are not only increasingly embedding ESG into their investment beliefs, but many of them also have a separate RI policy that sets out in further detail the goals and mechanisms that put those beliefs in action.

The reason why this is a significant industry development is that it means the industry is putting the building blocks in place to widen the interpretation of fiduciary duty to include behaving as a long-term responsible investor. By including ESG

as part of a trustee board's investment beliefs, the legitimacy of these issues with respect to their fiduciary duty increases. All investment beliefs have an element of subjectivity and require a judgment call (passive versus active investing; the long-run equity risk premium and so on) and hence by including ESG into beliefs it is treating the issue with the same degree of commitment and acknowledgement as the other investment issues that frame decision-making.

Evidence from the field on investment beliefs

I have two stories or pieces of evidence to share about how this works in practice and the challenges that remain. One is an example of the investment beliefs and integration of ESG factors by a mid-sized pension fund. The second relates to some research findings from a few years back that found even when beliefs exist there can still be a gap in action and follow through. So after trustee boards move to the first stage of legitimizing ESG issues within their internal processes, they still have a lot of work to do in ensuring they give due care and attention to those issues and treat them ultimately as part of their fiduciary duty.

Let's start with the good news story first. The fund in question is not dissimilar to many other asset owner investors that have signed up to the PRI and other related initiatives and so it provides a good example of how ESG can fit into investment beliefs and processes. The fund has embraced the notion that long-term investing that embeds ESG issues is about better risk management and return enhancement. In its investment beliefs as part of its investment policy it documents that the trustees:

> believe that responsible corporate behavior with respect to ESG factors will act to reduce investment risk and can generally have a positive influence on long-term corporate performance ...
>
> As a long term investor and near universal owner, [the Fund] believes that it can enhance members' interests by contributing to the effective operation of financial markets, quite apart from risks and opportunities arising from specific ESG issues.

In the RI policy, the fund goes further to explain the motivation for embracing ESG, where it states that the trustees:

> believe that markets are generally focused on a time horizon which is much shorter than it should be, and that this results in inefficient allocation of capital at the overall market level as well as excessive costs in management of institutional investment portfolios …
>
> [The Fund] will seek to ensure that its own behaviour does not reinforce this short term focus. The Fund will also seek where possible to have a positive influence on overall market behaviour.

A clearly worded set of investment beliefs that articulate the trustees' views on these issues is an important step towards legitimizing ESG as an integral part of fiduciary duty. It requires the trustees to discuss the issue and ratify any required changes to the investment beliefs that are core to the investment governance of the fund.

The gap between investment beliefs and decision-making

The murky area is the translation of the investment beliefs into action. At some funds this has resulted in an implementation plan on ESG that clearly sets goals and actions for different parts of the investment portfolio. For funds that have not yet developed such a plan, there is a risk that when push comes to shove, the ESG issues could get sidelined behind what are considered to be more "core" investment issues. This implementation gap is one of the key challenges facing the industry and highlights the role that ESG specialists play within asset owner and asset manager firms in integrating their function into the core investment decision-making process.

The disconnect between high level beliefs and investment decision-making is made clear by the results of a survey I conducted on behalf of the Marathon Club[1] a few years back. I will not go

into the detail of the survey but in essence it was designed to ask trustees and their advisors about their beliefs on ESG issues alongside other investment considerations and to see how these issues ranked in terms of priority and interpretation of fiduciary duty.[2]

Environmental and social issues considered less legitimate than governance

One of the key findings on the fiduciary question (as shown in Figure 25.2) was that issues around corporate governance were considered to be more legitimate than social or environmental issues (the latter defined in the survey as corporate responsibility). A small proportion of respondents were unsure or disagreed that these issues were compatible at all, but the majority was supportive.

Relative returns to a benchmark dominate priorities

But when we went on to link the goal of long-term responsible investing to core investment objectives and gauge priorities, Figure 25.3 shows that relative returns to a benchmark came to dominate. Engagement success with companies was in the top five and ranked above minimizing tracking error, which suggests that there is an understanding of the role that corporate engagement can play in evaluating pension fund performance. Nevertheless, the tension between return expectations and ESG considerations is starting to reveal itself as the returns relative to a benchmark dominate priorities.

---

[1] The Marathon Club was established in 2005 in the UK to stimulate pension funds, endowments and other institutional investors ("Institutional Funds") and their agents to be more long-term in their thinking and actions, encouraging more

emphasis on being responsible and active owners with a view to increasing knowledge about how their investment strategy and process could improve the long-term financial and qualitative buying power of fund beneficiaries. The Marathon Club no longer exists but materials that it produced are available on the USS website. www.uss.co.uk/UssInvestments/Responsibleinvestment/marathonclub/Pages/default.aspx.

[2] The full survey description and results can be found at http://papers.ssrn.com/sol3/papers.cfm?abstract_id=1911821.

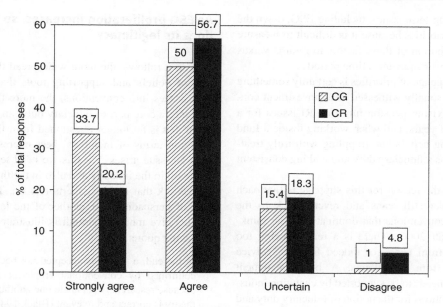

Figure 25.2 Promoting CG and CR is compatible with fiduciary obligations.
Source: Guyatt (2006); CG = corporate governance; CR = corporate responsibility.

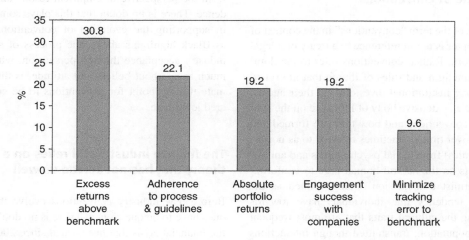

Figure 25.3 Percent of responses ranked as being *most important* when reviewing a pension fund's
performance on a quarterly and annual basis.
Source: Guyatt (2006).

On the whole, the conclusion from the research
was that relatively favorable shared beliefs regarding ESG factors can give way to dominant industry conventions that are more implicit and assumed

across the wider market. Based on the result of that
particular survey, relative returns to broad market
indices has become the most important consideration when evaluating portfolio performance. This

pushes long-term issues, including ESG, down the scale of priorities because it is difficult to measure the contribution of these factors to returns versus an index over short-term time periods..

This slippage of priorities is certainly something I have personally witnessed as an investment consultant advising pension funds on RI issues for a number of years, and when working inside a fund with strong beliefs but grappling with truly treating ESG as a fiduciary duty and making consistent decisions.

Part of the reason for this slippage is that each asset owner still leans and reverts back to the industry conventions that dominate current thinking (Guyatt 2006). There is a fear of being too different from peers, or indeed from the advice received from consultants. A belief statement therefore needs to be supported by changing industry conventions for the notion of fiduciary duty and interpretation of prudence to truly incorporate ESG issues.

The role of conventions

The use of the term "conventions" in the context of this chapter is not in reference to a treaty or a legal framework. Rather, conventions refer to the dominant paradigm and rules of thumb that are relied on among institutional investors and their agents. There is an extensive body of literature on the subject of conventions and how they are formed and evolve over time (sometimes referred to as norms, social rules) from social psychologists and anthropologists on the natural human urge to conform.[3] "Conformist transmission" being defined as the natural tendency that individuals have towards adopting the cultural traits that are most frequent in the population, transmitted though interactions within cultural groups.

[3] The human urge to conform is a powerful and natural one (Asch 1952; Deutsch and Gerard 1955; Epley and Gilovich 1999; Chartrand and Bargh 1999). Anthropologists Henrich and Boyd (1998) built a model of conformity that suggested a synergistic relationship exists between the evolution of imitation and the evolution of conformism and the transmission of conformist behavior.

As ESG proliferation increases, so too does its legitimacy

And so it follows, the more widespread the adoption of beliefs and supporting tools that embed ESG issues into conventions, the more that ESG becomes a core part of fiduciary duty; an industry norm that is no longer questioned from first principles in terms of members' best interests every time an issue arises. For this we need legitimacy both within the industry and also in the theoretical framework that insider experts rely on. This process of persuading one another of the legitimacy of alterative modus operandi is illustrated by the following quote:

> In the end, a theory is accepted not because it is confirmed by conventional empirical tests, but because researchers persuade one another that the theory is correct and relevant (Black 1986: 537).

Many people that work in the finance industry as ESG specialists, myself included, have spent a lot of time attempting to legitimize ESG issues from the perspective of empirical results and evidence. There is no doubt that this plays some role in supporting the evolution of conventions, but as Black highlights above, the process of shared industry acceptance through persuasion, which is much more about beliefs and attitude, is the ultimate turning point for conventions to be considered legitimate.

The finance industry still relies on a theory that has not served us well

Before new industry conventions evolve the old ones have to be questioned. There is no doubt that the financial crisis that has ensued since 2008 has taken its toll on the standing of mainstream finance across many parts of society. But the disturbing element of this is that the finance industry itself has not altered course in the sense that it still relies on a theory that has not served us well and there is little evidence that open-minded questioning of the assumptions and industry conventions that helped to perpetuate the crisis is taking place (Guyatt 2009).

Deep assumptions driven from teachings of neoclassical economics and modern portfolio theory continue to plague conversations that investors have with each other on a day-to-day basis. There is no alternative theory for them to turn to yet. The behavioralists provide the biggest challenge to conventional economic wisdom but those insights struggle to be willingly embraced by financiers as it requires them to accept that they are not infallible, rational utility maximizers but are rather emotional, shortsighted and overconfident, prone to errors of judgment and herding. Behavioral finance has also been marginalized by the finance industry as an opportunity for "smart money" investors to exploit, as the clever investors can take advantage of the biases that have been identified. The problem of course is when the market is collectively pricing assets and behaving in a way that impacts on the integrity of the whole market leading to outcomes that are not in the best interests of pension fund beneficiaries. Questioning the theory and assumptions that the finance industry has come to depend on when there are signs that things have gone awry, as is presently the case, is integral to fiduciary duty and adhering to the prudent person rule.

Different types of conventions need different types of people

As well as the theory and tools, changes in conventions will require changes at the individual and organizational level. It will mean a different type of person that works inside the finance industry, more diversity not just in gender and nationality but also in the values that they hold. The best way to challenge groupthink and challenge the status quo is to ensure that there is sufficient representation from different people with different skills and perspectives to contribute. It will also mean a different reward system at the organizational and industry level, one that encourages individuals to work together to solve common problems, to question and propose new solutions, to reward imagination and innovation and discourage short-term decision-making that does not at all times consider the knock on consequences and long-term impact

on the end beneficiary whose money is being invested.

Why are we stuck in our dysfunctional ways?

At this stage you might ask yourself, if it is so obvious that the existing conventions are failing us, why do they persist? There are a few possible explanations for this. First, within the game theory framework, conventions exist, in part, as a solution to the coordination problem faced by individuals in the formulation of expectations and decision-making under uncertainty (Schelling 1960; Lewis 1969). An individual's desire or preference to adhere to conventions is partly driven by a conscious need to manage the risks faced when making decisions under uncertainty, including tangible risks (such as fear of losing their job or getting a lower bonus payment) and less tangible risks such as reputational damage from behaving unconventionally and getting it wrong (Keynes 1936; Scharfstein and Stein 1990). Second, adherence to conventions can reflect an underlying reflexive form of mimicry that is more automatic in response to observing signals from the behavior of others (Devenow and Welch 1996). This human urge or need to adhere to conventions may produce suboptimal behavior and outcomes. While many conventions are essential to the efficient functioning of an economy, not all conventions will produce an optimal outcome in terms of agent behavior or market efficiency, as the following quote illustrates:

> One implication of evolutionary theory is that conventions can be evolutionarily stable even if they are not Pareto-efficient ... once established, the inefficient convention is self-perpetuating: no individual or small group can gain by deviating from it (Sugden 1989: 93).

Finally, Elster (1989: 108) discussed the idea that conventions may not always produce Pareto-efficient outcomes in the context of social norms. Elster suggested that some norms do not make everybody better off and, indeed, could actually make everybody *worse* off even when it is obvious to many that the norms of behavior are outdated (see further discussion below). While the process of adhering to conventions might provide some benefits to a particular group (such as lower transaction costs, lower search costs and lower perceived risks by way of "inclusion" in a group), the consequences of adhering to conventions in terms of the behavioral outcomes could be detrimental to the group overall. The challenge is therefore to consider if/how the dominant conventions that prevail might adapt in response to the changing needs and demands of institutional investors, their beneficiaries and society, and hence the industry's interpretation of fiduciary duty.

The need for fiduciaries to adapt and evolve

So where does that leave us as an industry? The core message is that those with fiduciary responsibility need to be constantly evolving, responding and challenging themselves to ensure that they are indeed acting in the best interests of their beneficiaries (Hawley et al. 2011).

North (1999) argued that societies that are most efficient at adapting to change will be the most prosperous and enduring over the long term. This so-called "adaptive efficiency" condition is relevant both at the individual level (such as individual beliefs, behavior and recognizing local conditions and differences) but also at the institutional level (such as government policies, economic systems and firm/institutional policies and practices). Therefore, for industry conventions to produce efficient economic and allocative outcomes, fiduciaries need to adapt and evolve in response to the continuously changing world environment.

This process of adaptation has been discussed in the context of an evolutionary stable strategy (ESS) by Maynard Smith (1982) on the subject of animal behavior, and by Sugden (1989), Boyer and Orlean (1992) and Young (1996) on the subject of how conventions evolve. The notion of an ESS goes beyond conventional game theory in studying human behavior, since it removes the assumption that individuals are always rational enough to work out optimal strategies by deductive reasoning but rather posits that strategies (or stable conventions)

may also be the result of imitation and trial and error. The implication of the ESS approach to the study of conventions is that an economy need not be locked into a Pareto-inferior convention indefinitely. The evolutionary theorists contend that conventions (and their inputs) are not static or permanent but rather they evolve over time (Young 1996: 106).

Learning from "deviants" who challenge the dominant paradigm

It follows that through this evolution, conventions have the potential to become unstable when there are deviants within the group, whereby the greater the number of deviants, the greater will be the incentive for others not to conform and the conventions become unstable. Choi (1999) described this in terms of the process of constant learning and adaptation that individuals undergo in response to observing the signals from the behavior of others. This learning process, according to Choi, is not a rapid one but rather one that takes time. Nevertheless, the presence of deviants in itself challenges existing conventions and potentially introduces a new "paradigm" or way of thinking:

> At any moment in a community, there is bound to be a number of people who have not quite learned to conform to conventions, or rather, who have adopted a different set of paradigms ... Each deviant represents a new inference, a new paradigm, and a new way of doing things (ibid.: 256).

The importance of collaboration in supporting change

The adaptation of conventions can emerge under different conditions (Boyer and Orlean 1992: 170), such as a result of:

(1) a general collapse, whereby the existing convention collapses is a very short period in response to some external shock or event;
(2) external invasion, where a new group adopts an alternative convention and creates instability in the existing convention;

(3) translation, whereby a new convention becomes interspersed with an old convention, causing some transformation; and

(4) Collective agreement/collaboration, where the group as a whole recognize the superiority of an alternative convention over the existing one, resulting in a deliberate and coordinated change in behavior.

It is the latter three conditions – external invasion, translation and collective agreement – that are most relevant for considering the adaptation of conventions for institutional investors and their agents, since the industry is by nature conservative and mindful of fiduciary obligations to beneficiaries, making a slow process of change more likely than an abrupt abandonment or collapse of existing practice.

The importance of legitimacy also makes collaboration preferable to going alone (Guyatt 2007). Hence the power of the collaborative networks that have come into being over the past decade in moving towards ESG becoming integral to how a trustee thinks about his/her fiduciary duty. It is an ongoing process of change through learning, sharing, researching and adapting. While it might seem like slow movement for the insiders, the combination of developing new tools, adapting investment beliefs and altering industry conventions through collaboration are forces that will allow a wider interpretation of fiduciary duty to sustain.

Conclusions

I have attempted to paint an honest and as it turns out, less bleak picture of the state of play than my day-to-day experiences as an industry ESG insider might lead me to conclude. There has been enormous progress on advancing the integration of ESG into institutional investors' processes over the past decade and, while it has a long way to go, the pendulum of momentum is swinging in favor of further movement away from the status quo. I am not naïve enough to think that this has happened entirely from our collective efforts, but rather it has taken place as a series of events and

crises within the finance industry have lined up to make it an obvious conclusion that the investment world needs to rethink what it does and how it does it.

Many of the decision-makers and influencers in investment firms today are of the generation that was raised on neoclassical economics and modern portfolio theory. The implicit assumptions are that the market knows best, individuals are mostly self-interested and rational utility maximizers and –in simplistic terms – the best we can do for pension funds members is diversify our asset allocation, pick smart investment managers and stay attuned to our performance versus a benchmark over a relatively short period of time. The long run will take care of itself.

In this narrow worldview, the bigger questions around the efficient allocation of capital, how short-termism can perpetuate underinvestment and increase systemic risks, the lack of effective stewardship and analysis of ESG risks and opportunities are not issues that institutional investors need concern themselves with. The outdated theories have come to provide a comfort zone and rationale for maintaining the status quo. As an industry we have collectively maintained blind faith in a set of assumptions that fail to hold in the real world. Consequently, the sooner they are called into question the faster will be the process of adapting to a changed environment within the institutional investor community. At that point, the conversation about whether ESG is compatible with fiduciary duty will cease to exist; it will have become internalized into the conventions of the day.

References

Ambachtsheer, K. 2007. *Pension Revolution: A Solution to the Pensions Crisis*. New Jersey: John Wiley & Sons.

Amenc, N. and L. Martellini. 2011. "In Diversification We Trust?" *The Journal of Portfolio Management* 7 (2): 1–2.

Asch, S. E. 1952. *Social Psychology*. Englewood Cliffs, NJ: Prentice-Hall.

Black, F. 1986. "Noise," *The Journal of Finance* 41 (3): 529–43.

Boyer, R. and A. Orlean. 1992. "How Do Conventions Evolve?" *Journal of Evolutionary Economics* 2 (3): 165–77.

Chartrand, T. L. and J. A. Bargh. 1999. "The Chameleon Effect: The Perception-Behavior Link and Social Interaction," *Journal of Personality and Social Psychology* 76: 893–910.

Choi, Y. B. 1999. "Conventions and Economic Change: A Contribution toward a Theory of Political Economy," *Constitutional Political Economy* 10 (3): 245–64.

Deutsch, M. and H. B. Gerard. 1955. "A Study of Normative and Informational Social Influences Upon Individual Judgements," *Journal of Abnormal and Social Psychology* 51: 629–36.

Devenow, A. and I. Welch. 1996. "Rational Herding in Financial Economics," *European Economic Review* 40 (3–5): 603–15.

Elster, J. 1989. "Social Norms and Economic Theory," *Journal of Economic Perspectives* 3 (4): 99–117.

Epley, N. and T. Gilovich. 1999. "Just Going Along: Nonconscious Priming and Conformity to Social Pressure," *Journal of Experimental Social Psychology* 35: 578–89.

Galer, R. 2002. "Prudent Person Rule: Standard for the Investment of Pension Fund Assets," OECD Working Paper Series.

Guyatt, D. 2006. "Behavioural Impediments to Investing in a Long Term Responsible Way," unpublished PhD thesis. http://ssrn.com/author=1134463.

2007. "Identifying and Mobilising Win-Win Opportunities for Collaboration between Pension Fund Institutions and their Agents." Rotman ICPM funded research. http://ssrn.com/abstract=2033516.

2009. "Beyond the Credit Crisis: A Responsible Investment Perspective," http://ssrn.com/abstract=2033536.

Hawley, J., K. Johnson and E. Waitzer. 2011. "Rethinking Fund Governance, Structure and Pension Design," *Rotman ICPM* 4 (2).

Henrich, J. and R. Boyd. 1998. "The Evolution of Conformist Transmission and the Emergence of Between-Group Differences," *Evolution and Human Behavior* 19: 215–41.

Ibragimov, R. and J. Walden. 2007. "The Limits of Diversification When Losses May Be Large," *Journal of Banking and Finance* 31 (8): 2551–69.

Keynes, J. M. 1936. *The General Theory of Employment, Interest and Money.* New York: Cambridge University Press.

Lewis, D. 1969. *Convention: A Philosophical Study.* Cambridge, MA: Harvard University Press.

Markowitz, H. 1952. "Portfolio Selection," *Journal of Finance* 7 (1): 77–91.

1959. *Portfolio Selection: Efficient Diversification of Investments.* New York: John Wiley & Sons.

Maynard Smith, J. 1982. *Evolution and the Theory of Games.* Cambridge University Press.

Mercer. 2011. "Climate Change – the Implications for Strategic Asset Allocation," www.mercer.com/ri.

Myners Review. 2001. "Institutional Investment in the UK: A Review," study commissioned by the UK government, www.hm-treasury.gov.uk.

North, D. C. 1999. "Understanding the Process of Economic Change," *IEA Occasional Paper* 106: 1–24.

Scharfstein, D. S. and J. C. Stein. 1990. "Herd Behaviour and Investment," *American Economic Review* 80 (3): 465–79.

Schelling, T. C. 1960. *The Strategy of Conflict.* Cambridge, MA: Harvard University Press.

Sugden, R. 1989. "Spontaneous Order," *Journal of Economic Perspectives* 3 (4): 85–97.

Young, H. P. 1996. "The Economics of Convention," *Journal of Economic Perspectives* 10 (2): 105–22.

PART V

Beneficiaries' roles and viewpoints

CHAPTER 26

The voice of the beneficiary

CHRISTINE BERRY AND CHARLES SCANLAN

Introduction

This chapter outlines the case for pension fund beneficiaries to have a greater say in investment policy – both proactively, by having their views taken into account in the formulation of policy, and reactively, by being empowered to hold fiduciaries to account for decisions made on their behalf. We address various common legal and practical objections to such involvement and explore how these play out in practice through real-world case studies. We argue that existing fiduciary law allows more scope than is often supposed for such beneficiary engagement and, moreover, for this to extend beyond purely financial matters. None the less, we conclude that there is a need for legislation both to clarify the law and to change it in certain respects.

The case for beneficiary engagement

What do we mean by "beneficiary engagement?"

It is important to be clear from the outset about what we do and do not mean by "beneficiary engagement," since objections to the idea often appear to stem from misunderstandings and straw men. First, we are not suggesting that beneficiaries should have the right to "instruct" trustees but rather that they should have the right to be consulted and have their wishes taken into account as part of the trustees' decision-making process. Second, we are not suggesting that trustees should be required to consult beneficiaries on the day-to-day minutiae of investment decision-making. We envisage that input from beneficiaries would relate mainly to general *policy* on investment and engagement rather than to "any tedious case-by-

case consideration of ... individual investments" (Richardson 2011a: 11). In relation to individual decisions, we see a role for retrospective transparency and accountability to beneficiaries about the decision taken and the reasons for it. Of course, this should not preclude beneficiaries from making their views known in advance where they feel particularly strongly about a particular question (see, for example, Case Study 26.4).

The legal case

Pension scheme beneficiaries are fundamentally different from beneficiaries of traditional family trusts because *they have paid for their benefits*. Consequently, "the concept of a settlor acting out of bounty, which underlies much trust law, has no application [to pension schemes]" (Browne-Wilkinson 1992: 126) and "[p]ension trusts ... should be recognised as a sui generis species of trust where trustees need to have a different mindset from trustees of traditional trusts" (Hayton 2005: 229). Accordingly, each scheme member can be regarded as "the settlor of a separate settlement ... whose expectations ... need very seriously to be taken into account" (Hayton 2005: 230).

This should mean that pension scheme beneficiaries are not expected to accept what Benjamin Richardson has described as the *passive* role of beneficiaries in traditional private trusts. In reality, however, this culture of passivity has been carried over to institutional investments (Richardson 2011a: 6–8; 2011b: 601–6). As an early commentary on the celebrated English case of *Cowan* v. *Scargill*[1] pointed out, in pension schemes "the strict operation of private trust principles can limit the rights of participation and control" (Farrar and

---

[1] *Cowan* v. *Scargill* 2 All ER 750 (1984), Ch 270 (1985).

Maxton 1986: 33–4). According to David Hayton, the trustees of a family trust have been traditionally seen as the successors of a "patriarch" settlor and any "whining, whingeing" beneficiaries "are not intended to have much scope to complain" and are "expected to accept the decisions of their trustees as if decisions of family umpires" (Hayton 2005: 230–1). Unfortunately, this picture will be all too familiar to many beneficiaries who have sought to engage with their pension fund regarding the investment decisions made on their behalf.

Such paternalism is at least understandable when it comes to defined benefit (DB) schemes, where employers shoulder the investment risk on their employees' behalf, and with it the responsibility for guaranteeing them a certain level of income in retirement. But the shift, in the UK and elsewhere, to defined contribution (DC) schemes makes this attitude even less defensible. Beneficiaries of DC schemes bear all the investment risk: their retirement income depends entirely on net investment returns on their contributions, and hence on the trustees' management of those investments. In today's changing pensions landscape, the assumption that beneficiaries should remain passive is increasingly hard to maintain.

Legal barriers explored

It is sometimes argued that the concept of the active, engaged beneficiary is fundamentally self-contradictory. This objection is encapsulated in the Ontario Law Reform Commission's claim that "to allow beneficiaries to direct the ongoing administration of the trust confuses the role of trustee and beneficiary and is inconsistent with the trust concept" (Richardson 2011a: 8) To reiterate, in this chapter we are suggesting only that fiduciaries *have regard to* their beneficiaries' views (as per FairPensions 2012a: 15, 22–3; a similar approach is considered in Richardson 2011a: 14). Trustees' discretion to decide how far these views can or should be reflected in the fund's investment policies or practices would remain unfettered. In any case, consultation with beneficiaries is not incompatible with the fiduciary relationship; indeed, there are examples of statutory provisions requiring this in various jurisdictions

(Richardson 2011a: 13). An example specifically in the UK pensions context is that trustees with powers to amend schemes cannot do so unless the employees have consulted with beneficiaries on the amendments.[2]

A related objection is that the beneficiary's *dependence* on the fiduciary is at the core of their relationship and is the reason why fiduciary obligations are so strict. In other words, beneficiaries are by definition unqualified to express views on how the fiduciary should discharge their obligations. Certainly, there are highly technical areas of investment decision-making, such as asset allocation, where most beneficiaries are wholly dependent on their fiduciary's expertise. Equally, though, there are many aspects on which beneficiaries *are* competent to ask questions or contribute views: for instance, risk appetite, shareholder engagement and ethical questions (Berry 2011: 98–9).

Without complete openness from fiduciaries there can be no effective participation by beneficiaries. As argued by Peter Morris (2012), the existence of a fiduciary relationship is not in and of itself a case against such openness. Morris makes a useful analogy with company directors: nobody assumes that the imposition on directors of a fiduciary duty to promote the success of the company precludes the need for them to be held to account for their discharge of this duty. On the contrary, we give shareholders extensive rights for this purpose. Although legally speaking the analogy is not perfect, intellectually it is difficult to see why the relationship between pension fund trustees and beneficiaries should be fundamentally different in this respect.

Yet, under the *"Londonderry"* rule (*Re Londonderry's Settlement, Peat v. Walsh*),[3] trustees do not have to disclose to their beneficiaries why they exercised their discretion in a particular way. The rule evolved in the context of private trusts, with a view to avoiding personal embarrassment or family discord. Despite this, the English courts

---

[2] The Occupational and Personal Pension Schemes (Consultation by Employers and Miscellaneous Amendment) Regulations 2006, SI 2006/349.
[3] *Re Londonderry's Settlement, Peat* v. *Walsh*, CA 768 (1965).

have sometimes applied it to pension schemes (for example, *Wilson* v. *Law Debenture Trust Corporation*; *Edge* v. *Pensions Ombudsman*[4]). It has been suggested that this may run counter to the general need to distinguish between "the basic principles of trust law" and "those specialist rules developed in relation to traditional trusts ... the rationale of which has no application to trusts of a quite different kind" (Lord Browne-Wilkinson in *Target Holdings* v. *Redferns*,[5] p. 362, cited in Walker 1996: 131).

The *Londonderry* rule has been described as "an insurmountable barrier to effective scrutiny of the trustees' decision-making" which should no longer apply to, at least, quasi-public trusts (Pearce et al. 2010: 841). Critics have also argued that, again because pension scheme beneficiaries have paid for their benefits, there are "strong arguments that ... [pension scheme] trustees should be ready to justify their decisions to those whose interests they represent, subject to protection for what is truly confidential" (Walker 1996: 130) and that "[s]uch a rule is wholly inappropriate to schemes which should be transparent and where an essential requirement must be the right of the members ... to a full account of the trustees' stewardship" (Browne-Wilkinson 1992: 125; see also Hayton 2005: 234–7). There is thus a compelling case for legal change to require fiduciaries to disclose their reasons for investment and engagement decisions at beneficiaries' request (see also Berry 2011: 100–1; Richardson 2011b: 602–3).

It is often argued that taking account of the views of any beneficiaries in the absence of complete consensus is a breach of the fiduciary duty of impartiality. This objection is explored at length below and so is not discussed further here.

The practical case

Aside from the moral argument that individuals should have the right to hold to account those entrusted with their interests, there are various practical arguments for greater accountability to

beneficiaries. As the Kay Review of UK Equity Markets put it: "[i]n the last five years, there has been a wide erosion of trust in financial intermediaries and in the financial system as a whole. This erosion is not the result of misplaced public perception ... it is based on observation of what has happened" (Kay 2012: 44). The pensions industry has not escaped this loss of trust: In their spring 2012 workplace survey, the UK's National Association of Pension Funds found that mistrust of the industry had overtaken affordability as the number one reason for opting out of the government plan to auto-enrol workers into pension schemes (NAPF 2012: 7).

The Kay Review attributed this collapse in trust to the "replacement of a culture based on relationships by one based on trading increasingly characterised by anonymity, and the behaviours which arise from that substitution" (Kay 2012: 44). Greater accountability to beneficiaries would not only help to restore their faith in the system – an essential prerequisite for the sustainability of private pensions – but could also help to bring about the *cultural shift* the Review calls for: to a true *relationship* between financial fiduciaries and their beneficiaries (see also Richardson 2011a, 2011b). Furthermore, increasing beneficiary participation would complement efforts to protect beneficiaries' interests through regulation, with scrutiny from below reinforcing supervision from above. In particular, greater voice for beneficiaries offers a potential counterweight to "regulatory capture" by the financial services industry (Miller and Dinan 2009).

Again, the analogy with the relationship between companies and shareholders is useful here. The UK corporate governance regime – which has been widely emulated in Europe and beyond – relies heavily on the "comply-or-explain" Corporate Governance Code. This form of "soft law" effectively gives shareholders the responsibility for enforcing good practice: Shareholders are the audience for companies' explanations under the Code, and are expected to scrutinize companies whose explanations for departing from its principles are inadequate – although the extent to which they do so appears to be extremely variable (Arcot et al. 2005). In 2010, the UK introduced a Stewardship

[4] *Wilson* v. *Law Debenture Trust Corporation*, 2 All ER 337 (1995); *Edge* v. *Pensions Ombudsman*, Ch 512 (1995).
[5] *Target Holdings* v. *Redferns* 3 WLR 352 (1995).

Code for institutional investors, modeled on and complementing the Corporate Governance Code. Again, this approach is now being emulated in other jurisdictions. The Code makes clear that the intended audiences of institutional investors' disclosures under the Stewardship Code are their clients and beneficiaries (FRC 2012: 4, 9). The assumption that beneficiaries will remain passive is therefore at odds with emerging corporate governance practice and, if unchallenged, seems likely to impede the success of the stewardship agenda.

Taking beneficiaries' views into account: views about what?

Once the principle of the active, engaged beneficiary is accepted, on what issues should engagement take place? This is equivalent to asking what the scope is of the fiduciary's duty to act in the beneficiaries' "best interests" or for their "benefit." Many of the common legal and practical objections to beneficiary engagement hinge on this question, since they amount to an argument that there are no issues on which beneficiaries' views should be taken into account: Financial matters are outside the beneficiary's expertise, while nonfinancial matters are outside the fiduciary's remit.

Such objections also reflect the mutation of the concept of duty to beneficiaries into that of duty to the fund or to the portfolio (Lydenberg 2012; also in Chapter 22 of this volume). This assumes that any views or interests of beneficiaries that are external to the performance of the portfolio are automatically ineligible for consideration by fiduciaries. In consequence, the beneficiary is either dehumanized – replaced with an archetypal "rational economic man" whose only interest is in the maximization of investment returns – or written out of the equation altogether. As we shall argue, such an interpretation is deeply flawed.

Financial interests

In a trust for the provision of financial benefits, "the best interests of the beneficiaries are normally their best financial interests."[6] Beneficiaries

should therefore be able to engage with their fiduciaries on any matters that may be relevant to their financial interests. Examples might include: the choice between active or passive investment policies; the investment philosophy of any active funds; risk appetite; engagement and voting policies; environmental, social and governance (ESG) considerations; and the approach to conflicts of interest throughout the investment chain. As above, it may be said that beneficiaries lack the expertise to engage on such matters. We have already argued that this is not necessarily true. Moreover, as the case study below demonstrates, members' views can have important implications for schemes even when those views are not well-informed.

All the above matters relate to *investment return*. We suggest, however, that while this will normally be the primary consideration in deciding what is in the beneficiaries' financial best interests, it may not be the only one. For example, at a seminar hosted by UK charity FairPensions (now called ShareAction) in 2012,[7] it was recounted that on one occasion legal advice had been sought by a pension scheme on whether, when voting on a hostile takeover, account could be taken of the fact that some of its beneficiaries might lose their jobs. The advice was that, in such cases, the fiduciary's sole consideration must be the share price. This further exemplifies the attitude that the fiduciary's duty is to the portfolio rather than to the beneficiaries, even where the collateral financial damage to a significant number of beneficiaries may far outweigh any putative benefit to the fund. We see no good reason why fiduciaries should have to take such a blinkered approach.[8]

There may be other cases where a fiduciary's investment or engagement activities could have a

---

[6] *Cowan* v. *Scargill*, p. 760.

[7] The authors are both affiliated with ShareAction and draw on this experience throughout this chapter. However, as stated in the disclaimer at the foot of this chapter, the views expressed here are their own.

[8] Naturally, the fiduciary should carefully balance all relevant interests before taking a decision (FairPensions 2012a: 14) but the question at issue here is whether the collateral financial effects of the takeover should be taken into account *at all*.

financial effect (negative or positive) on some or all of the beneficiaries, especially if they are concentrated in a particular locality or industry. In all such special circumstances, it is particularly appropriate that the views of the beneficiaries be both heard and heeded.

Case Study 26.1: National Employment Savings Trust

The National Employment Savings Trust (NEST) is a new DC scheme set up by the UK government for low-paid workers hitherto underserved by the pensions market. In designing its investment approach, NEST sought to understand the attitudes and preferences of its potential members. Since its membership did not yet exist, it conducted a survey of its target demographic (consisting of some 80% of the UK workforce). The survey covered a range of issues, from risk appetite to ethical preferences. One key finding was that the group exhibited a lower tolerance for downside risk: traditional approaches to DC investing were therefore unlikely to meet their expectations or needs. A decline in the value of their investments early on "may be unacceptable for some members and could lead to increased opt-out" (PADA 2009: 35). This has been used to inform the fund's investment strategy, which attempts to ensure sustainable real growth whilst reducing the likelihood of extreme shocks which could put members off saving altogether.

To be clear, this is not a case of a scheme deferring to its members' relatively less well-informed views on investment strategy. Rather, it reflects recognition that members' attitudes ultimately matter because "persistency in contributions has more of an influence than investment performance in ensuring that member returns are maximised at retirement. Encouraging members to save and maintain persistency in contributions is therefore crucial to delivering better retirement outcomes" (PADA 2009: 35). By understanding its beneficiaries, NEST has been able to tailor its offering in a way calculated to optimize outcomes in their interests – which may not always be identical with maximizing the performance of the fund.

Broader welfare interests: beneficiaries' quality of life

It is commonly asserted that since the purpose of a pension scheme is to deliver financial retirement benefits, any "nonfinancial" considerations are extraneous. We would argue, however, that this view is too narrow an interpretation of the principle that "[t]o decide whether a proposed course of action is for the benefit of the beneficiaries or is in their best interests, it is necessary to decide first what is the purpose of the trust and what benefits were intended to be received by the beneficiaries" (Nicholls 1995: 74).

We submit that one needs to go further and consider the *underlying* purpose of the trust. In relation to investments by charitable trusts, the courts have recognized that, while the immediate purpose that the trustees must pursue is to generate returns, the underlying purpose of generating those returns is to further the charity's objectives. In deciding whether to make particular investments, the trustees can – indeed, must – consider whether they conflict with the aims of the charity or may hamper the charity's work.[9] Yet pension funds are not devoid of an underlying purpose: generating returns for the fund is not an end in itself, but a means to the end of giving beneficiaries a better standard of living in retirement. Thus an investment policy which has negative implications for beneficiaries' future quality of life could be said to undermine that ultimate purpose (Berry 2011: 89–90).

As the Foreword to the Freshfields Report puts it:

> Many people wonder what good an extra percent or three of patrimony are worth if the society in which they are to enjoy retirement and in which

---

[9] *Harries* v. *Church Commissioners for England*, 2 All ER 300 (1993), pp. 304–5.

their descendents [sic] will live deteriorates. Quality of life and quality of the environment are worth something, even if not, or particularly because, they are not reducible to financial percentages (Freshfields Bruckhaus Derringer 2005: 3).

It was confirmed in *Cowan v. Scargill* that "'benefit' is a word with a very wide meaning."[10] Further, the judge made clear that he was "not asserting that the benefit of the beneficiaries which a trustee must make his paramount concern inevitably and solely means their financial benefit, even in a trust for the provision of financial benefits." On this basis alone, we suggest that there should be no difficulty in principle in recognizing that the promotion of the beneficiaries' wider well-being is a "benefit" for the purposes of a pension scheme and that, therefore, the beneficiaries have every right to express their views on matters relating to their broader interests. This may include the impact of investments on the environment (for example, climate change could affect beneficiaries through reduced food security or more frequent natural disasters) and on the economies or communities in which beneficiaries live.

Where fiduciaries, *acting alone*, cannot have a measurable influence on such impacts, legislation could usefully confirm that they may pursue socially responsible policies, including collective action with other investors, which in their view promote the enlightened self-interest of their beneficiaries, thus helping to save them from a "tragedy of the commons." This would remove any doubts on this score, including those arising from some observations in the judgment in *Cowan* v. *Scargill*.[11]

Such legislation should expressly preserve the principle that a fiduciary's duties are owed exclusively to the beneficiaries (FairPensions 2012a: 15–16, 22–3). It would therefore constitute neither an expansion of the group of beneficiaries nor an imposition of independent social or environmental obligations of the kinds discussed by Joakim Sandberg in Chapter 23 of this volume.

It is unfortunate that debates about the scope of beneficiaries' "best interests" have tended to neglect broader welfare considerations,[12] focusing instead on ethical issues. It is this more familiar territory that we turn to next.

Moral benefit: beneficiaries' ethical views

The *Cowan* v. *Scargill* judgment was clear that "benefit" can also include moral benefit – although it is noteworthy that the case in fact concerned a policy which purported to deliver socio-economic benefits to beneficiaries, rather than to accommodate their ethical views. As such, many of the arguments discussed in this section are also applicable to the "welfare interests" discussed above. In relation to moral benefit, the judge gave the example that where all the beneficiaries had strict views on moral and social matters it could be for their benefit "to receive less than to receive more money from an evil and tainted source."[13] He did, however, emphasize that such cases were likely to be very rare and that there would be a heavy burden on anyone who asserted that to receive less money through excluding possibly more profitable forms of investment would be for the benefit of the beneficiaries as a whole.[14]

In line with this observation, it is often argued that since ethics are subjective, in practice it will be impossible to secure consensus among all beneficiaries on a particular ethical stance. To the extent that upholding that stance compromises financial return, considering the ethical views of some beneficiaries is therefore said to be a breach of the duty of impartiality.

The *Cowan* v. *Scargill* judgment does imply that where a proposed ethical investment policy will likely entail financial disadvantage, the consent of all actual and potential beneficiaries will be required. While this condition may sometimes be met in a private trust, this will almost never be possible in a pension scheme (Scanlan 2005: 97). Indeed, one reason for the rejection of the union

---

[10] *Cowan v. Scargill*, p. 761.
[11] Ibid., pp. 764, 767.

[12] Although these are addressed by Sandberg in Chapter 23 of this volume.
[13] *Cowan* v. *Scargill*, p. 761.
[14] Ibid., p. 762.

trustees' policy of not investing overseas or in competitors to the coal industry was that the only beneficiaries who could even potentially have benefited from the policy were those still employed in the coal industry, whereas the judge considered that the restrictions would prejudice the financial performance of the fund, which was held for the benefit of all beneficiaries.[15] This would have been in breach of the trustees' duty of impartiality.[16]

But what if there were no prejudice to financial return? In a subsequent paper on the *Cowan* v. *Scargill* case, the judge, Sir Robert Megarry, considered what the position would have been if the union trustees had abandoned their policy of "total prohibition" for one of "preference," based on an "other things being equal" principle, so that "no investment should be made overseas or in oil if any other investment of equal merit were available." Sir Robert considered that this would have been "by no means a like case" and that it might "well be contended that an investment in A Ltd instead of in B Ltd made because the great majority of beneficiaries oppose investment in B Ltd and so gratifying the majority, will neither harm nor benefit the minority, and so will be for the benefit of the beneficiaries at large" (Megarry 1989: 157–8). There would thus be no breach of the duty of impartiality.

The same reasoning would seem to apply where any significant number of beneficiaries, even if not a majority, can be so "gratified" without harming any other beneficiaries (Scanlan 2005: 98; Freshfields Bruckhaus Deringer 2005: 97; Richardson 2011b: 610). Although the Megarry paper explicitly refrained from expressing a view on what the outcome of *Cowan* v. *Scargill* would have been if it had been fought on this "less stringent policy," the case is plainly no authority for ruling out such an "other things being equal" policy, or, as it is often

called, the "ethical tie-break" (since, as observed, this concept has wider applicability, one could also refer to a "social" or "welfare" tie-break).

A similar approach was approved in the leading charity case of *Harries* v. *Church Commissioners for England* previously mentioned. This concerned the commissioners' investment policy, which stated that while "financial responsibilities" remained of "primary importance," the commissioners also took "proper account of social, ethical and environmental issues." This entailed negative screening of some market sectors (around 13 percent of UK listed companies by value), monitoring of and engagement with investee companies, and a small amount of community-focused property development. The issue was whether the commissioners were right to reject a more stringent policy proposed by the then Bishop of Oxford and others, which, by tightening the existing restrictions on investment in South Africa, would have excluded about 37 percent of UK listed companies by value.

Approving the commissioners' stance, the judge, Sir Donald Nicholls, said that trustees might accommodate moral views that a particular investment would conflict with the objects of a charity; so long as they are satisfied that this would not "involve a risk of *significant* financial detriment."[17] Thus, the commissioners were right not to prefer the Bishop of Oxford's views on South African investment to the views of others "beyond the point at which they would incur a risk of significant financial detriment."[18]

Although some of the considerations in this judgment were specific to charitable trustees, the judge stated that he saw "nothing" in the commissioners' ethical policy that was inconsistent with the general principles of trustee investment,[19] and that he believed his views to be in accordance with the judgment in *Cowan* v. *Scargill*.[20] Likewise, an early, authoritative commentary on the case took the view that the above reasoning was not applicable only to charity trustees but was "compelling in

---

[15] Ibid., p. 764.

[16] In any case, however, the judge found that the union trustees "were mainly, if not solely, actuated by a desire to pursue union policy, and they were not putting the interests of the beneficiaries first, as they ought to have done" (p. 766). This clear breach of fiduciary loyalty is one of the several special features that make *Cowan* v. *Scargill* of less general relevance than is sometimes supposed (Scanlan 2005: 104–5; Freshfields Bruckhaus Deringer 2005: 88–89, 101).

[17] *Harries* v. *Church Commissioners for England*, p. 305 (emphasis added).

[18] Ibid., p. 309.

[19] Ibid., pp. 306–7.

[20] Ibid., p. 305.

relation to *all* trustee investment powers" and that "provided the ethical and social considerations do not prejudice the proper investment of the fund so as to produce profit, such considerations can properly be taken into account" (Browne-Wilkinson 1992: 123, emphasis added).

Moreover, in a later article, Lord Nicholls (as he had then become), writing explicitly in relation to pension schemes, stated:

> The range of sound investments available to trustees is so extensive that very frequently there is scope for trustees to give effect to moral considerations ... without thereby prejudicing beneficiaries' financial interests ... When this is so, there is no reason in principle why trustees should not have regard to moral and ethical considerations ... The trustees would not be departing from the purpose of the trust or hindering its fulfilment ... in other words, in most cases trustees may adopt an ethical investment policy (Nicholls 1995: 75).

The next question is whether an ethical investment policy that meets the terms of the "ethical tie-break" is possible in practice. The *Harries* judgment suggested that the Church commissioners' approach was indeed an example of such a policy. Nonetheless, critics such as Rosy Thornton have argued that this aspect of the judgment was misguided, since according to modern portfolio theory (MPT), "any restriction adopted on ethical or other grounds will necessarily have an effect, however small, upon efficiency" (Thornton 2008: 407).[21]

The financial crisis reinforced pre-existing concerns both about MPT as a technique at the individual portfolio level and about its perceived contribution to systemic risk. This has increased interest in other investment philosophies, such as holding concentrated, "stewardship" portfolios. Yet even if one suspends all skepticism about MPT, a policy of maximum diversification may not always be in the beneficiaries' best financial interests. First, research suggests that the benefits of diversification tail off dramatically above around thirty stocks (Elton and Gruber 1977). It

could therefore well be that the negligible extra benefit (or, in Thornton's words, the "effect, however small") of holding a larger number of stocks would be less than the increase in long-term value that an investor might achieve by engagement as a more significant shareholder in a smaller number of companies. Second, according to the efficient markets hypothesis, "every stock (of the same risk class) is an equally good investment ex ante" (Langbein and Posner 1980: 92). Consequently, assuming no *sector* exclusions, conventional wisdom dictates that the expected return on a portfolio with an ethical or social bias will be the same as that on one managed solely for wealth maximization.

Moreover, to ignore the clear message in the *Harries* judgment that an ethical policy is permissible provided it does not entail *significant* financial detriment amounts to interpreting "best interests" as meaning *exclusively* rather than just *primarily* "financial best interests." That precludes any assessment of whether some *in*significant financial benefit may not be outweighed by benefits of another kind, whether material or moral. These considerations should allay concerns that, because of MPT, the "tie-break" principle (or similar approaches) in practice leaves little or no room for ethical or social factors to be included in pension schemes' investment policies (e.g., Sandberg 2011: 148–50).

Unease about ethical investment often appears to stem from concerns that it amounts to trustees imposing their own moral agendas on beneficiaries. Naturally, the only ethical views that fiduciaries should take into account in their investment or engagement policies, are those of the beneficiaries themselves (Scanlan 2005: 99; Richardson 2007: 166; Berry 2011: 85). The fiduciary duty of undivided loyalty to the beneficiaries applies as much to this species of benefit as to any other.[22] Consequently, including an ethical dimension does not license fiduciaries to pursue their own moral agenda. On the contrary, in the case of moral benefit the voice of the beneficiary is

---

[21] It is important to note here that a "best-in-class" ethical strategy need not reduce diversification and is not inconsistent with MPT (Richardson 2007: 167).

[22] See also *Re Clore's Settlement Trusts, Sainer* v. *Clore*, 2 All ER 272 (1965), p. 275.

ultimately the *only* voice that counts, as the role of the fiduciary is to give best effect to that voice, so far as is compatible with their other fiduciary duties. Fiduciaries adopting an ethical policy must therefore have good grounds for believing that it reflects the views and values of the beneficiaries. They should also, however, retain a wide discretion as to how they discharge this duty in any given circumstances (FairPensions 2012a: 19, 22–3).

Case Study 26.2: tobacco investments

In August 2011, UK campaign group Action on Smoking and Health (ASH) released figures on investments in tobacco by local authority pension funds, who manage the pensions of council workers. Local newspapers pointed out that such investments directly undermine the work of council staff involved in public health activities, such as anti-smoking initiatives or dealing with the public health implications of smoking (see, for example, *Hackney Citizen* 2011). This, along with the potential impacts of smoking-related illnesses on members' own quality of life, adds a new dimension to the more familiar ethical arguments about tobacco investments.[23]

Kent County Council became the focus of publicity after topping the table with £24 million in four tobacco firms. The council responded that it had a "responsibility to obtain the best possible return on investments ... To meet this responsibility, we do not impose restrictions on the companies that our external investment managers can or cannot invest in" (BBC News 2011). This response was echoed by other local authorities – for instance, Hackney Council stated: "The Council's Pensions Sub-Committee has a duty to maximise returns for its pension fund. As a result, our external fund managers will explore investing in a wide range of investment opportunities to ensure the committee's responsibilities are fully met" (*Hackney Citizen* 2011). These responses typify the conventional view that pension funds' fiduciary duties prohibit them from considering beneficiaries' ethical views. They also contain echoes of Rosy Thornton's argument that any restriction of the investment universe constitutes a breach of fiduciary duty.

The debate resurfaced in January 2012 after FairPensions and ASH released a briefing discussing some of the legal and financial issues around ethical screening in general and tobacco investments in particular (FairPensions and ASH 2012). The briefing explored the notion of the "ethical tie-break" and encouraged funds whose beneficiaries had raised concerns about tobacco to assess the risk of significant financial detriment that would occur from excluding these stocks. The aim was to move the debate on from a simplistic interpretation of fiduciary duty to a more nuanced discussion of whether and how ethical concerns might form part of fiduciary investors' assessment of their beneficiaries' best interests.

Yet the response to the briefing from local authority pension funds was largely unchanged from that of six months earlier. For instance, West Yorkshire Pension Fund responded to press enquiries with a statement that "the fund has a legal duty to maximise its investment returns ... When councillors are involved with a pension fund they act as trustees and their sole responsibility is to beneficiaries of the fund and they should not have any political influence" (*Yorkshire Post* 2012). This illustrates a tendency to conflate the distinction between financial and nonfinancial interests with the distinction between beneficiaries' interests and trustees' own political concerns. Paradoxically, this characterization often justifies the dismissal of ethical concerns even when they are raised by beneficiaries themselves.

---

[23] It should be noted that UK local authority pension funds also have statutory duties to local taxpayers. However, they nonetheless have fiduciary duties to their members under common law, and it is these duties which we focus on here.

Beneficiary accountability in practice

Proactive accountability: taking beneficiaries' views into account in policy formation

When it comes to efforts to canvass beneficiaries' views and incorporate them into investment policies, legal objections about the duty of impartiality merge into practical objections about the impossibility of identifying a clear set of shared priorities among a diverse beneficiary base (Thornton 2008: 421; Sandberg 2011: 153–4). Such objections often arise in the context of debates on ethical investment, but the arguments have potentially broader applicability to beneficiary engagement on other matters. In our view, these objections are not insurmountable, for several reasons.

First, on many subjects beneficiaries will likely have not so much conflicting opinions as varying degrees of awareness and concern. For example, it seems fanciful to suggest that there are beneficiaries who are *morally committed* to environmental degradation, the violation of fundamental human rights, or forced labor in the developing world (Scanlan 2005: 98; Richardson 2007: 166). Joakim Sandberg (2011: 154) is no doubt right in saying that "even though most pension fund members may think that environmental degradation is ethically problematic to at least some extent, they will probably disagree about precisely how unethical it is, what institutional investors should do about it more exactly, and to what extent it is adequate to sacrifice financial returns in order to avoid supporting it." None of the three factors in this example, however, should pose insuperable difficulties for fiduciaries trying to formulate or implement an ethical investment or engagement policy: They can take note of the general consensus that environmental degradation is undesirable; they can decide how best to give practical effect to this sentiment in particular cases; and they can then act accordingly, so long as this will not, in their judgment, entail significant financial detriment to any beneficiary.

Second, the fact that beneficiaries will have *different* ethical priorities (Sandberg 2011: 153) should not be a problem if these are not *conflicting*. Fiduciaries could take into account whatever number of these matters they think practicable,

perhaps giving preference to the most "popular" issues among the beneficiaries. That is not unlike how *individual* investors prioritize their various ethical concerns when deciding how to invest.

Third, even where beneficiaries do have conflicting views, there could be circumstances in which fiduciaries could properly prefer one view to another. Suppose, for example, that there were a standing procedure under which beneficiaries could participate in an advisory vote (which the fiduciary would have to take into account) before any ethical preference could be incorporated into the investment or engagement policy. That would confer an equal, ongoing benefit on every beneficiary, which could outweigh any "harm" the beneficiary might suffer by being in a minority on a particular occasion. Furthermore, expressing even a minority view might have some effect. It could influence the fiduciary to modify the policy favored by the majority or even to abandon it on the grounds of an insufficient degree of consensus. Such an approach would reflect both the *continuing* and the *collective* nature of pension schemes and other forms of long-term saving through common funds. It would be a way of respecting the full property rights of settlor-beneficiaries (as per Langbein and Posner 1980: 104–5) by pooling their individual decision-making powers in return for a voice in far more influential combined policies.

The alternative is to deny *all* beneficiaries *any* say on the management of their investments. Disempowering *everyone* in this way may be "impartiality," but of a singularly negative kind: it is a highly impoverished concept of the term that demands all beneficiaries be ignored equally. In our view, arguments of this sort often disguise a status quo bias. After all, beneficiaries do not have identical *financial* interests, albeit financial interests are clearly less subjective than ethical views. Younger beneficiaries with longer time-horizons may have different interests from older beneficiaries: it may not be possible to devise an investment policy that optimizes the interests of both. Yet it would be an odd trustee that threw up their hands and concluded that this made it impossible for them to take investment decisions. The duty of impartiality does not paralyze trustees from acting where beneficiaries have divergent interests. Rather, it exists precisely in recognition of the fact that differing interests will sometimes need to be balanced, and that in doing so trustees ought to "[hold] the scales impartially between different classes of beneficiaries."[24] A prudent trustee should be able to discharge this duty in relation to their beneficiaries' views just as they do in relation to their financial interests.

It is worth noting that concerns about consensus and impartiality should be lessened in DC schemes where members are given a choice of funds in which to invest. For example, if a DC scheme offers an ethical fund that reflects concerns held by a substantial minority of its beneficiaries, the interests of the majority are unaffected even if this fund delivers substantially lower returns, since they are not obliged to invest in it. The only cost that could conceivably be borne by the membership at large, is that of establishing and administering this alternative option. It would seem difficult to object to such a course of action solely on this basis: if, for the reasons advanced in this chapter, giving effect to members' ethical views is a legitimate objective for the fiduciary, this implies some proportionate allocation of resources to achieve that end (Scanlan 2005: 101).

Of course, none of this affects the case for DC schemes to engage with beneficiaries' views in relation to their default fund, where similar issues of impartiality may still arise. Likewise, investment in an ethical or socially responsible fund only strengthens the case for continuing beneficiary engagement *within* that fund, given the interest in fund policy implicit in the initial selection. Thus we think that an increase in the choice of funds available to beneficiaries, although much to be welcomed, would not amount to a fundamentally different vision of impartiality and consensus, as is suggested by Sandberg in Chapter 23 of this volume.

Case Study 26.3: member surveys

Notwithstanding the practical objections discussed above, there are numerous examples of successful initiatives to canvass beneficiaries' views and incorporate them into investment policies.

The Pensions Trust, a UK multi-employer pension scheme for the charitable sector, undertook a survey based on a representative sample of scheme members to determine its beneficiaries' attitudes to ethical investment and the ethical issues that mattered most to them. The results were illuminating – the issues of greatest concern to beneficiaries were environmental sustainability, human rights and child labor. By contrast, "sin stocks" such as gambling and alcohol – which, perhaps because of the SRI movement's roots in religious communities, are a heavy focus of many ethically screened funds – were of relatively little concern. These preferences were echoed in NEST's research into its target demographic, referred to in Case Study 26.1 (PADA 2009). NEST is now incorporating the findings of its research into its ethical policy.

Yet initiatives such as these are still held back by supply-side problems: For instance, NEST has not been able to translate its detailed research on the issues that matter to members into a bespoke ethical fund, offering instead an existing "off-the-shelf" product from F&C (see also FairPensions 2012c). It is to be hoped that, as more schemes seek to understand and incorporate their members' preferences, the market will respond by refining the standard products available and offering more bespoke alternatives.

Reactive accountability: accounting to beneficiaries for investment decisions

As we have argued above, ongoing transparency and accountability to beneficiaries regarding decisions made on their behalf is vital, regardless of whether or not a fund engages with its beneficiaries *ex ante* in developing policies and practices. ShareAction works to promote such accountability by providing beneficiaries with opportunities to question their funds about investment decisions that are of particular concern to them. Although some pension funds consistently respond well, overall ShareAction's experience reinforces the picture of a culture of

---

[24] *Cowan* v. *Scargill*, p.760.

paternalism and passivity inappropriately carried over from private trusts (see FairPensions 2012b for an analysis of responses to an initiative which allowed beneficiaries to contact their funds about votes on executive pay).

In addition, the fact that day-to-day investment decisions are generally delegated to asset managers all too often appears to represent a broken link in the chain of accountability to ultimate beneficiaries. Many savers who contact their funds about specific decisions do not receive a meaningful answer but are simply informed that the relevant powers have been delegated. Yet delegation is not the same thing as abrogation. Fiduciaries remain responsible for overseeing external service providers on behalf of their beneficiaries. It is therefore not unreasonable to expect that queries from beneficiaries about outsourced activities should either be discussed with the relevant service provider or passed on to them to respond directly.

Case Study 26.4: tar sands resolutions

In 2010, a group of institutional investors, coordinated by FairPensions, tabled shareholder resolutions at the Annual General Meetings of BP and Royal Dutch Shell concerning their Canadian tar sands projects. The resolutions expressed concerns about the implications of these projects for the long-term success of the companies, and requested that they commission a report into their underlying risk assumptions. Using an email tool developed by FairPensions, around 6,000 members of occupational pension schemes contacted their funds asking them to support the resolutions and to let them know how they had voted. This was the largest ever mobilization of its kind in the UK. Although the campaign was primarily UK-based, some emails were also sent by members of overseas pension funds with holdings in BP and Shell. FairPensions requested those taking action to inform the charity of any responses received from their provider. Around forty-three different email responses were forwarded to FairPensions and the analysis, which follows, is based on that sample. Where direct quotes from responses have been used, all identifying information has been redacted.

There was enormous variation in the quality of responses. The best provided detailed explanations of their position on tar sands, their engagement with BP and Shell, their governance process for making voting decisions and their position on the resolutions in question. Where the fund did not have an internal governance capability, it made enquiries of its fund managers and relayed their responses to the beneficiary concerned. This demonstrates that effective accountability to beneficiaries is possible even where the decisions in question are outsourced by trustees.

However, these were a minority of all responses. Of the forty-three responses analyzed, only fifteen provided any substantive response to their beneficiaries' specific query. Of the remainder, many simply referred beneficiaries to general policy documents that were highly unlikely to deal with the specific issues raised and that provided no transparency to beneficiaries about the fund's holdings or voting intentions. A typical example is reproduced below.

> Subject: Thank You For Your Enquiry
> The XXX and XXX Trustees' policies on Corporate Governance and Socially Responsible Investment are set out in the Schemes' Statements of Investment Principles (SIPs) which are available on the member website. The Fund Manager implements the policies and reports to the Trustees with reports to members also being provided on the member website.
> This information can be found on [web address].
> Best Regards
> XXX Pension Fund

In only seven out of the forty-three cases did the fund confirm how its fund manager or managers intended to vote on the resolutions. In many cases, this was in part because no voting decision had yet

Case Study 26.4: (cont.)

been made; however, in only two such cases was a promise made to follow up with beneficiaries letting them know the decision in due course. In other cases, either the fund or its fund managers declared that it was not their policy to disclose voting intentions before AGMs. Again, in only a few cases was this followed by a promise to disclose their vote retrospectively. The minority of funds who were willing to disclose their voting intentions belie the arguments made by others that disclosing this information would be commercially sensitive or lead to conflicts of interest.

Eleven responses made reference to the trustees' fiduciary duties, in almost all cases as a factor militating against support for the resolutions or attention to beneficiaries' concerns:

- "The Trustees have a legal duty to not only invest, but to actively seek the best possible financial return … even if it is contrary to the personal, moral, political or social views of the trustees or beneficiaries. This was demonstrated in the *Cowan* v. *Scargill* (1984) court case."
- "We also have as our main duty the financial interests of our members and so must not be seen to be making decisions based on other criteria."
- "You are reminded that the Fund has to balance the financial interest of the Fund with environmental considerations and throughout, it has a legal obligation to try not to compromise financial returns to the detriment of its membership."

This is particularly disappointing given that the resolutions were firmly focused on the *financial* risks of tar sands projects to the companies concerned – and that this was made clear in beneficiaries' emails. In addition, as with Case Study 26.2 above, the first of these responses conflates the distinction between financial and nonfinancial considerations with the distinction between trustees' personal views and beneficiaries' views – incorrectly concluding that case law prohibits trustees from having any

regard to beneficiaries' views. *Cowan* v. *Scargill* confirmed the important principle that trustees cannot pursue a personal crusade with their beneficiaries' money. Its invocation to justify ignoring beneficiaries' own views about the management of their money represents a different principle altogether.

It is also noteworthy that in no case did any fund refer to its duty of impartiality as a reason for not engaging with individual beneficiaries' concerns. Instead, appeals to fiduciary duty were widely made in terms of a straightforward trade-off between a "duty to maximize returns" and the incorporation of beneficiaries' wider concerns. This suggests that the more sophisticated arguments made in the academic literature (and explored in this chapter) about the fiduciary implications of beneficiary involvement are not reflected in the attitudes and approaches of pension funds on the ground.

Indeed, a striking aspect of the experience of this campaign was the hostility displayed by some funds to the idea of being scrutinized by their members. This was sometimes linked to an implicit assumption that members had been "put up to it" by FairPensions and that their concerns were therefore inauthentic. One particularly terse response opened, "Thank you for your e-mail – as you can imagine I have received a number of identical ones from other members of the Scheme." In another case, the chair of a pension fund board memorably remarked that whoever had encouraged members to send the emails "should be taken out and shot." Yet it is difficult to see why NGOs acting as a conduit for like-minded individuals to express their concerns – a staple feature of democratic dialogue in the political arena – should become illegitimate when applied to investments (see Mount 2012: 108). In fact, it is hard not to conclude that disdain for this method of campaigning often disguises a rejection of the basic principle that members of a pension scheme have the right to ask questions about their investments and to have their views taken into account.

Case Study 26.5: PKA

The Danish occupational pension fund system offers an interesting contrast to the UK in relation to both proactive and reactive accountability. The example of healthcare sector fund PKA, which administers five pension schemes with 250,000 members, draws together many of the themes of this chapter and shows how a committed and thoughtful approach to member engagement can overcome assumed legal and practical barriers.

Member engagement is much more widely accepted in Denmark than in the UK: most industry wide and professional pension funds have some kind of established mechanism for member involvement. Of particular interest are the "Pensionskasser," a type of Danish pension fund owned and controlled by its members. These funds are obliged to account to members through annual meetings, usually through the election of delegates who attend and vote at AGMs and scrutinize the board on behalf of the membership at large. The board can choose not to act on delegates' concerns but is expected to explain why. This demonstrates that fiduciaries can be accountable to beneficiaries for their decisions without this usurping their status as decision-makers.

PKA's member delegates are elected from among the membership at large and are then given two and a half days of intensive training to equip them with an understanding of pensions and investment, in order that they can ask intelligent questions and engage with debates about fund policy. Delegates hold the board accountable for its decisions at the AGM, where they approve the annual report and accounts and have the opportunity to ask questions. They also participate in discussions with both members and fund decision-makers. This dialogue is two-way, helping delegates to understand the fund's approach as well as informing it: For instance, delegates have been engaged in "dilemma discussions," using role play to explore the relative merits of exercising "voice" versus "exit" when faced with unethical behavior by investee companies. PKA reports that this has helped to build understanding and support among delegates for the fund's engagement-led approach (interviews with PKA staff, April 27, 2012, and May 8, 2012). Such a representative model is one solution to the problem of insufficient expertise on the part of beneficiaries.

PKA staff observe that their delegates take a particular interest in socially responsible investing, since – as we have suggested might be expected in theory – this is an area which they understand and can relate to. The scheme's socially responsible investment policy was initially drawn up through a series of delegate seminars. Staff acknowledge that disagreement between members was the biggest challenge in developing the policy, noting that any ethical principles agreed upon had to be broadly acceptable, since members are not able to leave the fund. Part of the solution lay in making use of international norms and standards, such as the Geneva Convention on Forbidden Weapons and the UN Global Compact. (This illustrates that there need be no conflict between referring to such norms and giving effect to the views of beneficiaries, a concern expressed by Sandberg in Chapter 23 of this volume.) The process did identify a core of unacceptable investments – initially involving weapons, and expanded in 2005/6 to include tobacco – which the fund now screens out. It also showed that delegates were particularly interested in protecting labor rights and in seeking out socially or environmentally positive investments.

This demonstrates that concerns about impartiality are real, but can be overcome with a careful and intelligent approach. When asked to comment directly on these concerns, PKA staff articulate something very similar to the ethical tie-break: They are legally obliged to seek the best possible return for members, but their current screening policies (which exclude around eighty-three companies in total) do not compromise the fund's ability to do this.

Conclusions: a pragmatic approach

We accept that one should try to set beneficiary engagement within a coherent legal, and even philosophical, framework. None the less, the question of whether such engagement can work in practice is essentially *empirical*. We suggest, therefore, that even a fairly few examples of successful participatory procedures (such as those outlined above) already provide a definitive, affirmative answer. Conversely, the fact that most schemes have not initiated similar processes is no evidence that they could not do so.

While academic analysis of all the theoretical problems in this field is clearly desirable, we think that there is some risk that this may generate more angst than action and may even be seized on by industry practitioners as an excuse to do nothing. This further illustrates the need for legislative reform that would remove barriers, real or perceived, to beneficiary participation across the full range of their "best interests" and that would encourage fiduciaries to promote such engagement in whatever ways are most practicable in their own particular circumstances. FairPensions (2012a: 22–3) contains some indicative draft legislation, which reflects many of the matters discussed in this chapter.

Disclaimer

ShareAction (formerly known as FairPensions), a UK registered charity established to promote responsible investment practices by pension schemes and fund managers, has engaged extensively with the topic of this chapter and was actively involved in the campaigns described in Case Studies 26.2 and 26.4. The chapter also draws on various FairPensions publications (especially Berry 2011 and FairPensions 2012a) and on the charity's other experiences in advocating the rights of beneficiaries. In view of their respective connections with the charity, the authors wish to make it clear that the views expressed in this chapter are their own and not necessarily those of ShareAction.

References

Arcot, S., V. Bruno and A. Faure Grimaud. 2005. "Corporate Governance in the UK: Is the Comply-or-explain Approach Working?" LSE Corporate Governance Discussion Paper No. 581.

BBC News. 2011. "Kent Council Criticised over £24m in Tobacco Shares," August 22.

Berry, C. 2011. *Protecting Our Best Interests: Rediscovering Fiduciary Obligation*. London: FairPensions.

Browne-Wilkinson, Lord. 1992. "Equity and its Relevance to Superannuation Schemes Today," *Trust Law International* 6 (4): 119–26.

Elton, E. J. and M. J. Gruber. 1977. "Risk Reduction and Portfolio Size: An Analytic Solution," *Journal of Business* 50: 415–37.

FairPensions. 2012a. *The Enlightened Shareholder: Clarifying Investors' Fiduciary Obligations*. London: FairPensions.

2012b. *The Missing Link: Lessons from the Shareholder Spring*. London: FairPensions.

2012c. *Ethically Engaged? A Survey of UK Ethical Funds*. London: FairPensions.

FairPensions and ASH. 2012. *Local Authority Pension Funds and Investments in the Tobacco Industry*. London: FairPensions.

Farrar, J. H. and J. K. Maxton. 1986. "Social Investment and Pension Scheme Trusts," *The Law Quarterly Review* 102: 32–5.

Financial Reporting Council. 2012. *The UK Stewardship Code*. London: FRC.

Freshfields Bruckhaus Deringer. 2005. *A Legal Framework for the Integration of Environmental, Social and Governance Issues into Institutional Investment*. Geneva: UNEP Finance Initiative.

Hackney Citizen. 2011. "Hackney Council Pumps Taxpayer Millions into Tobacco Firms," August 18.

Hayton, D. 2005. "Pension Trusts and Traditional Trusts: Drastically Different Species of Trusts," *Conveyancer and Property Lawyer* 69: 229–46.

Kay, J. 2012. *The Kay Review of UK Equity Markets and Long-Term Decision-Making: Final Report July 2012*. London: HM Government.

Langbein, J. H. and R. A. Posner. 1980. "Social Investing and the Law of Trusts," *Michigan Law Review* 79 (1): 72–112.

Lydenberg, S. 2012. *Reason, Rationality and Fiduciary Duty*. New York: IRRC Institute.

Megarry, R. 1989. "Investing Pension Funds: The Mineworkers Case," in T. G. Youdan (ed.) *Equity, Fiduciaries and Trusts*. Toronto: Carswell, pp. 149–59.

Miller, D. and W. Dinan. 2009. *Revolving Doors, Accountability and Transparency – Emerging Regulatory Concerns and Policy Solutions in the Financial Crisis*. Paris: OECD.

Morris, P. 2012. "Keep a Beady Eye on Big Investors," *Financial World*, July/August: 39–40.

Mount, F. 2012. *The New Few: Or, a Very British Oligarchy*. London: Simon & Schuster.

National Association of Pension Funds. 2012. *Workplace Pensions Survey*. London: NAPF.

Nicholls, Lord. 1995. "Trustees and their Broader Community: Where Duty, Morality and Ethics Converge," *Trust Law International* 9 (3): 71–7.

Pearce, R., J. Stevens and W. Barr. 2010. *The Law of Trusts and Equitable Obligations*, 5th edn. Oxford University Press.

Personal Accounts Delivery Authority. 2009. *Building Personal Accounts: Designing an Investment Approach*. London: HM Government.

Richardson, B. J. 2007. "Do the Fiduciary Duties of Pension Funds Hinder Socially Responsible Investment?" *Banking and Finance Law Review* 22 (2): 145–201.

2011a. "From Fiduciary Duties to Fiduciary Relationships for Socially Responsible Investment: Responding to the Will of Beneficiaries," *Journal of Sustainable Finance and Investment* 1: 5–19.

2011b. "Fiduciary Relationships for Socially Responsible Investing: A Multinational Perspective," *American Business Law Journal* 48 (3): 597–640.

Sandberg, J. 2011. "Socially Responsible Investment and Fiduciary Duty: Putting the Freshfields Report into Perspective," *Journal of Business Ethics* 101: 143–62.

Scanlan, C. 2005. "Socially Responsible Investment by Pension Schemes," in C. Scanlan (ed.) *Socially Responsible Investment: A Guide for Pension Schemes and Charities*. London: Key Haven.

Thornton, R. 2008. "Ethical Investments: A Case of Disjointed Thinking," *Cambridge Law Journal* 67 (2): 396–422.

Walker, R. 1996. "Some Trust Principles in the Pensions Context," *Trends in Contemporary Trust Law 1996*, 123–34.

Yorkshire Post. 2012. "Region's Fund Attacked Over Tobacco Investment," January 25.

Understanding the attitudes of beneficiaries: should fiduciary duty include social, ethical and environmental concerns?

JOAKIM SANDBERG, MAGNUS JANSSON, ANDERS BIEL AND TOMMY GÄRLING

Introduction

There is currently a heated debate among fund managers, academics and stakeholders alike concerning to what extent institutional investors like pension funds should take social, ethical and environmental (SEE) considerations into account in investment decisions. Proponents argue that "with great power comes great responsibility," that is, that pension funds in industrialized nations – which today hold assets equivalent to (on average) 76 percent of the GDP of their respective countries (IFSL 2009) – for this reason also have a responsibility to care about the long-term prosperity and well-being of their countries' populations (Sethi 2005; Viederman 2008). By integrating SEE concerns, it is argued that pension funds would incentivize companies listed on the stock market to promote sustainable development and more long-term growth (Kiernan 2009; Woods 2009). This is then, it is said, what a responsible pension fund ought to do. But is it really asset owners' role to take a stand on such nonfinancial issues?

A central point of discussion in this context concerns how to understand the legal responsibilities owed by trustees to their beneficiaries; their so-called fiduciary duties. Pension trustees are under a legal obligation to manage their funds in the best interests of the ultimate recipients of the funds, that is, the future pensioners (Freshfields Bruckhaus Deringer 2005; Whitfield 2005). "Interests" have over time become equated with short term

"financial interests," as captured by prevailing finance theories, and has been thought to preclude fiduciaries from taking SEE concerns into account in investment decisions (Hawley et al. 2011; Hess 2007). However, this view is now being challenged on many fronts. A common argument in the debate is that "interests" can be understood more broadly to also include, for instance, beneficiaries' ethical interests or welfare interests (Lydenberg 2012; Sandberg 2013). As Richardson (2007: 158–9) argues: "If beneficiaries share a moral objection to a particular form of investment, it could be construed as for their benefit if the trust avoided that investment, possibly even at the cost of a lower financial return."

Previous research on these issues has mainly focused on financial aspects – most commonly, researchers have inquired into the financial cost for beneficiaries of integrating SEE concerns in investment decisions (for overviews, see UNEP FI 2009; UNEP FI and Mercer 2007). There are also some studies that take a top-down political or philosophical approach, giving normative arguments for why beneficiaries' "best interests" should be understood in a certain way (Lydenberg 2012; Sandberg 2013). In the present chapter we report on our recent research that takes a bottom-up approach. The chapter describes the results of a survey aimed at understanding the motives of the beneficiaries of pension funds. Our general interest is in how beneficiaries themselves define their "best interests," and what they believe that the managers of their pension funds should consider in investment decisions – for instance, should managers take SEE concerns into consideration even to the point of substantial financial cost? But we are also interested in identifying the psychological determinants of these beliefs and attitudes; that is, we test a model incorporating psychological factors that can explain why beneficiaries are positive or negative towards an extended fiduciary duty that includes SEE concerns.

The chapter is structured as follows. First we give a brief description of the survey method and sample. We thereafter outline our main descriptive results, that is, how respondents themselves define their "best interests" and how they reason concerning the fiduciary duty of their pension funds. A description then follows of the results of our statistical analyses aimed at identifying the psychological determinants of beneficiaries' attitudes in this regard. We discuss these determinants in three separate sections: first we focus on economic factors, then value-based factors and finally an integration of these two groups of factors. The chapter closes with a discussion of some implications of our research for the contemporary debate on fiduciary duty.

Method and sample

In order to get first-hand information on the relevant attitudes, a large-scale survey was conducted of the future beneficiaries of the mandatory pension system in Sweden. We chose the mandatory system in order to ensure a sufficiently large sample (the system covers all people of working age), and also to minimize any possible biases that may exist in specific groups of beneficiaries (such as the beneficiaries of a certain occupational or private pension fund). However, it may be noted that many respondents are likely to be covered by other pension plans as well, and may well be thinking of those plans when answering our questionnaire. Using a national sample has both advantages and disadvantages from a statistical point of view. We acknowledge that our results may not generalize beyond national borders. However, our belief is that they would still be indicative for a wide range

of countries with roughly similar financial systems and cultural norms.

A random sample of 3,500 Swedish residents of appropriate ages (that exclude pensioners) was obtained from the official tax payer register, and a mail-back questionnaire was sent to them by regular mail including a free-reply envelope. After two reminders, we received 1,119 usable questionnaires, corresponding to a response rate of 33.2 percent. The questionnaire consisted of sixteen (groups of) questions that we estimate took between fifteen and twenty minutes to answer. Judging from socio-demographic information reported in the questionnaire, our respondents did not deviate significantly from the general Swedish population with regard to sex and income distribution. However, they were slightly older and more educated than the population at large.

Beneficiaries' attitudes towards an extended fiduciary duty

Judging from how the respondents' answered our survey questions, we conclude that there is large individual variation in the sample. However, by and large, it is interesting to note that very few of our respondents expressed support for the traditional and strictly financial conception of fiduciary duty. Instead, most of them answered in ways that seem more consistent with the idea of pension funds having an extended fiduciary duty that includes SEE concerns.

For example, a central variable was respondents' own definition of their "best interests" as pensioners. Respondents were asked to grade on five-point scales the importance of various factors for their having a good retirement. We may call this their pension-related welfare interests (for further discussion of this variable, see Sandberg 2013). The results are reported in Table 27.1. Note that we here distinguish between three groups of factors: those that chiefly concern oneself (at the top), those that concern oneself as well as others (in the middle), and those that chiefly concern others (at the bottom). Interestingly, we found that respondents gave the lowest grades to factors in the first group and, in particular, the least important factor was personal wealth. This is interesting because, as noted above, the traditional

Table 27.1 Beneficiaries' "best interests."

Now think of the life that you want to lead as a pensioner. How important do you think that the following factors are for your having a good retirement?	
High personal wealth (money, belongings)	3.2
High social status (being liked, respected)	3.3
Good personal relationships (friends, family)	4.6
Safe neighborhoods (low criminality, well-functioning integration)	4.1
Well-functioning healthcare system (short queues, plenty of staff)	4.5
Green immediate environment (limited pollution, pristine nature)	4.2
Social justice (equality between sexes and social classes)	4.0
Stable climate (no climate change, few environmental disasters)	4.1
International stability (few wars, well-functioning UN)	4.2
Global justice (less poverty, respecting human rights)	4.0

conception of fiduciary duty equates beneficiaries' "best interests" solely with their financial interests, that is, their interest in a high pension amount.

The highest grades were given to factors in the second group, which we understand to concern both oneself and others. However, the factors in the third group also received fairly high average grades. On one understanding, both groups contain interests which can be connected to SEE issues and therefore to SEE investments (although this connection obviously is more pronounced with regards to the third group). All in all, as many as 78 percent of respondents gave a higher average grade to such factors (factors in the second and third groups) than to personal wealth. Correspondingly, less than 1 percent indicated that personal wealth was their single most important concern for having a good retirement life.

Respondents were also asked more directly about their understanding of the fiduciary duty of their pension funds and its limits. We may call

this their ethical interests (or ethical attitudes) with regards to pension investments. Some of the results are reported in Table 27.2. Interestingly, only one of five (19 percent) favored the traditional and strictly financial conception of fiduciary duty. Thus most respondents favored an extended conception; indeed as many as 20 percent indicated support for the rather radical view that pension funds have fiduciary duties not only towards beneficiaries but also to society in general (for more discussion on this, see Sandberg 2013). On a direct question, as many as 95 percent of respondents answered that their pension funds should consider SEE issues in investment decisions. A majority said that this holds even though such consideration may not guarantee higher profits. However, we did not find overwhelming support for the idea that it is worth substantial financial sacrifices.

Finally, the questionnaire included some more elaborate scenarios related to the investment choices of pension fund managers. For example, in one scenario respondents were asked to imagine that one of their pension funds owned shares in a mining company recently exposed as using deadly poisons to extract metals and bribing local authorities to avoid criminal prosecution. They were then asked what advice they would give to their fund manager: either to sell the shares immediately (which likely would incur heavy costs on the fund), to wait until a sale would be less financially detrimental to the fund or to do nothing as long as the scandal did not affect the company's share price.

The scenarios unveiled some further structures in respondents' ethical attitudes. For example, while very few (only 2–6 percent) were entirely unmoved by SEE concerns, the others' assessment of the importance of selling the shares immediately seemingly varied with the gravity of the company's unethical behavior (83 percent favored this option in the scenario above, but the figures were lower in other and less radical scenarios). Furthermore, when given the option of starting a shareholder dialogue with the company (instead of immediately selling the shares), around 50 percent of respondents preferred to give this advice. Finally, it was seemingly more important to respondents that their fund managers sell the shares of unethical or environmentally problematic companies, than that they (also) buy shares in

Table 27.2 Beneficiaries' attitudes towards fiduciary duty and SEE concerns.

What should the fund managers focus on when investing your pension money? Choose one of the following alternatives.	
The fund managers should only focus on maximizing financial returns to beneficiaries	19%
The fund managers should put much focus on financial returns, but also consider the ethical concerns of beneficiaries	27%
The fund managers should focus on what benefits beneficiaries in general, not just financially but also socially and environmentally	34%
The fund managers should focus on what benefits society in general, not just the beneficiaries	20%
What is your opinion about fund managers who include social, ethical and environmental concerns in investment decisions? Choose one the following alternatives.	
Fund managers should not consider social, ethical and environmental aspects	5%
Fund managers should only consider social, ethical and environmental aspects if it is relevant for increasing investment returns	35%
Fund managers should consider social, ethical and environmental aspects even if it does not increase investment returns	48%
Fund managers should consider social, ethical and environmental aspects even if it leads to lower investment returns	12%

morally or environmentally exemplary industries, such as "cleantech." In one scenario involving the latter, as many as 17 percent would not recommend buying such shares at all if it would not be profitable in the short term, while 73 percent recommended buying a limited amount of "green" shares and then wait and see how they fare on the market.

The influence of beneficiaries' economic thinking

While the results above are telling in many ways, it may be noted that they are only a snapshot of the current attitudes of beneficiaries limited by time, space and sample. In order to better understand these attitudes and how they may evolve in the future, the main thrust of our research has been to identify their psychological determinants; that is, what it is that makes beneficiaries positive or negative towards an extended fiduciary duty that includes SEE concerns (henceforth EFD). In what follows, we discuss our results concerning the influence of two main groups of determinants: economic factors and values-based factors.

A first and seemingly natural hypothesis in the present context is that beneficiaries' attitudes towards EFD are likely to be influenced by self-regarding or economic factors, that is, roughly what they stand to gain or lose from their pension funds' accepting social and environmental constraints. A number of more specific factors can be associated with this hypothesis. According to standard theories of finance, private investors will only chose a given investment if it provides higher or equivalent returns at lower or equivalent levels of risk compared to alternative investments (Nagy and Obenberger 1994). This is probably the strictest view, which seems to imply that the only relevant determinants of beneficiaries' attitudes towards EFD should be their beliefs about the financial risk and expected return of investments that include SEE concerns.

In order to evaluate this view, we performed a number of statistical tests on both individual factor correlations and more elaborate multifactorial models. We found that our respondents' beliefs about the expected risk and expected return of SEE investments, taken separately and over both the short and long term, indeed influence their attitudes towards EFD. That is, respondents who believe that integration of SEE concerns in investment decisions either reduces risk or improves returns (perhaps because it involves trading on additional relevant information), or both, indeed have a more positive attitude towards EFD. Beliefs about risk were correlated with beliefs about returns, but they both had explanatory power in their own right. However, we also found that these are far from the only relevant determinants.

A further interesting factor is beneficiaries' general attitude towards risk. Previous psychological research has shown that people vary in how they

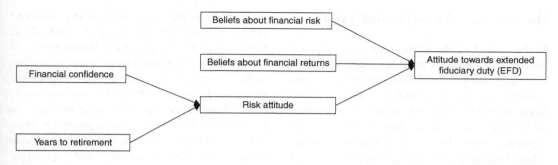

Figure 27.1 The economic model.

perceive the risks associated with different kinds of activities, as well as in their attitude towards these risks (Weber et al. 2002). We are not familiar with any previous studies on SEE investments in particular in this regard. However, inspired by standard theories of finance, one would expect that people that are more risk-averse with regards to investments – that is, those who have a more negative attitude towards risk-taking in this context – also should be more negative towards EFD, since it departs from strictly financial thinking in investment decisions (by restricting the investment universe). At the very least, this relationship could be expected to hold for people who regard SEE investments as more risky than conventional investments.

Interestingly, we found the opposite to be true. That is, respondents that are more risk-averse are generally more positive towards EFD, and this holds true irrespective of their beliefs about the risks associated with SEE investments. We return to discuss this finding some more below.

We also investigated the determinants of respondents' risk attitude – that is, why are some people gamblers, while others prefer safety and stability? Consistent with the predictions of financial theory, we found that age is negatively correlated with risk attitude – that is, respondents get more risk-averse the closer they get to retirement age. (This is rational in an investment setting, since one has increasingly less time to regain losses.) Furthermore, we found that risk attitude is closely connected to what one may call financial confidence; that is, respondents who feel like they know very little about stock markets and/or that seldom make active choices in their pension investments are also more risk-averse

in this area. Previous research has shown that lack of financial confidence and knowledge is a major source of seemingly irrational retirement planning behavior among the general public (Clark et al. 2004; MacFarland et al. 2004). Moreover, some groups of investors seemingly act irrationally due to "overconfidence" effects (Statman et al. 2006).

A final interesting economic factor is beneficiaries' dependence on the investment returns. Previous research on so-called ethical investors – that is, private investors with holdings in retail funds with an SEE profile – has shown that they typically put only a small fraction of their investments in such funds. A frequently suggested explanation for this is that investors only are prepared to take SEE concerns with their "surplus money," that is, money that they do not "need" for essential parts of their life and therefore can afford to lose (Mackenzie and Lewis 1999). This explanation is inspired by psychological research in other areas (Lopes 1987). We performed a number of statistical tests in order to find a similar effect in our sample, but we were unable to do so. That is, we found no evidence for any effect of respondents' (self-reported) dependence on the investment returns on their attitudes towards EFD.

When we put all of the above together – that is, when we construct a model involving both beliefs about risk and return of SEE investments as well as people's more general risk attitude and its determinants, age and financial confidence (see Figure 27.1) – we are able to explain a large proportion of the individual variance in the attitude towards EFD. However, the model does not fit the data perfectly. This indicates that we are still missing some important determinants.

The influence of beneficiaries' values

In the context of discussing what may influence beneficiaries' attitudes towards an extended fiduciary duty that integrates SEE concerns, it seems plausible that, besides economic beliefs and attitudes, central determinants are also beneficiaries' social and ethical values. That is, besides self-regarding factors, there may be important factors related to beneficiaries' regard for others. We tested a number of such factors on our sample.

Previous research on ethical investors has shown that their commitment to integrating SEE concerns in investment decisions partly depends on the existence of "pro-social" or "pro-environmental" attitudes, that is, their commitment to SEE concerns in society in general (Jansson and Biel 2011; Lewis and Webley 1994; Nilsson 2008, 2009). In order to test the corresponding hypothesis in our sample, we asked respondents to grade how important they think it is that society (individuals, companies and authorities) invest time and effort to reduce emissions of greenhouse gases, to counteract the acidification of lakes and rivers, to reduce global inequalities and eradicate world poverty, to reduce alcohol's negative effects on our society, to control the international arms trade and several other similar goals. Consistent with our expectations, we found a strong correlation between respondents' general concern for SEE issues and their attitude towards EFD. Indeed this correlation was stronger than for any of the economic factors.

But what can in turn explain people's general SEE concern? An interesting line of psychological theorizing and research concerns people's fundamental value orientations. According to Schwartz (1992), one of the central value differences between people is that some orient towards "self-transcendence" values such as benevolence and universalism, whereas others orient towards "self-enhancement" values such as achievement, power and hedonism. In laypeople's terms, we may call this altruism versus egoism. Schwartz' schema has been empirically confirmed in a number of domains (see, for example, Stern 2000). Furthermore, it has been shown that people with a self-transcendent (altruistic) value orientation are

more likely to engage in pro-environmental and pro-social behaviors (Hansla et al. 2008, 2013; Stern et al. 1999; Thompson and Barton 1994).

We measured our respondents' value orientation in the way suggested by Schwartz. Consistent with the research above, we found that self-transcendence (altruism) had a positive direct influence on respondents' SEE concern, and a positive indirect influence (through SEE concern) on their attitude towards EFD. What this means is that respondents who are more altruistic on average are more concerned about SEE issues in society, and also more positive towards EFD. We will say more about value orientation in the next section.

A final interesting factor in this context is political orientation. Some of the authors who have been most critical towards EFD have argued that it is essentially a "socialist" idea; that is, that it involves promoting the "special interests" of unions and other organizations to the detriment of other groups of beneficiaries with their own ideas and/or interests (Entine 2005; Rounds 2005). We therefore wanted to test whether attitude towards EFD is correlated with respondents' political orientation, as measured by their self-assessed placement on a unidimensional scale from the political left to right. We found that respondents that identified with the political left indeed had a more positive attitude towards EFD, whereas respondents that identified with the political right had a more negative attitude. However, these correlations also seem to stem from the importance of people's more fundamental value orientations as discussed above. Respondents that identified with the political left were namely more altruistic and had a greater concern for SEE issues in general. This is then what we believe explains their more positive attitude towards EFD.

When we put all of the above together – that is, when we construct a model involving both SEE concern and value orientation (see Figure 27.2) – we are once again able to explain a large proportion of the variance in attitude towards EFD. However, again the model does not fully account for respondents' attitudes in this regard. This suggests that not everything can be explained with reference to values.

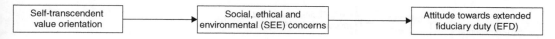

Figure 27.2 The values-based model.

Interaction between economic thinking and values

Our discussion above suggests that both economic and values-based factors are relevant for understanding beneficiaries' attitudes towards EFD, but that a model incorporating only one group of determinants does not statistically give the best fit to the data. An obvious final step is then to appeal to some combination of both economic and values-based thinking. Indeed, it may be noted that this is where many other studies on various kinds of pro-social and pro-environmental behavior ultimately have landed (Kaiser et al. 2005; Stern et al. 1999). This includes some previous studies on more direct private and professional investment decisions (Hong and Kacperscszyk 2009; Jansson and Biel 2011; Lewis and Webley 1994; Nilsson 2008, 2009).

In line with these studies, we found that we were able to explain more of the variance in the sample with a model integrating both economic and values-based factors. More specifically, we found the strongest statistical support for a model with the following mix of determinants: respondents' beliefs about the returns on SEE investments, their general risk attitude (which in turn is influenced by their age and financial competence) and their general SEE concern which is influenced by their value orientation (see Figure 27.3). We have submitted this model to a large number of tests and find that it comes out significantly better than the other models.

But how do these different factors relate to each other, and which is really the most important one? Interestingly, when we further investigated the interaction between economic and values-based factors, we found some unexpected correlations. First, we found a positive correlation between respondents' value orientation and their beliefs about the returns on SEE investments (the dotted line in Figure 27.3). What this means is roughly

that people with a self-transcendent value orientation also have a stronger faith in the positive returns of SEE investments. This is a kind of wishful economic thinking that ultimately is based on value orientation. Previous psychological studies have confirmed similar phenomena in other domains (Krueger and Dickson 1994; Stern et al. 1995) and the suggested rationale is that individuals tend to interpret information in accordance with their values in order to avoid cognitive dissonance, that is, incoherence between their values and beliefs (Festinger 1957). Wishful thinking thus helps beneficiaries to avoid a conflict between their moral convictions and their financial beliefs.

Second, we found a negative correlation between respondents' self-transcendent value orientation and their risk attitude. This correlation is more difficult to interpret. If we allow ourselves to speculate, it seems possible to understand both risk attitude and financial confidence as indirect proxies for the opposing value-orientation of self-enhancement – or greed. Some previous studies have suggested that people who are self-confident gamblers tend to score higher on such values (Campbell et al. 2004; Fritzsche and Oz 2007). Furthermore, this would indeed explain our finding that those who are more risk-averse generally are more positive towards EFD, which holds true irrespective of their beliefs about the risks associated with SEE investments. On this interpretation, risk attitude tracks greed and nothing else, and it seems natural that it is negatively correlated with attitude towards EFD.

If the speculations above are true, it seems that the most important determinant of beneficiaries' attitudes towards EFD actually is a relatively deep feature of their psychological make-up, namely their fundamental value orientation or, put simply, to what extent they are egoistic or altruistic. This factor influences all other determinants: general SEE concern, beliefs about the returns on SEE investments and general risk attitude. We close by

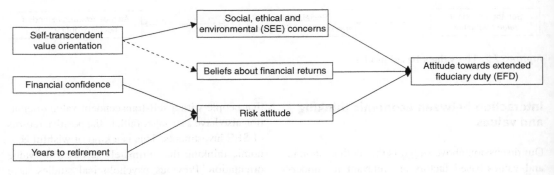

Figure 27.3 The integrated model.

Implications for the debate on fiduciary duty

discussing some implications of our results for the contemporary legal debate.

A great number of fund managers, lawyers and academic commentators assume that institutional investors' legal responsibility to manage assets in the best interests of their beneficiaries – that is, their fiduciary duty – implies that only short-term financial returns should be maximized. And this, it is often thought, rules out integrating social, ethical and environmental (SEE) concerns into investment decisions. But this view is now being challenged. A pertinent counterargument is that beneficiaries' best interests can be understood more broadly to also include, for instance, their ethical or welfare interests. In this chapter, we have reported on our research that seeks to contribute to resolving this controversy by asking beneficiaries themselves how they define their best interests and what they think that managers of their pension funds should consider in making investments. More specifically, we have reported on the results of our attempts to identify the main psychological determinants of beneficiaries' attitudes in this regard; that is, factors that can explain why beneficiaries are positive or negative towards an extended fiduciary duty that includes SEE concerns.

We want to highlight two findings which are particularly relevant if beneficiaries' attitudes should have any bearing on how fiduciary duty should be interpreted. One finding is that the attitudinal differences between individuals go deeper than previously assumed – individuals not only differ in their attitude towards extended fiduciary duty as such, but also in their underlying value orientations; for instance, they seemingly vary on a continuum from being solely concerned about SEE issues to being solely concerned about economic benefits. This finding is relevant to the issue of how fund managers should go about interpreting their beneficiaries' will, and especially to the issue of what more specific SEE issues fund managers may consider and how. According to standard interpretations of fiduciary duty, namely, fund managers need to be able to point to a consensus among beneficiaries in order to include a given nonfinancial concern (Freshfields Bruckhaus Deringer 2005).

Sandberg (2011) has recently argued that the prospects of finding any SEE issue on which all beneficiaries of a large pension fund can agree seem extremely slim. In a reply, Richardson (2011: 10) argues that legislative changes aimed at making beneficiaries more directly involved in their pension funds' decision-making processes may lead to increased consensus on many issues. This is so because "theories of ethical and democratic deliberation suggest that social values can evolve among participants through appropriately structured forums for reasoned discussion." While we are unable to evaluate all of the details of Richardson's suggestion here, it seems fair to say, based on the results of our studies, that it faces a number of major challenges. The relevant disagreements are not simply situational and one-dimensional. Rather, they are comprehensive and located deeply in people's self-images.

The other finding that we wish to highlight is the importance of values-based motivations among beneficiaries more generally. As noted at the outset of the chapter, previous research in the area has mainly focused on financial aspects – most commonly, researchers have inquired into the financial cost for beneficiaries of integrating SEE concerns in investment decisions. But according to our results, beneficiaries are not only interested in financial costs versus gains, but also in SEE aspects in their own right. Indeed, judging from some of the finer details of our results, there are clear indications that the values-based motives ultimately are the most important ones. Respondents' value orientation is a major part of the explanation of their (supposedly strictly financial) beliefs about the returns on SEE investments, and it is also connected to their attitude towards investment risk.

Our overarching hope is that these results will help pension fund managers to better understand their beneficiaries' expectations about their job and responsibilities; especially their expectations about including SEE concerns in investment decisions. An overwhelming majority of beneficiaries are clearly positive towards including such concerns, although there are important nuances in their attitudes in this regard. Our research thus provides a basis upon which fund managers can begin to design alternative portfolios that better match their beneficiaries' nonfinancial values. More specifically, being aware of the great differences between segments of beneficiaries could be an inspiration for funds that want to create a more differentiated supply of investment opportunities for future pensioners. Such funds could design a greater range of options for beneficiaries so that they can select investment strategies that better fit their own self-determined interests.

Acknowledgements

This chapter builds on manuscripts currently under academic review. Interested readers may contact Joakim Sandberg for more information.

Our research was financially supported by the Swedish Foundation for Strategic Environmental Research (Mistra) through the Sustainable Investment Research Platform (SIRP), and by a grant from the Rotman International Centre for Pension Management. We thank Anders Carlander and Daniel Peterson for assistance in collecting and entering the data.

References

Campbell, K., A. Goodie and J. Foster. 2004. "Narcissism, Confidence and Risk Attitude," *Journal of Behavioral Decision Making* 17: 297–311.

Clark, R. L., M. B. d'Ambrosio, A. A. McDermed and K. Sawant. 2004. "Sex Differences, Financial Education, and Retirement Goals," in O. S. Mitchell and S. P. Utkus (eds.) *Pension Design and Structure*. New York: Oxford University Press, pp. 185–206.

Entine, J. 2005. "The Politicization of Public Investments," in J. Entine (ed.) *Pension Fund Politics*. Washington, DC: American Enterprise Institute, pp. 1–12.

Festinger, L. 1957. *A Theory of Cognitive Dissonance*. Stanford University Press.

Freshfields Bruckhaus Deringer. 2005. "A Legal Framework for the Integration of Environmental, Social and Governance Issues into Institutional Investment," report from the UNEP Finance Initiative.

Fritzsche, D. and E. Oz. 2007. "Personal Values' Influence on the Ethical Dimension of Decision Making," *Journal of Business Ethics* 75 (4): 335–43.

Hansla, A., A. Gamble, E. A. Juliusson and T. Gärling. 2008. "The Relationship Between Awareness of Consequences, Environmental Concern, and Value Orientations," *Journal of Environmental Psychology* 28: 1–9.

Hansla, A., T. Gärling and A. Biel. 2013. "Attitude towards Environmental Policy Measures Related to Value Orientation," *Journal of Applied Social Psychology* 43 (3): 582–90.

Hawley, J., K. Johnson and E. Waitzer. 2011. "Reclaiming Fiduciary Duty Balance," *Rotman International Journal of Pension Management* 4 (2): 4–16.

Hess, D. 2007. "Public Pensions and the Promise of Shareholder Activism for the Next Frontier of Corporate Governance," working paper, Ross School of Business, University of Michigan.

Hong, H and M. Kacperscszyk. 2009. "The Price of Sin: The Effects of Social Norms on Markets," *Journal of Financial Economics* 103: 1–19.

International Financial Services London (IFSL). 2009. *Fund Management 2009*. London: IFSL.

Jansson, M. and A. Biel. 2011. "Motives to Engage in Sustainable Investment: A Comparison between Institutional and Private Investors," *Sustainable Development* 19: 135–42.

Kaiser, F. G., G. Hübner and F. X. Bogner. 2005. "Contrasting the Theory of Planned Behavior with the Value-Belief-Norm Model in Explaining Conservation Behaviour," *Journal of Applied Social Psychology* 35: 2150–70.

Kiernan, M. 2009. *Investing in a Sustainable World*. New York: Amacom.

Krueger, N. and Dickson, P. 1994. "How Believing in Ourselves Increases Risk Taking: Perceived Self-Efficacy and Opportunity Recognition," *Decision Sciences* 25 (3): 385–400.

Lewis, A. and P. Webley. 1994. "Social and Ethical Investing: Beliefs, Preferences and the Willingness to Sacrifice Financial Return," in A. Lewis and K.-E. Wärneryd (eds.) *Ethics and Economic Affairs*. London: Routledge, pp. 171–82.

Lopes, L. 1987. "Between Hope and Fear: The Psychology of Risk," in L. Berkowitz (ed.) *Advances in Social Psychology*. London: Academic Press, pp. 255–67.

Lydenberg, S. 2012. "Reason, Rationality and Fiduciary Duty," *Pensions & Investments*, February 21.

MacFarland, D. M., C. D. Marconi and S. P. Utkus. 2004. "'Money Attitudes' and Retirement Plan Design: One Size Does Not Fit All," in O. S. Mitchell and S. P. Utkus (eds.) *Pension Design and Structure*. New York: Oxford University Press, pp. 97–120.

Mackenzie, C. and A. Lewis. 1999. "Morals and Markets: The Case of Ethical Investing," *Business Ethics Quarterly* 9 (3): 439–52.

Nagy, R. and R. Obenberger. 1994. "Factors Influencing Individual Investors' Behavior," *Financial Analysts Journal* 50 (4): 63–8.

Nilsson, J. 2008. "Investment with a Conscience: Examining the Impact of Pro-Social Attitudes and Perceived Financial Performance on Socially Responsible Investment Behavior," *Journal of Business Ethics* 83: 307–25.

2009. "Segmenting Socially Responsible Mutual Fund Investors: The Influence of Financial Return and Social Responsibility," *International Journal of Bank Marketing* 27: 5–31.

Richardson, B. J. 2007. "Do the Fiduciary Duties of Pension Funds Hinder Socially Responsible Investment?" *Banking and Finance Law Review* 22 (2): 145–201.

2011. "From Fiduciary Duties to Fiduciary Relationships for Socially Responsible Investment," *Journal of Sustainable Finance & Investment* 1: 5–19.

Rounds, C. E. 2005. "Why Social Investing Threatens Public Pension Funds, Charitable Trusts, and The Social Security Trust Fund," in J. Entine (ed.) *Pension Fund Politics*, Washington, DC: American Enterprise Institute, pp. 56–80.

Sandberg, J. 2011. "Socially Responsible Investment and Fiduciary Duty: Putting the Freshfields Report into Perspective," *Journal of Business Ethics* 101 (1): 143–62.

2013. "(Re-)Interpreting Fiduciary Duty to Justify Socially Responsible Investment for Pension Funds?," *Corporate Governance: An International Review* 21 (5): 436–46.

Schwartz, S. H. 1992. "Universals in the Content and Structure of Values," in M. P. Zanna (ed.) *Advances in Experimental Social Psychology*. New York: Academic Press, vol. 25, pp. 1–65.

Sethi, S. P. 2005. "Investing in Socially Responsible Companies is a Must for Public Pension Funds – Because There is no Better Alternative," *Journal of Business Ethics* 56: 99–129.

Statman, M., S. Thorley, and K. Vorkink. 2006. "Investor Overconfidence and Trading Volume," *The Review of Financial Studies* 19 (4): 1531–45.

Stern, P. C. 2000. "Toward a Coherent Theory of Environmentally Significant Behavior," *Journal of Social Issues* 56: 407–24.

Stern, P. C., T. Dietz, L. Kalof and G. A. Guagnano. 1995. "Values, Beliefs and Proenvironmental Action: Attitude Formation Toward Emergent Attitude Objects," *Journal of Applied Social Psychology* 25: 1611–36.

Stern, P. C., T. Dietz, T. Abel, G. A. Guagnano and L. Kalof. 1999. "A Value-Belief-Norm Theory of Support for Social Movements: The Case of Environmentalism," *Human Ecology Review* 6: 81–97.

Thomson, S. and M. Barton. 1994. "Ecocentric and Anthropocentric Attitudes toward the Environment," *Journal of Environmental Psychology* 14: 149–57.

UNEP FI. 2009. *The Materiality of Climate Change*. Geneva: UNEP FI.

UNEP FI and Mercer. 2007. *Demystifying Responsible Investment Performance*. Paris: UNEP FI and Mercer.

Viederman, S. 2008. "Fiduciary Duty," in C. Krosinsky and N. Robins (eds.) *Sustainable*

Investing: The Art of Long-Term Performance. London: Earthscan, pp. 189–99.

Weber, E., A. Blais and N. Betz. 2002. "A Domain Specific Risk Attitude Scale: Measuring Risk Perceptions and Risk Behaviours," *Journal of Behavioural Decision-making* 15: 263–90.

Whitfield, J. 2005. "Trustees' Investment Duties," in C. Scanlan (ed.) *Socially Responsible Investment: A Guide for Pension Schemes and Charities*. London: Key Haven, pp. 27–52.

Woods, C. 2009. "Funding Climate Change: How Pension Fund Fiduciary Duty Masks a Collective (In)Action Problem," working paper, Oxford University.

Operationalizing socially responsible investment: a nonfinancial fiduciary duty problem

RALF BARKEMEYER, FRANK FIGGE, TOBIAS HAHN,
ANDREAS G. F. HOEPNER, ANDREA LIESEN AND
AGNES L. NEHER

Introduction

The fiduciary duty principle has taken center-stage in the debate concerning the integration of environmental, social and corporate governance (ESG) performance. For decades, it has been widely agreed that "trustees or fiduciaries [are to manage] assets in the best interests of the individual beneficiaries or investors: the ultimate recipients or owners of the funds" (Chapter 1 of this volume). The "best interests" of the beneficiaries or investors have typically been reduced to their *financial* interests (Langbein and Posner 1980; Sandberg 2011). Addressing this fiduciary duty problem is seen as pivotal for future development of the socially responsible investment (SRI) market in general (e.g., Richardson 2009). As a result, an ever-increasing body of literature has focused on the analysis of the financial implications of incorporating nonfinancial interests into investment decision-making. Over the past three decades, several thousand "does it pay to be green?" or "does it pay to be responsible?" studies have been published with the aim to shed light on this relationship (for excellent – albeit slightly contradictory – overviews see, for example, Margolis and Walsh 2003; Orlitzky et al. 2003; Salzmann et al. 2005). It is generally agreed that the inconclusiveness within this body of literature is a result of the diversity of the underlying measures of financial performance, the methodologies applied, the sample sizes analyzed, the time horizons under investigation, the respective industries analyzed and, most importantly, the operationalization of the environmental or social performance of the companies under investigation (cf. Horváthová 2010; Ullman 1985).

At the same time, much has been written about the complex undertaking of integrating environmental and social aspects in financial decision-making, and more generally about sustainable development and corporate social responsibility. Sustainable development as a broad societal concept is difficult to break down to the level of individual actors (Robinson 2004). In addition, it embraces a multitude of complex, context-specific environmental and socio-economic problems. As a result, it remains difficult to reach any meaningful consensus about what these concepts should entail and what their implications should be (Barkemeyer et al. 2011; Redclift 2005; Robinson 2004); analogously, the same applies to the specific responsibilities of business in a given context (Moon 2007). Hence, what we mean by sustainable development and corporate social responsibility is often only revealed through specific operationalization in a given context. The multifaceted nature of sustainability, CSR and consequently ESG integration is also reflected by the heterogeneity of SRI products available in the market (Sandberg et al. 2009). Clearly, different market participants have different understandings of what sustainability, CSR and ESG integration should constitute in the context of SRI.

Interestingly, this insight is hardly reflected upon in the SRI literature on fiduciary duty. It is safe to assume that many investors have more than financial interests. Surprisingly little has so far been written about the duty of SRI funds to represent these social and environmental interests of their investors. Whenever ESG criteria are integrated in investment decisions to purely maximize profits, there is strictly speaking no need for trustees to take into account the social and environmental interests of the investors. However, "value-driven investors" (as opposed to "profit-seeking investors," see Derwall et al. 2011) continue to form a significant part of the market. Beal et al. (2005) summarize that the vast majority of SRI investors can be expected to have at least a certain degree of ethical motivations – whereas the "pure" profit-driven investor represents a minority view.

In this chapter, we extend the fiduciary duty concept to the level of nonfinancial interests of beneficiaries and investors. In other words, rather than investigating the relationship between the integration of ESG into financial decision-making and the financial interests of beneficiaries and investors, we focus on the link between the integration of ESG into the investment decision and the environmental and social interests of beneficiaries and investors. Based on a survey of SRI practitioners, we show that their sustainability-related perceptions and priorities are unlikely to match with those of the beneficiaries; instead, the perceptions and priorities of SRI practitioners seem to reflect a relatively homogeneous epistemic community across national borders. For the integration of ESG issues into financial decision-making, this circumstance creates an agency problem. Along the lines of the fiduciary duty to manage funds in ways that best represent the financial interests of their investors, trustees can be argued to also have a nonfinancial fiduciary duty to manage funds in ways that best represent the nonfinancial interests of their investors.

There are numerous approaches with which ESG aspects can be incorporated into investment products by SRI practitioners. For ease of argument, in this chapter we distinguish between ESG integration and screened approaches. In the case of screened approaches we refer to positive screening approaches (i.e., including best in class, thematic funds) and negative screening approaches (i.e., the investment universe that is used for portfolio construction has been previously filtered

based on value or ethically based exclusion criteria) (Eurosif 2010). Screened approaches usually allow the investor/beneficiary to determine whether an investment product corresponds to his or her specific values, for example based on a list of excluded sectors or positive screening criteria. Approaches of ESG integration oftentimes do not allow for such an instant assessment. ESG integration refers to the practice of incorporating ESG factors in the analysis and portfolio construction process. Eurosif (2010: 15) summarizes that the methodologies "and depths of the approach may vary significantly." Often, the specific ESG criteria applied are only reflected implicitly in the final investment product and – as it will be shown below – are rarely communicated by SRI practitioners explicitly in a transparent manner. In terms of investment approaches, the nonfinancial fiduciary duty problem, as evidenced in this chapter, is consequently mainly relevant for approaches of ESG integration, and only of limited relevance in the case of screened approaches.

The remainder of this chapter is structured as follows: in the next section, we provide an overview of the current state of the pension fund market with regard to ESG reporting, with particular emphasis on the UK, the USA and Australia as the regions that are commonly perceived as the most mature (Haigh and Hazelton 2004). The following section serves to shed light on the interests and intentions of beneficiaries, both in terms of financial and nonfinancial motivations underlying their engagement with SRI. Subsequently, a survey of SRI practitioners reporting on their sustainability-related perceptions and priorities is presented. Building on the results of this survey, we discuss potential agency problems linked to nonfinancial fiduciary duty problems. We conclude by developing recommendations for practitioners.

Information transparency of pension funds

To illustrate the potential relevance of the nonfinancial fiduciary duty problem, an in-depth assessment of the ESG-reporting of the 1,000 largest pension funds worldwide has been undertaken.

Investments & Pension Europe (IPE), the leading European publisher for institutional investors and those running pension funds, collected the sample between 2009 and 2010. For the analysis, the existence of ESG reporting was examined first. Then, if a fund reported about ESG, either as part of its annual report or in a separate report, the information was screened with regard to eighteen detailed aspects, such as information about environmental or social activities or about human rights. For the purposes of this chapter, we focus on the pension funds from the USA, UK and Australia. A sample of 597 funds results, whereby 458 pension funds are based in the USA, 110 pension funds are from the UK, and 29 pension funds originate from Australia. It is striking that 37.9 percent of the Australian pension funds consider ESG criteria in their investments. In the UK, 25.5 percent of the pension funds report about their ESG activities, whereas only 2.8 percent of the American pension funds consider ESG criteria. This implies that 549 or 91.3 percent of the pension funds in our sample do not report at all about ESG criteria.

Table 28.1 shows the reported ESG issues addressed by pension funds in the USA, UK and Australia that do report on the use of ESG criteria. Of these funds, 79 percent consider "social issues" in general, such as community impact or workplace in the investment process. It follows proxy voting and the consideration of environmental issues with 75.8 percent, respectively. Animal testing and welfare as well as philosophical or religious screening are positioned at the bottom of the list with 4.8 percent. Overall, pension funds apply mainly conventional ESG criteria linked to ESG issues. Additionally, pension funds use their shareholder rights for proxy voting and engage actively with companies. It must be emphasized that these reporting/investment information only apply to 8.7 percent of the considered 597 pension funds. Also, the information of these 8.7 percent analyzed pension funds is at times patchy and largely limited to generic categories such as "social issues," rather than detailed information. It is commonly unclear how these broad categories are operationalized, i.e., which social issues are considered and how. However, pension funds do typically report very elaborately about their activities in regard to proxy

Table 28.1 ESG criteria of pension funds.

Issue	Rank	%
Social issues	1	79.0%
Proxy voting	2	75.8%
Environment	2	75.8%
Corporate governance	3	72.6%
Engagement/shareholder activism	4	69.4%
Integration	5	58.1%
Labor relations	6	48.4%
Ethics	7	40.3%
Human rights	8	37.1%
Foreign operations	9	27.4%
Alternative energy/ biotechnology	10	25.8%
Customer/product/employee advocacy	10	25.8%
Aerospace/defense/weapons	11	21.0%
Tobacco/alcohol	12	19.4%
Nuclear power	13	16.1%
Gambling	14	12.9%
Pornography/child labor	15	14.5%
Animal testing/welfare	16	4.8%
Religious/philosophical screens	16	4.8%

voting and engagement. Here, information about the specific companies, the problematic issues, its geographic location or the result of the vote is published. Analyzing the reports of pension funds, the explanation for this circumstantial reporting is the motivation of influencing the company's management for the better. As it can be seen in Table 28.1, religious or philosophical values play only a marginal role in ESG investment of pension funds.

Looking now at the selected country subsamples that are shown in Table 28.2, several differences can be pointed out among SRI activities. For example, Australian pension funds consider corporate governance most often in their investment decisions, whereas in the case of the UK and the USA, it is only on position 3. Every British pension fund that reported on the use of ESG criteria stated to be practicing proxy voting. In the UK, environmental

Table 28.2 ESG criteria of pension funds (selected country subsamples).

Issue	USA Rank	%	UK Rank	%	AUSTRALIA Rank	%
Environment	1	92.30%	2	96.40%	2	81.80%
Social issues	1	92.30%	2	96.40%	2	81.80%
Proxy voting	2	76.90%	1	100%	2	81.80%
Corporate governance	3	69.20%	3	92.90%	1	90.90%
Labor relations	3	69.20%	6	42.90%	2	81.80%
Engagement/shareholder activism	3	69.20%	2	96.40%	4	63.60%
Human rights	3	69.20%	7	32.10%	5	45.50%
Tobacco/alcohol	4	53.90%	11	7.10%	7	27.30%
Alternative energy/biotechnology	5	46.20%	9	25.00%	7	27.30%
Foreign operations	5	46.20%	8	28.60%	7	27.30%
Aerospace/defense/weapons	5	46.20%	10	10.70%	6	36.40%
Ethics	6	38.50%	5	57.10%	6	36.40%
Integration	6	38.50%	4	82.10%	3	72.30%
Gambling	7	30.80%	12	3.60%	7	27.30%
Pornography/child labor	7	30.80%	11	7.10%	7	27.30%
Nuclear power	7	30.80%	10	10.70%	7	27.30%
Animal testing/welfare	8	23.10%	13	0.00%	8	0.00%
Customer/product/employee advocacy	8	23.10%	8	28.60%	5	45.50%
Religious/philosophical screens	9	15.40%	12	3.60%	8	0.00%

and social issues are taken into account most often with 92.3 percent. This emphasizes the very different prioritizations in Australia, the UK and the USA. American pension funds most often apply negative screens in comparison to the two other country subsamples. In contrast, UK funds focus mainly on proxy voting, active engagement and ESG criteria. Australian funds concentrate on ESG criteria and thereby mainly on corporate governance. Additionally, they frequently practice proxy voting.

To summarize, some issues in SRI are more popular and widespread than others in the SRI activities of American, British and Australian pension funds. However, there are also several commonalities across country subsamples, such as the similar practice of proxy voting in the UK and Australia. After analyzing the subset of the 1,000 largest pension funds in the world, a SRI agenda can be identified that is mainly related to the three

ESG criteria and proxy voting. However, it is difficult to further specify the majority of criteria mentioned by pension funds. Instead, funds typically communicate the use of broad categories, referring to social or environmental issues rather than specifying specific criteria. This clearly demonstrates a lack of clarity and transparency. This would not be a problem as long as the only motivation for integrating environmental and socio-economic concerns was to maximize profits. If this was the case, it could be argued that there was no need to consider the nonfinancial interests of beneficiaries as they would ultimately serve as a distraction to the trustee's primary responsibility, i.e., to manage their funds in ways that best serve the financial interests of their beneficiaries (cf. Rhodes 2010). Yet, in the next section we will argue that this view fails to acknowledge the nonfinancial interests of a significant number of beneficiaries and the responsibilities that emerge from this.

The beneficiary: *homo economicus, homo sociologicus* or both?

Investors can have different motivations to integrate sustainability-related concerns in their investment behavior. In very general terms, their investment decisions can be based on either ethical considerations or profit-seeking behavior. Along these lines, two different types of responsible investors can thus be identified: value-driven and profit-seeking investors (Derwall et al. 2011). For profit-seeking investors, the importance of a social or environmental concern is determined by its relevance to the economic value of the firm. For value-driven investors, ethical rather than financial considerations shape the perception of the importance of this concern. This can be based on the desire for social change, and thus the prospect of changing the behavior of specific firms, or some sort of "psychic return," i.e., some sort of utility that goes beyond financial return (Beal et al. 2005). For example, a psychic return could be linked to the knowledge that money is invested ethically and that certain controversial products or practices are not supported through a specific investment.

The value-driven investor and the profit-seeking investor represent fundamentally different ideal-type models that reflect the discussion concerning the notions of "*homo economicus*" (or "economic man") and "*homo sociologicus.*" The behavioral model of *homo economicus* is built upon the notion of rationality. According to this model individuals are driven by narrow self-interest and seek to maximize private utility (Kirchgässner and Katterle 1994). Stemming from the field of political economy, the model of economic man has been widely used to model efficient (capital) markets where it is assumed that investors will behave in a self-interested way to maximize profits based on rational choice and full information. In contrast, the model of *homo sociologicus* assumes that actors' behavior is driven by social norms and roles. According to this model, individuals are not driven by narrow self-interest but they behave as prescribed by custom (Binmore and Samuelson 1994). From this perspective, investors will take into account institutionalized expectations and act according to

social roles that are ascribed to them. Social expectations and norms from outside the financial market sphere (that is itself an institutionalization of a set of norms, roles and expectations) are particularly relevant in the context of SRI where investments are supposed to contribute to some social cause or betterment as brought forward by societal stakeholders.

Arguably, in the context of SRI most investment decisions are likely to be influenced by a combination of both value-driven considerations and profit-seeking motives (cf. Beal et al. 2005). In other words, there is a role to play for both *homo economicus* and *homo sociologicus* in most SRI-related investment decisions. If one agrees that nonfinancial interests play a relevant role in SRI, then logically, extending the fiduciary duty rationale to nonfinancial interests of investors would mean that trustees are also to manage their funds in ways that best represent the nonfinancial interests of their investors. Hence, it would be the nonfinancial fiduciary responsibility of fund managers to address the nonfinancial concerns of their investors. As pointed out above, ESG criteria reflect specific prioritizations of perceptions and underlying values, making this nonfinancial fiduciary duty a difficult task to achieve in the first place. Given the relatively intransparent nature of SRI fund management identified above, investors – including institutional investors – will commonly not be able to actively choose those funds that best meet their nonfinancial interests.

It follows that there is a crucial role to play for SRI practitioners, as their actions will largely determine whether the nonfinancial interests of beneficiaries are met or not. Three general options are conceivable. First, fund managers could know the sustainability-related perceptions and priorities of their beneficiaries and act accordingly in their investment decision-making. Given the heterogeneous nature of individual as well as institutional investors, and the complex and multifaceted nature of ESG integration, it is fair to assume that this is a challenging task. Fund managers commonly do not systematically identify the nonfinancial interests of their beneficiaries. Second, although fund managers are not aware of the nonfinancial interests of their beneficiaries, their own perceptions may still match those of their beneficiaries. It could be assumed that both SRI practitioners and beneficiaries are typically based in the same institutional environment or setting. For example, in the context of sustainability and corporate social responsibility, previous research has identified distinct country-specific interpretations of sustainability as well as expectations regarding the social and environmental responsibilities of business (Hofstede 2006; House et al. 2004). Third, if fund managers do not know the sustainability-related perceptions and priorities of the beneficiaries and cannot act accordingly in their investment decision-making, a nonfinancial fiduciary duty problem exists. In the following section, we will approach this question through a more detailed analysis of the sustainability-related perceptions of SRI practitioners.

Perceptions of SRI practitioners

In light of the lack of transparency linked to SRI products and the potential scope of action given the multifaceted character of sustainability, a crucial question is whether the actions of SRI practitioners reflect the interests and perceptions of value-driven investors. As SRI practitioners typically do not systematically identify the nonfinancial priorities of their beneficiaries, it logically follows that the perceptions and decision-making of SRI practitioners largely correspond to the perceptions of their beneficiaries, or that a nonfinancial fiduciary duty problem exists. In this section, we present the results of a survey of SRI practitioners (n = 149) in order to shed light on their sustainability-related perceptions.

A range of individual and context-specific factors have long been known to impact the perceptions and decision-making of investment professionals. For example, previous studies have helped to shed light on the impact of gender on the way in which analysts perceive risk (Olsen and Cox 2001), the general impact of career pressures on the behavior of investment professionals (Dreman 2002) or the existence of cultural differences between investment professionals and policymakers (O'Barr and Conley 2000). For the case of US pension fund managers, a range of contextual, non-economic

factors have been identified that are likely to shape their investment strategies (Conley and O'Barr 1991; O'Barr and Conley 1992). It is safe to assume that the same also holds for SRI practitioners. After all, the potential mismatch between practitioners' interests and investors' interests represents the very foundation of the fiduciary duty literature.

A web-based survey was constructed with the aim of identifying general sustainability-related perceptions of SRI practitioners. These were asked to identify the three most urgent global sustainability challenges (unprompted), and then to rate a list of eighteen sustainability challenges based on their urgency and importance. The list of eighteen sustainability-related issues was compiled on the basis of a desk-based study of key international documents and initiatives in the context of sustainable development and corporate responsibility such as the Brundtland Report (WCED 1987), the OECD Guidelines for Multinational Enterprises, the UN Millennium Development Goals (UN Millennium Project and Sachs 2005) and the UN Global Compact (2004). Furthermore, documents related to the UN Millennium Ecosystem Assessment (2005) were reviewed in order to identify key global environmental challenges.

The survey was distributed via the social networking tool LinkedIn (www.linkedin.com); invitations were sent out through a number of groups of SRI professionals, targeting a total of approximately 2,700 SRI practitioners. Of these, 700 received personal invitations to respond to the survey. This generated 149 usable responses, reflecting a moderate response rate of 21.3 percent. Figure 28.1 shows that the clearly most urgent sustainability challenge identified by SRI practitioners was climate change, mentioned by 59 percent of respondents. Beyond climate change, a relatively diverse picture emerged with a wide range of challenges mentioned, the most frequent of which were water (25 percent) and natural resources (25 percent), as well as a number of challenges linked to global governance and the political system (19 percent), and inequality including gender-related challenges (19 percent). Five out of the ten most frequently mentioned challenges were explicitly environmentally oriented; of these ten most frequently mentioned challenges, only food security (10 percent)

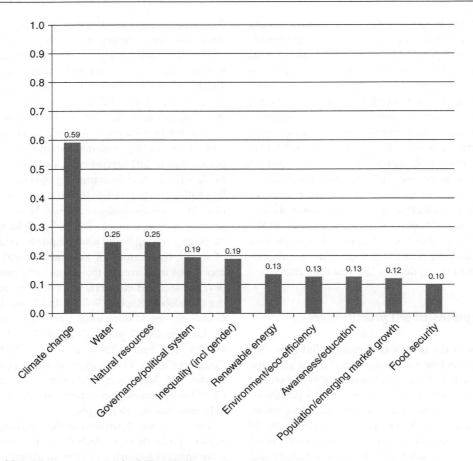

Figure 28.1 Most urgent sustainability challenges (unprompted).

emerged as a typical international development issue. Only four out of 149 SRI practitioners mentioned poverty or hunger as one of the three most urgent sustainability challenges we are facing.

When the same group of SRI practitioners were asked to rate a set of eighteen sustainability challenges on a six-point Likert scale, a more balanced picture emerged. As can be seen in Figure 28.2, climate change (5.10) still emerges as the most urgent challenge, with 52 percent of respondents awarding the highest score of 6. Again, water pollution (5.04) emerged as the second most urgent challenge. Not surprisingly, on average each of the eighteen issues received a score of at least 4.00; in other words, all eighteen issues were perceived as relatively urgent and important. Interestingly, a similar pattern emerges as in the case of the

unprompted responses: six out of the seven most highly rated sustainability challenges were environmental issues; six out of the seven challenges that received the lowest scores were socio-economic issues. One notable exception from this pattern is poverty and hunger (4.94; ranked third). Of the list of eighteen sustainability challenges, HIV/AIDS emerged as the issue receiving the lowest average score (4.00), with only 11 percent of respondents awarding it the maximum score of 6.

As can be seen in Table 28.3, this overall pattern also appears to be relatively consistent across the three largest country subsamples (Australia, UK and USA) within the sample of SRI practitioners. While a number of country-level differences can be identified (for example, poverty and hunger receive markedly lower scores in the Australian

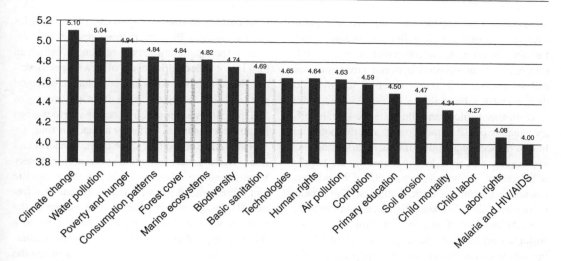

Figure 28.2 Urgency of eighteen sustainability challenges (rated on a six-point Likert scale).

Table 28.3 Survey of SRI practitioners: urgency of sustainability challenges (ranking of issues; selected countries).

Issue	Total Sample	USA	UK	Australia
Climate change	1	1	1	1
Water pollution	2	2	7	2
Poverty and hunger	3	3	4	13
Sustainable consumption	4	4	3	7
Forest cover	5	13	2	4
Marine ecosystems	6	7	4	3
Biodiversity	7	12	4	5
Basic sanitation	8	7	9	7
Human rights	9	5	11	15
Cleaner technologies	9	7	7	15
Air pollution	11	6	10	13
Corruption	12	10	12	7
Primary education	13	11	14	10
Soil erosion	14	15	14	6
Child mortality	15	14	13	10
Child labor	16	16	16	10
Labor rights	17	17	17	17
HIV/AIDS and malaria	18	18	18	18
Average rank socio-economic issues	12.44	11.22	12.78	12.22
Average rank environmental issues	6.56	7.44	5.88	6.44

subsample; US respondents awarded comparatively high scores for air pollution, but low scores for deforestation when compared to the overall sample), a clear division between environmental and socio-economic issues emerges again in all three country subsamples.

To further explore and illustrate the sustainability agendas of SRI practitioners and the potential link to respective agendas of beneficiaries, the survey results will now be compared to the results of a content analysis of a sample of broadsheet newspapers from the three countries. The Trends in Sustainability database (2012) contains average monthly number of articles reporting on various sustainability-related challenges across 185 leading international broadsheet newspapers. For the purposes of this analysis, average coverage levels over the years 2008–11 are calculated for a sample of twenty-three Australian, UK and US broadsheet newspapers.

The comparison is based on the underlying assumption that a relatively stable relationship exists between the coverage levels of broadsheet newspapers on specific issues and respective levels of public concern with regard to these issues in a given context. This relationship has long been established in agenda-setting research (Cohen 1963; Kiousis 2004; for exceptions see, for example, Neuman 1990), and has since been applied in the context of various sustainability challenges such as climate change (Boykoff 2007; Brossard et al. 2004) or HIV/AIDS (Dearing 1989). As a consequence, the Trends in Sustainability database lends itself as a proxy for general public concern with regard to various sustainability challenges in the three countries under review (Barkemeyer et al. 2009; Barkemeyer et al. 2013). Due to data availability, only thirteen of the eighteen sustainability challenges above are investigated and ranked according levels of coverage and their perceived importance, respectively (Table 28.4 below).

A first look at the results shows a certain degree of similarities with regard to country-level differences in both samples. For example, the US samples both show relatively low ranks for biodiversity and high ranks for air pollution, respectively; the Australian samples show comparatively low ranks for corruption and poverty. On the other hand,

clear outliers restricted only to one of the samples emerge, such as the very high scores for soil erosion in the Australian survey responses, which in turn is not reflected in levels of newspaper coverage. Most notably, while climate change emerged as the clearly dominant issue from the survey of SRI practitioners, respective newspaper coverage in the three countries varies by a factor of four.

It should be noted that some of the concepts and issues that are included in the analysis carry a very broad meaning, whereas others are more specific and therefore can be expected to appear less frequently in newspaper articles. For example, the terms poverty and hunger are likely to refer to a broader range of contexts than for example malnutrition. Therefore, general differences between the two samples should be interpreted with due care. Nevertheless, it is noteworthy that there is no case in which environmental issues receive lower ranks in the survey of SRI practitioners.

Although this type of analysis would ultimately need to be carried out at the level of individual funds, the marked differences that have been identified point towards differences in sustainability-related perceptions between SRI practitioners and beneficiaries in the respective contexts.

Discussion: a nonfinancial fiduciary duty problem

Given the patterns identified above, it is unlikely that the perceptions of SRI practitioners entirely match those of their beneficiaries. Instead, SRI practitioners appear to show characteristics of an epistemic community (Haas 1992; Knorr-Cetina 1999). An epistemic community has generally been described as "a network of professionals with recognized expertise and competence in a particular domain and an authoritative claim to policy-relevant knowledge within that domain or issue-area" (Haas 1992: 3). This can also be extended beyond direct policy relevance towards any group with a "sufficiently strong claim to a body of knowledge that is valued by society" (ibid.: 16; cf. Chilvers 2008).

Anecdotal evidence for this point was also provided by the free-text comments survey respondents

Table 28.4 Comparison of survey results with broadsheet newspaper coverage in the three countries (average number of articles 2008–11; Source: www.trendsinsustainability.com).

	TRENDS IN SUSTAINABILITY						SURVEY OF SRI PRACTITIONERS								
	USA		UK		AUSTRALIA		USA			UK			AUSTRALIA		
	Coverage	Rank	Coverage	Rank	Coverage	Rank	Score	Rank	Δ	Score	Rank	Δ	Score	Rank	Δ
Corruption	53.78	1	55.43	4	52.98	2	4.63	6	−5	4.52	7	−3	4.73	4	−2
Human rights	48.84	2	71.7	1	45.94	3	4.83	3	−1	4.56	6	−5	4.45	9	−6
Poverty	43.82	3	62.2	2	35.15	4	4.97	2	+1	4.96	2	±0	4.55	7	−3
Climate change	27.15	4	57.61	3	111.63	1	5.17	1	+3	5.4	1	+2	5.64	1	±0
HIV/AIDS	21.84	5	11.42	5	13.18	5	3.97	12	−7	3.88	12	−7	3.82	12	−7
Malaria	4.59	6	6.68	6	4.14	8			−6			−6			−4
Air pollution	4.28	7	1.96	10	2.19	10	4.8	4	+3	4.64	5	+3	4.55	7	+5
Labor rights	4.1	8	4.67	9	6.6	7	4.07	11	−3	3.88	11	−2	4.09	11	−4
Cleaner technologies	3.88	9	5.59	7	3.76	9	4.73	5	+4	4.84	4	+4	4.45	9	+3
Biodiversity	1.85	10	5.33	8	6.78	6	4.53	7	+3	4.96	2	+6	5.09	2	+4
Child labor	1.06	11	1.53	11	0.97	11	4.2	10	+1	4.04	10	+1	4.64	5	+6
Child mortality	0.31	12	0.62	12	0.49	12	4.37	8	+4	4.44	8	+4	4.64	5	+7
Soil erosion	0.3	13	0.39	13	0.36	13	4.23	9	+4	4.4	9	+4	4.82	3	+10

made at the end of the survey. For example, various respondents criticized the fact that the survey did not address the financial relevance of the sustainability challenges they were asked to rate. It should be noted that the research design might potentially have reinforced this view: while SRI practitioners were asked to complete the survey according to their own perceptions, they were contacted in their capacity as SRI practitioners. They might therefore intuitively have made the link to their professional context. Nevertheless, these responses arguably also show that respondents were indeed influenced by their professional background when they answered questions directed at their own perceptions and priorities.

Given the lack of transparency of SRI products identified above, investors and beneficiaries might be unlikely to be able to choose specific SRI products that match their own socio-economic and environmental interests and priorities. If SRI practitioners form an epistemic community and their perceptions are relatively homogeneous across country borders, then they are unlikely to reflect the typically heterogeneous and context-specific nature of sustainability-related values, perceptions and priorities of their beneficiaries. If the decision-making of SRI practitioners is shaped by their own perceptions and beliefs, then a nonfinancial fiduciary duty problem exists in these cases.

However, Table 28.5 below shows that this nonfinancial fiduciary duty problem is typically most pronounced in the case of ESG integration. As screened approaches usually provide the information necessary to allow the investor/beneficiary to determine whether an investment product corresponds to his or her specific set of values, at least in theory, investors and beneficiaries could act accordingly. ESG integration approaches oftentimes do not allow for this type of assessment. In addition, nonfinancial fiduciary duty responsibilities are not relevant in the case of a purely financially motivated SRI investor. In this case, it could even be argued that there is no need for the perceptions of investors and respective decision-making of SRI fund managers to match, given the information asymmetry between these two groups (cf. Rhodes 2010). As pointed out above, however, the purely profit-seeking investor can be assumed to be

Table 28.5 Investor/product matrix (categories based on Beal et al. 2005; Derwall et al. 2011).

	Value-seeking	Profit-seeking
Screening	OK	OK
ESG integration	Nonfinancial fiduciary duty problem	OK

a minority in the context of SRI: decision-making is typically influenced by both value-driven and profit-seeking motives, oftentimes characterized by trade-offs between these two dimensions. It should be noted that in the context of institutional investment, the link between SRI practitioner and beneficiary is further complicated through the passive role of the beneficiaries.

In recent years, and alongside the increasing popularity of ESG integration approaches, the discussion concerning the fiduciary duty principle has largely been narrowed down to purely financial considerations (cf. Richardson 2009). However, this discussion fails to acknowledge the interests of value-driven investors and beneficiaries as well as the ethical considerations of predominantly profit-driven investors and beneficiaries. Assuming further strong growth in the future as well as an increasing professionalization of SRI and ESG integration, the nonfinancial fiduciary duty problem sketched out above can be expected to become even more relevant.

There are a number of general ways to address this nonfinancial fiduciary duty problem. At the level of SRI products, increased transparency about the criteria applied in ESG integration would improve informed decision-making by investors and beneficiaries. At the level of institutional investment, a way of minimizing the mismatch of sustainability-related perceptions and values between SRI practitioners and beneficiaries would be the development of mechanisms that capture the perceptions and values of beneficiaries, and allow SRI practitioners to act accordingly. Beneficiaries should be enabled to exercise a minimum amount of choice that consequently should be reflected in portfolio construction. Given the projected future growth of SRI, failure to acknowledge and integrate the social and environmental concerns of beneficiaries – while overemphasizing the SRI business case – would put one of the main missions of SRI at risk: real social and environmental change, and driving businesses to act within the natural limits of the earth's carrying capacity.

Conclusions

In this chapter, we have extended the fiduciary duty concept to the level of nonfinancial interests of beneficiaries and investors. We have argued that in addition to the "conventional" fiduciary duty problem that has played a dominant role in the SRI literature, a nonfinancial fiduciary duty problem exists that has largely been ignored in the discussion on the responsibilities of fund managers. If trustees are to manage their funds in ways that best represent the interests of their investors, then this should not be reduced to purely financial interests but should also include the ethical considerations of these investors.

Based on an assessment of the information transparency of the 1,000 largest pension funds worldwide, we have showed that information on how social investment is reported by these funds is typically relatively scarce. As importantly, funds commonly only communicate the generic categories their social investment activities fall into. As a result of this lack of transparency, the actual operationalization of SRI remains unclear to the beneficiary. It should be noted that this part of the research only focused on ESG reporting of pension funds. Thus, we have only analyzed pension funds from an outside perspective; pension funds may provide more detailed information to their members. However, this type of information would not be available *before* the investment decision; therefore, ESG reporting remains as one of the main information sources in this context. Hence, the perceptions and decision-making of SRI practitioners are crucial for any operationalization of socially responsible investment. Subsequently, a survey of SRI practitioners helped to shed light on their sustainability-related perceptions and priorities. The survey results and subsequent comparison with Trends in Sustainability data suggested that SRI practitioners

appear to hold relatively uniform sustainability-related perceptions across national borders that are unlikely to match the perceptions and interests of their beneficiaries. As beneficiaries are typically not able to select SRI products according to their own sustainability-related perceptions – either as a result of the lack of transparency in the market, or as a result of the inability of beneficiaries to exercise choice related to social and environmental aspects in institutional investment – this creates a nonfinancial fiduciary duty problem.

This agency problem is mainly relevant for value-driven investors and ESG integration. However, given the increasingly important role of ESG integration approaches and the fact that few investors can be expected to engage in SRI purely on the basis of profit-seeking motives, this problem is likely to become more prominent in the future. Alongside the continued mainstreaming and maturing of SRI, practitioners will increasingly need to find ways to address these nonfinancial fiduciary responsibilities. In essence, SRI products need to become more transparent about the specific nature of ESG considerations linked to specific products, and beneficiaries need to be enabled to exercise more choice linked to their nonfinancial interests. Finally, future research will be needed to shed light on the relationship between financial and nonfinancial fiduciary responsibilities.

References

Barkemeyer, R., F. Figge, T. Hahn and D. Holt. 2009. "What the Papers Say: Trends in Sustainability. A Comparative Analysis of 115 Leading National Newspapers Worldwide," *Journal of Corporate Citizenship* 33: 69–86.

Barkemeyer, R., D. Holt, L. Preuss and S. Tsang. 2011. "What Happened to the 'Development' in Sustainable Development? Business Guidelines Two Decades After Brundtland," *Sustainable Development*, early view available online, DOI: 10.1002/sd.1521.

Barkemeyer, R., F. Figge and D. Holt. 2013. "Sustainability-related Media Coverage and Socioeconomic Development – a Regional and North/South Perspective," *Environment and*

Planning C: Government and Policy 31 (4): 716–40.

Beal, D. J., M. Goyen and P. Phillips. 2005. "Why Do We Invest Ethically?" *Journal of Investing* 14: 66–77.

Binmore, K. and L. Samuelson. 1994. "An Economist's Perspective on the Evolution of Norms," *Journal of Institutional and Theoretical Economics* 150: 45–63.

Boykoff, M. T. 2007. "Flogging a Dead Norm? Newspaper Coverage of Anthropogenic Climate Change in the United States and United Kingdom from 2003 to 2006," *Area* 39: 470–81.

Brossard, D., J. Shanahan and K. McComas. 2004. "Are Issue-Cycles Culturally Constructed? A Comparison of French and American Coverage of Global Climate Change," *Mass Communication and Society* 7: 359–77.

Chilvers, J. 2008. "Environmental Risk, Uncertainty, and Participation: Mapping an Emergent Epistemic Community," *Environment and Planning A* 40: 2990–3008.

Cohen, B. C. 1963. *The Press and Foreign Policy.* Princeton University Press.

Conley, J. M. and W. M. O'Barr. 1991. "The Culture of Capital," *Harvard Business Review* 69: 110–11.

Dearing, J. W. 1989. "Setting the Polling Agenda for the Issue of AIDS," *Public Opinion Quarterly* 53: 309–29.

Derwall, J., K. Koedijk and J. Ter Horst. 2011. "A Tale of Values-driven and Profit-seeking Social Investors," *Journal of Banking and Finance* 35: 2137–47.

Dreman, D. 2002. "Analysts' Conflicts-of-Interest: Some Behavioral Aspects," *Journal of Psychology & Financial Markets* 3: 138–40.

Eurosif. 2010. *European SRI Study 2010.* Paris: European Sustainable Investment Forum.

Haas, P. M. 1992. "Introduction: Epistemic Communities and International Policy Coordination," *International Organization* 46: 1–35.

Haigh, M. and J. Hazelton. 2004. "Financial Markets: A Tool for Social Responsibility?" *Journal of Business Ethics* 52: 59–71.

Hofstede, G. 2006. "What Did GLOBE Really Measure? Researchers' Minds versus Respondents' Minds," *Journal of International Business Studies* 37: 882–96.

Horváthová, E. 2010. "Does Environmental Performance Affect Financial Performance? A Meta-analysis," *Ecological Economics* 70: 52–9.

House, R. J., P. M. Hanges, M. Javidan, P. Dorfman and V. Gupta. 2004. *Culture, Leadership and Organizations: The GLOBE Study of 62 Societies.* Thousand Oaks, CA: Sage.

Kiousis, S. 2004. "Explicating Media Salience: A Factor Analysis of *New York Times* Issue Coverage During the 2000 US Presidential Elections," *Journal of Communication* 54: 71–87.

Kirchgässner, G. and S. Katterle. 1994. "Homo Oeconomicus," *Journal of Institutional and Theoretical Economics* 150: 570–5.

Knorr-Cetina, K. 1999. *Epistemic Cultures: How the Sciences Make Knowledge.* Cambridge, MA: Harvard University Press.

Langbein, J. H. and R. A. Posner. 1980. "Social Investing and the Law of Trusts," *Michigan Law Review* 79: 72–112.

Margolis, J. D. and J. P. Walsh. 2003. "Misery Loves Companies: Rethinking Social Initiatives by Business," *Administrative Science Quarterly* 48: 268–305.

Moon, J. 2007. "The Contribution of Corporate Social Responsibility to Sustainable Development," *Sustainable Development* 15: 296–306.

Neuman, W. R. 1990. "The Threshold of Public Attention," *Public Opinion Quarterly* 54: 159–76.

O'Barr, W. M. and J. M. Conley. 1992. "Managing Relationships: The Culture of Institutional Investing," *Financial Analysts Journal* 48: 21–7.

   2000. "When Cultures Collide: Social Security and the Market," *Journal of Psychology & Financial Markets* 1: 92–100.

Olsen, R. A. and C. M. Cox. 2001. "The Influence of Gender on the Perception and Response to Investment Risk: The Case of Professional Investors," *Journal of Psychology & Financial Markets* 2: 29–36.

Orlitzky, M., F. L. Schmidt and S. L. Rynes. 2003. "Corporate Social and Financial Performance: A Meta-analysis," *Organization Studies* 24: 403–41.

Redclift, M. 2005. "Sustainable Development (1987–2005): An Oxymoron Comes of Age," *Sustainable Development* 13: 212–27.

Rhodes, M. J. 2010. "Information Asymmetry and Socially Responsible Investment," *Journal of Business Ethics* 95: 145–50.

Richardson, B. J. 2009. "Keeping Ethical Investment Ethical: Regulatory Issues for Investing for Sustainability," *Journal of Business Ethics* 87: 555–72.

Robinson, J. 2004. "Squaring the Circle? Some Thoughts on the Idea of Sustainable Development," *Ecological Economics* 48: 369–84.

Salzmann, O., A. Ionescu-Somers and U. Steger. 2005. "The Business Case for Corporate Sustainability: Literature Review and Research Options," *European Management Journal* 23: 27–36.

Sandberg, J. 2011. "Socially Responsible Investment and Fiduciary Duty: Putting the Freshfields Report into Perspective," *Journal of Business Ethics* 101: 143–62.

Sandberg, J., C. Juravle, T. M. Hedesström and I. Hamilton. 2009. "The Heterogeneity of Socially Responsible Investment," *Journal of Business Ethics* 87: 519–33.

Trends in Sustainability. 2012. www.trendsinsustainability.com.

Ullman, A. A. 1985. "Data in Search of a Theory: A Critical Examination of the Relationships among Social Performance, Social Disclosure, and Economic Performance of U.S. Firms," *Academy of Management Review* 10: 540–57.

UN Global Compact. 2004. *The Global Compact: A Network of Networks.* New York: UN Global Compact Office.

UN Millennium Ecosystem Assessment. 2005. *Ecosystems and Human Well-Being: Current State and Trends. Findings of the Conditions and Trends Working Group.* Washington, DC: Island Press.

UN Millennium Project and Sachs, J. D. 2005. *Investing in Development: A Practical Plan to Achieve the Millennium Development Goals.* London: Earthscan.

WCED. 1987. *Our Common Future: The World Commission on Environment and Development.* Oxford University Press.

The preferences of beneficiaries: what can we learn from research on retail investors?

JONAS NILSSON

Introduction

During the last few years increasing attention has been given to the integration of environmental, social and governance (ESG) issues into various parts of the investment industry. While the fact that ESG issues often are debated, and that socially responsible investment (SRI) is a common phenomenon in the investment context, may come as a surprise to people who associate the finance industry with strictly utilitarian financial transactions, it is not particularly surprising given the amount and relevance of the environmental and social problems facing mankind. As a consequence of issues such as global warming, abuse of natural resources and global inequality, increasing corporate responsibility is now often demanded from several actors in society such as citizens, non-governmental organizations and consumers.

Even though ESG issues are becoming incorporated in both the institutional and retail investment sector, so far it seems like the institutional sector is leading the way. In Europe, for example, as much as 92 percent of the ESG-profiled assets under management are categorized as institutional (Eurosif 2010). Despite this positive development, however, the fact is that actors in the institutional investment context face specific obstacles for ESG integration that is not present in the retail context. Perhaps the most relevant of these obstacles, and the main topic of this book, is captured by the term fiduciary duty. Although the full meaning of this concept is perhaps explained better by legal scholars represented in this volume and elsewhere in the literature, a basic illustration of the impact of the concept for the purpose of this chapter is that while

retail investors are free to invest their money in the manner they best see fit, institutional investors such as large pension funds have fiduciary duties toward their beneficiaries that require them to manage their investments in the best interest of the final recipients/owners of the underlying money (e.g., Sandberg 2011; Stabile and Zanglein 2007).

What this "best interest" is, however, is debatable (Duska 2011; Richardson 2011a). Whereas some, given the necessity of an environmentally and socially sustainable future development, may argue that incorporating ESG issues is in the beneficiaries' best interest, many institutional investors have not interpreted their duties this way (e.g., Sandberg 2011). Instead, the interpretation that the best interest of beneficiaries is to maximize return (according to modern portfolio theory), and that institutional investors such as pension funds should solely focus on maximizing the pensions of their beneficiaries, has been common among investors (e.g., Sandberg 2011; Woods and Urwin 2010). Thus, despite the arguments about the benefits of long-term sustainable development, "best interest" has been defined in mainly financial terms. Institutional investors may therefore, due to their interpretation of their fiduciary duties, sometimes be prohibited from incorporating ESG issues into their investment processes.

What beneficiaries want

While institutional investors may sometimes not be allowed to integrate ESG concerns into their investment processes, the influential 2005 Freshfields Report argues that they are certainly not always prohibited from doing so (Freshfields Bruckhaus

Deringer 2005). According to the report, for example, ESG consideration is permissible (and sometimes mandatory) if positive financial consequences of doing so can be expected. However, the Freshfields Report also mentions one scenario where ESG concerns can be incorporated even when there are negative financial consequences of doing so: if beneficiaries agree and support the specific ESG initiative. Thus, if taking some form of ESG concern is in line with the preferences of the beneficiaries, it could fall within the fiduciary duties of the institutional investor to take these preferences into account (Richardson 2011a, 2011b).

However, although the idea that ESG concern may be incorporated into the investment process if beneficiaries support it is fairly straightforward, actually finding out which ESG issues and investment methods (if any) are supported by the beneficiaries of the institutional investor is much more difficult (Richardson 2011a, 2011b; Sandberg 2011). Given that the Freshfields Report outlines the preferences of beneficiaries as the only scenario where ESG concern could be incorporated into the investment process of institutional investors when it would not be financially beneficial to do so, this is problematic. If beneficiaries cannot agree, or if we do not know what they want, institutional investors could become severely limited in their decision-making. As a result, a genuine attempt to use institutional investments for the benefit of environmental and social sustainability may be difficult to pursue.

Given the importance of the preferences of beneficiaries to how institutional investors interpret their fiduciary duties, the aim of this chapter is to discuss what current knowledge on retail investors' views and preferences can add to this debate. As agreement among beneficiaries may be necessary in order for institutional investors to incorporate ESG factors in the investment process, the chapter will focus on discussing the potential for some sort of explicit agreement or consensus among beneficiaries of larger institutional investors, such as pension funds, based on this literature. While there are many ways to approach this topic, in this case it is done by reviewing previous research both on socially responsible (SR) and conventional private investors focusing on (1) the nature of retail

SR investors' ESG preferences and (2) whether we can expect beneficiaries of larger institutional investors, such as pension funds, to have stable and reasonable preferences in the complex environment that the investment context provides. By highlighting research from the consumer sciences on the preferences, attitudes and behavior of individual investors it is hoped that this chapter will contribute to the discussion on the preferences of beneficiaries of large institutional investors, such as pension funds.

Some initial specifications

While there are obviously many different perspectives on how to evaluate the preferences and desires of beneficiaries the focus of this chapter is to use knowledge of retail investors as indications on how we can expect beneficiaries of large institutional investors (such as pension funds) to think and act. In essence, the relevance of this perspective is dependent on three specific assumptions. The first of these is simply that there is value in using the private investor population to derive knowledge on beneficiaries of institutional investors. Although there are obvious differences between many of the different types of beneficiaries and more active individual investors, the fact is that in many Western countries, investing has become an activity that most people are exposed to.[1] While acknowledging that these groups are not entirely similar, this chapter therefore takes the position that there may be some value in looking to retail investors to get an insight into the attitudes and preferences of beneficiaries of larger institutional investors. Following on from this logic, the more detailed second assumption is that it is reasonable to use knowledge of private socially responsible investors to learn something about specific ESG preferences in the wider population of beneficiaries. While it is acknowledged that active SR investors are likely to be more involved with ESG issues than the larger beneficiary population, this chapter takes the position that the views of people that

[1] In Sweden, 98 percent of Swedish citizens are invested in mutual funds either directly or related to the Swedish pension system, PPM (Pettersson et al. 2009).

actually incorporate ESG issues into their investment behavior could still be used as an indication
of potential issues (and conflicts between issues)
relevant to beneficiaries. Finally, the third assumption in this chapter is that we approach agreement
or consensus in an explicit way, i.e., that a vast
majority of people *actively* agree and approve of
the issue. Thus, while there may be other ways of
addressing the notion of consensus or agreement
(such as for example through social customs or
stakeholders, e.g., Richardson 2011a), the topic of
this chapter is the actual *expressed* preferences of
the beneficiaries in question. Finally, having mentioned these three assumptions, it should also be
noted that they simultaneously serve as important
limitations of the chapter.

With these assumptions and limitations mentioned, the rest of the chapter focuses on the
behavior and preferences of both "conventional"
and "SR" private investors. First, in order to get
an insight into the issues and causes that may be
relevant in an institutional investment context, we
review the financial and ESG preferences of SR
investors. After this, we take a closer look at the
decision-making ability of investors in general
in order to scrutinize how the investment context
impacts the preferences of investors. Finally, these
reviews are discussed in the context of ESG integration and interpretation of fiduciary duty. Here
we focus on whether it is reasonable to expect that
beneficiaries of larger institutional investors can
agree on ESG issues.

What we know about the ESG preferences of private SR investors

The research on private SR investors is still in an
early stage. While there were virtually no studies
on the topic whatsoever a decade ago, there are
now a handful of studies that together form the
fundamentals of what we know about private SR
investors. In general, the studies are diverse, both in
topic and method. Moreover, given that the empirical phenomenon is relevant to a wide range of
academic disciplines, studies range from finance,
economics and consumer research. Although this
academic range makes the field somewhat difficult

to overlook, there are a number of conclusions
about the preferences of SR investors that can be
made. Some of these are presented below.

The importance of financial return

One of the major issues when discussing whether
beneficiaries support the integration of ESG issues
into the institutional investment process is the
question of whether they are willing to accept a
lower return for some sort of social or environmental initiative. If beneficiaries are willing to sacrifice
return for including ESG issues, the door is open
to address the issue further. However, if beneficiaries generally are unwilling to move away from the
notion of profit maximization, then there may be
little room for institutional investors to define the
"best interest" of beneficiaries in any other way
than in the financial sense.

The issue of the importance of financial return
has been the focus of much research on private SR
investors. However, while it has been dealt with
extensively, in many ways it fails to deliver a concrete answer. While it seems clear that many retail
SR investors (quite naturally) perceive financial
return as important (e.g., Nilsson 2008), the question of *how* important it is largely still remains. In
fact, many studies indicate that SR investors are
far from profit-maximizing people, often willing
to sacrifice part of their financial return for what
they perceive to be a good cause (e.g. Barreda-
Tarrazona et al. 2011; Lewis and Mackenzie 2000;
Lewis and Webley 1994; Webley et al. 2001).
Thus, while there seems to be little doubt that these
investors sometimes, to a certain extent, are willing
to forego the notion of profit maximization, it is
unclear exactly when and how much SR investors
are willing to trade away for ESG consideration.

Looking deeper into the financial preferences of
SR investors, several recent studies have also suggested that investors actually differ significantly
in their preferences regarding financial return
(Derwall et al. 2011; Nilsson 2009). These studies
highlight a significant heterogeneity in the financial
behavior and attitudes among investors. In many
ways, these studies provide a nuanced picture of
the financial preferences of SR investors and paint
a likely scenario that the financial preferences of

investors could be seen as a continuum from very financially oriented to less financially oriented.

In all, it seems that while financial return is quite naturally important to many investors, the notion that investors always attempt to maximize profits is largely incorrect. Instead, a heterogeneous picture emerges, where some investors hold financial return as very important and others seem more willing to sacrifice a significant part of it in order to support some form of ESG issue.

ESG issues that are relevant to SR investors

While the preferences regarding financial return may be the most important issue for how institutional investors interpret their fiduciary duties, another important factor is the actual issues that are to be supported and integrated into the investment process. Looking to the SRI industry, there are numerous issues that have been addressed in the ESG category. For example, on its website, the Forum for Sustainable and Responsible Investment outlines as many as fourteen different issues that are used by SRI funds on the US market (USSIF 2012). Looking at actual criteria used, Lönnroth et al. (2001) showed that as many as 330 different criteria are used to evaluate the socially responsible nature of companies.

While there is still a lack of research on how retail investors rate these issues, there are a number of studies that address the causes and issues of importance for SR investors. To get a quick overview of the current state of research, a summary of five published papers is presented in Table 29.1. Here, the five top issues mentioned in each study are categorized across the four categories present in the US Social Investment Forum information guidelines (environment, social, governance, products).

At first glance, Table 29.1 indicates a great deal of diversity. For example, the earliest study included in the table provides ESG issues that fit into all the four USSIF categories (Rosen et al. 1991). To the question "what factors are most important in determining whether a company's behavior is socially responsible?" the study found six overall categories of ESG issues. The environment and labor relations

proved to be the most important to the investors included in the sample, given by 28 percent each. This was followed by military (19 percent) and finance and marketing (14 percent) issues. Finally, political issues were mentioned by 8 percent of the respondents.

This diversity in preferences is also visible in other studies. For example, in Pérez-Gladish et al. (2012), there were no governance issues among the top five, but all the other three categories are represented in the top five issues that SR investors considered important. The environment was considered important to the 144 respondents in the sample as three of the top five issues belong to this category. Other important issues were human rights and nuclear power. In another study, by McLachlan and Gardner (2004), nuclear weaponry was ranked as important by investors. In addition to nuclear weapons, the fifty-four SR inventors included in the sample also ranked a number of industries including tobacco, weapons and pornography as important. In addition to these traditional negative screens, some social issues such as trade with oppressive regimes and exploitation of the developing world were also included in the top five.

Valor et al. (2009) studied demand for SRI in Spain and is thereby the only study based in the European market included in this review. In this study, the 400 respondents seem much more oriented toward social issues than in the other studies. Whereas the Australian studies above seem to give some support to issues usually associated with negative screening, it was the issues associated with positive screening that were more important here. For example, weapons and defense, that were in the top five important issues in all the three other studies (McLachlan and Gardner 2004; Pérez-Gladish et al. 2012; Rosen et al. 1991), was one of the least important issues here. Instead, issues such as labor conditions, policies and cooperation with the surrounding society were the ESG issues found important by the respondents.

The studies included in the review thus highlight many different ESG issues that SR investors consider to be important. However, taking this notion of diverse preferences further, there are also studies that indicate differing ESG preferences within the sample of respondents. One

Table 29.1 ESG issues perceived as important by SR investors (categorized by the USSIF categories).*

	Environment	Social	Governance	Products
Beal and Goyen (1998) **	- Conservation of endangered animals - Save endangered ecosystems - Conservation of endangered plants - Provision of sanctuaries - Protect ecosystems			
McLachlan and Gardner (2004)		- Trade with oppressive regimes - Exploits Third World		- Nuclear weapons - Pornography - Tobacco - Arms exporter
Pérez-Gladish et al. (2012)	- Climate change - Water pollution - Pollution	- Human rights		- Nuclear power
Rosen et al. (1991)***	- Environment (e.g., use solar energy, does not pollute)	- Labor relations (e.g., provides child care, no dangerous working conditions) - Politics (e.g., assist Third World countries, does not interfere in foreign government affairs	- Finance and marketing (e.g., no hostile takeovers, produces socially useful products)	- Military (e.g., supports peace initiatives, does not work on nuclear weapons)
Valor et al. (2009)		- Respect for human rights - Labor conditions - Labor policy - Cooperation with social and cultural community-based activities	- Transparency	

* The five most popular issues in each study are displayed here.
** The study sampled shareowners of an environmentally oriented company.
*** The authors made their own categories using positive and negative examples. In order to accurately represent the original study, the overall categories are used here. However, some of the examples that the authors included in their categories (such as "supports peace initiatives" and "produces socially useful products") would most likely belong to a different category if they were considered as separate entities.

example of this is a study by Statman (2008) who had "quiet conversations" with eight different people. While the respondents all had some form of ESG concern, the sample of (among others) a Catholic nun, an environmental planner, an owner of military-related companies, a graduate student and a member of the Church of the Brethren, clearly shows that ESG concerns are personal and related to the values of the individual. For example, in the study, the owner of the military-related companies believed that the industry or the products that companies produce is not an important indicator of socially responsible behavior. Instead, this particular respondent argued that socially responsible investment decisions should be based on supporting the companies that represent the best in terms of policies and practices in their particular field. On the other hand, other respondents in the Statman (2008) study argued that excluding certain companies based on the products they produce was a fundamental part of SR investment. The member of the Church of the Brethren, for example, is cited as saying that excluding companies is important as SRI is a matter of integrity.

To not support or profit from the activities of a perceived unethical company therefore becomes a fundamental part of this particular investor's ESG preferences.

In all, the Statman study, as well as the other studies reviewed above, shows that private SR investors have diverse ESG preferences. As with financial preferences, it seems that ESG preferences are highly personal. However, the results of this review should also be taken with a word of caution. As the research field is still new, existing studies focus on different geographical areas, use different research instruments and develop their own items. Under these circumstances, differing results should not come as a surprise. For example, while Beal and Goyen (1998) studied an explicitly environmental organization, the McLachlan and Gardner (2004) study hardly includes any items relating to the environment at all. Also, some studies focus more on general issues or concerns that investors may have, while others are more focused on actual grounds for screening. Thus, in many ways, we have a number of surveys that generate valuable information in themselves. However, at this stage, it is difficult to draw conclusions from all studies as a group. While each study indicates a great diversity of preferences, it may therefore be too early to draw any certain conclusions of a more general nature.

The impact of the investment context and decision-making ability

Given that the research on SR investors is still developing, it may be worthwhile to broaden the scope of the discussion to get a wider perspective on the possibilities of agreement among beneficiaries of larger institutional investors. In this section, we do this by addressing the decision-making ability of investors. Although the ability of beneficiaries to make appropriate decisions has not received much attention in the literature, it is crucially important in order to understand their preferences. In many ways, any form of explicit agreement requires that beneficiaries have the decision-making ability to make appropriate and reasonable decisions. If beneficiaries do not have the knowledge required or care enough about institutional investments

and ESG integration, an agreement in the explicit sense is difficult to achieve.

While it is common to assume that everyone has the capability to make appropriate decisions, this should not be taken for granted in the investment context. The investment context is highly complex, full of difficult terminology and is not very exciting to the average person (Kozup and Hogarth 2008; Kozup et al. 2008; Nilsson 2010). As such, it is not surprising that there is a plethora of studies that indicate that investors make some form of suboptimal investment decisions (Bateman et al. 2010; Lai and Xiao 2010). Although many reasons for this have been given in the literature, two of the most important are the lack of basic knowledge about investments and a limited involvement and interest in the topic. These two aspects of decision-making in the investment context are discussed below.

The knowledge of private investors

In consumer research on financial decision-making, the lack of basic financial knowledge among consumers is a frequently debated topic (Devlin 2003; Fonseca et al. 2012; Kozup and Hogarth 2008). The fact is that people today live in a world that expects them to take more responsibility for their own financial affairs (Atchely 1998). In many countries, the pension systems have been deregulated, putting responsibility of future financial well-being on the individual rather than the system. Having to invest for their own retirement, familiarity with the complex world of investing has become a necessity in order to get a high pension. Moreover, the recent credit crunch showed that the once fairly simple financial products of lending and credit have become increasingly complex and misunderstood by many people. In all, more is expected of people these days. The system requires people to have a high level of financial knowledge.

However, current consumer research indicates, time after time, the poor financial knowledge of the general population. For example, in a study of younger people, only 27 percent of respondents could answer basic questions on issues such as risk diversification, inflation and interest rates (Lusardi et al. 2010). Similarly, citing the 2006 Italian survey on household income and wealth, Monticone (2010) highlighted a lack in knowledge in the fact that the number of correct answers to six basic financial questions varied between 27 percent and 60 percent. Meanwhile, in a survey of 3,386 mutual fund investors, Capon et al. (1996) found that investors even had trouble understanding the mutual funds they had invested in. For example, as many as 75 percent of the sample did not know the investment style of their fund and 72 percent did not know if their funds focused on domestic or international investments.

In all, the financial literacy among the general public is low. In response, the governments of many Western countries have started policy initiatives in order to increase the knowledge of the public (Devlin 2003; Kozup and Hogarth 2008). However, although research has observed some positive effects of these initiatives, they are generally limited (Collins and O'Rourke 2010). Thus, it seems that even in the future, the simplest questions about personal finance are going to be a challenge for the average citizen.

Investor involvement

While knowledge is important, it alone does not guarantee decision-making ability. Another aspect that is fundamental to decision-making ability is to be involved in the decision. If the decision-maker does not care enough or spend sufficient time in processing necessary information, the decision is likely to be poor. As with financial knowledge, the lack of involvement and interest in financial services has been a major discussion point in consumer research (see, for example, Beckett et al. 2000; Harrison 1994; Martenson 2005, 2008).

While there are numerous examples of this lack of interest in personal finance issues, one of the most striking examples comes from the reformed Swedish pension system where, starting in the year 2000, individuals became responsible for investing part of their own pension. However, it seems that despite the direct personal consequences of the investment decisions made in the system, people are reluctant to put the effort into navigating it. While many people made a decision at the time of the introduction of the system, many have done little to follow up on this decision. Some people have even kept their money in the same investment

funds they chose more than ten years ago. One of the most remarkable examples of this apathy towards the system is one of the larger IT funds, which understandably was popular at the introduction of the system as it took place in the middle of the IT boom. However, even though the bubble burst many years ago and the fund has lost the majority of its value, many people have not been bothered to switch to a more suitable alternative. To this day, it is the fourth-largest mutual fund in the whole pension system (Andersson 2012).

Another example of the limited interest in the system is that a large number of people chose to let external advisors manage their investments. As such a large number of people chose to "outsource their transactions," and the companies involved with this activity grew, each individual trade by the advisors came to represent a large number of people. As large sudden transactions created problems for mutual fund companies, some of them even wanted to withdraw from the system. As a result, legislators had to step in to prevent advisors trading on the behalf of their clients (Larsson and Idling 2011).

While these two examples of the indifferent attitude towards the individually managed pension investment system in Sweden are interesting, they are not unique. Investments, personal finance and retirement savings are simply not something that the average person is interested in. In fact, many people remain passive, even when they suffer direct financial consequences of the decision. In more indirect contexts, in the role as a beneficiary for instance, this inertia is likely even stronger.

Involvement, knowledge and ESG

Up to this point, the review on investors' decision-making ability has indicated that for many (if not most) people, the area of personal finance is something that they are neither interested in nor knowledgeable about. This fact severely impacts their ability to make appropriate financial decisions. While most people would most likely prefer a high pension to a low one, it seems that they care too little about investments and personal finance to actually do the work that the investment context requires of them. Although there are few studies in this area, it is likely that this is also the case for ESG investments. While some people who are involved with issues such as social and environmental sustainability may care more about this specific investment topic, the finance and investment context is likely to keep most people as disinterested as they were for their regular pension savings. Given that the issue of ESG integration is also fairly complex, an informed opinion requires people to be involved and knowledgeable. While you may have a loose idea that tobacco is bad, actually having an opinion on what the institutional investor can do about this requires much more than just an instinct. As methods such as engagement and screening have completely different impacts on the investment portfolio, only the most involved and knowledgeable beneficiaries may have developed even a preference on the nature of ESG integration.

On this note, it has been shown empirically that investors have problems in understanding the strategies and methods of SRI as related to their own preferences. In a working paper focusing on the ethical preferences of retail SR investors, Sandberg and Nilsson (2010) highlight that investors often have conflicting preferences regarding how they want ESG issues to be incorporated into their mutual fund. Seen from an objective standpoint, the negative screening and engagement strategies are virtually impossible to combine (one excludes the company while the other includes the company). Despite this, many investors seem to want their mutual fund to use both methods. Thus, even the investors who have actively searched out an SRI alternative are confused about their preferences regarding ESG integration.

What insights can we get on the preferences of beneficiaries of large institutional investors?

In the introduction, this chapter set out to review the behavior of private investors to see if this body of literature can contribute to our understanding of the preferences of beneficiaries of large institutional investors such as pension funds. While it is up to each individual reader to judge the value of using private investors to say something about people in their role as beneficiaries of pension funds or other

institutions, the review above clearly shows two things about private investors. First, although it is difficult to evaluate the studies on retail investors' ESG preferences as a group (due to use of different research methods, items and contexts), there seems to be a wide range of ESG preferences that matter to investors. As displayed in Table 29.1, several studies highlighted both environmental and social, as well as product and industry issues. As suggested by the Statman (2008) study, this diversity in ESG preferences also seems to not only exist between studies (that are made in different countries and at different times), but most likely also *within* the samples of the studies. Thus, SR investors seem to care about different things. Second, the review also showed that people, for the most part, are not very interested in or knowledgeable about personal finance or their pension savings. This lack of interest and knowledge manifests itself through poor decision-making and dependence on external actors, such as financial advisors.

Taken in the context of the preferences of beneficiaries of large institutional investors, these insights on the attitudes and behavior of retail investors imply two things. First, it seems unlikely that beneficiaries of larger institutional investors can come to some form of *explicit* agreement on ESG issues, unless the issues are very general in nature. Of course there may be cases where the beneficiaries share some basic ESG preferences. However, it is likely that more often than not, ESG preferences will differ as they do so even among the people who have actively sought out investment products that take them into account. Thus, just like attitudes, political ideas and fundamental values, ESG preferences are highly personal and not something many people are likely to see eye-to-eye on.

While this insight is relevant, perhaps a more important insight from the realm of private investment is that this review questions whether the majority of people in their role as beneficiaries are interested and knowledgeable enough to be capable of even forming realistic context-specific ESG preferences. As displayed in the context of pension savings, the fact is that people for the most part do not care about how their retirement money is invested. Thus, the reality may very well be that most beneficiaries have no preferences other than a very general moral compass. When you ask them outright whether it is good to take some form of social or environmental responsibility, they may use this compass and answer yes. However, anything more than that in terms of ESG issues, methods (such as engagement or screening) and investment style, for instance, is going to be beyond the capabilities and interests of many people. Thus, if this is the case, achieving some sort of explicit agreement or consensus between beneficiaries will be difficult. After all, if you do not care or know about the issues you are supposed to agree on, how can you even begin to have an opinion about the specific issue?

Conclusions

In this chapter, two separate aspects of private investment behavior have been reviewed. The purpose of these reviews has not been to relate research directly to the issue of fiduciary duty as such, but rather to summarize some aspects that can be important to the discussion of how we can understand the preferences of "regular people" or beneficiaries in their relation to large institutional investors. This chapter contributes to the discussion by highlighting the fact that there seems to be a great lack of knowledge and involvement regarding investments and pension savings, and by showing that if there are any stable preferences, they are likely to differ between investors. While there are obvious limitations to the analysis as discussed initially, the chapter indicates that, from the perspective of the average person, the chances of an explicit agreement are small unless the population is very specific or the ESG issue is very general in nature.

That said, there may be other ways forward that are much more likely to be more realistic. For example, Richardson (2011b) highlights ways such as following social customs or third-party stakeholders. While discussing these is not within the scope of this chapter, against the background of the review above, they seem a much more suitable way forward than expecting some form of explicit agreement among a diverse population of beneficiaries.

References

Andersson, F. 2012. "Din IT-fond byter namn." www.avanza.se/aza/press/press_article. jsp?article=217666.

Atchely, R. C. 1998. "Financial Gerontology: Educating the Public about Personal Finance: A Call for Action," *Journal of the American Society of CLU & ChFC* 52: 28–32.

Barreda-Tarrazona, I., J. C. Matallin-Sáez and R. Balaguer-Franch. 2011. "Measuring Investors' Socially Responsible Preferences in Mutual Funds," *Journal of Business Ethics* 103: 305–30.

Bateman, H., J. Louviere, S. Thorp, T. Islam and S. Satchell. 2010. "Investment Decisions for Retirement Savings," *Journal of Consumer Affairs* 44: 463–82.

Beal, D. and M. Goyen. 1998. "'Putting your Money Where your Mouth is': A Profile of Ethical Investors," *Financial Services Review* 7: 129–43.

Beckett, A., P. Hewer and B. Howcroft. 2000. "An Exposition of Consumer Behaviour in the Financial Services Industry," *International Journal of Bank Marketing* 18: 15–26.

Capon, N., G. J. Fitzsimons and R. A. Prince. 1996. "An Individual Level Analysis of the Mutual Fund Investment Decision," *Journal of Financial Services Research* 10: 59–82.

Collins, J. M. and C. M. O'Rourke. 2010. "Financial Education and Counseling – Still Holding Promise," *Journal of Consumer Affairs* 44: 483–98.

Derwall, J., K. Koedijk and J. Ter Horst. 2011. "A Tale of Values-driven and Profit-seeking Social Investors," *Journal of Banking & Finance* 35: 2137–47.

Devlin, J. F. 2003. "Monitoring the Success of Policy Initiatives to Increase Consumer Understanding of Financial Services," *Journal of Financial Regulation & Compliance* 11: 151–63.

Duska, R. F. 2011. "Fiduciary Duty, Regulations and Financial Planning," *Journal of Financial Service Professionals* 65: 17–19.

Eurosif. 2010. *European SRI Study 2010.* www. eurosif.org.

Fonseca, R., K. J. Mullen, G. Zamarro and J. Zissimopoulos. 2012. "What Explains the Gender Gap in Financial Literacy? The Role of Household Decision-making," *Journal of Consumer Affairs* 46: 90–106.

Freshfields Bruckhaus Deringer. 2005. *A Legal Framework for the Integration of Environmental, Social and Governance Issues into Institutional Investment*. Geneva: United Nations Environmental Programme Finance Initiative.

Harrison, T. 1994. "Mapping Customer Segments for Personal Financial Services," *International Journal of Bank Marketing* 12: 17–25.

Kozup, J. and J. M. Hogarth. 2008. "Financial Literacy, Public Policy, and Consumers' Self-protection – More Questions, Fewer Answers," *Journal of Consumer Affairs* 42: 127–36.

Kozup, J., E. Howlett and M. Pagano. 2008. "The Effects of Summary Information on Consumer Perceptions of Mutual Fund Characteristics," *Journal of Consumer Affairs* 42: 37–59.

Lai, C. W. and J. J. Xiao. 2010. "Consumer Biases and Competences in Company Stock Holdings," *Journal of Consumer Affairs* 44: 179–212.

Larsson, L. and L. Idling. 2011. "Politikerna stoppar massbyten i PPM," *Dagens Nyheter*, April 5.

Lewis, A. and C. Mackenzie. 2000. "Morals, Money, Ethical Investing and Economic Psychology," *Human Relations* 53: 179–91.

Lewis, A. and P. Webley. 1994. "Social and Ethical Investing," in A. Lewis and K.-E. Wärneryd (eds.) *Ethics and Economic Affairs*. London, Routledge, pp. 171–82.

Lönnroth, M., S. Beloe and T. Linghede. 2001. *Screening of Screening Companies*. Stockholm: Mistra.

Lusardi, A., O. S. Mitchell and V. Curto. 2010. "Financial Literacy Among the Young," *Journal of Consumer Affairs* 44: 358–80.

Martenson, R. 2005. "Success in Complex Decision Contexts: The Impact of Consumer Knowledge, Involvement, and Risk Willingness on Return on Investments in Mutual Funds and Stocks," *International Review of Retail, Distribution and Consumer Research* 15: 449–69.

2008. "How Financial Advisors Affect Behavioral Loyalty," *International Journal of Bank Marketing* 26: 119–47.

McLachlan, J. and J. Gardner. 2004. "A Comparison of Socially Responsible and Conventional Investors," *Journal of Business Ethics* 52: 11–25.

Monticone, C. 2010. "How Much Does Financial Wealth Matter in the Acquisition of Financial Literacy," *Journal of Consumer Affairs* 44: 403–22.

Nilsson, J. 2008. "Investment with a Conscience: Examining the Impact of Pro-social Attitudes and Perceived Financial Performance on Socially Responsible Investment Behavior," *Journal of Business Ethics* 83: 307–25.

2009. "Segmenting Socially Responsible Mutual Fund Investors: The Influence of Financial Return and Social Responsibility," *International Journal of Bank Marketing* 27: 5–31.

2010. *Consumer Decision Making in a Complex Environment: Examining the Decision Making Process of Socially Responsible Mutual Fund Investors*, unpublished doctoral thesis, Umeå University.

Pérez-Gladish, B., K. Benson and R. Faff. 2012. "Profiling Socially Responsible Investors: Australian Evidence", *Australian Journal of Management* 37: 189–209

Pettersson, F., H. Helgesson and F. Hård af Segerstad. 2009. *Thirty Years of Investment Funds*. Swedish Investment Fund Association. www.fondbolagen.se.

Richardson, B. J. 2011a. "Fiduciary Relationships for Socially Responsible Investing: A Multinational Perspective," *American Business Law Journal* 48: 597–640.

2011b. "From Fiduciary Duties to Fiduciary Relationships for Socially Responsible Investing: Responding to the Will of Beneficiaries," *Journal of Sustainable Finance & Investment* 1: 5–19.

Rosen, B. N., D. M. Sandler and D. Shani. 1991. "Social Issues and Socially Responsible Investment Behavior: A Preliminary Investigation," *Journal of Consumer Affairs* 25: 221–34.

Sandberg, J. 2011. "Socially Responsible Investment and Fiduciary Duty: Putting the Freshfields Report into Perspective," *Journal of Business Ethics* 101: 143–62.

Sandberg, J. and J. Nilsson. 2010. "Conflicting Intuitions About Ethical Investment: A Survey Among Private Investors," *SIRP Working Paper* 10–16. www.sirp.se.

Stabile, S. and J. Zanglein. 2007. "ERISA Fiduciary Litigation: A Three-part Primer Part II: What Duties are Required of Fiduciaries?" *Journal of Pension Planning & Compliance* 33: 76–97.

Statman, M. 2008. "Quiet Conversations: The Expressive Nature of Socially Responsible Investors," *Journal of Financial Planning* 21: 40–6.

USSIF. 2012. "The Forum for Sustainable and Responsible Investment." www.ussif.org.

Valor, C., M. de la Cuesta and B. Fernandez. 2009. "Understanding Demand for Retail Socially Responsible Investments: A Survey of Individual Investors and Financial Consultants," *Corporate Social Responsibility and Environmental Management* 16: 1–14.

Webley, P., A. Lewis and C. Mackenzie. 2001. "Commitment Among Ethical Investors: An Experimental Approach," *Journal of Economic Psychology* 22: 27–42.

Woods, C. and R. Urwin. 2010. "Putting Sustainable Investing into Practice: A Governance Framework for Pension Funds," *Journal of Business Ethics* 92: 1–19.

PART VI

Fiduciary duty and governance

Investors and global governance frameworks: broadening the multi-stakeholder paradigm

JANE AMBACHTSHEER AND RYAN POLLICE

Introduction

Companies play an increasingly important role in the global economy.[1] With this growth has emerged a strong view that companies share in responsibilities traditionally assigned to governments – such as those relating to human rights and the environment (Ambachtsheer 2011).[2] A wide range of norms, codes of conduct and conventions have emerged to translate this broadening acceptance of extended corporate responsibility into policy and practice (see Appendix 30.1).

Traditionally, conventions were developed by multilateral institutions and targeted for ratification by national governments. More recently, a broader range of stakeholders have become involved in developing and supporting conventions under the espoused benefits of "multi-stakeholder processes" (Vallejo and Hauselmann 2004). This has resulted in a shift from legislative foundations towards the emergence of "soft law" approaches to regulating behavior, tending to take the form of nonbinding and voluntary codes of conduct. Multi-stakeholder processes have gained their standing as valid mechanisms to develop and implement codes of conduct in part because they include input from a broad range of stakeholders in their design, implementation and oversight. This chapter focuses on one stakeholder which is largely absent from the analysis of these processes – investors.

MIA: investors

The range of stakeholders in multi-stakeholder processes typically includes national, provincial and municipal government bodies; non-governmental organizations (NGOs) and other civil society actors; corporations; and individuals. In a smaller number of cases, financial institutions (pension funds, endowments, asset managers, banks and insurance companies) have also been involved.

This lack of investor involvement is changing, and investors are increasingly reflecting on their role in overseeing and influencing the companies in which they invest. This may be driven by one of two motivations: ethics, or a desire to behave in a manner which is consistent with the needs and view of beneficiaries; or risk management, stemming from a belief the consequences of a company's *not* adhering to certain standards could negatively impact on the investment performance of that security or investment.

Norms, codes and conventions support and influence these processes in a number of ways:

- They set standards for companies that, if adhered to, have a potential impact on the risk profiles of

---

[1] For example, a 2010 study of Fortune Global 500 and IMF data found that of the world's one hundred largest economic entities in 2009, forty-four were corporations. Together, the forty-four companies in our top one hundred list generated revenues of US\$6.4 trillion in 2009, equivalent to over 11 percent of global GDP. The largest in 2009, Walmart Stores, had revenues exceeding the respective GDPs of 174 countries. www.globaltrends.com/images/stories/corporate%20clout%20the%20worlds%20100%20largest%20economic%20entities.pdf.

[2] Much of this chapter draws from the previously published "The Missing Stakeholder: The Applicability of International Codes and Conventions to Institutional Investors" (Ambachtsheer 2011).

individual companies (e.g., through litigation or reputation risk).[3]

- They act as a compass, reflecting a level of international prioritization of, and consensus around, a range of issues, which create the backdrop against which long-term investors allocate capital.
- In some cases, they are bound by national and international law, and may legally extend to or govern the activities of specific public investment institutions (or, in other cases, safe harbor legislation may pave the way for investor consideration of the issue of focus[4]).
- Further, in addition to being influenced by these developments, investors are increasingly utilizing the content of the norms, codes and conventions in the context of their investment process.

Given the range of ways in which codes and conventions are relevant to – and increasingly utilized by – investors, it is puzzling that the academic literature analyzing the respective roles, relationships and power balances between these stakeholders involved in multi-stakeholder processes almost uniformly ignores the role of investors. The role that investors could (or should) play in the establishment, ongoing governance and enforcement of norms, codes and conventions across a range of social and environmental issues seems to have been given very little thought.

What is driving investor utilization of codes and conventions?

Investors are increasingly demanding (and being urged) to be more involved as owners of the capital under their control.[5] Coupled with growing

empirical evidence that suggests adherence to higher standards of corporate responsibility and sustainability can generate outperformance,[6] investors are increasingly reflecting on their role in overseeing and influencing the companies in which they invest. Further, a growing number of investors rely on international conventions and voluntary codes of conduct as standards and frameworks for assessing company performance. This is particularly common in Europe,[7] but can be expected to gain in popularity elsewhere.

How do norms, codes and conventions impact investor decision-making processes?

The ways in which norms, codes and conventions can be utilized by institutional investors in the context of current investment approaches can be categorized into three areas:

(1) **Avoiding investments** – investors may screen portfolios in a systematic way to avoid companies (or other investments) that related to a specific, unacceptable type of activity.

(2) **Ownership, stewardship and engagement** – referencing codes and conventions can support the execution of ownership rights as well as support engagement and dialogue with investee entities (directly and/or in collaboration with others).

(3) **Risk management and alpha generation** – there are a number of ways investors use codes and conventions to manage risk and/or generate alpha.

The first and second areas are utilized by investors with "ethical" objectives or motivations, while

---

[3] A 2007 survey by the European Centre for Corporate Engagement (ECCE) found that while ESG issues varied in importance in the analysis, valuation and recommendation of sell-side analysts, respect for human rights and the elimination of forced labor were rated as particularly important, behind corporate governance issues such as board composition, shareholder rights, and audit and internal controls. For an overview of academic and broker research on approaches to responsible investment, returns and impacts see Mercer (2009).

[4] For example, the South African Trust Investment Act in Ontario, Canada.

[5] For a review of international efforts to promote active ownership and "stewardship codes" see Espinosa and Pollice (2012).

[6] See, for example, Eccles et al. (2012) and El Ghoul et al. (2011).

[7] For example, in Sweden, an Ethical Council has been established by the four AP Funds and focuses on identifying violations of international conventions (signed by Sweden) in order to initiate a dialogue with the company around remedying the issue. Similarly, the New Zealand Superannuation Fund aims to adhere to international conventions to which New Zealand is a signatory, as well as significant policy positions of the New Zealand government.

Table 30.1 Avoiding investments.

Mechanism	Investment implications	Applications
Systematic negative screening: refers to the development of a disinvestment policy for an investor – identifying companies that undertake an unacceptable type of activity and/or are deemed to be involved in activities constituting an unacceptable level of risk. The focus here is on the consequences of the companies' production.	• High dependence on the interpretation of the state of noncompliance with convention(s). Range and depth of impact driven by extent of conventions applied / number of related companies, but typically relatively limited.	• Typically thought of in relation to public equity; also increasingly considered in relation to debt (corporate or sovereign, where the company or country in question is in breach). • Most applicable to conventions prohibiting certain easily identifiable products or activities.
Ad hoc negative screening: limit the universe of possible investments only on an ad hoc basis. The focus here is on the performance of a company around a specific issue. May relate to: • serious human rights violations and violations of human rights in war/conflict; • severe environmental damage; • gross corruption; • sanctions on countries; • other serious violations of conventions.	• Decisions will be made within context of existing policy guidelines. • More complicated and potentially with wider application than negative screening focused on excluding companies involved in producing certain products. • Equal treatment of companies may be difficult (and predictability for companies may be low), as exclusion is on a case-by-case basis.	• Applied to listed equities and to corporate and sovereign debt. • Also relevant to unlisted investments such as private equity and infrastructure (e.g., using Equator Principles). • Relevant to a broad range of conventions. • Can be used in conjunction with engagement (i.e., divest if unsuccessful, reinvest if successful).

the second and third areas reflect a more typical toolkit for "fiduciary driven risk managers."

The following tables explore these three mechanisms in further detail, including an assessment of the possible investment implications of each.

While currently outside mainstream investment practice, another possible approach involves reconceiving asset classes in the context of their social function and beyond their more narrow financial function (contribution to portfolio diversification and risk-adjusted returns). From a societal perspective, different asset classes serve different purposes: government fixed income investments typically fund public goods such as education and infrastructure; real estate investments create our built environment; venture capital promotes innovation and will be critical in tackling our resource constrained future; stock markets allow investors to access the growth associated with public companies.[8]

Thinking about asset classes – at least in part – in relation to their social utility (or detraction),

could be relevant in allowing investors to consider the ways different investments could enhance, or undercut, longer-term economic outcomes. Recently principles have emerged in relation to the role of certain asset classes in creating a more sustainable ecological and financial future. In 2011, a group of investors representing US$1.3 trillion in assets launched the Principles for Responsible Investment in Farmland (the "Farmland Principles") with the goal of improving the sustainability, transparency and accountability of investments in farmland.[9] There has also been a recent focus on the potential implications for investors of the risks associated with "land grabs" in emerging markets.[10] In the fixed income context, the Climate Bonds Initiative[11] is focused on scaling up investments in green fixed income to fund a transition to a low-carbon economy.

---

[8] This is an area of investigation by the Institute for Responsible Investment at Harvard University. See http://hausercenter.org/iri/publications/social-function-of-asset-classes.

[9] For more information see www.abp.nl/en/about-abp/press-service/principles-for-responsible-investment-in-farmland.asp and www.unpri.org/areas-of-work/implementation-support/commodities.

[10] For example, see http://farmlandgrab.org/post/view/21611.

[11] See http://climatebonds.net/ for more information.

Table 30.2 Ownership, stewardship and collaboration.

Mechanism	Investment implications	Applications
Exercise of ownership rights: a globally accepted practice for protecting and enhancing shareholder capital. Rights are exercised through voting on and participating in management and shareholder proposals.	• Practically, proposals can be screened for relevance or compliance to conventions. • UN Global Compact and/or OECD Guidelines can be used as a framework for exercise of ownership rights.	• Public equity. • Can be used in conjunction with engagement.
Engagement: dialogue is a major tool for investors on the application of conventions by investee entities. It can be applied by a single investor or as part of a group through various collaborative initiatives.	• Successful engagement relies heavily on research, risk assessments and skilled/experienced individuals. • Can be used as a tool to manage risk or unlock value. • Free-rider concern.	• To date, has largely focused on improving disclosure around adherence to a convention (versus advocating strict compliance). • Mostly focused on public equity, but now extending to some other asset classes (private equity, project finance, fixed income).

Table 30.3 Risk management and alpha generation.

Mechanism	Investment implications	Applications
Precautionary approach and guidelines: the precautionary principle means that where there is a threat of serious or irreversible damage to society or the environment, lack of full scientific certainty or of government policies shall not be used as a reason to postpone effective measures to avert these risks. A precautionary approach can drive the investment community to interpret and apply general conventions in concrete investment terms.[18]	• Active research into an understanding of how an investment relates to or affects both society and capital markets, and thus the long-term objectives of the investor. • Interpreted in the context of different levels of risk acceptance (unacceptable risk, acceptable but not recommended risk, tolerated risk). • A recent UK report modeled the impact of resource constraints on a pension fund and found that the financial impact could be profound (Jones et al. 2013).	• Relevant to risks emerging from a range of conventions and social issues (resource scarcity, climate change income inequality, etc.). • Across all asset classes in public and private markets; strategic asset allocation. • Investor principles recently introduced with regards to farmland.
Positive screening: positive investments are those that deliver strong environmental or social returns in addition to attractive (or sufficient) investment returns (depending on the investor's objective and the nature of the investment). Under this type of investing, research focuses on the risks but also the opportunities of investments identified as complying with (or exceeding) standards set by broad conventions.	• Rather than (or in addition to) screening companies, involves overweighting those that have the best performance relative to the convention(s) of relevance. • Systematic bias linked to risks and opportunities of the convention(s). • Specific strategic asset allocation may be set according to the convention's principles.	• Niche approach for thematic or targeted investments (such as microfinance or environmental investing). • Potentially wider application for "best-in-class" approach (e.g., using broad market ESG indices for passive investments. This is still quite uncommon, but has significant potential for growth).
Integrated analysis: investors can use information about company adherence to conventions as part of their investment research process.	• Additional input to analyze company performance and identify potential risk.	• While most research currently focuses on listed equity and debt, this is quickly broadening to focus on a broader range of asset classes. Private markets as conventions emerge or are applied to these areas.

Investor experiences to-date: two case studies

The following case studies have been included to provide illustrative examples of the ways in which norms, codes and conventions can be useful to investors to align with legal requirements; meet beneficiary requirements; manage risk and generate returns (alpha and beta). Case Study 30.1 on the Convention on Cluster Munitions discusses how international conventions may legally extend to or govern the activities of specific investment institutions and falls into the category of an "ethical" case study. In Case Study 30.2, the role of investors in enforcing the expectations of voluntary codes of conduct will be explored through a review of the UN Global Compact. Investor motivation for utilizing the UN Global Compact can be ethical and/or risk-related.

Case Study 30.1: Convention on Cluster Munitions

A cluster bomb is a weapon that can contain up to several hundred small explosive bomblets. Dropped from the air or fired from the ground, cluster bombs scatter these bomblets over a wide area. Anyone within the strike zone is likely to be torn apart, and because many bomblets fail to explode as intended, cluster bombs leave behind huge numbers of de facto landmines. Boer and Vandenbroucke (2011) report that civilians account for 98 percent of all victims of cluster munitions.

In 2008, governments negotiated an international treaty – the Convention on Cluster Munitions (CCM) – which bans the use, production, stockpiling and transfer of cluster bombs. The Convention entered into force on August 1, 2010, and 108 states have joined the Convention as states parties or signatories to date.[12] Article 1(1)c of the CCM states: "Each State Party undertakes never under any circumstances to assist, encourage or induce anyone to engage in any activity prohibited to a State Party under this Convention." Although countries that have signed the Convention must stop producing cluster bombs, these munitions continue to be produced by listed companies elsewhere (e.g., Lockheed Martin and Singapore Technologies Engineering).

Does the CCM affect investors?

The relevant question for investors in countries that have signed the CCM (particularly public pension systems and sovereign wealth funds) is whether they are contravening the Convention by investing in corporations that manufacture cluster munitions outside their borders. From a legal perspective, in most instances the answer would likely be "no," as the governance of these investment institutions will often be at arm's length from the signing authority of the country in question. However, one could reasonably interpret financing the production of cluster munitions as constituting "assistance" or "encouragement," also prohibited under the Convention. Thus, such investments by institutions responsible for public assets arguably undermine the commitment by signatory countries to ban these weapons and could run counter to their obligations under international law. Funds with divestment policies include the Irish National Pensions Reserve Fund, New Zealand Superannuation Fund, the Norwegian Government Pension Fund Global and Swedish Pension Funds AP 1–4.

From an implementation perspective, the challenge is lack of clarity; implementation by state parties does not automatically produce a ban on investing in cluster munitions. In October 2009, the Cluster Munitions Coalition set up the Stop Explosive Investments campaign[13] to help monitor and curtail the flow of funds to corporations that still manufacture cluster bombs. Through raising public awareness about the financial institutions investing in cluster bomb production, they aim to increase the number of financial

---

[12] See the list of ratifications and signatories of the CCM at www.clusterconvention.org/ratifications-and-signatures.

[13] The Stop Explosive Investments campaign has issued a 180-page report (Boer and Vandenbroucke 2011) that

Case Study 30.1: (cont.)

institutions adopting guidelines on cluster munitions and to urge governments to adopt legislation banning investment in cluster munitions. Because many signatory countries are now drafting

national implementation legislation (and/or have started to implement the CCM), the process of banning cluster munitions is in a crucial phase.

Case Study 30.2: investor activism and the UN Global Compact

Self-identified as a "global platform which convenes companies together with UN agencies, labor and civil society to support fundamental principles," the United Nations Global Compact is relevant to investors as a market-wide framework that articulates principles and practices related to human rights, labor, the environment and anti-corruption that companies are expected to adhere to. The Global Compact principles are derived from the Universal Declaration of Human Rights, the International Labour Organization's Declaration on Fundamental Principles and Rights at Work, the Rio Declaration on Environment and Development and the United Nations Convention against Corruption. The UN Global Compact aims to mainstream ten principles for business activities around the world while encouraging corporate behavior that supports broader UN goals, such as the Millennium Development Goals. It represents the world's largest "corporate social responsibility" (CSR) initiative and more than 5,625 companies from 130 countries currently have an Active Communication on Progress (COP) status.[14]

The UN Global Compact's system of reporting (COP) requires that business participants publicly disclose, on an annual basis, any relevant policies, procedures and activities that the company

has undertaken (and plans to undertake) to implement the Global Compact principles in each of the four issue areas. Through this public disclosure, the COP provides a means for the investment community to analyze a company's ability to manage and mitigate exposure to ESG risk. Where companies have committed to producing a COP but have not delivered, investors have used their collective influence to seek appropriate disclosure, reflecting the largest, most coordinated investor engagement to date around an international convention.

Investor activism based on UN global compact data

Since 2007, investors have engaged with participants in the UN Global Compact on their required public disclosure under the COP. Coordinated through the PRI Engagement Clearinghouse, Aviva Investors invites other PRI signatories to send joint letters to the CEOs of listed Global Compact signatories. The number of investors participating in the annual engagement has grown from twenty investors from ten countries in 2008 to thirty-eight investors from twelve countries in 2012, with assets represented growing from US$2.1 trillion to more than US$3 trillion.

provides much of the information included in Case Study 30.1. The report includes both a "Hall of Shame" (listing companies and investors involved in cluster munitions) and a "Hall of Fame" (describing financial institutions that are pioneering in disinvestment). It also includes a special focus on public pension funds.

[14] An Active COP status indicates that the company has made a public disclosure on progress made in implementing

the ten principles of the UN Global Compact and in supporting broad UN development goals. For details on the COP process, see United Nations Global Compact (2009). As of June 10, 2011, there are 1,549 business participants with a non-communicating COP status. A list of UN Global Compact participants is available at www.unglobalcompact. org/ParticipantsAndStakeholders/index.html. (For more information about this engagement, see Johnson 2010; United Nations Global Compact 2008; Wheelan 2010.)

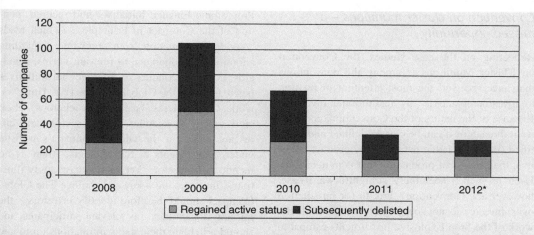

Figure 30.1 Engagement with Global Compact "laggards." *At the time of writing, final results have yet to be confirmed.

Investors use the Global Compact public database to identify companies for engagement, including those listed as "non-communicating" or "inactive" (termed "laggards" for failing to submit their COP or for poor performance) as well as those with particularly good reporting ("leaders"). The engagement serves to recognize leaders in disclosing their efforts to adhere with the Global Compact Principles while pressing laggards who have failed to report to improve the quality of their COP.

Between 2008 and 2011, the engagement has resulted in between 33 and 48 percent of non-communicating Global Compact participants subsequently submitting a COP, while at the same time, 272 "leader" companies have been acknowledged as advanced-level reporters. Since 2008, as Figure 30.1 illustrates, engagement with non-communicating Global Compact participants

has resulted in 115 participants' subsequently disclosing their activities and regaining Active COP status – approximately 40.7 percent of companies identified for engagement. At the time of publication, the ongoing 2012 engagement had resulted in 56 percent of laggard companies subsequently submitting a COP.[15]

Additionally, the PRI and Global Compact initiatives are engaged in a number of mutually reinforcing activities, including an investor engagement urging companies around the world to sign onto the UN Global Compact. As of November 2011, this engagement saw 211 of the targeted companies join the Global Compact. From September 2012, the PRI has announced a new collaborative engagement whereby signatories will have an opportunity to test engagement strategies, which will be used to support future investor-led collaborative engagements.

An imperative: embedding investors into convention and soft-law governance

Most norms, codes and conventions refer to general stakeholders and more specifically to corporations. Very few, however, include language specifically addressing their applicability to

investors or the role that investors can play in promoting or adhering to the provisions of the norm, code or convention.

---

[15] Data on the outcomes of past engagements was accessed via the PRI Secretariat at www.unpri.org/collaborations.

Convention on cluster munitions – a missed opportunity

Reflecting on the case studies, the Convention on Cluster Munitions is among the conventions that have received the most attention in relation to investment activity by institutional investors. Because of the nature of the Convention, companies in breach of it can be clearly defined and identified (that is, it is the nature of the product rather than the process of production that is in question). Even in such a seemingly straightforward case, however, the Convention's link to (or jurisdiction over) investors is not so straightforward. While the work of the Stop Explosive Investments campaign is thorough and has had a demonstrable impact, the need for such a group seems to have arisen because the CCM is unclear as to whether it was designed to prohibit financing and extend to investment pools over which signing countries have legal jurisdiction. This was arguably a missed opportunity.

Global Compact – not reaching its potential as an investor tool

The Global Compact has been an efficient means of improving corporate disclosure of information because it combines multiple underlying codes and international codes. Further, engagement around the Global Compact's Communication on Progress (COP) is an important way for the investment community to analyze a company's performance on these issues and for investors to communicate to management that corporate responsibility is considered highly relevant to long-term financial success.[16]

These points aside, there are notable missed opportunities within the Global Compact to include investors as a central stakeholder group. To its credit, the Global Compact jointly coordinated the development of the PRI (with the UN Environment Programme Finance Initiative) and secured mention of the Compact in Principle 3 (which reads "Ask for information from companies regarding adoption of / adherence to relevant norms, standards, codes of conduct or international initiatives (such as the UN Global Compact)"). However, while UN agencies, business associations, labor, civil society, academics, public sectors and cities are listed on the Global Compact's website under "Participants & Stakeholders," there is no mention of investors. Yet, as this case study illustrates, investors are a key stakeholder. The Global Compact should therefore identify investors – the missing stakeholder – as relevant participants, and should articulate their status in relationship to and their opportunities within the Global Compact initiative.

A diamond in the coal mine – EITI

A notable exception where investors have been embedded into a code or convention as a stakeholder is the Extractive Industry Transparency Initiative (EITI), which represents a coalition of governments, companies, civil society groups, investors and international organizations. The EITI sets a global standard for transparency in oil, gas and mining and aims to strengthen governance by improving accountability in the extractives sector. It supports improved governance in resource-rich countries through verification and full publication of company royalty payments through a set of principles. More than eighty global investment institutions have supported the EITI's Investor Statement on Transparency in the Extractives Sector.

Getting investors involved

There are both push and pull opportunities to have investors more fully embedded – alongside companies, NGOs and governments – as a fourth stakeholder in the evolving world of global multistakeholder governance frameworks.

Where the case is warranted (from an ethical or a risk-management perspective), the investment community needs to *push* itself into the relevant initiatives – at the outset (in the case of emerging

---

[16] In October 2008, a group of global investors representing US$4.4 trillion in assets signaled their endorsement of the UN Global Compact by announcing a collaborative effort to urge the CEOs of approximately 9,000 companies to commit to the UN Global Compact and its ten principles or to explain any decision not to do so (see United Nations Global Compact 2008).

initiatives), or later on (such as working with the Global Compact to make the initiative more attractive as a resource and framework for utilization by the investment community).

From the *pull* perspective, investors are providers of capital and as such, potential enforcers of standards. Given that many voluntary codes are criticized for lacking teeth, this lure of enforcement should prove large. Yet, very few groups actively reach out to investors and the reasons for this are worth probing. In some cases, it may relate to a lack of familiarity by the other stakeholders with the "world of investment."

Much of the high profile coverage we see (push or pull) centers on initiatives that call for divestment. For example, legislation has been introduced in a number of US states mandating public pension fund divestment from companies doing business in certain countries (such as Sudan, Iran or Iraq); Bill McKibbon's 350.org fossil fuel divestment campaign calls for divestment from the a list of companies having the largest proven fossil fuel reserves;[17] the Stop Explosive Investments Campaign calls for divestment from companies involved in cluster munitions production.

Although a straightforward objective such as divestment may be politically attractive, it may not always be the tool most appropriate for achieving the impact sought, in that divestment removes the ability for an owner to engage in dialogue with a company about their business practices. In the case of anti-apartheid divestment from companies doing business in South Africa, divestment was an effective tool, because the country's economy was effectively "ring-fenced." This will not be the case elsewhere, for example, large multinational companies will typically not feel the economic consequences of divestment, even if a significant number of high profile pension funds take part. There is also a difference between engaging a company to improve or discontinue a certain activity or policy indirectly related to

their core business (Sudan, ESG disclosure) versus engaging tobacco or gun manufacturers to change their core business. The lesson is that investors need to develop a strategic and well thought out approach to addressing the range of topics that they may be drawn in to, particularly as the process of divestment involves real costs (which might be better spent elsewhere, such as on engagement).

Conclusions

Looking ahead

Coming back to first principles, institutional investors are seeking to optimize risk-adjusted returns over a particular time frame, often the long term. Investment returns achieved today at the expense of future growth are unsustainable and at some point, will be curtailed. This poses both moral and financial risks.

Further, pensioners or other beneficiaries of investment pools tend not to want to see their capital used to fund activities or the production of services that are either illegal or morally unacceptable (assuming common ground such as on child and forced labor). It is also true that different people will have different views of what is morally unacceptable when it comes to their retirement income. Finally, the fact that behavior of global companies is increasingly watched by multi-stakeholder initiatives means that tracking company compliance with these provides an increasingly accepted means of identifying associated risks (reputation, litigation).

In the context of these drivers, what's the outlook on whether investors become fully engaged as a fourth stakeholder in the development, implementation and governance of international codes and conventions?

One the one hand, we have seen a tremendous growth of investor activity in this area over the past five years. On the other hand, it's probably fair to surmise that a solid proportion of the world's pension, sovereign wealth, insurance and mutual fund companies do not currently have the board commitment, resources and governance practices to respond to them. Nor, given the many challenges facing

---

[17] As identified by Carbon Tracker, www.carbontracker.org.
[18] For example, universal owners may adopt a precautionary approach in guiding market-wide engagements that seek to protect long-term value, such as on the topic of climate change. For discussion of universal ownership see Urwin (2011).

institutional investors (such as solvency risks and a low growth environment), it is not clear that a focus on this area will become a priority in the short term.

Some of the things that may change this include:

- More input from beneficial owners about their preferences and expectations in regards to investor adherence to or utilization of codes and conventions around environmental, social and governance factors.
- Safe harbors that provide the space for fiduciaries to consider issues that may not directly link to optimizing risk-adjusted return but that are important to the beneficiary.
- Better metrics that link company performance in these areas to investment analysis and performance.
- The growing acceptance (and push) for investors to enhance their engagement activities with companies. Given that investors often own hundreds or even thousands of companies, engaging in the development and applications of multi-stakeholder frameworks that govern company behavior is potentially more efficient than undertaking company engagements one firm at a time.
- At the systems level, more focus on ESG topics by stock exchanges and regulators will continue to drive focus in this area by investors, who may conclude that utilizing existing codes and conventions is a sensible way to set expectations for and measure corporate conduct with regards to a range of issues.

On the whole, the emerging role for investors in setting and enforcing global governance frameworks – for ethical and investment motivated purposes – is a fascinating one. It deserves far more attention by the academic and financial communities, and is a space we look forward to continuing to work on in collaboration with our clients and peers around the world.

Appendix 30.1: sample international codes and conventions

The following table lists a number of well-known international conventions, norms and codes of conduct. It categorizes these into formal, legal structures (conventions) or soft-law initiatives (codes of conduct and voluntary initiatives). The final column indicates cases where there is evidence that investors have utilized it for purposes of avoiding/screening investments, ownership and stewardship activities and/or risk management and alpha generation.

References

Ambachtsheer, J. 2011. "The Missing Stakeholder: The Applicability of International Codes and Conventions to Institutional Investors," *Rotman International Journal of Pension Management* 4 (2): 26–36.

Boer, R. and E. Vandenbroucke. 2011. "Worldwide Investments in Cluster Munitions: A Shared Responsibility," IKV Pax Christi and Netwerk Vlaanderen. www.stopexplosiveinvestments. org/uploads/REPORT%20May%202011%20 FINAL.pdf.

Eccles, R. G., I. Ioannou and G. Serafeim. 2012. "The Impact of a Corporate Culture of Sustainability on Corporate Behavior and Performance," Harvard Business School Working Paper No. 12–035. www.hbs.edu/ research/pdf/12–035.pdf.

Espinosa, D. and R. Pollice. 2012. "Stewardship Codes: An Emerging Global Phenomenon," Mercer Insights. www.mercer.com/articles/ stewardship-codes-emerging-global- phenomenon.

El Ghoul, S., O. Guedhami, C.Y. Kwok, and Dev R. Mishra. 2011. "Does Corporate Social Responsibility Affect the Cost of Capital?" *Journal of Banking & Finance* 35 (9): 2388–406.

Johnson, S. 2010. "Companies Fail UN's Global Compact," *Financial Times*, February 14.

Jones, A., I. Allen, N. Silver, C. Cameron, C. Howarth and B. Caldecott. 2013. "Research Report – Resource Constraints: Sharing a Finite World. Implications of Limits to Growth for the Actuarial Profession." www.actuaries.org.uk/ research-and-resources/documents/research- report-resource-constraints-sharing-finite- world-implicati.

Mercer. 2009. *Shedding Light on Responsible Investment: Approaches, Returns and*

Table A30.1 International conventions, norms and codes of conduct.

		Convention	Soft-law	Utilized by investors
Broad international conventions	Universal Declaration of Human Rights (1948)	✓		✓
	ILO Declaration on Fundamental Principles and Rights at Work (1998)	✓		✓
	UN Global Compact (2000)		✓	✓
	OECD Guidelines for Multinational Enterprise (rev. 2011)			✓
Human rights principles	The Sullivan Principles (1977)		✓	✓
	The MacBride Principles (1984)		✓	✓
	UN Human Rights Norms for Business (2004)		✓	
	Convention against Torture and other Cruel, Inhuman or Degrading Treatment or Punishment	✓		
	Voluntary Principles on Security and Human Rights		✓	✓
Labor standards	International Labour Organization (ILO) Conventions including • ILO Indigenous and Tribal Peoples Convention (ILO Convention 169) • Child Labour Convention (C138) • Worst Forms of Child Labour Convention (C182) • Forced Labour Convention (C105) • Equal Remuneration Convention (C100) • Discrimination (Employment and Occupation) Convention (C111) • Freedom of Association and Protection of the Right to Organize Convention (C87) • Occupational Safety and Health Convention (C155)	✓		✓
	UN Code of Conduct for Law Enforcement Officials (1979)		✓	
	ILO Tripartite Declaration of Principles Concerning Multinational Enterprises and Social Policy (2000)		✓	
Corruption	UN Convention against Corruption (2004)	✓		✓
Environment	Montreal Protocol on Substances that Deplete the Ozone Layer (1989)	✓		
	Rio Declaration on Environment and Development (1992)		✓	
	Convention on Biological Diversity (1992)	✓		✓
	ISO14000 series		✓	
	Kyoto Protocol (2005)	✓		

Table A30.1 (cont.)

		Convention	Soft-law	Utilized by investors
Weapons and military activity	Convention on the Prohibition of the Development, Production and Stockpiling of Bacteriological (Biological) and Toxin Weapons and on their Destruction (Biological Weapons Conventions) (1975)	✓		
	UN Basic Principles on the Use of Force and firearms by Law Enforcement Officials (1990)		✓	
	Convention on the Prohibition of the Use, Stockpiling, Production and Transfer of Anti-Personnel Mines and on their Destruction (Ottawa Treaty)	✓		✓
	Convention on the Prohibition of the Development, Production, Stockpiling and Use of Chemical Weapons and on their Destruction (Chemical Weapons Convention)	✓		
	Convention on Cluster Munitions (2008)	✓		✓
Health	Protocol on Water and Health to the 1992 Convention on the Protection and Use of Transboundary Watercourses and International Lakes (1999)	✓		
	ILO Code of Practice on HIV/AIDS (2001)		✓	
	World Health Organization Framework Convention on Tobacco Control (2003)	✓		
	Convention on the Rights to Persons with Disabilities (2008)	✓		

Impacts. www.mercer.com/attachment.
dyn?idContent=1357265&filePath=/
attachments/English/Shedding_light_on_
responsible_investment_free_version.pdf.

United Nations Global Compact. 2008. *Global Investors Urge 9000 CEOs to Join UN Global Compact.* www.unglobalcompact.org/ NewsAndEvents/news_archives/2008_10_27. html.

2009. *Investors Give New Twist to Good COP/ Bad COP.* www.unglobalcompact.org/ NewsAndEvents/news_archives/2009_01_12. html.

Urwin, R. 2011. "Pension Funds as Universal Owners: Opportunity Beckons and Leadership Calls," *Rotman International Journal of Pension Management* 4 (1): 26–33.

Vallejo, N. and P. Hauselmann. 2004. *Governance and Multi-stakeholder Processes.* New York: International Institute for Sustainable Development.

Wheelan, H. 2010. "UNPRI Coalition Targets 86 Major Companies on Global Compact Failure," *Responsible Investor*, February 15. www.responsible-investor.com/home/article/ unpri_coalition_targets_86_major_companies_ on_global_compact_failure.

Promoting corporate sustainability through integrated reporting: the role of investment fiduciaries and the responsibilities of the corporate board

ROBERT G. ECCLES, JOCK HERRON AND
GEORGE SERAFEIM

Introduction

While fiduciaries have various roles, they share a common obligation to act with care and loyalty to the beneficiary whose interests they serve. Fiduciaries that have control over a beneficiary's financial assets are generally held to the strictest standards of care and loyalty. The question then arises, "How can a fiduciary entrusted with someone else's assets make investment decisions that favor companies that promote sustainability over those that do not?" Unless the trust indenture explicitly directs the fiduciary to privilege sustainability, this conundrum has no definitive answer. However, we believe that by evaluating the activities and comparative due diligence of corporate boards, which are themselves fiduciaries, investment fiduciaries will gain valuable insights that enrich their own decision-making about companies committed to sustainable business practices.

Our argument has three legs to it. First, as discussed in the third section, corporations themselves have a broader mandate than is commonly recognized to serve various stakeholders in addition to shareholders. It is the role of the corporate board to reconcile the trade-offs implicit in this broader mandate and integrated reporting, discussed in the fourth section, is a key mechanism enabling them to do so. Second, as discussed in the fifth section, while fiduciaries may be held to a stricter standard, boards of directors must honor long-established duty of care and loyalty obligations to

act in the best interests of the corporation itself. Third, the investment fiduciary typically acts on behalf of diverse investors with a range of investment horizons, risk preferences and strategic objectives. That fact establishes some investment flexibility as long as the fiduciary is acting with demonstrable prudence when making decisions. In the sixth section we argue that when investing in companies that emphasize "sustainability" as integral to their business strategy, investment fiduciaries can rely on two underappreciated factors to support their decision-making. The first is to recognize that public companies have a broader legal mandate than to narrowly maximize shareholder wealth. The second is to establish that a corporate board is well informed and diligently acting in the best long-term interests of the company.

Why does this matter? As corporate sustainability – in our view a commitment to managing with long-term horizons that promote economic vitality along with environmental and social sustainability at an appropriate level of risk – becomes important on numerous global fronts, investment fiduciaries and corporations will be faced with both an opportunity and increasingly, we believe, a public mandate to play leading roles. If meaningful sustainability goals are to be achieved, the largest pools of capital and the largest companies cannot be on the sidelines. Examining what degrees of freedom fiduciaries have, be they board members or institutional investors, is a step in that direction and the aim of this chapter.

It is important to be clear at the outset that we believe that long-term profitability remains an essential attribute of the sustainable firm. However, we agree with an emerging critique (Blair 1995) that the premise that the *exclusive* mission of the corporation is to generate profits is a relatively recent ideological view. This critique holds that such a view has over-privileged short-term horizons and, when narrowly construed, is not well grounded in corporate law. On the contrary, boards of directors have the authority to broaden the mission of a corporation. This presumes that they are broadly and deeply informed about a full range of corporate operating performance. Although the essentials of our argument may apply to other social objectives, our focus in this chapter is on the prospects of the corporation as a sustainable entity. We strongly contend that more comprehensive and better integrated external reporting is an essential – and not a peripheral – step toward achieving this goal. The provision of more complete information to a wider range of corporate constituencies – shareholders, employees, suppliers and customers – is the forcing mechanism needed to promote more durable corporate sustainability.

We also note at the outset that evidence is emerging to support the notion that long-term corporate profitability and leadership in sustainability practices are convergent rather than divergent goals (Barnett and Salomon 2006; Ioannis and Serafeim 2011). Taking a long-term view, the same may be true when it comes to other social objectives, although stakeholder interests in some cases may be less well aligned. While addressing broader social and environmental questions lies beyond the purview of this chapter, the influence of the largest corporations in relation to the State, particularly in light of the State's failure to assuage such social concerns, makes further consideration of the role of the corporation as an instrument of social change both timely and important.[1]

After considering the evolution of the corporate form and discussing the re-emerging view that the role of the corporation is wider than conventionally understood, we focus on the contribution

to sustainability that can be made by expanding corporate accountability through "integrated reporting" – the public accounting of corporate performance across a wide range of metrics. The familiar adage, "can't manage what you can't measure," remains as relevant as ever. We then discuss the central role that the board of directors can play in promoting, measuring, and reporting on sustainability practices across the firm by adopting integrated reporting – a decision that would benefit a wide range of stakeholders that includes, but is not limited to, shareholders. We conclude by exploring what implications this has for investment fiduciaries.

Evolution of the corporation: a snapshot overview

In an era fixated on innovation, the institutionally flexible nature of the corporation as an instrument of change warrants more attention. The adaptability of the corporate form, combined with its procedural reliability, has created a social entity – the corporation – that has to varying degrees been an essential mediator in the progressive incorporation of new technologies, services, practices and expectations in economies throughout the world. We briefly consider that history as a reminder that the role of the corporation has never been fixed. Instead, it has co-evolved with other forces to meet the needs, desires and reigning political aims of society during particular historical eras.

The corporation is an unusually mutable form. As evidence we offer a snapshot of the evolutionary development of the corporation (Miranti 1999; Roy 1997; Smith and Dyer 1996). Our aim is to give some very rough context to the view that we are on the edge of a new way of thinking about the role of the corporation in the twenty-first century.

1600–1800: Colonial monopolies and the joint-stock company: The earliest large companies were privately funded corporations with geographic mandates awarded by sponsoring States interested in advancing their economic and political interests in colonial markets. Minimal information was supplied to investors and essentially none to the public. The East India Company (1600),

---

[1] For example, the world's largest corporation in terms of revenue, Wal-Mart, would rank 28th in GDP as a country. The 100th largest, Walgreen's, would rank 62nd.

the Virginia Company (1606) and, notoriously, the Mississippi Company (1684) are examples.

1725–1860: Industrial Revolution and private partnerships: Business partnerships with more functional and geographic latitude than State-chartered corporations were the preferred investment vehicles of the Industrial Revolution. Typically closely held by owner-operators, the partnerships had little public accountability. A famous example is the Birmingham partnership of Boulton & Watt, which commercialized Watt's steam condenser and also operated a coinage.

1840–1900: Railroads and the emergence of the modern corporation: The development and rapid expansion of railroads in both England and the United States required both complex business management and substantial external financing, much of it across international borders. Governments progressively increased the flexibility of corporate charters, and businesses began producing more sophisticated internal operating information to manage increasingly complex and geographically dispersed businesses. Credit analysts like Henry Varnum Poor supported investors by developing techniques to assess corporate performance, and the governments of England and the United States passed legislation during this period to increase the extent of public reporting and improve its reliability. The New York Central and the Pennsylvania Railroad are corporate examples. Periodically, railroad securities were subject to unscrupulous stock manipulation by financiers like Jay Gould, James Fisk and Daniel Drew.

1880–1950: Large domestic corporations and public accountability: Monopolistic trusts were created during this period in oil, steel, sugar, tobacco, meatpacking and other capital-intensive industries. While the Sherman Antitrust Act broke up some of the trusts, the era of big corporations with increasingly diversified ownership was in full force by the 1920s. The complex organizational structure, sophisticated internal management reporting and centralized control of Alfred P. Sloan's General Motors shaped and defined the modern corporation we recognize today. In a seminal book, Adolphe Berle and Gardner Means highlighted the consequences of the separation of ownership from control in large public corporations (Berle and

Means 1991) and, during the Depression, Merrick Dodd invoked two speeches by senior executives of General Electric and evolving case law to support his argument that corporate executives "are guardians of all the interests which the corporation affects and not merely servants of its absentee owners" (Dodd 1932). In other words, he rejected the concept of shareholder primacy. During the Great Depression, two legislative acts first created the Securities and Exchange Commission and subsequently mandated rule-based, external financial reporting with verification by independent auditors for all publicly traded securities.

1950–1980s: Multinational corporations and shareholder primacy: Following World War II, the United States emerged as the dominant national economy, leveraging its advantage through international trade and technological innovation. Domestic corporations that had anchored American war production quickly evolved into what became known as multinational corporations. These complex and legally opaque organizations typically consisted of an array of foreign subsidiaries designed to accommodate local regulatory, marketing and economic conditions. Economic growth generated surplus savings and accelerated the development of market-driven, institutional money management. This led to a sharper focus on short-term stock market performance and its corollary, short-term earnings. Philosophically, economists of the Chicago School became increasingly influential in establishing that the exclusive role of the corporation was to generate profits for the benefit of shareholders. In 1970, Milton Friedman asserted in a widely read essay that "there is one and only one social responsibility of business – to use its resources and engage in activities designed to increase its profits, so long as it … engages in free competition without deception or fraud" (Friedman 1970). This assertion was buttressed by Richard Meckling and Michael Jensen's much-cited paper on agency costs, which focused on the risks to shareholders of managers putting their own interests ahead of theirs (Meckling and Jensen 1976). This contributed to a dramatic change in executive compensation, with a far heavier weighting toward stock than cash. This seeming alignment of management and shareholder interests – in practice, an imperfect alignment – established shareholder primacy as a practical fact, if not a legal requirement. The greater complexity of multinational firms both in corporate structure and business diversity has created regulatory and market pressure for companies to provide more disaggregated information – especially at the business unit and country level.

1980s–current: Private equity and investor control: During the 1980s, large corporations with traditional franchises were put at risk by the weak performance of their own management, sharper foreign competition, the emergence of disruptive new technologies and the aggressive practices of financiers. The financial sector grew in prominence throughout the latter quarter of the twentieth century and into the early 2000s. MIT economist Simon Johnson estimated that financial sector profitability accounted for approximately 15% of total business profitability from 1973 to 1985, fluctuated between 21% and 30% during the 1990s and topped 40% before the crash in 2007 (Johnson 2009). The market for corporate control that began in earnest in the 1980s evolved from relatively straightforward merger battles between corporations to even more fractious contests between corporations and activist investors with access to large pools of capital. The leveraged buyout business grew from a small base in the early 1980s to become a pre-eminently important influence on corporate behavior. Large companies, even iconic ones such as Sears and Chrysler, were purchased by private equity funds. Shareholder primacy effectively became "controlling shareholder" primacy. Though private equity firms have very limited external reporting requirements, they must report portfolio performance to their limited partners. At the same time, the private equity firm can demand whatever information it wants from its portfolio companies.

2010–current: Sustainable corporations and stakeholder primacy: As noted above, the widely held view that the sole mission of the corporation is to maximize profitability in the interest of shareholders is an ideological view (e.g., Friedman 1970) – not a legal mandate. Discussed further in the section below, a debate with long historical roots has been resurrected as the role of the corporation is being re-examined anew from a legal perspective (Stout 2007). An emerging literature is developing that promotes the view that corporations have a central role to play in sustainability initiatives throughout the world.[2] Regulatory control over toxic emissions and other corporate externalities has been generally effective, but the case for embedding sustainability practices more deeply into corporate practice rests on three arguments. The first is self-interest: the premise that corporate sustainability leadership correlates well with better operating performance – an argument for which there is empirical support (Barnett and Salomon 2006). The second is the presence of "universal owners": the natural alignment corporate sustainability practice has with certain investors with long horizons due to their long-tailed liabilities (Hawley and Williams 2007). The third is predicated on social responsibility: the philosophical premise that a corporation needs to serve all of its stakeholders – shareholders, customers, suppliers and the public – equitably (Freeman 2010). The philosophical foundations of the sustainable corporation directly challenge the narrow view that the role of the corporation is strictly limited to maximizing profitability – a stark view now even rejected by Jack Welch (Financial Times 2009). Stakeholder, rather than shareholder primacy is now receiving the greater attention it deserves as a compelling corporate mandate – attention that first led to sustainability or corporate social responsibility reporting and, more recently, to integrated reporting.

The corporation today and the shareholder/stakeholder dilemma

Although much attention over the past decade has been devoted to new ventures and smaller companies, the fact remains that large corporations dominate the economic landscape. Enormous concentrations of economic activity are embedded in the largest Global 1000 companies and their

---

[2] Recent examples include Doppelt (2003); Eccles and Krzus (2010); Epstein et al. (2008); Savits with Weber (2006).

extensive supply chains. One measure of the scope of large corporations is that in 2009 a ranking of the top 100 economic entities in the world by revenue or GDP, as appropriate, included 44 companies. There were 59 corporations in the top 150 (Keys and Mainight 2010).

That said, the past decade has been rough on public corporations. A combination of corporate scandals, expensive regulations, investor-driven short-termism, the scaling-up of private equity, the growing influence of hedge funds, the emergence of state-owned enterprises in the developing world and the relative success of family-controlled companies has jarred the prestige of the public company and its broadly diversified investor base (Anderson and Reeb 2003; Sraer and Thesmar 2007). In the United States, the number of publicly listed firms has dropped 39 percent since 1997 and 48 percent in Great Britain (The Economist 2012).

While the number of public companies has declined, much activity has been devoted to crafting new legal entities to accommodate broader corporate missions.[3] These entities are designed explicitly to encourage broader social missions. They are likely a response to the prevailing and narrowly drawn ideological view that the sole purpose of a corporation is to maximize profitability, and the re-emerging appreciation that the corporation could be a very effective institutional tool for achieving broader social goals. Given our belief that the corporation as we know it today is well positioned to advance the interests of sustainability shared by a wider range of stakeholders – employees, customers, suppliers, the "community," as well as investors – rather than shareholders alone, our focus lies between these two extremes.

An elaborate analysis of the benefits of a stakeholder, rather than a purely shareholder-based perspective, is beyond our scope. However, there is a pragmatic way to look at the relationship between shareholders, other stakeholders and sustainability that may help sharpen and, in some cases, even resolve some of the issues involved. We begin with Milton Friedman's influential 1970 essay cited earlier on the role of the corporation that the *sole* mission of a company is to maximize profits while acting in full accordance with the law. In considering this assertion, two points should be kept in mind.

First, using as his example a "major employer in a small community," Friedman acknowledges that a company could subsidize local amenities if in doing so it made it easier to attract and retain employees. In other words, if a case can be made that a social contribution will eventually translate into increased corporate profitability, then Friedman was in favor of it. Second, while Friedman's view was that a company's purpose is limited to legitimately maximizing profitability, it is important to remember that his is a theoretical argument – a very influential argument that has shaped the debate about the role of the corporation – but in addition to being hard-to-define operationally, it is not an argument based on prevailing law in the United States.

The details vary somewhat across states, but as a strictly legal matter, directors have both the right and, in some cases, the obligation to take a broader view than immediate shareholder interest (Blair and Stout 1999; Stout 2003a). As discussed further below, directors must act with "loyalty" to the firm (i.e., not in a self-serving way) and exercise "duty of care" by using good business judgment in their deliberations. In most instances, this means that boards of directors are best understood as the group charged with mediating between various stakeholder interests for the long-term benefit of the firm – as opposed to narrow promoters of short-term shareholder interest.

These two points help frame an approach to determine whether and to what extent shareholders of publicly traded firms would benefit if those firms committed to their own sustainability pursued

[3] Examples include: "Maryland First State in Union to Pass Benefit Corporation Legislation." April 14, 2010. *CSR Wire.* Available online at www.csrwire.com/press_releases/29332-Maryland-First-State-in-Union-to-Pass-Benefit-Corporation-Legislation. Last accessed August 29, 2012; SB-201 "Flexible purpose corporations." (2011–2012) Senate Bill No. 201, Chapter 740. DeSaulnier. Approved by Governor October 9, 2011. *Legislative Counsel's Digest.* An act to amend Sections 102, 107, 158, 201, 1100, 1113, 1152, 1155, 1201, 5122, 7122, and 9122 of, to add Sections 171.08 and 1112.5 to, and to add Division 1.5 (commencing with Section 2500) to Title 1 of, the Corporations Code.

explicitly longer-term business strategies and provided richer sets of performance data of interest to a broad range of corporate stakeholders. There is a *strong* form, a *medium* form and a *weak* form of the argument.[4]

- The *strong* form establishes that shareholders are clear beneficiaries if corporate leadership in sustainability correlates with leadership in financial metrics, such as relative stock price performance and profitability.
- The *medium* form holds that shareholders are not discernibly worse off, while other stakeholders benefit from greater corporate commitment to sustainability practices and reporting.
- The *weak* form acknowledges that although shareholders may be worse off if a company commits itself to being more sustainable, other stakeholders are likely to benefit, including society at large. Profitability still matters in the *weak* form as a company cannot survive if it does not generate positive cash flows over time.

The *strong* form is a so-called "win-win" proposition in that it satisfies both Friedman's shareholder-centric view of corporate mission and a broader stakeholder perspective. It is not a fanciful proposition. A conceptual case can easily be made that the well-run firm effectively reconciles the interests of a broad range of stakeholders – employees, suppliers, customers and those affected by the firm's actions – and that this ultimately benefits shareholders. Better reporting makes for better informed stakeholders, including both investors and prospective investors. Sharpening up the research agenda to examine the evidence more deeply is essential: it would determine the type of data that is important to generate and indicate whether the *strong* form holds across industries or is more applicable in some cases than others.

The *weak* form presents highly contestable choices that raise hard-to-resolve questions

involving negative externalities, the social purpose of the firm, international trade competitiveness and trade-offs that must be made between the interests of various stakeholders. While not as conclusively compelling as the *strong* form, the *weak* form resurrects the discussion over Corporate Social Responsibility (CSR). While the *weak* form does not satisfy – it effectively violates – Friedman's narrowly drawn, if persuasively articulated imperative concerning the mission of the corporation, it is not inconsistent with state laws concerning the latitude directors have in shaping corporate strategy. Although the *weak* form would tend to allow various non-investor stakeholders to garner preferential gains over investors, in practice, shareholders would likely be protected by the unforgiving constraints on valuation and liquidity imposed by the market on all firms that depend on external financing.

Empirical evidence may ultimately tend to support the *medium* form, the middling version between the two extremes. In any event, framing the question in an empirically testable way will help shape the nature, quality and availability of information produced by intermediaries for various stakeholders. If evidence supports the *strong* form and there proves to be a high correlation between investment results and a firm's sustainability performance, then progress on integrated reporting, the best way to supply the information needed to test this hypothesis, should be less contentious and relatively quick. If evidence supports the *weak* form and investors must subsidize positive corporate contributions to sustainability and make various stakeholder accommodations, then the nature of the argument shifts and the path forward becomes more contentious. We cannot prejudge outcomes, but growing evidence favors the *strong* form or some version of the *medium* form (Cheng et al. 2011; Eccles et al. 2011; Ioannou and Serafeim 2010). As we will discuss in the conclusion, resolution of this issue will be of interest to investment fiduciaries.

Fortunately, this analysis will not be performed in a vacuum. A number of public firms already publish sustainability metrics that provide both anecdotal and, increasingly, statistical support

---

[4] This framing borrows from Fama (1970). Considerable work is needed to develop similarly robust hypotheses relating to corporate sustainability and share performance, taking into particular account uncertainty and time horizon.

for the relevance of the firm's performance on ESG (environmental, social and governance) issues and to stakeholders as well as investors. There are also efforts afoot to aggregate this data on a more consistent basis to facilitate more direct comparisons across companies and within industries.[5] While the formats and details of sustainability reporting are not standardized across firms or even consistent for a particular firm over time, the trend line is clear: more companies are providing ESG, often called nonfinancial information, to complement their accounting disclosures.

We believe that strong sustainability metrics for a company are apt to be a compelling proxy for the overall quality of management throughout a firm. Sustainability-oriented firms tend to have longer investment horizons and a more granular and comprehensive understanding of the operational workings of their businesses. For this information to be relevant, both companies and the information intermediaries who help them generate and disseminate high quality integrated reporting need to understand what customers, employees, NGOs representing various stakeholder groups, investors and regulators care about most. They need to understand the business models of different industries well enough to recognize which sustainability factors are material and which are not.

Stakeholder engagement is essential. The deeper that engagement is, the more likely it is that companies will quickly internalize externalities in the stock market. This will happen if information is both relevant and reliable. Credibility for company disclosures will be enhanced by robust auditing systems that more fully reflect the inputs, processes, outputs and overall sustainability performance of different firms.

[5] For example, a small consortium put together by the Canadian media company, Corporate Knights, has developed a list of the "Global 100" of so-called "World Leaders in Global Capitalism." Companies are ranked on a range of metrics including carbon productivity, percentage of tax paid, leadership diversity, employee turnover and safety. In 2010, over five thousand public companies reported some form of sustainability metrics for the year.

The role and importance of integrated reporting

History amply shows that the nature of corporate reporting for both external and internal purposes is dynamic rather than static. We are on the cusp of a new generation of corporate reporting that could enrich our collective understanding of how corporations perform along a range of dimensions relevant to an increasing number of stakeholders, including investors. Reporting standards, the type of information generated, the audiences for the information itself and the manner in which information is disseminated have evolved steadily over the past two centuries – a progression consisting of modest refinements punctuated by occasional spikes, like the Great Depression of the 1930s and the consequent creation of the Securities and Exchange Commission (SEC), which dramatically changed reporting standards. Similarly, the more recent financial deceptions of Enron, WorldCom and Tyco led to the passage of the Sarbanes-Oxley Act 2002.

Currently, corporate sustainability information is provided on a voluntary basis by an increasing number of firms who generate unaudited, or lightly audited, data for various constituencies. There appears to be some correlation between this type of performance information and overall corporate performance, so the information appears to be valuable. The questions become: a) How do we get from "here to there," from uneven and not necessarily reliable sustainability reporting to a more robust system, to the related question of b) What role will the corporate board have in guiding that transition? The evolution of public financial reporting and the development of managerial accounting offer some clues – promising ones if we can accelerate the process – for developing reliable integrated reporting that is meaningful to a broad range of corporate stakeholders and not just company managers and investors.

Historically, corporate reporting has focused on producing information for two related, but in practice quite different, purposes: internal managerial accounting data was aimed at improving operating performance, and external financial accounting data intended to protect the interests of those with external claims and obligations related to corporate performance – in particular, shareholders and lenders to the company. Integrated reporting represents a new generation of public corporate reporting because it includes aspects of both financial and managerial accounting. Similar to financial accounting, integrated reporting is public information developed on a basis consistent enough to facilitate cross-firm comparisons. Similar to managerial accounting, integrated reporting includes nonfinancial information that gives all stakeholders deeper insights into the operating characteristics of the company. Regulations need to be set to protect genuinely proprietary operating performance information. However, the fact that the market has succeeded in doing that with financial accounting leads one to believe that the issue would be easily addressed.

A blend of financial and sustainability information, integrated reporting has followed and likely will continue to follow a similar developmental path – spurred along by a mix of some enlightened managerial push (e.g., Dow Chemical, Philips and Novo Nordisk), greater stakeholder pull (e.g., Good Guide[6]), and, prospectively, greater support for mandatory reporting (Ioannou and Serafeim 2011). As discussed below, the path will be more or less passable depending on whether the evidence relating sustainability performance revealed in integrated reporting to investment performance supports a *strong* form, a *medium* form or a *weak* form of the argument as outlined above. Integrated reporting creates the opportunity for a substantial, cross-disciplinary research agenda that engages a wide range of assessment skills that complement, but are quite distinct from, financial expertise.

Integrated reporting presents several challenges. First, the company itself is uniquely positioned to create the primary data, some of which may be confidential. As the original and often sole source of information, the company may not be trusted if the information is not vetted by a disinterested third party. Second, the type of information

generated may differ materially across industries and even within an industry if geography (for example) plays a meaningful role in operations. Reporting standards, auditing procedures and disclosure protocols need to be set. Third, the question of who benefits from the information will continue to shape its scope, depth, frequency and quality. The quality of the information produced will be better if it has clear operational value for the company – a point important from a costing standpoint. If the information has real value to the company from the perspective of managerial accounting, then the information, filtered judiciously to protect what is legitimately confidential, will likely be of good quality and of interest to particular stakeholders.

Integrated reporting extends financial accounting and reporting practices, which were originally developed to meet the needs of investors. Led initially by the accounting profession, a robust social infrastructure has developed over the years to establish accounting standards, refine reporting requirements and update enforcement mechanisms on companies and auditing firms to promote improved financial measurement and reporting. The focus on financial accounting has tended to reinforce (and be reinforced by) ideological support for the preferences of shareholders over all other stakeholders. But, as outlined above, a shift is taking place that has been driven largely by public interest in sustainability.

Investors, as well as customers, suppliers and the public have shown greater interest in developing a better understanding of a company's environmental, social and governance performance. Though progress has been made in setting reporting standards for nonfinancial performance, the contributions of groups such as the Global Reporting Initiative and the Sustainability Accounting Standards Board have depended largely on voluntary participation. They have not yet had the support of government funding and mandate. As discussed in the next section, broadening perspectives on the role of the corporation and the consequent expectation that boards play a more active role in managing stakeholder interests is generating the need for improved nonfinancial reporting to complement the ongoing need for better financial information.

---

[6] GoodGuide is a venture-funded business that describes itself as "the world's largest and most reliable source of information on health, environmental, and social impacts of consumer products." www.goodguide.com.

Integrated reporting is the mechanism designed to do exactly that.

Changing social expectations and the role of the board

As noted above, history has shown corporations to be highly adaptive institutions that have co-evolved over the past several centuries with other forces ranging from technology to social philosophy. A natural consequence of this potency is the public expectation that the corporation has a broader contribution to make than maximizing short-term profitability for the exclusive benefit of shareholders, some of whom may prefer a longer-horizon commitment to sustainability. None of this, of course, diminishes the fundamental fact that corporations must be profitable in the long run if they are, themselves, going to be sustainable entities. Reconciling interests between different stakeholders for the long-run benefit of the corporation as a whole becomes the responsibility of the board of directors.

While substantial empirical work using further refined and more comprehensive integrated reporting data is needed to track the relationship between profitability performance and sustainability practices, much of the argument favoring stakeholder primacy is rooted in an understanding of how corporations work in practice. Lynn Stout frames the conundrum of why shareholders cede control of the public corporation to self-interested managers overseen by a corporate board with two very different hypotheses about the board's role (Stout 2003b). Predicated on concerns about agency costs raised most effectively by Meckling and Jensen, the first hypothesis holds that the board's primary role is to *monitor* executive performance to make sure that investors' interests are protected. The second hypothesis, and one that squares well with the view that corporate success depends fundamentally on stakeholder collaboration, holds that the role of the board is to *mediate* between various interested parties "as a means of attracting the extracontractual, firm-specific investments of such stakeholder groups as executives, creditors and rank-and-file employees" (Stout 2003b). While monitoring and

mediating are not necessarily mutually exclusive, an emphasis on the mediating hypothesis strikes us as being conceptually consistent with the type of stakeholder collaboration required to operate in a more genuinely sustainable manner.

In the case of public companies, the board of directors plays the central role in reconciling the sometimes-competing, sometimes-complementary interests of various corporate stakeholders. Specific rules and case law vary from state to state in the United States, but two overarching principles, shared to varying degrees by all fiduciaries, govern director responsibility: "duty of care" and "duty of loyalty" to the corporation. The former asserts that directors must be duly diligent in their deliberations, meaning that they must do their best to be well informed when making decisions. The latter asserts that each director must act in the best interests of the corporation, independent of the director's own personal interest. As long as there is no conflict of interest, directors are given wide latitude by the business judgment doctrine, which holds that directors will not be liable for bad outcomes from their decisions if they have been both dutiful and loyal in their decision-making (Lorsch 1989).

As the role of the corporation broadens to more explicitly incorporate the interests of all stakeholders, directors play the central role in managing an equitable reconciliation of those interests for the benefit of the corporation as an overall entity. Implicit in that reconciliation is the recognition that not all shareholders have identical interests or expectations of corporate performance. Some may well prefer investing in companies with long-term investment horizons and a commitment to broader support for all corporate stakeholders – including employees, customers, suppliers and the larger public. In any event, the board's effectiveness will turn in no small part on whether it has full access to the depth and rich variety of information generated through integrated reporting in order to help it set priorities and allocate resources across stakeholders over time.

Support for greater stakeholder primacy, as opposed to narrow shareholder primacy, is not based on a philanthropic view of the corporation. The sustainable corporation needs to generate long-term profits to attract and build capital – human, financial, intellectual and social. Long-term sustainability can only be achieved through sustained and self-interested coordination across the firm. The historian Dow Votaw observed that "the modern corporation has been aptly described as a 'constellation of interests'" (Blair 1995: 211). Financial expertise is part of that constellation, but so is a wide range of other skills that must be successfully melded together by management. As Frank Abrams, Chairman of Standard Oil of New Jersey, said half a century ago, managers must establish "an equitable and working balance among the claims of the various directly interested groups – stockholders, employees, customers and the public at large" (Blair 1995: 212).

The sustainable corporation is an entity that manages the full range of its resources in a highly coordinated way with a long eye to the future. It will most likely have a collaborative culture capable of making smart capital allocation decisions without relying exclusively on reductive financial techniques. Instead, the sustainable corporation will conform to what has come to be known as the "team production" theory of the corporation (Blair and Stout 1999: 247ff). Team production theory is compatible with both Robert Putnam's notion of "social capital" and Gary Becker's "human capital," as it recognizes the implicit equity contributions made by non-investor stakeholders in the firm. Imprecisely measured and present in varying degrees, stakeholder capital is an essential contributor to corporate performance. An employee with considerable experience who knows the corporate terrain well has accumulated "human capital," much of it firm-specific (e.g., uniquely related to the firm itself), that becomes more valuable when understood as an essential ingredient to effective team production across the firm.

In this more collaborative understanding of how firms operate – a view essential to achieving sustainable practices across the firm – the board of directors must mediate between the often poorly aligned interests of diverse stakeholders. As discussed earlier, integrated reporting that incorporates different and occasionally incompatible metrics that reflect the complex operating activities of a company, is an essential tool for directors, managers, shareholders and other stakeholders as they assess the performance, prospects and operating practices of the firm. Directors and senior managers charged with promoting collaborative behavior across the firm will be particularly dependent on integrated reporting to make difficult decisions that are hard to reduce to simple financial calculations.

While one should always be wary of facile analogies from the biological sciences, in studying the success of groups there is a steadily increasing appreciation of the evolutionary importance of "cooperation" as an alternative to zero-sum competition (Nowak and Highfield 2012). Commitment by the board of directors to effectively mediated stakeholder primacy is likely to create the type of well-informed, longer-term horizon, collaborative behavior within the competitive firm that ultimately leads to durable corporate sustainability – a goal that rewards investors as well.

Relevance to investment fiduciaries

After considering the evolving mission of the corporation, the role of the corporate board and the potential of integrated reporting, we return to the question of fiduciary investment responsibility. How many degrees of freedom do trustees and other managers of large pools of funds with diverse beneficiaries have when it comes to promoting a corporate commitment to sustainable business practices if it might come at the expense of short-term investor gain? As discussed earlier, all fiduciaries, and most especially investment fiduciaries, have to act with a duty of care, in addition to being loyal. When their beneficiaries are many and diverse, investment fiduciaries that would like to invest with a broadly defined sustainability theme may plausibly argue that that they are making decisions honoring the long-term horizons of some of their investors. They can also argue that they are on solid ground as long as they are making decisions that are free of any personal conflict of interest and a case can be made that their beneficiaries are better off through some combination of greater return or reduced risk.

These are credible arguments, but they are hard to make definitively. We believe that investment fiduciaries have an additional evidentiary source to consider: an informed assessment of the due diligence of the corporate board of the company in question. Investment fiduciaries would do well to focus on whether the corporate board of directors exercised the proper level of scrutiny and, ultimately, good judgment in reconciling the complex set of interests endemic to any corporate entity with an explicit commitment to sustainability. Of course, the decision is relatively straightforward if an empirical case can be established that investor returns are reliably correlated with sustainability leadership. That is the so-called *strong* form of the argument, but more work needs to done to convincingly make the claim. So investment fiduciaries with an interest in corporate sustainability are left in a gray zone and would benefit from complementary support.

We believe, and the body of this chapter argues, that properly informed corporate directors have the latitude to make long-term decisions that balance multiple stakeholder interests, sometimes at the immediate expense of shareholders. Investment fiduciaries would bolster their due diligence by spending time carefully examining how decisions are made in companies in which they might invest. A simple question to ask would be whether or not directors had access to high quality integrated reporting that would give them, and the public, multi-dimensional insights into corporate performance using a diverse range of firm-wide metrics. Were the right questions asked? Can directors and senior management make a convincing public case when they discuss stakeholder benefits accruing to sustainability practices?

Recalling how corporations have evolved over time, it is reasonable to expect that the mission and social expectations of corporations will continue to change. Co-evolving with those shifts, the quality, focus and extent of corporate reporting will change as well. We believe, for example, that integrated reporting will become a norm. Directors will also have to broaden their understanding of corporate performance. One thing that surely will not change – and should not change – is the duty of care and loyalty required of all fiduciaries, especially those with investment responsibilities. As we have argued, investment fiduciaries with an interest in sustainability have an opportunity to enrich their due diligence and re-enforce their loyalty in a steadily evolving world by closely examining the extent to which corporate boards make well-informed decisions. The availability and smart use of integrated reporting is the essential bridge between the duly diligent investment fiduciary and her closer to the front-line fiduciary cousin on the corporate board.

References

Anderson, R. C. and Reeb, D. M. 2003. "Founding-Family Ownership and Firm: Evidence from the S&P500," *Journal of Finance* 58: 1301–1328.

Barnett, M. and Salomon, R. 2006. "Beyond Dichotomy: The Curvilinear Relationship between Social Responsibility and Financial Performance," *Strategic Management Journal* 27.

Berle, A. and Means, G. 1991. *The Modern Corporation and Private Property*. New Brunswick, NJ: Transaction.

Blair, M. 1995. *Ownership and Control: Rethinking Corporate Governance for the Twenty-First Century*. Washington, DC: Brookings.

Blair, M. and Stout, L. 1999. "A Team Production Theory of Corporate Law," *Virginia Law Review* 85(2).

Cheng, B., Ioannou, I. and Serafeim, G. 2011. "Corporate Social Responsibility and Access to Finance," HBS Working Paper No. 11–130.

Dodd, E. M., Jr. 1932. "For Whom Are Corporate managers Trustees," *Harvard Law Review* 45(7): 1157.

Doppelt, B. 2003. *Leading Change Toward Sustainability: A Change-Management Guide for Business Government and Civil Society*. Sheffield, UK: Greenleaf.

Eccles, R. and Krzus, M. 2010. *Integrated Reporting for a Sustainable Strategy*. Hoboken, NJ: Wiley.

Eccles, R. and Serafeim, G. 2011. "The Role of the Board in Accelerating the Adoption of Integrated Reporting" *Director Notes*. The Conference Board.

Eccles, R. G., Ioannou, I. and Serafeim, G. 2011. "Culture of Sustainability on Corporate Behavior and Performance," HBS Working Paper No. 12–035.

Epstein, M., Elkington, J. and Leonard, H. 2008. *Making Sustainability Work: Best Practices in Managing and Measuring Social, Environmental and Economic Impacts*. San Francisco: Berrett-Koehler.

Fama, E. 1970. "Efficient Capital Markets: A Review of Theory and Empirical Work," *Journal of Finance* 25.

Financial Times. 2009. "Welch Denounces Corporate Obsessions," *Financial Times*, March 12, 2009.

Freeman, E. 2010. *Stakeholder Theory: The State of the Art*. Cambridge University Press.

Friedman, M. 1970. "The Social Responsibility of Business is to Increase its Profits," *The New York Times,* September 13, 1970.

Hawley, J. P. and Williams, A. T. 2007. "Universal Owners: Challenges and Opportunities," *Corporate Governance: An International Review* 15(3): 415–420.

Ioannou, Ioannis, and Serafeim, George 2010. "The Impact of Corporate Social Responsibility on Investment Recommendations," HBS Working Paper No. 11–017.

2011. "The Consequences of Mandatory Corporate Sustainability Reporting," HBS Working Paper No. 11–100.

Johnson, S. 2009. "The Quiet Coup," *The Atlantic Monthly*.

Keys, T. and Malnight, T. 2010. *Corporate Clout: The Influence of the World's Largest 100 Economic Entities*. Geneva: Strategy Dynamics Global Ltd.

Lorsch, J. 1989. *Pawns or Potentates: The Reality of America's Corporate Boards*. Boston, MA: HBS Press.

Meckling, R. and Jensen, M. 1976. "Theory of the Firm: Management Behavior, Agency Costs

and Ownership Structure," *Journal of Financial Economics* 3.

Miranti, P. 1999. *A History of Corporate Finance*. Cambridge University Press.

Nowak, M. and Highfield, R. 2012. *Super Cooperators: Altruism, Evolution and Why We Need Each Other to Succeed*. New York: Free Press.

Roy, W. G. 1997. *Socializing Capital: The Rise of the Large Industrial Corporation in America*. Princeton University Press.

Savits, A. with Weber, K. 2006. *The Triple Bottom Line: How Today's Best-Run Companies Are Achieving Economic, Social and Environmental Success – and How You Can Too*. San Francisco: Jossey-Bass.

Smith, G. D. and Dyer, D. 1996. "The Rise and Transformation of the American Corporation," in C. Kaysen (ed.), *The American Corporation Today: Examining the Questions of Power and Efficiency at Century's End*. Oxford University Press.

Sraer, D. and Thesmar, D. 2007. "The Performance and Behavior of Family Firms: Evidence from the French Stock Market," *Journal of the European Economic Association* 5(4).

Stout, L. 2003a. "On the Proper Motives of Corporate Directors (Or, Why You Don't Want to Invite *Homo Economicus* to Join Your Board)," *Delaware Journal of Corporate Law* 28.

2003b. "The Shareholder as Ulysses: Some Empirical Evidence on Why Investors in Public Corporations Tolerate Board Governance," *University of Pennsylvania Law Review* 152(2): 667.

2007. "The Mythical Benefit of Shareholder Control," *Virginia Law Review* 93(3): 789–809.

2012. *The Shareholder Value Myth: How Putting Shareholders First Harms Investors, Corporations and the Public*. San Francisco: Berrett-Koehler.

The Economist. 2012. "Briefing: The Endangered Public Company," *The Economist*, May 19, 2012.

Reporting and standards: tools for stewardship

MICHAEL P. KRZUS

Introduction

"Our Common Future," the 1987 report of the World Commission on Environment and Development and generally referred to as the Brundtland Report, implored each generation "to meet the needs of the present without compromising the ability of future generations to meet their own needs" (United Nations 1987: Chapter 2, para. 1). A critical question raised by the Brundtland Report definition of "sustainable development" is whether each generation and institutions established by society have an obligation, legal or moral, to address intergenerational responsibility.

The concept of intergenerational responsibility – like so many issues and problems that confront society today – is a classic collective action problem and no single group or person can solve the problem without help. Who will lead and what can an individual or group do?

The fiduciary duties of intergenerational impartiality and loyalty, i.e., duties that preclude fiduciary investors from using strategies that unreasonably transfer risk and returns between different groups of beneficiaries are found in law[1] and pension fund bylaws (CalPERS 2009). Under the universal owner concept, a fundamental characteristic is to care about economy-wide performance in addition to the performance of companies in a portfolio (Hawley and Williams 2000). Finally, the concept steward-ship, which dates back to the medieval era, refers to a duty to look after someone else's assets.[2]

Even though it may be possible to assert that every generation has a responsibility to each

succeeding generation, financial services and banks – organizations well-positioned to drive the concept of intergenerational responsibility though their investment policies – continue to be the least trusted sectors in the US and globally according to the 2012 Edelman Trust Barometer.[3]

This chapter discusses how private sector initiatives focused on integrated reporting and the development of sustainability accounting standards are relevant to the fiduciary duties of intergenerational impartiality and loyalty.

Integrated reporting

Integrated reporting is rooted in a view that a corporation's role in society is something more than generating short-term profits for shareholders.

> Integrated Reporting brings together the material information about an organization's strategy, governance, performance and prospects in a way that reflects the commercial, social and environmental context within which it operates. It provides a clear and concise representation of how an organization demonstrates stewardship and how it creates value, now and in the future (International Integrated Reporting Council 2011).

There is a profound difference between an "integrated report" and "integrated reporting." In simplest terms, an integrated report is a business communication; one report that presents a company's financial and nonfinancial (including environmental, social, governance, intangibles, and risks and opportunities) information. An integrated report enables the reader to better understand the cause-and-effect relationships between financial and sustainability

[1] Uniform Management of Public Employee Retirement Systems Act. www.nasra.org/resources/umpersa.pdf, accessed July 2012.
[2] www.forceforgood.com/userfiles/Why%20steward-ship%20matters%20L_FINAL.pdf.
[3] http://trust.edelman.com/trust-download/executive-summary.

performance. Put another way, an integrated report makes it possible for a reader to understand both the economic and societal benefits of sustainability initiatives.

Integrated reporting is the business process that makes publishing a truly integrated report possible. This process is the foundation for management's understanding that business models and corporate decision-making should reflect the complex and inextricably linked relationships between the economic, governance, environmental and social issues. The integrated reporting process also helps companies learn to balance the imperative for long-term viability – of the company and the world it relies on to create economic value – with the demands for short-term competitiveness and profitability. In this context, integrated reporting has the potential to drive a sense of responsibility not only for today, but also for the future.

"Sustainable Capitalism" a February 2012 paper by Generation Investment Management (2012) advocated for a shift to a more long-term focused form of capitalism. Sustainable capitalism, the paper argued, "seeks to maximize long-term economic value creation. It explicitly integrates environmental, social, and governance (ESG) factors into strategy, the measurement of outputs and the assessment of both risks and opportunities." Integrated reporting was identified as one of five ideas with the potential to accelerate a transition to sustainable capitalism.

Content of an integrated report

The building blocks of an integrated report are the guiding principles and content elements (International Integrated Reporting Council 2011). These items are directly related to transparency, which has been defined as "accessibility of information to stakeholders of institutions regarding matters that might affect their interests" (Tapscott and Ticoll 2003: 22).

Guiding principles

The guiding principles – strategic focus, connectivity of information, future orientation,

responsiveness and stakeholder inclusiveness, and conciseness, reliability and materiality – are the foundation of an integrated reporting. The complete definition of each of the guiding principles is in the IIRC Discussion Paper, which is part of an ongoing public consultation aimed at continuing improvement of the guiding principles to incorporate experience with using them.[4]

- **Strategic focus** is an explanation of how strategic goals and the business model link economic, governance, environmental and social considerations to enable long-term value creation.
- **Connectivity of information** demonstrates the relationships or connections between financial and nonfinancial performance as well as how the business model or external factors may force trade-offs that affect the organization's resources and relationships.
- **Future orientation** does not mean a forecast or projection.[5] Instead, the term refers to information that helps the reader understand management's expectations for short- and medium-term performance and the risks and opportunities facing the business.
- **Responsiveness and stakeholder inclusiveness** refers to discussion about how an organization manages its relationships with shareholders and other stakeholders. The discussion should also provide an understanding about how the business considers and responds to stakeholder needs and expectations.
- **Conciseness, reliability and materiality.** An integrated report is not intended to provide a discussion about thirty or forty "material" issues. A high-quality integrated report should focus on the issues that directly affect a company's ability to create and sustain value for shareholders and society over the long term. Because integrated reporting leverages the internet and Web 2.0 tools and technologies, such as wikis, blogs, podcasts and forums, it also serves as a platform to furnish

[4] International Integrated Reporting Council (2011); responses to the 2011 discussion paper were incorporated into International Integrated Reporting Council (2013).
[5] See Public Company Accounting Oversight Board (2008); www.ifac.org/sites/default/files/publications/files/B006%20 2012%20IAASB%20Handbook%20ISAE%203400.pdf.

more detailed data than what is available only in a paper or a downloadable PDF report.

Content elements

Content elements are linked to each other and, as a result, the IIRC envisions a robust and often overlapping narrative rather than presentation of six stand-alone sections. The following items were extracted verbatim from the IIRC Discussion Paper (International Integrated Reporting Council 2011).

Organizational overview and business model: The Integrated Report provides essential context by identifying the organization's mission, principal activities, markets, products and services; its business model, value drivers and critical stakeholder dependencies; and its attitude to risk.

Operating context, including risks and opportunities: To provide context, an integrated report identifies the commercial, social and environmental context within which the organization operates, including significant laws and regulations that affect the organization's ability to create and sustain value in the short, medium and long term; the resources and relationships that are key to the organization's success, including key stakeholders, their legitimate needs, interests and expectations, and their importance to the organization; and the organization's key risks and opportunities, including those that relate to its relationships and to its impact on, and the continued availability, quality and affordability of, relevant resources.

Strategic objectives and strategies to achieve those objectives: An integrated report describes the organization's strategic objectives and its strategies to achieve those objectives. It sets out how the organization will measure achievement and target outcomes for the short, medium and long term.

Governance and remuneration: An integrated report provides insight about the organization's oversight and tone at the top. It includes organization, including its culture, ethical values and relationships with key stakeholders; and how the remuneration of executives and those charged with governance is linked to performance in the short, medium and long term, including how it is linked to the organization's use of and impact on the resources and relationships on which it depends.

Performance: An integrated report includes qualitative and quantitative information, including key performance indicators (KPIs) and key risk indicators (KRIs) regarding the organization's performance against its strategic objectives and related strategies; the organization's impacts (both positive and negative) on the resources and relationships on which it depends; the significant external factors impacting performance; and how the organization fared against its targets.

Future outlook: Future outlook builds on other Content Elements to highlight anticipated changes over time. It provides information, built on sound and transparent analysis, about how the organization is currently equipped to respond to the operating context that it is likely to face in the future; how the organization balances short- and long-term interests; potential repercussions of where the organization expects it will go in the short, medium and long term; the actions needed to get there; and the associated uncertainties.

The capitals

The IIRC Discussion Paper introduces a concept called "the capitals." The capitals are the relationships and resources used by the business to create and sustain value for shareholders and all other stakeholders. The complete definition of each of the capitals is in the IIRC Discussion Paper (International Integrated Reporting Council 2011).

Financial capital is not only funds currently available for operations, but also is the ability of a company to continue to finance its operations and investments such as borrowing capacity/access to capital, quality of earnings, the character and reputation of the company's major debt and equity investors and the stability of the shareholder base.

Manufactured capital is comprised of physical objects such as buildings, equipment and infrastructure available to the entity and intangible aspects, such as a plant location, plant adaptability, raw material accessibility and reliance on strategic resources.

Human capital reflects the attributes of the workforce, both employees and contractors, and can be tangible, for example, employment contracts, and intangible, for example, education, skills and abilities, experiences, ability to lead and to collaborate, attitudes and accomplishments.

Intellectual capital provides competitive advantage and includes patents, trademarks, copyrights, formulas, databases, and methodologies and processes, all of which combine to enhance the brand and reputation of an organization.

Natural capital may be an input to the production of goods or services or an organization's impact on the air, water, land, minerals and forests, and biodiversity and eco-system health.

Social capital includes relationships with other organizations and third parties that it regards as important, such as contracts, license agreements, joint venture agreements, alliances, relationships with no contractual basis and personal relationships.

Describing and measuring how an entity's business model interacts with the capitals may lead to a thought process focused on enhancing, not simply protecting value. In other words, material risks and opportunities under each of the capitals could be the basis for thinking about how business creates value for shareholders and other stakeholders at the same time and over the long term.

The benefits of integrated reporting

It is important to reiterate the difference between an integrated report and the integrated reporting process when discussing the benefits of integrated reporting. An integrated report is a business communication. The integrated reporting process helps management understand the inextricable linkage between the economic, governance, environmental and social issues.

Companies don't benefit from combining an annual report to shareholders and a sustainability report into a single document. Companies benefit from learning to balance the imperative for long-term viability of the company and society with the demands for short-term competitiveness and profitability.

There is little, if any, research into the benefits of integrated reporting. This is not a surprise considering that the practice of integrated reporting

is little more than ten years old, with Novozymes publishing what is generally acknowledged to be the first integrated report in 2002 (Eccles and Krzus 2010a). In addition, even though the number of companies publishing integrated reports has grown significantly since 2002, the pool of such companies is relatively small; approximately 345 companies preparing GRI reports in 2012 declared that they were publishing an integrated report.[6]

Interviews with more than 200 people, including investors, standards-setters, companies, accounting firms and civil society identified four key benefits to a company when adopting integrated reporting (Eccles and Krzus 2010b). These benefits include: more clarity about relationships and trade-offs; improved decision-making; better stakeholder engagement; and enhanced risk management. These benefits are overlapping and mutually reinforcing.

More clarity about relationships and trade-offs

Implementing a strategy capable of creating value for shareholders and society over the long term is not easy. Management must understand the relationships between financial and nonfinancial information. It may be helpful to think about these relationships in terms of the financial statement line items. Will perceptions about "greener" or more energy efficient products create more customer demand and therefore increase revenues? Will taxes or other regulatory mechanisms to value carbon depress sales? What will be the effect of increasing scarcity of water and other finite resources on cost of goods sold? How much should research and development expenses increase to remain competitive in a given sector?

As a company achieves a better understanding of the relationships between financial and non-financial performance, its ability to re-evaluate categories of risks, opportunities and choices will

---

[6] Global Reporting Initiative, Sustainability Disclosure Database, www.globalreporting.org/reporting/report-services/sustainability-disclosure-database/Pages/Discover-the-Database.aspx. The most recent version of the comprehensive Global Reporting Initiative reporting guidelines was issued in May 2013: www.globalreporting.org/reporting/g4/Pages/default.aspx.

improve, which in turn supports development and implementation of sustainable strategies.

Improved decision-making

The body of work by Robert Kaplan and David Norton on the "balanced scorecard" provides much evidence supporting the assertion that better information and measurement leads to better decisions. Better-informed decisions about the relationships between financial and nonfinancial performance will improve the efficient and effective use of capital and other resources.

Management will find, however, that determining the relationship between financial and nonfinancial outcomes is easier said than done. Good metrics are very hard to develop. Christopher Ittner and David Larcker (2003) found that less than 25 percent of the companies they surveyed actually built and verified cause-and-effect diagrams necessary to identify relationships between for example, corporate governance, tolerance for risk and executive compensation. Difficulties such as this can serve as an excuse for not doing the hard analytical work necessary to specify and validate the relationships. A better response is to improve poor measurement methodologies and invent new ones for those useful metrics that do not yet exist.

Another obstacle to understanding relationships between financial and nonfinancial information and making more informed decisions possible is the need for collaboration between departments. Collaboration between accounting, finance, communications, investor relations, public policy, legal and regulatory affairs, sustainability, safety, marketing and line operations teams are critical to integrated reporting and will, in all likelihood, involve significant cultural change. However, one benefit of improved collaboration is a better appreciation by each function or unit of the consequences its decisions have on other parts of an organization.

Better stakeholder engagement

In leveraging the internet and Web 2.0 tools and technologies, integrated reporting drives a conversation about a company being able to furnish its stakeholders with more detailed data than what is currently available in a paper or a downloadable PDF report. Similarly, there is a need to think about meaningful engagement as much more than a focus group or a presentation to analysts.

The internet makes it possible to shift from a one-way push of information to an ongoing dialogue between a company and all of its stakeholders. This means a company's website should be simple and easy to navigate and permit visitors to perform their own analysis of information provided by the company. In addition, social media platforms, discussion forums, blogs and podcasts are likely to lead to richer stakeholder engagement, including user-generated content, comments and suggestions.

There are two tangible benefits of richer engagement with shareholders and other stakeholders. Shareholders will gain a more holistic perspective of a company; realizing that an organization's ability to earn profits over the long term will require short-term investments to not only mitigate environmental and social risks but also to drive the innovation necessary to take advantage of the opportunities presented by ever changing environmental issues and social trends. Conversely, NGOs and other stakeholders will learn that companies must make a profit in order to survive and grow, thereby making long-term value creating initiatives possible.

Enhanced risk management

Not only is integrated reporting the catalyst for incorporating economic, environmental, financial and social issues into business strategy, but integrated reporting can also push a company towards more integrated risk management processes. In driving better stakeholder engagement, integrated reporting can help companies more effectively focus on risk. Integrated reporting helps a company understand the effect of its strategic and tactical choices on society because internal and external dialogue ensures that a company's strategy is attuned to society's needs as a whole.

It is important to avoid overstating the case for integrated reporting as a risk management tool. For example, it would be absurd to claim that integrated reporting alone could have prevented the 2010 oil drilling rig explosion and fire in the Gulf of Mexico. That disaster was a reminder of the strong relationship between governance, appetite for risk and compensation, and the need to leverage those relationships to drive behavior. Integrated reporting has the potential to drive a chain of events that can help companies more effectively focus on risk. As discussed in the "Better stakeholder engagement" section above, the integrated reporting process helps a company understand the effect of its strategic and tactical choices on society because internal and external dialogue ensures that a company's strategy is better attuned to society's needs and expectations.

A fifth benefit of integrated reporting

Recent work identified more tangible considerations for companies thinking about adopting integrated reporting. Like the benefits described above, the argument is based on anecdotal information and on research into the benefits of sustainability reporting.

Eccles et al. (2011a) used a sample of 180 companies to study the effects of a commitment to sustainability and stock market performance. Companies that voluntarily adopted environmental and social policies many years ago were tagged as *High Sustainability* companies and those that adopted almost none of these policies were tagged as *Low Sustainability* companies. The authors identified several differences including evidence that *High Sustainability* companies significantly outperformed their counterparts over the long term.

In summary, the authors found:

The boards of directors of these companies are more likely to be responsible for sustainability and top executive incentives are more likely to be a function of sustainability metrics.

They are more likely to have organized procedures for stakeholder engagement, to be more long-term oriented, and to exhibit more measurement and disclosure of nonfinancial information.

… evidence that *High Sustainability* companies significantly outperform their counterparts over the long-term, both in terms of stock market and

accounting performance. The outperformance is stronger in sectors where the customers are individual consumers instead of companies, companies compete on the basis of brands and reputations, and products significantly depend upon extracting large amounts of natural resources (ibid.).

With respect to performance, the authors stated,

Investing $1 at the beginning of 1993 in a value-weighted (equal-weighted) portfolio of sustainable firms would have grown to $22.6 ($14.3) by the end of 2010, based on market prices. In contrast, investing $1 in the beginning of 1993 in a value-weighted (equal-weighted) portfolio of traditional firms would have only grown to $15.4 ($11.7) by the end of 2010 (ibid.).

A 2010 report by Accenture found that "companies that adopt sustainable business strategies and practices drive value by:

- Growing revenue through new products and services
- Reducing costs through efficiency gains
- Managing operational and regulatory risk more effectively
- Building intangible assets such as their brand, reputation and collaborative networks (Accenture 2010).

A research report published by Massachusetts Institute of Technology (2011) Sloan Management Review in collaboration with Boston Consulting Group found, among other things:

- Companies recognized the brand-building benefits of developing a reputation for being sustainability driven and respondents rated this benefit highest.
- Even the companies demonstrating the deepest commitment to sustainability struggled to develop financial measures for the more intangible business benefits of sustainability strategies (such as employee engagement, innovation and stakeholder appeal); those companies nevertheless assigned value to intangible factors when forming strategies and making decisions.

This demonstrates that a company can have a sustainable strategy without preparing an integrated report. However, if a company is committed a

Table 32.1 Obstacles to integrated reporting.

Entity-specific challenges	Collective-action problems
No clear understanding of what sustainability means	Materiality for nonfinancial information is not well-defined
Economics of sustainability initiatives not defined	Absence of generally accepted sustainability recognition, measurement, disclosure standards
Sustainability risks and opportunities not well-managed	Lack of robust assurance standards and methodologies
Weak controls over nonfinancial information	
Sustainability KPIs not in place or not monitored	

sustainable strategy and if a company is committed to transparent disclosure of its financial and nonfinancial performance, then there is a case to be made for integrating reporting. Reporting matters. When done right, reporting gives stakeholders a window to view the heart and soul of a company. Reporting provides insight into how a company views itself and its role in society. It communicates a company's performance, both good and bad. It creates commitments to improve in the future, both through specific targets and from the feedback a company gets from all of its stakeholders based on the information it is making available to them.

The nascent practice of integrated reporting will enable stakeholders to better evaluate the economic, environmental and social performance of a business, thereby facilitating a more effective assessment of a company's ability to create value over the long term. In this way, integrated reporting forms one of the cornerstones of corporate accountability and trustworthy markets.

Standards for nonfinancial information

High quality financial and sustainability reporting requires generally accepted standards for recognition, measurement and disclosure. Companies need standards to properly account for events and transactions and make appropriate disclosures to facilitate informed decision-making. Shareholders and other stakeholders rely on standards to drive consistency and comparability in reporting thereby enabling analysts to evaluate business performance within and across sectors. Standards for reporting

provide a benchmark that make it possible for auditors to give assurance that information "presents fairly" (Public Company Accounting Oversight Board 2008) or provides a "true and fair" (Financial Reporting Council 2008, 2011) view.

There are several obstacles to companies providing better information about how a company is mitigating risks or seizing opportunities related to economic, governance, environmental and social matters. See Table 32.1, which identifies several critical challenges to better reporting of nonfinancial information.

The foregoing issues plus other factors combine to prevent "the active and responsible management of entrusted resources now and in the longer term, so as to hand them on in better condition."[7] Some of these issues can be addressed on a company-by-company basis. However, the lack of generally accepted sustainability reporting standards and related assurance standards is critical to consistency and comparability in nonfinancial reporting.

A complicating factor is the sheer number of frameworks and guidelines. This creates complexity for companies trying to identify the framework best suited to communicating how a business model creates value for shareholders and society. National law and local stock exchange listing requirements mandate usage of some of these guidelines. Other guidance is widely used, often on a voluntary basis. However, neither country-specific requirements nor widespread voluntary adoption equates to being generally accepted on a global scale in the same sense that International Financial Reporting

[7] www.forceforgood.com/userfiles/Why%20stewardship%20matters%20L_FINAL.pdf.

Standards (IFRS) or US Generally Accepted Accounting Principles (US GAAP) are generally accepted for financial reporting. See Table 32.2, which identifies eighteen different reporting frameworks and guidance (Eccles et al. 2011b).[8]

Materiality

The importance of establishing globally accepted standards for nonfinancial information as a driver of consistency of approach and comparability across sectors can be illustrated by exploring the topic of materiality.

The concept of materiality for financial reporting has not only been evolving for decades, but is also the basis for most definitions of materiality for nonfinancial information. The most important materiality guidance has been promulgated by international and US accounting standards setting organizations, including the Financial Accounting Standards Board[9] International Accounting Standards Board,[10] Public Company Accounting

Oversight Board[11] and Securities and Exchange Commission.[12] Standards and guidance issued by the foregoing organizations are enforceable by law.

National and international regulators and standards setters and non-governmental organizations (NGOs) have issued guidance on materiality for nonfinancial information. Guidance published by regulators and standards setters include:

- Canadian Securities Administrators:

> The test for materiality is objective. Information relating to environmental matters is likely material if a reasonable investor's decision whether or not to buy, sell or hold securities of the issuer would likely be influenced or changed if the information was omitted or misstated. See Part 1(f) of Form 51-102F1 and Part 1(e) of Form 51-102F2.
>
> As noted in Form 51-102F1 and Form 51-102F2, this concept of materiality is consistent with the financial reporting notion of materiality contained in the Canadian Institute of Chartered Accountants (CICA) Handbook.[13]

---

[8] The list was adapted and updated from Lydenberg and Grace (2008).

[9] "Information is material if omitting it or misstating it could influence decisions that users make on the basis of the financial information of a specific reporting entity. In other words, materiality is an entity-specific aspect of relevance based on the nature or magnitude or both of the items to which the information relates in the context of an individual entity's financial report. Consequently, the Board cannot specify a uniform quantitative threshold for materiality or predetermine what could be material in a particular situation." Financial Accounting Standards Board. Statement of Financial Accounting Concepts No. 8, www.fasb.org/cs/Bl obServer?blobcol=urldata&blobtable=MungoBlobs&blobk ey=id&blobwhere=1175822892635&blobheader=applicati on%2Fpdf.

[10] "Omissions or misstatements of items are material if they could, individually or collectively, influence the economic decisions of users taken on the basis of the financial statements. Materiality depends on the size and nature of the omission or misstatement judged in the surrounding circumstances. The size or nature of the item, or a combination of both, could be the determining factor. If a line item is not individually material, it is aggregated with other items either on the face of those statements or in the notes. An item that is not sufficiently material to warrant separate presentation on the face of those statements may nevertheless be sufficiently material for it to be presented separately in the notes."

Deloitte IAS Plus, "Summaries of international financial reporting standards. Conceptual framework for financial reporting 2010." www.iasplus.com/standard/framewk.htm. Note: International Financial Reporting Standards are only available through a subscription service.

[11] In interpreting the federal securities laws, the Supreme Court of the United States has held that a fact is material if there is "a substantial likelihood that the … fact would have been viewed by the reasonable investor as having significantly altered the 'total mix' of information made available." As the Supreme Court has noted, determinations of materiality require "delicate assessments of the inferences a 'reasonable shareholder' would draw from a given set of facts and the significance of those inferences to him." Public Company Accounting Oversight Board, Auditing Standard No. 11, Consideration of Materiality in Planning and Performing an Audit, http://pcaobus.org/Standards/Auditing/Pages/Auditing_Standard_11.aspx.

[12] "Materiality concerns the significance of an item to users of a registrant's financial statements. A matter is 'material' if there is a substantial likelihood that a reasonable person would consider it important." Securities and Exchange Commission. SEC Staff Accounting Bulletin: No. 99 – Materiality, www.sec.gov/interps/account/sab99.htm.

[13] Canadian Securities Administrators. Staff Notice 51–333, Environmental Reporting Guidance, www.bcsc.bc.ca/uploadedFiles/securitieslaw/policy5/CSA%20Staff%20Notice%2051–333.pdf.

Table 32.2 Frameworks and guidance for nonfinancial information.

Organization	Initiative
Accounting for Sustainability	Connected Reporting
Alliance for Water Stewardship	AWS Standards
Australian Stock Exchange	Listing Rule 4.10.17
Buenos Aires City Council	Law 2598
Bursa Malaysia	Bursa Malaysia CSR Framework
Canadian Securities Administrators	Staff Notice 51–333 Environmental Reporting Guidance
Canadian Securities Administrators	National Instrument 51–102 Continuous Disclosure Obligations
China State-Owned Assets Supervision and Administration Commission	Directive
Climate Disclosure Standards Board	The CDSB Reporting Framework
Danish Commerce and Companies Agency	Parliamentary law
EFFAS-DVFA	KPIs for ESG Issues, Version 3.0
European Union	Business Review – Modernization Directive (4th and 7th Directives)
Extractive Industry Transparency Initiative	EITI Principles and Criteria
France	Grenelle 2
Germany	German Sustainability Code
Global Reporting Initiative	G3.1 Guidelines
International Accounting Standards Board	IFRS Practice Statement *Management Commentary*
International Integrated Reporting Council	Discussion Paper Towards Integrated Reporting: Communicating Value in the 21st Century
International Integrated Reporting Council	Draft Framework Outline
International Organization for Standardization	ISO 14000
International Organization for Standardization	ISO 26000
Johannesburg Stock Exchange	Listing requirements
Organisation for Economic Co-operation and Development	Reporting Guidelines on Multinational Enterprises
Singapore Stock Exchange	Policy Statement on Sustainability Reporting
Sweden	Parliamentary law
US Securities and Exchange Commission	Interpretive release – Commission Guidance Regarding Disclosure Related to Climate Change
UK Accounting Standards Board	Reporting Statement: Operating and Financial Review
United Nations	Global Compact
United Nations	Principles for Responsible Investment
Water Footprint Network	Water Footprint Assessment Manual

- International Federation of Accountants, ISAE 3000:

  Considering materiality requires the practitioner to understand and assess what factors might influence the decisions of the intended users. For example, when the identified criteria allow for variations in the presentation of the subject matter information, the practitioner considers how the adopted presentation might influence the decisions of the intended users. Materiality is considered in the context of quantitative and qualitative factors, such as relative magnitude, the nature and extent of the effect of these factors on the evaluation or measurement of the subject matter, and the interests of the intended users. The assessment of materiality and the relative importance of quantitative and qualitative factors in a particular engagement are matters for the practitioner's judgment.[14]

- Public Company Accounting Oversight Board:

    The practitioner should consider the concept of materiality in applying this standard. In expressing a conclusion, the practitioner should consider an omission or a misstatement to be material if the omission or misstatement – individually or when aggregated with others – is such that a reasonable person would be influenced by the omission or misstatement. The practitioner should consider both qualitative and quantitative aspects of omissions and misstatements.[15]

- Securities and Exchange Commission. Analyzing the materiality of known trends, events or uncertainties may be particularly challenging for registrants preparing MD&A disclosure. As the Commission explained in the 1989 Release, when a trend, demand, commitment, event or uncertainty is known, management must make two assessments:

    Is the known trend, demand, commitment, event or uncertainty likely to come to fruition? If management determines that it is not reasonably likely to occur, no disclosure is required.

    If management cannot make that determination, it must evaluate objectively the consequences of the known trend, demand, commitment, event or uncertainty, on the assumption that it will come to fruition. Disclosure is then required unless management determines that a material effect on the registrant's financial condition or results of operations is not reasonably likely to occur.[16]

Highly regarded NGOs have also offered definitions of materiality for nonfinancial information.

- AccountAbility:

    Materiality is determining the relevance and significance of an issue to an organization and its stakeholders. A material issue is an issue that will influence the decisions, actions and performance of an organization or its stakeholders (AccountAbility 2008).

- Carbon Disclosure Project/Climate Disclosure Standards Board:

    In financial reporting, information is material if its omission, misstatement or misinterpretation could influence the decisions that users make on the basis of an entity's financial information. Because materiality depends on the nature and amount of the item judged in the particular circumstances of its omission or misstatement, it is not possible to specify a uniform quantitative threshold at which a particular type of information becomes material. When considering whether financial information is a faithful representation of what it purports to represent, it is important to take into account materiality because material omissions, misstatements or misinterpretations will result in information that is incomplete, biased or not free from error.[17]

- Global Reporting Initiative:

    The information in a report should cover topics and Indicators that reflect the organization's significant economic, environmental and social impacts or that would substantively influence the assessments and decisions of stakeholders.[18]

---

[14] International Federation of Accountants. International Standard on Assurance Engagements (ISAE) 3000, "Assurance Engagements Other than Audits or Reviews of Historical Financial Information," www.ifac.org/sites/default/files/downloads/b012–2010-iaasb-handbook-isae-3000.pdf.

[15] Public Company Accounting Oversight Board. AT Section 101, Attest Engagements, http://pcaobus.org/Standards/Attestation/Pages/AT101.aspx.

[16] Securities and Exchange Commission. Commission Guidance Regarding Disclosure Related to Climate Change,

www.sec.gov/rules/interp/2010/33–9106.pdf. The CCRF's interpretation of the meaning of materiality is based on and reproduces IASB's ED 2008 paragraph QC28.

[17] Climate Disclosure Standards Board. "Climate Change Reporting Framework – Edition 1.0 September 2010," www.cdsb.net/file/8/cdsb_climate_change_reporting_framework_2.pdf, accessed July 2012.

[18] Global Reporting Initiative. "Materiality on the Context of the GRI Reporting Framework," www.globalreporting.org/reporting/guidelines-online/TechnicalProtocol/Pages/MaterialityInTheContextOfTheGRIReportingFramework.aspx.

• United Nations Conference on Trade and Development/Guidance on Corporate Responsibility Indicators in Annual Reports:

> Information is material if its omission or misstatement could influence users' decisions. Materiality depends on the size of the item or error judged in the particular circumstances of its omission or misstatement. Thus, it provides a threshold or cut-off point rather than being a primary qualitative characteristic which information must have if it is to be useful. If enterprises choose not to include an indicator due to materiality considerations, the enterprise is encouraged to state the reasons why (United Nations Conference on Trade and Development 2007).

The foregoing guidance is rooted in financial reporting approaches to materiality and, with the exception of the GRI's Sector Supplements, does not offer sector specific guidance.[19]

In 2010, a private sector initiative proposed sector specific materiality guidance for nonfinancial information and using key performance indicators (KPIs) to measure sustainability performance. In a paper published by the Initiative for Responsible Investment at Harvard University, the authors wrote:

> The definition of materiality is of crucial importance in all discussions of disclosure. Understanding the materiality of ESG issues and how materiality changes with respect to particular industry sectors is critical for successful implementation of a minimum ESG reporting scheme. Our working definition of materiality is a modified version of the materiality test developed by AccountAbility and advocated by the Global Reporting Initiative. Our major substantive revision to the AccountAbility definition of materiality was to increase the emphasis on positive material opportunities for sustainability innovation (in business models or offerings) that might bring competitive advantage.
>
> Our definition is broader in scope than the definitions of materiality historically used by financial regulatory parties, but by no means precludes definitions of financial materiality. Nor is it intended to replace corporate managers' responsibility to

report on all financially material issues, whether or not they conform with the ESG materiality tests identified through this process. This process results in a minimum set of material issues subject to mandatory KPI reporting.

> Our materiality test includes five categories of impact to be evaluated at a sector (or sub-sector) level. They are: Financial impacts/risks: Issues that may have a financial impact or may pose a risk to the sector in the short-, medium-, or long-term (e.g., product safety)
>
> Legal/regulatory/policy drivers: Sectoral issues that are being shaped by emerging or evolving government policy and regulation (e.g., carbon emissions regulation)
>
> Peer-based norms: Sustainability issues that companies in the sector tend to report on and recognize as important drivers in their line of business (e.g., safety in the airline industry)
>
> Stakeholder concerns and societal trends: Issues that are of high importance to stakeholders, including communities, non-governmental organizations and the general public, and/or reflect social and consumer trends (e.g., consumer push against genetically modified ingredients)
>
> Opportunity for innovation: Areas where the potential exists to explore innovative solutions that benefit the environment, customers and other stakeholders, demonstrate sector leadership and create competitive advantage (Lydenberg et al. 2010).

This approach offers an idea about how to identify sector specific ESG risks and opportunities that are relevant to shareholders and other stakeholders. If implemented, a process capable of providing comparable ESG information to those who analyze sustainability data within an industry could arise.

The Sustainability Accounting Standards Board, an investor-focused standards setting initiative, was launched in October 2011. SASB is a US-based nonprofit engaged in the creation and dissemination of sustainability accounting standards for use by publicly held corporations in disclosing material sustainability issues for the benefit of investors and the US capital markets. Over the next two and a half years, SASB will develop standards suitable for use in the SEC Forms 10-K and 20-F for eighty-nine industries in ten sectors. In using the SEC/US Supreme

---

[19] Global Reporting Initiative Sector Supplements for the G4 reporting format are available at https://www.globalreporting.org/reporting/sector-guidance/Pages/default.aspx.

Court definition of materiality – "material information" is defined as presenting a substantial likelihood that the disclosure of the omitted fact would have been viewed by the reasonable investor as having significantly altered the "total mix" of information made available – SASB is attempting to create a *de facto* mandatory reporting environment.[20]

Summary

International and US materiality guidance for financial and nonfinancial information are substantively the same. Fundamentally, materiality is a matter of professional judgment based on perceptions of the information needs of those who use the information. Without more rigorous standards for nonfinancial information, companies will not consistently identify critical issues, including opportunities for innovation and investors will face continued exposure to hidden risks.[21]

Standards are necessary to help companies and stakeholders develop a shared understanding of materiality, ensure consistency between issues identified as materiality in sustainability reports and issues disclosed as risk factors regulatory filings, and focus discussions about materiality to those issues that truly impact a company's business – or value creation – model. Failure to adopt standards for nonfinancial reporting puts all stakeholders at risk.

Conclusions

An argument can be made that integrated reporting and sustainability reporting standards are critical to widespread acceptance and adoption of stewardship. Integrated reporting supports understanding relationships between financial and nonfinancial performance, evaluation of trade-offs and making difficult decisions. Implementation of integrated reporting is certainly possible without generally accepted standards as evidenced by pioneers such as Natura, Novo Nordisk and United Technologies to name only three out of a few hundred integrated reporting companies. However, without standards, consistent and comparable reporting will be difficult and arguably impossible. In addition, standards are the basis for independent assurance, which give credibility to information.

Integrated reporting, sustainability reporting standards and stewardship itself depend on collective action. Who needs to do what? All the participants in the corporate reporting supply chain should support efforts to develop sector specific guidance on materiality and key performance indicators and sustainability reporting standards. In addition:

(1) Analysts and investors who believe that ESG information is critical to their decision-making should ask companies to provide integrated reports and tell regulators that integrated reporting "protects investors, maintains fair, orderly, and efficient markets, and facilitates capital formation."[22]

(2) Chief executive officers of companies voluntarily issuing integrated reports should be much more vocal about why their companies have chosen to issue "one report" (Eccles and Krzus 2010b).

(3) Regulators and standards setters should create environments that encourage innovative companies to experiment with integrated reporting by establishing projects similar to the Securities and Exchange Commission XBRL Voluntary Filing Program.

(4) Stakeholders must continue to challenge and ask hard questions of business to remind companies that their own interests are served when they learn to balance the demands of the capital markets and the demands of the society on which business entities rely to create value.

(5) Stock exchanges such as the five exchanges[23] (NASDAQ and stock exchanges in Sao Paulo,

---

[20] The Sustainability Accounting Standards Board is using an approach that creates unique materiality profiles for different industries. www.sasb.org/materiality/determining-materiality.

[21] For more discussion see Eccles et al. (2011b).

[22] www.sec.gov/about/whatwedo.shtml.

[23] www.bloomberg.com/news/2012–06–19/nasdaq-joins-four-exchanges-in-sustainability-effort.html.

Johannesburg, Istanbul and Cairo) endorsing paragraph 47 of "The Future We Want" (United Nations Conference on Sustainable Development 2012)[24] must move beyond simply urging their approximately 4,600 companies to produce sustainability reports, or explain why they don't. These exchanges should follow the lead of the Johannesburg Stock Exchange and amend their listing standards to require integrated reporting on a comply or explain why not basis.

A concentrated collective effort is needed to create an environment that encourages corporate stewardship and drives the understanding that business success is the ability to simultaneously create value for shareholders and society.

Disclaimer

The landscape of sustainability and integrated reporting is evolving at a rapid pace. Due to the lengthy timeline required to review and publish this comprehensive *Handbook*, several references herein have been superseded. This is particularly true of references to activities and publications of the Global Reporting Initiative, the International Integrated Reporting Council and the Sustainability Accounting Standards Board. While references to specific guidelines, frameworks and standards may be outdated, the fundamental arguments for widely accepted sustainability and integrated reporting standards – as well as the relationship of such standards to the fiduciary duties of intergenerational impartiality and loyalty – remain valid and unchanged.

[24] Paragraph 47 reads: "We acknowledge the importance of corporate sustainability reporting and encourage companies, where appropriate, especially publicly listed and large companies, to consider integrating sustainability information into their reporting cycle. We encourage industry, interested governments and relevant stakeholders with the support of the United Nations system, as appropriate, to develop models for best practice and facilitate action for the integration of sustainability reporting, taking into account experiences from already existing frameworks and paying particular attention to the needs of developing countries, including for capacity-building."

References

Accenture. 2010. *Driving Value from Integrated Sustainability: High Performance Lessons from the Leaders*. London: Accenture.

AccountAbility. 2008. *AA1000 AccountAbility Principles Standard 2008*. www.accountability. org/standards/aa1000aps.html.

CalPERS. 2009. "Total Fund Statement of Investment and Policy." www.calpers.ca.gov/ index.jsp?bc=/investments/policies/invo-policy-statement/home.xml.

Climate Disclosure Standards Board. 2010. "Climate Change Reporting Framework – Edition 1.0 September 2010." www.cdsb.net/file/8/cdsb_ climate_change_reporting_framework_2.pdf.

Deloitte IAS Plus. 2010. "Summaries of International Financial Reporting Standards. Conceptual Framework for Financial Reporting 2010." www.iasplus.com/standard/framewk. htm.

Eccles, R. G. and M. P. Krzus. 2010a. "A Chronology of Integrated Reporting." Harvard Business School Note 411-049, September.

2010b. *One Report: Integrated Reporting for a Sustainable Strategy*. New York: John Wiley & Sons, Inc.

Eccles, R. G., I. Ioannou and G. Serafeim. 2011a. "The Impact of a Corporate Culture of Sustainability on Corporate Behavior and Performance," Harvard Business School Working Paper No. 12–035, November, www. hbs.edu/research/pdf/12–035.pdf.

Eccles, R. G., M. P. Krzus and G. Serafeim. 2011b. "Market Interest in Nonfinancial Information," *Journal of Applied Corporate Finance* 23 (4): 113–27.

Financial Reporting Council. 2008. *True and Fair Opinion, Moore, 21 April 2008*. www.frc.org. uk/documents/pagemanager/frc/T&F%20 Opinion%2021%20April%202008.pdf.

2011. *Paper: True and Fair (July 2011) True and Fair Opinion*. www.frc.org.uk/images/ uploaded/documents/Paper%20True%20 and%20Fair1.pdf.

Generation Investment Management. 2012. "Sustainable Capitalism," February 15, 2012. www.generationim.com/media/pdf-generation-sustainable-capitalism-v1.pdf.

Hawley, J. P. and A. T. Williams. 2000. *The Rise of Fiduciary Capitalism: How Institutional Investors Can Make Corporate America*

More Democratic. Philadelphia: University of Pennsylvania Press.

International Federation of Accountants. 2004. "Assurance Engagements Other than Audits or Reviews of Historical Financial Information," www.ifac.org/sites/default/files/downloads/b012-2010-iaasb-handbook-isae-3000.pdf.

International Integrated Reporting Council. 2011. "Towards Integrated Reporting: Communicating Value in the 21st Century." www.discussionpaper2011.theiirc.org/towards-integrated-reporting.

—— 2013. "Consultation Draft of the International Integrated Reporting (IR) Framework." www.theiirc.org/consultationdraft2013.

Ittner, C. and D. Larcker. 2003. "Coming Up Short on Nonfinancial Performance Measurement," *Harvard Business Review* 81 (11): 89–91.

Lydenberg, S. and K. Grace. 2008. *Innovations in Social and Environmental Disclosure Outside the United States*. New York: Domini Social Investments.

Lydenberg, S., J. Rogers and D. Wood. 2010. "From Transparency to Performance: Industry-Based Sustainability Reporting on Key Issues." http://hausercenter.org/iri/wp-content/uploads/2010/05/IRI_Transparency-to-Performance.pdf.

Massachusetts Institute of Technology. 2011. *Sustainability: The 'Embracers' Seize Advantage*. Cambridge, MA: MIT Press.

Public Company Accounting Oversight Board. 2008. *The Meaning of Present Fairly in Conformity With Generally Accepted Accounting Principles*. http://pcaobus.org/Standards/Auditing/Pages/AU411.aspx.

Tapscott, D. and D. Ticoll. 2003. *The Naked Corporation: How the Age of Transparency Will Revolutionize Business*. New York: Free Press.

United Nations. 1987. "Report of the World Commission on Environment and Development: Our Common Future." www.un-documents.net/wced-ocf.htm.

United Nations Conference on Sustainable Development. 2012. Outcome of the Conference, "The Future We Want," https://rio20.un.org/sites/rio20.un.org/files/a-conf.2161-1_english.pdf.pdf.

United Nations Conference on Trade and Development. 2007. "Guidance of Corporate Responsibility Indicators in Annual Reports." http://unctad.org/en/docs/iteteb20076_en.pdf.

US corporate governance, fiduciary success and stable economic growth

CHRISTIAN E. WELLER

Introduction

Economic growth depends crucially on productivity growth – the rate at which businesses increase their efficiency. There are troubling signs for future productivity growth. The productivity acceleration that started in the mid-1990s eventually disappeared in the mid-2000s.[1] This productivity slowdown followed years of historically low levels of net corporate investment, which represents the actual additions to the country's capital stock after capital replacements have been accounted for.

Key business investments, such as equipment or workforce development, have languished. Investment has been low amid rising corporate profits. Corporations instead used their additional resources to increase share repurchases and dividend payouts.

The prioritization of share repurchases and dividend payouts over productive investments reflects a corporate penchant to pursue activities that boost share prices in the short run at the expense of long-term productivity growth.

This prioritization is partially related to the US corporate governance structure's short-run biases. US corporate governance institutions include corporate executives, shareholders and the board of directors. The board of directors and shareholders are supposed to provide checks and balances on managers. Managers nowadays have, by design, a short-term orientation in their resource allocation decision. And these corporate executives wield a disproportionate influence over corporate resource allocation because other stakeholders can currently

offer only a limited counterbalance. Executive performance measures are hence tilted toward short-run share price run-ups with limited countervailing forces in place. Corporations may hence reap short-term profits to boost their share prices, but slowly erode the basis for long-term productivity growth.

The threat of slower productivity growth requires policy attention. Finding a better balance in the pursuit of short-term and long-term goals in US corporate governance is one possible policy venue to boost productive investments. Policymakers can encourage the definition and emphasis of more long-term performance measures to counter the dominance of short-term share price gains and reduce the inherent biases that favor short-term stakeholders over longer-term ones.

This chapter briefly presents the challenges for productivity growth emanating from a biased corporate governance structure, shows the existing biases and discusses policies to overcome those biases. More specifically, the chapter first examines the macroeconomic links between productivity growth, investment and corporate resource allocation, then how these macroeconomic trends reflect the design of executive compensation. The chapter then offers evidence on the corporate governance structure's short-term biases that give rise to the existing executive compensation design, followed by potential policy responses to address the corporate governance structure's short-term biases.

Slowing productivity growth and low net investment

Productivity growth has swung over the past two decades. Productivity growth accelerated in the mid-1990s after more than a decade of very low productivity growth, but then slowed again after

---

[1] Gordon (2012) even suggests that US productivity growth may stall in the future in part due to inequality and a massive debt overhang.

2004. The initial acceleration, associated with the information technology boom of the late 1990s,[2] was remarkable both because of its strength and its durability (Gordon and Dew-Becker 2005). Long-term productivity growth, however, slowed again after 2004 (Kahn and Rich 2006).

The prospect for renewed productivity acceleration in the future hinges on strong business investments in the present (Weller and Reidenbach 2011). Productivity growth seems to follow investment – in this case investment net of depreciation – with about a seventeen-year lag.

Unfortunately, investment has been low for some time. Investment dropped sharply during the recession that started in March 2001 and remained subpar afterwards, averaging 10.3 percent of GDP between December 2007 and March 2012 – the lowest level of any business cycle since the early-1960s.[3] Net business investment – after accounting for the replacement of depreciated plant and equipment – dropped to its lowest average since World War II with 2.5 percent of GPD between March 2001 and December 2007 and averaged 1.4 percent from December 2007 through March 2012.

Productivity growth has been subpar during the business cycle that started in December 2007. Productivity was 6.8 percent higher in March 2012 than in December 2007, well below the 8.2 percent average for prior post-World War II expansions of similar length.[4]

High corporate profits and their allocation to short-term uses

Low investment reflects corporate priorities, not a lack of resources (Lazonick 2009; Weller and Bivens 2005; Weller and Reidenbach 2011). Corporate profits rose sharply after the recession

ended in November 2001 and again at the end of 2008, six months before the recession came to an end. Profit rates – profits to assets – had returned to the levels of early 2007 before the recession started by early 2010, despite weak economic growth in 2009 and 2010.

Corporations spent a growing share of rising profits on share purchases and dividend payouts to boost stock prices, leaving fewer funds for productive investments. When stock options and stock grants are issued to employees without any offsetting actions, a company's outstanding shares will rise and share prices will fall (Jolls 1998). Share repurchases offset this dilution by shrinking the supply of a company's shares in the market. Corporations often repurchase more of their shares than is necessary to avoid share price dilution and thus contribute to rising share prices (Lazonick 2009).

Dividend payouts also raise share prices by raising the demand for a company's share. Share repurchases and dividend payouts reward short-term stock market speculation since they drive stock prices higher without any change in long-term economic fundamentals. These price increases come at the expense of long-term productive investments since money spent on share repurchases and dividend payouts will no longer be spent on productive investments (Lazonick 2009; Weller and Bivens 2005; Weller and Reidenbach 2011).

This growing use of corporate resources directly linked to less productive investments as companies generated the means necessary to pursue share repurchases and dividend payouts through outsourcing, downsizing and hollowing out (Lazonick 2009; Weller and Bivens 2005). Companies invested less in physical capital and people to save money they could then use to prop up their share prices.

Share repurchases and dividend payouts have only increased in the twenty-first century. Corporations spent on average 125.2 percent of their after-tax profit on such resource allocations between March 2001 and December 2007, compared to an average 96.5 percent of the business cycle from December 1990 to March 2001 (Weller and Reidenbach 2011). Corporations continued to use on average all of their after-tax profits for share repurchases and dividend payouts after December

---

[2] A number of research studies have demonstrated the link between information technology investments and the productivity growth acceleration. See Brynjolfsson et al. (2007), Jorgenson et al. (2005, 2008) and Oliner et al. (2007).

[3] All figures are author's calculations based on Bureau of Economic Analysis (2012).

[4] Author's calculations based on Bureau of Labor Statistics (2012).

Table 33.1 Summary of key stakeholders in the corporate governance system.

Stakeholder	Goal orientation	Level of influence
Management	Short-term due to pay-for-performance incentives	High
Short-term oriented institutional investors such as hedge funds	Short-term due to own performance measures	High/medium
Long-term oriented institutional investors such as pension plans and mutual funds	Long-term due to benefit horizon	Medium/low
Board of directors	Both short-term and long-term	Medium

2007, allocating 109.4 percent of after-tax profits to these uses between December 2007 and March 2012.[5] Corporations had on average no profits left over to spend on investments during those years, requiring them to borrow additional money to pay for some investments.[6]

Executive compensation and short-term biases in corporate resource allocation

Managers nowadays have a short-term orientation in deciding corporate resource allocations. And they wield a disproportionate influence over corporate resource allocation because other stakeholders can currently offer only a limited counterbalance (Table 33.1).

The maximization of shareholder value has nominally been a top priority for corporate managers for the past three decades (O'Sullivan 2003) since maximizing returns on shareholders' equity holdings is supposedly equal to generating the strongest long-term productivity growth (Blair 2008). But the strict equation of profits and stock prices with productivity, ignoring the influence of fads, rumors and other factors, lead managers to increase

short-term profits to boost stock prices, even to the detriment of other productive investments.

Managers will pursue short-term profit opportunities due to a carrot-and-stick approach in their compensation. The carrot is performance-based compensation, such as stock options and stock grants and dividend incentives. The stick is a corporate takeover threat as poorly performing companies could see falling stock prices and thus become takeover targets (O'Sullivan 2003).

Both carrot and stick approaches assume that stock prices accurately reflect a company's performance. But, stock prices often follow fads, creating boom-and-bust cycles, rather than mirroring underlying economic fundamentals.[7] Corporate managers are thus rewarded or punished for results that they have little control over. They hence have an incentive to influence share prices. Share repurchases and dividend payouts can help boost stock prices in the short run.

Additionally, managers can use several short-term processes to their advantage. These processes include friendly compensation committees (Bebchuk and Fried 2005) or outright manipulation, such as backdating of stock options (Heron and Lie 2009).

Managers consequently prioritize short-term stock speculation over building a company's long-term productive base. In a 2004 survey of senior financial executives, for example, 80 percent of respondents said they would decrease discretionary spending, such as spending on research and

---

[5] Author's calculations based on Board of Governors, Federal Reserve System (2012).

[6] It should be noted that nonfinancial corporations also continuously increased their cash holdings since the early 1980s, growing from about three percent of total assets to about six percent in the Great Recession. This cash hoarding has typically been financed by additional borrowing. Author's calculations based on Board of Governors, Federal Reserve System (2012).

[7] See O'Sullivan (2003) for a summary of the literature and Shiller and Campbell (2005) for some additional evidence.

development and human resources, if their company's stock might come in below desired quarterly earnings targets (Graham et al. 2005).

And, managers can pursue short-term profit-seeking activities such as hollowing out the company's productive base to generate the resources for share repurchases and dividend payouts. Corporations also engage in mergers and acquisition activities to generate additional financial resources and gain access to talent and innovation, for example in the IT industry (Lazonick 2009). The result is less productivity growth for most corporations and for the US economy.

Ineffective checks and balances

Shareholders have voiced their concerns over investment decisions and other resource allocations. They can sue the company. They can engage in shareholder activism including but not limited to nominating alternative nominees for board of directors, withholding shareholder approval of the board of directors, opposing proposed executive compensation packages and directly changing corporate investment parameters by promoting sustainability standards. And, they can sell their shares, possibly incurring a loss. All of these three options are costly, and lawsuits and shareholder activism can be time-consuming and expensive, such that only the largest owners typically participate (CalPERS 2009; Council of Institutional Investors 2010).

Further, not all institutional shareholders have a long-term orientation. Many pursue their own short-term interests, thus diluting the influence of long-term oriented investors. Shareholders have consequently failed to provide an effective counterbalance to management's short-term orientation, even though the importance of institutional investors has grown over time (Aguilar 2009).

But the different objectives of institutional investors complicate the impact of shareholder activism

All institutional investors seek to maximize returns to shareholders. They often try to pursue various

intermediary steps that could increase the possibility of achieving higher share prices and dividend payouts over time. These steps include establishing independent compensation committees, removing poorly performing management and establishing an independent board of directors who can better oversee the company's investment decisions.

Yet the effectiveness of shareholder activism in pursuing these steps is generally limited. Shareholders may not be able to pursue all of their desired policies and management may be able to blunt the control such policies can exercise of their decisions (Council of Institutional Investors 2005).

The proxy process in particular poses a formidable hurdle to shareholder activism (CalPERS 2009). The proxy process is the primary tool for shareholder activists. Management can reject proposals, suggesting that they deal with the ordinary business of the corporation and are thus inappropriate for a shareholder vote. Votes cast against the proposal and abstentions can be considered as opposing the activists' proposal and favoring management. Moreover, all votes are nonbinding, even if a proposal receives a majority of the votes. And shareholder proposals can be very costly (CalPERS 2009). Shareholder activists consequently attempt to engage management on key issues before proposals opposing management and its decisions reach the annual shareholder meeting (Council of Institutional Investors 2005, 2010; Weller and White 2001).

Institutional investors are hardly homogenous, furthering weakening shareholder activism as institutional shareholders may pursue competing goals. Some are inactive in corporate governance. Mutual funds, for example, often refuse to engage management to try to influence returns at all (Taub 2009). And, short-term institutional investors, such as hedge funds and private equity firms, pursue competing interests from long-term investors.

Short-term institutional investors emphasize speculative investments, reinforcing short-term bias

Short-term institutional investors, especially hedge funds, are investors that seek immediate share value increase and place emphasis on quarterly profit gains. Hedge funds look to maximize shareholder value through short-term profit gains. They frequently demand that companies repurchase shares or pay out dividends. A 2008 study by New York University's April Klein and Emanuel Zur finds that, on average, activism targets of hedge funds doubled their dividends and significantly decreased their cash. Hedge funds had a success rate of 60 percent when they engaged management on these issues (Klein and Zur 2008).

Several factors give hedge funds outsized influence on corporate decisions. They face a more favorable regulatory environment than longer-term investors since they are largely exempted from the financial regulations, including parts of the Securities Act of 1944 and the Investment Company Act of 1940. For instance, hedge funds have more flexibility than many longer-term institutional investors on how to use their assets (ibid.), enabling them to concentrate more of their assets in one company and thus influencing one company's behavior.

Hedge funds also face no legal or regulatory incentives to diversify their stock holdings, giving them potentially considerable influence over their target companies. And hedge funds can make off-exchange stock trades to claim more company equity. Further, most hedge fund managers have personal stakes in going after short-term profits since their own compensation depends on a company's stock performance (Brav et al. 2008). Hedge funds' interests are already aligned with managers' short-term interests, reinforcing short-term biases in corporate resource allocations.

Short-term institutional investors also often band together. Such funds often collaborate and engage in "wolf pack" activity to minimize costs and increase effectiveness. Indeed, studies show that short-run institutional investors tend to have more information, often as a result of their stronger activism, than other institutional investors and thus are better equipped to target the weakest companies for the right underlying reasons in an effort to boost share prices in the short term (Yan and Zhang 2009).

Hedge funds are not significant as a share of total trading, but they wield significant shareholder

influence over key management decisions (Thomas 2008). The IRRC Institute for Corporate Responsibility reports that between 2005 and 2008, hedge funds led or initiated 89 percent of proxy battles (Cernich et al. 2009).

Long-term institutional investors are reluctant activists

Long-term institutional investors, mainly public pension plans, are the largest block of institutional investors. They pursue a long-term investment horizon because they need to pay benefits for decades to come,[8] making them primarily concerned with the long-term performance of the companies in which they are investing.[9] Pension funds seek governance solutions that preserve their long-term investments (Choi and Fisch 2008). Pension plan investments also have a signaling effect. Pension funds held 38.6 percent of total institutional assets at the end of 2009 (The Conference Board 2009). Other, smaller institutional investors will follow larger investors' decisions, thereby creating price swings and exacerbating losses, forcing larger investors to hold their investments and actively engagement in corporate governance.

One example of long-term institutional activism is how the California Public Employee Retirement System (CalPERS) has attempted to seek governance changes to protect its investments. It was the use of proxy votes by CalPERS that helped give institutional investors more influence over their portfolio companies (Monks and Minow 2001). CalPERS has augmented its influence further through the creation of the Council of Institutional Investors (CII), an influential shareholder advocacy

---

[8] Pension funds also use alternative investments such as hedge funds in their portfolio. This potentially creates a conflict for longer-term investment horizons pursued by pension funds.

[9] Another reason for pension funds to focus on the long term is that they often cannot unwind their holdings quickly without unduly influencing a company's share price. Pension funds and other institutional investors have very large holdings, which puts them in a leadership role. Their financial decisions will be imitated by other investors. Share sales by large institutional investors will thus result in disproportionately large price drops.

organization that advocates on behalf of institutions with a long-term investment horizon (Smith 1996). CalPERS has achieved periodic success in protecting its interests. Between 1987 and 1993, for example, CalPERS' activism increased its assets by almost $19 million at a total cost of $3.5 million (ibid.). The CalPERS effect is often larger than the numbers suggest since public funds more actively engage in corporate governance than private ones and since shareholder activists often engage with corporations in informal ways (Weller and White 2001).

Many long-term institutional investors face several obstacles to seeking widespread change in management decisions. Public pension funds have political considerations, making them more cautious about their activism (Kahan and Rock 2007). Public pension funds also face limits on the size of their investments in individual portfolio companies. Further, mutual fund managers often list a myriad of reasons for their disengagement from shareholder activism, such as legal obstacles, contractual obligations or lack of avid interest from shareholders (Taub 2009a, 2009b).

Importantly, long-term shareholder activism has achieved limited results (Black 1998; Gillan and Starks 2007; Smith 1996). Moreover, fiduciaries such as pension plan trustees have tried to shield themselves from liabilities, often shifting key investment functions to third-party service providers such as investment managers. This lowers the pursuit of long-term goals by long-term institutional shareholders (Hawley et al. 2011) as decision-makers at long-term institutional investors have become less engaged in investment decisions. Finally, long-term institutional investors often do not collaborate, citing regulatory hurdles that could require lawsuits and a long, drawn-out process (Black 1998; Council of Institutional Investors 2010). Shareholder activism may have had some desired effects on share price in the short run but fewer tangible results in improving the operating performance of targeted companies (Gillan and Starks 2007).

Furthermore, shareholder activism often requires substantial amounts of money to mount shareholder campaigns opposing management decisions (CalPERS 2009; Council of Institutional Investors

2010), occasionally reaching millions of dollars (McCracken and Scannell 2009). Funds such as CalPERS have shown the possibility of institutional activism by a long-term institutional investor, but CalPERS is also the biggest and most equipped to pursue these means. Most public pension plans lack the means to be as aggressive (Choi and Fisch 2008). The high cost of activism means that it has remained a "minority pursuit" (O'Sullivan 2003).

Long-term performance goal not well measured, discouraging long-term activism

Long-term shareholder activists also face a dual problem arising from long-term performance measures. They are hard to define and difficult to measure. Long-term performance measures, other than stock price gains, are hard to define (Gaspar et al. 2005). Shareholder activists thus often focus on measuring intermediate goals that could translate into longer-term productivity and profit gains. Such intermediate goals include the amount of capital expenditures (Weller and White 2001) and sustainable investments (CalPERS 2012).

More generally, CII and others produce a "Focus List" of firms that underperform and have weak corporate governance, which can make management of the targeted firms more responsive to shareholders (Ward et al. 2009). The effect has often been a change in corporate governance practices by the targeted companies, although the outcomes for long-term performance are unclear (Gillan and Starks 2007; Wahal 1996). And some time will have to pass before shareholders know that their interventions were a success or failure, even when long-term performance measures are well-defined (Dobbs and Koller 2005). Long-term institutional investors hence increasingly acquiesce to management's decisions or simply do not engage at all due to these obstacles to long-term shareholder activism.[10]

[10] It should be noted that there has been growing interest in defining long-term performance goals for long-term oriented investors since the mid-2000s that has accelerated in the wake of the financial crisis of 2008. Longer-term goals include a commitment by investors to incorporate environmental, social and governance (ESG) issues in their decision-

Boards of directors provide limited counterbalance to managers

Boards of directors also provide an ineffective counterbalance to the short-term goal orientation of corporate managers.[11] Boards theoretically hold poorly performing executives accountable and could steer a company in the right direction. But, they are often not truly independent from the company and its managers. Managers can curry favor with directors by influencing who gets on the board of directors, influencing the pay for the board of directors and interacting with board directors to entice favorable compensation packages. This means giving bonuses to helpful directors, donating to their charities or conducting favorable business dealings with firms owned by the directors. Bebchuk and Fried (2005) point out that in general directors and CEOs have a close relationship, both because they know each other from prior work and because they share much of the underlying values and preferences for corporate management and pay structures. More specifically, CEOs and managers often have a hand in drafting the compensation plans that they then present to their boards for approval, even influencing the nominally independent compensation committees (Jensen et al. 2004).

Corporations have tried to address boards' lack of independence with limited success. Independent directors have become increasingly common, with 19 percent of S&P companies having a completely independent board chair in 2010, up from 9 percent in 2005 (Spencer Stuart 2010). The rise of independent boards and independent directors was meant as a response to the Enron and WorldCom scandals in 2002 (Bebchuk and Weisman 2009).

The rise of independent directors, however, has not had a notable impact on long-term share value and executive compensation packages and speculative investments (Gordon 2006).

Boards also become entrenched as they have some protection from removal, reducing the penalty for siding with managers that may oppose longer-term interest. Boards can be unitary or staggered. Staggered boards reduce accountability since it is hard to replace the board in its entirety and they become entrenched. Entrenchment can lead to avoiding board duties. Boards will, for example, often bundle new charter provisions disliked by shareholders with well-liked measures to amend corporate charters in the board's favor, thus further entrenching their role by only pursuing little of what shareholders are seeking (Bebchuk and Kamar 2010).

Policy interventions start to help create more balance for long-term institutional investors

There have been several public policy changes related to corporate governance over the past two decades (Table 33.2). Public policy has gradually moved toward finding a better balance between short-term and long-term goals and investors. But policymakers have done so selectively – not using all of the tools at the disposal of policymakers – and not strategically. There is, for instance, so far no clear development of affirmative long-term performance goals.

The policy balance has gradually shifted away from state to federal ones. Most states give corporations flexibility in establishing their own governance provision, including the selection of boards (Glassman 2006).[12] But, new federal legislation, particularly Sarbanes-Oxley and DFA are examples of federal policymakers asserting a larger role in this area.

---

making process (Principles for Responsible Investing 2012). The United Nations-backed Principles for Responsible Investing (PRI) collaboration has the potential to create operationalizable long-term performance standards that differ from long-term stock price gains, which still leaves the imbalance between long-term and short-term owners in pursuing their goals to be addressed.

[11] The financial crisis of 2008 has put the role of boards and the incentives in executive compensation in focus. The Wall Street Reform and Consumer Protection Act of 2010, commonly known as Dodd Frank Act (DFA) started to address some of the perceived problems, as discussed in the policy section below.

[12] It should also be noted that Delaware plays a disproportionate role in corporate governance since many large corporations are chartered there. That is, policy changes in other states will have little effect on the US corporate governance system.

Table 33.2 Summary of select policy changes affecting corporate governance.

| Policy venue | Policy measure | Long-term performance measure | | Balance between stakeholders |
		Stock prices	Other performance measures	
Federal regulation	SEC "safe harbor" rule for stock repurchases to not count as stock manipulation in 1982	No, does not establish performance criteria	No, does not establish performance criteria	No, makes it easier to satisfy stock options and stock grants
	SEC deems stock options derivatives in 1991, shortening the required holding period after exercising options	No, does not establish performance criteria	No, does not establish performance criteria	No, makes it easier to gain short-term profits with stock options for executives
	SEC disclosure requirements	Yes, disclosure of long-term stock price performance	Yes, detailed cost of executive compensation	Yes, through greater transparency
	SEC narrowing of "ordinary business" rule	No, does not establish performance criteria	No, does not establish performance criteria	Yes, makes it easier for shareholders to introduce proposals for shareholder votes at annual meeting
Federal legislative requirements	Sarbanes-Oxley	Yes, greater oversight role for SEC	Yes, increased transparency to identify risk-taking	Yes, through greater transparency
	Dodd-Frank Wall Street Reform and Consumer Protection Act	Yes, disclosure of long-term stock price performance	Yes, details on independent compensation committees, risk-taking incentives in compensation packages, among others	Yes, through required votes by shareholders on executive compensation packages and through stricter regulations of less regulated entities, such as hedge funds
State legislative requirements	Stakeholder legislation	Yes, some states encourage managers to consider long-term share performance, but these are generally nonbinding	Yes, disclosure of impact on communities, but these are generally nonbinding	Yes, requires consideration of interests of communities in decision-making
Federal tax policy	Omnibus Budget Reconciliation Act of 1993 limits deductibility of executive wages	No, did not specify time frame for performance measures	No, focused just on executive compensation	No, tax changes only incentivize pay for performance for executives.
	American Job Creation Act of 2004	No, did not specify time frame	Yes, limits use of profits in 2005 for share repurchases and dividend payouts	No, only changes tax incentives for corporate resource allocation

Federal policy venues include regulatory policy, increasingly federal legislation on corporate governance and tax code changes. The Securities and Exchange Commission (SEC) is the most prominent federal regulatory agency. A number of SEC regulations have increased the short-term bias in corporate governance, but others have established broader disclosure rules and given more voice to shareholders – two changes that could allow for a better definition of long-term performance measures and create a better balance between short-term and long-term investors. Changes in the interpretation of SEC rules have facilitated share repurchases and thus enhanced the attractiveness of short-term speculative resource allocations (Hudson 1982; Lazonick 2009). And, new disclosure rules have centered on executive compensation and stock price performance. Corporations have to disclose more about the cost of executive compensation, including the cost of stock options (Securities and Exchange Commission 2009a). Finally, the SEC also has increasingly narrowed the definition of the "ordinary business rule," under which management may reject shareholder proposals for proxy votes (O'Sullivan 2000; Securities and Exchange Commission 2009b; Weller 2000).

Regulation is not the only federal policy venue. Federal legislators have occasionally weighed in on corporate governance issues. In the wake of the Enron scandals, the Sarbanes-Oxley Act of 2002 gave the SEC broad new authority to enforce new accounting and transparency rules (Kuschnik 2008). The Dodd-Frank Wall Street Reform and Consumer Protection Act of 2010 (DFA) establishes additional transparency guidelines on executive pay, mandates that federal regulators evaluate whether executive compensation packages at regulated banks encourage excessive risk-taking and requires regulators to devise rules to reduce such risk-taking (Congressional Research Service 2010). DFA also increases transparency, especially of executive pay (ibid.). Much of these past legislative efforts have been aimed at increasing disclosure and thus possibly giving longer-term oriented institutional investors a venue to better define longer-term performance measures.

DFA has also attempted to establish a greater balance between short-term and long-term interests. It requires that compensation committees are comprised of only independent directors and gives committees the authority to hire outside consultants and it extends oversight over hedge funds (ibid.).

Congress also has looked at the tax code as the third possible policy venue. First, Congress limited the corporate deduction of executive pay to $1 million per year in 1993. But, the tax changes incentivized companies to offer a larger share of executive compensation in performance-based pay (Cox 2006). Second, the American Job Creation Act of 2004 tried to move corporations away from short-term speculative toward long-term investments. It granted a tax holiday to corporations for repatriating overseas profits in 2005. The repatriated profits could not be used for share repurchases and dividend payouts (Lazonick 2009). But repatriating corporations appear to have repurchased their own stock at a higher rate than non-repatriating corporations (Blouin and Krull 2007). These examples highlight that tax policy is a potential venue to impact the balance between short-term and long-term oriented investments, but that policymakers need to be mindful that corporate funds are fungible.

States have also implemented policies to tip the balance toward long-term goals and investors, particularly so-called stakeholder legislation, whereby corporations chartered in the state would be required to consider the impact of their decisions on workers and communities (Adams and Matheson 2000). But, these statutes are generally nonbinding and have proven to be mostly ineffective (Singer 1993). And the policy space for states has been shrinking with greater federal policy attention to corporate governance.

Policy only creates a framework for fiduciaries to act

Policies have moved toward longer-term goals and given more say to longer-term investors. But, even though policy has gradually given a greater voice to shareholders and started to level the regulatory playing field between long-term and short-term investors, it has not yet affirmatively identified performance criteria that could be linked to faster long-term productivity growth.

It is up to long-term institutional investors to identify and define their own long-term performance criteria (Council of Institutional Investors 2010). CalPERS (2012), for example, has worked on considering ways for investors to influence climate change with their investments. The underlying logic is that climate change will create long-term unpredictable liabilities for corporations and that addressing the causes of climate change will consequently translate into long-term value creation for long-term investors. CalPERS partnered with other institutional investors to study ways that institutional long-term investments can influence climate change-related decisions and it has taken steps to influence corporate decisions that affect climate change through investments, procurements, and voting and engagement with managers (ibid.).

But different investors may emphasize different and possibly conflicting goals, reducing the effectiveness of long-term shareholder activism, unless long-term investors coordinate goals with each other. Long-term institutional investors have, for example, coordinated efforts around environmental, social and governance (ESG) work (ibid.). CalPERS coordinates its efforts with other long-term institutional investors, through the Ceres Coalition of more than 130 institutional and socially responsible investors and other public interest organizations advocating for sustainable leadership and the adoption of sustainable business practices.

This coordination between institutional investors has two limitations. First, long-term institutional investors may coordinate on some issues, but not on all issues of concern to them. And second, many long-term institutional investors may still be reluctant to coordinate with each other out of fear of running afoul of legal and regulatory restrictions, even though courts and regulators have clarified that coordination is acceptable (Council of Institutional Investors 2010).

Moving toward policy reform

There are two policy goals: better definition of long-term performance measures and a better balance between short-term and long-term investors.

Short-term versus long-term performance measures

Defining performance as shareholder value creation has succeeded in part because it provides an easy, low-cost and accessible metric by which to assess management operations (Rappaport 2005).

Efforts to tip the balance toward long-term investors should look at better defining long-term oriented metrics. These metrics could include spending on research and development, the level of capital expenditures for new ventures, customer satisfaction and the treatment of workers, specifically through investments in training and professional advancement.[13]

One policy option may be to establish regulatory practices to emphasize long-term productivity growth. The DFA may be a first step in this direction since it requires regulators to identify incentives for risk-taking by banks. It may be worth considering if this approach could be expanded to define long-term, productive practices, rather than to just prevent speculative ones for financial and nonfinancial corporations.

Balancing shareholder activism

The DFA may have started to lay the foundation for a greater balance between short-term and long-term corporate pursuits in relevant regulations, as discussed in the preceding section.

Tax policy may open another venue to incentivize corporate managers to pursue a better balance between short-term, speculative and long-term, productive goals. After all, tax policy is already designed to create a compensation structure that holds executives accountable. One possibility may be to impose an excise tax on short-term speculative activities, such as share repurchases, which add little long-term productive value to a corporation. Additional steps to consider could include lower costs for waging proxy fights that oppose corporate managers and possibly effective stakeholder

---

[13] Efforts under way to also understand how climate change and sustainability relate to investors' portfolios may offer a model for incorporating long-term performance goals in investment decisions, but more research linking these performance goals with corporate productivity is necessary.

legislation that creates formal voices for workers and communities in corporate resource allocation decisions.

Conclusions

The discussion in this chapter shows that corporate decisions are a critical ingredient for productivity growth. Corporate decisions tend to overemphasize short-run speculative investments over long-term investments, potentially hampering long-term growth.

Better definitions of long-term performance measures and reducing existing short-run biases could create a better balance between short-term and long-term investors. These goals could be pursued in a variety of ways. One is through federal legislation, for example by extending the recently enacted financial regulatory reform legislation to include all public corporations. Then there's federal regulation, which could require greater disclosure requirements or listing requirements for publicly held companies. And tax policy could offer long-term investments favorable tax treatment relative to short-term speculative activities.

But public policy can only set the framework for long-term investors to act more effectively in the corporate governance realm. Long-term investors will have to take the initiative afforded to them by new policy initiatives. This means defining long-term performance measures, coordinating with other long-term investors, acting on long-term goals and possibly engaging on new policy initiatives. Policy alone cannot change the *de facto* corporate governance balance towards longer-term investments and faster productivity growth.

References

Adams, E. and J. Matheson. 2000. "A Statutory Model for Corporate Constituency Concerns," *Emory Law Journal* 49(4): 1085–135.

Aguilar, L. 2009. "Speech by SEC Commissioner: Remarks at the Investment Company Institute's Board of Governors' Winter Meeting." Washington, DC: Securities and Exchange Commission.

Bebchuk, L. and J. Fried. 2005. "Pay Without Performance: Overview of the Issues," *Journal of Applied Corporate Finance* 17 (4): 8–23.

Bebchuk, L. and E. Kamar. 2010. "Bundling and Entrenchment." Harvard Law School, Discussion Paper, No. 659.

Bebchuk, L. and M. Weisman. 2009. "The State of Corporate Governance." Harvard Law School, NBER Working Paper, No. 15537.

Black, B. 1998, "Shareholder Activism and Corporate Governance in the United States," *The New Palgrave Dictionary of Economics and the Law* 3: 459–65.

Blair, M. 2008. "Testimony on American Decline or Renewal," testimony before the House Committee on Science and Technology, May 22. Washington, DC: Vanderbilt University Law School.

Blouin, J. and L. Krull. 2007. *Bringing it Home: A Study of the Incentives Surrounding the Repatriation of Foreign Earnings under the American Jobs Creation Act of 2004.* Unpublished manuscript, Wharton School, University of Pennsylvania, Philadelphia, PA.

Board of Governors, Federal Reserve System. 2012. *Release Z.1 Flow of Funds Accounts of the United States.* Washington, DC: BOG.

Brav, A., W. Jiang, F. Partnoy and R. Thomas. 2008. "Hedge Fund Activism, Corporate Governance, and Firm Performance," *Journal of Finance* 63 (4): 1729–75.

Brynjolfsson, E., A. McAfee, M. Sorell and F. Zhu. 2007. "Scale without Mass: Business Process Replication and Industry Dynamic," Harvard Business School Working Papers, 7–16.

2010. *National Income and Product Accounts 2010.* Washington, DC: Department of Commerce.

Bureau of Economic Analysis. 2012. *National Income and Product Accounts.* Washington, DC: BEA.

Bureau of Labor Statistics. 2012. *Productivity.* Washington, DC: BLS.

CalPERS. 2009. *Comment Letter to Elizabeth Murphy, Secretary, and Commissioners, Securities and Exchange Commission.* Sacramento, CA: California Public Employee Retirement System.

2012. *Towards Sustainable Investment: Taking Responsibility.* Sacramento, CA: California Public Employee Retirement System.

Cernich, C., S. Fenn, M. Anderson, and S. Westcott. 2009. *Effectiveness of Hybrid Boards.* Washington, DC: IRRC Institute.

Choi, S. and J. Fisch. 2008. "On Beyond CalPERS: Survey Evidence on the Developing Role of Public Pension Funds in Corporate Governance," *Vanderbilt Law Review* 51 (2): 315–54.

Congressional Research Service. 2010. *Summary: H.R. 4173 Wall Street Reform and Consumer Protection Act*. Washington, DC: Library of Congress, Congressional Research Service.

Council of Institutional Investors. 2005. *Portfolio Risk Reduction and Performance Enhancement: A Spectrum of Activism Practices for Institutional Investors*. Washington, DC: CII.

  2010. *Getting Involved in Corporate Governance: A Guide for Institutional Investors*. Washington, DC: CII.

Cox, C. 2006. "Testimony of Christopher Cox, Chairman of US Securities and Exchange Commission, 'Options Backdating,'" *Testimony before the Senate Committee on Banking, Housing, and Urban Affairs*, September 6. Washington, DC: SEC.

Dobbs, R. and T. Koller. 2005. "Measuring Long-Term Performance," *McKinsey Quarterly. 2005 Special Edition: Value and Performance*, 2005: 16–27.

Gaspar, J., M. Massa and P. Matos. 2005. "Shareholder Investment Horizons and the Market for Corporate Control," *Journal of Financial Economics* 76 (1): 135–65.

Gillan, S. and L. Starks. 2007. "The Evolution of Shareholder Activism in the United States" *Journal of Applied Corporate Finance* 19 (1): 55–73.

Glassman, C. 2006. "Corporate Governance in the United States," *Remarks before the ECGI/ALI 2006 Transatlantic Corporate Governance Conference*, June 27.

Gordon, J. 2006. "The Rise of Independent Directors in the United States: 1950–2005: of Shareholder Value and Stock Market Prices." ECGI – Law Working Paper No. 74/2006; Columbia Law and Economics Working Paper No. 301.

Gordon, R. 2012. "Is US Economic Growth Over? Faltering Innovation Confronts Six Headwinds," NBER Working Paper No. 18315, National Bureau of Economic Research.

Gordon, R. and I. Dew-Becker. 2005. "Where Did All the Productivity Go? Inflation Dynamics and the Distribution of Income," *Brookings Papers on Economic Activity* 2: 67–127.

Graham, J., C. Harvey and S. Rajgopal. 2005. "The Economic Implications of Corporate Financial Reporting," *Journal of Accounting and Economics* 40: 3–73.

Hawley, J., K. Johnson and E. Waitzer. 2011. "Reclaiming Fiduciary Duty Balance," *International Journal of Pension Management* 4 (2): 4–16.

Heron, R. and E. Lie. 2009. "What Fraction of Stock Option Grants to Top Executives Have Been Backdated or Manipulated?" *Management Science* 55 (4): 513–25.

Hudson, R. 1982. "SEC Eases Way for Repurchase of Firms' Stock," *Wall Street Journal*, November 10.

Jensen, M., K. Murphy and E. Wruck. 2004. "Remuneration: Where We've Been, How We Got to Here, What are the Problems, and How to Fix Them," Harvard NOM Research Paper No. 04–28; ECGI-Finance Working Paper No. 44/2004.

Jolls, C. 1998. "Stock Repurchases and Incentive Compensation," NBER Working Paper No. 6467, National Bureau of Economic Research.

Jorgenson, D., M. Ho and K. Stiroh. 2005. *Information Technology and the American Growth Resurgence*. Cambridge, MA: MIT Press.

Kahan, M. and E. Rock. 2007. "Hedge Funds in Corporate Governance and Corporate Control," *University of Pennsylvania Law Review* 155: 1021–93.

Kahn, J. and R. Rich. 2006. "Tracking Productivity in Real Time," *Current Issues in Economics and Finance* 12 (8).

Klein, A. and E. Zur. 2008. "Entrepreneurial Shareholder Activism: Hedge Funds and Other Private Investors," *Journal of Finance* 64 (1): 187–229.

Kuschnik, B. 2008. "The Sarbanes Oxley Act: 'Big Brother is Watching You' or Adequate Measures of Corporate Governance," *Rutgers Business Law Journal* 5: 64–95.

Lazonick, W. 2009. *Sustainable Prosperity in the New Economy? Business Organization and High-Tech Employment in the United States*. Kalamazoo: W. E. Upjohn Institute.

McCracken, J. and K. Scannell. 2009. "Fight Brews as Proxy Access Nears," *Wall Street Journal*, August 26.

Monks, R. and N. Minow. 2001. *Power and Accountability*. New York: Harper Business.

Oliner, S., D. Sichel and K. Stiroh. 2007. "Explaining a Productive Decade," *Brookings Papers on Economic Activity* 1: 81–137.

O'Sullivan, M. 2000. "The Innovative Enterprise and Corporate Governance," *Cambridge Journal of Economics* 24 (4): 393–416.

2003. *Contest for Corporate Control: Corporate Governance and Economic Performance in United States and Germany*. New York: Oxford University Press.

Principles for Responsible Investing. 2012. *Annual Report 2012*.

Rappaport, A. 2005. "The Economics of Short-Term Performance Obsession," *Financial Analysts Journal* 61 (3): 65–79.

Securities and Exchange Commission. 2009a. "Staff Legal Bulletin No. 14E (CF)," Washington, DC: SEC.

2009b. "Proxy Disclosure Enhancement," *Fed. Reg.* 70 (245): 68334.

Shiller, R. and J. Campbell. 2005. "Valuation Ratios and the Long Run Stock Market Outlook: An Update," in R. H. Thaler (ed.) *Advances in Behavioral Finance II*. Princeton University Press.

Singer, J. W. 1993. "Jobs and Justice: Rethinking the Stakeholder Debate," *Toronto Law Review* 43 (3): 475–505.

Smith, M. 1996. "Shareholder Activism by Institutional Investors: Evidence from CalPERS," *Journal of Finance* 51 (1): 227–52.

Spencer Stuart. 2010. *Spencer Stuart Board Index (SSBI)*. New York: Spencer Stuart.

Taub, J. 2009a. "Able But Not Willing: The Failure of Mutual Fund Advisors to Advocate for Shareholders' Rights," *Journal of Corporation Law* 34 (3): 349–76.

2009b. "It's a Wonderful Lie: Mutual Fund Advocacy for Shareholders' Rights, Part 2,"

The Race to the Bottom, August 17. www.theracetothebottom.org.

The Conference Board. 2009. "The 2009 Institutional Investment Report," New York: The Conference Board.

Thomas, R. 2008. "The Evolving Role of Institutional Investors in Corporate Governance and Corporate Litigation," *Vanderbilt Law Review* 61 (2).

Wahal, S. 1996. "Pension Fund Activism and Firm Performance," *Journal of Financial and Quantitative Analysis* 31 (1): 1–23.

Ward, A., J. Brown and S. Graffin. 2009. "Under the Spotlight: Institutional Investors and Firm Responses to the Council of Institutional Investors' Annual Focus List," *Strategic Organization* 7: 107.

Weller, C. 2000. "Understanding the Challenges and Opportunities of Increased Shareholder Activism for Workers," *Proceedings of the 52nd Annual Meeting of the IRRA, Boston, MA, January 7–9*, Champaign-Urbana, IL: IRRA.

Weller, C. and J. Bivens. 2005. "The Causes of the 'Job Loss' Recovery," *Challenge*, March–April.

Weller, C. and L. Reidenbach. 2011. "On Uneven Ground: How Corporate Governance Prioritizes Short-term Speculative Investments, Impedes Productive Investments, and Jeopardizes Productivity Growth," *Challenge* 54 (3): 5–37.

Weller, C. and D. White. 2001. "The New Kid on the Block: Unions are Playing their Institutional Investor Card," *Social Policy* 31 (3): 46–52.

Yan X. and Z. Zhang. 2009. "Institutional Investors and Equity Returns: Are Short-term Institutions Better Informed?" *Review of Financial Studies* 22 (2): 893–924.

Fulfilling fiduciary duties in an imperfect world – governance recommendations from the Stanford Institutional Investor Forum

CHRISTOPHER W. WADDELL

Introduction

From the perspective of a full-time practitioner in US pension and fiduciary law, debate and discussion over the future direction of the law of fiduciary duty and/or the governance structures of pension funds is extremely important. However, in the here and now, under existing fiduciary duty and plan governance constructs, US public pension board members and their staffs are making decisions concerning complex issues that affect the retirement security of more than 28 million Americans covered by public sector defined benefit plans (US Census Bureau and Becker-Medina 2012). They are often doing so in a highly charged environment. While many US systems are well-funded, in a significant number of highly publicized cases systems face the unprecedented twin challenges of coping with unfunded liabilities resulting from market conditions not seen since the Great Depression coupled with plan sponsors that are under tremendous financial pressure to maintain essential public services in the face of declining revenues and are not in the position to provide the increased employer contributions necessary to restore fiscal stability to the funds. Making things even more difficult is the drumbeat of those who would benefit either politically or financially from the demise of defined benefit pension plans for US public employees.

The overwhelming majority of the approximately $2.7 trillion held by 3,400 US state and local public pension plans (ibid.) is managed by lay boards consisting of from seven to thirteen individuals that come to their position by one of three ways: they are either appointed by the plan sponsor, elected from the plan membership or are "ex officio" members that become a member of the pension board because they have been elected or appointed to another public office, such as state treasurer (National Association of State Retirement Administrators 2013). In meetings that are generally open to the public, save for matters involving litigation, personnel or (sometimes) investment matters, these boards consider, discuss and act upon the plan administration, investment and actuarial matters that bear directly upon the system's ultimate objective of ensuring that sufficient plan assets are available to provide for the prompt and accurate payment of benefits to their existing and future retirees.

For most of these systems, the essential governance structure (board construct, qualifications, etc.) is set forth in state or local statute. Frequently, key aspects of the governance structure are provided for either in state constitutional or local city or county charter provisions that may only be changed by a vote of the applicable electorate. As such, the boards of US public pension systems lack control over significant governance issues such as the number of board members, their qualifications and so forth. While boards can and sometimes do choose to become involved in the legislative or electoral process relating to their governance structure, because they are public entities such participation is subject to constitutional limits on the expenditure of public funds for political purposes. As a result, ultimately they must "work within the system" that is determined for them by some combination of the plan sponsor and the general electorate.

While it has been argued that this political overlay is inconsistent with effective pension plan governance, its existence is hardly surprising given the US tradition of representative democracy and the large pools of money involved. Given such dynamics, proposals to shift the governance of US public pension plans from lay boards that reflect a diverse stakeholder base to so-called "expert" boards partially if not entirely comprised of those with backgrounds in investments, finance and/or actuarial matters, with few exceptions, have not found immediate traction. Proposals to change public pension board composition to include individuals with investment expertise have been attacked in some instances as a move to decrease pension member (employee/retiree) influence over system governance.[1] And experience has shown that getting such experts to serve on boards that are regularly in the public eye, require public disclosure of personal financial interests (including client relationships) and provide little or no trustee compensation can be difficult.

It is likely that the governance of US public pension funds will, at least for the foreseeable future, remain primarily in the hands of lay boards. How, then, should such boards organize their governance structures so as to ensure compliance with their fiduciary duties? Trustees do not calculate and pay benefits or manage investment portfolios. Instead, the principal function of a public pension fund trustee in the US is to work with his/her peers on the board to establish the strategic direction of the system, to hire the necessary staff and consultants with the expertise necessary to carry out that direction and administer the system on a day-to-day basis, and then to oversee the work being done to ensure that the board's direction is carried out. For the most part, board competency involves a different skill set than those of professional investment manager, actuary or auditor.

All boards benefit from diversity of member backgrounds and experience, and under the right circumstances it is helpful for some members to have a pre-existing familiarity with pension administration and/or investment matters. Irrespective of whether a board member comes into the position with a given level of experience in pension or investment matters, once they are on the dais all board members are subject to the same standards of fiduciary conduct. In the United States, through some combination of provisions in applicable state or local law, plan documents and/or the common law of trusts, trustee fiduciary conduct is evaluated primarily under the duties of care and loyalty.

The duty of care

In fulfilling its responsibilities, a public pension board must act with the "care, skill, prudence and diligence under the circumstances then prevailing that a prudent person acting in a like capacity and familiar with these matters would use in the conduct of an enterprise of a like character and with like aims."[2] The focus is on the conduct of the fiduciary and the extent of his/her diligent investigation and performance of acts consistent with the specific purpose and circumstances of the plan. This is referred to as "procedural prudence." In the context of an investment transaction, the duty has been described as follows:

> the ultimate outcome of the investment is not the yardstick by which the prudence of the fiduciary is measured; the court must consider the conduct of the fiduciary not the success of the investment, and the court must evaluate the fiduciary's conduct at the time of the investment decision rather than from the vantage point of hindsight.[3]

---

[1] *Panel Discussion on Composition of Public Pension Boards*, California State Teachers' Retirement System, Board Governance Committee, November 3, 2011 meeting, Item Number 3.

[2] See, for example, Cal. Const. Art. 16 §17. A broader discussion of the fiduciary duties applicable to US public pension plans may be found at www.nctr.org/pdf/INTROPrtctgRetMoney.pdf.

[3] *GIW Industries, Inc.* v. *Trevor, Steward, Burton & Jacobsen, Inc.*, 11 Employee Benefits Case, (BNA) 2737 (11th Cir. 1990).

Comment d. to Sec. 227 of the *Restatement (Third) of Trusts* summarizes these objective criteria for a trustee's conduct:

> The trustee must give reasonably careful consideration to both the formulation and the implementation of an appropriate investment strategy, with investments to be selected and reviewed in a manner reasonably related to that strategy. Ordinarily this involves obtaining relevant information about such matters as the circumstances and requirements of the trust and its beneficiaries, the contents and resources of the trust estate, and the nature and characteristics of available investment alternatives. To the extent necessary or appropriate to the making of informed investment judgments by the particular trustee, care also involves securing and considering the advice of others on a reasonable basis.

Application of this standard is not a "one size fits all" process. One commentator has observed that:

> Retirement systems differ on a wide variety of parameters and the prudence standard is sensitive to factors such as the size, complexity, and purpose of each system. Fiduciaries should be evaluated, not against a single prudent expert, but in terms of the actions of prudent fiduciaries for other systems facing similar circumstances.[4]

The duty of loyalty

A fiduciary's duty of loyalty is generated by an agreement to enter into a fiduciary relationship. In California, for example, a public pension fund trustee manifests that "agreement" by acceptance of their appointment.[5] Perhaps the most famous description of the duty of loyalty was written by Chief Judge (later Supreme Court Justice) Benjamin Cardozo, who stated:

> A trustee is held to something stricter than the morals of the market place. Not honesty alone, but the punctilio[6] of an honor the most sensitive,

is then the standard of behavior. As to this there has developed a tradition that is unbending and inveterate.

Uncompromising rigidity has been the attitude of courts of equity when petitioned to undermine the rule of undivided loyalty by the "disintegrating erosion" of particular exceptions. Only thus has the level of conduct for fiduciaries been kept at a level higher than that trodden by the crowd.[7]

Put more simply (albeit less eloquently) the duty of loyalty requires a board member to abstain from harming the interests of system members and beneficiaries by doing any of the following:

- Acting in the fiduciary's own interests (duty to refrain from self-dealing).
- Acting in the interests of a third party (for example, the employer and/or the plan sponsor.
- Acting in a way that favors the interests of one group of members/beneficiaries over those of another group (duty of impartiality).

The duty of loyalty is the "most fundamental" of fiduciary duties.[8] Laby (2004) has posited that, in the language of philosopher Immanuel Kant, the duty of loyalty is a "perfect" negative duty not to harm the interests of the beneficiaries to whom the fiduciary owns the duty. Such duty is unambiguous and "permits no exception in the interest of inclination" (ibid.: 106–7). Conversely, Laby characterizes the duty of care as a positive duty to act for the benefit of beneficiaries that is "open-ended," "uncertain" and "judgment-based" (ibid.: 120–2). As an "imperfect duty" under Kant's theory, Laby concludes that the duty of care is incremental and in situations where following the duty of care may harm beneficiary interests this creates conflict with the duty of loyalty, which must take precedence (ibid.: 124–5).

Duty of impartiality

The duty of impartiality has been described as follows:

---

[4] Uniform Management of Public Retirement Systems Act (1997), drafted by the National Conference of Commissioners on Uniform State Laws, 415 PLI/Tax 439, 466.

[5] *Hittle* v. *Santa Barbara County Employees Retirement Association*, 39 Cal. 3d 374 (1985), pp. 392–3.

[6] A minute detail of conduct in observance of a code. Merriam Webster Online Dictionary.

[7] *Meinhard* v. *Salman*, 249 NY 458, 464, 164 NE (1928), pp. 545–6.

[8] In Re Enron Corp. Securities, Derivative & ERISA Litigation (2003) 284 F. Supp. 2d, pp. 511, 546.

The duty of impartiality … derives from the duty of loyalty. A fiduciary for a retirement system owes a duty of loyalty to all participants and beneficiaries; respecting that duty requires the fiduciary to be impartial among any differing interests of participants and beneficiaries. The duty is well-recognized in trust law. Restatement of Trusts 2d Sections 183, 232; Uniform Prudent Investor Act Section 6.

Differing interests are inevitable in the retirement system setting. Differences can arise between retirees and working members, young members and old, long-and short-term employees, and other groupings of those with interests in the retirement system. The duty of impartiality does not mean that fiduciaries must accommodate such interests according to some notion of absolute equality. The duty of impartiality permits a fiduciary to favor the interests of one group of participants and beneficiaries over another in particular circumstances, but requires that such decisions be made carefully and after weighing the differing interests.[9]

What do these duties mean in practical terms for pension fund trustees? From a legal perspective, one question is what happens if a given issue requiring a decision results in a conflict between the duties of care and loyalty, i.e., when following the duty of care would yield one course of action while following the duty of loyalty would result in another. As noted above, Laby (2004) is of the view that the duty of loyalty takes precedence. He went on to analyze a number of cases in several areas of fiduciary law and determined that courts' resolutions to cases where the duty of loyalty and care conflicted could be accounted for by the principle that the "absolute" duty of loyalty "would not permit exceptions to provide an incremental benefit to be obtained … The duty of loyalty prevails over the duty of care as the fiduciary first must 'do no harm'" (ibid.: 125). At least one jurisdiction, California, makes this a constitutional imperative: "A retirement board's duty to its participants and their beneficiaries shall take precedence over any other duty."[10] Another question faced by pension fund trustees in light of these duties is what factors

should they be concerned with as they exercise their decision-making authority? The next section attempts to address this question.

The duties of care and loyalty as manifested in the board room

In the US, public pension boards typically meet on a regular basis, usually but not always monthly, to address the full range of issues involved in administering a pension system. The most important and sensitive issues include, but are not limited to, matters such as: determining the system's investment plan, including asset allocation; adopting actuarial assumptions that are fundamental to evaluating the financial health of the system and to setting plan sponsor contribution rates; selecting key service providers, such as consultants, investment managers, the system actuary and the system's outside auditor; and selecting and monitoring the performance of key executives such as the chief executive officer and chief investment officer. Ultimately, these issues require a trustee to cast a vote. What questions should a trustee ask his/herself in order to be satisfied that this vote is compliant with applicable fiduciary duties?

The California Public Employees Retirement System (CalPERS 2012) recently asked itself this very question and settled on the following:

1. Do the agenda materials and presentation/discussion at the meeting provide all of the information necessary for a proper understanding of the issue so that we can make a sound, informed decision?
2. Have all of the potential benefits and risks resulting from this decision been appropriately identified and analyzed?
3. Have all viable alternatives to this proposal been appropriately identified and analyzed?
4. Are staff and the outside expert (where applicable) in agreement on the recommended course of action?
    *   If not, are the bases for disagreement adequately explained?
    *   Are both recommendations reasonable (so that I can reasonably choose/decide between them), or do we need to seek another opinion?

[9] Uniform Management of Public Employee Retirement Systems Act (1997), 415 PLI/Tax 439, pp. 467–8 (citations omitted).
[10] Cal. Const. Art. 16, sec. 17(b).

5. Were any questions that we had before and during the discussion of the item sufficiently addressed?

6. Do I have any actual or potential conflicts of interest that prevent me from participating in this decision or make it advisable for me not to do so?

7. Does my intended vote reflect what I feel to be in the best interests of the system's members, beneficiaries and retirees as a whole, without regard to the interests of any constituency or appointing power responsible for my position as a board member?

8. Will the results of the board's decision favor the interests of one group of the system's members, beneficiaries or retirees over those of another group?

A review of these questions suggests that they are structured to address both the duty of care (#1–5) and the duty of loyalty (#6–8). From my twin perspectives as a practitioner of fiduciary law and a former public pension board member, these are the right questions. How, then, do we place trustees in a position to be able to ask them and, more importantly, be able to answer them competently and confidently? In my view, the solution lies in large part on the development, implementation and oversight of best practice governance policies. Such policies can: (1) clarify the roles and responsibilities of board members, staff and outside consultants and thereby provide a sound framework for effective decision-making; (2) define the system's expectations with respect to board member attributes and core competencies; (3) establish an educational curriculum designed to help trustees develop and maintain these attributes and core competencies; and (4) through the adoption of strong conflict of interest and disclosure provisions, provide deterrence against bad conduct.

The Clapman Report

In 2007, the Committee on Fund Governance of the Stanford Institutional Investors' Forum, chaired by Peter Clapman, retired senior vice-president and chief counsel for TIAA-CREF, issued a report recommending five best practice governance principles for pension, endowment and charitable funds.

Membership of the committee consisted of current and former representatives of large public and private institutional investors as well as academic and corporate governance practitioners. They were motivated by then-recent governance failures at several prominent private and public institutional investors, which raised concerns about the lack of adequate fiduciary protections on the one hand, and the potential for burdensome regulation on the other.

The report recommended best practice principles in the following areas:

- Transparency of a fund's rules and governance structure.
- A fund's leadership: the governing body and executive staff.
- Trustee attributes and core competencies.
- Approach to addressing conflicts of interest and related disclosure policy.
- Delegation of duties and allocation of responsibilities among relevant authorities.

The report summarized each of the five principles as follows:

1. **Transparency of a fund's rules and governance structure**
   - A fund should **clearly define** and make publicly available its **governance rules ...**
2. **A fund's leadership: the governing body and executive staff**
   - A fund should **identify and disclose its leadership structure** and all persons in positions of senior responsibility.
   - A governing body should **consist of appropriately qualified, experienced individuals** dedicated to fulfilling their fiduciary duties to fund beneficiaries.
   - A governing body should **promote policies that strengthen fiduciary principles in the selection and monitoring of trustees** and that enable trustees to fulfill their fiduciary responsibilities. When trustees are elected to a board to represent a class of fund beneficiaries, the elected trustee should take reasonable steps to acquire the skills to serve appropriately as a fiduciary.
   - A fund should **establish clear lines of authority** between its governing body and

its staff that reflect a commitment to representing beneficiary interests. Delegations of authority from a governing body to its staff should be clearly defined and regularly reviewed.

- A governing body should have **authority to select or dismiss key staff** and independent advisors and counsel. Trustees should establish regular processes by which staff performance is measured. The standards governing staff evaluation should be clearly communicated to the staff ...

3. **Trustee attributes and core competencies**

- Each trustee should **have a thorough understanding of the fund's obligations** to its beneficiaries, the fund's economic position and strategy, and its relevant governing principles. Each trustee must be able to make decisions based solely on the objective requirements of the trustees' fiduciary duties to fund beneficiaries. Each trustee should be inquisitive and should appropriately question staff, advisors, and fellow trustees as circumstances require. Each trustee should also contribute to a balanced set of skills that enables the board, acting as a collective body, to execute successfully its obligations.
- The board should at all times **include individuals with investment and financial market expertise** and experience relevant to the fund's ability to exercise its fiduciary obligations to its beneficiaries.
- Trustees, on a regular basis, should **obtain education that provides and improves core competencies,** and that assists them in remaining current with regard to their evolving obligations as fiduciaries.
- Trustees should be able **to obtain intelligible explanations** of recommended actions from staff, advisors, or colleagues.
- The fund should **engage in an annual evaluation of trustee skills** and, where appropriate, should develop a plan for improving and expanding the board's competencies ...

4. **Approach to addressing conflicts of interest and related disclosure policy**

- A fund should establish and publicly disclose its policy for dealing effectively and openly with situations that raise either an actual conflict of interest or the potential for the appearance of a conflict of interest. A fund should clearly identify the persons subject to its conflict policy ("covered persons") and should provide appropriate training to those covered persons.
- In order for a conflict of interest policy to be effective, appropriate authorities with the ability to act independently of any potential conflict must have access to information that adequately describes trustee and staff interests and relationships that could, at a minimum, give rise to an appearance of impropriety. A fund should therefore establish a regular, automatic process that requires all covered persons to report and disclose actual or potential conflicts of interest.
- Trustees and staff should periodically affirm and verify compliance with conflict rules, regulatory reporting requirements, and other policies intended to protect the fund against the actuality or appearance of self-interested transactions and conflicts.
- Trustees and staff should under no circumstances pressure anyone, whether or not a covered person, to engage in a transaction that creates an actual conflict or an appearance of impropriety. Trustees and staff should be required to disclose any such attempts to a proper compliance authority as determined by the board.
- A fund should publicly disclose necessary information as specified below to ensure that trustees and staff are fulfilling their fiduciary duties to beneficiaries ...

5. **Delegation of duties and allocation of responsibilities among relevant authorities**

- A governing body should be **permitted to rely on the expertise and advice of appropriately selected and unconflicted consultants and staff**. Trustees should also be permitted to delegate responsibilities, subject to appropriate oversight, to unconflicted consultants and staff.
- A fund should **require that any consultants or staff** from material advice is requested or received, or to whom material responsibility

is delegated, **comply with the funds conflict of interest and ethics policies.**

- A fund **should institute an evaluation process that assesses proposed fund expenditures** and weighs the benefits to fund beneficiaries generated by those expenditures against the cost and quality of the service for which funds are expended.
- A fund should **establish an effective and objective monitoring policy for all service contracts** including those for asset manager and investment consultants (Committee on Fund Governance 2007: 6–17, emphasis in original).

The Clapman Report's recommendations provided an important benchmark for large institutional investors, including public pension funds, against which to assess the scope and strength of their existing governance structure and policies. Many US public pension systems used the report as a reference point for updating their own governance policies. However, developing such policies "from scratch" involves a significant commitment of personnel and financial resources that may not always be within the means of systems with budgetary constraints on hiring internal staff and/or engaging outside governance consultants.

The AFSCME Report

Because of that concern, and a desire to enhance the retirement security not only of its own members but of public employees and retirees generally, the American Federation of State, County and Municipal Employees (AFSCME) commissioned a study of the governance policies of leading US public pension funds. Its report, entitled *Enhancing Public Retiree Pension Plan Security: Best Practice Policies for Trustees and Pension Systems* (AFSCME 2009) focused on the Clapman Report's recommendations in the areas of trustee core competencies and addressing conflicts of interest, and includes recommended best practice policy language in the areas of board member responsibilities and core competencies; board member education; and ethical and fiduciary conduct.

One thesis of the AFSCME report is that pension boards comprised of trustees that understand their responsibilities and possess the requisite core competencies will be able to evaluate effectively the complex issues presented to them and be much more immune to efforts made by those who would have them make decisions that are not in the best interest of the members, retirees and beneficiaries of the system. The AFSCME model policies follow the recommendations of the original 2007 Clapman Report, and are designed to ensure that each trustee has a thorough understanding of the funds obligations to its beneficiaries, its economic position and investment strategy and its relevant governing principles. For example, the recommended policies describe responsibilities and competencies such as inquisitiveness, integrity, collegiality and independence. The policies further specify requisite areas of knowledge such as:

- public pension plan governance;
- asset allocation and investment management;
- actuarial principles and funding policies;
- financial reporting, controls and audits;
- benefits administration;
- vendor selection;
- open meeting and public records laws;
- fiduciary responsibility; and
- ethics and conflicts of interest.

Tied to this is a board member education policy that, following the principles of the Clapman Report, "provides and improves core competencies, and that assists them in remaining current with regard to their evolving obligations as fiduciaries" (Committee on Fund Governance 2007: 10). While the AFSCME Report observed that abundant educational opportunities exist for pension trustees, it is important that such education be tied to developing the requisite knowledge, skills and abilities, and referring to previous research (Por and Ianucci 2001), noted that many existing programs "focus on investments," and that such programs as a rule "neither encourage trustees to develop the broad vision they need to set policy, nor do they provide the practical grounding a board needs to oversee a fund's operations" (AFSCME 2009: 6).

The comprehensive education policy recommended by the AFSCME report includes:

- an orientation process and curricula for new board members;
- a mentoring process for new board members;
- a general curriculum for trustees in the first and second years of service;
- ongoing training in areas such as fiduciary responsibility and conflicts of interest;
- a trustee self-assessment tool to enable trustees to identify their own areas of educational need, enabling them to work with system staff to obtain training that is targeted to their individual needs.

Following the recommendations of the Clapman Report, after extensive research the AFSCME Report also provided a comprehensive set of policy language addressing the area of ethical and fiduciary conduct. The language covers ten areas, including but not limited to fiduciary duties, ethical conduct, receipt of gifts policy, no contact/disclosure of communications, limitations on campaign contributions by system vendors and disclosure of placement agent relationships. One novel recommendation of the report is that current and former board members be permanently banned from providing placement agent services in connection with their system. AFSCME developed this recommendation as an alternative to the complete ban on placement agent activity with public pension systems that was then under consideration. In AFSCME's view, its policy proposal targeted more specifically the potential for abuse and/or undue influence when a current or former board or staff member seeks, on behalf of a client investment manager, an investment relationship with his or her former system. One of AFSCME's stated goals in developing its report was to provide a "one-stop-shopping" approach combining all potentially applicable laws, rules and policies into one place in order to facilitate "a comprehensive analysis of an issue or concern" so as to minimize the potential for inadvertent wrongful conduct (ibid.: 8).

The AFSCME Report served as a reference in the development by the Governance Finance Officers Association (GFOA) of their 2010 best practice recommendations for "Governance of Public Employee Post-Retirement Benefits Systems." The GFOA recommended the establishment of "rules of governance for … post-retirement benefit systems that define the key elements necessary for trustees and other fiduciaries to fulfill their fiduciary responsibilities, in accordance with fiduciary standards" (GFOA 2010). GFOA recommended the following as best practices:

- The adoption and maintenance of a written governance manual, including the authority under which the system operates, the roles and responsibilities of the board, administrator and staff, all board policies and applicable statutes and regulations, committee structure and charter.
- An optimal size of governing boards between seven and thirteen, composed of members with a mix of skills, competencies and behaviors that includes plan participants and retirees, citizens, plan sponsor officers and independent members that participate in specified orientation and education.
- Governance policies including a code of ethics, succession planning, investment policy, contracting for professional services and monitoring of governance policies.

The Clapman 2.0 Report

The GFOA recommendations align not only with the recommendations of the AFSCME Report but more broadly with the five areas addressed by the Clapman Report. Within the same timeframe, Peter Clapman felt that sufficient time had passed that an updating and refreshing of the original report was warranted. The Committee on Fund Governance of the Stanford Institutional Investors' Forum was reconvened, including a mix of original and new committee members. The Committee's goal was to provide recommended policy language and governance tools for all five or the areas covered by the original report. Building on the recommendations of the AFSCME report, the "Clapman 2.0 Report," first released in July 2012, provided recommendations for the three areas not addressed in the AFSCME report: (1) transparency of a fund's rules and governing structure; 2) fund leadership – the governing body and executive staff; and (3) delegation of duties and allocation of responsibilities among relevant authorities. In addition, Clapman 2.0 updated the recommendations of the AFSCME Report in the areas of board member core competencies/education and conflicts of interest where appropriate given intervening developments such as the SEC's adoption of "pay-to-play" regulations.

Source material for these recommended policies was obtained from a number of US state and local pension funds that have devoted considerable time and effort to governance issues. The Clapman 2.0 Report identifies a number of issues and concerns that a board must address in drafting governance documents that identify clear lines of decision-making authority, including the roles and responsibilities of the board, its leadership, board committees and senior management (Committee on Fund Governance 2012). A unique aspect of the report is that it includes a template for a summary of trustee duties and responsibilities that can be provided to individuals that are considering candidacy for elected trustee positions as well as to the appointing authorities of appointed trustee positions. This is a practice that had already been adopted by some systems, and is designed to ensure that prospective trustees approach potential office with "eyes wide open" with respect to the demands and responsibilities of the position. The template articulates not just the time demands of preparation and attendance at board and committee meetings but also includes a discussion of fiduciary responsibility, the commitment necessary to participate in necessary education and training, and the obligation to file public statements of financial interests pursuant to applicable conflict of interest laws.

Significantly, in the area of conflicts of interest the Clapman 2.0 Report addresses the importance of "tone at the top" to the effectiveness of a system's ethics policies. As noted in the discussion of fiduciary duties applicable to US public pension funds, the duty of loyalty includes a prohibition on self-dealing. Similarly, the common denominator to all conflicts of interest and disclosure policies is the prevention of various forms of self-dealing. Therefore, effective conflict of interest and disclosure policies serve not only to ensure compliance with federal, state and local laws but also align with the trustees' ultimate fiduciary obligations. The Report cites research by the Center for Audit

Quality (2010: 10) that "tone at the top" cascades down through the entire organization to create a "mood in the middle" and a "buzz at the bottom" that reflects and reinforces an organization's operating values. The Center further notes that:

> A strong ethical culture creates an expectation to "do the right thing" and counteracts pressure and incentives to commit fraud. An ethical culture also supports well-designed, effective controls that diminish opportunities for fraud and increase the likelihood that fraud will be detected quickly. In addition, a culture of honesty and integrity severely limits an individual's ability to rationalize fraudulent actions (ibid.: vi).

A common theme of the past high-profile scandals affecting a handful of US public pension funds is that the personal failings of a single board member or member of a system's senior management can undermine the system's ethical culture and open the door to devastating harm that can take years and large sums of money to fix. As observed in the Clapman 2.0 Report, a strong ethical culture supported by sound policies serves both to deter such conduct and enhance the likelihood that potential wrongdoers are caught before any harm is done.

Conclusions

Best practice governance policies can provide US public pension funds with the foundation necessary to ensure that fund trustees are fulfilling their responsibilities in a manner that is fully compliant with applicable fiduciary duties. The original Clapman Report, as augmented by the ensuing AFSCME and Clapman 2.0 Reports, provide a template for the consideration and adoption by US systems of such policies.

References

AFSCME. 2009. *Enhancing Public Retiree Pension Plan Security: Best Practice Policies for Trustees and Pension Systems.* Washington, DC: AFSCME. www.afscme.org/news/publications/for-leaders/pdf/AFSCME-report-pension-best-practices.pdf.

CalPERS. 2012. "Fiduciary Duty Questions for CalPERS Board Members," Fiduciary Training Workshop, December 7.

Center for Audit Quality. 2010. *Deterring and Detecting Financial Reporting Fraud: A Platform for Action*. Washington, DC: Center for Audit Quality.

Committee on Fund Governance. 2007. *Best Practice Principles*. Stanford Institutional Investors' Forum. www.directorsandboards. com/DBEBRIEFING/July2007/ FundGovernanceReport.pdf.

Committee on Fund Governance. 2012. *Clapman Report 2.0: Model Governance Provisions to Support Pension Fund Best Principles*. Stanford Institutional Investors' Forum. www.law. stanford.edu/sites/default/files/event/392911/ media/slspublic/ClapmanReport_6-6-13.pdf.

GFOA. 2010. "Governance of Public Employee Post-Retirement Benefits Systems." www.gfoa. org/index.php?option=com_content&task=view.

Laby, A. B. 2004. "Resolving Conflicts of Duty in Fiduciary Relationships," *American University Law Review* 54: 106–25.

National Association of State Retirement Administrators. 2013. *Composition of Public Retirement System Boards*. www.nasra.org/ governance.

Por, J. and T. Ianucci. 2001. "Good Pension Governance: An Advocate's Guide for Improvement," *The NAPPA Report* 13 (5).

US Census Bureau and E. Becker-Medina. 2012. *Public-Employee Retirement Systems State- and Locally-Administered Pensions Summary Report: 2010*. Washington, DC: US Census Bureau.

Addressing the participation gap in institutional investment: an assessment framework and preliminary results

TIM CADMAN AND TEK MARASENI

Introduction

This chapter shows how fiduciary duty and the governance quality of investment can be understood using a stakeholder-based approach. In the past, stakeholders were effectively passive economic actors, who were supposed to just sit back and reap rewards. This view is increasingly being challenged by the assertion that large investors should care about governance as well as economic outcomes, and have both a right and a responsibility to ensure that assets are managed in a way that is socially and environmentally beneficial for all stakeholders. Contemporary governance theory argues for a wider understanding of stakeholders, which, in the case of investment, encompasses both financial and nonfinancial interests. This chapter examines the changing nature of "stakeholderism," and explores its tensions and contradictions, using responsible investment as a case study. A survey of stakeholders involved in responsible investment follows. The results reveal interesting views about the governance quality of some central aspects of the sector's architecture, and thus provide useful learning points for institutional investment and fiduciary duty in general.

Changing conceptions of stakeholder rights and responsibilities

It has been argued that developments in institutional governance in the wake of the 1992 Rio "Earth" Summit, with its emphasis on sustainable development, necessitate a fundamental rethink of what constitutes a "stakeholder" in investment that claims to be truly "responsible." The definition has become far more all-encompassing, and now includes non-governmental organizations (NGOs, sometime also referred to as civil society or civil society organizations – CSOs), the general public and local communities, unions, private business, ethical shareholder groups and small shareholders, as well as traditional interests such as governments, regulatory authorities and large-scale investors (Cadman 2011a). If it is accepted that the investment community is made up of a wide range of participants, from traditional "internal" interests (e.g., banks, financial advisors and asset managers) to "external" groups in civil society, and that these interests all have a "stake" in investment activities, it is necessary to look beyond "corporate" governance as a means of determining the legitimacy of current financial practice (Cadman 2011b).

A well-established literature suggests that a stakeholder-based approach can be useful in understanding the governance quality of institutional investment and fiduciary duty (Donaldson and Preston 1995; Hamilton and Erikson 2010). In the past, certain stakeholders – for example, pension funds – were not seen as central to investment decisions; this is now changing. The "universal owner" hypothesis argues that such large investors, who have a stronger role in global economic activity than individual shareholders, are more concerned with minimizing investor risk than with making a quick profit (Hawley and Williams 2000). Hence, such investors pay more attention to matters of governance, and have become active around corporate behavior and investment practices (Yaron 2003). This engagement is leading to changes in corporate behavior, as companies seek to sell themselves to responsible investors by demonstrating their environmental or social credentials. In 2005, the influential Freshfields Report argued that responsible investors could go so far as to instruct trustees to make investment decisions on environmental or social grounds, rather than strictly on financial grounds (Freshfields Bruckhaus Deringer 2005). This has had legal repercussions, because there is now some uncertainty as to whether instructions that supersede financial considerations are contrary to fiduciary duty; determinations in different jurisdictions have gone either way. As a result of these developments, commentators are beginning to prefer the term "fiduciary responsibility" to "fiduciary duty" (Richardson 2010).

Regardless of the legal issues, institutional investors and shareholders are increasingly becoming involved in the decision-making that underpins investment activities, and influencing the deliberations made by financial planners and advisors. Civil society interests, most notably NGOs, are also playing an increasing role (Ransome and Sampford 2010). Yet the role afforded to such parties is generally a passive one of being consulted about investment decisions, rather than one of active participation; thus, they are considered important only in so far as they provide knowledge that is material to such decisions. Engagement, in the sense discussed above, is usually nonexistent or indirect; and creates, in terms of internal and external interests, what is referred to in public policy as a participation gap (Fiorino 1996).

Mitchell et al.'s theory of stakeholder salience explains stakeholder relations within an organization in terms of power (extent of influence), legitimacy (degree of status or acceptance) and urgency (ability to initiate a response) (Mitchell et al. 1997). This theory helps to explain why external interests are generally considered less salient to investment decisions than internal interests, but it does not provide any suggestions as to how to address this participation gap. An examination of developments in the sphere of corporate governance can shed some light on the incipient social relationships in

contemporary investment practice. The efforts of NGOs to change the behavior of companies has, for example, resulted in improvements in the human rights record of certain companies, or led them to address issues such as climate change. Indeed, it has been suggested that improved social and environmental performance can boost financial success. External parties such as NGOs may not yet have legally enforceable claims, but trustees may nevertheless have the mandate to take third-party interests into account (Richardson 2010). Thus, responsible investment has the potential to provide lessons for investment practice more generally. Given the evolving relations between internal and external stakeholders, it is necessary to recast the analytical basis on which the quality of investment governance is evaluated.

Background to the development of responsible investment

"Responsible investment" can be understood as investment practices that deliver sustainable returns in economic, social and environmental terms. Although related to the older concept of corporate social responsibility (CSR), with its historical links to human rights and the struggle for racial equality in countries such as South Africa, CSR is more closely tied to the discourse of sustainable development as it has emerged over the past two decades. Since the UN Conference on Environment and Development (UNCED) in 1992, sustainable development has been promoted through a range of global public–private initiatives, including the Global Compact, initiated in 2000. UNCED was central to the development and promotion of voluntary methods of environmental problem solving as an alternative to governmental regulation (Clapp 2005). Such methods are implemented through a range of private sector, market-based mechanisms, such as emissions trading and ecolabelling (Falkner 2003; Jordan et al. 2005). Through these mechanisms, a range of actors – state, civic and business – have come together in a series of multiscalar, multi-stakeholder initiatives that are "conducive to inclusive development" (Utting and Marques 2010: 17).

In 1999, the World Bank and the Organisation for Economic Co-operation and Development cofounded the Global Corporate Governance Forum (GCGF) as a facility of the International Finance Corporation. The aim of the GCGF is to encourage companies to invest and behave in a socially responsible manner (Global Corporate Governance Forum 2010). Between 2003 and 2005, the United Nations Environment Programme Finance Initiative engaged with the UN Global Compact and investment industry representatives to create a global body to promote sustainable financial practices: the Principles for Responsible Investment (PRI) (Global Compact and UNEP FI 2009a). The PRI initiative is aimed at integrating environmental and social governance (ESG) issues into financial management (Global Compact and UNEP FI 2009b). The principles cover the elements required for reporting on environmental and social performance, referred to as "sustainability reporting" (UNEP FI 2009a). Such reporting functions within a context of transparency about economic, social and environmental impacts, and is a "fundamental component in effective stakeholder relations, investment decisions, and other market relations" (Global Reporting Initiative 2008: 1). These elements were identified and developed between 2003 and 2005, in collaboration with the Global Reporting Initiative, and built on the 2002 social performance indicators of SPI Finance. *Environmental reporting* concerns elements such as materials, energy, water, biodiversity, emissions, compliance and transport. *Social reporting* covers four subthemes: labor and work practices, human rights, society and product responsibility. *Economic reporting* is also included; it concerns such issues as financial performance, market presence, indirect economic impacts and investment in the community. In each type of reporting, activities are reported against a series of performance indicators (ibid.). Such initiatives are understood as examples of "soft" law, based around "aspirational voluntary declarations of intent" (UNEP FI 2009b). Here, compliance occurs in the context of self-regulation against standards that concern such areas of corporate activity as accountability, responsibility and implementation (Clapp 2005).

As a financial product, responsible investment is governed by a plethora of initiatives that have arisen in the absence of any formal global system. Various models are available for determining the social and environmental sustainability of investments; however, with no consistent rules or standards, there is an urgent need for some level of consolidation (Waddock 2008; Whitman 2005). The problem of competing approaches to evaluating sustainability is evident in this sector. For example, there is an evolving debate over which method is best for screening "responsible" enterprises for their investment potential. Some companies use negative screens (e.g., no alcohol, tobacco or firearms), some use positive screens (best-in-class), and others simply screen on the basis of the degree to which a company engages and involves multi-stakeholders (UNEP FI and Mercer 2007). Hence, overall, there is uncertainty about the legitimacy of the evaluation methods being used and the entities being evaluated.

Analytical perspective on evaluating governance quality

This chapter contends that the term "stakeholders" now covers a diverse set of interests that collectively shape the institutions with which they interact. This interpretation allows for a more integrative conception than is possible in more strictly neo-utilitarian theory, in which "stake" effectively relates to "stock." Such developments require new approaches to evaluating the frameworks through which governance is legitimated; for example, universal ownership can be extended to include interests traditionally seen as peripheral to business practice. Traditional economic preferences for maximizing shareholder returns are now increasingly being supplemented by recognition of ESG (Hawley and Williams 2005). This results in a move away from traditional practices of corporate governance, and allows for a more ethical and less functionalist model for determining governance quality (Ruggie 1998). NGOs and other stakeholders are increasingly demanding governance systems that have a wider focus than those found in traditional "top-down" institutions. The trend towards greater levels of multi-stakeholder collaboration is generating new partnerships between businesses,

NGOs and governments, and is creating new services and products (Global Corporate Governance Forum and International Finance Corporation undated). Emergent contemporary social initiatives and movements focused on the environment are triggering more inclusive forms of governance based on the "dynamic interplay between civil society, business and public sector over the issue of corporate social responsibility" (Ruggie 2003: 95). It is now possible to speak of a "new corporate governance" within finance that includes a focus on environmentally and socially oriented values (Hilb 2009).

Commentators and theorists are preoccupied by various issues concerning the quality and legitimacy of this "new" approach to governance, whether in the responsible investment sector or more broadly within the arena of sustainable development. Institutional arrangements – that is, the mechanisms of governance that underpin the interactions between stakeholders – have a bearing on governance quality (Koenig-Archibugi 2006: 24). These arrangements most commonly refer to interest representation, aspects of responsible organizational behavior, decision-making and implementation. The foremost issue is organizational responsibility, usually understood in terms of accountability and transparency, both internally and externally to the public at large (Garten 1999; Hawley and Williams 2005; Detomasi 2006; Waddock 2008; UNGC and GCGF 2009). Another significant issue is the representation of different stakeholder interests within a given institutional context. Here, the discussion is largely about issues of inclusiveness and equality, focusing particularly on whether all interests enjoy the levels of influence and access to resources currently enjoyed by economic interests (Jänicke 1992; Stiglitz 2003; Kerwer 2006; Koenig-Archibugi 2006; Global Corporate Governance Forum and International Finance Corporation undated). A third concern is decision-making, particularly the presence or absence of institutional democracy, and the methods by which agreements are reached and disputes are settled (Ostrom 1990; van Vliet 1993; Jänicke 1996; Meidinger 2006; Bebchuk and Hamdani 2009). The fourth major issue is effective implementation, which has been identified as relating to both the behavioral and problem-solving abilities of an institution (Skjærseth et al. 2006). In

the context of responsible investment, behavioral change refers specifically to changing behavior around financial market activities, to lead to environmentally and socially sustainable outcomes. The problem that responsible investment seeks to address is the negative externalities (e.g., deforestation) associated with unsustainable investment. Given the inherently dynamic nature of social and ecological systems (and related markets), there is an implicit need for resilience in the face of changing external circumstances, such as climate change or market conditions (Folke et al. 2005). Another component of effective implementation is *durability*; in the context of responsible fiduciary activity, this refers to long-term investment practices that are based on environmentally and socially sustainable practices. Although emphasis is placed on social and environmental viability, implicit in this understanding is the recognition that an activity that is not economically viable will not be durable.

Previous work has brought these concerns about governance quality into a coherent analytical approach to evaluating sustainable development and, in particular, responsible investment (Cadman 2011a, 2011b, 2011c). A framework for evaluating the quality of governance of responsible investment, using a series of principles, criteria and indicators (PC&I) is presented here. The use of PC&I was popularized by UNCED, and has been generally applied to the sustainable development of natural resources. The approach has now spread to different fields, including stakeholder engagement in the corporate sector (Accountability 2005).

A problem common to studies of institutional governance is that the arrangements investigated are usually not tackled holistically; they tend to reflect the disciplines of the scholars researching governance quality, or to be drawn from professional organizations that provide governance-related services. For example, there is a current focus (almost an obsession) on accountability and transparency, with organizations devoted to providing advice or services concerning these arrangements, to the exclusion of other key governance arrangements. Alternatively, scholars and organizations studying governance may look at a variety of arrangements through the lens of one particular attribute, making evaluation somewhat confusing. A more

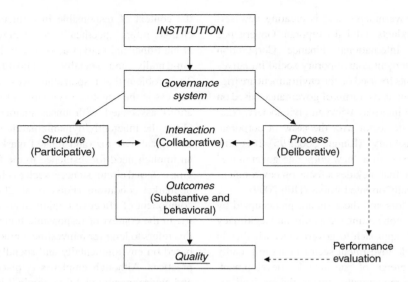

Figure 35.1 Theoretical model for evaluating institutional governance quality (Cadman 2011c: 5 – adapted. Reproduced with permission of Palgrave Macmillan).

comprehensive analytical approach understands governance on the basis of two central organizing principles: *structure* and *process* (Pierre and Peters 2000: 14). It has recently been suggested that contemporary institutional "new" governance systems, with their emphasis on collaboration, are more appropriately conceived of in terms of structure as it relates to stakeholder participation ("participation as structure"), and process in terms of the arrangements for stakeholder deliberation ("deliberation as process") (Cadman 2011c: 4–5). In this conception, participation and deliberation are "physical" aspects of institutional design – the extent to which institutional design facilitates participation and deliberation determines the effectiveness of its governance. It is the interactions within a given institution rather than the institution per se that determine governance quality, and ultimately, institutional legitimacy, as expressed in Figure 35.1.

Two normative values are attributed to the principles underpinning participation and deliberation: participation should be *meaningful* (i.e., stakeholder engagement is real, not tokenistic) and deliberation should be *productive* (i.e., produce genuine outcomes). These two principles are expressed through related criteria (i.e., categories associated with the relevant principle) and indicators (i.e., points of reference for measurement). Principles and criteria are usually difficult to measure; therefore, they are linked to *indicators* for determining the state of the governance system in question. Such indicators can provide either quantitative or qualitative information. Placing PC&I within a hierarchical framework ensures that a consistent analysis can occur at the appropriate level (Lammerts van Bueren and Blom 1997). Without such a hierarchy, some elements may be given undue attention (e.g., accountability and transparency, as has been discussed), and others that are of fundamental importance may be overlooked. For example, there is no point in focusing on inclusiveness if there is no meaningful stakeholder participation.

Implicit in this framework is the assumption that accountability and transparency, for example, are indicators of the degree of responsible organizational behavior; in turn, such behavior is one aspect of (hopefully genuine) participation. An organization that is neither transparent nor accountable is not behaving responsibly, and stakeholder participation is meaningless (since the entity in question is not answerable to stakeholders, and its actions are not visible to them). If this were the case with a given share portfolio, for example, it would be difficult to assert that the service provider (e.g., an asset manager or trustee) could really be considered a "responsible" investor.

Table 35.1 Hierarchical framework for the assessment of governance quality.

Principle	Criterion	Indicator
Meaningful participation	Interest representation	Inclusiveness Equality Resources
	Organizational responsibility	Accountability Transparency
Productive deliberation	Decision-making	Democracy Agreement Dispute settlement
	Implementation	Behavioral change Problem solving Durability

Source: Cadman (2011c: 17).

Two criteria are associated with participation: *interest representation* and *organizational responsibility*. Interest representation is almost universally linked to three aspects of "good" governance: *inclusiveness*, concerning the breadth of those interests that participate within the governance system and the degree to which their issues are taken into consideration; *equality*, demonstrating the quality of the relationship among stakeholders; and *resources*, referring to the economic, technical or institutional capacity of a particular participant or group to have their interests addressed by the system.

Organizational responsibility, as referred to above, consists of two indicators: *accountability* and *transparency*. These indicators are usually linked in the literature, and concern the degree to which stakeholder organizations or groups within the institution (and indeed, the institution itself) can be called to account internally (by shareholders, the board, other organizations and so on) and externally (by the public at large.) Transparency concerns the visibility of behavior, and the extent to which actions are open to scrutiny by other actors within the institution and beyond, and to the public at large. Consequently, the internal and external aspects of these two indicators are discussed separately in the results section.

The criteria connected to deliberation are *decision-making* and *implementation*. Decision-making is associated with three indicators: *democracy*, which concerns whether a system functions in a manner that is procedurally fair to those involved, rather than any particular type of institutional democracy; *agreement,* which refers to the methods used to reach decisions (e.g., casting of ballots, show of hands or consensus); and *dispute settlement*, which demonstrates that the system is able to manage conflict or handle disagreements in situations where no agreement can be reached or a decision is challenged. Implementation is associated with a further three indicators: *behavior change*, which signifies whether the agreements reached or substantive outcomes generated actually result in changed behavior (e.g., in the case of responsible investment, an example could be microfinance resulting in the empowerment of women); *problem-solving*, which is discrete from behavior change, and concerns the extent to which the problem the institution was created to address is actually addressed (e.g., whether emissions trading actually reduces emissions); and *durability*, which refers to adaptability, flexibility and longevity of the solution to the problem (e.g., that an emissions trading scheme does not collapse after a few years due to issues such as lack of interest, corruption or poor design). Table 35.1 summarizes these PC&I.

Together, PC&I may be used as the basis for standards that serve as a reference for monitoring, reporting and evaluation (Lammerts van Beuren and Blom 1997). Standards determine how the substantive outcomes of a given system are formulated and applied, thereby delivering both legitimacy (which can also be equated to effectiveness) and quality (Kooiman 1993).

Methodology

Using the analytical framework outlined above, a survey of stakeholders was developed to provide some insights into perceptions regarding the governance quality of various aspects of responsible investment among participants in the sector. The research was undertaken with the assistance of the PRI, which provided advice on what it thought were some of the most important aspects of the responsible investment "universe." The stakeholders contacted were sourced from two distinct groups. The largest group was from the Database of Contacts in the Field of Socially Responsible Investment, which is prepared annually by Emerging Markets ESG.[1] The 2010 list comprised approximately 1,500 named individuals and companies. A second group was sourced from the Responsible Investment Association of Australia (RIAA) website,[2] which in 2010 had a published list of 134 members.

The survey was conducted online, using the internet tool Survey Monkey.[3] It was anonymous, and was divided into two sections. The first section comprised a preliminary demographic survey designed to get a general feel for the makeup of stakeholders in the investment sector. Seventy-three respondents completed this section. Survey respondents were asked to select from a revised list of categories under the headings shown in the "Type" column of Table 35.2. The financial institutions were further asked to identify themselves as either institutional investors (thirteen respondents) or "other" (eleven). Those who selected "other" identified as consultant (two respondents), connector for social investors and social entrepreneurs (one), financial planner (five), financial adviser (three), financial service (one), industry body (one), issuer (one), network (one), not for profit trust/foundation (one) and proxy agent (one).

Respondents indicated that they were active on a range of levels: international (thirty), regional (eight), national (twenty-four), state/provincial (four), local (four) and other (three). Geographical spread was largely from developed countries (sixty-eight versus five from developing countries), with

[1] www.emergingmarketsesg.net.
[2] www.responsibleinvestment.org.
[3] www.surveymonkey.com.

Table 35.2 Description of survey cohort by type.

Type	Number
Academia	1
Company	11
Financial institution	22
Governmental organization	1
Media	3
Non-governmental organization	2
Professional association	6
Rating agency	6
Researcher	6
Other	15
Total	73

the highest number of respondents from Western Europe (twenty-eight), followed by Australasia (twenty-seven) and North America (twelve), with none from Latin America.

The second section of the survey comprised questions about perceptions of the governance quality of the sector, based on the eleven indicators of Table 35.1. The indicators "accountability" and "transparency" were expanded to allow respondents to take internal and external considerations into account, as shown in Table 35.3.

On the advice of PRI, the responsible investment "universe" was broken down into a number of specific subsectors to allow for a more comprehensive analysis. The subsectors of responsible investment identified for the purposes of comprehensive analysis were: services and products (responsible investment goods available in the market); sustainable investment organizations (associations representing the views of members); government regulation (i.e., state-based regulatory mechanisms); PRI (to provide an anecdotal perspective on a single organization active in the responsible investment space); and other reporting frameworks (i.e., nonstate and voluntary mechanisms). The intention here was to see whether any of these subsectors was viewed more or less favorably by respondents.

Perceptions of the governance of the responsible investment sector were evaluated using the eleven indicators in Table 35.1. Respondents were asked to rate each of the indicators using a one- to

Table 35.3 List of survey questions following the indicators of Table 35.1.

Do you think responsible investment includes, or takes into consideration, the issues and concerns that are most important to you?

Do you feel your issues and concerns are treated equally to the views of others with whom you work on responsible investment (RI) activities?

Are you adequately resourced to participate in RI-related activities?

Do you think the organizations you work with act in an accountable manner?

Do you think RI institutions/bodies are accountable to the general public?

Do you think the interests involved in RI act in a transparent manner?

Do you think the interests involved in RI act in a transparent manner towards the general public?

As far as is possible, given that responsible investment is not necessarily "democratic," do you feel that decision-making within RI organizations is procedurally fair?

Do you feel the way RI organizations reach agreement (i.e., make decisions) is effective?

Do you think dispute settlement in RI organizations is effective?

Do you think RI organizations play an effective role in changing behavior?

How would you rate the problem-solving capacity of RI organizations?

Do you think RI organizations are resilient (i.e., durable, flexible and capable of responding to change)?

five-point (Likert) scale of "very low," "low," "medium," "high" and "very high." Likert scales are used to assess respondents through structured questions in which respondents specify their level of perception on a given statement. The average of all respondents' ratings captures the collective perception per question (Burns and Burns 2008). The language used for choices within the survey was designed to address perceptions of governance *quality* (from "very high" to "very low") rather than agreement or disagreement. "Low" and "very low" are not strictly negative positions, but in the context of governance quality they can be interpreted as such. The overall average value of "medium" represents a neutral perception on the indicators. The ratings at the indicator scale were aggregated under the relevant criterion; in turn, the relevant criteria were combined to provide a result at the principle level. These principle-level results were summed to provide an overall "quality score" out of sixty-five. Opportunities for qualitative comment were also provided for each indicator, and respondents had the option of adding further general comments at the end of the survey. The results from the surveys were analyzed using Statistical Package for the Social Sciences (SPSS).

There are shortcomings associated with online surveys. Such surveys generally have much lower participation rates than other forms of survey technique (Van Selm and Jankowski 2006). In many developing countries, the internet is unreliable and subject to frequent interruptions, due to power shortages. Also, the survey questions related to the indicators of Table 35.1 were compulsory. This approach to obtaining statistically relevant results can result in a high drop-off rate. The survey could also take more than an hour to complete if stakeholders felt the need to provide extensive comments, which may also have led to incomplete responses. In our survey, thirty-four respondents commenced the second section, but only twenty-seven (i.e., 37 percent of the original seventy-three) completed it. Compulsory questions can increase the degree of ownership of the survey by respondents, and result in higher quality responses; nevertheless, the "science" of online surveys is still evolving (Manfreda et al. 2002).

Preliminary results and discussion

The comprehensive results across all eleven indicators, and their associated criteria and principles, are given in Table 35.4. It should be stressed, however, that a survey of this type is largely anecdotal, for a number of reasons. With such a small cohort

Table 35.4 Survey of stakeholder perceptions of the governance quality of responsible investment by subsectors.

	1. Interest representation Maximum score: 15 Minimum: 3				1. Meaningful participation Maximum score: 35; Minimum: 7 2. Organizational responsibility Maximum score: 20 Minimum: 4				
	Inclus-iveness	Equal-ity	Resour-ces	*Criterion* score	Account-ability (internal)	Account-ability (external)	Trans-parency (internal)	Trans-parency (external)	*Criterion* score
Services and products (27)	3.2	3.1	2.9	9.2	3.4	2.8	3.0	3.0	12.2
Sustainable investment organizations (27)	3.7	3.4	3.0	10.1	3.6	3.0	3.2	3.2	13
Government regulation (27)	2.8	2.6	2.3	7.7	3.0	2.7	2.8	2.7	11.2
Principles for Responsible Investment (27)	3.2	3.3	2.8	9.3	3.5	2.9	3.3	3.2	12.9
Other frameworks (27)	3.1	2.9	2.6	8.6	3.2	2.9	3.0	2.9	12
Average	3.2	3.1	2.7	9.0	3.3	2.9	3.1	3.0	12.3

of respondents, the survey cannot purport to be a definitive representation of views across such a large pool of potential participants. Also, the survey does not wholly reproduce the large cross-section of interest groups, institutions and other multi-stakeholders who make up the responsible investment sector. Finally, those who responded to the survey did not specify whether they were speaking on behalf of their particular organization or as individuals; rather, they provided their own unique perceptions. Low numbers of respondents can also produce "outlier" effects, whereby a few respondents giving a score of "very high" or "very low" can overly influence the results. In addition, many of the respondents were from Australasia, which may also have influenced the results. Thus, the survey cannot be used to make any definitive claims about the governance quality of responsible investment as a whole, nor about perceptions from

a given organizational viewpoint (institutional investor *contra* financial planner, for example). Consequently, the results presented are tentative and mainly useful for exploratory discussion only. Nevertheless, a few interesting observations can still be made, which it is hoped will encourage others to further investigate the perceptions of stakeholders directly or indirectly involved in, or affected by, institutional investment.

Looking at the average total for responsible investment as a whole, and for each of the identified subsectors, all passed with relatively similar scores. The weakest performer was government regulation, while sustainable investment organizations were the strongest. This may indicate that respondents have more confidence in the ability of the representative associations within responsible investment to govern the sector than of government; but this is speculative. The PRI performs relatively

Table 35.4 *(cont.)*

| | 2. Productive deliberation Maximum score: 30 Minimum: 6 | | | | | | | | | |
| Principle score | 3. Decision making Maximum score: 15 Minimum: 3 | | | | 4. Implementation Maximum score: 15 Minimum: 3 | | | | Principle Score | Total (out of 65) |
	Demo-cracy	Agree-ment	Dispute settle-ment	*Criterion* score	Behav-ioral change	Problem solving	Dura-bility	*Criter-ion* score		
21.4	3.0	2.8	2.7	8.5	3.2	3.0	3.1	9.3	17.8	39.2
23.1	3.4	3.1	2.9	9.4	3.2	3.0	3.1	9.3	18.7	41.8
18.9	2.7	2.3	2.6	7.6	3.0	2.5	2.6	8.1	15.7	34.6
22.2	3.2	3.0	2.9	9.1	3.3	3.0	3.1	9.4	18.5	40.7
20.6	3.1	2.9	2.8	8.8	3.0	2.7	2.9	8.6	17.4	38
21.2	3.1	2.8	2.8	8.7	3.1	2.8	3.0	8.9	17.6	38.9

well, and outperforms other reporting frameworks; however, the somewhat nebulous nature of "other frameworks" does not yield sufficient information to comment further. It is worth noting that the governance quality of the services and products offered by responsible investment were also looked on relatively favorably. At the principle level, all subsectors passed. Once again, government regulation did not perform as well as other subsectors, and only just passed the principle of productive deliberation. At the criterion level, respondents' perceptions about government regulation become more pronounced. In this regard, decision-making and interest representation failed. No other subsectors failed any of the criteria. These trends are reflected at the indicator level. Governmental regulation failed two indicators – resources and dispute settlement. The sustainable investment organizations achieved the highest single score for any indicator

(inclusiveness). This level of performance was repeated across most other indicators, but PRI was rated highest for its degree of internal transparency and its contribution to behavioral change. There are some indicators across all subsectors that are also worth commenting on. Resources, agreement, dispute settlement and problem-solving were the lowest performing indicators, with resources being the lowest of these. Of further interest is the consistent rating of the internal and external aspects of accountability and transparency. In both instances, it appears that respondents felt that all the sectors of responsible investment were less accountable and transparent to the public than they were to their own internal interests.

The comments from individual respondents make for interesting reading. Despite the high rating for inclusiveness overall, one respondent who identified as "professional organization" commented about "losing faith" and being "not sure" that either individuals or organizations went "deep enough" in taking issues and concerns into account; most individuals or organizations, the respondent felt, were "superficial." One company respondent provided an alternative perspective, pointing to the extent to which some companies had established "links" to "NGOs like Amnesty International." A financial adviser was particularly negative about the level of equality between the interests involved in responsible investment associations, commenting that "money talks and within organizations the 'power' follows the money. So fund managers will dominate RI associations because they can fund the running of that group, with hard or soft dollar support." With regard to accountability, two respondents were of the opinion that the general public had little interest in responsible investment. Looking beyond responsible investment as a sector to investment more generally, one institutional investor commented that "Lack of accountability on RI [responsible investment] by the investment industry is a major bug bear and risk for the industry." In terms of transparency and the general public, one financial adviser commented that:

> In the finance area of RI the need for transparency is extreme through government regulation, codes of ethics of financial associations, etc. However, there is always room for people to take advantage of the public. The government should be transparent, but I have found that the RI industry (especially alternative energy and technology) get badly treated by governments.

Few comments concerned either democracy or agreement, although one respondent who self-identified as a "small sustainability consultancy" felt that the way agreements were reached within the responsible investment sector placed it "a long way ahead of other businesses." In terms of dispute settlement, thirteen respondents noted that they had been involved in dispute settlement, and eight were of the view that these disputes had been settled effectively. A number of substantive comments were made concerning the indicator of behavior change. One professional association member made the observation that "Compared with conventional investment RI plays a huge role

in changing behavior." Another company representative commented that:

> Because of the lack of transparency often the role played in changing behavior is behind closed doors, which means in effect both the organizations who are not impacting change (and just have a marketing campaign saying they do) are placed in the same category as those who are impacting change.

Another financial adviser explored the links between governmental regulation, personal action and behavior change:

> It is really either government regulation as a macro change or behavioral change. But the regulations are scattered and some changes are unintentional. It is only at the one-to-one level that the real changes happen. Where people understand what their money is doing and then amend their ways accordingly.

Comments about the problem-solving capacity of responsible investment related to concerns about a "lack of means" according to one professional association respondent, but two other respondents saw responsible investment as a better performer than others, with one financial adviser stating that "RI looks further into peoples' needs and makes them confront what they really want." No comments were provided about the durability of responsible investment.

Conclusions

This chapter has looked at the development of the responsible investment sector, its relationship to the emerging concept of environmental and social governance, and the degree to which responsible investment can be seen as contributing to sustainable development. The transition of global financial markets towards investment models that incorporate environmental and social dimensions is now well underway. The previous assumption that governance quality was based on fiduciary *duty* alone has given way to recognition of the need for greater fiduciary *responsibility*. Such responsibility brings with it a need to facilitate more meaningful engagement of external parties in investment decisions.

Even if external parties are still seen as less salient in terms of power, there is growing recognition that their needs are legitimate and urgent. Both stakeholder engagement and stakeholder analysis need to be expanded to fit these developments. Here, there are some lessons to be learned from responsible investment, which is ahead of conventional investment practices and has notions of fiduciary duty that are far more socially and environmentally encompassing. At this stage, the contribution of responsible investment to improving social and environmental performance is evident, but based on preliminary investigation of the perspectives of some stakeholders from within the sector, there is still a way to go.

References

Accountability. 2005. *Stakeholder Engagement Standard Exposure Draft*. London: Accountability.

Bebchuk, L. and A. Hamdani. 2009. "The Elusive Quest for Global Governance Standards," *University of Pennsylvania Law Review* 157 (5): 1263–317.

Burns, A. and R. Burns. 2008. *Basic Marketing Research*, 2nd edn. New Jersey: Pearson Education.

Cadman, T. 2011a. "The Legitimacy of ESG Standard as an Analytical Framework for Responsible Investment," in W. Vanderkerckhove, J. Leys, K. Alm, B. Scholtens, S. Signori and H. Schäfer (eds.) *Responsible Investment in Times of Turmoil*. London and New York: Springer, pp. 35–54.

2011b. "Evaluating the Governance of Responsible Investment," *Journal of Sustainable Finance and Investment* 1 (1): 19–29.

2011c. *Quality and Legitimacy of Global Governance: Case Lessons from Forestry*. Houndmills and New York: Palgrave Macmillan.

Clapp, J. 2005. "Global Environmental Governance for Corporate Responsibility and Accountability," *Global Environmental Politics* 5 (3): 23–34.

Detomasi, D. 2006. "International Regimes: The Case of Western Corporate Governance," *International Studies Review* 8: 225–51.

Donaldson, T. and L. E. Preston. 1995. "The Stakeholder Theory of the Corporation: Concepts, Evidence, and Implications," *Academy of Management Review* 20 (1): 65–91.

Falkner, R. 2003. "Private Environmental Governance and International Relations: Exploring the Links," *Global Environmental Politics* 3 (2): 72–87.

Fiorino, D. 1996. "Environmental Policy and the Participation Gap in Democracy and the Environment," in W. M. Lafferty and J. Meadowcroft (eds.) *Democracy and the Environment: Problems and Prospects*. Cheltenham: Edward Elgar Publishing, pp. 194–201.

Folke, C., T. Hahn, P. Olsson and J. Norberg. 2005. "Adaptive Governance of Social-ecological Systems," *Annual Review of Environment and Resources* 30: 441–73.

Freshfields Bruckhaus Deringer. 2005. *A Legal Framework for the Integration of Environmental, Social and Governance Issues into Institutional Investment*. Geneva: UNEP FI.

Garten, J. 1999. "Lessons for the Next Financial Crisis," *Foreign Affairs* 78 (2): 76–92.

Global Compact and UNEP FI. 2009a. *The Principles for Responsible Investment*. www.unpri.org/principles.

2009b. *Signatories to the Principles for Responsible Investment*. www.unpri.org/signatories.

Global Corporate Governance Forum. 2010. *Global Corporate Governance Forum: Better Companies, Better Societies*. www.gcgf.org.

Global Corporate Governance Forum and International Finance Corporation. Undated. *Stakeholder Engagement and the Board: Integrating Best Governance Practices*. Washington, DC: Global Corporate Governance Forum and International Finance Corporation.

Global Reporting Initiative. 2008. *Sustainability Reporting Guidelines & Financial Services Sector Supplement*. Amsterdam: GRI.

Hamilton, I. and J. Eriksson. 2010. *Influence Strategies in Shareholder Engagement – A Study of Five Swedish National Pension Funds' Approaches to Responsible Investment*. Paper presented at PRI Academic Conference, May 5–7, Copenhagen Business School, Copenhagen, Denmark.

Hawley, J. and A. Williams. 2000. *The Rise of Fiduciary Capitalism: How Institutional*

Investors Can Make Corporate America More Democratic. Philadelphia: University of Pennsylvania Press.

2005. "Shifting Ground: Emerging Global Corporate-governance Standards and the Rise of Fiduciary Capitalism," *Environment and Planning* 37: 1995–2013.

Hilb, M. 2009. "New Corporate Governance in the Post-crisis World," *Private Sector Opinion* 16: 3–11.

Jänicke, M. 1992. "Conditions for Environmental Policy Success: An International Comparison," *The Environmentalist* 12: 47–58.

1996. "Democracy as a Condition for Environmental Policy Success: The Importance of Non-institutional Factors," in W. M. Lafferty and J. Meadowcroft (eds.) *Democracy and the Environment: Problems and Prospects*. Cheltenham: Edward Elgar Publishing, pp. 71–85.

Jordan, A., R. Wurzel and A. Zito. 2005. "The Rise of 'New' Policy Instruments in Comparative Perspectives: Has Governance Eclipsed Government?" *Political Studies* 53: 441–69.

Kerwer, D. 2006. "Governing Financial Markets by International Standards," in M. Koenig-Archibugi and M. Zürn (eds.) *New Modes of Governance in the Global System: Exploring Publicness, Delegation and Inclusiveness*. Basingstoke and London: Palgrave Macmillan, pp. 77–100.

Koenig-Archibugi, M. 2006. "Introduction: Institutional Diversity in Global Governance," in M. Koenig-Archibugi and M. Zürn (eds.) *New Modes of Governance in the Global System: Exploring Publicness, Delegation and Inclusiveness*. Basingstoke and London: Palgrave Macmillan, pp. 1–30.

Kooiman, J. 1993. "Social-Political Governance: Introduction," in J. Kooiman (ed.) *Modern Governance: New Government Society Interactions*. London: Sage, pp. 1–8.

Lammerts van Beuren, E. and E. Blom. 1997. *Hierarchical Framework for the Formulation of Sustainable Forest Management Standards*. Leiden, Netherlands: The Tropenbos Foundation.

Manfreda, K. L., Z. Batagelj and V. Vehovar. 2002. "Design of Web Survey Questionnaires: Three Basic Experiments," *Journal of Computer-Mediated Communication* 7 (3).

Meidinger, E. 2006. "The Administrative Law of Global Private-public Regulation: The Case of Forestry," *European Journal of International Law* 17 (1): 47–87.

Mitchell, R. K., B. R. Agle and D. J. Wood. 1997. "Toward a Theory of Stakeholder Identification and Salience: Defining the Principle of Who and What Really Counts," *Academy of Management Review* 22 (4): 853–86.

Ostrom, E. 1990. *Governing the Commons: The Evolution of Institutions for Collective Action*. Cambridge University Press.

Pierre, J. and B. Peters. 2000. *Governance, Politics and the State*. Houndmills: Macmillan.

Ransome, W. and C. Sampford. 2010. *Ethics and Socially Responsible Investment*. Farnham and Burlington, VT: Ashgate.

Richardson, B. 2010. *From Fiduciary Duties to Fiduciary Relationships for Socially Responsible Investment*. Paper presented at PRI Academic Conference, May 5–7, Copenhagen Business School, Copenhagen, Denmark.

Ruggie, J. 1998. "What Makes the World Hang Together? Neo-utilitarianism and the Social Constructivist Challenge," *International Organization* 52 (4): 855–85.

2003. "Taking Embedded Liberalism Global: The Corporate Connection," in M. Koenig-Archibugi and M. Zürn (eds.) *New Modes of Governance in the Global System: Exploring Publicness, Delegation and Inclusiveness*. Basingstoke and London: Palgrave Macmillan, pp. 93–129.

Skjærseth, J., O. Stokke and J. Wettestad. 2006. "Soft Law, Hard Law, and Effective Implementation," *Global Environmental Politics* 6 (3): 104–20.

Stiglitz, J. 2003. "Globalization and Development," in M. Koenig-Archibugi and M. Zürn (eds.) *New Modes of Governance in the Global System: Exploring Publicness, Delegation and Inclusiveness*. Basingstoke and London: Palgrave Macmillan, pp. 47–67.

UNEP FI. 2009a. *Sustainability Reporting*. www.unepfi.org/work_streams/reporting/index.html.

2009b. *Our Signatories*. www.unepfi.org/signatories/statements/index.html.

UNEP FI and Mercer. 2007. *Demystifying Responsible Investment Performance*. Geneva: UNEP FI and Mercer.

UNGC and GCGF. 2009. *Corporate Governance: The Foundation for Corporate Citizenship and Sustainable Businesses.* New York and Washington, DC: UNGC and GCGF.

Utting, P. and P. C. Marques. 2010. "Introduction: The Intellectual Crisis of CSR," in P. Utting and J. C. Marques (eds.) *Corporate Social Responsibility and Regulatory Governance.* London and Basingstoke: Palgrave Macmillan, pp. 1–25.

Van Selm, M. and N. W. Jankowski. 2006. "Conducting Online Surveys," *Quality and Quantity* 40 (3): 435–56.

Van Vliet, M. 1993. "Environmental Regulation of Business: Options and Constraints for Communicative Governance," in J. Kooiman (ed.) *Modern Governance: New Government Society Interactions.* London: Sage, pp. 105–18.

Waddock, S. 2008. "Building a New Institutional Infrastructure for Corporate Responsibility," *The Academy of Management Perspectives* 22 (3): 87–108.

Whitman, J. 2005. *The Limits of Global Governance.* Abingdon: Routledge.

Yaron, G. 2003. "Canadian Institutional Shareholder Activism in an Era of Globalisation," in J. P. Sarra (ed.) *Corporate Governance in Global Capital Markets.* Vancouver, BC: UBC Press.

The costs of fiduciary failure – and an agenda for remedy

STEPHEN M. DAVIS

Introduction

Institutional investors occupy the fulcrum of two vital dimensions of modern capital markets: the value of public corporations they own, and the financial security of the citizen-savers they serve. Yet for as much effort as policymakers around the world have spent modernizing corporate structures, they have devoted comparatively little attention to institutional investors.

Consequences for companies are profound. Regulators count on institutional investors to help police the market against the risk of repeat systemic crises and fraud, CEOs pay for failure and anemic value creation. In fact, a host of archaic barriers prevent all but a handful of funds from meeting the high expectations placed on them as owners of public corporations. Some observers even contend that the consequence of decades of governance reinvention must now be seen as deeply harmful. Yes, these critics assert, reform succeeded in making corporate boards responsive – but to funds that are habitual short-term traders, not long-term capital stewards. If that is true, policy has unwittingly put company directors and CEOs under more pressure than ever to pursue speedy profit over long-term value and social responsibility. "Corporations continue to place a strong emphasis on quarterly returns, because investors do," notes governance thought leader Ira M. Millstein.[1] As one key report concluded, "The obsession with short-term results by investors, asset management firms, and corporate managers collectively leads to the unintended consequences of destroying long-term value, decreasing market efficiency, reducing investment returns, and impeding efforts

to strengthen corporate governance" (CFA 2006). Similar charges are common in Europe, where the highly contentious – and ultimately catastrophic – Royal Bank of Scotland-led consortium takeover of ABN-Amro in 2007 prompted widespread calls to curb alleged investor short-termism (see also Keay 2011).

Consequences for the millions of citizens who entrust their savings to brokers and funds are equally weighty. An antiquated framework of fund governance, fiduciary duty and regulation has permitted material leakage in value for savers in many jurisdictions. "If a typical British and a typical Dutch person save exactly the same amount for their retirement, the Dutch person will end up with a 50% larger pension," found a Royal Society of Arts report, citing collective, low-cost, high-governance features of Dutch plans (Pitt-Watson 2010).

This chapter integrates research developed in recent years to extract policy ideas mirroring corporate governance reforms but aimed at institutional investors. Specific remedies address the US, as it is the largest capital market with among the starkest gaps in prudent ownership. Similar agendas to mobilize capital stewardship, tailored to conditions in other jurisdictions, may be equally timely and constructive. The objective is to strengthen the capacity of shareholders to act as responsible agents of beneficiaries as well as prudent long-term owners of equity. To identify reforms to shareholding institutions requires, first, an inquiry into the costs of and impediments to responsible stewardship.

Legacy practices

Hidden legacies have a way of swaying modern behavior. Today, rules and practices inherited from

---

[1] Ira M. Millstein speech at PLI Ninth Annual Directors' Institute on Corporate Governance, September 7, 2011.

a largely obsolete capital market haunt the investment world's ability to assume stewardship duties.

In 1950 institutions owned just 6.1 percent of US equities (Gilson and Gordon 2012). Dominant investors were wealthy families. Corporate boards were often supine. Pension plans offered by companies and public agencies were almost all "defined benefit," promising members a fixed amount of income upon retirement. Investments were largely in debt instruments or blue chip domestic stock, yielding unexciting but steady returns. Desultory investing made actuarial sense: current workers generating savings far outnumbered pensioners needing cash, especially as average life spans kept retirement relatively short. Few funds paid attention to share voting, which was considered not a guardian of value but rather a quaint formality allowing portfolio companies to enact routine matters such as ratifying director appointments. Those few engaged funds that did pay attention, having meager rights under US law, were forced to raise alarms about corporate conduct through the surrogate process of filing shareholder resolutions.

Today, investors owning most of US corporate equity form a vast panoply of funds representing, in the main, assets of millions of working- and middle-class citizens at home and abroad who are saving for retirement and health care expenses (Heineman and Davis 2011). In 2009 the US featured more than 700,000 pension funds, 8,600 mutual funds, 7,900 insurance companies, 6,800 hedge funds and 2,200 funds of funds. Defined benefit schemes are dying out, replaced by "defined contribution" (DC) plans that shift risk to individuals typically invested in mutual funds. In 2009, an estimated 60 million US workers had more than $2.4 trillion of their savings in more than 460,000 separate DC 401(k) plans, according to the Government Accountability Office (GAO 2012). Three years later the number of plans jumped to 483,000 covering as many as 72 million (Morgenson 2012). These accounts hold roughly $3 trillion. Once at the margins of the US investing world, mutual funds have become behemoths critical to the long-term wealth potential of individuals. Complexity rules; one study tracked no fewer than sixteen different intermediaries escorting – each for a price – the citizen-shareowner's

money to a company's stock.[2] Portfolios may contain everything from hedge funds to plain-vanilla equity, covering multiple markets and asset classes spread across the globe. Demographics place a new urgency on high returns: current workers are fewer in number while the universe of retirees is ballooning and people live longer than ever. Share voting is now often required and disclosed, as regulators consider the ballot a means to protect the interests of beneficiaries. And the powers US investors now enjoy to sway board composition and compensation are unprecedented.

For all that sweeping change, the market lives with practices and a culture shaped to a now-disappeared era. Problems may be found in three major baskets: misgovernance, fiduciary duties and regulation.

Misgovernance

Take governance – that is, how transparent an institutional investor is, and how accountable to and aligned it is with the ultimate beneficiaries it serves. Mounting evidence suggests that a fund's governance is perhaps the single most critical factor in predicting its performance *both* as a savings vehicle *and* as a prudent owner of equity. Why? An institution's governing body oversees strategic judgments such as time horizons, fee structures, agent and advisor hiring, conflicts of interest and whether to compensate fund managers for long- or short-term results. The governing body is also responsible for decisions around how a fund – or its agent – acts as an owner of corporate equity to enable or inhibit bad behavior by public company boards. High quality governance appears to be a prerequisite for meaningful long-term strategy, according to a 2012 World Economic Forum study authored by Josh Lerner (2012).

Yet US law in recent years has largely failed to address the governance of institutional investors. Corporate plans are still typically overseen by a single fiduciary who is a company executive; there is generally no trustee board such as exists at cross-industry ("Taft-Hartley") funds or in markets such

---

[2] Private study prepared for HM Treasury, November 2011.

as Australia or Britain. Indeed, the last major legislative effort to provide for accountability in defined contribution plans failed in a Senate committee as long as a decade ago.

Most mutual funds do have boards of directors with duties and features prescribed by the Securities Acts. But members are rarely subject to election even though they are meant to serve as agents of citizens who invest with the fund company. For their part, hedge funds – under the Dodd-Frank Act – need reveal only token details about themselves. US public employee funds are subject to state laws, which vary greatly in what disclosure they require and how boards are composed. Where trustees do exist, skill requirements in statute are minimal, and many boards are seen as captive to professional advisors or to constituents who appointed them.

In sum, even though the security of retirement plans and the behavior of public companies both increasingly hinge on the behavior of investment agents, governance at the top of these institutions can be deeply archaic. Does that matter?

The risk of weak oversight by governing bodies of institutional investors has received comparatively little research attention. But studies that do exist suggest that implications for savers can be serious. Several have found that, as one put it, mutual funds, apparently unchecked by boards, place "important business interests ... in asset gathering ahead of their fiduciary duties" to grassroots savers (Taub 2009). Funds may also make investment allocation decisions designed to help gain and retain 401(k) corporate clients even at a substantial financial penalty to savers (Cohen and Schmidt 2007). According to Vanguard founder John C. Bogle (2009: 82), over the twenty-five years ending in 2005 mutual funds reaped $500 billion in fees while delivering returns less than one third of the figure investors would have made had they put savings into an index. A 2009 Aspen Institute report agreed.

We have already noted data suggesting the annual leakage of value when beneficiaries entrust their money to agents that are out of synch with savers' interests. The GAO found evidence of this – "adverse effects on the plan sponsor and participants" – in its 2012 survey of sample retirement savings plans offered by corporate employers, who are by law the fiduciaries (GAO 2012: 24, 27, 35).

Inadequate oversight exacerbated by misalignment of interests carries material implications for savers. *New York Times* columnist Gretchen Morgenson put it this way: "If plan sponsors don't even know that fees are levied, they are surely not putting any effort into aggressively managing the costs that their employees are paying in their 401(k)'s" (Morgenson 2012). She quoted consultant Brent Glading: "The reality is, most of the fiduciaries of these plans ... say, 'It doesn't save money for the company, so why do I care?' There has to be a groundswell from the employees" (ibid.). Australia's 2010 Cooper Review into fund governance came to similar conclusions: The investment industry is "purpose-built for ambiguity and lack of accountability ... a condition that favors the interests of everyone but the [beneficiaries]."[3]

By contrast, research led by Keith Ambachtsheer finds that well-governed funds outperform bottom-ranked counterparts by as much as 2.4 percent per year (Ambachtsheer et al. 2008; see also Thornton and Fleming 2011).

While costs of misalignment may be gauged in lower returns for beneficiaries, they may also be felt by public corporations when institutions that own them feature imprudent ownership. Investor conflicts of interest, for instance, seem to disarm engaged monitoring even when a portfolio company's management is going wrong – say, with a dodgy takeover. One notorious example, exposed through rare leaks and court challenges, occurred in 2002. Hewlett-Packard threatened to drop business with Deutsche Bank's investment banking arm unless the bank's asset management unit switched 17 million proxy votes to back HP's controversial merger with Compaq Computer. Deutsche complied (SEC 2003). The takeover has since been widely viewed as a failure. But conflicts of interest short-circuited at least one investor's initial message at the time to halt.

At the market-wide level, unchecked conflicts may be behind the oft-cited statistic that not one US corporate fund has ever filed a shareholder resolution expressing dissent with another corporate

---

[3] www.supersystemreview.gov.au.

board. Conflicts work in other ways, too. Within a single investment house, asset managers eager to retain access to corporate executives may override the judgment of governance experts who may, for instance, want to vote against overpaying a CEO responsible for poor performance (Wong 2010, 2012; see also Clearfield 2005). In sum, an institutional investor's appetite to pursue its own commercial interests can trump its duty to grassroots investors, undermining its capacity to monitor portfolio company boards. The signals corporate directors then receive may enable poor, short-term or conflicted decision-making.

Yesterday's fiduciary?

Fund governance isn't the only weak link in the discipline of ownership. Today's fiduciary standards, the legal guardrails that determine what investors can and cannot do with respect to portfolio companies, are the product of a time when corporate value could best be gauged by calculating a company's stock of physical assets. In that earlier context, it was arguably rational that fiduciary rules should carve a narrow channel for investor action. Shareholders, as owners of public equity, could press companies solely on matters defined as strictly financial. The SEC enforced this as the gatekeeper of what shareowner resolutions it would approve or block. In the UK, readings of the Megarry judgment in *Cowan* v. *Scargill* (1985) kept investor action to within similar limits.[4]

Today's calculus is far more complex; corporate value rests as much on intangibles such as "human capital," that is, how employees are recruited, trained, motivated and retained; on reputation and brand identity; and on capacity to create applied knowledge. Consumer trust is understood as central to value. So is management of environmental risk. And in an age when social media empowers any whistleblower, information leaker or disgruntled neighbor to send complaints viral, the quality of risk oversight is critical to corporate welfare.

The international initiative to develop "integrated" reporting provides a window on just how profoundly lacking are conventional techniques of assessing corporate performance.[5]

For all the new insight into what makes companies valuable, fiduciary duty is largely stuck in a bygone era. Lawyers counsel, for instance, that funds act most prudently if they follow investment behavior commonly used by other institutional investors. That "prudent man" rule made sense in the 1960s, when the investment industry was immature as far as retail shareholders were concerned. Today such advice often overwhelms other duties and serves as a "lemming standard" which drives the market's "unrelenting focus on short-term results," observe analysts Keith Johnson and Frank Jan de Graaf (2009; see also Lydenberg 2012). The herd approach breaches the fiduciary obligation to impartially balance the divergent financial needs of all beneficiaries, whether they are first-year employees, middle-aged workers or elderly retirees. After all, an obsession with short-term investing may run counter to the institution's simultaneous responsibility to generate patient returns over decades. But this "duty of impartiality" is today largely ignored because it drew little attention in the years when funds were first created and workforce demographics were wholly different.

Copycat investment takes a further toll. It discourages a focus on extra-financial risks at portfolio companies because such factors fall outside of what shareholders favor under conventional interpretations of their fiduciary duty. At least three studies – two by Freshfields and one by FairPensions – make cases that an updated understanding of fiduciary duty legitimizes investor attention to extra-financial risks precisely because such risks relate directly to long-term value creation (Freshfields Bruckhaus Deringer 2005; FairPensions 2011). So far, however, these studies have not widely transformed practice. As a result, efforts to shift corporate purpose toward sustainable growth still run into resistance by mainstream investors who insist on capital allocated for

---

[4] Judge Sir Robert Megarry, VC, later observed that the investment industry's interpretation of his ruling was too narrow.

[5] See www.theiirc.org. Also see Calvello (2009).

maximum quarterly results. That's a message corporate boards are hearing on a regular basis.

Where are the regulators?

Another legacy which inhibits the rise of an ownership culture in the US may be found in Washington, DC. Capital market changes long ago escaped the once-rational boundaries of regulation, at least when it came to institutional investors. Consider the following two statutory pillars. In 1940 the Investment Company Act laid a framework for the then-new concept of the mutual fund, giving the SEC regulatory authority. Then, in 1974, Congress adopted the Employee Retirement Income Security Act (ERISA), naming the US Department of Labor (DOL) to oversee and safeguard most of the nation's retirement plans.

Today, of course, much of US retirement savings has shifted, for good or ill, from the archetypical defined-benefit ERISA fund to 401(k)-style collective savings in mutual funds. But regulation designed to protect citizen nest eggs has hardly budged.

Serial probes by the Government Accountability Office have found the US Department of Labor (DOL) deficient in enforcing ERISA rules on proxy voting (GAO 2004; see also GAO 2012). Despite the Reagan administration's 1988 milestone definition of the vote as an asset, the DOL has long signaled that this is far down its list of priorities. Further, there is a growing backlog of advancements that have surfaced in the capital market but that appear to receive scant attention at the DOL. Fiduciary duty reform is one; do current definitions safely allow ERISA funds to consider extra-financial risks when assessing whether to invest in companies? Shouldn't fiduciary standards apply to the array of intermediaries that have grown up in recent years to advise (some say control) retirement funds?[6] Stewardship is another; codes now in place in different markets suggest that safeguarding

assets hinges not just on voting but on more fulsome engagement by funds with corporate boards. And then there is fund governance; current regulations take little account of modern guidance on transparency and accountability – particularly as retirement plans migrate from defined benefit to defined contribution options, with higher fees and risks.[7]

The SEC, for its part, has no special obligation under legislation to protect retirement plans, even though long-term pension and health savings, having moved *en masse* into mutual funds, now lie within its jurisdiction. The Commission's charge is to protect investors as a whole. Yet arguably there are distinctive features that apply to retirement plans – where members may be classed, in Delaware Chancellor Leo Strine's words, as "forced capitalists" – as compared to individuals investing freely (Strine 2007). Retirees presumably deserve assurance that agents are using every tool in prudent fashion to manage risk and add value over time. Fund members may not have the right to move cash from one money manager to another if they are unsatisfied. So the same issues of fiduciary duty, stewardship and governance apply to their agent institutions here as at the DOL. But the two agencies appear to be looking elsewhere, leaving the unique interests of the population of retirement savers falling through a gap in regulation.

Two hands clapping: a policy agenda for prudent ownership

If corporate behavior hinges in large part on owner behavior, then it cannot be surprising that too many public companies run astray. Too many institutional shareholders are either failing to monitor portfolio company boards or are monitoring them in pursuit of quick returns. In fact, the surprise is the number and clout of funds that do follow a prudent stewardship approach to investment, despite all

---

[6] A 2008 industry survey by Create-Research found "a widespread perception in the pension world that the investment industry is perverse in one crucial sense: its food chain operates in reverse, with service providers at the top and clients at the bottom. Agents fare better than principals." www.create-research.co.uk. Quoted in ICGN letter to the

US Department of Labor, January 20, 2011, on Definition of Fiduciary Proposed Rule RIN 1210-AB32.
[7] Labor economist Teresa Ghilarducci is a leading critic of US 401(k) plans for retirement savings. Access her published research at http://teresaghilarducci.org/published-papers.html.

the formidable obstacles.[8] Research, while mixed, suggests that by doing so they enhance returns and better control risk (see, for example, Dimson et al. 2012; Claessens and Yurtoglu 2012). And these patient investors tend to be constructive partners with corporate directors in support of sustainable, long-term value creation. The policy challenge to consider, therefore, is straightforward. What tools are available to unlock prudent stewardship in the broader capital market?

First, one ground rule. Legions of experts have argued for a root-and-branch overhaul of the way retirement savings is managed in the US (Nocera 2012). Were that to happen, the shape of the capital market and institutional shareholders would presumably change. But steps outlined below envisage practical and achievable improvements working with the investors we have.

Disclosure

Lawmakers and regulators around the world have developed robust disclosure regimes covering the governance of corporations. Such transparency rules are recognized as motors of change; in fact, they are one of the SEC's main tools in investor protection. Regulators assume market participants will use information in making better decisions as traders and owners.

The contrast with institutional investors is striking. In general, they need do little reporting to beneficiaries on how they are run and overseen. This opacity limits individual shareholders, some of whom may already be restricted in where they direct their savings, in their ability to hold agents to account on costs, performance and stewardship. Transparency as a motor of change is disabled. One remedy, therefore, would be for authorities to apply the kind of reporting investors have long asked of corporations to retirement plans and other asset owners themselves. Institutions would issue a statement annually to their stakeholders on critical governance features. In effect, they could produce

the equivalent of a nutrition label on accountability. Members could theoretically use information to shop for better agents or, if they are locked in, raise their voice in house or in external channels. One UK-based investor initiative, titled 2020 Stewardship, made a start in this direction in 2012, releasing a voluntary disclosure recommendation.[9]

What should such a statement cover? For one, it should explain what governance arrangements ensure that decisions are made in alignment with the interests of beneficiaries. Australia, for instance, urges each retirement plan to feature a trustee board composed equally of sponsor corporations and plan members, and chaired by an independent non-executive. In the US, regulators could provide guidance on accountability principles without dictating specific structures. Alternatively, market participants could together craft a voluntary, but authoritative, national code of governance – with corporate and stewardship components – that embeds such guidance.[10] One minimum standard: beneficiaries should be given knowledge of not only who is serving as fiduciaries on their behalf, but also the fiduciaries' professional backgrounds, skill sets, potential conflicts of interest, independence – and how to contact them. Mutual funds now face such rules; most plan fiduciaries do not. Potential conflicts of interest should also be fully revealed.

Second, retirement plans should describe how governance arrangements are subject to regular independent review to ensure that they meet best-practice accountability principles. Mutual fund boards have to produce such reports already. And self-evaluations are spreading among US public funds, prompting accountability reforms as a result. State retirement systems in California, Massachusetts, New York and Oregon are among those adopting the practice. CalPERS, in a public

---

[8] For example, see the work of the Harvard Law School Shareholder Rights Project, accessible at http://srp.law.harvard.edu.

[9] www.forceforgood.com/Uploaded_Content/tool/2132012172742724.pdf.
[10] In 2011 the Yale School of Management's Millstein Center for Corporate Governance and Performance launched a multi-stakeholder research inquiry into the idea of an authoritative national governance code for the US. Nearly every other significant market has a corporate governance code of some kind.

description of its process, found that it improved board effectiveness.[11]

Third, plans should identify feedback channels appropriate to the era of social media. It should be easy for grassroots members to offer and petition ideas and opinion on aspects of the plan's operations just as shareholders of corporations and mutual funds may offer resolutions on strategic direction. Two-way communication is essential to modern accountability.

Fourth, plans should describe what steps they take to test the investment interests of beneficiaries. One example is the €100 billion Dutch health sector pension fund PFZW, covering 2 million members, and its asset manager PGGM. Starting in mid-2011 the duo began conducting a quarterly sample "Brand Tracker" survey of beneficiaries. Reports provide regular, unique data on how the fund is perceived and whether it is meeting the right needs.[12] Results are cycled into strategy; PGGM cites findings to support its profile as an advocate of long-term stewardship.[13]

Fifth, an asset owner statement should explain how pay for portfolio managers working on behalf of the fund aligns with beneficiaries' interests. If a pension fund expresses investment beliefs that include a long-term investment horizon while advisors and portfolio managers it selects are evaluated and compensated on short-term criteria, it should explain why. Having to supply such information could better alert fiduciaries to the issue and help beneficiaries and regulators gauge a plan's quality.

Sixth, and finally, investment savings plans should disclose every year how they or agents use ownership tools to protect assets – and not only by the narrow-gauge measure of how they vote shares. Ballot records are in themselves useful; they allow beneficiaries to "see who is voting to

enable dysfunctional board behavior."[14] But there is a lot more in the stewardship toolbox with the potential to affect assets and influence corporate behavior. Funds can engage with portfolio companies in a variety of ways. They can enroll in the Principles for Responsible Investment.[15] They can join with other funds to raise concerns at specific companies. They can collaborate with other investors on market-wide initiatives such as the Diverse Director Datasource, created by CalPERS and CalSTRS to improve US corporate boards.[16] They can integrate governance and extra-financial risks as part of portfolio management, including in due diligence research on companies before deciding to buy a stock, periodically while they own shares, and as part of decisions to hold or sell. Regulators, or a national code, could provide best-practice guidance on such disclosure. But if an asset owner uses only bare-minimum stewardship to safeguard beneficiary interests, it should have to disclose that and explain why.[17] A chief benefit: catalyzing fiduciaries to adapt from a bygone era of shareholder compliance and impotence to today's, when constructive stewardship is actionable.

Fiduciary duty

Legal expectations of fiduciaries have fallen well behind changes in the capital markets. So a policy agenda to unlock prudent stewardship must consider reforms in this area. Otherwise the market risks living with standards baked into investor behavior that encourage owner passivity or myopia. Prescriptions generally fall into the following categories:

---

[11] See CalPERS's discussion of the review and subsequent changes in the system's own governance at www.calpers.ca.gov/index.jsp?bc=/about/organization/board/governance-policies.xml.

[12] Reports provided to the author in April 2012 courtesy of PFZW and PGGM.

[13] One academic study found that Dutch beneficiaries would also accept a higher premium or lower retirement benefit if that is necessary to invest more responsibly (Erbé 2008).

[14] Nell Minow. Testimony before the US House Committee on Oversight and Government Reform, October 6, 2008.

[15] Some 900 institutions with more than $30 trillion under management are signatories as of the first quarter of 2012. See www.unpri.org.

[16] See www.gmi3d.com/home.

[17] The Sydney-based Asset Owners Disclosure Project, which focuses on climate change risks, is an example of a grassroots advocate of fund transparency. See http://aod-project.net.

- **Rediscovering the duty of impartiality.** As we have seen, duties as now widely interpreted compel fiduciaries to adopt lemming behavior, often short term in nature. An antidote is to resurrect the key, but long-ignored, "duty of impartiality," which obligates an institution to weigh the interests of different beneficiaries. The CFA Institute describes the duty this way: "engage in a delicate balancing act of taking sufficient risk to generate long-term returns high enough to support real benefit increases for active participants who will become future beneficiaries, while avoiding a level of risk that jeopardizes the safety of the payments to existing pensioners" (CFA 2008). In other words, combine patient capital with the need to make short-term payouts to retirees (see Hawley et al. 2011). The duty of impartiality could theoretically emerge organically through the courts, if cases asserting breaches produce judgments that re-emphasize it. But most advocates believe the vacuum may require legislation or regulation.
- **Apply fiduciary duty to intermediaries.** Statutes designed to safeguard retirement savings were designed well before today's complex market, where intermediaries with many functions touch on the value of fund member assets. Yet such middlemen normally do not fall under fiduciary duty standards applying to the home fund. So when they work for an asset owner, they have no obligation to do so in the ultimate interests of beneficiaries. An executive at TIAA-CREF, one of the largest and most owner-conscious fund companies in the US, even had to remind delegates to a conference in June 2012 that the firm was not covered by fiduciary duty.[18] John C. Bogle has long called for a fiduciary duty "establishing the basic principle that money managers are there to serve...those whose money they manage" (quoted in Davis et al. 2009). The US DOL is now considering whether to extend aspects of fiduciary duty to certain agents – but this, too, may require legislation and regulatory clarification.
- **Widen fiduciary duty to include extra-financial factors.** Current legal counsel encourages fiduciaries to downplay the investment relevance of key corporate drivers of value and risk because they fall outside the bounds of traditional, narrow financial measurement. So long as these factors are excluded from generally accepted investment responsibilities at portfolio companies, mainstream funds will steer clear of them for fear of running afoul of law. Most, therefore, would not signal concern about them in engagements with corporate directors. FairPensions has drafted fiduciary language for UK pension fund trustees that would broadly match more expansive obligations now in place for corporate board members. Similar legislation or regulation may be considered in the US.

Public policy

US regulation of investment today fails both corporations and savers. Oversight gaps opened over the years owing to tectonic shifts in the capital market have unintentionally enabled institutional shareholders to act short term even as their beneficiaries need them more than ever to behave long term. Several public policy steps, if implemented, have the potential to reverse course.

First comes a bedrock question: who should mind the industry? Oversight of long-term savings has become a regulatory orphan. The US Department of Labor, handed the job of supervising pension plans under the 1974 ERISA statute, is buffeted by politics. The agency is cosseted under Democratic administrations, starved under Republican ones, subject to budgetary torque where power is divided. In part for this reason, as we have seen, the DOL is an unreliable regulatory parent of retirement funds. At the same time the SEC, now the default guardian of savings thanks to the rise of 401(k)s, has myriad other securities market priorities – and no specific mandate to look after retirement plans. Again, a flawed parent.

One of two remedies would appear sensible. One would be to pull supervision out of the DOL into an independent, less politically charged agency dedicated to expanded oversight of long-term savings. The UK's Pensions Regulator is such

---

[18] Remarks by Jon Feigelson at the International Corporate Governance Network annual conference in Rio de Janeiro, June 26, 2012.

an approach.[19] Another less efficient but arguably more feasible option would be to create an independent overlay body charged with coordinating and harmonizing oversight of long-term savings in concert with existing agencies. Such a body could draw from other federal models, such as the Financial Stability Oversight Council. It could best address challenges if its structure included not only agency heads, but also individuals representing investing institutions and beneficiaries, who can supply continuing insight on market conditions. Structural reform would aim to house coordinated regulation fit for purpose for today's investment savings environment.

Then comes the question of content. What supervisory steps would help propel ownership behavior more aligned with long-term citizen shareholders – and more constructive for corporations?

Regulators should require retirement savings plans and other asset owners to produce an annual "nutrition label" of information on the six major governance and stewardship features noted above. Authorities can issue best-practice accountability principles to help frame such releases. Or regulators can press market participants to develop their own through a code that funds would have to apply, or explain why if they diverge. One model for fund governance is the guidance drafted in April 2012 by APRA, Australia's prudential regulator. Provisions set out the agency's expectations of fund board oversight in everything from fiduciary skills to portfolio manager compensation to whistleblower protection.[20] In the US, voluntary standards on fund governance were released the same month by the National Conference on Public Employee Retirement Systems, representing 500 funds with $3 trillion in assets.[21] Best practices for how

institutions should use ownership tools at portfolio companies may be found in stewardship codes in the UK, the Netherlands and South Africa.[22] A market-based international version covering both fund governance and stewardship was developed by the International Corporate Governance Network.[23] And the Organisation for Economic Co-operation and Development produced broad principles of fund governance in 2009.[24]

Whichever model US regulators adapt, the needs of modern transparency dictate that disclosures opt for plain English over jargon. This isn't just cosmetic. The UK's NEST retirement system discovered through surveys that technical language was a barrier to communication with prospective members, so it developed a glossary of commonly understood pension terms to use.[25] US governance disclosures, similarly, should be accessible online and written for easy comprehension by beneficiaries. Further, like a food nutrition label, any data required should follow a common format, so that individuals can readily make comparisons between institutions. An SEC example shows what not to do; the Commission rightly required mutual funds to release their share voting records, but then gave no guidance about how funds should do it.[26] Apps allow individuals using smartphones and tablets to compare doctors, restaurants and countless other services. Disclosures should allow social media to give similar services to individuals trying to assess the quality of their savings arrangements.[27] Scholars would also benefit; there

---

[19] See www.thepensionsregulator.gov.uk/index.aspx.

[20] See www.apra.gov.au/Super/PrudentialFramework/Documents/ Draft-Prudential-Standard-SPS-510-Governance- (April-2012).pdf. The UK's Stewardship Code is a related model, but it focuses more on fund engagement with portfolio companies than own governance.

[21] See www.ncpers.org/Files/2012_ncpers_best_governance_practices.pdf. See another set of best practice recommendations in the "Clapman Report" accessible at www.directorsandboards.com/DBEBRIEFING/July2007/ FundGovernanceReport.pdf.

[22] See the UK code at www.frc.org.uk/corporate/investor-governance.cfm; the Dutch at www.eumedion.nl/en/public/ knowledgenetwork/best-practices/best_practices-engaged-share-ownership.pdf; and South Africa's at www.iodsa.co.za/ PRODUCTSSERVICES/KingIIIReportPapersGuidelines/ CodeforResponsibleInvestinginSACRISA.aspx.

[23] See www.icgn.org/files/icgn_main/pdfs/best_practice/inst_ share_responsibilities/2007_principles_on_institutional_ shareholder_responsibilities.pdf.

[24] OECD Guidelines for Pension Fund Governance (June 2009), accessible at www.oecd.org/dataoecd/18/52/ 34799965.pdf.

[25] See www.nestpensions.org.uk/schemeweb/NestWeb/includes /public/docs/NEST-phrasebook,PDF.pdf.

[26] Form N-PX, accessible at www.sec.gov/about/forms/ formn-px.pdf.

[27] For example, see www.proxydemocracy.org.

is a need for solid, accessible data on fund governance to advance research in the area (Heineman and Davis 2011).

Regulators should also modernize fiduciary duty standards and apply them to intermediaries along the investment chain. In particular, they should make clear that voting proxies is not the only, or even always the most effective, expression of ownership. Agents responsible for long-term assets should be expected to make use of any and all stewardship tools, including voting, so long as options are practical and available, to safeguard the savings of beneficiaries. Similarly, supervisors should clarify that fiduciary duty permits institutions to take extra-financial factors into account when making investment and ownership decisions. And a duty of impartiality is critical to curb short-term decision-making at the expense of beneficiaries' with long-term interests.

The US Sarbanes-Oxley Act set skill standards for members of corporate board audit committees. In a similar way, authorities should examine what expertise and independence fiduciary entities should feature to carry out investment responsibilities, including as responsive agents of beneficiaries and prudent owners of public corporations. The CFA Institute offers one version of guidance in this area through a "Pension Trustee Code of Conduct."[28] Fiduciaries must be able to impose the interests of beneficiaries throughout the investment chain rather than be captured by advisors with other objectives.

Of course, these initiatives will fail to take hold if enforcement is lax, as it is today. Regulators should be on the beat, scrutinizing annual disclosure statements, testing whether fiduciaries are matching decisions to beneficiary interests, and checking if those tasked with overseeing plans know what they are doing. But supervision can be prophylactic, not just punitive. The Australian Treasury, for instance, provided start-up money for a Responsible Investment Academy, which now offers online training for asset managers

in ownership skills.[29] In 2012 the European Commission provided similar funds for courses leading to certification in prudent ownership (International Corporate Governance Network 2011). Public or semi-public bodies such as FINRA or the SEC could help stimulate training of fund trustees and asset managers as one means of instilling a culture of stewardship in investment.

Conclusions

If policy in recent decades has made corporations more a product of what their short-term owners allow them to be, systemic changes in company purpose can come about in one of two ways. Either policies aim to divorce boards from the sway of institutional investors, freeing directors to do what they think is best for companies. That is what aspects of the JOBS Act of 2012 started.

Or, policy can concentrate on measures to align investment agents with long-term beneficiaries, strip conflicts from the system and discard obsolete investment practices for those matched to today's market realities. That agenda is based on the premise that impediments have long disabled the ability of most funds – with a handful of exceptions – to exercise stewardship.

Prudent ownership, in effect, has not really been widely tried yet, at least in the era when collective investment bodies have largely replaced controlling entrepreneurs. That circumstance implies, in turn, that markets harbor an underpowered capitalism: public corporations are pressed to put short-term gain over long-term value, and savers find themselves with less wealth than they should.

Corrections to the world of institutional investment carry the potential of giving corporate boardrooms both capital and a license to innovate, embrace appropriate risk and address extra-financial drivers of value creation over the long term. The formula distills to this: reforms that put the interests of citizen-investors first hold out the prospect of making better citizens of corporations.

[28] See www.cfainstitute.org/ethics/codes/pension/Pages/index.aspx.

[29] See www.riacademy.org.

Acknowledgements

This chapter is based on *Mobilizing Ownership: An Agenda for Corporate Renewal*, Brookings Institution – Issues in Governance Studies (May 2012), accessible at www.brookings.edu/research/papers/2012/06/01-shareholder-davis.

References

Ambachtsheer, K., R. Capelle and H. Lum. 2008. "The Pension Governance Deficit: Still With Us," *Rotman International Journal of Pension Management* 1 (1). http://papers.ssrn.com/sol3/papers.cfm?abstract_id=1280907.

Aspen Institute. 2009. *Overcoming Short-Termism: A Call for a More Responsible Approach to Investment and Business Management*. www.aspeninstitute.org/sites/default/files/content/docs/bsp/overcome_short_state0909.pdf.

Bogle, J. C. 2009. *Enough*. New York: John Wiley & Sons.

Calvello, A. 2009. *Environmental Alpha: Institutional Investors and Climate Change*. New York: John Wiley & Sons.

CFA. 2006. "Breaking the Short-Term Cycle." www.cfapubs.org/toc/ccb/2006/2006/1.

2008. *Code of Conduct for Members of a Pension Scheme Governing Body*. CFA Institute Centre for Financial Market Integrity. www.cfainstitute.org/learning/products/publications/ccb/Pages/ccb.v2008.n3.1.aspx.

Claessens, S. and B. Yurtoglu. 2012. "Corporate Governance and Development: An Update," *Focus* 10. www.ifc.org/ifcext/cgf.nsf/AttachmentsByTitle/Focus10CG&Dev/$FILE/Focus10_CG&Development.pdf.

Clearfield, A. M. 2005. "With Friends Like These, Who Needs Enemies? The Structure of the Investment Industry and Its Reluctance to Exercise Governance Oversight," *Corporate Governance: An International Review* 13 (2). http://papers.ssrn.com/sol3/papers.cfm?abstract_id=684302.

Cohen, L. and B. Schmidt. 2007. "Attracting Flows by Attracting Big Clients: Conflicts of Interest and Mutual Fund Portfolio Choice." www.chicagobooth.edu/research/workshops/finance/docs/cohen_attractingflows.pdf.

Davis, S., J. Lukomnik and D. Pitt-Watson. 2009. "Active Shareowner Stewardship:

A New Paradigm for Capitalism," *Rotman International Journal of Pension Management* 2 (2). http://papers.ssrn.com/sol3/papers.cfm?abstract_id=1493279.

Dimson, E., O. Karakaş and X. Li. 2012. "Activism on Corporate Social Responsibility." www.inquire-europe.org/seminars/2012/papers%20Budapest/SRI%20-%20Dimson%20Karakas%20Li%20v42.pdf.

Erbé, D. 2008. "Stille Kapitalisten: Een sociologisch onderzoek over de invloed en controle van deelnemers op het beleggingsbeleid van hun pensioenfonds," University of Amsterdam.

FairPensions. 2011. "Protecting Our Best Interests: Rediscovering Fiduciary Obligation." www.fairpensions.org.uk/sites/default/files/uploaded_files/fidduty/FPProtectingOurBestInterests.pdf.

Freshfields Bruckhaus Deringer. 2005. "A Legal Framework for the Integration of Environmental, Social and Governance Issues into Institutional Investment," report produced for the United Nations Environment Programme Finance Initiative.

GAO. 2004. "Pension Plans: Additional Transparency and Other Actions Needed in Connection with Proxy Voting," Government Accountability Office GAO 04–749. www.gao.gov/assets/250/243646.pdf.

2012. "401(k) Plans: Increased Educational Outreach and Broader Oversight May Help Reduce Plan Fees," Government Accountability Office GAO-12–325. www.gao.gov/assets/600/590359.pdf.

Gilson, R. and J. Gordon. 2012. "Capital Markets, Efficient Risk Bearing and Corporate Governance: The Agency Costs of Agency Capitalism." https://coursewebs.law.columbia.edu/coursewebs/cw_12S_L9519_001.nsf/0f66a77852c3921f852571c100169cb9/C52A6786C57B3B52852579830053479F/$FILE/GilGor+Oxford+Prelim+Draft.Conf+Final.011012.pdf?OpenElement.

Hawley, J., K. Johnson and E. Waitzer. 2011. "Reclaiming Fiduciary Balance," *Rotman International Journal of Pension Management* 4 (2). www.reinhartlaw.com/Publications/Documents/art111020%20RIIS.pdf.

Heineman, B. and S. Davis. 2011. "Are Institutional Investors Part of the Problem or Part of the Solution?" Committee for Economic Development and Yale School of Management-

Millstein Center for Corporate Governance and Performance. http://millstein.som.yale.edu/sites/millstein.som.yale.edu/files/80235_CED_WEB.pdf.

International Corporate Governance Network. 2011. "European Commission Appoints ICGN, PRI and EFFAS to Build Capacity of Investors to Integrate ESG Information in Investment Decisions," September 27. www.icgn.org/press/item/1103-european-commission-appoints-icgn-pri-and-effas-to-build-capacity-of-investors-to-integrate-esg-information-in-investment-decisions.

Johnson, K. and F. Jan de Graaf. 2009. "Modernizing Pension Fund Legal Standards for the 21st Century," *Rotman International Journal of Pension Management* 2 (1).

Keay, A. 2011. "The Global Financial Crisis: Risk, Shareholder Pressure and Short-termism in Financial Institutions." http://papers.ssrn.com/sol3/papers.cfm?abstract_id=1839305.

Lerner, J. 2012. "Measurement, Governance and Long-term Investing," World Economic Forum. www3.weforum.org/docs/WEF_IV_MeasurementGovernanceLongtermInvesting_Report_2012.pdf.

Lydenberg, S. 2012. "Reason, Rationality and Fiduciary Duty," IRRC Institute. www.irrcinstitute.org/pdf/FINAL-Lydenberg-Reason-Rationality-2012-Winner.pdf.

Morgenson, G. 2012. "The Curtain Opens on 401(k) Fees," *New York Times*, June 2.

Nocera, J. 2012. "My Faith-Based Retirement," *The New York Times*, April 27. www.nytimes.com/2012/04/28/opinion/nocera-my-faith-based-retirement.html?_r=1.

Pitt-Watson, D. 2010. *Tomorrow's Investor: Building the Consensus for a People's Pension in Britain.* London: Royal Society for the Arts. www.thersa.org/__data/assets/pdf_file/0009/366948/RSA-TI-report-Pensions.pdf.

SEC. 2003. "SEC Brings Settled Enforcement Action Against Deutsche Bank Investment Advisory Unit in Connection with Its Voting of Client Proxies for Merger Transaction; Imposes $750,000 Penalty," Securities and Exchange Commission, August 19. www.sec.gov/news/press/2003-100.htm.

Strine, L. 2007. "Toward Common Sense and Common Ground? Reflections on the Shared Interests of Managers and Labor in a More Rational System of Corporate Governance," speech delivered at the University of Iowa, March 1. www.law.upenn.edu/academics/institutes/ile/CCPapers/040507/Strine%20Speech.pdf.

Taub, J. 2009. "Able But Not Willing: The Failure of Mutual Fund Advisors to Advocate for Shareholders' Rights," *Journal of Corporation Law* 34 (3).

Thornton, P. and D. Fleming (eds.). 2011. *Good Governance for Pension Schemes.* Cambridge University Press.

Wong, S. 2010. "Why Stewardship is Proving Elusive for Institutional Investors," *Butterworths Journal of International Banking and Financial Law*, July/August.

2012. "Barriers to Effective Investor Engagement," *Financial Times*, January 15.

Index